T0326336

The Sustainability Ethic in the Management of the Physical, Infrastructural and Natural Resources of Zimbabwe

Edited by

Innocent Chirisa

Langaa Research & Publishing CIG
Mankon, Bamenda

Publisher
Langaa RPCIG
Langaa Research & Publishing Common Initiative Group
P.O. Box 902 Mankon
Bamenda
North West Region
Cameroon
Langaagrp@gmail.com
www.langaa-rpcig.net

Distributed in and outside N. America by African Books Collective
orders@africanbookscollective.com
www.africanbookscollective.com

ISBN-10: 9956-550-45-0

ISBN-13: 978-9956-550-45-6

Note on Contributors

Abraham Rajab Matamanda holds a BSc Degree in Rural and Urban Planning and MSc in Social Ecology from the University of Zimbabwe. Currently, he is a PhD candidate in the Department of Urban and Regional Planning at the University of the Free State, South Africa. His study focuses on Applied Systems Analysis in planning with reference to urban dilemmas and emerging human settlements forms nexus. Abraham has published more than 10 articles and book chapters in national and international peer-reviewed journals that include Springer and two book chapters in Urbanisation and Its Impact on Socio-Economic Growth in Developing Regions. His research areas are urban sustainability, environmental planning and management, rural development and the planning of cities and towns.

Aurthur Chivambe is a Graduate of BSc Hons in Rural and Urban Planning, (University of Zimbabwe). His research interests include socio-economic development, project planning and management and urban and regional planning for sustainability.

Barbara Chibvamushure holds q Master's degree in Development Studies (NUST), BSc Honours Degree in Sociology and Gender Development Studies (WUA), Diploma in Industrial Relations (UZ) and Certificate in Monitoring and Evaluation (UZ). She has worked as a secretary and office management in various faculties and departments within the University of Zimbabwe.

Charles Chavunduka is a senior lecturer at the Department of Rural and Urban Planning, University of Zimbabwe. Currently he is the Chairman of the Department of Rural and Urban Planning. Dr. Chavunduka is a holder of the following qualifications: PhD in Development Planning (University of Wisconsin-Madison, USA) and, Masters in Business Administration, MSc Regional and Urban Planning, and BSc (Hons.) Geography, all from the University of Zimbabwe. He is a corporate member of both the Zimbabwe Institute of Regional and Urban Planners (ZIRUP) and the Royal Town Planning Institute (RTPI). After working with the Department of Physical Planning, Ministry of Local Government, Public Works and National Housing; Dr. Chavunduka worked with several international organisations, and was appointed senior lecturer in the Department of Rural and Urban Planning, University of Zimbabwe in 2017. His research interests are land reform, urban land management and policy, and decentralisation.

Charlotte Muziri is a student at the University of Zimbabwe. Currently a third year student studying BSc Honours in Rural & Urban Planning. She attended high school at Holy Cross High School.

Conillious Gwatirisa is a DPhil Student (Public Health Policies) with the University of Zimbabwe's Centre for Applied Social Sciences. Currently he is lecturing the Environment and Sustainable Development Courses at the Women's University in Africa. He holds a MSc in Environmental Policy and Planning, a BSc in Geography and Environmental Studies, and a Diploma in Education (Geography).All were obtained from the University of Zimbabwe.

Easther Chigumira (PhD) is a Political Ecologist who teaches human-environment courses to undergraduate and graduate students. Topics include social and cultural geography, political ecology, climate change, agricultural geography, environment impact assessments, environment policy and planning, natural resources, energy, society and the environment. Her current research interests are related to land and agrarian studies, the nexus of agriculture and mining, climate change and resilience, green growth and feminist political ecology

Henry Gurajena is an award winning realtor. He won the IHS Alumni International Urban Professional Youth Award 2018 in Rotterdam, Netherlands. He holds a Distinction in a Bachelor of Science Honours Degree in Real Estate Management from the University of Zimbabwe. He was also awarded the UZ Book Price. He also graduated from the YALI Regional Leadership Centre at University of South Africa with a Certificate in Business and Entrepreneurship. Henry was also awarded a First Price in Undergraduate Humanities for Entrepreneurship at the UZ Research Week. Henry was also a Finalist in the CBZ – Youth Entrepreneurship Programme 2018 walking away with a certificate, trophy and price money. Henry has 5 years' experience in the real estate industry. Henry doubles on the positions of Operations Officer at AHDT and Executive Director at Solinfra Zimbabwe.

Innocent Chirisa is a full professor at the Department of Rural & Urban Planning, University of Zimbabwe. Currently is the deputy dean of the Faculty of Social Studies at the University of Zimbabwe and is a Research Fellow at the Department of Urban and Regional Planning, University of the Free State, South Africa. He holds a DPhil in Social Studies, MSc (Planning), BSc Honours in Rural & Urban Planning all from the University of Zimbabwe and a post-graduate Diploma in Land Management and Informal Land Resettlement from the Institute of Housing and Urban Development Studies, Erasmus University,

The Netherlands. His research interests are systems dynamics in urban land, regional stewardship and resilience in human habitats.

Isheanesu Mpofu is a consultant at a local construction company, Ligerdom Projects. Its key services include but not limited to: town planning, draughting services, construction and project management. He holds a BSc Honours in Rural and Urban Planning. His research interests are urbanisation, densification and modernisation.

Liaison Mukarwi holds a BSc Honours Degree in Rural and Urban Planning from the University of Zimbabwe. He is currently practicing as a Town Planner at Human Settlements Experts (Pvt) Ltd in Zimbabwe. Liaison is a freelance researcher whose researches focus on Urban Management and Governance, Environmental Design, Urban Planning Practice, Housing and Community Issues and Transport and Sustainability issues. He had published more than several journal articles and book chapters. Liaison participated in various academic researches as a research assistant.

Liliosa Musiyiwa is a part time Quality Improvement Specialist at the Department of Community Medicine for CODAID project, she holds a MSc Degree in MCH and Midwifery obtained from the University of Zimbabwe College of Health Science, a BSc degree in Nursing Science from Zimbabwe Open University, a Diploma in Community Health Nursing from Parirenyatwa Post Basic School, a Diploma in Midwifery from Chitungwiza Central Hospital, a Diploma in General Nursing from Harare Central Hospital, a certificate in Family Planning from Seke North Clinic, and a certificate in Monitoring and Evaluation from University of Zimbabwe.

Oripha Chimwara is a part-time lecturer at the Department of Political and Administrative Studies, University of Zimbabwe (UZ). She has been lecturing at UZ since 2016. She holds a Bachelor of Science Honours Degree in Political Science and a Master of Science Degree in International Relations acquired from UZ. Her Masters research focused on natural resources and conflict. She is a member of the Organisation for Social Science Research in Eastern and Southern Africa (OSSREA). Her main academic interests are in political science and international relations focusing on democracy and governance (elections), gender politics as well as peace and security in Africa (conflict analysis).

Paidamoyo Maud Chikandiwa is a part time facilitator of Sociology at High Achievers International Academy. She holds a MSc in Development Studies from the Women's University in Africa, a Bachelor of Science Degree in Sociology and Gender Development Studies from the same University and a Certificate in Project Management, and a Certificate in Monitoring and Evaluation from the Catholic University.

Shamiso Hazel Mafuku is a lecturer in the Department of Rural and Urban Planning and a DPhil Student at the University of Zimbabwe. She holds a Master of Science Degree in Construction Project Management from the National University of Science and Technology (NUST) and a Bachelor of Science Honours Degree in Rural and Urban Planning from the University of Zimbabwe (UZ). Her research interests are peri-urban environments and sustainability, infrastructure and services planning, construction planning and management as well as urban regeneration and renewal.

Solomon Muqayi is a Senior Lecturer in the Department of Political and Administrative Studies, University of Zimbabwe. He holds a DPhil in Social Studies (International Relations), MSc (International Relations), BSc Honours in Public Administration all from the University of Zimbabwe. His research interests are: international relations, international political economy, politics and democracy, politics and development, and political parties.

Tamirirashe Banhire is a student at the University of Zimbabwe. Currently a third year student studying BSc Honours in Rural & Urban Planning. She attended high school at Midlands Christian College where she also attained an OCR Level 1 New Clait International Certificate for IT Users in File management and e-document production and an ICDL (International Computer Driving Licence) Certificate.

Tamuka Joel Mukura is a lecturer in the Department of Economics, University of Zimbabwe. He is currently pursuing a PhD (Economics) in the School of Accounting, Economics and Finance at the University of KwaZulu-Natal, South Africa. He holds an MSc and BSc Honours in Economics both from the University of Zimbabwe. His research interests are in agricultural and development economics.

Tatenda Z.K Chiwota is a graduate in BSc Honours in Real Estate Management from the University of Zimbabwe. His research interests are in sustainable real estate management.

Tsungai Mukwashi is the Programmes Director and founder of NDIRIMO Trust. She is a Disaster Management Expert with a passion for community development and poverty alleviation by building resilience in marginalised and vulnerable communities. Tsungai holds a MSc. Disaster Management (UFS), BA (Geography, Archaeology) UZ, Diploma in Marketing Management (IMM) and Certificate in Basic Counselling (UNISA).

Table of Contents

Chapter 1

Sustainability: An Overview

Innocent Chirisa

Introduction

Oftentimes the intricately-connected critical aspects of society, environment and technology appear incongruent and disconnected in policy and academic discourse in developing countries. A perpetuation of this omission in thinking is detrimental to the understanding of the dynamics transpiring in any economy. In effect, these aspects are the pillars of sustainable development and are often presented as equity, ecology and economy (3Es) or people, planet and production (3Ps), respectively. A fourth pillar to sustainable development has been added as institutions or governance. For sustainability to work, properly developed institutions and governance frameworks are necessary. However, this realisation is important when the interstitial interlinkages of the same have been properly understood. The present work is an attempt to discuss the interlinkages of the pillars of sustainability using Zimbabwe as a country of reference. The focal point of the debate is the interlinkages of the pillars of sustainable development and how the same are operationalisable on the ground to culminate in measurable benefits to the country and its citizens.

The contemporary society is increasingly taking deliberate efforts to protect the environment from continuous damage by human activities. In these efforts, there have been many proponents in favour of technology as one of the tools that can be used by societies to stop sustained environmental degradation (Humphrey *et al.* 2002). Indeed, environmental sustainability has been seen to exert serious burden on economic development but the current environmental catastrophes like climate change have eased the tension and help create considerable traction in this regard. Ruttan (1971:713) has argued that "… the environmental movement, in spite of its extra baggage (including its extensive 'demonology' and its resurrection of discarded concepts from the underworld of science), is contributing to the creation of a social and political environment in which it may become feasible to more adequately institutionalise the redirection of technological effort and carry through the re- forms necessary to redefine the ownership rights in an increasingly valuable set of common property resources." A look at the societal-environmental interaction, illustrates that environmental issues are global because both more developed countries

1

(MDCs) and less developed countries (LDCs) are faced by environmental problems. This then calls for a global drive, where societies can cooperate and collaborate to avoid further ecological problems. LDCs have not advanced in technological innovations hence a need for a global cooperation to allow easy and deliberate transmission of technologies that can help in the protection of the environment. Jokinen *et al.* (1998:495) have posited that, "new technology is basically a cultural product and a social undertaking, and, equally, some characteristics of society are primarily technological projects." This shows a symbiotic relationship among the three, namely society, environment and technology.

Society: Change with Continuity

Today's society is one situated in immense risk. There are so many side-effects of industrial production that have been recorded in the name of modernisation. These environmental hazards include climate change and its associated threats like droughts, floods, heat waves, and cyclones, among others. Beck (1986: 37) has argued that, "Risk society is uncovered society, in which insurance protection decreases with scale of the danger" The environmental dangers in this era affect all the protection mechanisms that may be available in society because of their high intensity. The El-Nino phenomenon which hit southern Africa in the 2015-2016 rain season has, for example, exposed many societies to not only limited water and food but also loss of jobs in the agriculture related industries. Combing terms, uncovered and comprehensively insured society, constitute the politically explosive force of risk society as civil strife is imminent in such societies. Wynne (2002:459) argues, "Risk has become the form of public discourse through which public meaning is given to technology and innovation, as defined in institutional discourses such as government, media, legal and commercial, all deriving from the scientific." However, necessity has always been a mother to invention; thus, highly risk societies have prompted scientific solutions through technology. For example, highly erratic rainfall has been met with cloud seeding.

Earlier Boserup (1976:34) observed the seemingly "… fairly close correlation between population size and density, on one hand, and the degree of stratification and complexity of the social system, on the other…" Taking cue from the above observation, as societies increased in size, indeed their social organisation, what they take from the environment and how they produce (ways of production-technology) change. Historically, hunting-gathering groups, for example, were usually small and scattered, and they had a simple social organisation. However, larger groups, with higher population densities are more

2

land-saving, as an example, compared to the former. With urbanisation, the size and density of urban population are increasing, the social organisation of such society becomes increasingly complex through the interplay of several factors, all of which seem to be related to population density. This may create or enhance social differentiation and a more centralised organisation of society either through warfare or through the appearance of a ritually sanctified social ranking. In this process, as population increases, the demand of services or goods from the finite environment grows, setting in the need for efficiency and effectiveness which can all be subsisted by technology.

Africa is rapidly urbanising though, globally, it is the least urbanised region at the moment. Chakrabarti (2001:260) asserts that, for example, "…In absolute terms, India's urban population is the second largest in the world after China's, and is almost twice the combined urban population of France, Germany, and the UK. Yet, in relative terms, India is still one of the least urbanised of the developing countries, with less than 30 percent of its population living in urban areas, compared with 80 percent in Brazil, 45 percent in Egypt, and 35 percent even in neighbouring Pakistan. But this scenario is changing fast ..." The rate of urbanisation also explains the intensity of societal problems faced. High rate of urbanisation is associated with inadequate development of attendant urban services leading to an increased environmental degradation. For example, the most urbanised societies in the developed countries have put in place measures, supported by their hi-tech industries, to deal with concentration of problems in one area. Consequently, their problems, let al.one with the environment, are getting lesser as compared to the development-trailing Africa.

The Environment

As far back as the early 1970s, Ruttan (1971:709) made this critical observation, "…We are now experiencing the effects of a rapidly rising demand for environmental services pressing against a relatively inelastic supply. The rising demand is derived from a growth in commodity production and consumption; the energy production and transportation services associated with commodity production and consumption; and a rapid growth in consumer demand for environmental amenities for direct consumption of environmental services such as freedom from pollution and congestion ..." This is real and the negative impact of the human society on the environment is now visible globally. For example, climate change effects have affected not only LDCs but also the MDCs. Gaseous emissions from industries and transportation (carbon mainly) have led to the depletion of the Ozone layer, with global warming being the immediate effect. Global warming has been punctuated with many problems

3

including rising sea level resulting from the melting of glaciers, and increased frequency and intensity of droughts, heat waves, cyclones and floods.

Camagni *et al.* (1998:106) argue that, "… In a city three different environments coexist, the physical (natural and built) environment, the economic environment and the social environment, each of them explaining in part or in combination the existence and continuity of a city. All three environments generate advantages and disadvantages for the city …" In all fairness, societies should consider all the three together because they deeply interact with one another and represent or express, at the same time, goals, means and constraints to human action in the city. At a global level, the holistic consideration of environmental issues has been the agenda of the 21st century as seen by a global ratification of the Millennium Development Goals (MDGs) and the post 2015 Sustainable Development Goals (SDGs). This was after the realisation that there has been a piecemeal approach or rather much emphasis on the economic environment. This has created known environmental problems which are even very difficult to deal with in the current development mode hence the call for sustainability.

Taking the modern city water subsystem as an example, the water stress is a growing environmental challenge begging for prudent measures in place. Pimentel *et al.* (1997:104) have concluded that, "…Water limits exist in many regions of the world even without the effects of the projected global warming. By causing changes in rainfall patterns and more rapid evaporation, global warming is likely to intensify the water crisis in many regions of the earth. Increased water stress, with or without global warming, is projected to have a negative impact on agricultural and forest production and other plant and animal species throughout the world ecosystem…" In this light, for human societies to avoid further water problems and lessen projected harsh outcomes for the future, they must conserve water and energy, and must protect land and biological resources, all of which are vital for a sustainable economy and environment. With technology, the humankind can manage water resources more efficiently in agriculture and in other activities. Conservation of water and pollution control by individuals as well as by society is essential for the protection of sustained water supply.

Building infrastructure is another city sub-system. Espinoza *et al.* (2012:32) observe that, "… Buildings are major contributors to the environmental effects of human activity; they consume about 30 percent of all raw materials, 42 percent of all energy, and 25 percent of all water claimed by human society and responsible for 40 percent of all pollution emissions …" Putting this into perspective, buildings in the Americas, for example, are the largest consumers of energy (39 percent), contribute 38 percent of the nation's total carbon dioxide emissions, and consume 12 percent of all water claimed by society (*ibid.*). This is a cause for concern where, in the interests to promote sustainable development, factors that contribute to the environmental performance of buildings like design, orientation, location, building materials, user behaviour, energy and water inputs during use, and demolition have to be redefined to reduce the carbon footprint of the same (Geng *et al.* 2012). This has motivated the emergence of the green building movement. According to the U.S. Environmental Protection Agency's (EPA), green building is "… The practice of creating structures and using processes that are environmentally responsible and resource-efficient throughout a building's life-cycle …" To enable the creation of environmentally responsible and resource-efficient buildings, green building ratings systems have been put into place in many countries worldwide to assess the environmental performance of buildings. The green building rating systems have guidelines for energy-efficient products, sustainable materials, and environmentally-friendly construction practices and promote the use of materials with recycled content. The Food and Agriculture Organisation (FAO) has identified green building practices and life cycle analysis as suitable strategies to improve the sustainability of human activity and to strengthen the profitability of the forest industry.

Technology and the Technological Question

The 21st century has been termed the information era, an attribution to technological innovations which seem to be advancing every day. To society and the environment at large, technology has advantages and disadvantages which then calls for an internal evaluation of various technological inventions to assess if they positively contribute to a sustainable society. As Wynne (2002:459) aptly asserts, "… given that technology and its instrumental culture are perhaps the pervasive issue in the attempted civilization of modernity, the idea that technology requires social assessment of some kind is hardly controversial …" He further observes that the latter half of the 20th century saw a succession of man-made technological disasters including Challenger, Bhopal, Chernobyl, BSE, and World Trade Centre among other. These branded into popular awareness an uncomfortable reality that, for all the formidable powers and benefits of modern science and technology, lack of full control is normal, including lack of intellectual control, that is, with unpredictable consequences (Chakrabarti, 2001). This same period saw many increasingly intense and persistent public controversies over new technologies, which can be seen as attempts at social assessment (Wynne, 2002). However, new technologies are critical in the face of challenges of, for example, cybercrime and cyberterrorism.

The evaluation of technology or technological innovation has been met with mixed reactions. As Jaffe *et al.* (2004:21-22) argue, "Policy experimentation would logically work hand-in-hand with systematic policy evaluation. On the ground, however, policy success is very difficult to measure, because the output or effect is often intangible, the expected benefits of technologies change with changing conditions, and the evaluation period must take place over a long time period ..." This leads some advocates of public investment in technology to resist quantitative evaluation of technology programmes because measurements of such intangible outputs will understate the benefits and hence undermine political support for such programmes (Hillier, 2008). However, it has also been observed that the danger of not even attempting to evaluate technological policies is that it can perpetuate ignorance and thereby fail to solve the problem, and consign technology policy forever to the realm of ideology (Jaffe *et al.* 2004). Rather, societies should embrace the fact that technological change is a long-term process, and ought to be willing to take a long-term view. The proponents of this view recommend that society should remain hopeful that, on the time scale of years and decades, systematic evaluation will eventually allow the creation of a solid empirical base for the design of technology policy to maximise its social returns (*ibid.*).

In other technological analysis, it can be seen that technology has negative side effects to society but has also potential to provide solution. Hillier (2008:76) observes, "...Mixed-use and high-density areas with less crime and greater traffic safety where children have access to recreation facilities promote physical activity...Media from TV to the Internet to computer games pervade their time, limiting their active and outdoor play and exposing them to messages promoting unhealthy foods .... To date, technology has contributed more to this problem than to its solution, but many technological innovations and applications hold promise for reversing this pattern. So how do researchers and public health advocates ensure that this happens?" These sentiments are also in line with other observations that the use of technology has also increased the capacity of human societies to cause harm to the environment through the use of machines, for example, forest clearance is accelerated by the invention of motorised chain saws (Espinoza *et al.* 2012). This has a negative impact on the environment since the forests act as carbon sinks with the potential to serve society from climate change. In the same vein, technology however offers opportunities which can serve humankind from the jaws of environmental change.

With respect to India, Chakrabarti (2001:260) has asserted that, "...Despite the constraints of poor urban governance, there has been some headway for adopting and propagating a few innovative, low-cost, and environmentally sustainable technologies for solving some of India's pressing urban problems..."

This has been made possible by a few individuals and organisations, and by grants from central government and soft credit from international financial institutions (*ibid.*). These sentiments are among other testimonies of the beauty of technology to the human society and the environment at large. In this regard, three major initiatives in India and world over are the techniques of low-cost sanitation, low-cost housing, and rainwater harvesting, and this has saved the Indian society by providing the basics and protected the environment through a responsible sanitation system. However, the spread of these technologies has been severely restricted in many African countries because of poor urban governance, an inefficient delivery system for extending the incentives, and the non-involvement of civil society in any meaningful manner in terms of creating awareness of the benefits and efficacy of these technologies (Hillier, 2008).

The Sustainability Dilemma

Sustainability is, and can mean the use of resources to meet the current generation's needs in a way that does not compromise future generations from getting the same benefits. The way to achieve this has been to balance economic, social and environmental concerns of this world when making development decisions. However, Giddings *et al.* (2002; 194-195) argue, "… The division of sustainable development into three separate sectors, environment, society and economy, which are only partially connected, does not produce an integrated or principle based outlook. This division reflects the common approach to the study and description of human life and the world around us, which is dominated by a multitude of separate disciplines …" In the view of Giddings *et al.* (2002), this separation has been shaped by the alienation of much of human life from the environment people live in, as well as the separation between the production and consumption of the means of life. Too many people today, goods just appear in a shop and there is little or no awareness of where they came from or how they were made. At the other end of a product's life, it disappears into another unknown black box labelled waste. The philosophy of the separation of mind and body is a fundamental conception of alienation and of separation. Technology is often seen as separate from society yet it only exists within social and cultural relationships (*ibid.*). This reinforces the need for a systems approach to sustainability.

Camagni *et al.* (1998:106) argue that, a 'sustainable city' is "… a city in which agglomeration economies should possibly be associated with positive environmental externalities and social network externalities, and in which at the same time negative effects stemming from the interaction of the three different environments are kept within certain threshold conditions associated with the urban carrying capacity on the urban environmental utilisation space …" This is true but the ways in to achieve this has been met with serious politicisation and finger pointing between the developed and developing nations with the latter blaming the former for pushing environmental sustainability to cripple the latter's prospect of achieving economic development. Schindler (2010:290) argues that, "… While the encouragement of green buildings at the local level is certainly a step in the right direction toward lessening the negative environmental impacts of buildings, ordinances that force private developers to comply with uniform standards developed by a private building-industry organisation are fraught with practical and legal problems that have not been fully explored in scholarly literature …." In the developing countries, the green buildings movement has not made significant inroads because of the cost involved in building such structures. There are contradictions as to what constitutes sustainable development signifying that it is contextually defined rather than a globally prescribed concept. This is from a realisation that the economic, social, environmental and technological resources are not uniform the world over, warranting a context defined approach to sustainable development (Espinoza *et al.* 2012).

Still on green buildings, Schindler (2010:299) argues that, "… a city, once having adopted a LEED-based green building ordinance, will falsely believe that it has sufficiently addressed its environmental concerns. In reality, this "solution" sticks a band-aid on a major wound, calls the process successful, and stops there." To avoid such a problem, Schindler suggests that if cities are going to create a green building regime based on requirements, rather than incentives, they should promulgate those requirements locally, taking into account specific local building-related and environmental concerns. Moreover, the development should take place under the auspices of public governmental bodies, not private, industry-based organisations. This points to the context definition of sustainable development. Using these methods will result in a green building requirements regime that ensures stronger protection against climate change and local environmental harms, as well as a transparent and democratic governmental process resistant to industry capture.

It has been observed with concern that sustainability bears an added burden to the developer and, in developing nations, this would mean stifling development because of resources, financial and technical constraints (Wynne, 2002; Espinoza *et al.* 2012). Governments of developing nations are always in a dilemma on how they can foster economic development at the same time promoting environmental concerns as these cannot be achieved with the level of finances and technology available (Espinoza *et al.* 2012). With this in mind, the global community through the Agenda 21 agreed that the developed world must contribute financially to the developing world and help in the transmission of technology and knowledge to these countries for effective environmentally responsible development (*ibid.*). However, the transmission has been limited and many developing countries have started politicising the whole process of sustainability.

As recommendations, Leach (2010:6) argues that meeting sustainability challenges will require taking dynamic and diverse ways of understanding and experiencing these seriously. This includes moving beyond singular views of 'the problem' and 'progress', to recognise multiple possible goals and values and their contestation. Furthermore, it is moving beyond risk to recognise and respond to wider dimensions of incomplete knowledge and moving beyond stability/control to embrace strategies that respond to ongoing change. In brief, it is moving beyond a politicised perspective on sustainability.

Situating the Concept and Debate of Sustainability in Zimbabwe

1n 2013, the Government of Zimbabwe adopted the Zimbabwe Agenda for Sustainable Socio-Economic Agenda (ZimAsset). In 2015, the world adopted the Sustainable Development Goals (SDGs). There are a plethora of documents, plans and programmes of which the catchphrase "sustainable" is the focus of description and locus of operation. There is even a "sustainable livelihoods framework" (SLF) which is a reference of many development actors when they assess context, vulnerabilities and assets in the communities and localities of their foci. The buttressing question for scholarship and policy debate becomes: How are individuals, households, firms, sectors, communities, countries and regional blocs, to name these few, planning and programming for and implementing sustainability?

Evidently, the concepts of "sustainability" and "sustainable development" have become the axioms of planning and management of development at several levels and platforms where human progress is being discussed. Literature generally points to the fuzziness and fluidity of the notions and their difficulty in implementation. Manjengwa (2007) argues that the application of the concepts is easier said than done. The documented pillars of sustainable development are people, production and planet which some scholars speak of as equity, economy and earth. The fourth pillar or anchor now added is governance of which the most important argument around its inclusion to the traditional three is that institutions that govern the processes to ensure striking a balance between the three must be in existence. Otherwise, sustainable development will not be possible without the necessary structures and processes including participation of the local and interested communities. In other words, regarding the fourth pillar of "people", their active engagement is possible if it is directed and well managed. On the same note, with respect to production, structures must be there in place to ensure that things like appropriate technology, strategies and policies are in place. Regarding the natural environment (earth or planet), monitoring mechanisms and tools must be applied but government must be responsible or must be in a position to monitor, direct and enforce these. For example, before development projects take root, it is mandatory that they must be subjected to impact assessments including environmental, social, strategic structures, institutions and protocols become the overarching referents for the effectuation of sustainable development and sustainability and making communities, developers and producers account for their actions in so far that they do not harm the environment. For example, houses or industries on wetlands in Harare is one sign that sustainability is posing as threat to social and economic development of the Zimbabwean society.

Structure of the Book

Sustainability is a crosscutting issue. The book focuses on the sustainability debate with particular reference to Zimbabwe in as far as households, firms and sectors planning, programme and implement it. The book anchors on various themes on the planning, programming, and implementation for sustainability in Zimbabwe are being sought:

- Participation of people (households) in their pursuit for sustainable livelihoods,
- Appropriate technology, tools and techniques for environmental protection and stewardship,
- Structures, institutions, policies and processes of governance and sustainability,
- Ethics, laws and indigenous technical knowledge for sustainability,
- Capacity building and education plans and programmes (formal, non-formal, informal) for sustainability,
- Population and demographic determinants, processes and outcomes for sustainability,
- Literature, media and politics and sustainability, and
- Production including (mining, farming, manufacturing, urban and housing development) and sustainability.

References

Beck, U. (1986). Risk Society and the Provident State. Chapter 1 in: Lash S, B Szerszynski and B Wynne (Eds.). *Risk, Environment and Modernity - Towards a New Ecology*, SAGE Publications: London (pp. 27-43).

Boserup, E. (1976). Environment, Population, and Technology in Primitive Societies. *Population and Development Review* 2(1) pp. 21-36.

Camagni, R., Capello, R., and Nijkamp, P. (1998). Towards sustainable city policy: an economy-environment technology nexus. *Ecological economics, 24*(1), 103-118.

Chakrabarti, P. G. D. (2001). Urban Crisis in India: New Initiatives for Sustainable Cities. *Development in Practice* 11(2/3):pp. 260-272.

Espinoza, O., Buehlmann, U., and Smith, B. (2012). Forest certification and green building standards: overview and use in the US hardwood industry. *Journal of Cleaner Production, 33*, 30-41.

Geng, Y., Dong, H., Xue, B., and Fu, J. (2012). An overview of Chinese green building standards. *Sustainable Development, 20*(3), 211-221.

Giddings, B., Hopwood, B., and O'Brien, G. (2002). Environment, economy and society: fitting them together into sustainable development. *Sustainable development, 10*(4), 187-196.

Hillier, A. (2008). Childhood Overweight and the Built Environment: Making Technology Part of the Solution rather than Part of the Problem. *Annals, AAPSS*, 615: pp.56-82.

Humphrey, C. R., Lewis, T. L., and Buttel, F. H. (2002). *Environment, Energy, and Society: A New Synthesis* Belmont, CA: Wadsworth Group.

Jaffe, A. B., Newell, R. G., and Stavins, R. N. (2004). A Tale of Two Market Failures: Technology and Environmental Policy, Harvard University and Resources for the Future: Washington, DC.

Jokinen, P., Malaska, P., and Kaivo-oja, J. (1998). The Environment In an 'Information Society' – A transition stage towards more sustainable development? *Futures* 30(6): pp. 485–498.

Leach, M. (2010). Dynamic Sustainabilities: Linking technology, environment and social justice. Seminar Presentation, CES, Surrey, 27 May 2010.

Pimentel, D. J. Houser, E., Preiss, O., White, H., Fang, L., Mesnick, T., Barsky, S., Tariche, Schreck, J., and Alpert, S. (1997). Water Resources: Agriculture, the Environment, and Society: An assessment of the status of water resources. *BioScience* 47(2): 97-106.

Ruttan, V. W. (1971). Technology and the Environment. *American Journal of Agricultural Economics* 53(5): pp. 707-717.

Schindler, S. B. (2010). Municipal Adoption of Private Green Building Standards. *Florida Law Review* 62(2): 285-350.

Wynne, B. (2002). Risk and Environment as Legitimatory Discourses of Technology: Reflexivity Inside Out? *Current Sociology* 50(3): pp. 459–477.

Chapter 2

Emerging Settlement Planning and Development Paradigms with Reference to Zimbabwe

Innocent Chirisa and Liaison Mukarwi

Summary:

This chapter is an attempt to provide a rich discussion of the new and emerging paradigms set in the sustainable development goals (SDGs), particularly Goal 11 which spells out the need for the creation of cities and human settlements that are inclusive, safe, resilient and sustainable. The chapter challenges this phraseology by asking: Is this not another rhetoricisation that should warrant some tangible results on the ground? Is Zimbabwe able to deliver? This chapter seeks to advance the argument that without context-specific definition of the terms of reference which resonate with the overarching goals of the global agenda, efforts and direction are lost and that programmes, projects and plans that are conceived and implemented without accurate understanding of the overall SDGs will fall short of expectations. For the methodology, the study engages the review of relevant literature tying up the notions of inclusivity, safety, resilience and sustainability as cornerstones for planning cities and human settlements. In addition, the study reviews statutory, policy and official reports of the Zimbabwean planning system. Data were collected by interviews, especially with the planning practitioners. The study recommends a collaborative planning approach for everyone to own the process as well as achievements that come by accomplishing the intended goals. This would assist practitioners to convert the 'abstract' into 'concrete' realities.

Introduction

One major pitfall in development practice is to do the same thing repeatedly by just putting different labels; reinventing the wheel. This can be a source of confusion, lethargy and ill-targeting. It can also create serious conflict between the thinkers, the doers and the researcher who may form, among themselves critics, heretics and loyalists all pulling into different directions at the expense of real development on the ground (Muggah 2012; Mansor *et al.* 2004). In contemporary human settlements, issues of social exclusion, informality and urban poverty, among other misdemeanours, continue to be seen despite the presence of many planning institutions and a vast literature on human settlements planning. Perhaps planners in these institutions must do introspection and answer the question: How are we planning? In answering this question, the global community have sought to address the ills of social exclusion, the incidence of poverty, insecurity, growing informality and climate change through sustainable development goals as a post 2015 agenda, that is, to guide development up to 2030. The chapter is a study on the achievement of targets set out under the Sustainable Development Goal 11 in the context of Zimbabwe (see Box 2.1). The study argues that global conventions or polices enacted without local commitment will not achieve much. This observation therefore warrants a local enquiry.

The debate in this article is based on three critical methodologies. The first is the discussion of meanings, dimensions and issues that define inclusivity, safety, resilience and sustainability in cities and human settlements. Second, the study engages document review involving a keen scrutiny of the various policy documents, statement, statutory and legislative instruments and ministerial directives that have shaped the planning of human settlements in Zimbabwe. Third, and as a matter of cross-validation of the facts garnered through the preceding methodologies, the study engages the opinions and views of various pundits (academic, research and practising planners and related personnel) on the issue at hand.

> **Box 2.1: SDG 11: Make cities and human settlements inclusive, safe, resilient and sustainable**
>
> **The targets under this Goal are:**
>
> 11.1 By 2030, ensure access for all to adequate, safe and affordable housing and basic services and upgrade slums.
>
> 11.2 By 2030, provide access to safe, affordable, accessible and sustainable transport systems for all, improving road safety, notably by expanding public transport, with special attention to the needs of those in vulnerable situations, women, children, persons with disabilities and older persons.
>
> 11.3 By 2030, enhance inclusive and sustainable urbanisation and capacity for participatory, integrated and sustainable human settlement planning and management in all countries.
>
> 11.4 Strengthen efforts to protect and safeguard the world's cultural and natural heritage.
>
> 11.5 By 2030, significantly reduce the number of deaths and the number of people affected and decrease the economic losses relative to gross domestic product caused by disasters, including water-related disasters, with a focus on protecting the poor and people in vulnerable situations.
>
> 11.6 By 2030, reduce the adverse per capita environmental impact of cities, including by paying special attention to air quality and municipal and other waste management.
>
> 11.7 By 2030, provide universal access to safe, inclusive and accessible, green and public spaces, in particular for women and children, older persons and persons with disabilities.
>
> 11.8 Support positive economic, social and environmental links between urban, peri-urban and rural areas by strengthening national and regional development planning
>
> 11.9 By 2020, increase the number of cities and human settlements adopting and implementing integrated policies and plans towards inclusion, resource efficiency, mitigation and adaptation to climate change, resilience to disasters, develop and implement, in line with the forthcoming Hyogo Framework, holistic disaster risk management at all levels.
>
> 11.10 Support least developed countries, including through financial and technical assistance, in building sustainable and resilient buildings utilizing local materials.

The chapter covers the theoretical framework, methodology, results and discussion, the conclusion and policy recommendations.

Inclusivity, Safety, Resilience and Sustainability in Cities and Human Settlements: An Overview

Inclusivity can mean social inclusion (UNHABITAT, 2009). Social inclusion is described as the practice of including all people, irrespective of race, gender, disability or other attributes which can be perceived as different. Inclusivity enables all people to participate actively in the social, political, cultural and economic life of their community. Exclusion leads to increased urban poverty (World Bank, 2007; 2008). An important observation on the costliness of urban poverty is expressed by Mcgranahan *et al.* (2016:7) who argue that informal systems are more costly to residents than those in formal systems. For example slum residents in Eldoret, Kenya, pay over five times more for water from kiosks than residents in formal urban areas pay for municipal council water. The informal settlements are usually located in urban peripheries where the cost of transport excludes them easy access to urban labour markets. Due to undesirable and precarious spaces the informal settlers often face disproportionate risks posed by environmental disasters (*ibid.*). More often they fall victim to evictions and displacements mainly due to their insecure tenure in contested urban spaces.

Globally, it has been observed that without deliberate efforts to address the questions of safety and security, the prospects of future development and poverty reduction are limited (World Bank, 2006; Muggah, 2012). In global cities, safety is the condition of being protected against physical, social, economic, and environmental consequences of failure, damage or harm. It is acknowledged that urbanisation, particularly in the developing world, has been accompanied by increased levels of crime, violence, and lawlessness. For example, it is said 60% of all urban residents in developing countries have been victims of crime at least once over the past five years, 70% of them in Latin America and Africa (UNHABITAT, 2009). The growing violence and feeling of insecurity that city dwellers are facing daily is one of the major challenges around the world. In some countries, crime and violence have been exacerbated by the proliferation of weapons, substance abuse, and youth unemployment (*ibid.*). Crime and violence impact on everyday life of residents; and women and children are often the most affected, especially when fear hinders their access to services. The impact of crime and insecurity restricts urban social and economic development, and often jeopardizes opportunities and pro-poor policies.

Goldstein (2008:1) argues that resilience is the ability or capacity for speedy return to normalcy in a more innocent time. Given that urban areas in Africa are increasingly becoming hotspots for disasters or environmental shocks like floods, the encouragement is to promote resilience. To achieve this, the residents must be collaborative to come up with their own understanding of resilience, with possible ways and means to promote the same (*ibid.*). Collective efforts are essential in soliciting best ideas, pooling of resources and accountable management of such resources given that corrupt practices are now the norm rather than exceptions (Zurawski and Czerwinski, 2008). Collaboration is effective in participatory planning and management through reconciling the winners and losers, the rulers and ruled, the wealthy and the poor, the vocal and silent majority in consensus building for resilient city futures (*ibid.*).

Collaboration can also enable committed groups to challenge dysfunctional but durable institutions. Such a capacity is especially useful during times of rapid transformation when existing governance models often fail. In Zimbabwe, most local governments are divorced from the collaborative approaches in urban management. Consequently, the local governments are desperate for resources to address the cumulative infrastructure needs of the bulging resident populations (Chirisa *et al.* 2016). The inadequacies evident in the cities, in terms of finances, infrastructure, human capital among others, indicates that the same are not resilient (*ibid.*).

Sustainability is centred on social justice, economic growth and environmental integrity. A sustainable city is defined as one that is significantly decoupled from resource exploitation and ecological impacts and is socio-economically and ecologically justifiable in the long-term (UNEP 2007). Sustainable development notions hinges on long-term visions where resources must be used giving attention to the future needs of the same. Sustainable development is achievable when programme beneficiaries continue managing the same programme activities without need for additional assistance in funding or capacity building after the aid has ceased. Thus, in order to achieve city-wide development, McGranahan *et al.* (2016:14) advocate the need for decentralisation processes to build adequate capacity of local government units to be inclusive in managing their own affairs in collaboration with central government.

Urban Safety and Security as a Concern in Developing Resilient Cities

The image of urban insecurity is haunting cities in developing countries, and this is perhaps more pronounced in major cities than the smaller and inter-mediate ones. Yi-Fu Tuan (1974) describes *topophilia* as the affective bond between people and place. Much of that is devoted to biophysical elements of place including attachment and love to certain ecosystems (Ogunseitan, 2005; Cucu *et al.* 2011, Hadfield-Hill, 2013). The bond can be on selective artefacts of architectural merit, tourist resorts and or literary narratives (O'Hare, 2007; Lew, 2011; Selby, 2004; Renz, 1992; Kerstin-Verena, 2007). A real estate development and management perspective views "value-formation" of properties as a function of human behaviour in space (Kauko, 2004). Tidball (2012) has attempted an examination of ecological conservation from human-induced disasters in environments. Other studies (Busch, 2011) have attempted to tie urban grassroots movements to the development of *topophilic* cities. Overall, places are resisted, detested and desisted because they are in a 'pathological' state or because they have become open to vices and crimes, real or perceived (Jacob, 1961; Burton,2005; Greene and Greene, 2003).

In African cities, criticism has been levelled against colonialism which divided urban spaces along racial lines, making stark divisions of the city between Africans as the underclass and whites as the dominant class (Burton, 2005). The same spatial segregations have persisted along income lines in post-colonial Africa (Muggah, 2012). Kamete (2013:2) is of the view that urban planning, though a spatial technology of domination, has failed to produce cities in southern Africa as favourable spaces to be for Africans and other races. This is perpetuated by the elitist and modernist view of the city which detests informality. Unlike in the developed world where spatial technologies, like the closed-circuit television (CCTV), have been fully embraced to enhance urban security, urban security in developing world has not been fully embraced (Zurawski and Stefan, 2008; van Nes and López, 2007). The reasons for the declining 'sense of belonging' to African cities among their dwellers are many and varied. These reasons, among others, include derelict infrastructure systems, inconsistent energy supplies, poor sanity and poor designs. The signs of lack of citizenry pride or bond to their places include increased vandalism of public property, and poor citizen support in community development, for example, non-payment of rates and fees (Abdul and Mariapan, 2009). For Gibbons (2013), vandalism of property is symptomatic of urban decay sometimes leading to the development of locally unwanted land-uses (Steelman and Carmin, 1998).

Results and Discussion

Five underlying facts emerge from the discussion. First, the statutory instruments of planning in both colonial and post-colonial Zimbabwe have been heavy-handed, rigid and a barrier to inclusivity of cities in the city. Reference in point is the Regional, Town and Country Planning Act of 1976 (revised 1996) which represents the grinding stone of any debate regarding urban, country and regional planning in the country. The preamble of the Act reads, in part,

"…provide for the planning of regions, districts and local areas with the object of conserving and improving the physical environment and in particular promoting health, safety, order, amenity, convenience and general welfare, as well as efficiency and economy in the process of development…" (RTCP Act, 1996)

No doubt the planning concerns of inclusivity, safety, resilience and sustainability are highlighted and emphasized. For example, Magwaro-Ndiweni (2011:45) observes that in managing settlements during the pre-colonial era, protecting the health and safety of people was the main objective of governance, spatial organisation and physical development. During the colonial period the prevailing ideology was that of white racial superiority such that it significantly influenced spatial planning (*ibid.*).

Inclusivity in regional and urban planning in Zimbabwe

Before independence in 1980, the colonial governments emphasised separate development (Muchadenyika, 2015). After independence, the new African majority government under the current and still ruling Zimbabwe African National Union – Patriotic Front (ZANU-PF) led by Robert Mugabe set to break this racist separatist urban development by infusing some schemes, and the repulsion of pass laws (Kamete, 2005). In the rural areas, the socialist inclined government embarked on massive rural development programmes with emphasis on infrastructure development and provision of public services like schools, hospitals, clinics and hospitals. The government also mobilised land re-distribution programmes to reduce overcrowding in the impoverished communal lands where the majority indigenous Africans had been forced to live, reduce poverty and increase agricultural productivity in efforts to improve living conditions of the rural people (*ibid.*). The growth point strategy designed for the impoverished communal lands and adopted under the purview of the Growth with Equity policy sought to stimulate economic development and a balanced development through the decentralisation of industrial development to the under-developed rural areas via massive public capital investment in growth point centres to attract private investors.

In the domain of urban planning, the government made several inroads in promoting inclusive designs. Taking note of the home ownership schemes, low income housing initiatives, housing cooperatives and slum upgrading were other efforts implemented since independence to accommodate those of the lower income strata (Chatiza, 2010). The Housing Standards Circular Number 70 of 2004 reduced tremendously the cost of construction through a downwards review of the building standards (GoZ, 2004). In response to informal settlements and to promote inclusion, the government, civil society and the concerned local authorities went on a drive to formalise such developments through slum upgrading.

There have been, however, issues of income, individual choices, and poor performance of the economy in the recent years. These have militated against efforts to ensure inclusivity of largely the poor and disenfranchised ordinary citizens in the country. The government and business sectors alike, have not been able to generate the much-needed corpus of critical resources to make this possible. In summarising some of the handicaps in creating a robust local government system, Chatiza (2010:26) presented a critical synopsis of the realities pointing out that an unrelenting culture of abusing public office, corruption and inefficiency, political patronage, financial constraints and weak civic-mindedness militate against sound and sustained positive change in local government. The capture of the powerful organs of state by the new black ruling elite and the growing comprador bourgeoisie is increasingly perpetrating the exclusion of the majority urban poor in service delivery and sources of decent livelihoods.

Consequently, the story of the urban poor in Harare and other cities throughout the country is largely one of episodic evictions, fear, and misery, unsanitary living conditions and poor living standards. Town planning standards have been castigated as very high, very elaborate, rigid and not amenable to the changed physical, and climatic conditions, irresponsive to end users with planners criticised for planning for themselves (Muchadenyika, 2015). Further, the urban planning system is inherently technocratic, robustly bureaucratised, and manifestly modernist and has not responded adequately to changes over time (Kamete, 2006). This has resulted in social exclusion since many people in the informal settlements have no access to urban services and generally incur more costs to participate in the labour market due to long distances travelled (Muchadenyika, 2015).

Safety in regional and urban planning in Zimbabwe

While the existing spatial planning legislation and policies point to the promotion of safety of inhabitants, orderliness and amenity in the use of space, the other intervening factors including corruption and non-performing economy, have created loopholes in the system (Kamete, 2013). The current economic and political situation in the country affects the achievement of safety in Zimbabwean settlements. The vulnerability of the Zimbabwean citizens owing to floods, heat waves and droughts has increased due to climate change. Though the government has been making public statements on the improvement of the same, the situation on the ground indicates a sad story. Corruption by public officials is robbing the country the much-needed financial resources to boost the safety of human settlements. Corruption, together with financial challenges, has stagnated rural or urban development as evidenced by a deterioration in the once available infrastructure due to lack of maintenance, inadequacy of the infrastructure and a near collapse of service delivery (Chatiza, 2010; Kamete, 2009, 2013). This has increased economic, environmental and social vulnerability of both rural and urban residents, hence making the settlements unsafe.

In spatial planning, the statutes provide adequately for the creation of safe settlements. For example, by providing minimum distances away from water sources or rivers, prohibiting developing on wetlands, and providing the minimum allowable building standards and the quality of the attendant services required for any settlement. However, due to the factors mentioned above, many settlements have been developed without some or all spatial planning requisites, for example, the rampant growth of slums on wetlands, open spaces and land zoned for institutional purposes. Settlements developed using the illegal means are not safe to residents as they do not observe all the planning standards. Consequently, they become hotspots for waterborne diseases, and are at risk for flooding as witnessed in Harare and Chitungwiza in the 2016/2017 summer season. Many settlements on wetlands were submerged by floods leading to losses of property, food and many other social problems. Also, settlements of slum nature breed high rates of criminality, further worsening the safety of such settlements. High risks of theft and burglary makes a settlement unsafe for human habitation.

Resilience in rural, regional and urban planning in Zimbabwe

Third, the notion of resilience as it applies to human settlements in the rural, urban and peri-urban areas of Zimbabwe is a fluid one given that a planned urban area will obviously be resilient to environmental vagaries including flooding and fire outbreaks. On the other hand, in rural areas, resilience might mean use of seed varieties that are resistant to droughts or moths which makes communities safe against vices including thefts. It may also mean, in this setting, the viability of safety nets and social protection mechanisms in the event of disasters.

The rural and urban planning regime has not been up to the task of delivering resilient cities. The dominant development control procedures in Zimbabwe have been implicated in delaying development projects, promoting high prices on properties, using archaic legislation like the RTCP Act (1976). Under similar attack are the rigid modernist structure plans instead of incremental process plans and the high building standards that the low-income earners can scarcely afford (Kamete, 2013). The issuance of permits takes long and costly, thus, instead of encouraging formal development, it is encouraging informal developments. In addition, planning standards are set are too high as compared to the social-economic conditions. Given that design standards have implications on affordability and availability, high standards have led to overcrowding and shortage of housing, which is a sign of poor urban management (*ibid.*). However, all the criticisms on development control do not necessarily mean that development control should be thrown away in a dustbin, but only highlight areas of improvement.

Sustainability in regional and urban planning in Zimbabwe

Sustainability is a multifaceted concept to achieve stability of communities through balancing the three facets of urban development, namely economy, social and environment. Sustainable settlements are a product of deliberate poverty reduction strategies, conservation of natural resources and climate change adaptation and mitigation, among other initiatives. In terms of planning, the area of sustainability in Zimbabwe is the major push by planners but there are other diverging interests to the good intent. There are several challenges which inhibit sustainable development. These include lack of political will, bad governance, lack of financial resources, lack of technical skills, and rigid policy and legal framework.

The policies or strategies aimed at addressing housing problems in Zimbabwe have been on quantity not quality which, according to Kamete (2005), is not sustainable. Sustainability also consider structural quality/durability of dwellings. A house is considered as 'durable' if it is built on developable land and has a structure permanent and enough to protect its inhabitants from extreme weather conditions. On the contrary, in most urban areas of Zimbabwe houses are being built on wetlands, near toxic waste and trunk sewer or electricity servitude to say the least. This is not sustainable. The current planning system, despite the zeal to promote sustainable urban development, cannot translate intentions to actual urban forms, as shown by continuance of urban sprawl, development on wetlands, destruction of open spaces, and increased disposal of waste on undesignated sites (sewer and solid waste). Evidently, there is need to incorporate aspects of sustainability such as upgrading, promoting and encouraging transformation in urban planning principles and practices that are realistic and in keeping with current development trends to avoid informal settlements which are known for non-compliance to building codes. Due to poor economic growth experienced in Zimbabwe over the past two decades, issues of affordability of housing has become topical. There is urgency of pro-poor housing policy strategies such as provision of on-site services by governments, differentiation of building and planning standards, cascading them across staggered income levels, and capacity building of beneficiary households to plan their neighbourhoods.

Environmental consciousness in building designs is very important to reduce carbon emissions. In Harare, the Eastgate Mall typifies green architecture and ecologically sensitive adaptation (Doan, 2012). The Eastgate Mall complex has no conventional air-conditioning or heating which translates to less energy consumption, a positive note in environmental sustainability. However, Zimbabwean government has no incentives and or sanctions to take up green buildings. USA, Malaysia and South Africa, among other countries, provide some incentives in form of grants, tax rebates and prize awards for green buildings. In terms of sanctions, the planning statutes can make it mandatory to produce green buildings, failure of which should be punishable. In other countries, the Green Building Council is a mother body that is responsible for spearheading the adoption of the green buildings.

The proverbial challenges of capacity, finance, political will and peace in Zimbabwe

The emerging paradigms on urban development and management are generally a constellation of the development efforts that have already been in place. Chakaipa (2010:68) points out that Zimbabwe has a robust local government system with institutions and sound governance structures in place. However, he is concerned that the system needs to be properly nurtured through the current challenges by a combination of legislative reforms, capacity building, institutional strengthening, and injection of financial resources (*ibid*: 68). The authorities must put in place measures or strategies to ensure quality services are delivered to communities. With respect to local government finance in Zimbabwe, Coutinho (2010:71) observes that almost all local authorities have been facing insurmountable challenges in raising sufficient funding to support efficient service delivery ever since independence in 1980. Most of these challenges revolve around a failure to ensure effective financial management systems that result in the levying of sub-economic tariffs, failure to ensure cost recovery on essential services, such as, water and sewer provision, failure to recover debts owed, lack of skilled and qualified staff due to skills flight to the private sector and to the diaspora, and generally poor financial accounting systems (*ibid.*). Ndudzo (2016), in light of the challenges mentioned, has suggested that government offices and local councils must be staffed with appropriately skilled, enthusiastic and professionally inclined people who are committed to deliver. The growth of illegal settlements must be met with provision of the necessary infrastructure and, in future, the requisite infrastructure must come ahead of the superstructures. Public private partnerships could help in this regard. There must be harmonisation of laws with the new constitution and other government policies like Zimbabwe Agenda for Socio-economic Transformation to promote institutional coherence. There must be rule of law where the land barons, corrupt people or officials must face the full wrath of the law. These groups should be made accountable, even in retrospect, for financial misconduct as defined in the Public Finance Management Act.

Progress towards implementing the SDG 11 in Zimbabwe

The general observation is that Zimbabwe, in terms of legislative and regulatory framework, is favourably positioned to achieve the global development goal (SDG11). However, much work is still needed to expedite and promote transparency and earnest implementation or crafting of support programmes and activities for sustainability. The major worry is political patronage wherein the policies or legislation amendment is done with political intents rather than genuine commitment to make cities and human settlements inclusive, safe, resilient and sustainable.

Taking for example the provision of adequate, safe and affordable housing and basic services and upgrade slums, as a target set out by the SDG 11. The new constitution, Chapter 2, Section 28 mandates the State and all institutions at every level to take reasonable legislative and other measures, within the limits of the resources available to them, to enable every person to have access to adequate shelter. Also, the government's Zimbabwe Agenda for Socio-economic Transformation set out to provide at least 300 000 housing stands by 2018. The Housing Standards Circular Number 70 of 2004 reduced the housing standards to accommodate low income households to have accommodation. At a local level, various local authorities are instituting efforts to increase the housing stock for example the City of Harare targets to service not less than 3 000 stands each year and to build not less than 1 000 housing units yearly. However, these activities tend to have political overtones where members of the ruling party are the major beneficiaries of such programmes. For attainment of these targets, there must be continued commitment by the local leadership and politicians in investment in housing, engaging in public-private partnerships for infrastructure development, reforms in the ease of doing business to attract investments, promotion of self-help housing projects and introduction of new long term funding options among other initiatives.

Moreover, the efforts in the promotion of access to safe, affordable, accessible and sustainable transport systems for all and improving road safety have been observed. The National Transport Policy of 2012 advocates for inclusive public access wherein there must be public transport to cater for people of different incomes and those with disabilities. It also calls for integrated public transport system wherein transport modes will be complementing each other (road, rail, and air) to enable people of different incomes and those living with disabilities to participate in the development of their persona and communities. At a local level, Harare has the Harare Combination Master Plan that also advocates for inclusive public transport systems. The Harare Combination Master Plan promotes inclusivity in the transport by advocating for designs that accommodate pedestrians and people with disabilities. It speaks

24

to the provision of pedestrian/cycle tracks and pedestrian malls to cater for the travelling needs of urban residents. The plan also supports public transport that is composed of high passenger vehicles like buses. However, the policies and proposal of the plan have not been implemented to the full because of financial challenges, corruption and unnecessary delays. Corruption also leads to financial shortages as resources meant for infrastructure development can be diverted to personal use. The Harare Airport Road took nearly 10 years to complete due to financial problems after the responsible authorities awarded the tender to undeserving companies.

To promote sustainable urbanisation in Zimbabwe, the government, with the support of other development agents, has made significant headways. Chapter 2 Section 79 of the constitution of Zimbabwe, states that every person has the right to an environment that is not harmful to their health or well-being, and to have the environment protected for the benefit of present and future generations. This makes it mandatory for every economic player to protect the environment on which he/she is operating from to avoid infringing other people's environmental rights. It also gives the supreme power to the Environmental Management Agency (EMA) to act on behalf of the state in the protection of the people's environmental rights. Also, in a bid to reduce the adverse per capita environmental impact of cities, the Environmental Management Act mandates all, including urban planners and managers, to protect the environment. The Environmental Impact Assessment Policy allows impacts of any development observed and measures proposed to reduce the same before commencement. This allows preventative measures to be taken on activities that damage the environment. However, environmental laws, nationally or locally are on many cases have not be observed. The non-compliance to the environmental statutes has led to environmental degradation. Pollution (water, air and land), loss of vegetation due to sprawl development, construction on wetlands and destruction of open spaces continue to be environmental malpractices committed by cities in Zimbabwe.

On governance, the constitution vests power in the people by allowing people to contribute in making decisions that affect their lives. The Constitution of Zimbabwe charges that a people centred government must prides itself in promoting equitable development and prosperity for all Zimbabweans (GoZ, 2013). In this way, all regions and their residents deserve equitable development and prosperity thus inclusive development being enshrined in the supreme law of Zimbabwe. The Urban Councils Act and the Regional Town and Country Planning Act also mandate local authorities to engage the public on any decisions in their jurisdiction; this is a clear testimony on the participatory human settlement planning and management. However, the statutory instruments have not effectively been honoured to influence or achieve the sustainability evidenced by continued construction on wetlands, growth of informal settlements unserved with attended services and sprawl development which lead to loss of biodiversity. Participation in national decision-making and local planning continue to be nominal with no real or genuine public participation. A simplified checklist of the Zimbabwean government's standing on SDG11 can be seen in Table 1.

Conclusions, policy options and practical implications

The chapter concludes that in as far as Zimbabwe ratified to work towards the SDGs, and despite the several statutes and programmes which implicitly and explicitly promote the attainment of the targets set out by the SDGs, the country is not genuinely committed to achieving the goals as shown by the sluggish implementation of the statutes. The constitution and laws such as the Urban Councils Act, Environmental Management Act and Regional Town and Country Planning Act have been mere expression of aspirations with little on the ground that shows compliance. The study therefore recommends a collaborative approach in urban development. In the collaborative approach, every citizen owns the process as well as the celebrations that come by achieving the intended goals. There should be political will and leadership commitment from the highest level to promote strong collaborative partnerships among government agencies, the private sector, citizens and other stakeholders. Human capital development programmes should be put in place enhance the acquisition of requisite skills and, above all, macroeconomic stabilization. The collaboration of various development actors is essential in bringing out best workable ideas, mobilising resources and instituting accountability in the development process. In spatial planning, there is need for such collaborations, for example, it is essential to have working relations between planners in practice and planners in the academia, or between planners in the public sector and planners in the private and voluntary sectors given that a divided house will not stand.

The study also recommends that there is need to reform urban planning to transform urban forms. The planners should resort to compact settlements. Compact settlement curb sprawling and many of the ills associated with urban development starting with loss of biodiversity loss. Compact city development reduces air pollution related to transportation as these discourage the use of automobiles by shortening distances travelled. The smart growth concepts are entrenched in the use of non-motorised transport including walking or cycling and promote the use of public transport. Promotion of green designs through policy incentives and sanctions will help improve building energy efficiency, a positive in reduction of buildings' carbon footprints, for example, the Eastgate

Shopping Mall that uses less energy hence less carbon emission. This reduces per capita environmental degradation as a result of urban growth or development.

The chapter also recommends that there is need to revisit the growth point project. The plan adopted by the government prior did not yield the expected results due to several reasons hence the need to revisit and structure this noble strategy grounding on potential basis rather than the need basis. The Zimbabwean government must engage in a comprehensive plan to incentivise development in such growth points through public private partnerships in infrastructure financing, providing financial incentives like tax holidays and import exemption as incentives for investment in the selected growth points. The initial growth point strategy had problems of suggesting the way forward without pointing to the pool of resources or at least means of generating such resources for implementation of the provision. These are gaps that need to be addressed for the success of this strategy.

Table 2.1: A Checklist for action in Zimbabwean Planning towards SDG 11

Target	Where are we now? (Policies, Statutes, Plans, Targets, Programmes, etc.)	What will take us there?
Adequate, safe and affordable housing and basic services and upgrade slums	National Level • The Zimbabwe New Constitution • National Housing Policy (2012) • Zimbabwe Agenda for Socio-economic Transformation (ZIMASSET) • Zimbabwe National Housing Delivery Programme • Housing Upgrading Programme • Housing Standards Circular Number 70 of 2004 • Urban Councils Act • Regional Town and Country Planning Act Local Level • City of Harare targets to service not less than 3 000 stands each year and to build not less than 1 000 housing units yearly. • Slum Upgrading Programme	National Level • Public-Private partnerships • Reforms in the ease of doing business to attract investments. • Promotion of self-help housing projects • Lowering of housing and planning standards • Direct government investment • Slum or informal settlements upgrading • Introduction of new long term funding options (new banks for example National Building Society by NSSA) • International financial assistance for housing development (examples from Infrastructure Development Bank of Zimbabwe, African Development Bank) Local level • Resuscitation of land servicing by local authorities like Harare. • Public-Private partnerships

		• Lowering of housing and planning standard • Slum or informal settlements upgrading
Access to safe, affordable, accessible and sustainable transport systems for all, improving road safety, notably by expanding public transport, with special attention to the needs of those in vulnerable situations, women, children, persons with disabilities and older persons	**National Level** • The Zimbabwe New Constitution (2013) • National Transport Master Plan (2016) • National transport Policy (2013) • Zimbabwe Agenda for Socio-economic Transformation (ZIMASSET) • Road Traffic Act • Statutory Instrument 129 of 2015 – the Road Traffic (Construction, Equipment and Use) Regulations. **Local Level** • Harare Combination Master Plan • City Traffic By-laws	**National Level** • Public-Private Partnerships for transport infrastructure development. • Promotion of public transport through the introduction of high passenger vehicles in cities. • Introduction of cheap airlines for example Fast-jet. • Strict and religious implementation of the Road Traffic Act for road safety. • Transport infrastructure refurbishment and expansion especially road. • Resuscitation of National railways of Zimbabwe. • International financial assistance for transport infrastructure development (examples from Infrastructure Development Bank of Zimbabwe, African Development Bank). • Adoption of Intelligent Transportation Systems (ITS) for road safety for example traffic and road conditions updates. **Local Level** • Redesign of public transport facilities to accommodate people of different abilities (Harare Combination Master Plan). • Adoption of Intelligent Transportation Systems (ITS) for road safety for example traffic and road conditions updates. • Public-Private Partnerships for transport infrastructure development. • Promotion of public transport through the introduction of high passenger vehicles in cities. • Promotion of integrated public transport system (National Transport Policy, 2012) • Promotion of sidewalks/ways, pedestrian and cycle tracks for easy access in urban areas (in the Harare Combination Master plan)

Inclusive and sustainable urbanisation and capacity for participatory, integrated and sustainable human settlement planning and management in all countries	**National Level** • The Zimbabwe New Constitution. • Zimbabwe Agenda for Socio-economic Transformation • Regional and Country Planning Act (RTCP Act). • Urban Council's Act. • Information and Communication Technology Policy (2015). • National Housing Policy (2012). • Housing Standards Circular Number 70 of 2004. **Local Level** • Participatory Budgeting • E-governance Policy (websites, online bill enquiries, Facebook pages) • Slum Upgrading Programmes	**National Level** • Devolution of power by the central government to the local authorities. • Public participation in decision-making • E-governance through the use of Information and Communication Technologies (ICTs) • Pro-poor planning initiatives like lowering of housing and planning standards and slum upgrading. **Local Level** • Decentralisation of functions to district offices by municipalities • Public consultative meetings • E-governance through the use of ICTs • Pro-poor planning initiatives like lowering of housing and planning standards and slum upgrading. • Mixed use and compact development (mixed density residential)
Protect and safeguard the world's cultural and natural heritage.	**National Level** • The Zimbabwe New Constitution • Traditional Leaders Act • National Cultural Policy • National Culture Fund • Education Amendment Act • National Museums and Monuments Act • National Archives Act • The Parks and Wildlife Act • The National Arts Council of Zimbabwe Act • The National Gallery of Zimbabwe Act • Zimbabwe Copyright Act • Zimbabwe Tourism Act • Environmental Management Act • Local Harare Control of Worship in Open Spaces (2016)	**National** • Education and promotion on indigenous language • Promotion of traditional dances and poems in schools • Abolition of immoral activities • Protection of national heritage and monument sites. • Guaranteeing freedom of expression • Capacity building and local empowerment programmes • Government financial support for cultural development **Local Level** • Provision of cultural centres in urban centres

Reduce the number of deaths and the number of people affected and decrease by [x] percent the economic losses relative to gross domestic product caused by disasters, including water-related disasters, with a focus on protecting the poor and people in vulnerable situations.	National • Zimbabwe New Constitution • Zimbabwe Agenda for Socio-economic Transformation • Civil Protection Act (Chapter 10:06) • Disaster Risk Management Policy • National Civil Protection Fund. • Meteorological Services Act [Chapter 13:21] • Awareness Programmes through the media • National Insurance Policy Local • Fire brigade drills • Ambulance and Emergency services • Disaster sensitisation programmes	National • Promoting the National Civil Protection Fund. • Awareness campaigns and risk communication. • Increased investment in disaster response and recovery equipment. • Integrating efforts of different stakeholders in disaster management. • Smooth synergies between the Meteorological Services Department and the Department of Civil Protection. • Resourcing the Meteorological Services Department for proper weather warning systems. • Resourcing, financially and technically, rural local authorities for disaster management. • Refurbishment and expansion of transport infrastructure for increased accessibility during disaster response reactions. • Strengthening insurance policies and reviewing insurance premiums to accommodate the generality. Local • Awareness campaigns and risk communication. • Increased investment in disaster response and recovery equipment. • Integration of efforts of different stakeholders in disaster management. • Refurbishment and expansion of transport infrastructure for increased accessibility during disaster response reactions.

Reduce the adverse per capita environmental impact of cities, including by paying special attention to air quality and municipal and other waste management.	National • Zimbabwe New Constitution • Environmental Management Act • Regional, Town and Country Planning Act. • Urban Councils Act. • Regional Town and Country Planning Act. • Environmental Impact Assessment Policy • National Transport Policy • Environmental Management Atmospheric Pollution Control Regulations Statutory Instrument 72 of 2009. • National Energy Policy • Atmospheric Pollution Prevention Act of 1971. • Statutory Instrument 7 of 2007 (general guide to environmental management), • Statutory Instrument 6 of 2007 (water and effluent, solid waste and industrial and mining waste) • Statutory Instrument 10 of 2007 (hazardous substances) • Statutory Instrument 12 of 2007 (hazardous substances like fuels and chemicals) Local • Harare (Protection of Marginalised Land) By-laws, 2014.	National • Promotion of ICTs in environmental management • Solid waste grading and recycling. • Strict enforcement of the EMA Act • Public awareness on environmental protection. • Promotion of renewable energy and energy efficiency in designs. • Promotion of public transport • Strict enforcement of the emission regulations for industries. • Introducing incentives for clean production and installation of pollution prevention technologies • Government investment in renewable energy sources and public transport. Local • Promotion of ICTs in environmental management • Solid waste grading and recycling. • Public awareness on environmental protection. • Promotion of renewable energy and energy efficiency in designs. • Promotion of public transport • Strict enforcement of the emission regulations for industries. • Introducing incentives for clean production and installation of pollution prevention technologies • Good urban designs like compact city development
Provide universal access to safe, inclusive and accessible, green and public spaces, in particular for women and children, older persons and persons with disabilities.	National • The Zimbabwe New Constitution • Environmental Management Act • Regional, Town and Country Planning Act. • Urban Councils Act • Statutory Instrument 7 of 2007 (general guide to environmental management), • Statutory Instrument 6 of 2007 (water	National • Promotion of good urban planning • Strict enforcement of the environmental and the built-up environment laws (Urban Councils Act, RTCP Act). • Increased investment in public infrastructure • Promotion of inclusive and affordable public transport systems • Promotion plural institutionalism in management of the open spaces

	and effluent, solid waste and industrial and mining waste) **Local** • Harare Combination Master Plan • Harare Control of Worship in Open Spaces By-laws (2016) • Harare (Protection of marginalised land) By-laws (2014).	**Local** • Inclusive urban planning and urban design • Good environmental protection • Provision of accessible open spaces • Increased investment in public infrastructure • Promotion of public security for all in open spaces. • Promotion plural institutionalism in management of the open spaces • Investing in public facilities that caters people of all abilities. • Promotion of inclusive and affordable public transport systems • Promotion of good sanitation and hygiene in urban areas.
Support positive economic, social and environmental links between urban, peri-urban and rural areas by strengthening national and regional development planning.	**National** • Zimbabwe New Constitution. • Zimbabwe Agenda for Socio-economic Transformation • Environmental Management Act. • Local Government Amendment Bill. • National Land Policy • Land Acquisition Act • Peri-urban Subdivision Policy • Transitional Development Plans **Local** • Harare Combination Master Plan of 1992. • Peri-urban Agriculture Policy	**National** • Devolution of power • Promotion of institutional pluralism • Effective regional planning • Public participation • Decentralisation • Promotion of sustainable development • Increased government investment in rural infrastructure • Capacity building in the countryside for institutional pluralism **Local** • Promotion of institutional pluralism • Effective regional planning • Public participation • Decentralisation of functions to district offices • Promotion of sustainable development • Increased investment in infrastructure

| Increase the number of cities and human settlements adopting and implementing integrated policies and plans towards inclusion, resource efficiency, mitigation and adaptation to climate change, resilience to disasters, develop and implement, in line with the forthcoming Hyogo Framework, holistic disaster risk management at all levels. | National
• Zimbabwe New Constitution
• Zimbabwe Agenda for Socio-economic Transformation
• Environmental Management Act
• Local Government Amendment Bill.
• Environmental Management Act
• Regional, Town and Country Planning Act.
• Urban Councils Act.
• Provincial Councils Act.
• Indigenisation and Black Empowerment policy.
• Civil Protection Act (Chapter 10:06)
• Disaster Risk Management Policy
• National Civil Protection Fund.
• Meteorological Services Act [Chapter 13:21]
• National Agriculture Policy.
• National Insurance Policy.
Local
• Harare Combination Master Plan of 1992.
• Peri-urban Agriculture Policy
• Disaster sensitisation programmes | National
• Devolution of power
• Promotion of institutional pluralism
• Effective regional planning
• Public participation
• Reforms in the ease of doing business to attract investments for economic growth
• Promotion of agricultural productivity through green revolution.
• Investing in disaster and risk management
• Strengthening insurance policies and reviewing insurance premiums to accommodate the generality
• Promotion of irrigation development for climate change effects in agriculture.
• Adoption of ICTs in agriculture production and weather forecasting
• Enhancing local empowerment programmes
• Promotion of the national civil protection fund for swift disaster response mechanisms.
Local
• Enhancing urban and peri-urban agriculture
• Accommodating informal business in the mainstream urban planning for economic emancipation of the people
• Investing in public infrastructure.
• Risk and disaster sensitisation programmes. |
| Support least developed countries, including through financial and technical assistance, in building sustainable and resilient buildings utilizing local materials | National
• Zimbabwe New Constitution
• Zimbabwe National Foreign Policy
• The Look East Policy | National
• Promotion of good international relations
• Normalisation of relations with the West.
• Continued participation in international conventions and groupings |

References

Audirac, I. (2005). Information Technology and Urban Form: Challenges to Smart Growth. *International Regional Science Review, 28*(2), pp119–145

Burton, A. (2005). *African Underclass: Urbanisation, Crime and Colonial Order in Dar es Salaam1919-1961.* Oxford: James Currey.

Busch, A. (2011). Whose "Sense of Place"? Topophilia, the Grassroots, and Urbanization in Austin, Texas. *American Quarterly 63*(2), 399-408.

Castillo, D. R. and Nelson, B. J. (Eds.). (2011). *Spectacle and Topophilia - Reading Early Modern and Postmodern Hispanic Cultures.* Vanderbilt: Vanderbilt University Press:

Chakaipa, S. (2010). Local government institutions and elections. In J. de Visser, N. Steytler and N. Machingauta (Eds.), *Local government reform in Zimbabwe: A policy dialogue* (pp. 31-70). Cape Town: Community Law Centre University of the Western Cape.

Chatiza, K. (2010). Can local government steer socio-economic transformation in Zimbabwe? Analysing historical trends and gazing into the future. In J. de Visser, N. Steytler and N. Machingauta (Eds.), *Local government reform in Zimbabwe: A policy dialogue* (pp. 1-30). Cape Town: Community Law Centre University of the Western Cape.

Chirisa, I., Bandauko, E., Mazhindu, E., Kwangwama, A. N. and Chikowore, D. (2016). Building resilient infrastructure in the face of climate change in African cities: Scope, potentiality and challenges. *Development Southern Africa, 33*(1), 113-127.

City of Harare. (2016). Harare Control of Worship in Open Spaces By-laws. Harare: City of Harare.

City of Harare. (2016). Harare Protection of marginalised land By-laws, 2014. Harare: City of Harare.

Coutinho, B. (2010). *Sources of local government financing.* Chapter 3 in: de Visser, J, Steytler, N, and Machingauta, N. (Eds.) Local government reform in Zimbabwe: A policy dialogue, Cape Town: Community Law Centre University of the Western Cape, 71-86.

Cucu, L. A., Ciocănea, C. M. and Onose, D. A. (2011).Distribution of Urban Green Spaces – an Indicator of Topophobia – Topophilia of Urban Residential Neighbourhoods - Case Study of 5th District of Bucharest, Romania. *Forum geografic. Studii și cercetări de geografie și protecția mediului,* 10(2), 276 – 286.

Doan, A. (2012). *Biomimicry's Cool Alternative: Eastgate Centre in Zimbabwe. Inhabitat, 29 November 2012.* Available online:
http://inhabitat.com/building-modelled-on-termites-eastgate-centre-in-zimbabwe/

Goldstein, B.E. (2008). Introduction: Crisis and Collaborative Resilience. In B.E. Goldstein (Ed.), *Collaborative Resilience: Moving through Crisis to Opportunity* (pp.1-15).

Government of Zimbabwe. (1977). Model Building Bylaws. Harare: Government Printers.

Government of Zimbabwe. (1996). Urban Council Acts [Chapter 29:15]. Harare: Government Printers.

Government of Zimbabwe. (1997). Regional, Town and Country Planning [Chapter 29:12]. Harare: Government Printers.

Government of Zimbabwe. (2002). Environmental Management Act [Chapter 20:27]. Harare: Government Printers.

Government of Zimbabwe. (2004). Housing Standards Circular Number 70. Harare: Government Printers.

Government of Zimbabwe. (2012). National Housing Policy. Harare: Government Printers.

Government of Zimbabwe. (2013). Constitution of Zimbabwe. Harare: Government Printers.

Government of Zimbabwe (2013). Zimbabwe Agenda for Socio-economic Transformation. Harare: Printflow.

Government of Zimbabwe. (2015). Information and Communication Technology Policy. Harare: Printflow.

Greene, M., and Greene. R. (2003). *Urban safety in residential areas - Global spatial impact and local self-organising processes.* Proceedings. 4th International Space Syntax Symposium London 2003. URL: http://www.spacesyntax.net/symposia-archive/SSS4/fullpapers/52Greene-Greenepaper.pdf, Accessed on 10 January 2013.

Jacobs, J. (1961). *The Death and Life of Great American Cities,* Penguin Books, Singapore.

Kamete, A. Y. (2013). Missing the point? Urban planning and the normalisation of 'pathological' spaces in southern Africa. *Transactions of the Institute of British Geographers, 38*(4), 639-651.

Kamete, A. Y. (2005). Revisiting the urban housing crisis in Zimbabwe: Some forgotten dimensions?. *Habitat International, 30*(4), 981-995.

Kauko, T. (2004). Sign value, topophilia, and the locational component in property prices. *Environment and Planning* (36), 859-878.

Kerstin-Verena, M. (2007). (De) colonization through topophilia: Marjorie Kinnan Rawlings's life and work in Florida. Accessed 10 January 2013 at http://ubm.opus.hbz-nrw.de/volltexte/2007/1293/pdf/diss.pdf.

Lew, A. A. (2011). Topophilia and Emotional Geographies in Tourism Destinations. Accessed 10 January 2013 at http://hospitality.blognotions.com/2011/12/20/tourism-topophilia-and-emotional-geographies/.

Magwaro-Ndiweni, L. (2011). Contestation in the Use of Residential Space: House Typologies and Residential Land in Bulawayo, Zimbabwe. *African Review of Economics and Finance, 3*(1), 40-56.

Mansor, S. M., Shariah, L., Billa, I., Setiawan, D., and Jabar, F. (2004). *Spatial Technology for Risk Management*. Paper prepared for the FIG Working Week 2004, Athens, Greece, May 22-27, 2004.

McGranahan, G., Schensul, D., and Singh, G. (2016). Inclusive urbanization: Can the 2030 Agenda be delivered without it? *Environment and Urbanization, 28*(1), 13-34.

Muchadenyika, D. (2015). Slum upgrading and inclusive municipal governance in Harare, Zimbabwe: New perspectives for the urban poor. *Habitat International* (48), 1-10.

Muggah, R. (2012). Researching the Urban Dilemma: Urbanization, Poverty and Violence. Accessed 10 January 2013 at http://www.issafrica.org/crimehub/siteimages/Researching-the-Urban-Dilemma-Baseline-study.pdf.

Ndudzo, E. (2016). Getting our cities to work again: *The Sunday Mail*, 12 June 2016. Available Online: http://www.sundaymail.co.zw/getting-our-cities-to-work-again/

Ogunseitan, O.A. (2005). Topophilia and the Quality of Life. *Environ Health Perspectives* 113(2): 143–148

O'Hare, D. (2007). Not another Waikiki? Mobolizing topophilia and topophobia in coastal resort areas. In, Ruan X and P. Hogben (Eds.). *Topophilia and topophobia: Reflections on twentieth-century human habitat*. London: Routledge.

Renz, D. (1992). Topophobia, topophilia: Environmental perspectives in selected writings. Accessed 13 September 2013 at summit.sfu.ca/system/files/iritems1/3691/b14223405.pdf

Ruan, X, and Hogben, P. (Eds.). (2007). *Topophilia and topophobia: Reflections on twentieth-century human habitat*. London: Routledge.

Selby, M. (2004). *Understanding Urban Tourism: Image, Culture and Experience*. New York: IB Tauris and Co Limited.

Stedman, R.C. and Ingalls, M. (2012). *Topophilia, biophilia and greening in the red zone*. In K. G. Tidball, M., and Krasny, E., (Eds.) *Greening in the red zone: disaster, resilience, and community greening*. New York: Springer.

Stedman, R.C. and MIngalls, C. (2007). Topophilia, Biophilia and Greening in the Red Zone, Draft Chapter Submitted for Consideration in KG. Tidball and ME. Krasny (Eds.), *Greening in the Red Zone: Vulnerability, Resilience, and Urgent Biophilia*. URL: www.sci-links.com/files/Stedman_and_Ingalls.docx, *Accessed on 10 January 2013*.

Steelman, T. A. and Carmin, J. (1998). Common Property, Collective Interests, and Community Opposition to Locally Unwanted Land-uses. *Society and Natural Resources, 11*(6), 485-504.

Suvorova, A. (2012). *Lahore - Topophilia of Space and Place*. Oxford: Oxford University Press.

Tidball, K.G. (2012). Urgent biophilia: human-nature interactions and biological attractions in disaster resilience. *Ecology and Society* 17(2), 16-35.

Tuan, Y. (1974). *Topophilia: A Study of Environmental Perceptions, Attitudes, and Values*. New Jersey: Prentice-Hall.

UNEP (2007). *Liveable Cities. The Benefits of Urban Environmental Planning: A Cities Alliance Study on Good Practices and Useful Tools*. Washington DC: The Cities Alliance.

United Nations Human Settlement Programme (UNHABITAT). (2009). *Planning sustainable cities: Global report on human settlements* 2009. London: Earthscam.

Van Nes, A. and López. M.J.J. (2007). *Micro-scale spatial relationships in urban studies: the relationship between private and public space and its impact on street life*. Proceedings, 6th International Space Syntax Symposium, İstanbul. Accessed 10 January 2013 at
http://www.spacesyntaxistanbul.itu.edu.tr/papers%5Clongpapers%5C023%20-%20VanNes%20Lopez.pdf.

World Bank. (2006). *World Development Report 2007: Development and the Next Generation*. Washington, D. C: World Bank.

World Bank. (2007). *Tackling the Shelter Challenge of Cities, Thinking it Through Together*. Cairo: World Bank.

World Bank. (2008). *World Development Report 2009: Reshaping Economic Geography*. Washington, D. C: World Bank.

Zurawski, N., and Czerwinski, S. (2008). Crime, Maps and Meaning: Views from a Survey on Safety and CCTV in Germany. *Surveillance and Society 5(1)*: 51-72.
Government Publications and Sources

Chapter 3

Ecological Footprint Analysis for Gletwyn, Chishawasha Hills, Harare

Timothy Mawere

Summary:

This study examines the adoption of the ecological footprint analysis (EFA) as a planning tool to effect sustainable urban development entailing development and resource consumption within nature's reproductive capacity. It also focuses on the effects of new residential developments on landscape ecological processes in urbanising conservation areas through a case study of Gletwyn, Chishawasha Hills in Harare. The ecological footprint measures if a country, region, or the neighbourhood is living within its ecological means. This chapter examines Gletwyn's ecological footprint in relation to its bio capacity. It also examines some of the challenges and opportunities Zimbabwe faces in decreasing its ecological footprint intensity to strengthen its ecological security and reduce risks in a world facing ever growing pressure on natural resources. Reflecting the growing influence and occurrence of Gletwyn and related emerging developments in an increasingly interconnected system, Chapter 3 of the report further highlights the role that ought to be played by Gletwyn in helping sustain the country's environment. This chapter further develops the methods and data from the "Report on Ecological Footprint in Gletwyn" published in 2008 (which used data from 2003). The current edition is based on 2015 data for Gletwyn.

Introduction

The world today is resource constrained and many nations are living beyond their means. As of 2008, uncurbed urbanisation has been increasing at an alarming rate creating adverse effects along the way the world over (Clancy, 2008). Urban sprawl has emerged thus, and has seen the total bio capacity of the planet being excessively exploited to support humanity's ever growing resources demand. This exceeds the planet's capability to rejuvenate resources and absorb the wastes we produce resulting in an ecological footprint [18.2 billion Gha, equivalent to 2.7 gha per capita hence an overshoot] (Global Footprint Network, 2012). The overshoot of approximately 50% means that in 2008 alone an equivalent of 1.5 earths was used to support our consumption

(Using time, it would have taken at least one and half years for the earth to regenerate the waste produced by people). Civilization's demand on the world's living resources has more than doubled since 1961 and now overshoots the planet regenerative capacity by about 50% (Kitzes, 2009). Africa is not yet in bio capacity deficit as its ecological footprint exceeds available bio capacity (Africa Development Bank, 2012). However, this may not be true for all African nations and cities. Continuing with the current consumption patterns and rate of urbanisation will lead it into deficit within a generation if not accounted for. Africa had an ecological surplus in 1996 of 0.40 area units per person (a footprint of 1.33 units and an available biological capacity of 1.73 area units) (WWF, 2006). The ecological footprint of all African countries increased by 240% between 1961 and 2008 as a product of mounting populations, unsustainable planning practices as well as increased per capita consumption in a minority of countries.

People depend on ecosystem products such as water, trees and air, the ability to absorb waste together with space to host urban development and infrastructure (WWF, 2006). The earth provides all citizens' needs for survival, but the critical issue is what it will take for humanity to live within the means of one planet with who using which resources and with what resultant consequences. There is necessity to make ecological limits central to the day-to-day planning and decision-making of urban areas in Zimbabwe, individuals, households, neighbourhoods, LPAs and different institutions as well. Urban sprawl both in low and high- density suburbs is rife in Harare, advocating for the adoption of principles such as new urbanism to curb and control urban sprawl. However, to achieve this, a tool to measure the current state of sustainability of our urban practices is required. This chapter seeks to apply the ecological footprint analysis as a tool that may assist in measuring and recommending on new urban developments' and practices' ecological impacts and consumption patterns in relation to the capacity of the ecosystem to sustain and support those patterns.

This study seeks to assess how the concept of ecological footprint analysis may be adopted and applied in new urban developments as a planning tool to measure the sustainability of urban practice. The specific objectives of the study are to:

1) explore the usefulness of the ecological footprint analysis tool to planners, administrators, and community residents;

2) assess the spatial and temporal land-use changes in Gletwyn from 2005 to 2015;

3) estimate the ecological footprints of individuals, households, and neighbourhood;

4) describe ecological footprint as a tool for developing sustainability, discuss its rationality and to review its intellectual context;

5) propose measures to minimise footprints/overshoot within neighbourhood areas.

Theoretical framework

This section's main aim is to discuss the theoretical underpinnings of ecological footprint and the possible human urban related developments associated with overshoot. The ecological footprint analysis (EFA) tool developed by Rees and Wackernagel in 1990 (Global Footprint Network, 2012; 2) forms the theoretical framework of this research. It is a tool formulated for the purposes of identifying bio-sphere demand of people versus the ability of the ecology to support that demand, regenerating the resultant wastes as well (Rees and Wackernagel, 1994). The EFA tool, from a bio-sphere perspective, informs human activity from recognition that human activities one way or the other depend on the bio-capacity. The major driving force behind the EFA is that the bio-sphere is limited and does not replicate exponentially as the human activities does and its draw down reduces its productive capacity (Folke *et al.* 1994; 5). Consumption under EFA is divided into five land-uses or categories namely food, housing, transportation, consumer goods, and services (Lenzen and Murray, 2003). Eight categories of land are forwarded, namely energy land, built land, gardens, cropland, pastures, forests, and land of limited availability, which is considered to be untouched forests and non-productive areas. The non-productive areas are not included nor talked about further for the purpose of this research. The ecological footprint is calculated by compiling a matrix in which a land area is allocated to each consumption category. In order to calculate the per-capita ecological footprint, all land areas are added up, and then divided by the population, giving a result in hectares per capita. For example, the land that was needed in 1991 to support the lifestyle of an average Canadian was calculated by Wackernagel and Rees (1995: 83) to be 2.34 ha energy land, 0.2 ha degraded land, 0.02 ha garden, 0.66 ha crop land, 0.46 ha pasture, and 0.59 ha forest, giving a total ecological footprint of 4.27 ha per capita. The total ecological footprint for a population may also be subtracted from the productive area that population inhabits. If this gives a positive number, it is taken to indicate an ecological remainder, or remaining ecological capacity for that population. A negative figure indicates that the population has an ecological deficit.

Land-use and land cover are at the core of urban ecosystem change. Alberti (2009) outlines that land cover and land must be handled as discrete components only linked and bound by combined human-biophysical procedures. The insufficiable human demand on land resources compels changes in land-use and these involve conversion and alteration (Riebsame *et al.* 1994). Alberti (2009) describes conversion as the change intended or unintended from a certain state of land-use to another, with land modification being the change of state within the same land-use type. This chapter, however, is concerned mostly with land conversion from farmland to residential.

Land development behaviours, dynamic models, physical dynamics and hierarchical organisation are the four relevant points of note discussed by Alberti (2009). However, only two of the four are of importance to this chapter. These are land development and ecosystem processes. In most cases, as argued by Erle and Pontius (2007), most studies that focus on land cover/land-use changes usually do not embrace the use of computer-aided programmes such as Google Earth, Google Maps and GIS. Such tools/programmes, if well manipulated, can aid in resource management and planning hence reducing overshoot and footprint. However, spatial planners in Zimbabwe are lagging behind in embracing these tools (Booth *et al.* 2004; Carter *et al.* 2009). Rapid unchecked urbanisation, as argued by Mohan (2005), is the major contributor towards land-use/ land cover changes, ecology loss and fragmentation.

Ecological footprint accounts are comprehensive, credible, conservative, concise and flexible in their findings providing key advantages to policymakers if adopted (Redefining Progress, 2002). The EFA tool may be used to inform policy by examining to what extent does Gletwyn use more (or less) than is available within its territory, or to what extent the neighbourhood's lifestyle would be replicable citywide or nationwide. The ecological footprint answers significant questions in more than just one specific way. For instance, it answers the question: Which activities are occupying or in need of how much of the biosphere's regenerative capacity? (Redefining Progress, 2002). The EFA, as a tool, allows policy makers to make holistic decisions from a systems approach view. The EFA may help policy makers and implementers to analyse the compound effect of resource consumption pressures related to the ecology and urbanisation. Derivatives from EFA calculations are useful to planners as they help compare humans 'demand on the ecology to the earth's regenerative capacity hence informing sustainability.

In 1992, the Earth Summit took place in Rio de Janeiro Brazil (Redefining Progress, 2002). It is at this conference where the United Nations raised the idea of nations embracing the concept of sustainability. The driving force behind sustainability is ensuring that the current generations live well within their means using what nature may support without compromising future generations. However, sensible and appealing this idea may be, there have been no reliable and comprehensive methods to evaluate progress towards this goal (Redefining Progress, 2002). The introduction of the EFA largely came because of a lacking tool to measure sustainability (Wackernagel and Rees, 1996). Redefining Success (2002) describes the EFA tool as a panacea for developing the sustainability call because it utilises available data sets to unpack, simplify and communicate the vague concept of sustainability into a measurable goal (Redefining Progress, 2002). Governments are fast realising that the contemporary advances, especially in economic prosperity, require complementary contemporary urban planning tools for measuring it. For instance, to measure economic growth and the performance of economies, the EFA may be one 21st century planning tool to facilitate the drive towards sustainability in an ever-changing 21st century context.

It will be of no use and relevance to only discuss and depict the human actions culminating to ecological footprint without being able to recommend on how to minimise it. Lawrence *et al.* (1998: 12) suggests the adoption of the eco-efficiency approach which is largely being promoted by the World Business Council for Sustainable Development and the UN Environment Cleaner Production Programme to minimise the ecological footprint of neighbourhoods and cities. Eco-efficiency, as a strategy, advocates for both financial and ecological productivity. This is whereby monetarily, there will be consumption of less assets and delivering less waste mean sparing dollars, and producing benefits. Ecologically, which as reiterated by this exploration, this involves less waste and less assets inside our methods and securing nature by rationing non-renewable characteristic assets and making less contamination (Lawrence *et al.* 1998). Eco-efficiency advocates for thinking not only about preventing imminent pollution reaching the environment once it has been produced but also about rather creating less waste from start to finish. This then calls for revisiting our production processes in different sectors, from the moment raw materials are keyed in and extracted from the land up to the disposal of the final product. This will go a long way even in minimising the waste produced during the life cycle of the product such as packaging.

At the centre of our day-to-day lives and practice, technological advancements must be of paramount importance. Making technology more efficient will play a pivotal role in making society take a closer step towards attaining sustainable development and consumption (Lawrence *et al.* 1998). Technology, however, must be closely regulated. If technology is to profit us, our efforts need to go far beyond technological innovation. A good example is technological innovations in cars which gave people more kilometres per litre of fuel and lower emissions, but we have since replaced and responded to these improvements by driving more kilometres each day and year and even a sharp increase in motorists and car ownership (Wackernagel, 1998). For example, Harare's carbon footprint is largely from the driving populations which drive to work, shopping, churches, schools from distant residential suburbs such as

Gletwyn, Borrowdale Brooke and Glen Lorne. To make matters worse, most of the rich driving population in Harare are in a sort of habit of driving new, highly fashionable four-wheel drive vehicles for city driving, vehicles that are markedly less efficient than sedans (Lawrence *et al.* 1998). The transition to sustainable urban practice and ending overshoot will mean making different choices.

Recycle, reuse and reduce are the three R's related to consumption patterns advocated for by the eco-efficiency concept to try and minimise overshot (Lawrence *et al.* 1998). Lawrence *et al.* (1998), argue that the same way people contemplate about their health and bank accounts should be the same way in which consumers can start contemplating on their consumption patterns on the environment, legal, and health concerns in their day-to-day decision-making. At the end of it all, the ecolabels from the research to inform the citizens and public must eventually lead to questions like: Can one take the bus/train or the car, use a plastic bag or a string bag, heat the house with a cleaner renewable energy like solar and natural gas or use oil and electricity? A cost benefit analysis, as in economics, is largely required when it comes to humanity urban practices in relation to costs to the environment measured in footprints providing a complete picture by profiling for the natural capital component (Lawrence *et al.* 1998). Civilisation still has choices to make concerning the future; to live in a reasonably large human society sustainably or to risk flop of ecosystems and our populations followed by a sequence existence in an impaired environment.

An urban ecosystem may be defined as a composite of the natural environment, the built environment and the socio-economic environment (Clark, 2009). Urban ecosystems are not separate entities as they have direct and indirect impacts on immediate and wider (global to local) environments hence planners must note. The ecological footprint analysis underpins that because of the massive increase in per capita energy, material and resource uptake required mostly by technology, ever increasing rates of urbanisation, and population growth rates, the ecological locations of cities, and new neighbourhoods that no longer coincide with their geographic locations (Rees, 1996). In most twenty first neighbourhoods, cities and new industrial regions such as Gletwyn and Sandton, there is an alarming emerging trend of a dependency syndrome for their survival and growth on the urban fringe and hinterland. However, they resort to depending on the ecologically productive global hinterland, if the urban fringe hinterland is not accessible (Rees, 1996).

Rees (1996) points out a reality that sustainability cannot be attained independently as no household, neighbourhood, city or nation can attain sustainability on its own. Regardless of the fragility of urban land-use and environmental policies to ecological concerns, the sustainability of the countryside and hinterland neighbourhoods must be a prerequisite of urban sustainability (Rees, 1996). Increase in resource demand resulting from rapid population growth mostly because of mass rural-urban migration has turned urban regions into nodes of intense consumption. The wealthier the neighbourhood and the more connected it is to the rest of the city, nation and world at large, the greater the entropic load it is able to impose on the bio-sphere through trade and other forms of economic leverage. However, most biophysical resources and life-support services are produced outside the cities, in the areas that are again being exploited through the emergence of new residential suburbs such as Gletwyn, which can be described as sprawling in nature. Seen in this light, and contrary to popular understanding, the seeming depopulation of many rural areas does not necessarily mean the latter are being abandoned in any functional sense. While most of the people may have moved elsewhere, rural lands and ecosystem functions are being exploited more intensely than ever in the service of newly urbanized populations. Indeed, while the countryside could sustain themselves without the city, it is difficult to have a city without the countryside.

Methodology

This section discusses the methodologies used to address the aim and objectives of the chapter, as well as analysing the data. It dwells on the research design aspect and approaches to the research. Data collection methods, tools, research paradigms, ethical considerations and methods used, are discussed in this section. This chapter was based on a mixed methods research paradigm. Mixed methods research adopted entailed dialectical logicality whereby methods specifically for the Gletwyn community in specific context were used. Combining quantitative (mostly from Gletwyn) and qualitative (mostly from interviews with key informants) research study helped the chapter to be objective and subjective at the same time resulting in the best of results. The main emphasis of this chapter aimed at provision of subjective insider and objective outsider viewpoints, presentation and integration of multiple dimensions and perspectives. Only 60 questionnaires were administered and 15 key informants interviewed rather than a survey of the whole Gletwyn population. Twenty-five (25) key informants were drawn from the spatial planning field. In Gletwyn, 100 questionnaires were distributed using stratified random sampling for the residents in order to derive their consumption patterns and lifestyles. ZIMSTATS was used for the population and development trends, City of Harare for their views and relevant information on sprawl and the currently practised planning, the Gletwyn Park developer and other relevant stakeholders. Purposive sampling was used to identify specific knowledgeable urban planning and environment stakeholders in local planning authorities, professional consultants and practitioners, the developer, beneficiaries of the accounts to be derived mostly residents of Gletwyn. The questionnaire survey, key informant interviews, field observations are among the instruments that were used. In assessing the spatial and temporal land-use/land cover changes of Gletwyn from 2000 to 2015, aerial photos as well as maps were acquired from Google Earth and the surveyor general. These were scanned, geo-referenced and analysed using Google Earth and Geographic Information System (GIS). On screen digitising was conducted on geo-referenced aerial photos so as to classify the study area into built-up land, forest land and bare ground. Microsoft office excel was then used to produce bar graphs after the statistics had been entered. Statistical data were analysed using matching spreadsheet packages such as those presented in the article Calculation Methodology for the National Footprint Accounts (2010 Edition), and MS Excel, graphic presentations, mathematical graphs were viewed to be suitable. Model systems and software such as Statistical Package for the Social Sciences (SPSS) were also used accordingly where they were required. For text data, it was analysed largely using tables and graphic presentations, synthesising the data making it more meaningful and easier to understand.

Results and discussion

Usefulness of the ecological footprint analysis tool to planners and community residents

The first objective of this chapter is to assess the usefulness of the ecological footprint analysis as a planning tool to planners, administrators, and community activists and residents. The major units of analysis are mainly derived from the key informants and respondents. Planning instruments and tools largely have a relationship with the perception attached to it by the policy makers, users and formulators, for instance, if they develop a negative attitude towards a certain tool it will be slowly implemented, if at all. As the interviews confirmed, if adopted as a planning tool, the EFA may provide various features that makes it attractive and assert its potential as a tool for planning towards sustainability. However, if the EFA is to be effective in the Zimbabwean context, are clearly some aspects of the tool requiring further development and contextualisation. This was proposed by interview participants. The major concern raised was that the EFA tool is not yet central to practitioners' everyday decision-making. Potential users in particular still lack sufficient examples and calculation procedures. Communication is therefore critical for establishing confidence into the model to make the tool considerations and implications more accessible to the public. An example can be derived from the way EIAs at first were being conducted in Zimbabwe. They were only applicable to certain projects and were initially regarded as a luxury one could afford to forego. With time, however,

EIAs evolved into becoming a necessity for every development which has an impact on the environment. The EFA, hence, may perhaps be adopted into the day-to-day operations of planners, individuals and decision makers, and not viewed as a luxury.

The EFA tool translates global ecological constraints to the local scale, demonstrating the need for planners to adopt appropriate local socio-economic adjustments. As derived from the Environmental Management Agency (EMA) the carrying capacity in Harare is being surpassed by land-uses, and ecological productivity has become a limiting factor for aggregate human activity. EMA further highlights that, if adopted, the EFA may be useful to Zimbabwean practitioners as in Canada whereby it may be used to show that the carrying capacity appropriated by one person, group or neighbourhood like Gletwyn diminishes the carrying capacity that may be appropriated by other people. In short, human uses of nature compete against each other, and to planners, this has implications for global development strategies. To both planners and administrators, the EFA is useful and essential as it links social and ecological concerns raised in the sustainability debate. From the study, it was derived that the tool clearly illustrates how competing uses of nature may translate into social conflicts and how conventional economic development strategies are at odds with preserving ecological integrity, thereby compromising future wellbeing. The EFA then becomes a tool to visualise these conflicts and provides a framework for alternate approaches to development which interrelates to the goal of living within neighbourhood/city, and country/global carrying capacity. From the interviews with key informants, it was revealed that the tool may aid politicians in making political decisions as it offers a relatively simple, transparent approach for comparing sustainability impacts of human activities just like how the Gross Domestic Product is used in economics. This may be achieved or done either on municipal level or rather national level. By raising ethical questions such as how much of my share am I using, and translating them into concrete terms, the EFA could make the trade-offs decisions more visible. For instance, it might assist developing nations like Zimbabwe when making consumer choices from the community or household scale up to the global scale and in their negotiation for more ecological space, and the relaxation of misinformed legislations which might inhibit development.

For Zimbabwean spatial planners who for long have been lacking futuristic oriented tools, a key informant from the Department of Physical Planning (DPP) pointed out that the EFA comes in as an essential heuristic tool. This is whereby the tool is built on present knowledge, stimulating future oriented thinking and action oriented planning. The tool at first seemed too abstract to some informants but after explanation the interviewees appreciated that it rather deals with generalisations. If adopted, it may also help planners to sharpen the debate between conflicting assumptions and beliefs around such issues as decoupling, ecological efficiency, growth management and impact assessments. From the conducted interviews, it is clear that the EFA, if adopted, has the potential to aid and improve the cross-paradigm communication between planners and society. This is because the EFA provides the imagery about the impacts of people's individual decisions without necessarily confronting the individual; rather than pointing fingers it shows the connectedness of life and the human dependence on nature. The EFA, as a tool, respects the reluctance and anxiety of people to accept sustainability challenges by providing a non-threatening communication tool. By addressing all these aspects, the EFA tool ties together multiple facets of the sustainability crisis rather than fragmenting it into separate issues. This inherent holism most likely enhances the effectiveness of the tool for planning towards sustainability.

Gletwyn Land-use Changes from 2000 to 2015

2005	2014

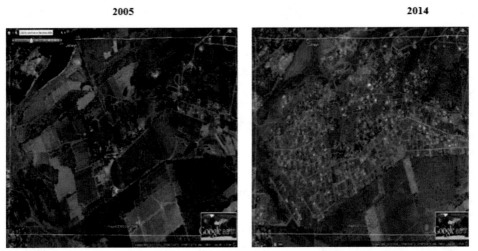

Figure 3.1: Gletwyn Spatiotemporal Land-use/Cover in 2000-2014 Source: Google Earth

Objective 2 of this research entailed assessing the spatial and sequential land-use/land cover variations in Gletwyn from 2000 to 2015. Three key land cover classes were analysed and these are cropland, forestland and built-up area. Figure 3.1 above illustrates the results from the Google Earth and Computer Aided Design (CAD) based analysis. The key result area is that the built-up area in Gletwyn covered at least 10% in 2000 and shot alarmingly to 75% in 2015, sparse forestland was 50%, while bare ground was 22% as of 2000 (see Figure 3.1). This gives support to the claims made in the literature review and introduction that unchecked population growth is culminating into the loss of vegetation and forest cover. The 41% decrease in forest area and 21% decrease in crop/pasture land can largely be attributed to development and conversion of Gletwyn from farmland to residential land. This conversion came along with increase in population, and with the people also requiring social and economic services. In 2005, infrastructure in Gletwyn only constituted 10%, which was largely in the form of farm-buildings. Ten years later in 2014 infrastructure levels leap-frogged to an astonishing 75%, recording a 65% increase in infrastructure. A decade and half later from 2000, by keeping the land cover classes constant, the results for the same study area indicates that there is a significant increase of built up area to 25%, bare ground to 12% and a general decrease in sparse woodland to 63% (see Figure 2). This, by far, is unsustainable as per World Wildlife Fund (WWF) standards whereby a conversion of 20% is allowable in 10years. Unless something is done and developments continue to emerge at this rate, soon one planet will not be enough for all of us.

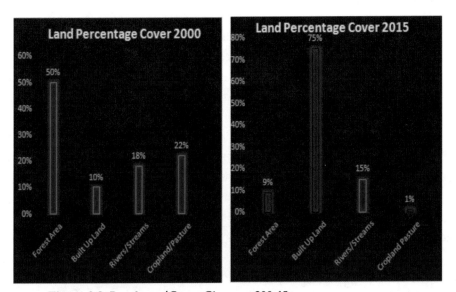

Figure 3.2: Land-use/Cover Changes 200-15
Source: Research Findings 2015

Figure 3.3, illustrates some amalgamated results for the decade under study. For example, there was a substantial tremendous increase of built up area by 65%, from 10% in 2000 to 75% in 2015. Crop land decreased by 9% from 3% in 2000 to 12% as of 2015, and forestland showed a marked general decrease by 41% from 50% in 2000 to 9% as of 2015.

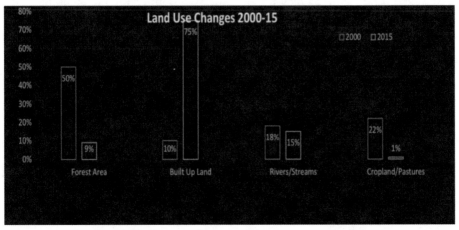

Figure 3: Amalgamated Results: Land-use/Cover Changes 2000-2015
Source: Research Findings: 2015

These findings indicate that, in relation to spatiotemporal land-use land cover dynamic forces, there is tremendous growth in terms of the built-up space in Gletwyn in relation to the past land cover. This is a true picture of all new developments whereby there is a manifestation and upsurge in the spatial magnitude and development density in the area. Main land-uses dominant in this growth are housing and accompanying ancillary services which constitute the built-up area such as roads and pavements creating hard impervious surfaces and other infrastructure developments. What may be deduced from this is that the average rate of landscape alteration is too high and future projections of this trend points to a significant loss in vegetation cover. Unless measures are taken to curtail this trend, Gletwyn's loss of its lungs for the city character is inevitable.

Ecological Footprints of Gletwyn Individuals and Households

Gletwyn is sparsely populated in relation to its geographic area. Equating this to its resource consumption and constitution of residents, Gletwyn is one of Zimbabwe's wealthiest high spending neighbourhoods. Gletwyn residents by far, are consuming resources at a faster rate than nature can regenerate. As of the time of this research, to support the demands of Gletwyn's population, an average of 23.08gha was required and this included 10.5 hectares for carbon dioxide assimilation from automobiles alone. Thus, the per capita ecological footprint of a Gletwyn resident is almost fifteen times their "fair Earth-share" of 1.5 hectares. As shown in Figure 3.4, from a sample size of thirty households the ecological footprint of Gletwyn was calculated and estimated, recording an alarming 23.08gha/household, a footprint far above the world average of 2.7gha. Zimbabwe's average ecological footprint currently stands at

1.25gha/person. The ecological footprint of Gletwyn being far above the world and country's averages means that Gletwyn residents and community are using way in excess of their share or what nature may provide. This can be attributed to their lifestyles and consumption patterns because the residents are largely wealthy.

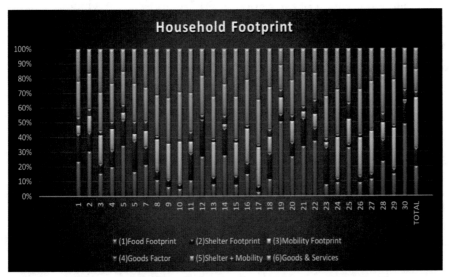

Figure 4: Consolidated Ecological Footprints of Gletwyn Households
Source: Fieldwork 2015

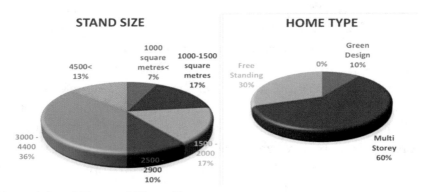

Figure 5: Stand Sizes and Home Types
Source: Fieldwork 2015

From the findings, it was established that shelter and mobility footprints combined and produced the highest value of footprints as illustrated in Figure 3.4 above. Shelter footprint entailed the stand size, house type, energy efficiency and the number of people living within one household, with the mobility footprint dealing largely with the car ownership and travel, fuel type and amount used public transit and distances travelled and air travel respectively.

51

The above illustration (Figure 3.5), is showing the different stand sizes and home types found within Gletwyn. In terms of stand sizes, there is evidence of land usage and wastage as residents are taking up huge pieces of land for residential development. From the area sampled, 60% of the home types are multi-storey. This, if not analysed properly, can entail vertical expansion which is sustainable. It is, however, observed from the survey that it is the stand sizes that are unsustainable. Much of the stand is used for landscaping which is usually for self- appeasement. For instance, one stand owner even went to the extent of installing an artificial lake within his +4500square meter stand, a feat exacting the ecological footprint with huge percentages. Of the sampled population, only 10% had green design homes which have designs minimising energy usage hence footprint such as solar passive designs/wind powered homes and lighting a well.

Ecological footprint as a tool for developing sustainability

From the interviews, it was found out that not only can the EFA stimulate lively discussion on the issue of sustainability and its barriers in Zimbabwe, but it also managed to reveal the key informants' attitude towards the topic and their perceptions as well in relation to decisions and strategies to attain sustainability. Using the ecological footprint as a tool for developing sustainability is informative as the EFA informs households, municipalities and nations at large of the acts, consumption patterns, development patterns which must be avoided if we are to achieve sustainability. From the study, it was established that in order to attain sustainability, wealthier neighbourhoods such as Gletwyn and wealthier industrialized nations have to cut their consumption lifestyles. If adopted, the EFA as a tool is very essential in informing how sustainable our development patterns and lifestyles are. From the study, it is evident that, although there is so much gospel on sustainability and sustainable development today, society still seems to be ignorant of that as the subject seems too abstract to them. However, the EFA brings a viewpoint whereby the sustainability responsibility is brought to the doorstep and lifestyle of an individual hence demystifying it and making it more understandable even to a layman.

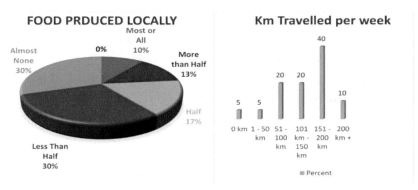

Figure 6: Household Produced Food and Mileage/Individual/Week
Source: Fieldwork: 2015

Figure 3.6 above shows the amount of food locally produced in Gletwyn and the distance travelled by an average resident of Gletwyn to acquire varying services. Trends shown in Figure 6 above indicates an intensifying impact on the environment whereby by locally producing food, the grown crops can act as carbon sinks and breathing lungs of the neighbourhood hence diffusing the different emissions. By locally producing food, it also means cutting on the distance travelled to supermarkets and markets hence reducing a substantive amount of the carbon and mobility footprint.

From the study, it may be deduced that urban development related land-use changes are becoming the norm unsustainable as they are. It was also revealed that using the EFA may indeed inform lifestyles, and policy on how sustainable current human activities are and what it would take, not only for the Gletwyn residents to reduce their footprint and live/develop sustainably within the confines of what the ecology may support, but rather the city and nation as a whole. The following section seeks to give the key lessons derived from the study and propose recommendations informing policy.

Conclusion

The main aim of this chapter was to assess how the concept of ecological footprint analysis can be adopted and applied as a planning tool to measure and check on sustainability of new urban residential developments. This entailed analysing the perceptions of all stakeholders involved, tracking the land cover changes over the recent years and calculation of households' footprints. Perceptions of residents, planners, administrators, community activists and environmental specialists were analysed, revealing their willingness to accept the EFA as a planning tool. However, it emerged from the study that stakeholder engagement and educating still needs to be done to effectively communicate the tool. The land-use cover changes from 2005 to 2015 were also traced and analysed, revealing the largely unsustainable spatial changes in Gletwyn.

Seven critical aspects from which crucial lessons and conclusions were established emerged from the study. First, unchecked rapid urbanisation and population growth are the major drivers towards land-use changes. These create the need for resources to support this ever growing and expanding urban population, especially for housing and infrastructure development, putting pressure on the ever-shrinking ecology. Second, planners within local authorities and government administrators in Zimbabwe acknowledge the need for adopting sustainability check tools such as the EFA in the quest to attain sustainability. However, in the current Zimbabwean context, they feel that time is still needed to embrace the EFA as they still have a lot of issues on their plates to deal with such as the erratic service delivery system, harsh economy and mismatching legislation. Tools such as the EIA are taking longer to be embraced hence a new tool might prove too much to handle if not appropriately embraced. This group of planners and administrators still view sustainability as a luxury which may be sought after when all the issues have been dealt with. Environmentalists, community activists, and planners in consultancy and private sector, unlike their counterparts in government, feel that sustainability is a priority as prevention is much more effective than restoration.

The fourth critical aspect drawn is that achieving the common goal of sustainable development requires public support and participatory planning. However, there is little evidence that currently the general residents understand the sustainability crisis. Most people are aware of the challenges but a few understand the implications and connections between their actions and the impact they have on nature. Stakeholder collaboration is key to planning as a step towards attaining sustainable urban development. Before every new development, it is best to have the input of environmental specialists, community activists, planning experts, economists, politicians and the targeted residents themselves. Economic motives and opportunities such as profiting from land sales for development are forcing all levels of decision-making to be profit oriented hence choosing unsustainable development options which are financially lucrative and attractive today but catastrophic in the near future. Developers think every piece of land has to be maximised on, every development option has to be seized hence leading to the alarming rate of land-use/cover changes. Lastly, the sixth objective of the research was to propose means to reduce overshoot. From the research, it was observed that a cut in resource consumption and a downward change in lifestyle is only acceptable to the public if it brings identifiable benefits otherwise it will face stiff rejection.

Recommendations

From the chapter objectives and conclusions outlined in the preceding section, the recommendations are in two categories. Recommendations are at the strategic and the operational levels. This in the form of recommendations to better communicate the EFA as planning tool towards attaining sustainable development and measures to minimise the overshoot in neighbourhood areas and respectively. At the strategic level, the EFA is still new a concept. There is therefore need for it to be effectively communicated to the different stakeholders (planners, environmentalists and general citizenry). Local authorities and government through its ministries must make initiatives to educate people on the methodology, limitations, assumptions and benefits of the EFA as a tool to check and inform on how sustainable our actions are. This may be achieved through organising seminars, workshops and even including EFA education in school curricular as in other nations such as Canada which took the same course. Methodologically, if local authorities and planners are to adopt the EFA, improvements and modifications will have to be made to the tool. This is to make it suit the local Zimbabwean context and make it as robust as other widely accepted indicators such as the Gross Domestic Product. To make it more robust, the EFA tool may be combined with the EIA hence widening the scope. Local authorities and legislators must put in place complementary legislation and align it with the EFA. For instance, a provision in the development permit that no development or layout is to be approved or implemented before a projected EFA is carried out and a probable effect of the development on the ecology is established. If the footprint is above average the tolerated footprint, then the development is totally abandoned or better be modified and altered to reach the acceptable footprint in relation with the available resources. For the footprint calculations to be more comprehensive, omitted categories in the research such as water footprint and carbon footprint emanating from industries and fuels must be included.

After the strategic level, the recommendations are operationalised at the operational level where measures to reduce footprints are outlined from the household level up to the global level. In order to minimise overshoot, sustainable consumption must be promoted at the household level. This may be achieved by encouraging low carbon and resource efficient consumption patterns and selection of environmentally friendly goods and services such as vegetables produced at the household level. On the neighbourhood level, promoting residences with locally available facilities and services will go a long way in minimizing footprint. New developments must give incentive to transit oriented development which promotes walking and cycling as opposed to driving. To reduce overshot, local authorities must aim at improving the ecological base and ecological security of neighbourhoods. This may be accomplished by implementing ecological restoration and nature conservation practices such as afforestation hence increasing ecologically productive areas to compensate for the ecology lost during the development stages and increasing the pollution absorption capacity.

On a city level, local authorities and the government must enforce strict but enforceable land-use planning policies. There is need for strict but enforceable restrictions and regulations on new residential developments to curb sprawling and rapid urbanisation. There must be development ceilings whereby overdevelopment simply because one may afford, should not be the determinants and order of the day in emerging low-density neighbourhoods such as Gletwyn. Rather, there must be limits to what is acceptable to keep sustainability in check. Enacting appropriate transportation systems such as the principle of sustainable urban polycentric development which reduces vehicle emissions in cities will go a long way in reducing the footprint of cities. Public transportation and its upgrade, highly taxing private car owners so that at least a large population resorts to public transportation may also go a long way in reducing overshoot. Local authorities must control the sprawling of cities and towns. Apart from using legislation, this may be achieved by adopting appropriate design measures promoting sustainable urban forms. Sustainable urban forms are characterised with mixed land-uses, compactness, diversity, density, and greening.

To curb expansion of cities, pieces of legislation such as the Harare Combination Master Plan which back development patterns such as densification need to be revisited and applied. Floor area ratios of buildings also need to be increased promoting vertical as opposed to horizontal expansion. For example, differences between Gletwyn in 2017 versus Gletwyn in 2005 illustrate dwindling natural resources on a per capita basis. Improving ecological base throughout Zimbabwe must be made a key strategy to ensure national ecological security. Local authorities, environmentalists, EMA and relevant stakeholders should strengthen ecosystem management and increase bio capacity through maintaining a healthy natural environment and preserve biologically productive areas.

As a country with vast but poorly managed and fast disappearing ecological resources, it is vital that Zimbabwe preserves its existing natural ecosystems for future generations. It is important to account for regional development and consumption levels when formulating plans for encouraging changes in carbon footprint. In neighbourhoods such as Gletwyn where per capita GDP is high, the plan should focus on changes in consumption patterns to slow down or freeze the increase in their ecological footprint. Government must set a nationwide example through establishing green procurement policies and low carbon policies. No single policy may single-handedly address the decision-making need. This calls for complementing indicators that cover a wide spectrum of sustainability issues. Research must be done on how to best use the EFA in multi-criteria, integrated assessments which will be key in the adoption of the EFA. Planners should focus on building low carbon cities / eco-cities in Zimbabwe's urbanisation.

Although urbanisation is associated with higher ecological footprint, there are ways this relationship may be optimised. Urbanisation process in Zimbabwe should follow a low carbon, environmentally friendly approach to urban planning. High carbon emissions have become the primary force driving the increase in Gletwyn and largely Zimbabwe's ecological footprint and any effort to reduce ecological footprint must therefore focus on reducing carbon footprint. Zimbabwe may reduce carbon footprint through establishing and promoting a low carbon economy by increasing the proportion of renewable energy in the national budget's energy portfolio. The ecological footprint analysis tool still needs to be refined, modified, and adjusted to specifically fit the Zimbabwean context as it is a tool being adopted from the developed nations, specifically originating from Canada. It will be welcome if in the methodology for calculating the footprint of neighbourhoods if all other footprints are included, that are, water footprint, carbon footprint and the complex chlorofluorocarbons.

References

African Development Bank. (2012). Rio+20, How May an Ecological Footprint Contribute to Green Economy in Africa? Abidjan: African Development Bank.

Clark, A. L. (2009, September). Environmental challenges to urban planning: Fringe areas, ecological footprints and climate change. Paper presented at Key Challenges in the Process of Urbanization in Ho Chi Minh City: Governance, Socio-Economic, and Environmental Issues Workshop 16-18 September 2009 Ho Chi Minh City, Vietnam. Available online: https://www.eastwestcenter.org/fileadmin/resources/seminars/Urbanizat ion_Seminar/HCMC_Workshop/Papers_and_Presentations/Allen_Clark __HCMC_Workshop_Final_Paper__formatted_version_.pdf

Hepinstall-Cymerman, J., Coe, S., and Alberti, M. (2009). Using urban landscape trajectories to develop a multi-temporal land cover database to support ecological modelling. *Remote Sensing*, 1(4), 1353-1379.

Booth, D. B., Karr, J. R., Schauman, S., Konrad, C. P., Morley, S. A., Larson, M. G., and Burges, S. J. (2004). Reviving urban streams: Land-use, hydrology, biology, and human behaviour 1. *JAWRA Journal of the American Water Resources Association*, 40(5), 1351-1364.

Carter, S., Manceur, A. M., Seppelt, R., Hermans-Neumann, K., Herold, M., and Verchot, L. (2017). Large scale land acquisitions and REDD+: a synthesis of conflicts and opportunities. *Environmental Research Letters*, 12(3), 035010.

Erle, E., andPontius, R. (2007). Land use and land cover change. In J. Cutler (Ed.), *Encyclopedia of Earth* (1-4). Cleveland, Washington, D.C: Environmental Information Coalition, National Council for Science and the Environment.

Folke, C., Larsson, J. and Sweitzer, J. (1994). *Renewable Resource Appropriation by Cities.* Paper presented at "Down To Earth: Practical Applications of Ecological Economics," third international meeting of the International Society for Ecological Economics, San José, Costa Rica, 24-28 October.

Global Footprint Network. (2012). *Advancing the Science of Sustainability.* Available online: http://www.footprintnetwork.org/en/index.php/GFN/page/calculators. [Accessed 04/10/2014].

Kitzes, J., Galli, A., Bagliani, M., Barrett, J., Dige, G., Ede, S., Erb, K.H., Giljum, S., Haberl, H., Hails, C., Jungwirth, S., Lenzen, M., Lewis, K; Loh, J., Marchettini, N., Messinger, H., Milne, K., Moles, R., Monfreda, C., Moran, D., Nakano, K., Pyhälä, A., Rees, W., Simmons, C., Wackernagel, M., Wada, Y., Walsh, C. and Weidman, T. (2009). A Research Agenda for Improving National Ecological Footprint Accounts. *Ecological Economics,* 68(7), 1991-2007.

Onisto, L., Krause, E. and Wackernagel, M. (1998). *How Big Is Toronto's Ecological Footprint: Using the Concept of Appropriated Carrying Capacity for Measuring Sustainability, Toronto, Canada.* Toronto: Centre for Sustainable Studies.

Lenzen, M., and Murray, S. A. (2003). *The Ecological Footprint: Issues and Trends.* University of Sydney, Australia.

Mohan, M. (2005). Urban Land-use/Land cover change detection is National Capital Region Delhi: A study of Faridabad district. Available online: https://www.fig.net/resources/proceedings/fig_proceedings/cairo/paper s/ts_24/ts24_05_mohan.pdf

Rees, W. E. (1996b). Ecological Footprints and the Imperative of Rural Sustainability. In I. Audirac (Ed.), *Rural Sustainability in America* (pp. 41-78). New York, USA: John Wiley and Sons.

Rees, W. E. (1992). Ecological footprints and appropriated carrying capacity: what urban economics leaves out. *Environment and urbanization*, 4(2), 121-130.

Rees, W., and Wackernagel, M. (1996). Urban ecological footprints: why cities cannot be sustainable—and why they are a key to sustainability. *Environmental impact assessment review*, 16(4-6), 223-248.

Progress, Redefining, and Earth Day Network. (2002). Sustainability starts in your community: a community indicators guide. Oakland: Redefining Progress.

West, R. and Turner, L. (2010). *Understanding Interpersonal Communication: Making Choices in Changing Times. Boston, USA: Wadsworth.*

Riebsame, W. E., Meyer, W. B., and Turner, B. L. (1994). Modelling land-use and cover as part of global environmental change. *Climatic change*, *28*(1-2), 45-64.

Wackernagel, M. and Rees, W. (1996). *Our Ecological Footprint: Reducing Human Impact on the Earth.* Gabriola Island, BC. New Society Publishers.

WWF (WWF International, Global Footprint Network, ZSL Zoological Society of London). (2006). *Living Planet Report, Gland, Switzerland.* Available online: http://www.panda.org/livingplanet

Chapter 4

Shifting Physical Boundaries and Implications for Harare since 1890

Innocent Chirisa, Abraham R. Matamanda and Liaison Mukarwi

Summary:

The chapter is based on a study that sought to decode the meanings associated with the centrifugal shifting of urban boundaries as a city grows outwards. It is a phenomenological inquiry into urban sprawl using Harare as a case study. The study advances the argument by Home that underscores that the spatial expansion of cities is a threat to natural resource-based and primary industries particularly agriculture as abutting farms are transformed into urban space. Besides traditional livelihoods being affected, communities are also displaced and replaced with suburbs and townships and, overall, the lifestyles transformed immeasurably. Harare, the capital city of Zimbabwe, established in 1890 by the British, has expanded significantly since then with the greatest growth being witnessed since 2005. There are several reasons for the shifting boundary of Harare, of which this particular study observes five key ones. First, the shift of the boundary of Harare implies that more people are flocking to the city (ahead of other urban centres hence urban primacy). Secondly, the peri-urban interface of the city is urbanising faster than ever before. Thirdly, the fast-track land resettlement programme in the year 2000 was a landmark event that has now seen the city borders assuming greater shifts as negotiations for urban expansion have become easier than before land nationalisation. Fourthly, the constituency boundaries, according to the 2013 National Constitutional provisions, are a source of greater political stability during election times because this translates into more voters. Lastly, the city is increasingly networking and linking with its satellites, namely Chitungwiza, Norton, Epworth, Ruwa and Mazowe hence becoming a metro. Overall, these emerging developments are important for urban discourse, particularly urban sustainability which is placed at the centre of urban planning agenda for Harare.

Introduction

The spatial configuration and physical boundaries of cities in most parts of the world, particularly the global south has shifted immensely over the last years.

The re-configuration of these cities, for example, Cairo, Lagos, Abuja, Harare and Johannesburg, is characterised by population growth as well as shifting of cities' boundaries (Du *et al.* 2014). This shift of boundaries is synonymous with cities that usually develop from a single node such as Nairobi whose initial size was little more than 20 square kilometres, however, the boundary of the city at present has shifted greatly (UNHABITAT, 2006: 7). Cairo is another city that is currently experiencing shifting boundaries that are encroaching into productive agricultural land and desert (Hasan, 2011; Sejoume and El Shorbag, 2011). Evidence shows that the urban area of Cairo increased from 233,78km^2 to 557,87km^2 between 1973 and 1996 of which 136,75km^2 of the increase were from agricultural lands (Hereher, 2012). In China, it is estimated that physical expansion accounts for 40-50 percent of urban growth in the country (Yue *et al.* 2010). According to Chabra (1985), approximately 1.5 million hectares of land (mostly productive agricultural land) in India was lost to human settlements between 1955 and 1985. The main problem with such development is that such physical expansion of the cities encroaches onto productive agricultural lands, yet cities rely on farmlands for the various goods and services especially food (Home, 2001). Above all, the land-use zones automatically change when the city boundary shifts, meaning that some land-uses become illegal within the new urban boundaries. Land-uses and activities related to farming are not always tolerated in urban areas as they are considered as undesirable in cities yet they act as the major livelihood sources for both urban and rural communities (Marongwe, 2003). As a result of the physical expansion of cities, the livelihoods of the communities that reside in the way of the physical expansions and who face displacements are evidently compromised (Melesse, 2005; Wei and Ye, 2014). Furthermore, the natural environment is disturbed in one way or the other as farmland and open spaces pave way for urban land-uses; a situation which ultimately compromises sustainability.

The situation for Harare, the capital city of Zimbabwe, is very interesting because some proponents, such as Mbiba (2017:12), observe that the 2012 census did not capture the urban demographic growth the spatial expansion has caused. The implication is that boundaries in Zimbabwe have remained static while urban sprawl and urban populations in rural jurisdictions have expanded (Mbiba, 2017:12). Some critics such as Feresu (2010), however, argue that Harare has been experiencing shifts of its boundaries so as to accommodate the growing urban population, particularly through housing development. Moreover, from the time the city was established in 1890 to date the boundaries of the city have shifted markedly and this shift is attributed to a number of factors. Political interference, housing shortage and institutional dynamics are among the critical factors that influence shifts in boundaries for Harare (Muronda, 2008; Muchadenyika and Williams, 2017; Chirisa and Matamanda,

2016). Much of the physical expansion occurs on the city's fringe or peri-urban areas which is a zone of contestation (Marongwe, 2003; Chirisa, 2013; Mbiba, 2017).

DFID (1999) argues that, if the dynamics of urbanisation and peri-urban development are to be fully understood and the processes proceed in a sustainable manner, planners and policy-makers have to understand the scale and nature of urban expansion. Although various studies have been undertaken to document the physical expansion of the City of Harare (Muronda, 2008), it seems there is a dearth of researches with regards the physical expansion of the city and livelihoods of the displaced communities. Therefore, this study focuses more on the implications of such physical expansion of the City of Harare on livelihoods of those communities residing in the city's periphery as well as the impacts on the natural ecosystems and landscape which support the environmental integrity of the city. Moreover, this study is critical in informing urban policy on urban and peri-urban development since Marongwe (2003) argues that the rural-urban nexus is an important area for urban development policy and research. Overall, this study advances the argument by Home (2001) that asserts that the physical expansion of cities outwards is a threat to natural-resource-based and primary industries particularly agriculture as abutting farms gradual gets engulfed into urban space. Besides traditional livelihoods being affected, communities are also 'uprooted' and replaced with suburbs and townships and, overall, the lifestyles transformed immeasurably (Du *et al.* 2014; Fazal, 2000).

Literature review

Urbanisation is occurring at unprecedented rates in the global south, specifically in Africa. In parallel with this urbanisation, cities, for example, Abuja, Cairo, Kinshasa, Harare and Nairobi are constantly growing both in terms of population together with the shift of city boundaries (officially and unofficially) (Chirisa *et al.* 2018; Hassan, 2011). This growth and shift of boundaries is attributed to various factors which all usually result in the demand for more land to accommodate the increasing population in the urban areas through housing development (Munzwa and Jonga, 2010). The shift of boundaries in urban centres is usually a product of rapid urbanisation which creates housing shortages in the city (Melesse, 2005; Muchadenyika, 2015). On the other hand, the shift in boundaries is a result of several institutional and economic factors that include globalisation, rural industrialisation, improvement in transportation and land management systems (Wei and Ye, 2014). Moreover, Clark (1968) argues that urban expansion is best explained using two major theories, namely primacy of economic benefits and the role of urban social production. The former involves the agglomeration of different economic activities which eventually attracts migrants from rural areas and other small towns and cities (Clark, 1968). It follows that the shift of the cities' boundary is a driver and product of economic growth (Bai *et al.* 2012). On the other hand, the urban social production theory argues that urban areas are concentrated and congested with people and are also denser than rural areas and still continue to attract more people (Clark, 1968: 576). In the end, there is increased demand for more land to accommodate these new urbanites which may result in shift of cities' boundaries. In the developing world, the manner of the physical expansion of cities is such that there is unplanned and uncontrolled expansion of built up areas at the expense of agricultural land and areas of natural landscape (Hasan, 2011: 1).

An improvement in local transportation also contributes to the physical expansion of boundaries of cities (Mbara, 2015: 3). This improvement may be in the form of reduced commuting costs which eventually results in the huge influx of people into the urban areas, especially in the urban fringes where land is usually cheap or where they tend to establish informal settlements. Moreover, reliable transport systems usually result in the establishment of satellite cities which eventually results in the development of urban metropolitan regions and urban conurbation, examples being the Greater Cairo region and cities in China such as Shangai (Hereher, 2012; Du *et al.* 2014).

Globalisation in recent times has strengthened the linkages between small towns and rural areas resulting in metropolitanisation of the world economy. The phenomenon of globalisation is best described as "... spatial-temporal processes of change which constitutes the fundamental transformation of human concerns in an organisation...without referring to the expansion in space of the connections, there can be no clear coherent formulation of the term globalisation" (Cuterela, 2012:138). In this vein, globalisation will be contextualised along the thoughts of Beerkens (2004:13) who postulates that it is the interconnectedness between nation-states due to acceleration, massification, flexibilisation and expansion of transnational flows of people, products, finance, images and information. Within the African context, technological advances in information and communication technologies are the main factors fuelling this network between settlements (Boateng, 2012; Verma, 2012). Advances in transport systems are also another contributing factor to the connection of these settlements because people can travel longer distances within short spaces of time (Mbara, 2015). Ultimately, metropolitan regions emerge, and this connection eventually results in the physical expansion of cities as they end up being connected with these small towns and urban centres (Knieling, 2014).

The advancements in transportation infrastructure greatly plays a role in the shifting of city boundaries because travelling times are lowered; an example being the Rapid Transit system in South Africa that has been influential in the metropolitisation of the Gauteng Metro Region (Greenberg, 2010). However, there is need for policies and legislations which will guide the success of such developments; hence we consider such policies and strategies hereunder. Metropolitisation is thus a product of metropolitan regions. Such regions are described as highly urbanised, city-regional areas that are characterised by a high population density, as well as concentration of economic, political and cultural activities (Knieling, 2014: 9). Considering that the shift in the boundaries of a city results in the formation of an urban syntax, metropolitan regions are usually created, for example, the Gauteng Metro Region in South Africa (Greenberg, 2010).

From the perspective of Hardboy *et al.* (2001), the physical expansion of cities in the developing world is mainly because of lack of appropriate policies and strategies to guide new development and not the lack of vacant land for urban development. This is so because overcrowding and new developments usually occur in urban fringes where the land is fertile and idle while large amounts of land remain vacant or partially developed in other parts of the city (Kamete, 2002: 14). This situation is typical of Cairo and Addis Ababa where physical expansion of cities encroaches onto arable lands, yet greater part of the cities' developable lands remains undeveloped (Melesse, 2005; World Bank, 2015: 25). Furthermore, central and local governments usually influence the extent of the physical expansion of urban areas through policies and land-use management plans that may either be restrictive or accommodating. In such cases, migratory laws may be relaxed, which is usually the case in most developing countries where rural-urban migration was heavily controlled by the colonial masters. Once these countries gained independence, they was an exodus of rural-urban migration that was followed by physical expansion that took place in an unplanned manner while their administrations also failed to keep pace with and track the growth related processes (Griffiths *et al.* 2009; Daniels, 1999). This situation is synonymous with most African cities as they seek to do away with the colonial laws that restricted mostly Africans to migrate to urban centres. The inception of independence in Africa came with the migration of large numbers of people into cities that were historically the enclave of colonial masters and a few workers who served them.

Most of the physical expansion of city boundaries takes place in the peri-urban areas, yet these are sites where much urban agriculture is practised. Urban agriculture is a livelihood strategy that sustains the most vulnerable citizens in urban areas (Mbiba, 1994). Urbanisation in most African countries is associated with limited economic opportunities that often translate into urban poverty

(Manjengwa *et al.* 2016). Structural adjustments programmes in most African states have also contributed to increased poverty among the urban dwellers through massive retrenchments that were associated with these programmes (Heidhues and Obare, 2011). Also, the cash-based economy that characterise urban areas and the limited wages that most migrants earn leaves them with great financial burdens with some households struggling to get adequate food. Furthermore, the urban landscape is also improved through activities such as tree planting and the vegetation cover. A good example is Lusaka where 78 percent of the garden plots are in peri-urban areas and create an aesthetically pleasing environment which has resulted in Lusaka being labelled the world capital of urban cultivation (Sanyal, 1986). However, the physical expansion of cities results in the emergence of new land-uses that usually have an impact on peri-urban agricultural activities, the environment and ultimately the livelihoods of the urban poor (Mbiba,2017).

Physical expansion of urban area in developing world is characterised by multiple undesirable physical and socio-economic impacts that include scattered development, excessive commuting and transportation costs, socio-economic segregation through inequitable land and housing markets and increasing utilisation of natural open space and ecological sensitive sites (Matamanda and Chirisa, 2014; Matamanda *et al.* 2014; Carruthers, 2002). Scattered development is usually perceived as undesirable, yet it emerges as the product of the shift in city boundaries as is the case in cities such as Nairobi, Abuja and Kinshasa (Chirisa *et al.* 2018). Muderere (2011) also demonstrates how open spaces and ecologically sensitive sites are utilised and degraded as a result of the physical expansion of Harare. According to Long *et al.* (2011), the rapid urban expansion and disappearance of cultivated land in Chinese cities has imposed serious challenges for food security, social management and economic polarisation. The disappearance of such land means that there will be less land to cultivate; hence productivity is reduced such that less food will be available for the urban dwellers that rely on the food produced in these farms.

Various policies and strategies have been implemented in both the developing and developed world to protect farmland and open spaces (Bergstorm and Ready, 2009). For example, the government in Egypt has made attempts to implement decentralisation policy so as to reduce the population pressure in greater Cairo and ultimately reduce the physical expansion of the city (Hereher, 2012). However, such initiatives by the government have proved to be futile since the cost of living in small towns has remained higher and the lack of modern services and infrastructure also results in people favouring the capital city. Furthermore, the Egyptian government introduced a law that prohibits building upon productive agricultural land (Sims, 2012: 95). This strategy failed to be successful because there were little deterrent actions that were in existence to guard and regulate the actions of offenders who constructed on agricultural lands and thus infringed this law (Hereher, 2012). Another example is Nigeria which resorted to the relocation of the capital city from Lagos to Abuja so as to relieve the pressures of growth in the primate city. In some instances, and usually borrowing from Western urban planning ideologies, the physical expansion of cities has been controlled through the establishment of green belts around major urban areas. Such a strategy is aligned to the 'garden city' approach envisioned by Ebenezer Howard (Howard, 1902). This strategy was adopted in Seoul, Republic of Korea in 1971 where a green belt was established around the city to restrict any further physical expansion (Melesse, 2005).

Efforts to contain the rapid urbanisation and physical expansion of cities in developing world are inevitable considering the ecological footprint associated with these processes. However, some of the foregoing strategies are not implemented in the developing world because of the lack of resources that haunt government and inability to control land-uses. Furthermore, the failure of strategies in developing countries is attributed to the fact that some of the policies and strategies are politically oriented and imposed by the state without consulting various stakeholders in the cities such as urban planners and public officials (Muchadenyika, 2015). Porter (2007) argues that managing urban expansion should be centred on formulation of strategies and programmes for future development but also aligning political decisions and community demands towards a consensus.

The legislative and institutional framework

The Regional Town and Country Planning (RTCP) Act (Chapter 29:12) of Zimbabwe specifies the requirements that apply when state land is to be subdivided. In section 43 of the RTCP Act it is mentioned that state land may be subdivided for various reasons, but this has to be done after a proposed layout plan is prepared for the subdivision and has to be approved by the Minister of Lands after consulting the responsible local authority. It follows that before any state land is occupied in the city, a layout plan must be prepared which shows that the emerging land-uses will be planned and regulated by the local authority. The same applies for private land which may not be subdivided without the authority of the responsible local authority as outlined in section 39(1)(a) of the RTCP Act. The Urban Councils Act, in section 155, focuses on encroachments that may occur on council land. According to section 155(1), the relevant council may take necessary actions to remove or regularise the encroachment of human settlements onto state land. This may be done through selling the land concerned to the offender, granting him/her a servitude or removal of the encroachment. Removal is usually undertaken when the land is an ecological sensitive site which needs to be preserved as espoused in the RTCP Act section (31).

City of Harare, as the local authority, is mandated to undertake the physical development for the city. This follows the powers conferred on the local authority by the RTCP Act and Urban Council's Act. However, planning decisions made by the local authority may be superseded by the Ministry of Local Government, Public Works and National Housing which at times disregard the authority and power of the councils. Such situations occur when councils are given mandates and orders by the responsible minister to undertake certain initiatives. A good example being the cancellation of all arrears owed by rate payers in 2013, a move that was initiated by the then Minister Chombo, yet it was against the wish of the local authorities. At times the ruling party [ZANU (PF)] has had a major influence in decision-making. This has been evident in situations where decisions made by the local authorities tend to be overridden by the ruling party.

The Harare case study

Harare lies in the north-east part of the country and is characterised by four seasons, namely summer, autumn, winter and spring (see Figure 4). There is also large inventory of wetlands as well as underground water sources in Harare (Matamanda *et al.* 2014). These conditions are suitable for agricultural activities which resulted in some colonial masters practising various types of agricultural activities in the city's fringes during the colonial times. According to *The Patriot* (2016), at least 414 016 hectares of land in Harare had been physically occupied by European settler-farmers because the region was almost entirely agricultural. Market gardening was traditionally practised around the city which provided a ready market for the farmers produce. Most parts of the present-day Harare was farmland and, as highlighted by *The Patriot* (2016), Borrowdale, Hatfield and Prospect (now residential suburbs in the present day Harare) were all farms. Other farms in Salisbury (Harare) that were owned by settlers included Mt Pleasant Farm, Mabelreign Farm, Willowvale Farm and Lochnivar Farm in the north and western parts of the city (Figure, 2). In this way the land surrounding the city was protected since no development was allowed on these farms which fed the urbanites. However, these areas were recently turned into residential suburbs where urban agriculture is an illegal activity now.

In-migration/population growth and shifting boundaries in Harare

There are several meanings attached to the shifting boundaries in Harare. This study observes five key ones. First, the shift of the boundary of Harare implies that more people are flocking to the city (ahead of other urban centres hence urban primacy). Prior to independence in 1980, the occupation of land in the City of Harare was controlled by the white colonial government which used strict planning laws to guide the development of the city. The city developed on the basis of separate development wherein Africans were allocated land in designated areas and there was no room for unplanned physical expansion of the city during this era. However, a new wave was ushered in at independence when the migration laws that restrained Africans from migrating to urban areas were relaxed. The colonial laws that restricted the migration of mostly African women into urban areas were abolished in the new Zimbabwe. Therefore, there was massive rural-urban migration, with Harare absorbing the greater part of these migrants.

Harare has continued to attract more people since independence as evident from the 2012 national population figures which show that the population for Harare was 2,1 million, a figure which constitutes 16,3% of the country's population (ZIMSTATS, 2013). Clearly, Harare is the most populous city in the country and emerges as a primate city. However, when the colonial settlers established Harare they had designed it to accommodate a mere 300 000 people, a figure which is way less than the current population of the city. Therefore, the city has failed to accommodate this excess population which has resulted in the physical shift of the city's boundary to create space for new migrants to the city as well as for the development of other urban services. This has seen new settlements being established in areas such as Chitungwiza, a dormitory town for Harare; Ruwa and Epworth. Slowly, the farms were converted into residential areas so as to accommodate the growing population in the City of Harare. Correspondingly, the increase in value of urban land also resulted in the conversion of farmland for human settlements.

Urbanism in the City of Harare

Secondly, the peri-urban interface of the city is urbanising faster than ever before. The population pressure in Harare, a city that was initially designed to accommodate a mere 300 000 people and now has a population in excess of 2 million, has greatly contributed to the housing shortages in the city. The result has been the concentration of people in the periphery of the city. Furthermore, the shift in the boundaries of Harare is also attributed to inefficient land-use planning resulting from too much political interference in land allocation which has resulted in people settling in the urban fringes such as Caledonia and Whitecliffe (Chirisa *et al.* 2011; Muchadenyika, 2015) Housing development is increasing in the peri-urban areas of Harare, a situation which is associated with multiple challenges, chief among these being the loss of sensitive ecological sites such as wetlands. Muderere (2011) narrates how biodiversity has been lost through the peri-urban development of housing units. Furthermore, the peri-urban areas are not adequately serviced with water and sanitation facilities, considering that some of these settlements are illegal and not connected to the council system. This then forces the residents to extract water from underground sources such as shallow wells as well as Blair toilets and pit latrines which compromise public health. The problem is mainly attributed to the failure of the local authority to expand its infrastructure resulting in negative effects of disease outbreaks in areas such as Caledonia and Hatcliffe.

Fast-track land resettlement programme (FTLRP)

Thirdly, the fast-track land resettlement programme (FTLRP) in the year 2000 was a landmark step that has now seen the city borders assuming greater shifts. The FTLRP of 2000 resulted in the occupation of both rural and urban land. The initial chaotic nature of the programme resulted in most vacant land in the peri-urban area of Harare being occupied by people in need of land for housing (Chitiga and Chigora, 2010). Moreover, some farms were also occupied for residential purposes yet rural land in the peri-urban areas were supposed to be considered for peri-urban agriculture (Marongwe, 2003). Examples of such farms include Retreat Farm located between Harare and Chitungwiza. Prior to FTLRP, this farm was used for crop production and livestock production (cattle ranching), poultry production and citrus production. Although most of the settlers were allocated big plots of land, few have engaged in agricultural activities as they only required affordable land. Ultimately, the occupation of this farm has resulted in many farm workers losing their jobs as well as failing to get any land which then compromised their livelihoods. Furthermore, the environment has been jeopardised through the FTLRP as evident from Whitecliffee Farm which was also occupied for residential purposes. Developments on all these farms reflect activities that are skewed towards residential than agricultural use. The environment has thus been degraded in various ways due to the FTRLP. Examples of environmental peril include land degradation, water pollution and deforestation (Feresu, 2010).

Political boundary shifts

Fourthly, the constituency boundaries, according to the 2013 National Constitutional provisions, provide political stability during election times because this results in increased electorate. Despite the negative implications associated with unplanned and unregulated physical expansion of cities, it seems the trend always continues in Harare where land allocation is used by political leaders to gain support from the masses (Muchadenyika, 2015). In this way, untitled land in the peri-urban areas is usually parcelled out to 'homeless' party supporters, especially during and towards election times. The result is land degradation as the people allocated the land often indulge in unsustainable practices such as sand mining and quarrying as well as deforestation (Feresu, 2010; Kamete, 2002). Furthermore, these settlements rarely have services such as water which forces the residents to resort to ground water sources (Chirisa *et al.* 2014).

The Metropolitanisation of Harare

Fifthly, the city is realising a greatly networked syntax with its satellites—Chitungwiza, Norton, Epworth, Ruwa and Mazowe hence metropolitanisation (see Figure 4.1). Harare is increasing getting connected with its satellite settlements through the reduction in commuting costs and increase in car ownership. Most of the satellite settlements are now dormitory towns as most people commute and come to the City of Harare to engage in various economic activities. This is so because Harare urban emerges as the core metropolitan as it has industries and services that offer several economic opportunities for citizens. Industrial development in these satellite towns has been affected by the economic malaise in the country which has seen most of them ceasing operations. The result is that settlements continue to develop further reducing farmlands and number of family farms as the demand for housing increases. Although these satellite towns may appear as independent settlements, they are actually a part of single urban entity. Through this metropolitanisation of Harare and its satellite towns, these satellite settlements are slowly being absorbed into the City of Harare. For example, Epworth is also being incorporated into the sphere of the city's daily activities. Ultimately, the traditional land-uses that have been synonymous with these areas have been lost paving way for human settlements. The other reason is that the cost of living is low in these small towns where accommodation is less than in the capital city, yet commuting expenses remain the same.

Figure 4.1 shows the boundaries of Harare for different periods beginning in 1973. The physical space that was bound in 1973 was smaller giving an indication that few people and residential suburbs were in existence at the time. Furthermore, these neighbourhoods were concentrated in the centre of the city with few centres found close to the city's boundaries. This was meant to safeguard the city boundaries and the green that was synonymous with this area as well as promoting the greening of the city. It is also in these areas that much of the market gardening was practised hence the scattered nature of the settlements along the city's balance which ensured a balance between nature and the population. Furthermore, the road network was also less dense which implies that much of the land remained undeveloped (see Figure 4.2).

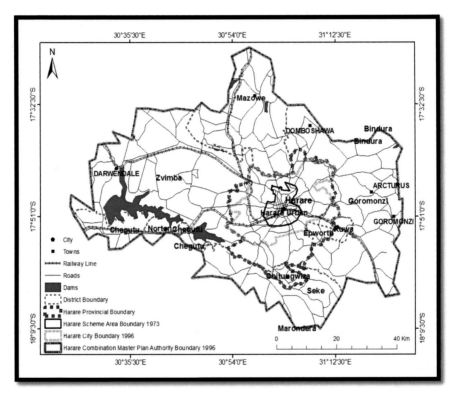

Figure 4.1: The Boundaries for Harare from 1973 to date
Source: Authors Creation (2017)

Figure 4.2 shows how the city's boundary was in 1996. There were few suburbs in the city as shown on the map (see Figure 4.2). Currently, this has shifted resulting in the concentration of residential suburbs in the eastern and western parts of the city. The nothern part may have been spared because of the existence of Borrowdale a residential suburb for the elites while the southern parts have been spared due to the existence of the Harare International Airport.

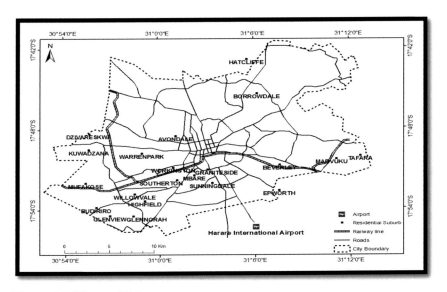

Figure 4.2: Harare 1996
Source: Authors Creation (2017)

Figure 3 shows the Harare Metropolitan region which shows an increased coverage of suburbs in the city indicating the increased concentration of people in Harare. The residential suburbs are also densely spread all over the city including along the periphery of Harare where there are suburbs such as Stoneridge, Tynwald and Gleneagles. This is a clear indication that the physical boundary of the city has shifted and encroached on productive farmlands that were previously shown on the Harare map of 1996 (Figure 4.1 and 2).

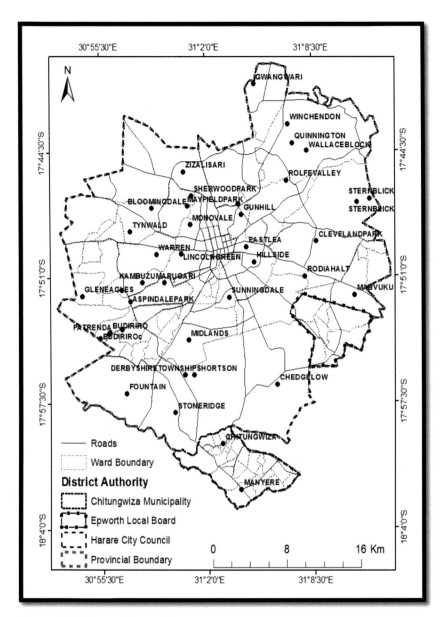

Figure 4.3: Harare Metropolitan
Source: Authors Creation (2017)

Figure 4 shows the official boundary of the City of Harare in relation to Harare Combination Master Plan. The Harare boundary is within the Harare Combination Master Plan Boundary which shows how the city is connected with its satellite towns. Currently, most of these towns are increasingly connecting with Harare with some of these depending on Harare for services. Moreover, the developments of roads and housing infrastructure in these small towns have resulted in the loss of open spaces and biodiversity.

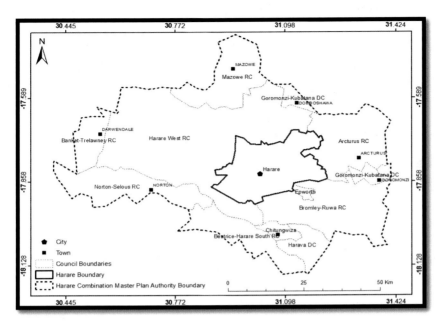

Figure 4.4: Harare Combination Master Plan Boundary
Source: Authors Creation (2017)

Figure 4.5 is a comprehensive diagram that shows the physical boundary of Harare in relation to the Harare Scheme of 1973, Harare City boundary of 1996 as well as the boundary for the Harare Combination Master Plan of 1996. The city is surely expanding outwards and with time Harare will become a metropolis because of the large network of road systems which makes it easier for people to commute from various places around Harare to the city centre. Eventually, as the boundaries shift outwards, land-uses are converted to residential use which then compromises the vegetation and biodiversity in these areas.

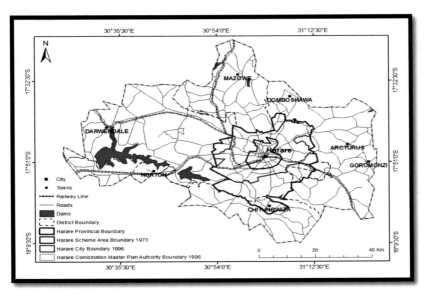

Figure 4.5: The physical shifts of the city's boundaries over the years

Source: Authors Creation (2017)

Discussion

The phenomenon of physical expansion being experienced in Harare, Zimbabwe, is a similar trend to what is occurring in cities in other developing countries such as Egypt and Ethiopia where much of the encroachment is onto farmland (Hereher, 2012; Melesse, 2005). In Cairo the rapid shift of the city's boundary has been mainly a result of increasing concentration of people in the capital city which has resulted in increase in the demand for cheap accommodation. The same applies for Harare where rapid population growth has been experienced in the city after independence owing to relaxed migration laws which then resulted in huge influx of people into the city. Ultimately, the experiences from Harare highlight a highly urbanising city that owes its growth mainly to population growth from natural increase and rural-urban migration which has resulted in an increase in urban population and escalating demand for urban housing and other services. The events in Harare concur with studies from Cairo, and Nairobi where the rapid rates of urbanisation has increased the demand for more land which has resulted in the outward expansion of the city onto fertile lands which were used by the colonial settlers for farming.

For Harare, the extension in the city's boundary is also attributed to the FTRLP which was spearheaded by the government mainly as a strategy to gain political support from the masses. The manner in which the resettlement was implemented differs from the programme in China which was organised and controlled by the state. The result in Zimbabwe was that people ended up encroaching into ecologically sensitive sites in the quest for residential areas.

76

Harare possesses fertile lands and a climate that sustains agricultural activities, yet the physical expansion of the city has led to the conversion of most of these lands into residential areas much to the detriment of the livelihoods of households who depended on this land for their livelihoods. To make matters worse, once the boundaries of the city shifts officially, the local authority does not consider urban agriculture as a legitimate activity in urban areas hence households who once survived on this livelihood strategy are thus denied the opportunity to continue farming. Besides the negative implications on the traditional rural livelihoods in areas such as Epworth and other peri-urban areas, the environment has also been compromised due to the physical expansion of Harare. It emerges from this study that there is little or no operational models that exist in Harare to guide the implementation of land development policies and to regulate and check the urban expansion processes. Furthermore, the unrestrained physical expansion of Harare in an unplanned and poorly managed manner greatly undermines the environment, economy and society through loss of nature and livelihoods.

Policy options and recommendations

According to the European Environmental Agency (2006), policy coherence in land-use planning is recommended as a solution to urban sprawl in Europe. In this chapter, the authors also make the same recommendation for Harare where land-use and planning decisions have to be coherent rather than being politically motivated. Policy coherence may be of importance in the context of Harare because it is rooted in rationality and diverges from being politically driven. Hence, such a situation may enable effective land-use initiatives to be implemented rather than have a situation where politicians determine what has to be done. The land-use policies and decisions to be made for Harare must be holistic rather than being sector specific. Sector specific policies usually result in disintegrated planning hence it would be critical to consider a holistic approach to land-use planning that looks at the various needs of the people as well as nesting these into the complex web that involves socio-economic, environmental and political landscape. Holism allows for the integration of all problems associated with the shift in city boundaries rather than simply focusing on certain issues which does not fully address the negative impacts related to this process. It is also important for local authorities to effective monitor the performance of various stakeholders who are engaged in the development of the city as well as have as the oversight to establish the potential growth of the city. In this regard, it is recommended that the local authority makes use of technology such as Landsat, Geographic Information Systems and Remote Sensing to identify and monitor land-uses in the city and facilitate the regulation of any unplanned developments. The planners and decision-makers need to be proactive to local conditions when formulating and implementing development plans for Harare rather than being rigid and adopting colonial legislations. This means that there is need for more flexibility in addressing issues such as urban agriculture which supports livelihoods in Harare, yet the activity is deemed illegal by City of Harare since there is no piece of legislation that says anything about urban agriculture. There may be initiatives to integrate such activities into the city's land-use planning and development schemes.

Conclusion

The focus of this study has been on defining the meanings that are related to the outward expansion of the land spaces of cities using Harare as a case study. The central argument advanced in the study is by Home (2001) who argues that much of the extension of the boundaries of cities encroaches onto productive farmland resulting in the threat to natural resource-based and primary industries, especially agriculture. Subsequently, the environment is also degraded. From the findings of the study, the same issues raised by Home (2001) are identified in Harare where the shift of the physical boundaries of the city is evident. There are five key factors relating to the shifts of the boundary in Harare. These include rapid expansion of the city due to rural-urban migration from various areas to Harare, the peri-urban interface of city is urbanised, the fast track resettlement land programme also significantly resulted in the shifts of the city boundaries, and the metropolitanisation of Harare.

References

Bai, X.M., Chen, J., and Shi, P.J. (2012). Landscape urbanisation and economic growth in China: Positive feedbacks and sustainability dilemmas. *Environ SciTechnol*, 46(1), 132-139.

Beerkens, H.J.J.G. (2004). *Global Opportunities and Institutional Embeddedness: Higher Education consortia in Europe and Southeast Asia*. Centre for Higher Education Policy Studies, University of Twente.

Bergstrom, J. C., and Ready, R.C. (2009). What have we learned from over 20 years of farmland amenity valuation research in North America? *Rev. Agric. Econ*, 31, 21–49.

Boateng, M. S. (2012). The Role of Information and Communication Technologies in Ghana's Rural Development. *Library Philosophy and Practice (e-journal)* Paper 871.

Carruthers, J. I. (2002). The Impacts of State Growth Management Programmes: A Comparative Analysis. *Urban Studies,* 39(11), 1959-1982.

Chabra, R. (1985). *India: Environmental Degradation, Urban Slums, Political Tension.* Draper Fund Paper

Chirisa, I., Matamanda, A. and Bandauko, E. (2014). Ruralised Urban Areas vis-a-vis Urbanised Rural Areas in Zimbabwe: Implications for Spatial Planning. *Regional Development Dialogue, 35*, 65-80.

Chirisa, I. and Matamanda, A.R. (2016). Addressing Urban Poverty in Africa in the Post-2015 Period: Perspectives for Adequate and Sustainable Housing. *Journal of Settlements and Spatial Planning, 7*(1), 79 – 87.

Chirisa, I., Mukarwi, L. and Matamanda, A.R. (2018). Social Costs and Benefits of the Transformation of the Traditional Families in an African Urban Society. In U, Benna and I, Benna, *Urbanization and its Impact on Socio-Economic Growth in Developing Regions* (Chapter 9). Hershey: IGI Global.

Chitiga, G., and Chigora, P. (2010). An Analysis of the Implications of the Fast Track Land Reform Program on Climate Change and Disaster Management in Zimbabwe: A Case of Chegutu District. *Journal of Sustainable Development in Africa, 12(2),* 124-143.

Clark, T. (1968). Community Structure, Decision-making, Budget Expenditure and Urban Renewal in 51 American Communities. *American Sociological Review*, 33, 576-580

Cuterela, S. (2012). Globalisation: Definition, Processes and Concepts. *Revista Romana de Statistica – Supliment Trim* iv/2012, 137-146.

Daniels, T. (1999). *What to do About Rural Sprawl?* Paper presented at the American Planning Association Conference.

DFID, 1999. *Sustainable Livelihoods Guidance Sheets.* London: DFID.

Drakakis-Smith, D.W. (1994). Food Systems and the poor in Harare under conditions of structural adjustment. *Geografiska Annaler,* 76B, 3-20.

Du, S., Peijun, S., and Rompaey, A.V. (2014). The Relationship between Urban sprawl and Farmland Displacement in the Pearl River Delta, China. *Land, 3*, 34-51.

Fazal, S. (2000). Urban expansion and loss of agricultural land – a GIS based study of Saharanpur City, India. *Environment and Urbanisation,* 12(2), 133-149.

Feresu, S.B (Ed.). (2010) *Zimbabwe Environmental Outlook: Our Environment, Everybody's Responsibility. Executive Summary. Government of the Republic of Zimbabwe.* The Ministry of Environment and Natural Resources Management, Harare.

Greenberg, S. (2010). *The Political Economy of the Gauteng City-Region.* Gauteng City Region, Pretoria.

Griffiths, P., Hostert, P., Gruebner, O. and Linden, S. (2009). Mapping mega city growth with multi-sensor data. *Remote Sensing of Environment*, 114: 426-439.

Hasan, A.A.M. (2011). *Dynamic Expansion and Urbanisation of Greater Cairo Metropolis, Egypt*. Proceedings from REAL CORP 2011.

Hereher, M. E. (2012). Analysis of urban growth at Cairo, Egypt using remote sensing and GIS. *Natural Science*, 4(6), 355-361.

Hiedhues, F. and Obare, G. (2011). Lessons from Structural Adjustment Programmes and their Effects in Africa. *Quarterly Journal of International Agriculture*, 50, 55-64.

Home, R. (2001). *"Eating farmland, growing houses": Peri-Urban settlements and customary land tenure in Botswana, Southern Africa*. Available online: http://n-aerus.net/web/sat/workshops/2001/papers/home.pdf. Accessed on 22 July 2016.

Howard, E. (1902). *Garden Cities of Tomorrow*. Faber and Faber, London

Kamete, A.Y. (2002). *Governance for sustainability? Balancing social and environmental concerns in Harare*. Bergen, Chr. Michelsen Institute, Development Studies and Human Rights.

Knieling, M.A.J. (2014). *Metropolitan Regions: Definitions, Typologies and Recommendations for Development Cooperation*. Eschborn: Internationale Zusammenarbeit (GIZ) GmbH.

Long, H., Zou, J., Pyket, J. and Li, Y. (2011). Analysis of rural transformation development in China since the turn of the new millennium. *Appl Geogr*, *31*(3), 1094–1105.

Manjengwa, J., Matema, C., and Tirivanhu, D. (2016). Understanding Urban Poverty in two High –Density Suburbs of Harare, Zimbabwe. *Development Southern Africa, 33*(1), 23-38.

Marongwe, N. (2003). *The Fast Track Resettlement and Urban Development Nexus: a case of Harare*. Paper Presented at the Symposium on Delivering Land and securing Rural Livelihoods: Post Independence Land Reform and Resettlement in Zimbabwe, Mont Clair, Nyanga, 26-28 March 2003.

Matamanda, A., and Chirisa, I. (2014). Ecological planning as an Inner – city revitalization planning agenda for Harare, Zimbabwe. *City, Territory and Architecture, 1*, 14.

Matamanda, A., Chirisa, I. and Mukamuri, B. (2014). Stakeholders' Awareness and Perceptions on Ecosystem Services Provided by Wetlands in Harare, Zimbabwe. *Zambezia, 41*(1/2), 107 – 122.

Mbara, T. (2015). *Achieving Sustainable Urban Transport in Harare, Zimbabwe: What Are the Requirements to Reach the Milestone?* Paper presented at CADATU2015, 2-5 February 2015, Istanbul-Turkey

Mbiba, B. (2017). *On the Periphery: Missing Urbanisation in Zimbabwe*. Africa Research Institute, London.

Melesse, M. (2005). City Expansion, Squatter Settlements and Policy Implications in Addis Abeba: The Case of KolfeKeranio Sub-City, Working papers on population and land-use change in central Ethiopia, nr. 2, Serie A, Nr. 9, Trondheim.

Muchadenyika, D. (2015). Land for Housing: A Political Resource-Reflections from Zimbabwe's Urban Areas. *Journal of Southern African Studies*, 41(6): 1219-1238

Muchadenyika, D. and Williams, J.J. (2017). Politics and the Practice of Planning: The Case of Zimbabwean Cities. *Cities*, 63, 33 – 40.

Muderere, T. (2011). Natural Co-Existence or Confinement: Challenges in Integrating Bird-Life Concerns into Urban Planning and Design for Zimbabwe. *Journal of Sustainable Development in Africa, 13*(1), 162-183.

Muronda, T. (2008). Evolution of Harare as Zimbabwe's Capital City and a major Central Place in Southern Africa in the context of Byland's model of settlement evolution. *Journal of Geography and Regional Planning*, 1(2), 34-40.

Porter, D.R. (2007). *Managing Growth in American Communities*. Washington DC: Island Press.

Sanyal, B. (1987). Urban cultivation amidst modernisation: how should we interpret it? *Journal of Planning Education and Research*, 6, 197-207.

Sejoume, M. and El Shorbag, M. (2011). *Urban Slums Report: The Case of Cairo Egypt.* Available online: https://www.ucl.ac.uk/dpu-projects/Global_Report/pdfs/Cairo.pdf.

Sims, D. (2012). *Understanding Cairo: The Logic of a City Out of Control*. Oxford: Oxford University Press.

The Patriot. (2016). The Struggle for Land in Zimbabwe (1890 – 2010)…..Borrowdale, Hatfield, Prospect were all farms. Available online: http://www.thepatriot.co.zw/old_posts/the-struggle-for-land-in-zimbabwe-1890-2010-borrowdale-hatfield-prospect-were-all-farms/ [Accessed on 3 August 2016]

Verma, R. (2012). Project Report on Role of Information Technology in Development of Rural Himachal.

Wei, Y.D. and Yu, X. (2014). Urbanisation, urban land expansion and environmental change in China. *Stoch Environ Res Risk Assess, 28,* 757-765.

Wolch, J.R., Byrne, J. and Newell, J.P. (2014). Urban green space, public health, and environmental justice: The challenge of making cities 'Just green enough'. *Landscape and Urban Planning, 125*(2014): 234-244

World Bank. (2015). *Addiss Ababa, Ethiopia: Enhancing Urban Resilience*. Washington, D.C: The World Bank Group.

Yue, W., Liu, Y. and Fan, P. (2010). Polycentric urban development: the case of Hangzhou. *Environ Plan A*, 42(3): 563-577.

Zimbabwe National Statistics Agency (ZIMSTATS). (2013). *Census 2012: Provincial Report Harare*. Harare: ZIMSTATS.

Chapter 5

Prospects for a Sustainable Rail Commuting System in Harare

Tafadzwa Dube

Summary:

This chapter sought to reveal the opportunities, challenges, the potential role and impact, and options for a better and sustainable rail commuting system. Cities around the world are experiencing a rapid increase in population without adequate resources to cater for that population. This has seen a rampant growth of settlements (planned and unplanned) without social facilities and services like water, sewer, transport and health services. Due to the chaos in transportation systems in human settlements in Zimbabwe, this chapter examines the feasibility of re-utilisation of public urban rail transport system as a means of commuting in Harare metropolitan. Urban transport in Harare seems to be relying more on road transport despite the challenges associated with it that include traffic congestion, poor road maintenance and pollution. The rail system, as a means of commuting, has been a forgotten dimension in urban public transport. The idea of urban rail commuting seems far-fetched given that the existing rail network is currently underutilised. However, it is a reality that the growth of Harare requires a new approach oriented towards improving affordability, environmental sustainability and transport safety.

Introduction

Public transport is the backbone of urban life as it also determines the form and socio-economic development of a city. This study sought to investigate the feasibility of utilising public rail transport as an alternative way of urban commuting and to propose an enabling approach to its sustainability. As the world is fast getting urbanised, the United Nations is emphasizing on sustainable urban mobility and accessibility (UNHABITAT, 2013). However, mobility and accessibility in Zimbabwe have remained a challenge in most urban areas, specifically in Harare. The thrust of the provision of public transport in Zimbabwe since the start of the 21st century has relied more on road service than other forms of transport like rail transport. This thrust, therefore, was the impetus of this article which sought to gauge the feasibility of utilising rail commuting system as an alternative way of public transport provision in urban areas using the case of Harare Metropolitan area. Kanyepa (2014) suggests that the provision of bus rapid transport (BRT), as a form of public transport that would act towards effective urban commuting in Zimbabwe, is not feasible at the moment. This present study looked into urban commuting by means of rail system. The study explored the various means of urban commuting in order to understand the challenges currently being faced by commuters, examined the current state of rail transport in Harare Metropolitan, investigated the current operating cost /profit on passenger coaches as well as mapping out existing and possible routes for urban rail commuting in Harare Metropolitan.

Background and overview

Since the 1970s, there has been a considerable increase in urban rail ventures with new urban rail systems and light rail systems being built worldwide (Babalik, 2000). These investments were planned as possible infrastructure to solve transport and land-use problems allied with the wide-ranging use of automobiles. Rapid urbanisation in developing countries has resulted in transport facilities and infrastructure failing to handle the huge demand of road usage. This has resulted in traffic congestion, delays in movement, high travel costs, noise and air pollution as well as road carnage, all of which have negatively affected the pace of economic development (Adesanya, 2012). It has also been observed that most urban areas in developing countries are now linked with more road networks compared to rail system, especially in new and up-coming suburban areas (Cervero, 1991). Consequently, the cities have become the worst cities considering their development into traffic jungles. This is largely attributed to the increase in personal income which translates to a rapid growth in the number of vehicles on the streets. However, this growth is not being matched with infrastructure development, soft and hard infrastructure (Bouqet, 2010:3). This can be seen in Harare where road usage, especially during peak hours has outstripped the supply of road space thus leading to serious traffic jams. The ex-Japanese cars that have flooded the streets of Harare are contributing to the difficulties in managing road space (Bouqet, 2010). It is further mentioned that there has been reluctance in most developing countries to invest on rail urban commuting system as transportation solutions are mainly road based (Adesanya, 2012). Transport solutions are thus biased toward road systems which are marred by problems, for example, the demand for road space is outstripping road space supply creating serious traffic jams as witnessed in cities such as Bangkok, Manila, Cairo, Lagos, Sao Paulo and Mexico City (Cervero 1991; Bouqet 2010).

Small (2006) alludes to the defining trait of urban areas as the density of people, activities and structures while the defining trait of public urban transportation as the ability to cope with this density while moving people and goods. Density creates challenges for urban transportation because of crowding and the expense of providing infrastructure in built-up areas. However, density can also create certain advantages because of economies of scale whereby transportation activities are cheaper when carried out in large volumes. In South Africa, urban public rail commuting is one of the key pillars of transport provision and the system is operated in 6 metropolitan areas transporting 2.2 million passengers daily. The three major metropolitan commuter networks, namely Johannesburg, Cape Town and Pretoria, are together responsible for about 2 million of these movements. The majority of passengers (84%) are working people (South African Rail Commuter Corporation, 2007).

In Zimbabwe, the National Railways of Zimbabwe (NRZ), formerly called the Rhodesia Railways (RR), is a government owned and controlled rail company since the colonial era under the Rhodesian government before 1980 and then the new Zimbabwean government from 1980 until today (Mbara, 2006). According to Mbara (2006), the rail transport was mainly used to ferry agriculture and mining resources while the passenger train was operating on major routes such as Bulawayo, Mutare and Gweru. In 1991, the Government of Zimbabwe adopted the Economic Structural Adjustment Programme (ESAP) aimed at improving the economy. This led to the deregulation and privatisation of some public transport operators except for ZUPCO and NRZ. These remained under government control. The deregulation increased competition and, with less operating efficiency from NRZ, it led to passengers moving away from rail to road transport. This in turn affected NRZ operations faced by dwindling sources of finance to run the coaches. Mbara (2006:10) states that, as urban transport problems continued to escalate, the NRZ provided the suburban commuter services in Harare and Bulawayo in 2002. However, the expansion of these services caused shortages of locomotives for the freight traffic. From peak passenger traffic of 17.4 million in 2007, the number of passengers declined to about 2 million in 2009 who were used ferried on the intercity service. From this view, it can be observed that much emphasis was on intercity linkage not intra-city. Little regard has been put forward to consider urban rail commuting system as a sustainable way of transport provision given that it has merits socially, economically and environmentally.

Conceptual framework

The conceptual framework below indicates the available transport mode used by the public for urban commuting and the challenges emanating from such transport options. The concept points to the possible alternative, which is the rail transport, and the benefits of switching to a rail commuting system. Having all these benefits, the concept exhibits the final results of having a reliable, efficient and sustainable public transport system for urban commuting.

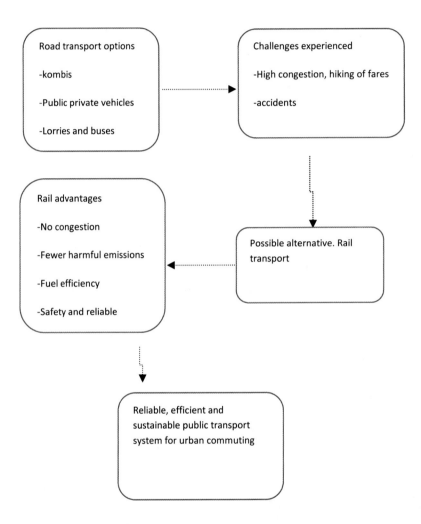

Figure 5.1. Conceptual Framework
Source: Authors (2015)

Literature review

Rail transport systems is viewed as one of the economically and friendly mode of transport for urban commuting if well managed (Cervero, 2011). In a quest to make any city liveable with a proper means to public transport and aspiring to greater sustainability, the way the responsible authority envisions its future and in particular the way it plans its future transport systems in relation to land-use, will be critical. According to Kenworthy (1998:72) it is stated that more centralized cities tend to have less central city parking, stronger rail systems and more use of public transport for radial trips. Western and Eastern European cities, high-income Asian and Latin American cities provide the greatest amount of public transport service. However, it is argued that European and high-income Asian cities offer 46% to 62% public transport services by rail, and this arguably is more competitive to automobiles due to high reliability and speed compared to African cities were most of the operations of public transport providers are not well registered and monitored (Kenworthy, 1998). Only the Western, Eastern European and high-income Asian cities have public transport systems that capture a large share of the overall transport market, and these are cities where urban rail systems are strongest. Regarding the statistics and views above, there is a need to correlate some of these factors when considering public transport for urban commuting.

Public transport in commuting is supported by various theories. Buchanan (1991) proposes a public choice theory which evaluates societal preferences basing on behavioural choices. This present study is hinged on this theory. The public choice theory serves the philosophical desire of a rational account of societal preferences on behavioural choices. The theory states that there is a relationship between the workings of society in common and of public choice in particular in terms of rational choices in decision-making (Buchanan, 1999). The theory further states that the operation of societies is perhaps strongly affected by social situations in which private interests are at odds with collective interests (Van Lange *et al.* 1996). In relation to public transport commuting, the theory can fit well in trying to understand the commuter's rationality on deciding modes of transport. The theory aids in describing the relationship between social human behaviour to public transport selection; and explains the basis for choices between private transport and public transport. In the context of commuter decisions, one relevant attribute that defines utility for most commuters is travel time. Indeed, prior studies revealed that commuter decisions are influenced by time considerations, with individuals preferring the option that is least costly in terms of average travel time (Kropman and Katteler, 1993; Loos and Kropman, 1993). The decision to commute by a private car or public transportation does not only affect the well-being of the individual commuter but also the well-being of others. The public choice theory is therefore crucial in describing how society changes in terms of commuting either in urban areas or on long distances.

A General view of rail commuting system

Public rail commuting is regarded as one of the key contributing factors to economic vibrancy of most economies in the developed countries, and those countries in transition to higher economic development (Simpson, 1994, Babalik, 2000, UNHABITAT, 2013). Relating to urban transport commuting, the European Commission issued the Green Paper which addresses the main challenges related to urban mobility through five core themes. The themes include free flowing towns and cities, green towns and cities, smarter urban transport, accessible urban transport as well as safe and secure urban transport. These are the cornerstones that can promote or spearhead liveable communities with sustainable urban public transport (Antoniou, 2012).

Rail commuting system has been looked upon with favour by regional and national governments due to its capabilities of increasing attractiveness and quality of urban public transport (Du and Malley, 2006). Rail commuting is a high-profile alternative to private motor vehicle and is radial (Newman and Kenworthy, 1996; Mees, 2000). The rail commuting system is also associated with the capability of attracting residential and commercial development resulting in high density nodes (Gibbons and Machin, 2005). Under normal circumstances and well managed environments, rail system is renowned for its reliability, as can be seen in developed countries such as South Korea and Japan, among others. Reliability is an important consideration in ensuring the success of any public transport system (Annabel and Gatersleben, 2005).

Rationale for urban rail commuting system as a public transport

Historically, low and middle-income cities have high density because people needed to remain compact in order to get access to services through non-motorized modes and low-cost public transport (Barter, 2000). However, higher incomes have allowed more people to buy private vehicles to increase their mobility although the city transport networks are not enough to handle this vehicle boom. To cope with motorization, it is evident that low and middle-sized cities are duplicating the past errors of Western cities by resorting to the construction of more road space. Literature has shown that this is not a sustainable solution as this perpetuates private car ownership (Dimitriou, 2006). The realisation of the dangers of private car ownership drives the affinity for higher capacity public transport systems like buses and rail system.

The concept of sustainable development in relation to urban commuting

In order to understand sustainable transport, the concept of sustainable development should first be explained. According to the Brundtland Commission (1987), sustainable development aims to meet the needs of the present generation without compromising the ability of future generations to meet their own needs. The interest in sustainability foremost highlights the concern about long-term risks of over consumed resources reflecting the goals of being fair to future generations. In other words, sustainable decisions can be described as planning that considers goals and impacts regardless of how difficult they are to measure (Litman and Burwell, 2006). Concerning public transport, it is of great importance to decide upon modes that are environmentally friendly.

Case studies in which rail commuting system was successful

The Zurich model is used as one of the examples that managed to promote a lucrative passenger rail commuting system in an urban area. One of the reasons for its success was the manner in which the model uses a well-structured grid network to increase densification that promoted high mass transit. The success of the Zurich rail commuting is attributed to the organisation of integrated public transport system where inter-changes of different modes from place to place were very easy. Buses feed waiting high speed rail services forming a 'pulse' network capturing an average of 500 trips per resident per year (Mees, 2000: 124). Zurich's rail commuting transport patronage levels are second only to Hong Kong and are attributable to decades of integrated transport policy through the establishment of a central planning agency (*ibid.*).

Another example of successful public rail commuting transport is the urban commuting rail in Freiburg, Germany. According to Pedro and Pablo (2011), the area consists of a population of about 250 000 people. Buses and passenger rail commuting system are the main means of public transport for urban commuting. There was an increase in service frequencies due to an efficient economic function which led to high demand for travelling. There was discouragement for private car users through high parking charges. It was also observed that pedestrian friendly urban planning increased attractiveness of public rail transport (Fitzroy and Smith, 1995). The achievement of Freiburg's rail commuting system was one of the reasons for achieving an efficient transport system and is regarded as one of the best in the world.

Methodology

The study adopted mixed research methods in which qualitative and quantitative data were used. It also made use of primary and secondary data. For primary data, the study used questionnaires, observations and key informant interviews. The targeted population in this research study included passengers who use public transport, motorists, government agencies such as the Ministry of Transport that have been involved in railway transport strategies, and the Harare city council. To gather data from respondents using questionnaires, convenience sampling and purposive sampling technique was used to select interviewees. On questionnaire surveys, the idea was to get the views of the commuters. Major bus termini/ranks were identified, and these included Coppa Cabbana, Market Square, Charge Office, Fourth Street rank as well as public spaces such as Africa Unity Square and Harare Gardens. With the haphazard movement in the rank, random convenient sampling was used for easiness in identification of respondents. The reason for selecting the areas was to ensure a good coverage of the sample since these bus terminuses accommodate people from various residential areas. The idea was to obtain information from commuters travelling from distant residential areas such as Chitungwiza, Mabvuku, Tafara, Norton, Ruwa, Dzivarasekwa, Kuwadzana, Glenview, Budiriro and Marondera, all surrounding Harare metropolitan area. In terms of the state of the rail system infrastructure, observation technique was used. The observation included taking photographs using a digital camera. Key informant interviews were conducted with selected personnel from participating organisations. The organisations included the Ministry of Transport and Infrastructure Development, Municipality of Harare, Municipality of Chitungwiza, Marondera Town Council, and the National Railways of Zimbabwe. Secondary data were collected form textbooks, journal articles, theses and dissertations, newspapers and other public documents. The qualitative data were analysed through content or discourse analysis. The quantitative data were analysed using statistical packages that include Statistical Package for the Social Science (SPSS) and MS Excel. Quantitative data were presented using charts and graphs while the qualitative data were presented using text with direct quotations to empathize on certain points.

Results

The essence of collecting data pertaining to income and choice of mode on the questionnaire was to gather information to understand whether a train system is of significance to public commuters. From this information, commuters who use private cars to travel into town are those employed though some use public transport. Dominating the result is the undisclosed range perhaps due to privacy as explained after a discussion with some individuals saying,

> *"Mari inonetsa kungoudza munhu wese wese shamwari yangu kunyanya yakawanda nekuti nyika yatiri kurarama iyi unozobvunzwa uri kuiwanepi iwe usina basa svinu raunoshanda"* (It is difficult to disclose my income to you especially considering the tough economy we are having thus you are prone to be questioned where you are getting that lot of money without proper formal work.)

Income variability helps to determine the need of public transport. The National Transport policy section 1.4 policy goal describes the provision of adequate public transport to the vulnerable groups of the society including the urban and rural poor. Having low income may highly point to those commuters using public transport mainly and a rail system is one of the modes which can accommodate transportation in large numbers and provide affordable fares for the poor.

Challenges experienced in using road transport

The data obtained indicates that congestion, police road blocks, accidents and above all hiking of fares are the major challenges currently experienced when commuting using road transport. These inconveniences prompt the option of finding alternatives that best provide good public transport to commuters. The National Transport Policy section 1.4 states the need for safety, reliability, efficient and promotion for all modes of transport and this paves way for utilisation of rail commuting system as a viable option. From the research, the commuters are dissatisfied by the prevailing transportation modes as one respondent went on to say,

> *"Mufanami isu toda kufamba zvisina kumbunyikidzwa kwete zvatinoitwa nevanhu vemakombi ava kutounza chitima sesu vanobva kuChitungwiza hurumende inenge yatigonera nekuti kufamba kwatirikuita hausi hupenyu uyu."* (Young man, we want to travel safely not the harassment we often face from these kombi drivers, if the government brings the train to Chitungwiza route the life of travelling will be safe because this kind of commuting is not favourable.)

Moreover, other challenges were bad customer care services by rank marshals. Several women who participated in the study cited the behaviour of rank marshals as a troubling issue when using commuter buses. A common complaint was the way the rank marshals would whistle all over the rank at women dressing. Participants were therefore supportive of bringing a good rail system that would allow them to move freely.

From the findings, critical issues were cited as pivotal to the idea of introducing an urban rail commuting system and these are efficiency, safety, affordability, reliability as well as new models of train coaches. In terms of preferences, if all the stated conditions mentioned above were considered and improved upon, the majority of participants were willing to use the rail system. The current state of coaches and station is shown in Figures 5.1, 2 and 3.

Figure 5.1: The Locomotive at NRZ
Source: Fieldwork (2015)

Figure 5.2: The Locomotive at NRZ
Source: Fieldwork (2015)

Figure 5.3: The Locomotive at NRZ
Source: Fieldwork (2015)

Views from different departments of the government

The study, through interviews, sought the views of the organisations below and the information is as presented in the following sections.

Ministry of Transport and Infrastructure Development

The Ministry of Transport, as the mother body of the transport sector, hinted on several issues which have affected the national railways and the reasons why many no longer consider commuting using public rail. In an interview, one of the Engineers opined that many of these problems emanate from sanctions. The Engineer stated that NRZ is still relying on over aged coaches, and with difficulties currently facing the economy, most of the materials for repairing comes from abroad. Reeling under sanctions, the responsible ministry is facing difficulties to import equipment from abroad. Another point stressed by the Engineer was that, even though the responsible ministry want efficient public rail system for commuting, the returns are normally below profit margins hence it would be better to concentrate on goods train. The Engineer elaborated that NRZ fares are highly controlled by government hence the profit return is very low since fares are charged to accommodate the poor. The best option for the responsible ministry would be operating and managing goods train. In terms of goods transport, they used to ferry on average 12 million tonnes to 18 million tonnes per annum and that could rip an amount of 1.4 billion dollars. However, current operations carry 6 million tonnes per year. From the above statistics, it clearly shows that the ministry prefers goods train operations compared to passenger.

National Railways of Zimbabwe

From the NRZ perspective, they stated that they are experiencing challenges in management and resuscitating the infrastructure. As per interview, it was discovered that the NRZ has for a long-time experienced funding, technical and operational problems arising from poor corporate governance and inadequate investment. The status of the railway system was described as difficult to manage with the amount of finance required for new coaches and servicing of rail lines totalling the range of $3 to $4 billion dollars for them to provide quality services. The registration service manager affirmed that passenger train contributes only 5% to their coffers hence requires subsidies they used to have from the government for them to be able to fight stiff competition from road transport. Another issue was the need to engage in partnerships with both local and foreign companies to reduce the workload on operational costs. The major downfall of previously commuting train was blamed on the economic downturn. For example, the interviewee noted that before the collapse of the rail transport industry most commuters were using the train for commuting. Having gathered all the data, the major challenge which currently faces the NRZ such as old dilapidated coaches and lines highly hinges on the assistance of the financial factor.

Harare City Council

The city of Harare Chief Traffic and Transportation personnel hinted that the city council is willing to cooperate in resuscitating the rail commuting system with the NRZ. This was mentioned as a boost in trying to decongest the city centre and bring order to the CBD since it will reduce the volume of traffic entering the CBD. From the City of Harare standpoint, resuscitating the rail system for urban commuting was a noble idea. However, through further discussion, the researcher observed that the local authority prefers to bring its own public buses rather than re-establishing the rail system. The researcher believes this is due to revenue earning issues since the city council will not gain much in the case of re-establishing the rail system. With their own public buses, the city council would generate more revenue for their coffers hence they were not clearly in support of the rail system. However, the council is aware that the rail system can be a good way to manage the problems of road and parking spaces in the CBD.

Marondera, Bindura and Chitungwiza local authority's responses

In one of the interviews, a health officer representing the local authority of Marondera, highlighted that re-establishing the rail commuting system in Harare metropolitan is long overdue. The interviewee expressed that the NRZ is currently sitting on opportunities, especially with the poor conditions of the road network. Furthermore, the health officer cited examples of other developing countries that have established the rail system as a major means of public transport for both intercity linkages and urban commuting. Brazil and South Africa were some of the countries mentioned, with reference to the Gauteng train in South Africa.

The views of these local authorities were generally supportive in comparison to the Harare City Council. One interviewee from the local authority of Chitungwiza expressed that a rail system will allow residents to have more development projects in their areas of location since transport will be available easily. The participant further opined that this could help to develop some surrounding local authorities of the Harare metropolitan. One of the officials from Marondera local authority further stated that an efficient rail system could reduce the cost of road maintenance since commuters would use better means of commuting. The official further expressed that this could allow local authorities to increase investments of funds in other pressing issues.

The research's respondents comprised 50 respondents with 33% male compared to 17% female. This can be attributed to the security factor as male were more open to express their views as compared to females. The researcher also observed that one of the major issues cited was the inability of women to sometimes withstand the pressure to hustle for transport during peak hours.

The women, especially those who depend on informal business of vending and have kids, often opt to commute at a time when there is little pressure. The essence of this demographic analysis is to clearly understand that, in terms of public transport provision, there is a need to provide a rail transport system which offers security and safety. This is succinctly explained by one female participant that,

"*mukwasha kufamba nechitima hakutomboite nekuti hamuna order sesu vanhukadzi hatimboonekwa sevanhu nekuda kwezvidhakwa security yako chaiyo panenge pasimborina kunyanya tikatarisa malong journeys chaiwo ekuenda kunana Mutare environment yemuchitima inoita vanhukadzi vanyanyofarira kufamba havo nemakombi or mabhazi for security reasons*" (It is much better to continue using buses or kombi's because at least they have a bit of some security and order compared to the suggestions of train where by the touts don't have any respect in those train coaches especially considering those which used to be for long journey like Mutare).

From the previous statement, it can be observed that a public transport must offer an environment conducive to commuting for both females and male commuters. The re-establishment of rail commuting as a means of urban public transport thus requires addressing security issues for it to be successful. The other reason might be the convenience and easy navigation on the road as commuter bus drivers can manoeuvre in any kind of road hence this choice of transport by commuters. One respondent elaborated further that,

"*shamwari yangu papeak hour mabhazi nemota dzemushikashika iwaya maLorry netuma private ka ndizvo zvandinotokwanisawo kuafforder nekuti makombi anenge ava $1.50 kuenda kuChitungwiza instead of $0.50*" (My friend on peak ours i can only manage to board these private cars and lorries from undesignated places because they are affordable and one can pay normal fee of $ 0.50 compared to a hiked fee of $1.50 by kombis)

All these factors were pointed as critical in what determines the choice of public transport currently utilised by commuters in in the Harare metropolitan.

Discussion

Rail commuting system in urban areas is regarded as a key factor to the current global efforts of sustainable public transport (UNHABITAT, 2013). Literature has revealed that a rail commuting system in an urban area with increasing population can reduce congestion and promote a liveable environment which is pollution free. However, to have such a system working perfectly it is imperative to improve the quality of the passenger rail system to counter some of the challenges faced by using road transport. This goes in tandem with the data that was obtained from the field as public commuters in Harare welcomed the idea of rail commuting system with some citing the main challenges they are currently facing on day to day commuting. The challenges were cited as mainly hiking of fares, police roadblocks, congestion, accidents and other behavioural concerns such as the rowdy rank marshals.

From the public's opinion, and basing on the data, the researcher found that hiking of fares was the major worry for commuters, especially with the current economic downturn. This typifies the state of public transport for urban commuting as there is no clear pricing policy existing in the current public transport system. Commuters who use commuter buses daily to and from Harare CBD have experienced unfair hiking of bus fares.

Literature based on World Bank (2002) reveals that one of the Millennium Development Goals (MDGs) hinges on eradication of poverty through a sustainable public transport that would improve mobility and accessibility. From the statistics of data collected, the reason why commuter buses occupy the greatest concerns of respondents might be due to the fact that there is lack of good public transport alternatives. This reveals the limited choices of commuters to choose other means of commuting and the poor transport scenario therefore needs alternatives. This lack of alternatives contradicts one of the national transport goals, which states the provision of public transport from all modes of transport.

The existence of challenges faced by commuters is a clear sign that there is greater need for revitalization of public transport. In their response to the research questionnaires, participants expressed that reutilisation of a rail commuting system would be a cornerstone towards solving public transport woes in Harare metropolitan area. According to Mees (2000), a well-monitored, efficient, fast and reliable passenger rail train for urban commuting is a recipe to achieve the level of quality public transport that can provide benefits to members of the public and can help towards the growth of an economy since transport is one of the key facilitators to economic development. Basing on the data findings, most urban commuters in Harare expressed that the chaos of public transport, especially in the CBD during peak hours, is a choker blocker due to the haphazard and disorder on roads which reflects the unsustainability of urban expansion.

Besides the issues of safety, efficiency, reliability and security, there is also the view from literature about collection cost and waiting time as factors that can make commuters willing to use rail system as a good alternative mode of urban commuting. This also concurs with the results from this research. Warner and Baumol (1969) revealed that relative time and money costs can provide explanations of modal choice and estimated that enormously large amount of money cost and time differentials may produce a significant change in ways of deciding a modal choice. Basing on the issue that the last journey to the doorstep is made on foot, it may now depend on the time taken to travel that distance from the rail station to home or to work place. In relation to the reutilisation of rail commuting system as means of public transport, it may now require an effective shuttle from the rail station to the homestead hence a greater need for an effective integrated system. In this case, one of the goals of National Transport Policy (2012-2016) will be fulfilled, that is, enhancing and providing all modes of transport in urban commuting.

As per interview with personnel at the Ministry of Transport, the issue of sanctions was blamed as one of the challenges faced by the NRZ. Sanctions were blamed for restricting the ministry to acquire rail materials as well as funding to resuscitate the system. However, the downfall and poor operation of the rail system might not sorely be blamed on sanctions. The researcher also observed that poor organisational management which include nepotism and corruption might have been one of the root causes contributing to underutilisation and the below par performance of the rail transport system. Another issue the researcher established is that the NRZ is controlled so much by national party politics to the extent that every decision concerning the running of the organisation is scrutinised from a political angle. Potential investors might be willing to invest. However, the high bureaucratic structure and unfavourable national investment policies can discourage any potential investors. The argument that sanctions are the main hindrance to the efficient operation of the NRZ is therefore an overstatement.

The information obtained from City of Harare, highlights that the idea of reutilising the urban rail commuting system is a noble idea, however, the government has failed to help the NRZ and the local authority to resuscitate the rail system back to a reliable and organised means of public transport. As a result, the City fathers were in support of an effective urban transport and preferred the use of buses such as the BRTs of Bogota in Colombia and Curitiba as a perfect example of how the local authority could solve the existing problem of public transport in Harare. The city council was in favour of buses since they will earn income to balance and improve their budgetary coffers. The idea of buses would enable them to have their own buses and by that possess firm control over management of such facilities than if the rail system is operating. From this viewpoint, it can be seen that there is a tug of war on the issue of public transport provision in Harare.

In addition, major factors that have affected the rail system are lack of appropriate technology, absence of political will and inconsistent government policies. For example, the lack of appropriate technology has jeopardized the rapid expansion of the commuter services. This is coupled with lack of funding by the government to invest in research and new technologies. Furthermore, the existing transportation policies favour road transport at the expense of rail transport. More funding and investment are directed to building new roads while none is set aside for railway line expansion. According to the NRZ official, currently the road system is benefiting from toll-fees and the resurfacing of major roads including the Beitbridge-Harare-Chirundu are all projects aimed at improving the road network system but rarely has this been the case for the rail system. Most commuters cited lack of political will as a crippling factor that has affected the operations so the NRZ, leading to the collapse of the rail services. An NRZ official interviewed highlighted that besides interfering in the regulations of fares, the goods train has also suffered from other political decisions such as the introduction of heavy trucks on the road to transport heavy goods traditional ferried by goods train. To the NRZ official, this policy inconsistency had political backing and, consequently, had a negative impact on rail freight services. The respondent further remarked that there was a deliberate effort to convince industries to transport their goods through the road network instead of the rail transport as revealed by lack of interest by government in remodernising the rail system and purchasing of new coaches. The management of the rail services also suffered from political interference as they are under the scrutiny of various stakeholders. This has inhibited some investors from putting their trust and commit their funds and machinery to operate in partnership with the NRZ.

Conclusion, policy and recommendations

To sum up this study, revitalizing the rail commuting system for urban public transport provision is not a viable idea with the current environment. This requires a lot of resources, ceteris paribus. For example, funds needed to purchase modernised coaches would be close to US$4 billion. The revitalization of the rail system would thus be a farfetched idea to achieve in the current economic environment in which the government is struggling with the maintenance of roads and attempting to address other economic pressing issues. The emphasis should therefore be on the bus rapid transport (BRTs). The BRT is an idea that could be achieved if there is commitment in terms of planning, investment, policy implementation and management. The following recommendations are therefore based on the results from this study,

- Public private partnerships between the government and external private companies should not be stifled but rather promoted to enhance funding.
- It was also found that the NRZ has got vast land which is in form of buffers to the rail line. As per study some suggestions were that the NRZ could make use of those

large buffers through leasing them to generate income rather than letting the land lie idle while there is a potential for small marketing projects in the buffer areas.

- There is need to create an integrated public transport system which would allow utilisation of both modes of transport. The current scenario does not promote such a function hence the need to come up with a strategy transport plan for Harare metropolitan encompassing all surrounding towns. This plan ought to provide the best urban commuting transport by first consulting stakeholders in different sectors of the economy through strategised researches.

There is also need for education regarding the importance of public transport so as to reduce individual car usage. Education of citizens through environmental awareness on the benefits of mass transport to the environment has a positive bearing towards achieving a sustainable urban mass transport.

References

Asare - Akufo, F. (2014). *Evaluating the Effectiveness of Urban Planning and Administration in Taming Urban Sprawl IN TAMING URBAN SPRAWL.* Alabama: Unpublished Msc Thesis (University of Alabama).

Department for International Development. (2015). *Urban infrastructure in Sub-Saharan Africa —Harnessing Land Values, Housing and Transport.* Harare,: African Centre for Cities.

Mwaura, A. M. (2006). Policy Review for Zones 3, 4 and 5, Nairobi, Kenya. *42nd ISoCaRP Congress*, (pp. 1-13). Nairobi.

(2017, February). Retrieved from Zimbabwe Classifieds: http://www.classifieds.co.zw

(2017, March). Retrieved from Property 24: http://www.property.co.zw/

Agency, Z. N. (2015). *Zimbabwe 2012 Population Census Population Projections Thematic Report.* Harare: Government of Zimbabwe.

Ajzen, I., and Fishbein, M. (2000). Attitudes and the attitude-behavior relation: Reasoned and automatic processes. In W. Stroebe, and M. Hewstone, *European Review of Social Psychology* (pp. 1-33). John Wiley and Sons.

Amoako, C., and Cobbinah, P. (2014). Urban Sprawl and the Loss of Peri-Urban Land in Kumasi, Ghana. *International Journal of Social, Behavioral, Educational, Economic, Business and Industrial Engineering*, 313-322.

Annez, P. C., and Buckeley, R. M. (2009). Urbanization and Growth: Setting the Context. In M. Spence, P. C. Annez, and R. M. Buckley, *Urbanization and Growth.* Washington: The World Bank.

Arman, M., Zuo, J., L. W., Zillante, G., and Pullen, S. (2009). Challenges of responding to sustainability with implications for affordable housing. *Ecological Economics.*

Babbie, E. (2002). *Social research* (2nd ed.). United States of America: Wadsworth Group.

Basawaraja, R., Chari, K. B., Mise, S. R., and Chetti, S. B. (2011, August). Analysis of the impact of urban sprawl in altering the land-use, land-cover pattern of Raichur City, India, using geospatial technologies. *Journal of Geography and Regional Planning, Vol.* 4(8), 455-462.

BBC. (2014). *Geography.* Retrieved from GCSE Bitesize: http://www.bbc.co.uk/schools/gcsebitesize/geography/

Bekele, H. (2005). *Urbanization and Urban Sprawl.* Stockholm: Unpublished Thesis.

Bhatta, B. (2010). *Analysis of Urban Growth and Spraw from Remote Sensing Data: Advances in Geographic Information Science.* Berlin Heidelberg: Springer-Verlag.

Briassoulis, H. (2010). Who plans whose sustainability? Alternative roles for planners. *Journal of Environmental Planning and Management.*

Brinkhoff, T. (2013). *SOUTH AFRICA: City of Tshwane / .* Retrieved from City Population: https://www.citypopulation.de/

CDC. (2013). *Sexually Transmitted Disease Surveillance 2013.* CDC.

Chirisa, I. (2008). Population growth and rapid urbanization in Africa: Implications for sustainability. *Journal of Sustainable Development in Africa*, 10(2), 361-394.

Chirisa, I. (2010). Inner-City Revitalization and the Poor in Harare: Experiences, Instruments and Lessons from Mbare. In A. Ayala, and E. Geurts, *Urbanising Africa: the city centre revisited Experiences with inner-city revitalisation from Johannesburg (South Africa), Mbabane (Swaziland), Lusaka (Zambia),Harare and Bulawayo (Zimbabwe)* (pp. 58-67). Rotterdam: IHS.

Chirisa, I. (2013). *Housing and Stewardship in Peri-urban Settlements in Zimbabwe: A Case Study of Ruwa and Epworth.* Harare: University of Zimbabwe, Faculty of Social Studies (Unpublished).

Chirisa, I. (2014). Building and Urban Planning in Zimbabwe with Special. *Consilience: The Journal of Sustainable Development*, 1-26.

Chirisa, I., and Mlambo, N. (2017, February 20). *Situating Morality in the Housing Debate in Harare: Case of Matapi Hostels.* Retrieved from Research Gate: https://www.researchgate.net/publication/45713937

Chirisa, I., Gaza, M., and Bandauko, E. (2014, December). Housing Cooperatives and the Politics of Local Organization and Representation in Peri-Urban Harare, Zimbabwe. *African Studies Quarterly*, pp. 37-53.

Chirisa, I., Gaza, M., and Bandauko, E. (2014). Husing Cooperatives and the politics of local organization and representation in Peri-urban Harare, Zimbabwe. *African Studies Quarterly.*

Chitura, M., and Manyanhaire, I. O. (2013). Preferences for complementary and alternative HIV and AIDS treatment among rural residents in Zimbabwe. *E3 Journal of Environmental Research and Management,* 4(6), 0275-0292.

City of Capetown. (2012). *Capetown Densification Policy.* Capetown: City of Capetown.

City of Tswane. (2014). Mayoral Committee. City of Tswane.

Clarke, S., and Ginsburg, N. (1984). *THE POLITICAL ECONOMY OF HOUSING.* London: SAGE.

Cobbina, P. B., and Nsomah Aboagye, H. N. (2017). A Ghanaian twist to urban sprawl. *Elsevier,* 231-241.

Cobbinah, P. B., and Amoako, C. (2014). Urban Sprawl and the Loss of Peri-Urban Land in Kumasi, Ghana. *International Journal of Social, Behavioral, Educational, Economic, Business and Industrial Engineering,* 8(1), 313-322.

Cooke, R., and French, D. P. (2008). How well do the theory of reasoned action and theory of planned behaviour predict intentions and attendance at screening programmes? A meta-analysis. *Psychology and health,* 23(7), 745-765.

Crowley, S. (2003). The Affordable Housing Crisis: Residential Mobility of Poor Families and School Mobilityof Poor Children. *The Journal of Negro Education.* Retrieved from Linked references are available on JSTOR for this article:http://www.jstor.org/stable/3211288?seq=1andcid=pdf-reference#references_tab_contents.

Cseh, K., and Terebessy, A. (2005). *Introduction to demography. Presentation and calculation of basic demographic indicators.* Retrieved from University of Hungary: http://semmelweis.hu/nepegeszsegtan/files/2015/05/1415_Introduction-to-demography1.

Curley, A. M. (2005). THEORIES OF URBAN POVERTY AND IMPLICATIONS FOR PUBLIC HOUSING POLICY. *Journal of Sociology and Social Welfare,* 1-24.

Department of Physical Planning. (1999). *Layout Design Manual.* Harare: government Publications.

Appiah, D. O., Bugri, J. T., Forkuor, E. K., and Boateng, P. K. (2014). Determinants of peri-urbanization and land-use change patterns in peri-urban Ghana. *Journal of Sustainable Development,* 7(6), 95.

ECDC. (2012). *European Centre for Disease Prevention and Control. Evaluating HIV treatment as prevention in the European context.* Stockholm: ECDC.

European Environment Agency. (2006). *Urban sprawl in Europe: The ignored challenge.* Copenhagen,: EEA.

Fishbein, M. (1967). Attitude and the prediction of behavior. In M. Fishbein, *Readings in attitude theory and Measurement* (pp. 477–492). New York: Wiley.

Fishbein, M. (2000). The role of theory in HIV prevention. *AIDS Care,* 12, 273–278.

Freire, M. E., Somik, L., and Leipziger, D. (2014). Africa's Urbanization: Challenges and Opporttunities. Washington DC: The Growth Dialogue.

Gahadza, N. (2016, August 2). *CABS to launch rent-to-buy Scheme.* Retrieved March 14, 2017, from The Herald: http://www.herald.co.zw/cabs-to-launch-rent-to-buy-scheme/

Gelfand, M., Mavi, S., Drummond, R., and Ndemera, B. (1985). *The Traditional Medical Practitioner in Zimbabwe: His Principles of Practice and Pharmacopoeia.* Gweru, Zimbabwe: Mambo Press.

Githira, D. N. (2016). Growth and Eviction of Informal Settlements in Nairobi. Enschede, Netherlands.

Governement of Zimbabwe. (2002). *Rural District Councils Act 29:13.* Harare: Governement of Zimbabwe.

Government of Zimbabwe. (1998). *Regional, Town, Country and Planning Act (chapter 29:12).* Harare: Government of Zimbabwe.

Government of Zimbabwe. (2005). *Urban Councils Act (Chapter 29:15).* Harare: Government Publications.

Government of Zimbabwe. (2016). *Ministry of Lands and Rural Resettlement.* Retrieved from Ministry of Lands and Rural Resettlement: http://www.lands.gov.zw/

Green, E. (1994). *AIDS and STDs in Africa: Bridging the gap between traditional healing and modern medicine.* Scotsville, Pietermaritzburg, South Africa: Westview Press, Inc., Boulder, Colorado / University of Natal Press.

Group, W. B. (2012). *Independent Evaluation Group (IEG).* Rctrieved April 13, 2017, from The World Bank group:
http://lnweb90.worldbank.org/oed/oeddoclib.nsf/DocUNIDViewForJav aSearch/4EF67E4EE2EE239C852567F5005D8BAE

Henderson, P. (2011). *A kinship of bones: AIDS, intimacy and care in rural KwaZulu-Natal. South Africa:* . KwaZulu-Natal. South Africa: University of KwaZulu-Natal Press.

Hofstad, H. (2012,). Compact city development: High ideals and emerging practices. *European Journal of Spatial Development*, 1-23.

Housing Department. (2015). Retrieved from City of Harare: www.hararecity.co.zw

Hudson, B. M., Galloway, T. D., and Kaufman, J. L. (1979). Comparison of current planning theories: Counterparts and contradictions. *Journal of the American Planning Association*, 45(4), 387-398.

Jijide, J. (1994). Community-based AIDS Prevention and Care in Africa. In A. Leonard, *Building on Local Initiatives, Case Studies from Five African Countries* (pp. 2-8). New York: Population Council.

Johnson, M. P. (2006). Decision Models for Affordable Housing and Sustainable Community Development. *Journal of the American Planning Association: The futures of housing*, 1-26.

Kamusoko, C., Gamba, J., and Murakami, H. (2013). Monitoring Urban Spatial Growth in Harare Metropolitan Province, Zimbabwe. *Advances in Remote Sensing*, 322-331.

Katz, B., Turner, M. A., Brown, K. D., Cunningha, M., and Sawyer, N. (2003). Rethinking local affordable housing strategies: Lessons from 70 years of policy and practice. *The Brookings Institution centre on urban and metropolitan policy and urban institute.*

Kent, A., and Sepkowitz, M. D. (2001). The New England Journal of Medicine. *The New England Journal of Medicine*, 344, 1764-1772.

Kiai, S. K. (2013). Sustainable Housing Densification in Kileleshwa: Nairobi, Kenya. Nairobi, Kenya.

Kippler, C. (2010). Exploring Post Development: Politics, the state and emancipatiion. the question of alternatives. *POLIS*, 1-38.

Langley, P. (2006, September). Securitising Surburbia: The transformation of Anglo-American Mortgage Finance. *Competition and Change*, 10(3), 283-299.

Lindsay, C. M., and Feigenbaum, B. (1984). Rationing by waiting lists. *American Economic review*, 404-417.

Lucci, P., Bhatkal, T., Khan , A., and Ber, T. (2015). *What works in improving the living conditions of slum dwellers: A review of the evidence across four programmes.* London: Overseas Development Institute.

Macherera, M., Moyo, L., Ncube, M., and Gumbi, A. (2012). Social, Cultural, and Environmental Challenges Faced by Children on Antiretroviral Therapy in Zimbabwe: a Mixed-Method Study. *International Journal of MCH and AIDS*, *1*, 83-91.

Magwaro-Ndiweni, L. (2011, Dec). Contestation in the Use of Residential space: House Typologies and Residential Land in Bulawayo, Zimbabwe. *African Review of Economics and Finance, Vol. 3*(1).

Makoshori, S. (2014, October 30). Harare approves cluster houses. *Financial Gazette* .

Manikela, J. S. (2008). *Understanding the Peripheralisation of Low-Cost Housing Delivery in the Mbombela Local Municipality.* Johannesburg: University of the Witswatersrand.

Mansoori, M. J. (undefined). Government Low-Cost Housing Provision in the United Arab Emirates. *Implications of standards of construction and conditions of tenure* , 1-6.

Mayer, H., and Venkatesh, K. (2011). Promoting Public Health Research, Policy, Practice and Education. *American Journal of Public Health*, 101(2), 199-200.

McGranahan , G., and Satterthwaite, D. (2014). *Urbanisation concepts and trends.* London: International Institute for Environment and Development.

Mengya, Y. (2013). *To analyze urban sprawl using remote sensing : a case study of London, Ontario, Canada.* Hong Kong: Unpublished Dissertation.

MLGPWNH. (2004, December). Circular 70 of 2004. Government Records.

Mohajeri, N., Gudmundsson, A., and Scartezzini, J.-L. (2015). *Expansion and Deensification of Cities: Linking Urban Form to Urban Ecology.* Lausanne: CISBAT.

Moyo, W. (2014). URBAN HOUSING POLICY AND ITS IMPLICATIONS ON THE LOW-INCOME EARNERS OF A HARARE MUNICIPALITY, ZIMBABWE. *International Journal of Asian Social Science.*

NAC. (2006). *National HIV/AIDS Behavior Change Strategy and Priorities.* Harare: National AIDS Council. Ministry of Health and Child Welfare (MOHCW), Health Information and Surveillance Unit, Department of Disease Prevention and Control, AIDS and TB Programme.

Newman, W. (2011). *Social research methods; Qualitative and quantitative approaches.* Boston: Allyn and Bacon.

Nyakazeya, P. (2010, January 14). *Building Residential Properties Expensive.* Retrieved March 13, 2017, from ZIMBABWE INDEPENDENT: http//www.theindependent.co.zw/2010/01/14/building-residential-properties-expensive/

Oyewole, C. (2016). Rapid Urbanization and Sustainable Food Security: Africa's Dilemma. *Journal of International Scientific Publications*, 261-266.

Pei, S. (2001). Ethno botanical approaches of traditional medicine studies: Some experiences from Asia. *Pharmaceutical Biology*, 39, 74-79.

Peng, X., Chen, X., and Cheng, Y. (2012). *Urbaniisation and its Consequances.* Beijing: Unesco.

Potsiou, C. (2010). *Rapid Urbanization and Mega Cities: The Need for Spatial Information Management.* Copenhagen: The International Federation of Surveyors (FIG).

Potts, D., and Mutambirwa, C. C. (2006). *High Density housing in Harare: Commodification and Overcrowding.* London: Liverpool University Press.

Rakodi, C., and Mutizwa-Mangiza, D. N. (1990). *Housing Policy and Production in Harare.* Undefined.

Reporter, M. (2016, July 20). *Council loses thousands to corrupt employee.* Retrieved March 24, 2017, from The Herald: http://www.herald.co.zw/council-loses-thousands-to-corrupt-employees/

Rights, H. (2005, July). Housing Rights in Zimbabwe. *Human Rights Monthly Number 37.*

Rojas, E., and Greene, M. (1995). Reaching the poor: lessons from the Chilean housing experience. *Environment and Urbanization*, 7(2), 31-50.

Ruwende, K. (2015, February 27). *CABS slashes deposit for Budiriro Scheme.* Retrieved April 10, 2017, from The Herald: http://www.herald.co.zw/cabs-slashes-deposits-for-budiriro-scheme/

Sanderson, C. (2004). *Health Psychology.* John Wiley and Sons. Inc.

Scheidel , W. (2006). *Population and demography.* Stanford: Stanford University.

Shava, T. (2013, November 12). *Urban poverty increase in Zimbabwean Cities* . Retrieved March 13, 2017, from VOA: http://www.voazimbabwe.com/a/urban-poverty-increases-in-zimbabwe-study/1788633.html

Skovbro, A. (2002). Urban densification --a sustainable urban policy? *The Sustainable City, II.*

Smith, J., and Osborn, M. (2003). Interpretive Phenomenological Analysis. In J. Smith, *Qualitative psychology: A practical guide to research methods.* London: Sage Publications.

Smith, J., Flowers, P., and Larkin, M. (2009). *Interpretative Phenomenological Analysis: Theory, Method and Research.* London: SAGE Publications Ltd.

Taylor, T., Dolezal, C., Tross, S., and Holmes, W. (2008). Comparison of HIV/AIDS-specific quality of life change in Zimbabwean patients at western medicine versus traditional African medicine care sites. *Acquired Immune Deficiency Syndrome, 15 49(5),* 552-556.

Tighe, J. R. (2010). Public Opinion and Affordable Housing:A Review of the Literature. *Journal of Planning Literature.*

Toriro, P. (2008). Town Planning in Zimbabwe: History, Challenges and the Urban Renewal Operation Murambatsvina. In F. Maphosa, K. Kujinga, and S. Chingarande (Eds.), *Zimbabwe Development Experiences since 1980: Challenges and Prospects for the Future* (pp. 164-181). Harare: OSSREA.

Trussel, B. (2010). The bid Rent Gradient theory in Eugene Oregon:An impirical investigation. *University of Oregon,* 4-28.

UN-Habitat. (2015). *Planned City Extensions: Analysis of Historical Examples.* Nairobi: UN-Habitat.

UN-Habitat. (2016). *Guide Lines for Urban Planning: Preparing for the Republic of the Union of Myanmar.* Nairobi: UN-Habitat.

United Nations. (2015). *World Population Prospects, The 2015 Revision, Volume II: Demorgraphic Profiles.* New York: United nations.

United Nations. (2015). *World Urbanization Prospects: The 2014 Revision.* New York: United nations.

University of Otago. (2013). *Urban Intensification in Auckland.* Retrieved from GEOG397 Topics: https://geog397.wiki.otago.ac.nz/index.php/Main_Page

Unkown. (2016, May 30). *Chombo and the rot at Harare City Council.* Retrieved April 10, 2017, from New Zimbabwe: http://www.newzimbabwe.com/news-29466-corruption+chombo+and+hre+city+council/news.aspx

WHO. (2003). *Fact sheets.* Retrieved March 16, 2012, from WHO: http://www.who.int/mediacentre/factsheets/fs134/en/print.html

Williams, K. (2007). Can Urban Intensification Contribute to Sustainable Cities? Retrieved from http://www.urbanicity.org/

Willig, C. (2013). *Introducing Qualitative Research in Psychology* (3rd ed.). Open Univesity Press.

ZIMSTATS. (2012, May). *ZIMSTATS.* Retrieved October 2, 2016, from ZIMSTATS: http://www.zimstats.co.zw

ZIMSTATS. (2014, May). *ZIMSTATS.* Retrieved September 18, 2016, from ZIMSTATS: http://www.zimstats.co.zw

Zwinoira, T. (2017, January 30). NBS to rollout 10 000 housing units in 2017. *Newsday.*

Chapter 6

Diagnosing the 2014 Flood Disaster of Tokwe-Mukosi in Search of Sustainable Solutions

Tsungai Mukwashi

Summary:

Due to the need for infrastructural development, there have been discussions on 'development versus disasters' showing that some developments have led to disruptions as well as changes and or disruptions on people's livelihoods and in the way people live. In many countries, floods triggered during new dam construction have led to the displacement of communities, many deaths, destroyed livelihoods, people's homes and caused economic setbacks. This chapter seeks to discuss underlying causes of the calamity that befell the Tokwe-Mukosi community and to enquire from a range of stakeholders whether construction of the Tokwe-Mukosi dam in Zimbabwe achieved its intended purpose of enhancing community livelihoods. The chapter explores the impact of the 2014 flood on the Tokwe-Mukosi community and analyses community vulnerability before and after the flood revealing the underlying factors that caused the disaster. The chapter proposes how local, provincial and national authorities and communities can reduce vulnerability and increase resilience in the face of floods.

Introduction

To improve the economy of Masvingo Province through increased agricultural production, mainly sugarcane, the Government of Zimbabwe embarked on constructing the Tokwe-Mukosi Dam in Chivi district (ZINWA, 2015). Mazara (2015) states that dam construction project had been on the table as far back as 1955 but a number of hindrances such as economic challenges due to the Rhodesian unilateral declaration of independence in the 1960s, the liberation war in the 1970s, other post-independence developmental priorities in the 1980s, to high construction costs resulting from the fall of the Zimbabwean dollar against major currencies in 1998 delayed the completion of the dam. Salini Impregilo began the construction of the dam in 2011 funded by the Government of Zimbabwe (Gumindoga, 2011). Figure 6.1 shows the location of the Tokwe-Mukosi dam.

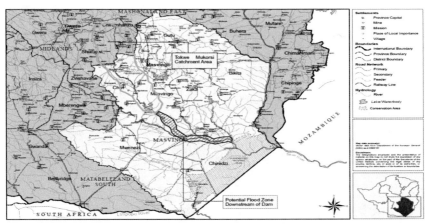

Figure 6.-1: Masvingo Province Map – Showing Tokwe-Mukosi Dam Catchment and Flood Risk Area

Source: Reliefweb.int

The Tokwe-Mukosi dam is in Chivi district, whose average rainfall is 400mm per year (World Weather Information Services, 2017). Historically, the rainfall is erratic and minimal (Moyo, 2000). However, from February to March 2014, Chivi received above average rainfall of up to 850mm (Gumindoga, 2014). The persistent heavy rains led to an increase in the reservoir water, putting pressure on the dam wall whose sluice gates could not be opened as the dam was still under construction. Consequently, the pressure resulted in the partial collapse of the dam on 4 February 2014, releasing a lot of water downstream (Zimbabwe National Water Authority, 2015). Floods were experienced upstream due to rising reservoir water levels and downstream due to the breached dam wall affecting hundreds of households (Tarisayi, 2015). This marked the beginning of a catastrophe whose impact the Tokwe-Mukosi inhabitants continue to shoulder to this day. Many households, according to Mudzingwa (2015), lost their crops, livestock, homes as well as their livelihoods.

Background and Overview

The 2014 Tokwe-Mukosi floods caught the Government of Zimbabwe and the Tokwe-Mukosi community by surprise and affected hundreds of people in Chivi, an area where "meteorological drought and not floods are the most frequently experienced natural hazard" (Chineka, 2016). The community could not cope with the floods and they are still not coping as others have not been able to return to their homes and "re-start" their lives (Mukwashi, 2017). The floods resulted in the displacement of people from their homes, loss of property, livestock and sources of income and making them vulnerable and susceptible to any hazard (International Confederation of the Red Cross, 2017).

On 9 February 2014, the Zimbabwe government declared the Tokwe-Mukosi flood a national disaster and appealed for US$20 million for humanitarian assistance and relocation of those affected (Human Rights Watch, 2015). The Zimbabwe National Army and Civil Protection Unit (CPU) relocated over 20,000 people (around 3,300 families) from the flooded Tokwe-Mukosi Dam basin to Chingwizi Camp on Nuanetsi Ranch in Masvingo's Mwenezi District (Human Rights Watch, 2015). Figure 6.2 shows the areas affected by flood and where flood victims were relocated to.

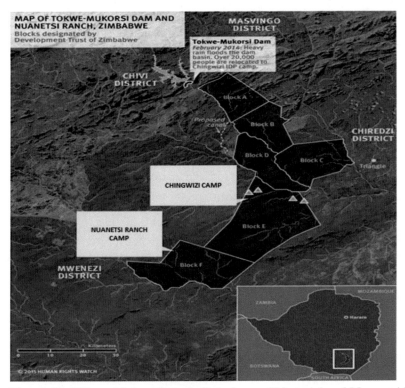

Figure 6.2: Tokwe-Mukosi Dam in Relation to Chingwizi and Nuanetsi Ranch Camps
Source: Human Rights Watch (2015)

The welfare of Tokwe-Mukosi community, now the Chingwizi residents, has deteriorated since the 2014 flood displaced them from their land. The community, whose livelihood depended largely on subsistence crop production such as maize, millet and leafy vegetables such as kale and cabbage were now confined to temporary holding camps, Figure 6.3, that did not enable them to conduct their usual livelihood activities (Human Rights Watch, 2015).

Figure 6.3: Chingwizi temporary relocation camp in 2015
Source: Human Rights Watch (2015)

According to Human Rights Watch (2015), loss of livelihoods such as market gardening and chicken rearing in households displaced by the Tokwe-Mukosi flood may have brought about poverty in the community. Some of the displaced flood victims were moved to Chingwizi Camp. This was to be a transit camp where more than 3,000 families (about 20,000 people) from Chivi were to be housed before they were moved to permanent homes (International Confederation of the Red Cross, 2017). Human Rights Watch (2015) described the Chingwizi Camp residents as "homeless, landless and destitute" as they had lost almost everything they owned. This suggests that there has been an increase in poverty levels due to lost livelihoods. The Chingwizi community's lack of access and control of productive capital has given rise to permanent and irreparable decline in living standards affecting household food security leading to undernourishment of the sick, old and young (UNICEF, 2014).

Finding out why the disaster occurred and taking a risk reduction approach will assist mitigation against similar recurrence of such events in areas with dam construction projects. It will also assist in the development of coping strategies, building of resilience and the reduction of risks in flood prone areas. Lessons can be learnt prior to and in the aftermath of dam failures, as factors which may assist in the prevention and/or reduction of risk for communities that are living in dam catchment areas are identified.

Theoretical Framework

According to the United Nations Office for Disaster Risk Reduction (2015), disaster risk reduction (DRR) is the "concept and practice of reducing disaster risks through systematic efforts to analyse and reduce the causal factors of disasters". Activities that may be undertaken in DRR include "reducing exposure to hazards, lessening vulnerability of people and property, responsible management of land and the environment, as well as improving preparedness and early warning for adverse events" (United Nations Office for Disaster Risk Reduction, 2015). The response to flooding in most instances is mostly reactive as authorities try to evacuate communities who have already been affected by floods. The study took the DRR approach which seeks to prevent and raise awareness to disasters rather than to react when they occur. DRR aims to minimise losses in cases where there is a hazard impact. It is important not to focus only on the hazard, but to consider human factors that may line up to cause a disaster when there is a hazard impact. Human factors may include how susceptible the community may be to the hazard as well as resources that the communities may have in place to withstand or recover from the impact. Risk identification and assessment, prevention and mitigation, preparedness as well as the recovery process, if there is to be a hazard impact, should all work together to reduce disaster risks rather than to respond to disasters (Figure 6.4).

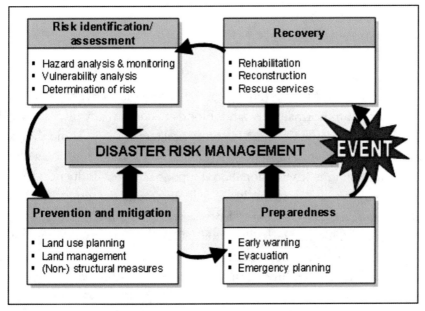

Figure 6.4: Process of Disaster risk management
Source: International Confederation of Surveyors 2014

In assessing resilience, the study took the sustainable livelihood framework approach (Figure 6.5).

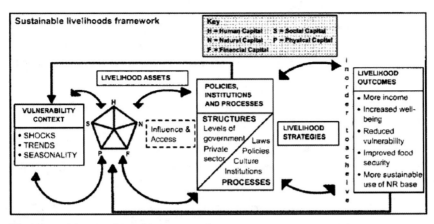

Figure 6.5: The livelihood Framework
Adapted from Farrington *et al*. (2002:8)

The livelihood framework considers the types of work that people in a community are pursuing to earn a living. This may include the agricultural sector, formal or informal employment or a combination of different income generating activities (Farrington *et al*. 2002).

Literature Review

A flood, according to Madaan (2016), can be defined as an overflow of large quantities of water onto normally dry land. Floods occur in many places around the world, in some communities they become disasters while in some they are just events which disrupt the normal functioning of a community for a short while. The United Nations International Strategy for Disaster Reduction (2007) describes a hazard as a threat to life, wellbeing, material goods and the environment caused by extreme natural processes or technology. Floods can thereby be classified under hazards. Pimentel (2013) states that when there is a hazard, impact disasters may be experienced. This can be due to "an act of nature", or it can be an anthropogenic hazard or a combination of both (Pimentel, 2013).

Floods have social, economic, and environmental consequences to individuals, communities and society at large. The impact can either be positive or negative depending on flood location, extent of flood, duration of the flood event, depth of the water, speed of the water as well as vulnerabilities of communities in which the floods have occurred (State of the Queensland, 2016). Floods may be positive such as on the agricultural plans of Saskatchewan and Manitoba in Canada where flood waters sometimes leach the soil of nitrogen but also bring in a good variety of nutrients in the soil for agriculture (Guenther,

2012) When the flood waters are deep and have great speed they carry a lot of debris which in many instances cause injuries and fatalities

The disaster theory formulated by Blackie *et al.* (1994), the pressure and release (PAR) model (also known as the crunch model) maintains that a disaster does not only occur because of the presence of a hazard but because of vulnerability. The root causes are historical causes that are imbedded in society and these include limited access to power, society structures and resources as well as ideologies of political and economic systems. Sarewitze *et al.* (2003) consider the root causes of disasters as systems that go beyond human control, calling it "the physical aspect of an event". Figure 6.6 shows the progression of vulnerability and how it eventually leads to a disaster.

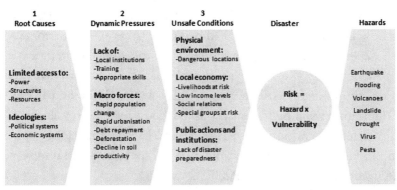

Figure 6.6: The Pressure and Release (PAR)
Source: Blackie *et al.* (1994)

When applied to the Tokwe-Mukosi disaster, the hazard, that is, the flood, may have 'met with the vulnerability' of the community leading to the 2014 disaster as indicated in Figure 6.7.

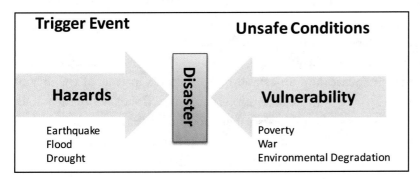

Figure 6.7: The Crunch Model
Source: Smyth 2012

The negative effects of disasters may remain if response and recovery outrank risk reduction. Responding to disasters has been a major part of disaster management as it took more of a humanitarian relief angle, rather than reducing the disaster risks that existed in communities. The development of the post-2015 development framework which succeeded the Hyogo Framework for Action calls for risk reduction in all countries and, if followed, development and disasters can remain more in a positive relationship (UNISDR, 2005). Disaster risk reduction was considered seriously in the Rio+20 Document, calling on countries to address the issue of disasters with urgency. The Rio+20 Document called upon disaster risk reduction to be included and integrated into policies, plans, programmes and budgets of national, provincial and local levels since sustainable and significant reduction of disaster risk can only be achieved by working across policy frameworks (Hillier *et al.* 2013).

In the past, disasters were seen as once-off events that governments and relief agencies would respond to in order to give relief to victims and they did not consider how and why the disaster had occurred (International Federation of Red Cross, 2000). One of the components of the disaster preparedness framework is vulnerability. Research has shown that the rise in disasters and their impact on communities is linked to people's vulnerability and if this is eradicated, communities will be less susceptible to disasters. With vulnerability assessments, disasters are no longer seen as natural hazard impacts that occur on their own but are now seen as a combination of the hazard and unresolved problems of development (Yodmani, 2000:2).

This transition of dealing with disasters from response and recovery to preparedness, prevention and mitigation has begun to influence the way disaster managers are planning and financing management programmes. Disaster preparedness planning as part of DRR, takes into consideration the resources available, allocation of roles and responsibilities of different organisations as well as the development of policies and procedures on how disaster management activities are to be carried out. During pre- or post-disaster, the plans on paper are then implemented in order to reach specific goals (International Federation of Red Cross, 2000:5).

Institutional framework, according to Kent (1994:23), centres on efforts of disaster management working in established structures instead of the creating new ones. The capacity of these institutions to manage floods lies in their ability to define roles and responsibilities so that each organ knows what to do and when (Label, 2006:407). Successful prevention and disaster mitigation activities may be realised if there is cooperation and coordination between communities, the government, and other agencies in disaster risk reduction. Pimentel (2013:30) states that disasters do not occur because of the presence of poverty only but also because people do not know "how to get out of harm's way or take preventative or protective measures". For people to know how to get out of harm's way it is imperative that training and education against hazards be introduced in communities. Pimentel (2013:30) states that response to flooding should be proactive rather than reactive so that lives can be saved. A proactive approach focuses on eliminating problems before they arise, and a reactive approach is based on responding to events after they have occurred.

For disaster risk reduction activities to be efficient and effective there must be good communication and information management systems. This includes the collection of disaster activity related information, analysis of the information, development of a database as well as dissemination of the information (Pimentel, 2013:38). The availability or lack of resources is critical in DRR. In its training manual, the International Red Cross and Red Crescent (2000) looks at resources as being important in coping with disasters.

In the Hyogo Framework of Action (UNISDR, 2005:5) resilience is described as the capacity of communities that are exposed to any kind of hazard to adapt to the conditions they are exposed to, or by changing their society so that they may reach or remain at an acceptable level of functioning and structure. A community may be termed resilient depending on the resources that are available within and without the community to withstand the impacts of hazards. These may be insurance schemes which make reconstruction of property and infrastructure affordable and easier (Surminski, 2014). In the livelihood framework presented by Care Livelihood Toolkit (Farrington *et al.* 2002), the "asset pentagon" (Figure 6.5) shows how households in different communities have access to both tangible and intangible assets that is, financial assets, social assets and human assets. Having a steady source of income may be a form of resilience as one is able to "bounce back" to an acceptable level of functioning after a hazard impact. Figure 6.5 shows the livelihood framework. The different asset categories help people meet their needs. Livelihood strategies consider options of jobs that households ought to pursue in order to get an income. If there is a wide choice of livelihood strategies, communities develop resilience to the shocks, trends and seasonality concerns and the success of one's pursuit of a livelihood strategy can be measured by the livelihood outcome (Farrington *et al.* 2002).

According to Pimentel (2013), disasters are considered as *"agents of destruction"* while developments are usually seen as positive. Both the development and the disaster sectors have been viewed by Pimentel (2013) as having both a positive and a negative sector which are woven together, as in some instances a disaster or development can be positive while in some instances development or disasters can be negative. Figure 13.8 shows how disasters can either be regarded as positive or negative depending on the situation.

Figure 6.8: Disasters and development
Source: Pimentel (2013)

The positive sector, Figure 6.8, indicates that development can reduce vulnerability. Development programmes can be designed to make communities less vulnerable to disasters and move towards a goal of resilience. According to Jha (2010), disasters can provide development opportunities. After the Tokwe-Mukosi disaster government can take the disaster as a way of developing structure villages with amenities such as schools, clinics, portable water and electricity for relocated flood victims. Development in some instances can therefore increase vulnerability. According to Pelling (2003:7), "urbanisation affects disasters just as profoundly as disasters affect urbanisation". Due to construction of tarred roads and concrete pathways, urbanisation may increase runoff and cause rivers to overflow causing floods. Disasters are not inevitable, while development is a necessary facet of society. The link between the two has led the United Nations to steer countries into sustainable development. This led to the Agenda 21 document in 1992 followed by the Johannesburg Summit in 2002. Sustainable development centres on reducing the causal factors of disasters such as poverty, rapid population growth, rapid urbanisation, environmental degradation, and others.

International Rivers (2017) states that dam construction can be regarded as risky business as there are technical as well as environmental problems that investors can face. Because of such risks, finance can be said to be 'the weakest link" in many dam projects as whoever is the investor may decide which projects advance as well as the standards that have to be met (International Rivers, 2017). The construction of Tokwe-Mukosi Dam according the main contractor's report (Salini-Impregilo, 2016) as well as media reports The Sunday News

(2015); The Herald, (2015) was mainly funded by the Government of Zimbabwe. The project as stated by Chitagu (2015) had already started in 1998 and stopped in 2008 due to the economic difficulties the country was facing resulting in lack of funds for the Tokwe-Mukosi project.

Methodology

The population of the study included all people affected by the 2014 Tokwe-Mukosi floods. A sample was drawn from the population as it was impractical to attempt to study or survey every unit of the population. According to the United Nations Office for the Coordination of Humanitarian Affairs (OCHA) (2014), the population of Tokwe-Mukosi comprised 3,125 households. The researcher used judgmental and convenient non-probability sampling technique. The use of judgmental and convenient sampling ensured optimisation of time and resources. This ensured that quicker interviews were done as meetings were conducted with people with information and knowledge about the Tokwe-Mukosi flood disaster. The researcher took advantage of food distributions meetings of flood victims to distribute questionnaires.

One hundred and ten (110) households' representatives were interviewed. The researcher tolerated a margin of error of 10% and a confidence level of 95%. Of the 110 respondents interviewed 49% were women, 18% of whom were older than 50 years and 14% between 40-49 years old. Slightly more than half (51%) of the respondents were men most of whom are in the 40 to 49-year category (16%) followed by those older than 50 years which had 15% of all men interviewed. The highest percentage of the females interviewed was in the 50 plus years' category which is at 18%. Figure 13-7 shows the age and gender of the respondents.

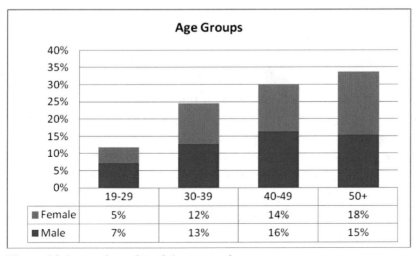

Figure 6.9 Age and gender of the respondents

The research design chosen for this study was both descriptive and exploratory. Descriptive research design, according to Anastas (1999), looks at a research problem and assists in providing answers to the questions of *who*, *what*, *when*, *where* and *how*. Questionnaires and interviews are the two methods that were used to elicit information in the descriptive research. The descriptive research design allowed in-depth analysis of variables and elements of the Tokwe-Mukosi population in the study.

An exploratory design is conducted for a research problem when there are few or no earlier studies to refer to or rely upon to predict an outcome, in a particular area or study field (Cuthill, 2002). The exploratory research design in the study allowed insights for later investigation. The exploratory research gave a well-grounded picture of the situation being developed, generation of new ideas and assumptions in the Tokwe-Mukosi area. The use of exploratory research enabled issues to get refined for a more systematic investigation and formulation of new research questions while direction for future research and techniques got developed (Cuthill, 2002).

A multi-disciplinary approach was used in this study comprising:
- Literature review
- Questionnaires
- Site Observation
- Interviews
- Focus group discussions
- Geographic Information Systems

Literature was reviewed on general flooding and the Tokwe-Mukosi flood. A questionnaire was designed and peer reviewed in order to remove difficult or ambiguous words that could confound respondents concerning what they are being asked. Permission was sought from the Ministry of Local Government in Zimbabwe to conduct research in the Chingwizi camp. To gain community trust, the researcher started with a meeting with local administrators and community leaders to explain the purpose of the research. The researcher and three assistants interviewed respondents and completed a questionnaire which was retained for analysis and record preservation.

Key informant interviews were conducted to identify the causes and sources of vulnerability to floods in the Tokwe-Mukosi area, assess the level and adequacy of disaster preparedness as well as assess levels of adaptation and resilience within the community. The key informants were interviewed with the expectation that they were directly involved in the Environmental Risk Assessment and the monitoring of the dam while it was being constructed. In addition, they would be aware if there were any flood preparedness training that were being done, if any, and would be aware of early warning systems that should be in place.

Observation, which is a systematic data collection approach (Robert Wood Johnson Foundation, 2008), was used. Observations were used to get a picture or images of the impact of the flood and how the former Tokwe-Mukosi community is living now. Figure 6.10 shows the pole and dagga houses that some of the flood victims built after the tents from the United Nations had worn out.

Figure 6.10: Pole-Dagga Homestead and Tuck-shop

Geographic Information Systems (GIS) are systems designed to capture, store, manipulate, analyse, manage, and present spatial or geographic data (Esri, 2017). Spatial data including aerial photographs and images were used in the study. GIS with mapping capabilities, assisted in visualizing, questioning and interpreting data to understand patterns and trends in flooding and vulnerability in the Tokwe-Mukosi area as seen in Figure 6.11 which shows farmland which is part of the dam now.

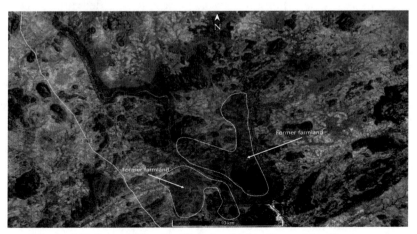

Figure 6.11: Image Showing Farmland Now Part of the Dam
Modified from Google Earth

Two focus groups were held in Chingwizi. The focus group for women had 11 participants and a men's focus group had 8 participants. A third focus group was held the following day at Zunga village in the Tokwe-Mukosi (Chivi) area. Figure 6.12 shows the areas were focus groups were done as well as the key discussion areas.

Figure 6.12: Location Map Showing Key Discussion Areas (Red Labels) Modified from Google maps

The FGD brought the flood victims together to discuss their experiences about the flood. The group was guided by a moderator who, in line with the objectives of the study ensured the discussions, stayed in line with key questions that had been developed. The discussion was meant to know the respondents' views on what they perceive as being the cause of the flood disaster, why they think the 2014 flood affected them in the way it did, how participants perceive the government, how other role players fared in meeting their needs in times of distress as well as gain an understanding of how the victims of the flood disaster would want future developments in their areas to be handled. The discussion was recorded so as not to miss some important issues. The focus group discussion assisted in bringing meaning to survey findings that cannot be explained statistically.

Results and discussion

Causes of the vulnerability

The collapse of the dam and not the cause of the collapse of the dam has been blamed for the catastrophe. It appears convenient for the authorities to focus on the dam collapse and avoid exploring the underlying causes. Results from the research indicate that the 2014 disaster was not only due to heavy rains but a product of the social, political and economic environment that existed in the Tokwe-Mukosi area at that time. In such an environment the community lacked the "capacity to anticipate, cope, resist and recover from the impact of a hazard" (World Health Organisation, 2017). Disaster risk is a result of the presence of a hazard, the vulnerability of the community as well as the coping capacity that the community has. Flood risk in Tokwe-Mukosi was there because of the presence of the hazard (flood), the vulnerability of the community as well as low community coping capacity.

The 2014 floods resulted in evacuations of families living both upstream and downstream (Kadzatsa, 2014). Human Rights Watch (2015) estimates that around 4,500 villagers with homes along and in the flood basin were evacuated in February 2014. The flood victims were evacuated to Gunikuni and then relocated to Chingwizi Transit Camp which is a site in the Nuanetsi Ranch in Mwenezi District (Figure 13-2). The sites were meant to be temporary before relocation to permanent homes (Tarisayi, 2015). The flood victims were promised compensation for their losses and to be relocated to other areas (Hove, 2016).

The research points to poverty as a significant causal factor of the Tokwe-Mukosi disaster. It should be observed, however, that lack of access to information created a high degree of exposure to risk. Slightly less than half (47%) of the respondents indicated that they knew about the Tokwe-Mukosi dam construction through word of mouth and 44% expressed that they saw the builders working at the construction site but there was no communication from the government, ZINWA to be specific, that a dam was to be constructed in the area. With all 4 key informants interviewed indicating that there was no public participation in the EIA, the community was not aware of the gravity of the flood risk that surrounded them. It does not appear there were any mechanisms for construction progress updates to be provided to the community. Without progress updates on the dam construction and subsequent increasing risk, the Tokwe-Mukosi community was oblivious to the impending disaster to proactively relocate to safety. Lack of access to information prevents people from getting out of harm's way, even for retrospectively "obvious" hazards.

Lack of efficient early warning systems increases vulnerability in communities as it reduces the ability of people to make decisions and to respond appropriately in emergencies. This was lacking in the Tokwe-Mukosi flood disaster. There was no early warning system in place so that people could avoid the flood. This was made worse as there were no established emergency response protocols for envisaged project risks such as flooding. The lack of early warning systems and emergency plans suggest inefficiencies in disaster management guidelines or policy enforcement. These inefficiencies cause communities to be vulnerable as they become "sitting ducks" to hazards.

Impact of flood on the community

The Tokwe-Mukosi community is poor, dependent on peasant agriculture and the flood was a huge shock from which they are struggling to recover. Due to poverty, the research revealed that the Chingwizi community is struggling with recovery and reconstruction in the aftermath of the 2014 flood. The poorer the community is, the more sensitive or vulnerable households are to the impact of hazards. Poverty or being poor means that households have a low threshold for withstanding any or most shocks. They are therefore less able to respond, cope with and/or adapt to disaster.

In line with the pressure and release (PAR) model, the Tokwe-Mukosi flood impacted on a vulnerable community resulting in a disaster. There was flooding in an area where 51% of the population had secondary education as the highest qualification and the rest had primary school education (39%) and no schooling (10%). This, together with the livelihoods that were pursued in the community, provided very little income. With low household incomes (85%, no income and 14% less than US$100 per month), the community was not able to deal with the impact of the flood. 89% of households had five or more persons. Through livelihoods pursued, living conditions as well as educational levels (using international benchmarking of poverty datum line), the study classified the Chingwizi community to be poor. Poverty, according to Bolin and Stanford (1999), makes communities more vulnerable to hazards than richer communities.

The 2014 flood disaster can be said to be a cause or source of poverty in Chingwizi as most households do not have the income or capacity to rebuild homes, replace lost assets as well as meet basic needs. The research reveals that disasters can induce and/or increase poverty, especially in communities marginally above or below the poverty datum line. This is because some households or the entire community may not be able to recover from losses incurred in disasters. Change of livelihoods (Figure 6.10) and the change of house construction materials (83% changed from brick and zinc to pole and dagga huts) reveal that the Chingwizi community are now living in worse conditions than before the flood. Figure 6.10 shows the change of livelihoods pre and post disaster. This change lowered incomes and increased poverty. Without significant humanitarian intervention, the Chingwizi community may take many years to recover from the aftermath of the 2014 flood disaster.

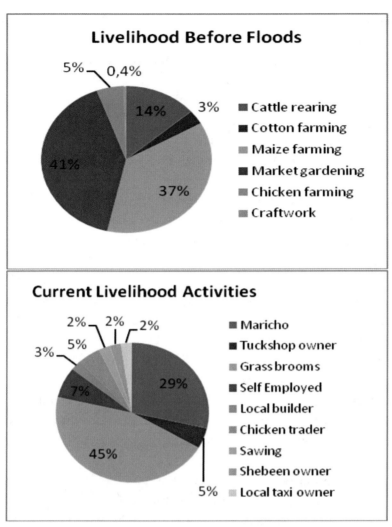

Figure 6.13: Livelihoods Before and after the Flood

Maricho is a Shona word which refers to a daily contract for weeding and seeding on another person's plot

Chingwizi community resilience to disasters

The Chingwizi community were vulnerable to floods and are still susceptible to the impact of hazards such as drought and floods. The community has a low resilience to loss. This is because they have very low incomes and no surplus capacity to 'cushion' themselves from losses let al.one recover. All (100%) are dependent on food handouts from humanitarian and government agencies. Disaster risk in Chingwizi is shaped by a range of social and economic factors that have erased their capacities to respond to disasters and thus create a more vulnerable community.

Man-made poverty

All respondents (100%) did not know where they were going to be relocated to. The community wanted to relocate but they would only do so if they knew exactly where they will be resettled and whether they will be provided with materials to reconstruct their homes. Most (97%) of the respondents in Chingwizi did not receive compensation to be able to rebuild elsewhere. By not comprehensively compensating the Tokwe-Mukosi community, the government made the community worse off than they were before the dam.

Intra community stress coping variances

Although the community's populace was exposed to the same stress factor, there are wide variances in how different inhabitants coped with the impact. The research indicated that households affected by the same flood cope differently depending on the resources each has. The respondents in Chingwizi who received some compensation from the government had better houses (brick and zinc), one owned a taxi, another tuck-shop and the other a tavern. All (3%) respondents that had received compensation fared better than those who had no compensation (ranging from US$2,000 to US$4,000). An orderly evacuation and/or relocation with coping capacities (compensation) are an important factor in areas where people ought to be moved in order for development to take place. Without compensation for households, the government itself became a source of vulnerability in the community.

Importance of preparedness in disaster response

A lack of planning and unpreparedness on the part of the responsible government departments made the Chingwizi community vulnerable to the 2014 flood. The Tokwe-Mukosi community was informed that they would be relocated to various farms around the province of Masvingo, but this was not done. The fact that an evacuation ended up being relocation to Chingwizi where there were no social amenities, shows that the government had not planned to relocate people to that area. Unpreparedness meant that, when there was a flood, the government had to take the people 'somewhere' and this 'somewhere' was not known or planned for. The study highlights that preparedness may be the most important phase in disaster management as the relief approach used by the Government of Zimbabwe seems not to have worked. Post-disaster relief is ineffective if there are no other measures taken to prepare for and mitigate the impact of a hazard.

The research reveals subtle political and administrative factors that may have contributed to the disaster of 2014. This may be inferred from the manner in which resources, such as knowledge, information and food are distributed in the Chingwizi community. The fact that the recipients of aid did not know the source of donations and that one had to be close to the community headman who distributed food along political party affiliation, shows the discrimination that occurred in welfare allocation and potentially information sharing. The 2014 floods may have been a result of heavy rains, but the broader pattern shows that vulnerability is brought out when both the natural environment and the social environment combine. Disaster mitigation may be difficult to implement if such a social environment continues to exist in Chingwizi.

Post disaster recovery

The government's approach of focussing on relief provision in lieu of resilient building continues to create a vulnerable community dependent on hand-outs. Relief provision without plans to restore and build community resilience is ineffective. All the research respondents in Chingwizi community were not aware of any plans by the government to enhance their livelihoods. Three years after the disaster, there are no indications of resilience building but just relief provision, which the community says is insufficient to meet their needs. The Government of Zimbabwe and donor partners are still treating the flood victims as if they are in the evacuation phase where they had to cope. They now need resilience building and adaptive capacity that are long term solutions in disaster management.

The 2014 floods had an adverse impact on the Tokwe-Mukosi community some of whom have moved to Chingwizi area. This is evidenced by more than 80% of respondents who indicated that they had lost all their possessions which included the homes, beds wardrobes, clothes, crops and livestock (cattle and goats) destroyed in the flood. Disaster risk reduction revolves around public information and education, existence of efficient warning systems, disaster preparedness, mitigation and coping mechanisms. The lack of these fundamental disaster management concepts in Zimbabwe made the Tokwe-Mukosi community vulnerable to the 2014 floods.

Conclusion

The study reveals that the 2014 Tokwe-Mukosi flood disaster is not due to a single cause but a complex mix of both the presence of a hazard and human action or inaction. Although dam constructions and dam failures are relatively common, disasters arise when there are social, political and economic issues that are deeply imbedded into the community 'fabric', for instance According to international benchmarking, the Chingwizi community can be classified as poor hence most likely to be affected by the impact of any hazard. With the highest level of education being secondary schooling, most in the community do not have formal skills and rely on communal farming which has not enabled them to build resilience. The material poverty and lack of higher education limited the community's awareness of their rights and recourse to effectively challenge shortcomings in project implementation in their area.

Inadequate funding for the dam construction project and poor planning on the part of the responsible government departments in terms of relocation modalities resulted in the community remaining in an evidently hazardous location. Regardless of financial constraints to compensate each affected household, it is evident that there was no plan on where to relocate this community. If the community had been empowered with the knowledge of their intended relocation site, some or most may have relocated at their own cost to flee the obvious impending danger, especially those who were located within the actual dam perimeter.

The dam constructors, Salini Impregilo (an Italian company) and the project sponsors, the Zimbabwe National Water Authority (ZINWA), did not engage the Tokwe-Mukosi community in the full processes of EIA and this resulted in them not being aware of the risk they faced from the dam construction. In the pre-disaster period, the community was vulnerable through lack of information on flood risks in the area. Where education on disaster risk reduction should have been the focus, the community was left to construe their own versions of risks and potential benefits, adding to their unwarranted exposure to the flood hazard. The absence of early warning system and the community's oblivion to emergency plans highlights deficiencies in disaster management guidelines or policy enforcement that resulted in more households than necessary being impacted by the flood.

The pre-existing socio-economic conditions in Chingwizi played a major role in highlighting how vulnerable the community was. Living in poverty in Tokwe-Mukosi made the community vulnerable to the flood. However, living in poverty in Chingwizi now makes them more vulnerable to various hazards including food shortages which may lead to acute malnutrition. The community was dependent on agriculture which means their livelihoods were destroyed. With negligibly low incomes and low educational levels, the community is not able to pursue other livelihoods to generate sustainable income.

The Department of Civil Protection in Zimbabwe coordinated evacuation of the flood victims saved lives as the flood victims lacked the capacity for self-evacuation. The material and food relief provided after the flood increased the coping capacity of the victims. The study reveals that the evacuation of Tokwe-Mukosi victims did not only end on being evacuations where the victims would later on come back to their homes. The evacuation turned into a permanent relocation as flood victims were moved to Chingwizi and are not able to come back to their homes as the area is now a dam. The Government of Zimbabwe had not planned on where the Tokwe-Mukosi community was to be moved so they moved. The flood victims were moved to Chingwizi, an area which has basic community amenities such as schools, clinics or potable water sources.

The flood victims were moved without any monetary compensation that would help them rebuilt their lives. This significantly reduced their coping capacity and resilience to disasters. Without compensation for their lost homesteads, the enshrined right to shelter will not be achieved in the short to medium term. The livelihoods adopted at Chingwizi generate less income than those pursued before the flood and there are no evident programmes to enhance community livelihoods at present.

The flood victims are now living in a social, economic, political environment that makes them more vulnerable than they were in Tokwe-Mukosi. In the absence of a well-planned and well-implemented intervention to promote sustainable livelihoods, the vulnerability to hazards may become imbedded in the community such that it will not only affect the current generation but those to come. Disaster risk reduction revolves around public information and education, existence of efficient warning systems, disaster preparedness, mitigation and coping mechanisms. The lack of or failure to apply these fundamental disaster management concepts in Zimbabwe made the Tokwe-Mukosi community vulnerable to the 2014 floods. The Government of Zimbabwe was not adequately prepared for the Tokwe-Mukosi dam project in terms of project financing, implementing legally prescribed community engagement and awareness through prescribed EIA processes.

Recommendations

Based on the research findings, the following policy options and recommendations may assist in improving disaster management strategies.

- Governments should start major development projects when all financing mechanisms are fully signed off and irrevocable. Costs for actual construction and associated social responsibilities such as relocation should be provided for to avoid situations like the Tokwe-Mukosi disaster.
- Major development approval processes should require and provide guidelines for hazard and risk assessments which should be gazetted and open to public scrutiny. Before commencement of development projects disaster management checklists to guide developers must be legally enforced. These checklists should require community representatives' signoff.
- EIAs should be available for public scrutiny in order to actively invite public comment for comprehensive stakeholder engagement. Knowledge of risks is itself a mitigation that encourages self-reactiveness instead of waiting for government intervention.

- Government communication strategies ought to be improved in order to reduce fatalities, avoid injuries and property damage during emergencies. People will listen to government instructions if they are clear, truthful and agreed upon by the affected parties.

- Basic early warning systems may be considered through community forums such as churches or schools. These can be in the form of project progress updates and risk rating boards to inform the community in real-time. Risk awareness creates hazard anticipation which improves the response reaction to a hazard.

- Communities facing relocation should be informed of the intended destination and progressively kept appraised of the challenges, progress plans and implementation schedule. This information should not be the preserve of a select few because relocating requires as much material and financial preparation as mental conditioning.

- Fairly and equitably settling all victims of the Tokwe-Mukosi disaster where they may benefit from the dam through fishing cooperatives or irrigation farming may appease their anger and frustration at losing their property and livelihoods. This increases their reliance and weans them from donor dependence. The required landholding per household significantly decreases as these new livelihoods have a higher cash generating capacity than their previous peasant farming.

- Direct interventions in disaster and post disaster situations from local and/or international donors should be allowed and encouraged. The government may establish a multi-party parliamentary committee to oversee relief efforts for a particular disaster. Such a committee will play a monitoring and coordinating role in relief efforts. This will assure donors that their funds and/or material donations are being used for the intended recipients regardless of political affiliation.

- Notwithstanding the risk of sensationalisation, mass media should not be used to investigate and report on both potential disasters and disasters which have occurred. Media should be allowed to report circumstances disaster victims face which will highlight relief requirements. Governments should allow media to tell the story of disaster victims so that they may be assisted, within the prescripts of the Code of Conduct of Zimbabwe Media Practitioners (2014).

- The research shows that the Civil Protection policy framework of Zimbabwe is on par with regional peers such as South Africa. However, the Tokwe-Mukosi disaster highlights shortcomings in implementation and enforcement which can be mitigated by holding responsible officials liable and accountable for such incidents.

References

Anastas, J. W. (1999). Flexible Methods: Descriptive Research, (Chapter 4) in: Anastas, J.W. (Ed.) *Research design for social work and the human services*. New York: Columbia University Press.

Blackie, P., Cannon, T., Davis, I. and Wisner, B. (1994). *At risk: Natural hazards, people's vulnerability and disasters.* Routledge, New York.

Bolin, R. and Stanford, L. (1998). *The Northridge earthquake: Vulnerability and disaster.* London and New York: Routledge.

Chineka, J. (2016). *Analysis of drought incidence, gendered vulnerability and adaptation in Chivi South, Zimbabwe* (PDF). Limpopo University of Venda. Available online: http://univendspace.univen.ac.za/handle/11602/616 (Accessed on 16 February 2017).

Chitagu, T. (2015). Government turns to China. *Newsday.* Available online: https://www.newsday.co.zw/2015/07/28/tokwe-mukosi-dam-government-turns-to-china/ (Accessed 1 June 2017).

Cuthill, M. (2002). Exploratory research: Citizen participation, local government, and sustainable development in Australia. *Sustainable Development, 10,* 79-89.

Esri. (2017). *What is GIS: Esri.* Available online: www.esri.com/library/fliers/pdfs/what_is_gis.pdf. (Accessed10 March 2017).

Farrington, J., Ramasut, T. and Walker, J. (2002). Sustainable livelihoods approaches in urban areas: General lessons with illustration from Indian cases. Available online: https://www.odi.org/sites/odi.org.uk/files/odi-assets/publications-opinion-files/2706.pdf

Guenther, L. (2012). *Flooding and soil fertility: Top crop manager.* Available online: https://www.topcropmanager.com/soil/flooding-and-soil-fertility-10936 (accessed 9 October 2017).

Gumindoga, W. (2014). *The spatio-temporal variation of the 2014 Tokwe-Mukosi floods: A GIS and remote sensing based approach.* Institutional Repository at the University of Zimbabwe. Available online: http://researchdatabase.ac.zw/3142/ (Accessed 2 December 2016).

Hillier, D. (2013). *How disasters disrupt development.* Oxford, UK: Oxfam International.

Hove, M. (2016). When flood victims became state victims: Tokwe Mukosi Zimbabwe. *Journal of Democracy and Security.* Available online: www.tandfonline.com. (Accessed 29 May 2017).

Human Rights Watch. (2015). *Homeless, landless and destitute: The plight of Zimbabwe's Tokwe Mukorsi flood victims.* Human Rights Watch (Pdf). Available online: https://www.hrw.org/report/2015/02/03/homeless-landless-and-destitute/plight-zimbabwes-tokwe-mukorsi-flood-victims (Accessed 21 February 2017).

International Confederation of Surveyors. (2014). *The contribution of the surveying profession to disaster risk management.* FIG Publication. Available online:

http://www.fig.net/resources/publications/figpub/pub38/figpub38.asp (Accessed 9 October 20147).

International Federation of the Red Cross and Red Crescent. (2015). *IFRC.* Available online: http://www.ifrc.org/en/news-and-media/news-stories/africa/zimbabwe/starting-again-after-the-floods-in-zimbabwe-69184/ (Accessed on 14 February 2017).

International Rivers. (2017). *Dams and dam builders.* Available online: https://www.internationalrivers.org/programmes/banks-and-dam-builders. (Accessed 17 February 2017).

Jha, A. (2010). Haiti earthquake: Out of great disasters comes great opportunities (Blog) Available online: http://blogs.worldbank.org/eastasiapacific/haiti-earthquake-out-of-great-disasters-comes-great-opportunity (Accessed 2 June 2017)

Kadzatsa, D. (2014). Tokwe-Mukosi disaster: Lessons learnt workshop (Pdf). Available online: http://www.drmzim.org/wp-content/uploads/2015/06/Tokwe-Mukosi-Lessons.pdf (Accessed 11 May 2017).

Kent, R. (1994). *Disaster preparedness: Disaster management training programme.* New York: UNDP.

Label, Y.L., Nikitina, E. and Manuta, J. (2006). Flood disaster risk management in Asia: An institutional and political perspective. *Science and Culture,* 72, 2-9.

Madaan, S. (2016). *What is flood and what causes flooding.* Earth Eclipse Available online: http://www.eartheclipse.com/natural-disaster/what-is-flood-and-what-causes-flooding.html (Accessed 2 November 2016)

Matonho. T. (2014). Coping with rural flooding: Lessons from Tokwe-Mukosi. *The Standard* Available online: https://www.thestandard.co.zw/2014/02/23/coping-rural-flooding-lessons-tokwe-mukosi/ (Accessed 14 March 2017)

Mazara, G. (2015). And 60 years later Tokwe Mukosi roars into life. *The Sunday Mail.* Available online: http://www.sundaymail.co.zw/and-60-years-later-tokwe-mukosi-roars-into-life-pictures-incl/ (Accessed 15 February 2017)

Mhofu, S. (2016). Zimbabwe flood victims still in camps: two years on. VOA. Available online: http://www.voanews.com/a/zimbabwe-flood-victims-still-camps/3197006.html (Accessed 22 February 2017).

Mudzingwa, D. (2015). *Homeless, landless and destitute: The plight of Zimbabwe's Tokwe Mukosi victims.* Human Rights Watch (PDF). Available online: https://www.hrw.org/report/2015/02/03/homeless-landless-and-destitute/plight-zimbabwes-tokwe-mukorsi-flood-victims (Accessed 14 February 2017).

OCHA. (2014). *Zimbabwe: Floods situation report No. 9* (as of 16 May 2014). OCHA. Available online:

http://reliefweb.int/report/zimbabwe/zimbabwe-floods-situation-report-no-9-16-may-2014 (Accessed 3 March 2017).

Pelling, M. (2003). *The vulnerability of cities: Natural disasters and social resilience.* Earthscan Publications Ltd. London. UK

Pimentel, E. (2013). *Risk assessment and monitoring. University of South Africa study guide.* Programme in Disaster Management. UNISA. Pretoria. South Africa.

Pimentel, E. (Ed.). (2013). *Introduction to disaster management. Study guide for DPDM01K.* Pretoria: University of South Africa.

Robert Wood Johnson Foundation. (2008). *Qualitative research guideline projects.* Available online: http://www.qualres.org/HomeObse-3594.html Accessed 6 October 2017

Sarewitz, D., Pielke, R. and Keykhah, M. (2003). Vulnerability and risk: Some thoughts from a political and policy perspective. *Risk Analysis, 23,* 805–810.

Shaping Policy for Development. (2009). *Research tools: Focus group discussion.* Toolkits: Shaping Policy for Development. Available online: www.odi.org/publications. (Accessed 10 March 2017).

Smyth, I. (2012). The disaster crunch model: Guidelines for a gendered approach. OXFAM (Pdf). Available online: www.alnap.org/pool/files/the-disaster-crunch-model-010512-en.pdf (Accessed 9 October 2017).

Southern Eye. (2014). Flood victims deserve better. *Southern Eye.* Available online: https://www.southerneye.co.zw/2014/09/25/flood-victims-deserve-better/ (Accessed 15 March 2017).

Surminski, S. (2014). *The role of insurance in reducing direct risk: The case of flood insurance. International Review of Environmental and Resource Economics, 7* (3-4). 241-278.

The International Confederation of the Red Cross. (2017). *The sphere.* Available online: http://www.ifrc.org/PageFiles/95530/The-Sphere-Project-Handbook-20111.pdf (11 March 2017).

The State of Queensland. (2004). *Understanding floods: Reports on floods by the office of Queensland chief scientist.* Available online: http://www.chiefscientist.qld.gov.au/publications/understanding-floods/flood-consequences (Accessed 2 November 2016).

UNEP. (2008). *Community vulnerability assessment guide.* Available online: http://www.unep.org/pdf/DTIE_PDFS/DTIx1054xPA-CommunityRiskProfile.pdf (Accessed 12 March 2017)

UNICEF. (2014). Situation report number 2. Available online: https://www.unicef.org/appeals/files/UNICEF_Zimbabwe_Sitrep_18Feb2014.pdf (Accessed 29 May 2017)

UNISDR. (2005). *The Hyogo framework for action (2005-1015).* Available online: http://www.unisdr.org/2005/wcdr/intergover/official-doc/L-docs/Hyogo-framework-for-action-english.pdf (Accessed 4 June 2017)

United Nations International Strategy for Disaster Reduction. (2007).
    Terminology. Available online:
    https://www.unisdr.org/we/inform/terminology (Accessed 2 June 2007).

Voluntary Media Council of Zimbabwe. (2014). *Revised code of conduct for
    Zimbabwean media practitioners*. Available online: www.vmcz.co.za (Accessed 4
    June 2017).

World Health Organisation. 2017. *Risk reduction and emergency preparedness*.
    Available online:
    http://www.who.int/hac/techguidance/preparedness/emergency_prepare
    dness_eng.pdf (Accessed 2 June 2017).

Yodmani, S. (2001). Disaster risk management and vulnerability reduction:
    Protecting the poor. Paper presented at the Asia and Pacific Forum on
    Poverty. Asian Development Bank.

ZINWA. (2014). Memorandum Tokwe Mukosi Dam. ZINWA. Available
    online: https://www.idbz.co.zw/downloads/Information-Memorandum-
    Tokwe-Mukorsi-Dam3.pdf (Accessed 22 February 2017).

Chapter 7

Rationality, Sustainability and the Planning of Human Settlements in Zimbabwe

Innocent Chirisa and Liaison Mukarwi

Summary:

The chapter is based on a study that interrogated the planning, development and maintenance aspects of human settlements in Zimbabwe. The study was inspired by a paucity of studies that can explain and interpret the meaning of processes and events witnessing the emergence of rural, urban, peri-urban and even peri-rural settlements in the country. The study reveals how planning has become its own worst enemy for failing to embrace innovative thinking in meta-planning and attending to the rapid changes over time and space. The planning profession thus still lacks an internal mechanism to readjust itself in response to the changing needs. Before and immediately after the country's independence from Britain in 1980, local authorities and the Department of Physical Planning used to gather, analyse and interpret data with a bid to create space for manoeuvring. Today, little or no research is taking place at all. Information is power for planning. Without information the urban planning profession has been ambushed, pushed and abused by the public, officialdom and politicians. Urban planning has tended to be more reactive than proactive. Political power has overridden the scientific and technical rationalities informed by economic rationality. The chapter provides evidence drawn from different rural, urban and peri-urban localities in the country to illustrate how the failure to reconcile the multiple rationalities threatens the sustainable development of urban settlements in Zimbabwe. The major outcomes of the threat manifest worsening delivery of infrastructure and basic services culminating in poor public health performance and environmental maintenance. The study recommends an urban planning system that creates space for corrective maintenance and proactive strategies for city-wide development. Urban planning should therefore take its position and assist in modelling the future based not so much on the whims of politicians but also on techno-managerial considerations of the planning profession.

Introduction

In Zimbabwe, spatial planning, like all other state functions, has fallen victim to systemic societal failures since the start of the new millennium when the country experienced major economic crises which peaked in 2009 (Makwara and Tavuyanago, 2012; Mapuva and Muyengwa, 2014). Key stressors included the rural and peri-urban land occupations since 2000, mid-2000s hyper-inflation, growth of urban informal settlements, fierce and often violent political contests, economic informalisation which led to urban miasma characterised by street vending in cities and political polarisation. This created uneven and shifting terrain for planning policy and practice in the context of reconciling professional standards with the expectations of society (Chirisa *et al.* 2016). Before and immediately after independence, local authorities and the Department of Physical Planning (DPP) used to gather, analyse and interpret data with a bid to create space for manoeuvring. Today, little research, if any, is taking place at all. Information is power for planning. Without information the profession has been ambushed, pushed and abused. It has become more reactive than pre-active and proactive; planners have become backbenchers in promoting development yet in actual sense they must be at the forefront (Kamete, 2010; *The Herald*, 2017, May 2). The considerations of political expediency have overridden the scientific and technical rationalities which, in most cases, should be informed by economic rationalities (Marongwe *et al.* 2011; Muchadenyika, 2015). Using document and literature review, the chapter seeks to illustrate how the irreconcilable multiple rationalities threaten sustainability in human settlements in Zimbabwe. The foregoing has been illustrated using evidence drawn from different locales in the country (rural, urban, peri-urban and even peri-rural). The study sought to document the impact of political rationality overriding planning rationality on the obtaining substructures, superstructures, infrastructure and services in human settlements. This chapter is motivated by an observation that the rot in professional planning translates to miasma and other debilitating outcomes including a compromise in public health and environmental maintenance.

Literature Review and Theoretical Underpinnings

Urban planning is a technical and political process concerned with the development and use of land, protection and use of the physical environment, public welfare and the design of the built environment, infrastructure including transportation, communication and distribution networks (Faludi, 2012; Maos and Charney, 2012). It influences the spatial distribution and rational organisation of land-uses and the linkages between them, balancing the demands of development with the protection of the environment in order to achieve the set social and economic objectives (Chirisa *et al.* 2016). This is an interventionist activity that coordinates and improves the spatial impacts of other sectoral policies so as to achieve a more balanced economic development within a given territory than would otherwise be created by market forces (*ibid.*).

Rationality of urban planning

Rationality is the quality or state of being reasonable based on facts or reason. Rationality implies the conformity of one's beliefs with one's reasons to believe, or of one's actions with one's reasons for action (Planning Tank, 2017; Maos and Charney, 2012). In this view, there are several rationalities which are based on one's beliefs, namely political, economic or social rationalities. Influenced by Max Weber, Allexander (1986), cited in the Planning Tank (2017) distinguishes between two types of rationalities in planning to include formal rationality and substantive rationality. Formal rationality involves separating means from given ends and systematically identifying, evaluating, and choosing means in a technical and apolitical way (Allmendinger, 2002:182). It focuses on the means rather than the ends, favours facts over values, and is often used in bureaucracies. A major problem with formal rationality is that it cannot show the goals that one ought to prefer. In using the example of robbing a bank, Faludi (1978), in Faludi (2012), proposes that there is a rational way to robbing a bank but the goal itself is wrong. Rationality is thus contextual. Substantive rationality is more concerned with ends and their evaluation rather than the means themselves (Allmendinger, 2002). It is less scientific than formal rationality and it considers more than simply efficiency and effectiveness. It involves values which are not based on 'blind faith' but are built up from the experience and the information available to the decision-maker (*ibid.*).

In planning theory, rational planning includes comprehensive, long-range view and a systematic, analytical approach in a planning process (Kamete, 2010; Maos and Charney, 2012). According to the rational planning model, planning is a process that include realizing a problem, establishing and evaluating planning criteria, creating alternatives, implementing alternatives, and monitoring progress of the alternatives (Faludi, 2012). This is used in designing neighbourhoods, cities, and regions signifying its importance to urban planning and transportation planning. Faludi (1986), cited in the Planning Tank (2017), argues that planning should be rational by evaluating comprehensively all possible actions in the light of their consequences, and ensuring that these considerations include alternative goals and that planning should also respond flexibly to new situations. In planning, efforts also need to make to relate operational decision to each other (*ibid.*). Rationality connotes specific cognitive skills which must be mastered, coupled with administrative expertise and appropriate aesthetic understanding for the planner to study options and present worked solutions to decision-makers for choice (Allmendinger, 2002).

In the above-mentioned sense, the idea is to give equal importance to all elements of the area of concern and the examination of these elements. Rational comprehensive planning is perceived as a necessary rational tool to safe guard public interest and guide communities into the desired long-range future (Faludi, 2012). It is important to verify, define, and detail the problem in order to come up with common goals and objectives; the process is important as it ensures that action is not without purpose. Having generated all possible solutions, planners enclose on a few final solutions to the problem (*ibid.*). The generation of alternative ways of achieving the desired goals is important in order to ensure that potentially useful plans are not overlooked (Planning Tank, 2017). The objective assessment is undertaken to determine success and failures of each alternative. This process contains secondary analysis and evaluation of the information and possible options to anticipate the consequences of every possible alternative that is thought of ensuring that the best option is identified and chosen (*ibid.*). The best solution having been chosen for implementation, different strategies of how to apply the solutions to the site are developed based on criteria assessment and analysis and finally implementation of the preferred alternative (Campbell and Fainstein, 2003). After implementation of the chosen alternative, monitoring and evaluation of outcomes and results is undertaken to ensure that the plan is on course.

Though rationality in planning seems to be a noble approach in human settlement development, it has several shortcomings. It is important to note that all activities directed towards allocation and reallocation of the scarce resources, like land, is essentially political (Kamete, 2010; Faludi, 2012). Rational decision-making tends to ignore this dimension of social planning. Decisions in the political arena are influenced far more by the perception of the situation than by any rational concept of objective reality (Raine, 2005). Critics argue that the lack of political interest and commitment to implement policies challenges the planner's agenda of rationality in planning. The assumption of comprehensive intellectual human abilities can also be questioned on the basis that human beings cannot comprehend everything, nor can they even fully comprehend one planning aspect (*ibid.*). No matter how rational planners would want, there is no way planners can gather all the facts and take into account every consideration. The nature of the problems and the complexity of the environment would generate an unmanageable number of alternatives to consider. Not all relevant information required for a decision can be acquired within a limited time frame and within confined budgets; this always cripple the whole process in most developing countries. Rationality in the planning process places power and trust in the hands of the planner who is seen as an expert bearing all the information required to solve problems; thus, it is technocratic (Faludi, 2012). This ignores the role of the public in decision-making which is paramount in creating sustainable inclusive cities. Planning rationality has been disregarded in most developing countries due to poor governance, lack of financial resources, rapid urbanisation makes planning institutions overwhelmed to allow much time to make decisions, and lack of political will by authorities to also allow the natural flow of planning systems (*ibid.*).

Politics in/and planning

Politics is the process of making decisions (Maos and Charney, 2012). It also refers to achieving and exercising positions of governance in an organised control over human community particularly a state (*ibid.*). A political system entails a framework which defines acceptable political methods within a given society. Urban planners are concerned with research and analysis, strategic thinking, architecture, urban design, public consultations, policy recommendations, implementation and management in an urban area (Planning Tank, 2017). Politicians are people that contest for public administrative positions in order to help the community they live in with good policies, initiation of developmental projects and decisions that could improve the local economy (Chirisa and Muzenda, 2013; Faludi, 2012). Urban planning and local politicians are supposed to work together since planning involves everything that affects the public good (Mapuva *et al.* 2014).

Many actors participate in the urban planning process, including planners, bureaucrats, politicians, entrepreneurs, as well as the general public. All these are mainly concerned about personal, group or institutional interests. Frequently they engage in persuasion, power struggles, and negotiations (Faludi, 2012). One must therefore focus not merely on the professional and technical aspects of planning but also on the impact of the involved interests on the planning process and its outcome (Maos and Charney, 2012). Urban planning is conducted in circumstances of scarcity of resources, in a complex system of pressures and conflicts, under tensions between political rationality and planning rationality.

In most African countries, political interference in urban planning is rife. Political interference in urban planning occurs when politicians use their power of influence to disturb or hinder the processes of urban planning and the control of development during plan implementation (Maos and Charney, 2012; Kamete, 2010). Politicians' involvement in the planning processes is motivated by political reward. Political interference in urban planning have its roots from the fact that politicians formulate decisions that affect the activities of urban areas and administer those decisions through governmental agencies and bureaucrats (Marongwe *et al.* 2011). Issues of political interference in planning leads to poor planning and decision-making, poor implementation of projects, loss of resources, bias in planning and unnecessary prolonging of planning process (Marongwe *et al.* 2011; Mapuva and Muyengwa, 2014). When a political party's interest does not tally with that of the city administration, they tend to stop any developmental programmes that are in place and propose their new concept and approach which in turn disturb the ongoing project. In some instances, it creates chaotic developments whereby people with political power may do as they please, normally disobeying planning standards (Maos and Charney, 2012). Planning is all about optimal use of resources but interference of politics in planning process may lead to resource waste. For example, when a project that is supposed to be completed in 5 years takes 10 years before its completion, the project cost will increase. This was the case of the dualisation of Harare' airport road. Politics creates room for corruption which is common in many African nations. Bogus land dealings, fraudulent tendering processes and deliberate abuse of public funds also put planning to shame (Kamete, 2010).

It is known that every government has its set of goals on which they base their manifesto on. Political parties always make certain promises to the electorate during campaign periods without actually knowing how those promises can be fulfilled. They consequently exert pressure on urban planners in order to fulfil those promises even though not feasible. For example, during the run-up to 2013 elections, the then minister of local government promised people in Harare residential stands which were supposed to be planned through fast-tracking and be allocated to supporters before the election day less than 2 months away. The minister advised the housing cooperatives aligned to his ZANU-PF party to identify the land they wanted so that he could simply write a letter to the councils to allocate them the land (*The Zimbabwean*, 2013, April 10). Under these conditions, planners have little room to manoeuvre or influence developments given the directive from the top. This creates settlements without services since the local authority will have increased its capacity to supply services to such land (Kawadza, 2017). In addition, political administrators sometimes complicate the planning process by demanding certain adjustments to the plan that may not be possible or may not comply with the concept of the plan. In such cases, the plans that will be generated by planners will lose vision due to political influence that would be targeting to achieve personal objectives or the interests of their constituencies/parties (*ibid.*).

Methodology

The study interrogated the planning, development and maintenance of human settlements in Zimbabwe. It sought to respond to the main research question: What is the role played by urban planning in shaping the obtaining urban landscape? In addition, the study sought to understand the type of rationality shaping the planning of human settlements in Zimbabwe. It also evaluated whether the present planning leads to sustainable development. In this quest, the study reviewed various textbooks, articles from academic journals, government documents and newspapers. It is understood that literature or document review is based on secondary data which is not specifically collected for this purpose. The danger is that this data can be over or under-rated thus affecting the validity of the results. However, there was cross validation where many articles on the same matter were reviewed to come to a conclusion that is close to reality. The study is buttressed by the examination of various examples in Zimbabwe. Several published texts and journal articles were engaged to inform the authors on the contemporary multiple rationalities that are threatening sustainability in human settlements in Zimbabwe. The use of published texts and data from academic journals also validated the information contained herewith since some of these publications are thoroughly reviewed before publication. The data or evidence on the presented scenarios were collected from newspapers. The newspapers gave a rich content of the current urban planning and infrastructure realties surrounding the country's human settlement developments and the coverage of the contest between political rationality and planning rationality. The data sought were gleaned, collated and presented in themes. Analysis was done using discourse analysis.

Results

The study was an interrogation of development planning and maintenance of human settlements in Zimbabwe. It touched on the effects of politics in the administration of planning in Zimbabwe which seem to compromise the sustainability and quality of the provision of infrastructure and services in settlements emerging around the country (rural, urban, peri-urban and even peri-rural). Political reasoning was established to be an overbearing influence over planning rationality hence a lack of foresight in plans and implementation of development projects.

Spatial planning and human settlements' development in Zimbabwe - An overview

Contemporary Zimbabwe's spatial planning is marked by unpredictability and uncalled for indecisiveness. Several communities have grown spontaneously rather being rationally planned (Kawadza, 2017). The problems faced by society in urban and peri-urban areas illustrate how the irreconcilable multiple rationalities threaten sustainability in human settlements development in Zimbabwe. The infrastructure and services have been on the receiving end of this decay in developmental planning and maintenance which results in miasma and many debilitating outcomes including a compromise in public health and environmental maintenance (*ibid.*). The realities in most urban areas have seen council officials, councillors and workers putting town planning to shame. Unapproved layouts are rising everywhere and implemented on open spaces which are haphazardly turned into housing. In rational town planning, open spaces are reserved for recreational purposes. Service capabilities of water supply, sewerage systems, drainage and road are stretched to the limit or hazardously outstretched (Kamete, 2010; Chirisa *et al.* 2016). The planning profession has been compromised such that it has become more reactive than pre-active and proactive (Kawadza, 2017). The political rationality has overridden the scientific and technical rationalities which, in most cases, should be informed by economic rationalities (Marongwe *et al.* 2011; Mapuva and Muyengwa, 2014). The cities have deteriorated in standards, fabric and services posing many problems. This obtaining situation indicates missing features in the planning of urban settlements in Zimbabwe and this has not done any good to the sustainability cause (Marongwe *et al.* 2011).

Master and local plans are the main tools that planners use to guide them in the development of urban settlements (Kamete, 2010). Though master plans are mainly used in urban areas, there are a lot of concerns for them (*ibid.*). Master plans are criticised as being rigid and inflexible. They are not routinely reviewed as should be done (Maposa and Chisango, 2016). The evidence can be deciphered from the City of Harare where the rigidity of the schemes including local and master plans resulted in many appeals against the granting or not granting of planning permission and, consequently, informality in housing, commercial and industrial sectors (Mapuva and Muyengwa, 2014). The Regional, Town and Country Planning Act (Chapter 29:7) was also used to justify the eviction of 700 000 squatters countrywide in a program called "*Murambatsvina*" (Murisa, 2010). This was been largely seen as a political move. For example, Muchadenyika (2015) contends that it was a ZANU-PF way of decongesting urban areas known to be supporting the opposition party, MDC. It was a calculated strategy against the opposition as it displaced perceived its supporters towards the 2005 harmonised elections; and many people who were displaced were not allowed to vote (*ibid.*). This needed a thorough thought, if there was no pressure on planning, planners could have used other means of cleaning the city. The lack of resources, lack of political will, political repression and polarisation, corruption and abuse of public funds were constantly named as culprits for the lack of review in plans guiding development in cities.

Politicians always take advantage of bad governance prevailing in most societies to breed havoc in human settlement development (Mapuva and Muyengwa, 2014). Corruption, fraudulent land deals and abuse of public funds meant for local development have been raised on several occasions to be the reason for the unplanned development in the country. For example, councillors in Chitungwiza allocated themselves land and duped the local authority of money from land sales through undercharging and or selling the stands for personal gains (*The Herald*, 2017, April 28). There are various corrupt deals that are happening across Zimbabwe which seem to emanate from politics. In addition to this, there is a sour centre-local relationship in the country which increase tensions in development administration thereby affecting effective and sustainable settlement planning. Most local authorities, in which local planning resides, are run by the Movement for Democratic Change (an opposition party) while the ruling government is ZANU-PF overseas the work of local authorities. This creates a room for push and shove between these two key stakeholders responsible for human settlement development (Ngwerume, 2014; Muchadenyika, 2015). The conflicts of control that happen between the centre and local also affect the long-term planning of the settlements in question. It appears the central government is constantly interfering with how local authorities are run and this creates much acrimony with local councillors (Mapuva and Muyengwa, 2014; Ngwerume, 2014). At the end of the day, it becomes politicking at the expense of service delivery and consequently the high levels of decay in infrastructure and service provision in most urban and rural centres (Mpofu, 2012). Some decisions made by politicians cost local authorities resources that can be channelled towards improving infrastructure and service delivery. For example, the Government of Zimbabwe suspended the Harare town clerk hired by the city citing that the local authority failed to follow the law in appointing the Clerk. In response, the local authority was adamant that it was above board. In all these skirmishes, because the hired clerk signed a contract, he is demanding about US$125 000 in salaries and benefits from the council as of March 2017 (*The Herald*, 2017, March 30). This will cost the local authorities a fortune which can be used for service delivery instead of paying an individual who has never worked at the Harare Town House.

Water management

Water is an essential resource for all life on earth. However, its supply in Zimbabwean urban areas is a problem (Mpofu, 2012). The water challenges faced by many cities in Zimbabwe are both of quantity and quality in nature. For example, the last quarter of 2016 was marked with erratic supply of water with many areas in Harare going for months without running water (Maposa and Chisango, 2016). In Bulawayo, the city has faced the problems of water supply for quite long time (Chirisa *et al.* 2016). The poor are the most vulnerable because they lack resources to acquire safe and clean water. Harare, among other cities, has become a hot bed of water borne diseases. The latest cases of water borne disease outbreak in Harare include the typhoid outbreak in Mbare that occurred in January 2017. The elites are better positioned as they can afford to drill boreholes or buy water from water vendors (Maposa and Chisango, 2016). Informal settlers are on a permanent danger without clean water supply as they are not recognised by the formal urban system. There is no formal water supplies therefore in the illegal settlements, and residents depend on shallow wells or polluted streams for survival. The present socio-economic and political environment in the country shows that the water problems are changing for the worse with continuous deterioration due to inadequate investment (Muchadenyika, 2015; Maposa and Chisango, 2016; Ngwerume, 2014). The macro-political cloud which is hanging over most local authorities proves to be working against the ethos of good governance and sustainable development.

The interference of the central government on local issues has on several occasions frustrated efforts to promote good governance (Ngwerume, 2014). For example, the suspension of Gweru councillors by the government was a clear destruction of a formal way through which locals may participate in the provision of services (Mapuva and Muyengwa, 2014). It was also alleged that the actions by the state were motivated more by political considerations rather than improving service delivery. In fact, there was a feeling that, by suspending all councillors, the minister was trying to undermine an opposition-dominated council other than improving service delivery (*ibid.*). However, there is rampant abuse of resources by the local authorities which leave nothing or little resources for water provision, and some of the perpetrators have a political blessing (Maposa and Chisango, 2016). The former Harare Town Clerk was blamed of abuse of council resources. For example, the allegations of abusing the loan facility meant for water and sewer plant upgrade to purchase executive cars indicates that the funds were entrusted to incompetent people. It took consented effort by the Harare mayor to end the tenure of the town clerk as he had a political blessing form the ruling government. The government rescinded his suspension to pave way for financial abuse investigations in 2014 following failure to provide a salary schedule to the councillors (*The Herald*, 2014, February 3). It was understood that Harare City Council had 8 directors gobbling US$500 000 per month. It was suspected that the minister had a lot to hide by trying to stop investigation into the matters raised (*ibid.*).

Through political patronage, politicians are known to allocate stands which are not serviced leading to increased number of stands not connected to water reticulation (Mpofu, 2012). The land barons and the expansion of the informal settlements ought to be blamed for the continued deterioration of planning standards and provision of water. The rate of urban sprawl has outstripped the capacity of local authorities to manage urban development and to respond to the needs for infrastructure, public services and land (*ibid.*). Poor waste management emanating from the uncontrolled and informal urban growth also increased the cost of water purification. Toward the elections in 2013, the government scraped all urban councils' rates and water bills in a populist strategy, and this affected water supply in cities. Recently, there is an impasse between Gwanda Town Council and Zimbabwe National Water Authority (ZINWA). ZINWA purifies water and sells it to Gwanda Town Council which then sells it to residents. The reason for the impasse is financial; the council is failing to pay ZINWA for bulk water. ZINWA is also up in arms with the Beitbridge local authority over water supplies which it had terminated. The local authorities are saying ZINWA did not write off bills in 2013 as was directed by the government and this made the councils' debt so untenable; they cannot pay for the residents since local authorities wrote-off debts. To confirm this, ZINWA charges that they did not receive any government directive for utilities to cancel debts equivalent to what their clients owed (*Newsday*, 2017, April 8). This creates an awkward situation given that local authorities wrote off debts owed by residents, yet they are still expected to pay for that water to ZINWA. In general, the scraping of bills affected negatively on all local authorities to raise revenue for the maintenance and construction of new water infrastructure that would increase the capacity of treated water production (Ngwerume, 2014). This constantly makes the supply fall short of the present water demand in all human settlements around Zimbabwe (*ibid.*).

Solid waste management

Solid waste management is a big problem in Zimbabwe as witnessed by high levels of littering and mounds of heaps of garbage (Maposa and Chisango, 2016). Poor waste management techniques have become the order of things in Zimbabwe's cities and towns, a major health hazard that has given rise to many disease outbreaks leading to the unnecessary death of hundreds of people every year (*Financial Gazette*, 2017, May 9). For example, the recent typhoid outbreak in Harare's Mbare suburb can be attributed to poor sanitation and solid waste management (*ibid.*). Most cities in Zimbabwe use huge bins as central garbage deposits points in their CBDs for forward dumping to dumpsites. However, due to resource constraints, most cities miss collection schedules resulting in the bins spilling over. The poor waste management increases water pollution; solid waste like used condoms, diapers and plastic bags among others are finding their way into the main water bodies affecting clean water supply (Makwara and Tavuyanago, 2012). The informality and decay of waste management infrastructure has accelerated the problem of waste management.

The resources generated in urban councils have not been used accountably and transparently. Corruption and plunder of such resources has affected trust and confidence of the institutions in charge of waste management to the extent of reduced cooperation from the public (Maposa and Chisango, 2016; Makwara and Tavuyanago, 2012). The previously noted writing-off of debts in 2013 created a wait and see attitude among residents; they are no longer paying their bills constraining the local authorities' capacity to provide solid waste management services (Muchadenyika, 2015). The local authorities are in the reactive mode, they are always following where development is happening instead of guiding such development (Kawadza, 2017). The occurrence of organic settlements (informal settlements) in the peri-urban areas has also increased the problems of waste management (*ibid.*). The growth of informal settlements and or unserviced land has a political blessing (Ngwerume, 2014). Recently, the Government of Zimbabwe, through the Ministry of Local Government began issuing stands to youths all over Zimbabwe. This has been fast tracked in areas which were having by-elections as a campaigning strategy. For example, the ministry handed over 5000 stands in Norton to the youths ahead of the parliamentary by-election in October 2016 (*The Herald,* 2016, October 20). This has a negative impact on forward planning given that planners are now being forced to subdivide and plan for residential development without capacity to provide services like waste management. With the obtaining socio-political framework, where trust between citizens, the corporate world and public authorities is sour, no meaningful resources can be mobilised from the non-state players (Kawadza, 2017). Accountability, transparency, efficacy and effectiveness are lacking in the current governance structure hence a major blow to effective solid waste management (*ibid.*).

Human habitat and housing issues

At the moment in Zimbabwe, there is a mismatch between demographic growth, economic opportunities, and the service, infrastructure and utility expansion, making the economy filled in by the informality and self-employment. These are short-term palliatives that only fuel poverty and socio-economic insecurity across generations (Chirisa *et al.* 2016). Informality is a problem; not a solution and has invaded the land markets. People have engaged in the self-provisioning mode with unapproved layouts being used to allocate stands in many suburbs (Kawadza, 2017). Pertaining to urban land markets, poor land administration and unresponsive public institutions are increasingly failing to track formal and informal land transactions, and this interferes with proper market mechanisms. This has seen the growth of land barons, for example, those that loom in Chitungwiza and Harare (*The Herald,* 2016, October 20). Responsive governance systems are flexible and robust to consciously recognise informal land markets to improve the administration, management and supply of urban land; however, politicisation of urban land and administration has increased this mayhem in housing supply (*ibid.*).

Inappropriate use of public office is one of the major factors behind the unequal distribution of incomes and rising urban poverty (Mapuva and Muyengwa, 2014). The illegitimate control of power, wealth and resources by a minority or, in other words, corruption, is obviously part and parcel of the larger process of underdevelopment. Where governance is weak and corrupt, public urban land is often captured by privileged individuals who are politicians and sold or illegally transferred for private gains (*ibid.*). Unless illegal transfer and sale of this non-renewable municipal resource is curbed, the outcome can only be the perpetuation of significant foregone municipal own-source funding. Even though there are efforts to regularise in Zimbabwe, overly cumbersome and time-consuming tenure regularisation procedures are linked with corruption and vested interests, turning land management and administration into a challenge. The politicians are grabbing many urban residential stands as mentioned earlier and witnessed in Harare, Chitungwiza, Gweru and many other towns in Zimbabwe (Chirisa *et al.* 2016).

Transport and mobility

The lack of economic growth and a rapid rise in urban population have created unintended consequences impacting on the economy, social fabric and the environment (Mbara, 2015:1). Transport has been one of the problems facing Zimbabwean urban communities owing to lack of infrastructure, affordability of transport, accidents and convenience of such transport. The twin factors of increasing population and the deterioration of the conventional public transport stimulated the growth of the informal public transport and private car ownership which again increased the transport commuter service impasse (*ibid.*). This has also led to congestion which is impeding rather than facilitating the urban population's ability to access the required social and economic services (*The Herald*, 2015, November 26). A clear mismatch between the demand for traffic space and its availability is evident; and this mismatch is resulting in severe congestion (Kamete, 2010; Muchadenyika, 2015). The traffic is considerably higher due to the increase in the number of vehicles (usually the ex-Japanese cars) and the deteriorating infrastructure characterised by potholes and malfunctioning traffic signals (Mbara, 2015). The solution to this is close to impossible. The fashion in which most urban areas are growing has little regard to transport as a substantive matter (*ibid.*). There is no integration of land use and transport planning.

Due to rapid urbanisation, mostly in major cities of Zimbabwe, the uncontrolled urban sprawl has not done any good to the demand for good transportation network. These settlements in the peri-urban areas are having transport challenges in terms of cost, convenience and safety (Mpofu, 2012). However, due to the lack of foresight in planning such settlements, those developed through housing cooperatives or land barons are automobile dependent which has created problems socially, economically and environmentally. In addition to being far from the city centres, the locations cannot support operation of sustainable conventional public transport due to low patronage; many people staying in these areas are in the informal sector and some do not travel much. Funds for infrastructure development are allegedly being swindled and abused (Musandu-Nyamayaro, 2008). There is limited regard to sustainable transport planning given that most of the settlements are growing spontaneously, or by government directive with little regard to all factors that promote sustainable development. The stands given to the youths or people are fairly distant form the economic activities in the central business districts. These new settlements need to be planned well so that sustainable public transport can be thoroughly investigated and consciously implemented (*ibid.*). Given that this is done to please the electorate, some of the considerations in the areas are road provision with little regard to traffic movement hence increased congestion and air pollution.

Street trading and vending

Existing policies on street vending in the cities of Zimbabwe do not reflect the economic context of the country. Politicians are heard making public pronouncements which serve to either please vendors (who form part of the electorate) or to supposedly promote order and cleanliness in cities (Chirisa *et al.* forthcoming). Saungweme *et al.* (2015) have estimated that unemployment ranges between 85% and 90%, and this calls for alternative means of employment for citizens. The cumulative result has seen the growth of informal enterprises as urban populations seek various ways of eking out a living, thereby spreading 'informality' (Ngwerume, 2014). This reflects the incapacity of the formal economy to generate adequate private and public resources for housing, infrastructure and urban employment. The economy is not sufficiently developed enough to create employment opportunities for the teeming masses of urban unemployed, a situation further compounded by high levels of rural-urban migration (*ibid.*). This has contributed to the invasion of city pavements by street vendors seeking a livelihood. Many local authorities pointed out that illegal vending is a major problem in the cities, and that vendors should move to designated vending sites in the CBD. This is in line with planning principles and the existing legal framework for vending, Vendors and Hawkers' Bye-laws of 2014, the Regional Town and Country Planning Act, and the Urban Council's Act mong other statutes.

Street vending is proving to be unavoidable, so if urban planning is to be sustainable, it needs to devise best strategies for sustainably incorporating it into the existing urban system (Kamete, 2010). Street vending is an example of micro-entrepreneurship and constitutes a solution to urban poverty. However, the efforts to accommodate this phenomenon as an urban land-use has created some kind of confusion with political connotations (*ibid.*). Some political figures advocate for a complete removal of the street vendors from the street and some calling for their rescue. To illustrate this controversy, the former Vice President of Zimbabwe, Mphoko, mocked vending in 2015, indicating that able-bodied men must find better things to do (*Daily News*, 2015, January 27). The then Minister of Local Government, also gave local authorities an ultimatum to deal with vendors in February 2015 (*Dailynews*, 2015, February 1). The push was to get rid of street vendors; this was in line with the laws governing urban areas.

The former First Lady, Grace Mugabe, also made remarks shaming the running battles between police and street vendors in the same year (2015) (*Dailynews*, 2015, March 7). The Grace Mugabe's views were political considering the venue, a rally; her position and her assumed interests in the ruling political party (ZANU-PF) and her lack of background in urban systems, urban economics and urban planning principles. The views of the Grace Mugabe on vending were contrary to the utterances by the Vice-President Mphoko. The vendors at undesignated space welcomed her statement as it informally legalized their activities. This necessitated growth of such activity neutralising even the local authority's power to act on them. Any action considering street vending was assessed from a political angle and political rationality prevailed at the expense of urban planning. When the City of Harare announced a temporary ban of street vending of foods in January 2017 following the outbreak of typhoid in Mbare, there were a lot of political statements which undermined these efforts. For sustainable human settlement development, there ought to be a unity of purpose where people participate and collaborate for the common good (Faludi, 2012; Mapuva and Muyengwa, 2014). The political disorder in the country has been transferred to service delivery and city administration, and this is very unwelcome in the interest of sustainability (Ngwerume, 2014; Muchadenyika, 2015).

Conclusions and Policy Recommendations

The study exposed that the spatial planning profession has been ambushed, pushed and abused by the public, officialdom and politicians. The political power has overridden the scientific and technical rationalities informed by economic rationality. Political survivalism in Zimbabwe has worsened the situation in urban areas where politicians do all they can to remain in office at the expense of economics and professionalism at large. Such short-term, and selfish politicking is to the detriment of professional conduct not just in the planning profession but in other disciplines. The spatial planning institutions suffer more than others to the political situation largely because their agenda is long-term, requires stability and predictability, observance of the rule of law, particularly security of tenure and a focus on sustainability. Consequently, the profession is now more reactive than proactive. It also emerged that the major outcomes of the present planning rationalities are manifesting in worsened service delivery; poor infrastructure and basic services culminating in poor public health performance and environmental maintenance. The plans created to guide long-term development have been contradicted if not overrun by short-term political ambitions constructed in relation to brief political cycles and built on the notion of quick fixes and the science of muddling through, for example, the growth of informality with political blessings. The issue of giving residential stands in undesignated places towards the election puts so much pressure on the planning systems ending up overriding the operative master and local plans. It is recommended that the urban or rural systems must give due space to, not only, corrective maintenance but also preventive and predictive maintenances of which planning is the tool that drives them all.

Planning should take its prime position and assist in modelling the future, not based on the whims of political control but technocratic and scientific power of the profession. The issue of following land-use allocation done by politicians that are specifically meant to lure the electorate must end as this often overrides planning laws. Political interference in urban planning comes with an adverse effect on the development of any urban area as it completely disturbs the flow of planning work. It also renders the urban planning profession's relevance insignificant. To achieve a steady and effective urban development through optimal allocation and distribution of resources, the planning profession must readjust itself in response to the changing needs. Before and immediately after the country's independence from Britain in 1980, local authorities and the Department of Physical Planning used to gather, analyse and interpret data with a bid to create space for manoeuvring. Today, little research, if any, is taking place at all. Information is power for planning; thus, the planning profession must be effective in information systems.

References

Chirisa, I. and Muzenda, A. (2013). Environmental rights as a substantive area of the Zimbabwean constitutional debate: Implication for policy and action. *Southern Peace Review Journal*, 2(2), 104-121.

Chirisa, I., Maphosa, A., Zanamwe, L., Bandauko, E. and Mukarwi, L. (2016). *Past, present and future population growth and urban management in Zimbabwe: Putting institutions in perspective.* In U.G. Benna, A.S. Bello and S.B. Garba (Eds.),

Population growth and rapid urbanisation in the developing world (pp. 64-81). Pennsylvania: IGI Global.

Daily News (2015, January 27). *Vice-President Mphoko slams vendors.* Harare: Alpha Media Holdings.

Daily News. (2015, March 7). *Grace, Chombo on collision path.* Harare: Alpha Media Holdings.

Daily News. (2015, February 1). *Chombo wants vendors off the streets.* Harare: Alpha Media Holdings.

Faludi, A. (2012). *Rational comprehensive theory of planning.* Accessed 7/5/17 at http://theenviro.blogspot.com/2012/11/rational-comprehensive-theory-of.html.

Kamete, A.Y. (2010). Defending illicit livelihoods: Youth resistance in Harare's contested spaces. *Int. J. for Urban and Reg. Res, 34*(1), 55-77.

Makwara, E.C. and Tavuyanago, B. (2012). Water woes in Zimbabwe's urban areas in the midst of plenty: 2000 – present. *European Journal of Sustainable Development*, 1(2), 2239-5938.

Maos, J.O. and Charney, I. (2012). Urban planning: Politics vs. planning and politicians vs. planners. *Horizons in Geography, 79*(80), 49-69.

Maposa, A. and Chisango, F.F.T. (2016). Impact of water-rationing on Zimbabwe's high density suburbs: A case of Harare (capital city). *Greener Journal of Environmental Management and Public Safety*, 5(1), 007-012.

Mapuva, J. and Muyengwa, L.M. (2014). The citizen participation/democracy dichotomy. *International Journal of Politics and Good Governance*, 5(5.2), 0976 – 1195.

Marongwe, N. (2003). *The fast track resettlement and urban development nexus 1: The case for Harare.* Paper Presented at the Symposium on Delivering Land and Securing Rural Livelihoods: Post Independence Land Reform and Resettlement in Zimbabwe in Nyanga.

Marongwe, N., Mukoto, S. and Chatiza, K. (2011). Scoping study governance of urban land markets in Zimbabwe. Harare: Urban Land Mark.

Mbara, T. (2015). *Achieving sustainable urban transport in Harare, Zimbabwe: What are the requirements to reach the milestone?* Paper presented to a conference on Energy, Climate and Air Quality Challenges in Istanbul- Turkey (2-5 February 2015).

Mpofu, B. (2012). Perpetual 'uutcasts'? Squatters in peri-urban Bulawayo, Zimbabwe. *Afrika Focus, 25*(2), 45-63.

Muchadenyika, D. (2015). Land for housing: a political resource–reflections from Zimbabwe's urban areas. *Journal of Southern African Studies, 41*(6), 1219-1238.

Murisa, T. (2010). Social development in Zimbabwe. Discussion paper prepared for the Development Foundation for Zimbabwe.

Musandu-Nyamayaro, O. (2008). The case for modernisation of local planning authority frameworks in Southern and Eastern Africa: A radical initiative for Zimbabwe. *Habitat International, (32)*, 15–27.

Mutembedzi, J. (2012). *Housing land allocation in Kadoma: Implication for low-cost housing provision* (Unpublished MSocSCi dissertation). University of Zimbabwe.

Newsday. (2017, April 8). *ZINWA refuses to write-off 2013 Bills.* Harare: Alpha Media Holdings.

Ngwerume, E.T. (2014). *Independent but destitute: the challenges to decent housing and human security in urban Zimbabwe.* Bindura: IDA Publishers.

Planning Tank (2017). *Rational Planning Model.* Accessed 7/5/15 at http://planningtank.com/planning-theory/rational-planning-model

Saungweme, T., Matsvai, S. and Sakuhuni, R. (2014). *Economic analysis of unemployment, output and growth of the informal sector in Zimbabwe (1985-2013).* Masvingo: Great Zimbabwe University.

Financial Gazette. (2017, May 9). *Poor Waste Management: Public Threat.* Harare: Alpha Media Holdings.

Herald. (2014, February 3). Chombo underfire over Mahachi. Harare: Zimpapers.

Herald. (2015, November 26). Efficient Public transport system overdue in Harare. Harare: Zimpapers. Available at http://www.herald.co.zw/efficient-public-transport-system-overdue-in-harare/

Herald. (2016, October 20). Zanu-PF hand overs 5000 Norton Stands. Harare: Zimpapers.

Herald. (2017, April 28). Chitungwiza Town Council Dissolved. Harare: Zimpapers.

Herald. (2017, May 10). Mushore's Salary Ballons. Harare: Zimpapers.

Zimbabwean. (2013, April 10). Chombo promises Zanu supporters land. Harare: Alpha Media Holdings.

Chapter 8

Parameters of Land-use Densification in Urban Zimbabwe: Lessons from Harare City

Isheanesu Mpofu and Charles M. Chavunduka

Summary:

Land-use densification has become an important tool for addressing the issue of urban sprawl. Developing countries such as Zimbabwe stand to benefit from densification given its potential to improve viability and functionality of cities. This chapter reviews the implementation of land-use densification in Harare and draws lessons of experience. It reveals that although provided in policy, the approach to land-use densification has been piecemeal and focused on housing development rather than the entirety of the city. The chapter recommends the adoption of a robust policy framework and guidelines for urban land-use densification.

Introduction

Densification is considered an effective tool of addressing human settlement in the wake of rapid urbanisation, given land is finite, and the need to protect the environment (Hofstad, 2012; Nordregio, 2012). Densification is the increased use of space, both horizontally and vertically, within existing areas and new developments, accompanied by increased number of units and population threshold (City of Cape Town, 2012). Williams (2007) and UNHABITAT (2016) have considered densification as the ultimate tool for addressing urban sprawl. Developing land at higher densities supports efficient infrastructure and improves energy efficiency of urban areas in the transport and energy sectors. Skovbro (2002) reckons there is no better solution for creating shorter distances between urban functions than compact cities. Moreso, UNHABITAT (2015) has observed that densification minimises transport and service delivery costs, optimizes the use of land, and supports the protection and organisation of urban open spaces. This is because in cities or towns where densification has been implemented successfully, public transport systems have been used efficiently, thus reducing greenhouse gas emissions from vehicles. As a concept, densification has been implemented by many planning authorities around the globe (see for example City of Harare, 1992; City of Cape Town, 2012; Kinyua, 2013; Nordregio, 2012).

The purpose of this chapter is to introduce the concept of land-use densification and explain how it has been used to improve the sustainability of cities. The chapter begins by giving a background on land-use densification. After the background section, a brief conceptual framework about densification is examined, followed by a review of the relevant literature. On the basis of data collected from observation of land-use densification projects, document reviews, City of Harare residents and key informant interviews. In addition, a discussion is presented on how densification has been implemented in Harare. Following the discussion, recommendations are made for improving the effectiveness of densification in Harare and other urban settlements.

Background and Overview

The need for densification has risen over the past half century because of the rapid increase in urban population (UNHABITAT, 2015). UNHABITAT (2015) observes the first 1 billion people were urbanised in 1960 and that from the 19th to the 21st century the percentage of people living in urban areas rose from 2% to 50% respectively. It is predicted that by 2050, 70% of the population will be living in urban areas (UNHABITAT, 2015). UNHABITAT (2016) has considered densification as one of the five principles of sustainable urban planning. The principles that guide densification of urban land-uses include availability of adequate space for streets, mixed land-uses, social mixes, and connectivity. For densification, the UNHABITAT recommends 15 000 people/km² as the minimum density to accommodate the rapidly growing population in cities. Over the years, various countries have managed to formulate infrastructure development policies that support densification although some countries have lagged behind in that respect.

Admittedly, sub-Saharan Africa lags behind other regions in terms of infrastructure development. The sub–continent has had to deal with many political, economic, religious, administrative, and social challenges. In recent years, sub–Saharan Africa experienced rapid urbanisation (United Nations, 2015b). The rate of urbanisation soared from 15% in 1960 to 40% in 2010 and by 2050 sub–Saharan Africa's rate of urbanisation is expected to reach 60% (Freire, Somik and Leipziger, 2014). Projections such as these serve to guide responsible authorities in formulating development plans that can address rapid urbanisation. One might consider densification as an appropriate tool that can address the ever-increasing demand for residential, institutional, commercial and industrial space associated with rapid urbanisation.

The World Bank (2013) pointed out how urban planners in Ghana had the chance to anticipate and plan, and not plan in retrospect. This shows the vast opportunities that sub–Saharan Africa has in terms of managing rapid urbanisation through densification. When attention is focused on the demand for housing in Harare, which is ever-increasing compared to the total number of housing units that are delivered by central government, local government, or private developers, the need for densification becomes imminent. In 2005, more than 150,000 people applied for housing in Harare while in 2004 only 220 housing units were delivered (Toriro, 2008). Toriro (2008) observes these figures are lower than the actual figures as some people are reluctant to apply or register on the housing waiting list. Following urban gentrification occasioned by Operation Murambatsvina (Operation Restore Order) 20,432 housing units were availed in Harare's Whitecliff, Hopley and Hatcliffe suburbs – a figure that barely satisfied the demand for housing (Ministry of Local Government, Public Works and National Housing, 2015). According to the City of Harare (2015), at the end of 2010, the council's housing waiting list had 49,672 applicants, a figure that has been barely satisfied to date if one looked at the property developments that have taken shape in the past five years.

Conceptual Framework

The section shows how various urban phenomena such as rapid urbanisation, urban sprawl and densification affect each other. One ought to note that rapid urbanisation and urban sprawl are the major causes of the rapid extension of boundaries and growth of city populations. Densification becomes a reliable tool for containing urban sprawl. Figure 8.1 shows the relationship between rapid urbanisation, urban sprawl and densification. Rapid urbanisation arising from natural growth and rural – urban migration has been accompanied by urban sprawl. Densification then becomes a tool adopted by planning authorities for purposes of dealing with urban sprawl. As a concept, densification is being treated within the context of rapid urbanisation and urban sprawl.

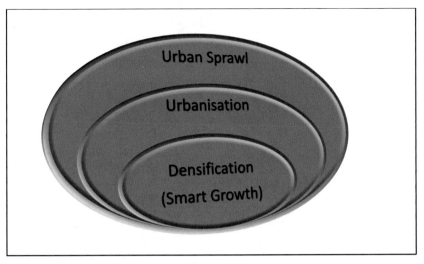

Figure 8.1: Conceptual Framework
Source: Authors

Literature Review

Urbanisation refers to the increase in the proportion of people living in urban areas. It involves the multiplication of points of population concentration and the individual growth of urban areas. In the former case, previously rural settlements become urban as people move from agricultural to non–agricultural occupations, while in the latter case urban areas grow through natural growth and rural – urban migration (Peng et al. 2011). McGranahan and Satterthwaite (2014) observe that urbanisation is accompanied by the transformation from rural to urban use of land in the peri–urban areas.

Global trends show that in 1950, 30% of the world's population was urban and by 2050, 66% of the world's population is projected to be urban (United Nations, 2014). Peng *et al.* (2011) identify modernisation, industrialisation, globalisation and migration as the main causes of urbanisation. The availability of modern technology, communication infrastructure, medical facilities and other social amenities attract people to urban areas where they expect to lead a better life. Through industrialisation, more people have been attracted to move from rural to urban areas on account of improved employment prospects. In the contemporary era, globalisation, a process supported by expanded transport and telecommunication systems as well as an environment favouring international trade has made use of the urban region as the competitive unit where businesses thrive on their comparative advantages of costs and innovative capabilities. The impact of modernisation, industrialisation and globalisation has been increased rural – urban migration. As an addition to these factors, Mbiba

(2017) observes the increasing contribution of natural growth to urbanisation in developing countries.

Sub–Saharan Africa is the world's most rapidly urbanising region. Africa's rate of urbanisation was 35% in 2005 and is expected to reach 60% by 2050 (UNHABITAT, 2016). A unique feature of Africa and other developing regions of the world is that urbanisation is taking place amidst poverty that expresses itself in the form of slums and informal settlements. In the developing countries, the UNHABITAT (2016b) has it that more than 1 in 5 people live on less than $1,25 a day. McGranahan and Satterthwaite (2014) note that cities in Africa are not serving as engines of growth and structural transformation. Instead, they are part of the cause and major symptom of the economic and social crises that have enveloped the continent. This claim is backed by Annez and Buckley (2009) who state that Kenya is one such country that fits the description of urbanisation occurring faster than economic growth. Figure 8.2 illustrates the problem.

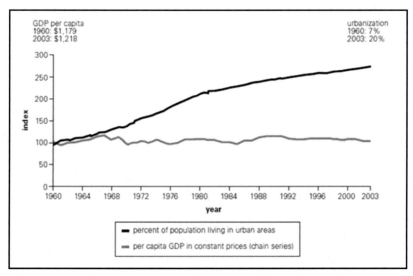

Figure 8.2: Urbanisation and Per Capita GDP in Kenya, 1960-2003
Source: Annez and Buckley (2009, p.7).

Urbanisation has been accompanied by an increase in urban sprawl, a trend that Litman (2015) has considered worrisome. Litman (2015) defines urban sprawl as relatively dispersed, homogenous, and automobile dependent development. Notwithstanding the benefits, such low-density communities that are car dependent tend to have negative economic, social and environmental consequences. They can lead to increased economic disparity as more affluent people relocate from the core to the fringe of urban areas. As poorer households are left behind, urban sprawl may enhance social stratification based on location. In terms of the environment, the rapid expansion of urban areas can lead to loss of biodiversity and increased air pollution from larger traffic volumes. The lower density development is characteristic of urban sprawl (Burgess, 1998; Bekele, 2005).

Mengya (2013) characterises urban sprawl as low-density sprawl, ribbon or linear sprawl and leap–frog development. Low-density developments take up too much space and lengthen commuting distances. Ribbon development often takes place when extensive commercial development occurs in a linear pattern along both sides of major roadways. It is a recipe for traffic congestion as workers and shoppers enter and exit the major streets in substantial numbers. Leap–frog development occurs when developers build on cheaper land away from an urban area than on more costly land closer to the city. Leap–frog development creates extra costs as infrastructure must be extended further and the longer distance creates more traffic and longer commutes into the city.

The causes of urban sprawl can be put to population growth, industrialisation, physical geography, government policy and, investment in infrastructure (Bhatta, 2010). As regional population increases, communities begin to spread further away from the city centre. Establishment of new industries in the countryside may be accompanied by the development of housing facilities in a large area that generally becomes larger than the industry itself. Sometimes sprawl is caused by unsuitable physical terrain such as wetlands, water bodies, or broken topography. This often leads to leap–frog development. Sprawl can increase where government policy does not promote the development of compact cities. Where municipalities subsidise the cost of infrastructure such as roads and sewers to undeveloped areas, such action provides an incentive for the creation of communities outside of city centres.

European cities such as Madrid, Barcelona, Istanbul, Paris, Lyon, Brussels and Munich are characterised by urban sprawl. The European Environmental Agency (2006) notes the causes of urban sprawl in Europe as low population pressure, globalisation, industrialisation and good infrastructure. These factors allow people to enjoy the life of the city at the expense of personal mobility (vehicles and bullet trains), improved transport infrastructure, and improved information and communication technologies. One can easily enjoy life in the main core of the city and yet live outside the core of the city thusly. Bhatta (2010) has also highlighted the above causes of urban sprawl but highlights the high costs of living in the main city compared to the countryside that acts as a push factor for people to promote urban sprawl. Another factor that has also enhanced urban sprawl in Spain is that of the physical geography where people prefer to settle along coastlines. This is because coastlines have been considered to provide better recreational amenities; however, the coastal ecosystems have been known to be vulnerable (European Environmental Agency, 2006).

While highlighting environmental effects, the European Environmental Agency (2006) observes urban sprawl increases the transport related consumption of energy, hence increasing greenhouse gas emissions. The Agency also observes woodlands disappear, thus compromising on carbon sinks. In terms of social and economic costs of urban sprawl, Bekele (2005) observes that rural dwellers get prejudiced of their land. Sprawl also increases the demand for services at the periphery of the city, a development that might burden local authorities. For example, sprawl increases the length of trips required to collect municipal waste at increasingly distant waste treatment plants. Given the numerous effects of urban sprawl, Bekele (2005) summarizes them in Figure 8.3.

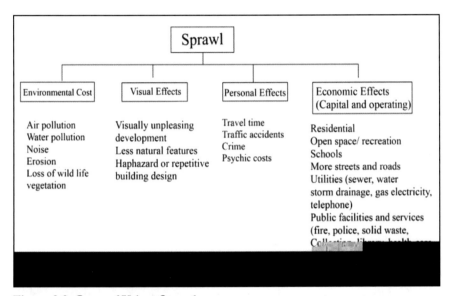

Figure 8.3: Costs of Urban Sprawl
Source: Bekele (2005), p15

In Africa, the City of Kumasi in Ghana can be used to illustrate the phenomenon of urban sprawl. With a population of about 2 million, Kumasi is the second largest city in Ghana (Cobbina and Amoako, 2012, Asare–Akufo, 2014). In Kumasi, sprawl has manifested in a way similar to its occurrence in both developed and developing countries. The morphology of Kumasi has been coupled with the various sprawl patterns. Cobbina and Amoako (2012) and Asare-Akufo (2014) have described this as clustered or nucleated sprawl; leapfrog development; ribbon development; and low-density development. Examples of nucleated developments in the city include Atafua, Breman, Atimatim and Pankrono. Asouyeboa, Buokrom, Apatrapa and Patasi are among developments that are classified as scattered or dispersed and are speckled, spread out and patchy in their characteristics. Dompoase serves as an example of leap-frog development in the city. Parts of Asawase have been considered as ribbon development. Asare–Akufo (2014) has ascribed much of the urban sprawl to poor planning and affordability of property development that has lured the poor and immigrants to peri–urban locations. Figure 8.4 illustrates the spatial distribution of urban sprawl in Kumasi, Ghana.

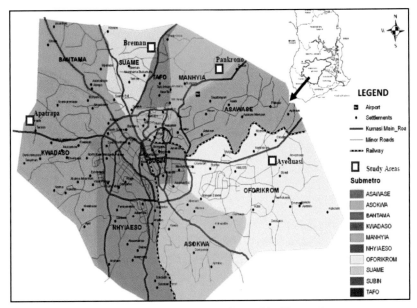

Figure 8.4: The Manifestation of Urban Sprawl in Kumasi
Source: Cobbina and Amoako (2012), p316

The major driver of urban sprawl in Kumasi has been rapid population growth (Asare-Akufo, 2014). In the context of weak land management systems, Asare–Akufo (2014) describes a peri–urban environment characterised by unapproved settlements and conflicting land-uses. In addition, Cobbina and Amoako (2012) note poor infrastructure and services, loss of agricultural land and destruction of the natural environment as some of the primary effects of urban sprawl in Kumasi.

Given the challenge of urban sprawl, Skovbro (2002) sought to establish whether the application of densification policies in Europe resulted in sustainable urban environments. It was found that high urban densities resulted in lower energy consumption for transport and heating. Furthermore, it was established that greenbelts in England were more valuable from a biodiversity point of view than green spots that mainly served a recreational function in an urban area.

In South Africa, one of the urban areas where densification has been implemented is Tshwane. Tshwane is a metropolitan municipality of nearly 3 million inhabitants and it encompasses Pretoria, Temba, Mamelodi,

Bronkhorstspruit, and Mabopane. In a 2014 document (Figure 8.5) the Tshwane Mayoral Committee approved a spatial development policy that included guidelines for densification. The spatial development policy sought to promote densification around rapid transit stations (Figure 8.5).

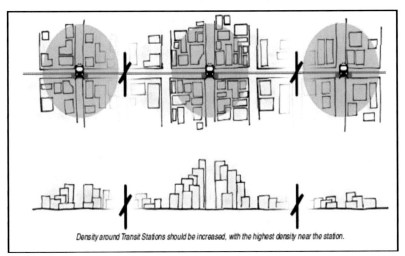

Density around Transit Stations should be increased, with the highest density near the station.

Figure 8.5: Urban Densification being promoted around Stations
City of Tshwane (2014)

Densification has been considered in matters of sustainability in as far as cities are concerned. In South Africa, densification has been considered for purposes of dealing with rapid population growth. The objective of densification has been the development of a compact city. Densification has been characterised by the development of tower blocks, terraced housing and perimeter blocks. Across the African continent, countries have been adopting densification as a policy for dealing with rapid urban growth. In Kenya, Kiai (2013) traced the role of the Nairobi City Council in promoting densification as a policy for sustainable development. Kiai (2013) established that as early as 2004 Zone 4 which contains areas such as Woodley, Thompson, Riverside, Kilimani, Spring Valley and Kileleshwa had been earmarked for high–rise developments. In 2011, the Nairobi City Council conducted studies on the feasibility of further densifying some areas including Zone 4; and over time Kileleshwa has been redeveloped with high–rise developments that accommodate higher population densities. The Nairobi case shows how some local authorities on the African continent have used densification to address urban sprawl.

In Zimbabwe, densification has been recommended for urban settlements (Ministry of Local Government, Public Works and National Housing and City of Harare, 1992). However, research carried out by Toriro (2008) and Chirisa (2014) would make one wonder whether policy makers have fully embraced densification. Toriro (2008) draws attention to the continued use by planning authorities of colonial standards that were generous in the provision of building space. Some properties in the low-density residential suburbs sit on 5,000m² plot in Hatfield and yet some high-density residential suburbs have 150m² plots as in Caledonia suburb. In summary, this section focused on the concepts of urbanisation, urban sprawl and densification in literature. The concepts were reviewed in relation to how they have been applied across the globe.

Methodology

The study made use of primary and secondary methods of data gathering. Since the 1980s, densification has been considered as a potential tool for managing urban sprawl in Zimbabwe. The study examined urban policy documents, planning laws and regulations, urban plans and design manuals to establish how planners have been addressing the issue of densification. Key documents that were examined included the Ministry of Local Government, Public Works and National Housing New National Housing Standards for High, Medium and Low-Density Areas – Circular Number 70 of 2004, the Zimbabwe National Housing Policy of 2012, Layout Design Manual of 1999, and the Harare Combination Master Plan of 1992.

Primary data was gathered from key informants and residents of Harare. Key informants included 3 planners each from Harare City Council, central government, academia, and the private sector. In addition to planning professionals, key informants also included a representative each from the Confederation of Zimbabwe Industries, National Chamber of Commerce and the Combined Harare Residents Association. For purposes of coming up with a sample of residents for primary data collection, the City of Harare was divided into four clusters, that is, north, south, west, and east cluster. In each cluster, two suburbs were randomly selected and in each suburb convenience sampling was used to select 15 households for interview. Site visits were made to observe three projects where the City of Harare has been implementing its densification policy. The use of different methods, that is, documentary reviews, interviews and observation increased the validity of the data that was gathered.

Results

The results of the study revealed that the main influences on urban land-use densification in Harare were the planning authorities, the legal mechanisms, and the residents. Although planning authorities differ with the setting (the ministries for agriculture, mining, tourism, and the environment), the Ministry of Local Government, Public Works and National Housing and local authorities, either urban or rural councils, were the most relevant in as far as densification is concerned. Within the Ministry of Local Government, Public Works and National Housing is the Department of Physical Planning that oversees the implementation of the Regional, Town, and Country Planning Act 29:13, and the planning activities of rural and urban councils. The planning functions of rural and urban councils are outlined in the Regional, Town, and Country Planning Act 29:12 and the Urban Councils Act 29:15 or the Rural District Councils Act 29:13. The policy framework for densification in Harare is outlined in various documents such as the Harare combination master plan, local development plans, the Layout Design Manual of 1999, and Circular Number 70 of 2004.

The operative master plan for Harare is the Harare Combination Master Plan of 1992, which is currently under review. The plan sought to promote densification in Harare as reflected in the Harare housing policy which stipulates that at least 30% of land zoned for residential purposes should be used for high-rise developments. Local development plans articulate in greater detail the provisions of urban master plans. In Harare, notable local development plans that have taken densification on board are the Central Business District local development plan, the Tynwald local development plan and the Borrowdale Brooke local development plan. The Avenues local development plan zoned the avenues for high-rise residential developments. The Tynwald local development plan earmarked plots in Tynwald North for subdivision and rezoning. High density residential subdivisions were reduced to 150m² while some portions of the area were zoned for development of flats. The Borrowdale local development plan has also implemented densification by allowing cluster units to be developed (*Financial Gazette*, 2014, October 30).

Circular Number 70 of 2004 is an important document that has influenced densification in Harare and Zimbabwe at large. The circular reduced the minimum standard requirements for planning, house construction, and infrastructure. Since 2004, layout plans and development schemes that do not comply with standards specified in the circular were not to be approved. For high density/ low cost housing, stand sizes were reduced from 150m²-300m2 to 70m²-200m². The circular specified that stand sizes between 70m²-89m² should be used for terraced and semi-detached housing only while those ranging from 90m²-200m² should cater for detached units. In addition, building lines were reduced from the conventional 1,5m side boundary to 1m. The front and rear building lines were maintained at 3m and 2m respectively. For the road widths and access, stands ought to have direct road access with the width of access roads being 8m and local distributors 10m-12m. For houses, the minimum room size was reduced from 7m2 to 6m2 with a minimum width of 2.1m. For medium density/ middle income housing, stand sizes range from 300m²-500m² with only a single dwelling unit permitted. The circular also reserves 10% of the land for medium and high-rise flats in residential estates close to town centres and 5% for garden and four storey flats in all other medium cost residential areas. The building lines are 5m from the front, 2m on the sides and 3m from the rear stand boundary. Access roads ought to be 10m and local distributors range from 12m-15m wide. For low density/high income housing, stand sizes range between 800m²-2000m². The circular also stipulates that all municipal areas, except those waivered by the Director of Physical Planning, shall set aside a minimum of 5% for garden and duplex flats on land designated for residential use. The building line was reduced from 10m to 5m on the front boundary and from 5m to 3m from the side and rear boundaries. Access roads ought to be 12m while local distributors 15m wide.

In this study, building design experiments were carried out in order to assess the feasibility of the standards contained in Circular Number 70 of 2004. The building designs focused on the minimum threshold for the stand size for high-density residential/ low-income residential areas as these are targeted at lateral densification. This helps to question the rationale of the densification policy prescribed by the Ministry of Local Government, Public Works, and National Housing. Plates 8.2 and 3 demonstrate building designs that a designer would typically come up with for construction on 70m² and 90m² residential stands. Residential stand sizes of 70m² prove to be the most efficient when one is attempting to build terraced or semi-detached houses. This is because when one attempts to design on such a stand size, one is forced to come up with two floors; one with the living room and kitchen and the other with toilet, bathroom and three bedrooms because not all rooms could fit on the same floor. However, two bedrooms are the most satisfying number of bedrooms as they offer more space for the inhabitants. Considering possible family structures, one ought to design for families that may have children of different sexes who may need separate bedrooms. A typical housing unit was therefore designed with three bedrooms.

For the minimum threshold of stands that allow detached houses, 90m² stands with dimensions of 9m x 10m prove not to be the most efficient way of densifying settlements. This is because the type of house that can be built when following the permissible building lines cannot accommodate an average household of 4.2 persons as indicated in the Census Report of 2012. Although Circular Number 70 of 2004 allows the alteration of building lines subject to approval by the Director of Physical Planning, 90m² seems inadequate for accommodating the recommended housing unit. The 90m² stands are suitable for the development of terraced or semi-detached houses that can utilise all the space on the side building lines and have an additional floor. That way, densification is permissible and rational.

An experimental building design was made on a stand that measures 9m x13m (see Plate 8.4). The building lines in Circular Number 70 of 2004 were retained, that is, 3m in front, 1m on the sides, and 2m from the rear stand boundary. The stand accommodated a house that has three bedrooms, a living room, kitchen, and a combined bath and toilet. The house covered 48% of the stand area. Designing a building for construction on such a stand size proves feasible as it can accommodate an average household of 4.2 people.

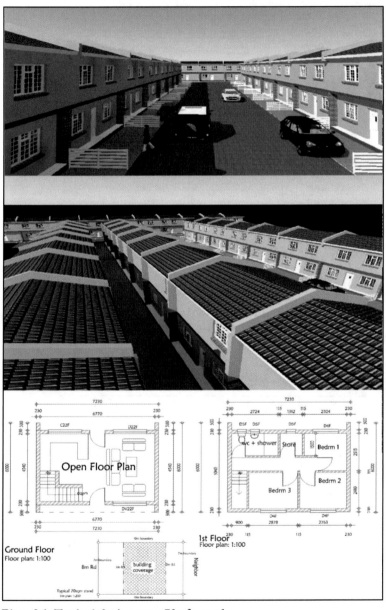

Plate 8.1: Typical design on a 70m² stand
Author's creation

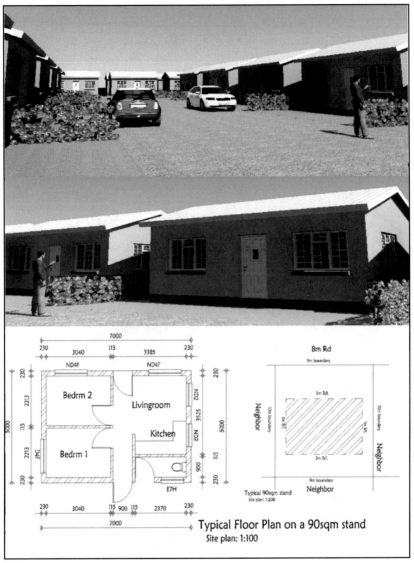

Plate 8.2: Typical design on a 90m² stand

Author's creation

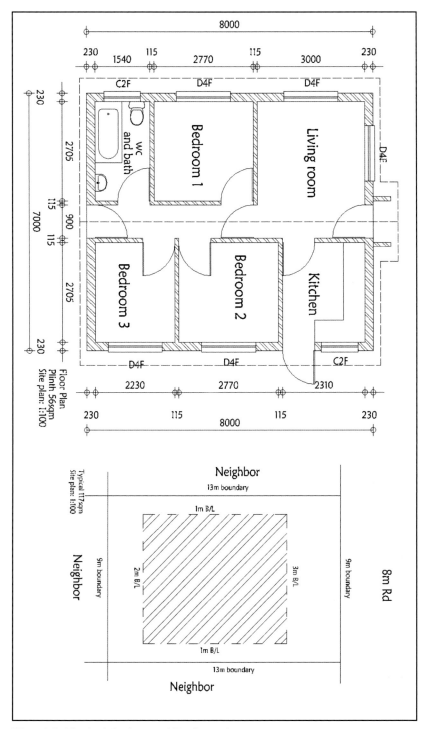

Plate 8.3: Typical design on 117m² stand
Source: Author's creation

Apart from the influence of planning authorities and legal mechanisms that have shaped densification, the residents' contribution is necessary. What makes the contribution of residents important is that it can guide decision and policy-making regarding densification. Although the Layout Design Manual of 1999 makes it clear that in urban areas, land should not be reserved for agriculture because of the demand, residents find a way of carrying out agriculture even on stands averaging 200m².

In interviews, residents were asked to indicate their preferred stand size for housing development. Most residents preferred 2000m² residential stands that provided space for farming activities such as market gardening and poultry. These are some of the common income generating projects that households embark on. Residents thus felt densification deprived them space for supplementary economic activities.

From observation, it was clear that Harare, like most developing cities in Africa, has a lot of greenfields rather than brownfields that are common in the more economically developed cities in Europe. The City of Harare is already expanding to adjacent districts yet the city itself has so many greenfields. This is something some personnel within the council have observed. What the local authority has failed to grasp is that service delivery is expensive when urban sprawl is the order of the day. Some of the land has been reserved as wetlands, while countries like the United Arab Emirates have developed infrastructure in the sea (the greatest irony).

In the City of Harare, although some land is not utilised for the reason of protecting the environment, a shopping mall like Avondale Shopping Centre was built on a stream and the Longcheng Plaza was built on a wetland. Protecting the environment goes beyond just reserving land. It calls for co-existence between the people and the environment. Wetlands should be made available for development, especially for institutional and public purposes because such land-uses often require large pieces of land and have the ability to sustain the environment. Institutional buildings usually occupy a small portion of the stand and the remaining land can be landscaped. For instance, instead of surfacing vacant space with concrete/tar, interlocking bricks or pavers; surfacing should be of two layers, one of quarry stones and the other of river sand to allow water to infiltrate to the underground instead of a quick run off.

Discussion and Recommendations

The findings from the study clearly show that densification of urban settlements in Zimbabwe has been dominated by implementation of the Ministry of Local Government, Public Works and National Housing Circular Number 70 of 2004. The circular provides new national housing standards for high, medium and low-density residential areas. An analysis of parameters for densification, that is, provisions, adequacy and rationale; shows planning authorities' focus on residential land-use and affordability for densification. This may not be surprising given that most urban spatial growth has been taking place in the housing sector. National housing standards are aimed at reducing the cost of housing delivery. A property near Sam Levy Village (a shopping mall in Borrowdale suburb, Harare) with 20 housing units sitting on one hectare was being sold for USD4,000,000.00; an average of USD200,000.00/unit on 500m² per unit (see Plate 5). Although the area in question is prime land that is highly sought after, unit prices for investment projects should consider affordability if densification is to be implemented at scale.

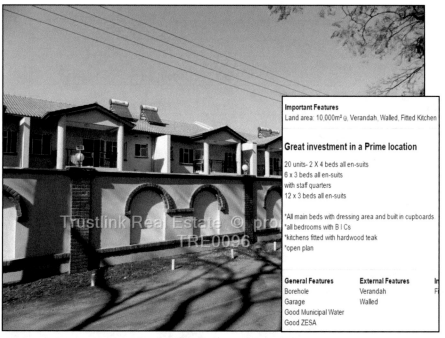

Plate 8.4: Showing the price of a townhouse property being sold for USD 4 000 000.00
Source: property.co.zw

Another case of affordability influencing the densification policy is the Budiriro low income housing development project, a partnership between City of Harare and the Central Africa Building Society. In the partnership, City of Harare provided land at a subsidised price and the Central Africa Building Society carried out the land and property development. The partnership developed about 2800 housing units which are core houses classified into 3 categories, type A, A⁺ and B. The houses are 2 bed-roomed, 2 bed-roomed with a slab and a 4 bed-roomed at the cost of USD 25,302.30; USD 27,451.65; and USD 31,262.75 respectively. Ironically, the cost of acquiring a single housing unit from Central Africa Building Society can buy a much-improved house in the same location, that is, Budiriro (see Plates 8.6 and 7). However, what has kept the scheme relatively afloat are the payment terms that are manageable to people with minimum gross incomes indicated in Table 1 cropped from a Central Africa Building Society pamphlet that shows the pricing and qualification scheme. However, it has been observed that the houses in the scheme are not selling well and this can only be attributed to the harsh economic environment that has seen many businesses closing down hence increasing the unemployment rate.

Table 8.1: Minimum Qualifications for the Mortgage to Buy a House under the Scheme

MINIMUM GROSS SALARIES			
Min. monthly gross income - 10 yr mortg. (90% loan)	850.00	922.00	1,050.00
Min. monthly gross income - 10 yr mortg. (100% loan)	945.00	1,025.00	1,167.00
Min. monthly gross income - 20 yr mortg. (90% loan)	652.00	708.00	806.00

Central Africa Building Society (2014)

Plate 8.5: Typical Budiriro house under the Central Africa Building Society housing scheme

Source: http://www.classifieds.co.zw

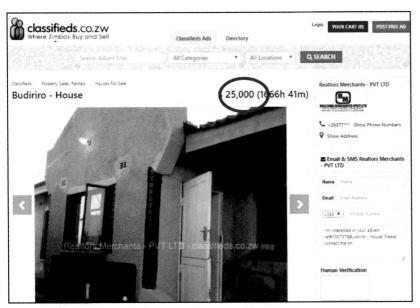

Plate 8.6: A house in Budiriro selling at the same unit price for a house under Central Africa Building Society's housing scheme

Source: http://www.classifieds.co.zw

Zimbabwe's national housing policy of 2012 mentions problems arising from generous stand sizes that were inherited from the colonial era and their contribution to urban sprawl. The policy provides for densification through vertical development but planning practice has been preoccupied with reducing stand sizes as a way of densification. The incoherence between policy and practice seems to rise from lack of a comprehensive approach and model of how Harare would look like when developed at higher density. Rather than basing densification policy on a vision or broader idea of a compact city characterised by increased population density, mixed land-use, reduced infrastructure and travel costs; the approach adopted in Zimbabwe has not been holistic. For example, unlike in South Africa, densification policy in Zimbabwe has not been related to mass transit. The narrow view and piecemeal approach have not been helped by donor funded urban programmes in support of densification and private sector investment in cluster housing because such efforts have not been coordinated in the context of an overall densification policy. As long as planning authorities continue to see densification of urban development as a planning standard issue in the context of uncoordinated housing infill and cluster housing projects; densification may not lead to the development of a compact city that it is meant to deliver.

This study has, among other things, examined the feasibility of densification through Ministry of Local Government, Public Works and National Housing Circular Number 70 of 2004. The study supports the promotion of semi–

detached and terraced housing as that significantly contributes to development at higher densities. The study recommends a model of semi–detached housing units as shown in Plates 8 and 9. The model allows four housing units on a 400m^2 stand with a plinth area of 149m^2, and at a total floor area of 298m^2. The stand allows 4 laundry lines and has enough room to accommodate more than 6 vehicles. The building design suits housing development by private and other institutional developers. For detached housing development, the study recommends that stands earmarked for high density/low income residential areas should have a minimum size of 117m^2. This arrangement holds if the side building lines are 1m, and the front and rear building lines are 3m and 2m respectively. The minimum stand size of 90m^2 as provided in the Ministry of Local Government, Public Works and National Housing Circular 70 of 2004 was found inadequate for accommodating an average household of 4.2 people. Beyond Circular Number 70 of 2004, it is recommended that planning authorities move away from the piecemeal approach to densification where at times it is variously viewed as reduction of stand sizes, vertical development, and cluster development; to a holistic approach. Viewed from a holistic perspective, densification becomes part of urban policy and is consciously related to other aspects of the city economy such as infrastructure, employment and recreation centres. Like the Harare Combination Master Plan of 1992, master plans of Zimbabwean cities contain densification policies. The master plans are mute on the meaning of densification and how it would be implemented. The omission becomes evident in the lack of guidelines for densification. On this aspect, the City of Tshwane case that was reviewed in this study provides some lessons. Most importantly, it is good to develop cities at higher densities, but it can be a big challenge to realize the objective of a compact city. In developing countries, the implementation of densification policy amidst the urbanisation of poverty can be an exercise in futility. It is incumbent upon governments to foster an environment that is conducive to employment creation for it is when individuals have a stable income stream that ideas about development reach fruition.

Plate 8.7: Typical proposed semidetached unit
Authors Creation

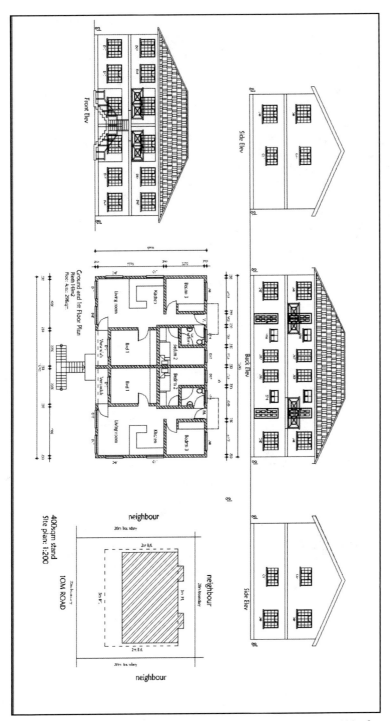

Plate 8.8: Design of typical semidetached housing unit on a 400m² stand
Author's creation

Conclusion

The chapter examined the parameters of land-use densification in terms of policy and legal provisions, adequacy and rationale applied in Harare. This arose out of the concern that global and African cities have been experiencing the problem of urban sprawl in the face of rapid urbanisation. In sub–Saharan Africa, the study reviewed the experiences of Kumasi in Ghana, Nairobi in Kenya, and Tshwane in South Africa with urbanisation, urban sprawl and land-use densification. The Nairobi experience focused on the development of high-rise buildings in some zones of the city as a means of addressing urban sprawl. Municipality of Tshwane seemed to approach land-use densification in a systematic manner that made use of spatial development policy. In Harare, the Combination Master Plan of 1992 provided for land-use densification but one of the limitations has been the lack of guidelines for implementing the policy. Densification has been implemented in an ad hoc manner mostly through residential infill and cluster housing developments. The Ministry of Local Government, Public Construction and National Housing Circular Number 70 of 2004 provides standards for increasing population density in urban areas but the circular's focus on the delivery of affordable housing renders it a partial effort. Lessons from Harare have highlighted the need for a holistic approach to land-use densification. Rather than thinking of it as a process that can be enabled through the review of planning standards as has hitherto been the approach by the Government of Zimbabwe, a systems approach that relates densification to other facets of the urban economy such as employment, infrastructure, and the environment is called for.

References

Agency, Z.N. (2015). *Zimbabwe 2012 population census: Population projections thematic report*. Harare: Government of Zimbabwe.

Akufo, F. (2014). *Evaluating the effectiveness of urban planning and administration in taming urban sprawl in Alabama* (Unpublished MSc thesis). University of Alabama.

Amoako, C. and Cobbinah, P. (2014). Urban sprawl and the loss of peri-urban land in Kumasi, Ghana. *International Journal of Social and Human Sciences, 6,* 313-322.

Annez, P.C. and Buckeley, R.M. (2009). Urbanisation and growth: Setting the context. In M. Spence, P.C. Annez and R.M. Buckley, *Urbanisation and growth* (1-45). Washington: The World Bank.

Arman, M., Zuo, J.L.W., Zillante, G. and Pullen, S. (2009). Challenges of responding to sustainability with implications for affordable housing. *Ecological Economics, 68(12), 3034-3041.*

Asare Department for International Development. (2015). Urban infrastructure in sub-Saharan Africa: Harnessing land values, housing and transport. Harare: African Centre for Cities.

Zimbabwe Classifieds. (2017, February). Property Sales, Rentals In Zimbabwe: Available online: Zimbabwe Classifieds: http://www.classifieds.co.zw.

Property 24. (2017, March). Property.co.zw: Property in Zimbabwe - Rent & Buy Real Estate Available online: Property 24: http://www.property.co.zw/

Basawaraja, R., Chari, K.B., Mise, S.R. and Chetti, S.B. (2011, August). Analysis of the impact of urban sprawl in altering the land-use, land-cover pattern of Raichur City, India, using geospatial technologies. *Journal of Geography and Regional Planning, 4*(8), 455-462.

BBC. (2014). *Geography.* Available online: GCSE Bitesize: http://www.bbc.co.uk/schools/gcsebitesize/geography/

Bekele, H. (2005). *Urbanisation and urban sprawl* (Unpublished Doctoral thesis). University, Stockholm.

Bhatta, B. (2010). *Analysis of urban growth and sprawl from remote sensing data: Advances in Geographic Information Science.* Berlin Heidelberg: Springer-Verlag.

Briassoulis, H. (2010). Who plans whose sustainability? Alternative roles for planners. *Journal of Environmental Planning and Management,* 42(6), 889-902.

Brinkhoff, T. (2013, October 5). *South Africa: City of Tshwane.* Available online: City Population: https://www.citypopulation.de/

Chirisa, I. and Mlambo, N. (2017, February 20). *Situating morality in the housing debate in Harare: Case of Matapi Hostels.* Available online: Research Gate: https://www.researchgate.net/publication/45713937

Chirisa, I. (2008). Population growth and rapid urbanisation in Africa: Implications for sustainability. *Journal of Sustainable Development in Africa, 10*(2), 361-394.

Chirisa, I. (2010). Inner-city revitalization and the poor in Harare: Experiences, instruments and lessons from Mbare. In A. Ayala and E. Geurts, *Urbanising Africa: The city centre revisited - Experiences with inner-city revitalisation from Johannesburg (South Africa), Mbabane (Swaziland), Lusaka (Zambia), Harare and Bulawayo (Zimbabwe)* (pp. 58-67). Rotterdam: IHS.

Chirisa, I. (2013). Housing and stewardship in peri-urban settlements in Zimbabwe: A case study of Ruwa and Epworth, Harare (Unpublished). Harare: Faculty of Social Studies, University of Zimbabwe.

Chirisa, I. (2014). Building and urban planning in Zimbabwe with special consilience. *The Journal of Sustainable Development, 2*(1), 1-26.

Chirisa, I., Gaza, M. and Bandauko, E. (2014). Housing cooperatives and the politics of local organisation and representation in peri-urban Harare, Zimbabwe. *African Studies Quarterly, 15*(1), 37-53.

City of Cape Town. (2012). *Capetown densification policy.* Cape Town: City of Cape Town.

City of Tshwane. (2014). *Mayoral committee.* City of Tswane.

Clarke, S. and Ginsburg, N. (1984). *The political economy of housing.* London: SAGE.

Cobbina, P.B. and Nsomah Aboagye, H.N. (2017). *A Ghanaian twist to urban sprawl. Land-use Policy, 61,* 231-241.

Cobbinah, P.B. and Amoako, C. (2014). Urban sprawl and the loss of peri-urban land in Kumasi, Ghana. *International Journal of Social, Behavioural, Educational, Economic, Business and Industrial Engineering, 8*(1), 313-322.

Crowley, S. (2003). The affordable housing crisis: Residential mobility of poor families and school mobility of poor children. *The Journal of Negro Education,* 72(1), 22-38.

Cseh, K. and Terebessy, A. (2005). *Introduction to demography: Presentation and calculation of basic demographic indicators.* Available online: University of Hungary:
http://semmelweis.hu/nepegeszsegtan/files/2015/05/1415_Introduction -to-demography1.

Curley, A.M. (2005). Theories of urban poverty and implications for public housing policy. *Journal of Sociology and Social Welfare,* XXXII (2), 97-119.

Department of Physical Planning. (1999). *Layout design manual.* Harare: Government Publications.

Divine O. Appiah, J. T. (2014). Determinants of peri-urbanisation and land-use change patterns in peri-urban Ghana. *Journal of Sustainable Development, 7*(6), 95-109.

European Environment Agency. (2006). *Urban sprawl in Europe: The ignored challenge.* Copenhagen: EEA.

Freire, M.E., Somik, L. and Leipziger, D. (2014). *Africa's urbanisation: challenges and opportunities.* Washington DC: The Growth Dialogue.

Gahadza, N. (2016, August 2). CABS to launch rent-to-buy scheme. *Herald.* Available online: http://www.herald.co.zw/cabs-to-launch-rent-to-buy-scheme/

Githira, D.N. (2016). *Growth and eviction of informal settlements in Nairobi.* Enschede, Netherlands: University of Twente Faculty of Geo-Information and Earth Observation (ITC).

Government of Zimbabwe. (1998). Regional, Town, Country and Planning Act (Chapter 29:12). Harare: Government of Zimbabwe.

Government of Zimbabwe. (2002). Rural District Councils Act 29:13. Harare: Government of Zimbabwe.

Government of Zimbabwe. (2005). Urban Councils Act (Chapter 29:15). Harare: Government Publications.

Government of Zimbabwe. (2016). Ministry of Lands and Rural Resettlement. Available online: http://www.lands.gov.zw/

Group, W.B. (2012). Independent Evaluation Group (IEG). Retrieved April 13, 2017, from The World Bank group: http://lnweb90.worldbank.org/oed/oeddoclib.nsf/DocUNIDViewForJavaSearch/4EF67E4EE2EE239C852567F5005D8BAE

Hofstad, H. (2012,). Compact city development: High ideals and emerging practices. *European Journal of Spatial Development, 49*, 1-23.

Housing Department. (2015). Available online: City of Harare: www.hararecity.co.zw

Hudson, B.M., Galloway, T.D. and Kaufman, J.L. (1979, 26 Nov 2007). Comparison of Current Planning Theories: Counterparts and Contradictions. *Journal of the American Planning Association, 45*(4), 387-398.

Johnson, M.P. (2006). Decision models for affordable housing and sustainable community development: The futures of housing. Journal of the American Planning Association, *Carnegie Mellon University, 5000,* 1-26.

Kamusoko, C., Gamba, J. and Murakami, H. (2013). Monitoring urban spatial growth in Harare Metropolitan Province, Zimbabwe. *Advances in Remote Sensing, 2*(04), 322-331.

Katz, B., Turner, M. A., Brown, K. D., Cunningha, M. and Sawyer, N. (2003). *Rethinking local affordable housing strategies: Lessons from 70 years of policy and practice.* New York: The Brookings Institution Centre on Urban and Metropolitan Policy and Urban Institute.

Kiai, S. K. (2013). *Sustainable Housing Densification In Kileleshwa: Nairobi, Kenya* (Doctoral dissertation, University of Nairobi)

Kippler, C. (2010). Exploring post-development: politics, the state and emancipation. The question of alternatives. *Polis journal, 3*(1), 1-38.

Langley, P. (2006, September). Securitising suburbia: The transformation of Anglo-American mortgage finance. *Competition and Change, 10*(3), 283-299.

Lindsay, C. M., and Feigenbaum, B. (1984). Rationing by waiting lists. *The American Economic Review, 74*(3), 404-417.

Lucci, P., Bhatkal, T., Khan, A. and Ber, T. (2015). *What works in improving the living conditions of slum dwellers: A review of the evidence across four programmes.* London: Overseas Development Institute.

Magwaro-Ndiweni, L. (2011). Contestation in the use of residential space: House typologies and residential land in Bulawayo, Zimbabwe. *African Review of Economics and Finance, 3*(1), 40-56.

Makoshori, S. (2014, October 30). Harare approves cluster houses. *Financial Gazette*.

Manikela, J.S. (2008). *Understanding the peripheralisation of low-cost housing delivery in the Mbombela Local Municipality. Johannesburg*. University of the Witwatersrand.

Al Mansoori, M. J. (1997). Government Low-Cost Housing Provision in the United Arab Emirates. *Age, 129*, 5546.

Mbiba, B. (2017). On the periphery: missing urbanisation in Zimbabwe. counterpoints, Africa Research Institute, London, counterpoints, Africa Research Institute, Available online:
http://www.africaresearchinstitute.org/newsite/publications/periphery-missingurbanisationzimbabwe/ (accessed 11 April 2017).

McGranahan, G. and Satterthwaite, D. (2014). *Urbanisation concepts and trends*. London: International Institute for Environment and Development.

Mengya, Y. (2013). To analyse urban sprawl using remote sensing: A case study of London, Ontario, Canada, Hong Kong. (Unpublished Doctoral dissertation. The University of Hong Kong, Pokfulam, Hong Kong.

Ministry of Local Government (MLGPWNH). (2004, December). Circular 70 of 2004. Government records.

Mohajeri, N., Gudmundsson, A. and Scartezzini, J.L. (2015). *Expansion and densification of cities: Linking urban form to urban ecology*. Lausanne: CISBAT.

Moyo, W. (2014). Urban housing policy and its implications on the low-income earners of a Harare Municipality, Zimbabwe. *International Journal of Asian Social Science, 4*(3), 356-365.

Mwaura, A. M. (2006). Policy review for Zones 3, 4 and 5, Nairobi, Kenya. 42nd ISoCaRP Congress (pp. 1-13). Nairobi.

Nyakazeya, P. (2010, January 14). Building residential properties expensive. Retrieved March 13, 2017, from Zimbabwe Independent:
http//www.theindependent.co.zw/2010/01/14/building-residential-properties-expensive/

Oyewole, C. (2016). Rapid urbanisation and sustainable food security: Africa's dilemma. *Journal of International Scientific Publications, 3*(1), 261-266.

Peng, X., Chen, X. and Cheng, Y. (2012). *Urbanisation and its consequences*. Beijing: UNESCO.

Potsiou, C. (2010). *Rapid urbanisation and mega cities: The need for spatial information management*. Copenhagen: The International Federation of Surveyors (FIG).

Potts, D, and Mutambirwa, C. C. (2006). High Density housing in Harare: Commodification and Overcrowding. London: Liverpool University Press.

Rakodi, C., and Mutizwa-Mangiza, N. D. (1990). Housing policy, production and consumption in Harare: A Review Part I. *Zambezia, 17*(1), 1-30.

Reporter, M. (2016, July 20). Council loses thousands to corrupt employee. Retrieved March 24, 2017, from The Herald:

http://www.herald.co.zw/council-loses-thousands-to-corrupt-employees/

Rights, H. (2005, July). Housing rights in Zimbabwe. *Human Rights Monthly, 37, pages.*

Rojas, E., and Greene, M. (1995). Reaching the poor: lessons from the Chilean housing experience. *Environment and Urbanization, 7*(2), 31-50.

Ruwende, K. (2015, February 27). CABS slashes deposit for Budiriro Scheme. Retrieved April 10, 2017, from The Herald: http://www.herald.co.zw/cabs-slashes-deposits-for-budiriro-scheme/

Scheidel, W. (2006). *Population and demography.* Stanford: Stanford University.

Shava, T. (2013). November 12). Urban poverty increase in Zimbabwean cities. Retrieved March 13, 2017, from VOA: http://www.voazimbabwe.com/a/urban-poverty-increases-in-zimbabwe-study/1788633.html

Skovbro, A. (2002). Urban densification: A sustainable urban policy? *The Sustainable City, II,* pages.

Tighe, J. R. (2010). Public opinion and affordable housing: A review of the literature. *Journal of Planning Literature, 25*(1), 3-17.

Toriro, P. (2008). Town planning in Zimbabwe: History, challenges and the urban renewal (Operation Murambatsvina). In F. Maphosa, K. Kujinga and S. Chingarande (Eds.), *Zimbabwe development experiences since 1980: Challenges and prospects for the future* (pp. 164-181). Harare: OSSREA.

Trussel, B. (2010). The bid rent gradient theory in Eugene Oregon: An empirical investigation. *University of Oregon,* 4-28.

UNHABITAT. (2015). *Planned city extensions: Analysis of historical examples.* Nairobi: UNHABITAT.

UNHABITAT. (2016b). *World cities report: Urbanisation and development* (Emerging futures). Nairobi: UNHABITAT.

UNHABITAT. (2016). *Guide lines for urban planning: Preparing for the Republic of the Union of Myanmar.* Nairobi: UNHABITAT.

United Nations. (2014). *World urbanisation prospects: The 2014 Revision.* New York: United Nations.

United Nations. (2015). *World population prospects: The 2015 Revision* (Volume II: Demographic profiles). New York: United Nations.

United Nations. (2015b). *World urbanisation prospects: The 2014 revision.* New York: United Nations.

University of Otago. (2013). *Urban Intensification in Auckland.* Available online: GEOG397 Topics: https://geog397.wiki.otago.ac.nz/index.php/Main_Page

Unknown. (2016, May 30). Chombo and the rot at Harare City Council. *New Zimbabwe.* Retrieved April 10, 2017 from http://www.newzimbabwe.com/news-29466-corruption+chombo+and+hre+city+council/news.aspx

Williams, K. (2007). Can urban intensification contribute to sustainable cities? Available online: http://www.urbanicity.org/

ZIMSTATS. (2012, May). *ZIMSTATS*. Retrieved October 2, 2016, from ZIMSTATS: http://www.ZIMSTATS.co.zw

ZIMSTATS. (2014, May). *ZIMSTATS*. Retrieved September 18, 2016, from ZIMSTATS: http://www.ZIMSTATS.co.zw

Zwinoira, T. (2017, January 30). NBS to rollout 10 000 housing units in 2017. *Newsday*.

Chapter 9

Infrastructure Maintenance for Sustainable Agriculture in Zimbabwe

Tamuka J. Mukura, Aurthur Chivambe
and Halleluah Chirisa

Summary:

The chapter aims to discuss infrastructure maintenance as a forgotten dimension of agricultural development in Zimbabwe and propose a model for ensuring sustainability. It enhances the argument that infrastructure is the bedrock of a successful agricultural system especially in developing countries. The fundamental premise of this argument is that the agricultural sector hinges on easily accessible markets, storage facilities and road networks. The decade after the fast track land resettlement programme (FTLRP) of 2000 saw a debilitating economic and climatic environment characterised by challenges of hyperinflation, and extreme weather events in the form of droughts and floods. This cocktail of challenges saw cross sectoral declines in output economy-wide due to forward and backward linkages among the different sectors, especially agriculture, manufacturing and mining. Despite several government input programmes that include the Government Input Scheme, Operation Maguta/Inala, and Presidential Input Scheme, among others, the country has failed to produce enough grain to reach self-sufficiency levels. This has resulted in the underutilisation and ultimate dilapidation of the country's grain storage infrastructure under the management of the Grain Marketing Board (GMB). Nevertheless, the closure of companies and the resulting spike in unemployment against a background of lack of access to international lines of credit, saw the government revenues plummeting thus constraining public investment in fixed capital formation, rehabilitation and maintenance. As a result, a deterioration of key infrastructure, especially the country's road network further exacerbated the poor performance of the country's agricultural marketing system. However, the 2016/17 agricultural season opened a new page in the Zimbabwean agricultural sector as the combination of good rains and the government's special input loan facility, the Command Agriculture initiative, put the country on the verge of an imminent bumper harvest, probably the first in more than 15 years. Unfortunately, it is at this point that the government just realised that the grain storage facilities are in a deplorable state and urgent rehabilitation is needed before harvest. Maintenance ought to be preventive or predictive. If it comes as an afterthought, it will result in a lot of unnecessary and avoidable costs. The lesson from this is that more costs are incurred if maintenance plans are non-existent. Always repairing is never a good form of maintenance. The chapter recommends the application of timely maintenance works as these are crucial to prevent unnecessary post-harvest losses.

Introduction

Agriculture is a major driver of economic growth in Zimbabwe and the greater part of Africa. The sector is critical for food security, poverty reduction and has strong forward and backward linkages with the manufacturing sector. In Africa, agriculture is one of the most important sources of livelihood, accounting for more than 70% of total employment (Morris, Hess and Posthumus, 2010). The chapter aims to discuss infrastructure maintenance as a forgotten dimension of agricultural development in Zimbabwe and to propose a model for ensuring sustainability. It argues that infrastructure is the bedrock of a successful agricultural system given that the sector depends on accessibility of markets, storage facilities and road networks.

Agriculture is said to be the backbone of Zimbabwe's economy (Chazovachii, 2012; Masaka, 2011; Chingono *et al.* 2009). On average, the sector contributes about 15% of Zimbabwe's GDP, 22.8% of export earnings and about 23% of total formal employment (Masiyandima *et al.* 2011: 8). The country has a total land area of 39.6 million hectares with 33.3 million hectares of the land being reserved for agriculture (Utete Presidential Commission, 2003). Major crops produced in Zimbabwe include maize, tobacco, cotton, soya bean, sorghum, and wheat.

Historically, the white large-scale commercial farmers, constituting 1% of the total population, owned 49% of the total agricultural land, while 51% was owned by African indigenous farmers, who constituted 99% of the population in the country (Masiyandima, 2011). The need to correct this historical imbalance and transfer land to the disadvantaged black majority was the driving force behind the liberation struggle which led to Zimbabwe gaining independence in 1980. According to Morales (1999), agrarian reform is recognised as a prerequisite for growth with equity in developing countries as evidenced in Japan, Republic of Korea, Taipei, China, and People's Republic of China, which have successfully implemented this reform (Morales, 1999). The redistribution of land therefore helps reduce poverty by granting full ownership and control to the farmer and providing the necessary support services and infrastructure to make the land productive, while laying the foundation for broad-based development. Through successful implementation of land reform programmes, these countries have achieved sustained economic growth and successfully reduced absolute material poverty among their populace.

In the case of Zimbabwe, in accordance with the Lancaster House Conference agreement, between 1980 and 1990, land was re-distributed on the basis of willing buyer willing seller, a process which was highly unsuccessful. Efforts were made to speed up this process between 1990 and 1997 through the Land Acquisition Act, but still no meaningful in roads were made. Mounting pressure from the now disgruntled liberation war veterans and their sympathisers, who initiated invasions of white owned farms, forced the Government of Zimbabwe to initiate the fast track land reform programme (FTLRP) in the year 2000. This sought to address these historical imbalances. According to Chisango (2010) and Obi (2010), these invasions were marked by violence as the war veterans and their sympathizers unleashed a wave of terror on the large-scale commercial farm sector.

To complement the new policy, the government introduced input support programmes such as the Government Input Scheme, Operation Maguta/Inala and the Reserve Bank of Zimbabwe led Farm Mechanization Programme targeted at beneficiaries of the land redistribution exercise and aimed at improving their agricultural productivity (FAO/WFP, 2007; Mugabe, 2007; The Final Call, 2008). Due to implementation inefficiencies, corruption and abuse of these facilities; coupled with climate change and other variable challenges in the form of droughts; it became clear not long after the launch of the FTLRP that expectations had been exuberant as production declined dramatically and only about 30-55% of the arable land was being cultivated (Chatizwa and Khumalo, 1996; Moyo, 2004; Fang et al. 2007). In the eyes of the donor community in Zimbabwe, this process had no goal, no plan, no timetable, no budget, no capacity and no transparency (Kinsey, 1999). While the FTLRP clearly led to substantial repossessions and transfers of land, it seemed to have created several other problems. At one level, the FTLRP is blamed for directly leading to a 30% drop in agricultural production, a hyper-inflationary situation, and 15% contraction of the economy that culminated in 2008, and to an unemployment rate estimated to exceed 80% (Zikhali, 2008).

The decade after the launch of the FTLRP saw Zimbabwe experiencing massive capital flight as several key multinational corporations relocated to other countries. In addition, the deteriorating economic environment characterised by hyperinflation forced companies to close thus driving unemployment up. The resultant shrinking tax base coupled with lack of access to international lines of credit severely narrowed the government's fiscal space. Efforts to finance the ballooning government budget deficit through seigniorage (money printing by the central bank) only fuelled hyperinflation. The crisis peaked in 2008 with hyperinflation reaching record levels of 231 million percent by July, leading to the rejection of the local currency, the Zimbabwean dollar, and the subsequent adoption of the multicurrency regime in early 2009. The dollarization process brought temporary relief to the country as it halted the hyperinflation and brought some short-lived improvement in economic growth as shown in Fig. 9.1. However, the ensuing liquidity challenges due to lack of international lines of credit reversed the momentum gained after dollarization, plunging the economy back into a crisis characterised by deflation, insufficient demand and persistent current account deficits. Company closures peaked and so did unemployment exerting pressure on government revenues.

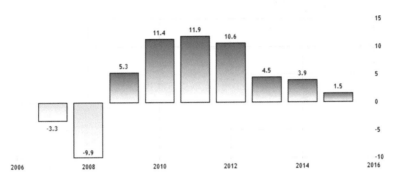

Figure 9.1: Zimbabwe GDP Annual Growth Rate (2007 – 2015)
Source: www.tradingeconomics.com

In light of the above developments, government capital expenditures plummeted with employment costs accounting for more than 80% of the budget for the greater part of the dollarization era. This negatively affected expenditure on infrastructure development, rehabilitation and maintenance. According to the African Development Bank-AfDB (2011), the level of investment in Zimbabwe has been below average since 2000, that is, around 19% of GDP, making it highly inadequate for the maintenance of the existing capital stock. After the FTLRP, much of the farm infrastructure and equipment that include dams and irrigation systems were vandalized and left in moribund state. Furthermore, despite several government input programmes meant to complement the land reform exercise, the country failed to produce enough grain to reach self-sufficiency levels resulting in the underutilisation and ultimate dilapidation of the country's grain storage infrastructure under the management of the Grain Marketing Board (GMB). The AfDB (2011) argues that Zimbabwean infrastructure faces five main challenges: (i) lack of maintenance due to financial constraints; (ii) accelerated deterioration through misuse; (iii) capacity constraints due to migration of skilled personnel; (iii) inadequate funding for infrastructure greenfield projects; (iv) high rates of accidents; and (v) lack of an integrated approach in infrastructure investment planning.

Theoretical Framework and Literature Review

The agriculture sector in Zimbabwe is the cornerstone of the economy (Campbell *et al.* 2001; Boserup, 2007; Skalnes, 2016). A major determinant of agricultural productivity growth is infrastructure (Gajigo and Lakuma, 2011). According to Intodia (2012), a close relationship exists between agricultural sector growth and investment in infrastructure through higher output and productivity, and increased horizontal and vertical integration of agricultural markets, and this improves price discovery and transmission of price signals from deficit to surplus areas. Agricultural infrastructure includes all basic services, facilities, equipment and institutions needed for efficient functioning of the food and fibre markets (Venkatachalam, 2003). The three types of agricultural infrastructure, according to Gajigo and Lakuma (2011), are road networks, irrigation technology and post-harvest storage technology. Empirical evidence suggests that a three to four-fold increase in infrastructure investment reduces poverty by 0.6 to 1 % annually (Besely and Byrgess, 2003). Clearly, more needs to be done to raise agricultural productivity to reduce the poverty and hunger among the rural people and to increase food production so as to bring down the cost of food and ensure sustainable food production and agricultural productivity. While a myriad of solutions is available to avert the Zimbabwean food crisis and attain sustainable food production (Munyanyi, 2013; Stringer, 2009; Margulis, 2014), this chapter seeks to establish the relationship between financing essential agricultural infrastructure and food production levels hence sustainable food production.

Figure 9.2 indicates the vital components of agricultural infrastructure maintenance which are critical for sustainable agriculture. First, are government and institutions which are responsible for policy-making such as giving land to the people. Secondly, is the agricultural financing component, the mother board which provides incentives and subsidies. Lastly, are private and public partnerships which are critical in fostering infrastructure maintenance through cooperation and integration in order to boost the agriculture sector.

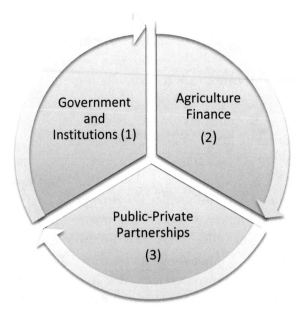

Figure 9.2: A schematic Model Indicating Various Components Needed for Agricultural Infrastructure

Source: United Nations (1987)

Access to affordable physical infrastructure is a major source of competitiveness in agricultural value chains and sustainable food production (Warner and Kahan, 2008). This includes infrastructure such as irrigation and energy which support on-farm production; transport and bulk storage to ensure efficient movement of commodities from the farm gate; and agro-processing and packaging facilities critical for value addition. Infrastructure in the agricultural sector enhances the comparative advantage of the region where infrastructural investment is made (Venkatachalam, 2003). Studies by Ahmed and Hussain (1990) demonstrated that fertilizer use in the agricultural sector increased with the improvement in the quality of roads. Fan and Hazell (2000) modelled agricultural output as a function of traditional farm inputs, technology, infrastructure and time. This is supported by Rostow (1960) who argues that improvement in infrastructure is considered as a necessary precondition for capital formation and increase in production and productivity. Boosting agricultural productivity can help to address a raft of problems such as food security and hunger, poverty and economic competitiveness besetting the African continent (Gajigo and Lukoma, 2011). Using aggregate agricultural production data from forty-seven developing and nineteen developed countries, Antle (1983) observed a strong positive relationship between infrastructure development and aggregate agricultural productivity. Bhatia (1999) also established a positive relationship between a composite index of rural infrastructure in 15 states of India and the level of per hectare yield of food grains and value of output from agriculture.

Infrastructure helps poorer individuals and underdeveloped areas to get connected to core economic activities, thus allowing them to access additional productive opportunities (Estache, 2003). Similarly, infrastructure development in poorer regions reduces production and transaction costs (Gannon and Liu, 1997). For example, in poor rural areas, infrastructure expands job opportunities for the less advantaged by reducing the cost of accessing product and factor markets (Smith *et al.* 2001; Renkow, Hallstrom and Karanja, 2004). Estache and Fay (1995) found that enhanced access to roads and sanitation has been a key determinant of income convergence for the poorest regions in Argentina and Brazil. Infrastructure access can raise the value of the assets of the poor. Improvements in communication and road services imply capital gains for these poor farmers (Jacoby, 2000). Some studies consider the issue of infrastructure efficiency. Hulten (1996) finds that differences in the effective use of infrastructure resources explain one-quarter of the growth differential between Africa and East Asia, and more than 40% of the growth differential between low and high-growth countries. Infrastructure development can have a positive impact on the income and welfare of the poor over and above its impact on average income (Lopez, 2004). Calderón (2004) found that inequality declines not only with larger infrastructure stocks but also with an improved quality of infrastructure services regardless of the econometric technique and the inequality measure employed.

Overall, agriculture is the driver for economic development in Zimbabwe as it leads to employment, improvement in living standards and reduction in inequality. After the FTLRP of 2000, and the economic crises that followed, most agriculture infrastructure that include roads, dams, storage facilities and irrigation deteriorated due , among other factors, vandalism and lack of rehabilitation and maintenance. Regardless of this, literature suggests that agriculture infrastructure development is the key to improve the socio-economic livelihoods of the people of Zimbabwe.

Methodology

Secondary sources of data were used in this chapter as they provide a quick and relatively easy method of obtaining a good overall understanding of agriculture infrastructure maintenance in Zimbabwe. First, literature review was used to identify the background of agricultural activities, especially in the three eras of pre-colonial period, colonial and post modernism. Secondly, content analysis was also employed as it can be used to make replicable and valid inferences by interpreting and coding textual material (Elo and Kyngäs, 2008).

This chapter also used documents relevant to agriculture and systematically evaluated different agriculture texts in order to have reasonable discourses on the topic discussed. Nevertheless, content analysis, as a method, has only recently become more prevalent in the arts and social studies despite its long usage history in other disciplines. Finally, document review was also used in this study because it quickly enables the writer and reader to find a knowledge gap.

Results and Discussion

At independence, in 1980, Zimbabwe inherited from Rhodesia an agricultural base characterised by a high degree of government intervention through indirect stimulation and interference (Makamure *et al.* 2001). The country was one of the most industrialised economies in sub-Saharan Africa, with an extensive agro-processing industry and a relatively diversified industrial sector (APRODEV, 2002; Carmody, 1998). Prior to attainment of independence, the colonial government established a prosperous commercial farming sector through financing essential infrastructure, providing direct and indirect subsidies, and creating supportive marketing and credit systems (Seidman, 1982). The new black government kept up the momentum in the early 1980s resulting in Zimbabwe being labelled the bread basket of Africa. However, by the late 1980s, the government was facing budgetary challenges which later culminated in the adoption of the International Monetary Fund (IMF) driven Economic Structural Adjustment Programme (ESAP) in 1991. ESAP sought to liberalise and open up the economy. Unfortunately, its launch coincided with the 1992 drought which decimated the country's agricultural sector causing the nation to appeal for international food aid. After wide-spread company closures and increase in unemployment, ESAP was abandoned in 1995 but its effects still linger on. In 1997, Zimbabwe was engaged in the DRC war which put a strain on the fiscus. To exacerbate the situation, mounting pressure from war veterans saw government awarding those Z$50,000 gratuities triggering inflationary pressures in the economy. The introduction of the FTLRP in 2000 attracted local and international criticism and catalysed the economic decline of the country. For the next decade after 2000, Zimbabwe plunged into arguably the worst economic meltdown in its history. The meltdown was characterised by widespread company closures, hyperinflation, shortages of basic commodities, fuel and foreign currency and the dilapidation of infrastructure owing to underutilization and lack of proper maintenance. The country went into a severe food crisis due to consecutive years of droughts, structural challenges, unreliable supply of low-cost inputs, limited access to credit, market information and research, and the land reform programme (United Nation, 2010). Average maize yields dropped to below half a tonne per hectare and total annual wheat output fell from 325 000 tonnes in 1990 to 18 500 tonnes in 2008, according to the Ministry of Agriculture, Mechanisation and Irrigation Development production statistics (United Nations, 2010).

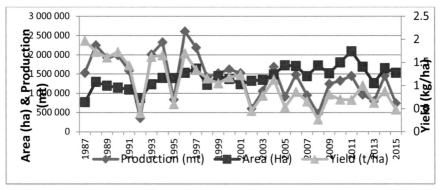

Figure 9.3: Evolution of Maize Production, Area and Yield, 1986-2015
Source: Agricultural Statistical Bulletin, MAMID

According to the UN (2010), the situation in Zimbabwe was exacerbated by the fast track land reform and the subsequent need for investment in the development and rehabilitation of irrigation systems, and post-harvest infrastructure that followed. The shortage of foreign currency that characterised the period affected the availability of repair and maintenance workshops close to the farmers, and supply of spare parts on the local market. The result was widespread hunger and increase in poverty levels. Low productivity was attributed to lack of capacity by the irrigation industry, equipment suppliers and contractors to provide services. Likewise, lack of postharvest infrastructure led to a high level of post-harvest losses. Existing literature supports that liberalization of the agricultural sector, accompanied by increased infrastructural development, can improve efficiency and equity in Zimbabwe. Fuglie *et al.* (2012) posit that technological innovations, investments in infrastructure and supporting policies, including subsidies, which were effective in some regions, were lagging behind, particularly in sub-Saharan Africa, Zimbabwe included.

State and condition of infrastructure supporting agriculture in Zimbabwe

This section examines and discusses the state and condition of infrastructure supporting agriculture in Zimbabwe. Following Gajigo and Lakuma (2011), focus is given on three types of agricultural infrastructure, that is, post-harvest storage technology, road networks and irrigation technology. These three types of agricultural infrastructure are discussed as follows.

Post-harvest storage technology (grain silos)

Inadequate and improper post-harvest handling of farm produce results in quantitative and qualitative losses, causing welfare loss to stakeholders in the form of reduced profitability for producers and higher prices for consumers (Khan, 2009). In Zimbabwe, the mandate for the storage of the country's grain lies with the Grain Marketing Board (GMB). GMB is a wholly state-owned enterprise established in 1931 with the main objective of ensuring national food security through production, procurement and management of the strategic grain reserve (SGR) and to transform the organisation into a commercially viable entity. The SGR is 100% run by government, with the GMB relying on Treasury for resources. The institution has over 80 depots around the country, 12 of them equipped with grain storage silos designed to hold up to 500,000 metric tonnes of maize. The Lion's Den silo, near Chinhoyi, is the second largest in Africa after Egypt and third largest in the world after Australia, with a 104,000-metric tonne holding capacity.

Since the year 2000, Zimbabwe has failed to reach self-sufficiency levels in grain production due to a multiplicity of factors including the fast track land reform programme (FTLRP), input availability challenges and extreme weather events, droughts in particular. Furthermore, the disincentive effects of low maize prices and non-payment of farmers for maize deliveries by the GMB also exacerbated the situation, and in some instances causing farmers to shun maize for more viable cash crops such as tobacco and cotton. In light of this, the capacity utilization of the GMB storage infrastructure drastically declined. The failure by GMB to pay farmers was due to government budgetary constraints. Unfortunately, the same budgetary constraints also meant that the GMB could not get enough funding for maintenance of the nearly 60 years old grain storage infrastructure. The silos have a normal lifespan of 10 to 15 years before reproofing but by 2010, the silos had gone for more than 15 years without major refurbishment. The resultant deterioration of the silos due to years of neglect saw 61,400 metric tonnes of maize destroyed between 2010 and 2012. In 2015, at Lion's Den, only 4 out of 29 silo bins were suitable for grain storage; the rest needing reproofing due to ageing. The silos, when in good condition, should store grain for at least 3 years without the grain losing its quality or grade. However, most of them have developed multiple cracks which allow water to seep through causing bin burn and cracking. Estimates put the repair costs at US$51 million but failure to raise a US$7.5 million deposit prevented the government from finalising a facility with the Export-Import Bank of China (China EximBank).

Even at the smallholder level, grain post-harvest losses remain a major concern to many smallholder farmers in Zimbabwe. According the Food and Agriculture Organisation (FAO) of the United Nations, -post-harvest losses, estimated at 20% to 30% in storage alone, can be as high as 40% when handling, transportation, and processing losses are included. In most communal areas of the country, including Zaka Jerera in Masvingo, grain production is characterised by one year of good production followed by two or three years of deficit. That is why long-term post-harvest storage is so important (Artés-Hernández *et al.* 2004). In light of this, FAO-Zimbabwe is implementing a project that promotes the construction of improved brick granaries and metal silos in rural areas with pilots having been carried out in Guruve and Gokwe. These innovations are more effective for preserving grain at the household level than the traditional storage structures (Nukenine, 2010).

The 2016/17 agricultural season opened a new page in the Zimbabwean agricultural sector as the combination of good rains and the government's special input loan facility, the Command Agriculture initiative has put the country on the verge of an imminent bumper harvest, probably the first in more than 15 years. The Command Agriculture scheme saw 240,000 hectares being put under maize by 36,000 contracted farmers who were expected to deliver 5 tonnes per hectare at US$390 per tonne. The farmers were assisted with maize seed, fertiliser, chemicals and diesel for tillage. The initial target was 2.2 million metric tonnes of maize from 400,000 hectares. Unfortunately, it is at this point that government realised that the grain storage facilities are in a deplorable state and urgent rehabilitation was needed before harvest. Failure to undertake timely rehabilitation works on the GMB silos against a background of lack of storage facilities at the farm level could result in unprecedented levels of grain post-harvest losses in the country. This development bears testimony to the lack of a holistic approach when addressing food and security issues by the authorities. Instead of a narrow production-oriented approach, a value chain integrated approach is critical for the revival of Zimbabwe's agricultural sector as the country battles to restore the country's status as the 'Bread Basket of Africa'.

Road network
Transport is critical for delivering r agricultural produce to markets, enhancing interaction among geographical and economic regions and opening up new areas to economic focus and hence agricultural development (Tunde and Adeniyi, 2012). According to Ajiboye (1994), availability of transport facilities is a critical investment factor that stimulates economic growth through increased accessibility. In a study on the relationship between transportation, underdevelopment and rurality, Ogunsanya (1988) observes that the greater the degree of rurality, the lower the level of transport development. Paul *et al.* (2009) pointed out that the impacts of road infrastructure on agricultural output and productivity are particularly important in sub-Saharan Africa for three reasons. First, the agricultural sector accounts for a large share of gross domestic product

(GDP) in most sub-Saharan countries. Secondly, poverty is concentrated in rural areas. Finally, the relatively low levels of road infrastructure and long average travel times result in high transaction costs for sales of agricultural inputs and outputs, and this limits agricultural productivity and growth.

Zimbabwe's road network was once considered to be among the best in Africa and it was a significant contributor to the growth of the economy (African Development Bank (AfDB), 2011). The network comprises 88,100 km of classified roads, and 17,400 km of which are paved. Just over 70% of this network comprises tertiary feeder and access roads that link rural communities to social economic amenities such as schools, health centres and markets, and enable government services to reach rural areas. The tertiary roads are managed by the District Development Fund (DDF) and Rural District Councils (RDCs) and connect rural areas to the trunk road system (primary and secondary roads). The trunk roads account for 70% of the vehicular traffic and are managed by the Department of Roads (DoR) which is responsible for their development and maintenance. Road development and rehabilitation is funded by the Road Fund which is administered by the Zimbabwe National Roads Administration (ZINARA). It is financed through fuel levy, toll gate fees, vehicle licence fees, and abnormal load and superload charges which are put in a consolidated revenue fund. Disbursement is then made to various road authorities. The road network is complemented by a rail network which connects the major mining, agricultural and heavy industrial centres to Zimbabwe's four neighbours, thus playing a key role in international trade while improving road safety and reducing road damage and congestion.

According to the AfDB (2011), the share of the total road network in fair to good condition declined from 73% in 1995 to about 60% for much of the 2000-2010 decade. Furthermore, an additional 12,800 km of road network that was reclassified to poor condition required US$1.1 billion for complete rehabilitation. The AfDB (2011) puts the replacement cost of the transport infrastructure and facilities at US$12 billion at 2009 constant prices, the rehabilitation cost at US$4 billion and the periodic maintenance at US$550 million annually. However, there was an estimated US$24 million, that is, 16% of annual maintenance requirements in 2009 only.

The railway network has a length of about 2,760 km, comprising 1,881 km mainline and 878 km of branch lines. While the rail network has a design capacity of 18 million tonnes per annum, the NRZ last highest achieved was 12.2 million tonnes in 1999. By 2009, volumes had declined to as low as 2.7 million tonnes, with improvements to 3.5 million observed from 2010 to date. This massive reduction in capacity utilisation resulted in fall in income which consequently led to serious deterioration in the state of the infrastructure and equipment. The track is marred with speed restrictions. This is further exacerbated by the Centralised Train Control System (CTCS) which is no longer functioning in most areas due to vandalism, obsolescence and lack of maintenance (Draft National Transport Master Plan, 2017).

The poor performance of the NRZ increased pressure on the country's roads as they were the only feasible alternative. Haulage trucks have done much damage to the country's road network which are now handling tonnage beyond their design capacity in the absence of proper rehabilitation and maintenance. The situation was exacerbated by the increase in passenger vehicle traffic fuelled by the massive importation of cheap second-hand Japanese cars since the dollarization of the economy. Although the government, through the Zimbabwe National Roads Administration (ZINARA), introduced toll gates under the user-pay principle for road development and rehabilitation finance, the realised revenues fall way short of the needs. The disbursements to the Departments of Roads and local authorities by ZINARA have not been adequate for meaningful maintenance and rehabilitation works. All over the country, the roads have developed potholes which have increased carnage and loss of lives. In 2017, Harare roads were declared a state of disaster prompting funds to be released from central government mainly for pot-hole filling.

Dams and irrigation facilities

A dam is a barrier built across a river or stream to confine and utilize the flow of water for human purposes such as irrigation and generation of hydroelectricity (Poff, 2002; Postel, 2012). While dam construction is done with positive intentions in mind, their adverse impacts on elements of biodiversity are threatening to outweigh the positive objectives for which they are built. As a result of this, throughout the past few years, the negative impacts of dams have become well documented that some countries have stopped building them altogether and are now forced to invest their money into fixing the problems created by existing dams (Collier, 2008). There are various dams in Zimbabwe, namely Tokwe Mukosi, Kariba Dam and Ruti Dam in Buhera district of Zimbabwe. Ruti Dam was constructed in 1976 to serve the local communities and the Chisumbanje Irrigation Scheme in the southeast lowveld of Zimbabwe. Due to the increased need for irrigation and the increased frequency of droughts, the capacity of Ruti Dam was increased by 25% through the installation of hydroplus fusegates on the 284m spillway sill in the year 2000 (Chikodzi et al. 2013). However, most of the dams in Zimbabwe are now in a deplorable state and need maintenance. Most of these dams are not maintained because of the socio-economic factors that include capital, corruption and lack of expertise to do the job.

Dams and irrigation facilities are intertwined in agriculture as a base for economic growth. Most large dam developments worldwide are either primarily for irrigation or hydropower. If the main use for the water is hydropower, then the water released from the power stations is used downstream for irrigation (Nhundu *et al.* 2010; Kates, 2003). Irrigation is therefore a very common benefit of these large dams such as Kariba Dam and Tokwe Mukosi. Considering that irrigation was not given prominence in the feasibility and design studies for Kariba Dam, it is not surprising that little irrigation development has occurred in Zimbabwe using Kariba Dam water. To date, only two irrigation schemes have been established which depend on Kariba Dam in Zimbabwe, and these are:

- Charara Estates, a privately-owned commercial irrigation scheme, with 50ha of irrigation for the production of bananas and horticultural crops;
- Gatshe-Gatshe community smallholder irrigation scheme, with an irrigated area of 18ha managed by 39 smallholder farmers. Main crops being grown are maize and vegetables.

Irrigation development continues to expand, but now the pace is slowing worldwide (Kates, 2003; Nhundu *et al.* 2010). In Zimbabwe, there are now challenges and constraints to irrigation development, particularly social and environmental concerns. Low productivity of many existing schemes has prompted a change in investment policy away from new infrastructure and toward programmes that improve the performance of existing schemes (Water Sector Board, 2007). Jones (1995) indicates that there has been a sharp decline in World Bank lending for new irrigation schemes. As a result of this, investments in irrigation systems in Zimbabwe are perceived to have failed to address the changing needs of irrigation services as rehabilitation of existing schemes was mostly carried out to restore original project objectives. However, this did not take into account or ignored the desirable changes in cropping patterns and irrigation techniques, thus allowing low water-productivity practices. The cost and time overruns in irrigation projects in Zimbabwe have therefore further eroded the confidence of funding agents in irrigation development.

In Zimbabwe, despite several government input programmes every year and then, the country has failed to produce enough grain to reach self-sufficiency levels resulting in the underutilisation and ultimate dilapidation of the country's grain storage infrastructure under the management of the Grain Marketing Board (GMB). Box 9.1 indicates the views and opinions surrounding the introduction of the Command Agriculture.

Box 9.1: The Introduction of the Command Agriculture in Zimbabwe

The idea and concept of Command Agriculture was spearheaded by Vice President Emmerson Mnangagwa. The Command Agriculture programme is under the Government and is also regarded as a booster model for agriculture production in Zimbabwe. Under the Command Agriculture programme, government was targeting to produce two million tonnes of maize on 400 000 hectares of land. 2 000 farmers were given inputs, irrigation and mechanised equipment. They were however required to give five tonnes per hectare to government as repayment. At the fourth Annual National Agribusiness Conference at the Exhibition Park, the Vice President said that:

"... successful agricultural performance would stimulate the agro-industry and create employment...I call upon right thinking Zimbabweans to invoke the spirit of patriotism and dedication to the welfare of the country by casting aside petty rivalries and joining hands in supporting this vital government initiative. The initiative has a potential to restore food security and nutrition, generate income and improve livelihoods of all our people including those in the diaspora irrespective of gender, religion, origin and political orientation...the Command Agriculture is aimed at raising maize production and reducing grain imports...."

It should be observed that the Command Agriculture is a national programme and has been occasioned by the declining trend in production and a steady increase in national food security. Source: Chikwati (2016)

Until recently Zimbabwe was one of the most industrialised economies in sub-Saharan Africa, with an extensive agro-processing industry and a relatively diversified industrial sector (APRODEV, 2002; Carmody, 1998). However, with the recent political and economic crisis, the country's agricultural sector and the economy in general suffered a lot of setbacks. Furthermore, it was discovered that more than 60% of the farms are inaccessible by road. The subdivisions that were done to the larger commercial farms to enable resettlements infringed negatively on the already established network systems. The failure to prepare land on time because of the shortage of tractors and machinery resulted in dwindling crop yields and consequently falling agricultural production. For years after the fast track land reform (FTLR), the absence of an effective mechanisation programme was seen as the major obstacle to increasing efficiency in crop production at the individual farmer level in Zimbabwe (Made, 2006).

Since the launch of FTLRP in around 2000, infrastructure maintenance has been low despite government efforts to develop and promote agriculture development. This was attributed to challenges and constraints as revealed by this research paper. It is therefore recommended that governments, in partnership with public and private institutions, work together in defining and implementing comprehensive strategies for infrastructure maintenance. Nhundu and Mushunje (2010) argue that such strategies should include the following components:

- Review of existing regulations and policies that influence agriculture development since the FTLRP introduced new farmers into the irrigation industry.
- Develop a legal framework to ensure land rights of farmers. This motivates farmers to invest in irrigation.
- The establishment of an adequate governance and institutional framework for service delivery, implying the need for integrated development approaches to provision of critical irrigation services, that is, widening the knowledge base with regard to irrigation service provision and accessibility.
- Institutionalisation of public–private partnerships in irrigation development, i.e. encouraging private investment in irrigation through provision of credit and financial incentives.
- Capacity building programmes for farmers to strengthen, support, and enlighten farmers and encourage farmer participation in irrigation development.
- Crop diversification to enhance farmers' incomes and viability levels and promote cost recovery from users, adequate to cover operation and maintenance costs.
- Promote harmonisation of scheme-wise development supported by economically sound, technically appropriate, sociologically sustainable, environmentally friendly and institutionally reliable medium.

Policy Options, Recommendations and Practical Implications

The chapter recommends the application of timely maintenance works as these are crucial to prevent unnecessary post-harvest losses. There is a need for a concerted effort from government to creating an appropriate land tenure system that makes it easy for farmers to borrow and invest on the land. At the same time, financial engineers should explore alternative agriculture financing models that facilitate access to credit by farmers at minimum possible risks and costs in order to improve productivity. There is a need therefore to emphasize the importance of information, social cohesion and peer loan guaranteeing in successful lending to agriculture. It is recommended therefore that institutions such as the Grain Marketing Board, with assistance from Government, ought to invest in establishing farmer data bases on past farmer loan performance, production performance and indebtedness that banks need in appraising loan applications from farmers. In line with the recommendation by United Nations

(2010) for Zimbabwe, there is an urgent need for development and rehabilitation of rural agricultural infrastructure, including storage facilities, roads, irrigation, dip tanks, handling pens and mechanisation.

Because of the persistent low level of annual harvest, over and above infrastructural development, there is a need for consolidation of the capacity for research, agricultural extension and policy analysis in the areas of crops, livestock, mechanisation, water resources development and irrigation, agricultural education, forestry, natural resources management, and climate change. Improved institutional capacity for research will provide a long-term solution to the problems that the farmers are facing in the rural areas. Research efforts should not be concentrated more particularly in one of the agricultural sectors (commercial and subsistence) to the detriment of the other. The task of maintaining a balance between both has become increasingly difficult since 1980 because, before this time, research was involved mainly with the large-scale farming sector and easier farming environments. A shift in emphasis ought to occur as it is now critical to solve the problems involved in small-scale and communal farming areas with the majority of farmers in Zimbabwe.

Conclusion

The results of the study clearly establish that investments in rural infrastructure like irrigation, rural markets, and roads increase the total factor productivity in agriculture. It is imperative that stepping up investment in rural infrastructure is not only essential to accelerate agricultural productivity but also to secure livelihoods for two-thirds of the population in the emerging global economic order. Thorat and Sirohi (2002) have used ten explanatory variables, namely transport, power, irrigation, tractors, research, extension, access to agricultural credit societies, regulated and wholesale markets, access to fertilizer sale points and commercial banks, covering physical, financial and research infrastructures. They have reported that transport, power, irrigation and research were the four critical components affecting agricultural productivity significantly. Maintenance ought to be preventive or predictive. If it comes as an afterthought, it will result in a lot of unnecessary and avoidable costs. The lesson from this is that more costs are incurred if maintenance plans are non-existent. Continuously repairing is never a good form of maintenance. At the time of independence, Zimbabwean agriculture was characterised by a distinct dualism. A high-yielding commercial sector with the capacity to produce a national surplus, on the one hand, was operated and managed by white farmers; alongside this affluent production power, a large African population of subsistence peasants struggled for small yields on poor soils. The agricultural sector in Zimbabwe is a critical sector in terms of economic growth and development. However, with the recent political and economic crisis, the country's agricultural sector and the economy in general suffered a lot of setbacks. The research revealed that infrastructure in the resettled farms is either dilapidated due to lack of maintenance or nonexistent. The fast track land reform programme implemented by the Zimbabwean government had a negative impact on farm infrastructure and equipment. An investment in infrastructure is thus required to ensure that there is improved agricultural productivity. In line with existing literature, the challenges that farmers face can be rectified by infrastructure development. A multi-sectorial participation in infrastructure development is thus required.

References

Ahmed, R. and Hussain, M. (1990). Developmental impact of rural infrastructure in Bangladesh, IFPRI. Research Report 83. Washington, D.C.

Antle, J.M. (1983). Infrastructure and aggregate productivity: International evidence. *Economic Development and Cultural Change, 31*(2), 609-620.

APRODEV. (2002). Women in Zimbabwe: Issues in future trade negotiations with the European Union. Available at: http://www.aprodev.net

Artés-Hernández, F., Aguayo, E. and Artés, F. (2004). Alternative atmosphere treatments for keeping quality of 'Autumn seedless' table grapes during long-term cold storage. *Postharvest Biology and Technology, 31*(1), 59-67.

Besley, T. and Burgess, R. (2003). Halving global poverty. *Journal of Economic Perspectives, 17*(3), 3-22.

Bhatia, M.S. (1999). Rural infrastructure and growth in agriculture. *Economic and Political Weekly, 34*(13), A43-A53.

Blakely, E.J. and Leigh, N.G. (2013). *Planning local economic development.* London: Sage.

Boserup, E. and Kanji, N. (2007). *Woman's role in economic development.* London: Earthscan.

Bunch, R. and López, G. (1996) Soil recuperation in Central America: sustaining innovation after intervention. Gatekeeper Series SA 55, Sustainable Agriculture Programme, IIED, London.

Campbell, B., Mandondo, A., Nemarundwe, N., Sithole, B., De Jong, W., Luckert, M. and Matose, F. (2001). Challenges to proponents of common property resource systems: Despairing voices from the social forests of Zimbabwe. *World development, 29*(4), 589-600.

Carmody P (1998). Neoclassical Practice and the Collapse of Industry in Zimbabwe: The Cases of Textiles, Clothing, and Footwear. Econ. Geo, 74(4): 31 9-343.

César, C. and Luis, S. (2004). The effects of infrastructure development on growth constraints. Research Series, No. 128, Facultis Universitaires Notre-Dame de la.

Chatizwa, K. and Khumalo, T. (1996). Weed management under different tillage systems and soil fertility levels. Report on the rapid rural appraisal for Chihota, Chivhu and Tsholotsho. Harare, Zimbabwe; IAE.

Chazovachii, B. (2012). The impact of small-scale irrigation schemes on rural livelihoods: the case of Panganai Irrigation Scheme Bikita District Zimbabwe. *Journal of Sustainable Development in Africa*, *14*(4), 217-231.

Chikodzi, D., Mutowo, G. and Makaudze, B. (2013). Impacts of dam construction on tree species diversity in semi-arid regions: The case of Ruti Dam in Zimbabwe. *Greener Journal of Environmental Management and Public Safety*, *2*(1), 16-21.

Chikwati, E. (2016, August 25). VP Mnangagwa calls for unity on the command agric. *Herald*. Accessed 20 February 2017 at: http://www.herald.co.zw/vp-mnangagwa-calls-for-unity-on-command-agric/

Chingono, M. and Nakana, S. (2009). The challenges of regional integration in Southern Africa. *African Journal of Political Science and International Relations*, *3*(10), 396-408.

Chisango, F.F.T. and Obi, A. (2010, September). Efficiency effects Zimbabwe's agricultural mechanization and fast track land reform programme: A Stochastic frontier approach. Poster presented at the Joint 3rd African Association of Agricultural Economists (AAAE) and 48th Agricultural Economists Association of South Africa (AEASA) Conference, Cape Town, South Africa, September (pp. 19-23).

Chiwara, D.C. (2014). *The role of the southern African development community on Zimbabwe's quest for food security*. Gweru: Unpublished Master of Arts in Development Studies Dissertation: Available online: http://ir.msu.ac.zw:8080/jspui/bitstream/11408/583/1/Dadirayi%20Chiwara%20R13705F%20MADS%20870-%20Dissertation%20FINAL.pdf

Collier, P. (2008). *The bottom billion: Why the poorest countries are failing and what can be done about it*. City, USA: Oxford University Press.

Cottrell, R.R. and McKenzie, J.F. (2011). *Health promotion and education research methods: Using the five-chapter thesis/dissertation model* (2nd edn). Massachusetts: Jones and Bartlett Learning.

DFID. (2000): Sustainable livelihoods guidance sheets. Department for International Development. http://www.livelihoods.org/info/info_guidancesheets.html (accessed: 23.07.2008)

Dixon, J.A., Gibbon, D.P. and Gulliver, A. (2001). *Farming systems and poverty: Improving farmers' livelihoods in a changing world*. City: Food and Agriculture Org.

Dobberman, A. and Nelson, R (201 3) Opportunities and solutions for sustainable food production. Sustainable Development Solutions Network, United Nations. Available online: http://unsdsn.org/wp-content/uploads/2014/02/130112-HLP-TG7-Solutions-for-sustainable-food-production.pdf

Estache, A. and Fay, M. (1995). *Regional growth in Argentina and Brazil: Determinants and policy options.* Washington, DC: The World Bank, Mimeo.

Estache, A. (2003). *On Latin America's infrastructure privatization and its distributional effects.* Washington, DC: The World Bank, Mimeo.

Fan, S. and Hazell, P. (2000). Should developing countries invest more in less favoured areas? *An Empirical Analysis of Rural India, Economic and Political Weekly,* (April), 1 455-1 464.

Fang, C., Sharma, R., Favre, R. and Hollema, S. (2007). FAO/WFP food security assessment mission to Nepal. Special Report. FAO, WFP.

Gajigo, O. and Lukoma, A. (2011). Infrastructure and agricultural productivity in Africa. Tunis: AfDB. Available online:
https://www.afdb.org/fileadmin/uploads/afdb/Documents/Publications/Infrastructure%20and%20Agricultural%20Productivity%20in%20Africa%20FINAL.pdf

Gannon, C. and Liu, Z. (1997). Poverty and transport". Washington, DC: The World Bank.

GLOPP. (2008). DFID's sustainable livelihoods approach and its framework. Available at
http://r.search.yahoo.com/_ylt=A0LEVi2ijK1YsfgAJmwPxQt.;_ylu=X3oDMTByOHZyb21tBGNvbG8DYmYxBHBvcwMxBHZ0aWQDBHNlYwNzcg/RV=2/RE=1487797539/RO=10/RU=http%3a%2f%2fglopp.ch%2fB7%2fen%2fmultimedia%2fB7_1_pdf2.

Hinchcliffe, F., Thompson, J. and Pretty, J.N. (1996). *Sustainable agriculture and food security in East and Southern Africa.* Report for the Committee on Food Security in East and Southern Africa. Stockholm: Swedish International Agency for International Cooperation.

Hulten, C. (1996). Infrastructure capital and economic growth: How well you use it may be more important than how much you have. NBER Working Paper 5847, December.

Jacoby, H. (2000). Access to rural markets and the benefits of rural roads. *The Economic Journal, 110,* 713-37.

Jayne, T.S., Chisvo, M., Rukuni, M. and Masanganise, P. (2006). Zimbabwe's food insecurity paradox: hunger amid potential. Harare: University of Zimbabwe (UZ) Publications.

Jones W.I. (1995). The World Bank and irrigation. A World Bank operational evaluation study. Washington, DC. World Bank.

Kanyenze, G. (2011). *Beyond the enclave: Towards a pro-poor and inclusive development strategy for Zimbabwe*. Harare: Weaver Press.

Kates, R.W. and Parris, T.M. (2003). Long-term trends and a sustainability transition. *Proceedings of the National Academy of Sciences, 100*(14), 8062-8067.

Kherallah, M., Delgado, C.L., Gabre-Madhin, E., Minot, N. and Johnson, M. (2000). *The road half travelled: Agricultural market reform in sub-Saharan Africa*. Washington, DC: Intl Food Policy Res Inst.

Kinsey, B. (1999). Land reform, growth and equity: Emerging evidence from Zimbabwe's resettlement programme. *Journal of Southern African Studies, 25*(2), 173-196.

Kollmair, M. and Gamper, St. (2002). *The sustainable livelihood approach*. Input Paper for the Integrated Training Course of NCCR North-South. Development Study Group, University of Zurich.

López, H. (2004). *Macroeconomics and inequality*. The World Bank Research Workshop, Macroeconomic Challenges in Low Income Countries, October, Paix, NAMUR, Belgium.

Made, J. (2007). Zimpapers. *Herald*.

Makadho, J., Matondi, P.B. and Munyuki-Hungwe, M.N. (2001). *Irrigation development and water resource management*. Harare: University of Zimbabwe (UZ) Publications.

Makamure, J., Jowa, J. and Muzuva, H. (2001) Liberalization of agricultural markets. Harare, Zimbabwe: SAPRI.

Margulis, M. E. (2014). Trading out of the global food crisis? The World Trade Organisation and the geopolitics of food security. *Geopolitics, 19*(2), 322-350.

Masaka, D. (2011). Zimbabwe's land contestations and her politico-economic crises: A philosophical dialogue. *Journal of Sustainable Development in Africa, 13*(1), 331-347.

Masiyandima, N., Chigumira, G. and Bara, A. (2011). Sustainable financing options for agriculture in Zimbabwe. Zimbabwe Economic Policy Analysis Research Unit Working Paper Series (ZWPS 02/10).

Morales, H.R. (1999). *When does agrarian reform work for the poor?* Speech delivered at the ADB, Manila Social Forum: The New Social Agenda for East and Southeast Asia. ADB, Manila, 10 November.

Morris, J., Hess, T. and Posthumus, H. (2010). Agriculture's role in flood adaptation and mitigation: policy issues and approaches. In Pariss K, (Ed.), *Sustainable management of water resources in agriculture*. Copenhagen: OECD Publishing.

Moyo, S. *et al.* (2004), Review of the Zimbabwean agricultural sector following the

implementation of the land reform, Harare, Zimbabwe: AIAS.

Mugabe, R.G. (2007). Zimpapers. *Herald*.

Munyanyi, W. (2013). Agricultural infrastructure development imperative for sustainable food production: A Zimbabwean perspective. *Russian Journal of Agricultural and Socio-Economic Sciences, 24*(12), pages.

Nhundu, K. and Mushunje, A. (2010). Analysis of irrigation development post fast track land reform programme. A case study of Goromonzi District, Mashonaland East Province, Zimbabwe. Poster presented at the Joint 3rd African Association of Agricultural Economists (AAAE) and 48th Agricultural Economists Association of South Africa (AEASA) Conference, Cape Town, South Africa, September 19-23.

Nukenine, E.N. (2010). Stored product protection in Africa: Past, present and future. Paper presented at the 10th International Working Conference on Stored Product Protection.

Obi, A. (2010). Impact of Zimbabwe's fast track land reform programme on the production and marketing of maize in the smallholder sector. Available online:
https://pdfs.semanticscholar.org/ca9f/c193cc0108b66ee43f05f53e47a5ed a36c92.pdf

Oluoch-Kosura, W. (2010). Institutional innovations for smallholder farmers' competitiveness in Africa. *African Journal of Agricultural and Resource Economics, 5*(1), 227-242.

Poff, N.L. and Hart, D.D. (2002). How dams vary and why it matters for the emerging science of dam removal. *BioScience, 52*(8), 659-668.

Postel, S. and Richter, B. (2012). *Rivers for life: Managing water for people and nature.* Washington DC: Island Press.

Pretty, J.N. (1995). Participatory learning for sustainable agriculture. *World Development, 23*(8), 1 247-1 263.

Pretty, J.N., Thompson, J. and Hinchcliffe, F. (1997). Sustainable agriculture: Impacts on food production and challenges for food security. International Institute for Environment and Development, GS No. 60.

Rakodi, C. (2002). A livelihoods approach–conceptual issues and definitions. In Rakodi, C. (Ed.). *Urban livelihoods: A people-centred approach to reducing poverty.* London: Routledge.

Renkow, M.D.G., Hallstrom, Initial. and Karanja, D.D. (2004). Rural infrastructure, transactions costs, and market participation in Kenya. *Journal of Development Economics, 74*(2), 349–367.

Report of the Presidential Land Review Committee (Chaired by Utete) (2003).

Rostow, W.W. (1960). *The stages of economic growth: A non-communist manifesto,* Cambridge: Cambridge University Press.

Schneider, K., and Gugerty, M. K. (2011). Agricultural productivity and poverty reduction: Linkages and pathways. *Libraries Test Journal, 1*(1), 56-74.

Seidman, A. (1982). A development strategy for Zimbabwe, *Zambezia, X*(i), 13-39.

Skalnes, T. (2016). *The politics of economic reform in Zimbabwe: Continuity and change in development.* City: Springer.

Smith, D., Gordon, A., Meadows, K. and Zwick, K. (2001). Livelihood diversification in Uganda: Patterns and determinants of change across two rural districts. *Food Policy, 26*, 421-435.

Stringer, L.C. (2009). Reviewing the links between desertification and food insecurity: From parallel challenges to synergistic solutions. *Food Security, 1*(2), 113-126.

Thompson, R.L. (2001). The World Bank strategy to rural development with special reference to the role of irrigation and drainage: Keynote address (pp. 2 – 17). 1st Asian Regional Conference and Workshop on the Occasion of 52nd IEC meeting of ICID, Seoul. New Delhi, ICID.

Thorat, S. and Sirohi, S. (2002). Rural infrastructure: State of Indian farmers, a millennium study. New Delhi: Ministry of Agriculture, Government of India.

UN. (2010). Country analysis report for Zimbabwe. Harare: United Nations.

United Nations General Assembly. (1987). *Report of the world commission on environment and development: Our common future.* Oslo, Norway: United Nations General Assembly, Development and International Co-operation: Environment.

Venkatachalam, L. (2003). *Infrastructure and agricultural development in Karnataka State.* Nagarbhavi, Bangalore: Institute for Social and Economic Change.

Warner, M., Kahan, D., and Lehel, S. (2008). *Market-oriented agricultural infrastructure: Appraisal of public-private partnerships.* Rome: FAO.

Water Sector Board Discussion Paper Series. (2007). Emerging public-private partnerships in irrigation development and management: Paper no. 10. The World Bank Group

Webersik, C. and Wilson, C. (2009). Achieving environmental sustainability and growth in Africa: The role of science, technology and innovation. *Sustainable Development, 17*(6), 400-413.

Zikhali, P. (2008). Fast track land reform and agricultural productivity in Zimbabwe. Discussion Paper Series, EfD DP 08-30, Environment for Development, Sweden.

Chapter 10

The Question of Sustainability and Dumpsites in Harare: A Case Study of Pomona

Barbara Chibvamushure

Summary*:*

Dumpsites, as disposal points of solid waste, if badly sited can be a major source of pollution that impacts negatively on the environment. The chapter assesses the location, quality and sustainability of the Pomona dumpsite in Harare. The chapter recommends ways of ensuring environmental sustainability in the face of the growing population and rapid sprawl of the city. Inefficiently managed dumpsites are a potential health hazard, thus alternative effective methods of disposing garbage are discussed suggesting sustainable mechanisms regarding dumping sites in Harare such as closed landfills. At present the city of Harare largely relies on the Pomona open landfill. However, there are a lot of hidden costs in service delivery amongst managing toxicity and transportation with particular reference to the maintenance of the fleet of vehicles used for waste disposal. Regardless of the city`s expansion, is there sustainability in the delivery of solid waste to Pomona dumpsite? Pomona has been a source of livelihood for various poor households that collect empty containers for resale. Although various studies on dumpsites have been done, there is a dearth of knowledge in the lessons learnt from the burning of the Pomona dumpsite. A qualitative study on Pomona dumping site was conducted after a literature review. The case study of Pomona dumping site used structured interviews with participants. The research indicates that Pomona dumpsite was dangerous to human health. This was caused by toxins produced from the chemicals which are disposed of at the dumpsite. The research found the Pomona dumpsite is not sustainable in view of the physical expansion of the city. The study recommends that enhanced quality on service delivery should be a priority in reducing threats to land, water and air pollution by shifting waste disposal from open dumping to closed landfills.

Introduction

Zimbabwe`s capital city Harare has Pomona dumpsite which has been in operation since 1988. Having been active since 1988 and receiving 36 000 tonnes of municipal solid waste, the Pomona dumpsite is a breeding ground for diseases such as cholera, typhoid, dysentery and various airborne and skin diseases which could affect residents of the surrounding settlements. Pomona is surrounded by residents of Hatcliffe Extension. The ground water is not very safe for drinking because of the toxins underground. Pomona dumpsite is the official landfill located 12 kilometres North from the City of Harare`s Central business district. It is one of the City of Harare`s biggest open dumpsite for disposing waste. The dumpsite is currently the only dumpsite in the City of Harare which has a population of 1.5 million (ZIMSTATS, 2016). This has resulted in the accumulation of solid waste crippling the city`s capacity operations. The rise in urbanisation has not been matched with the development of the city`s infrastructure. A landfill is defined as a site used to dispose solid waste that is licensed as a landfill under Zimbabwe's Environmental Management Agency (EMA) Act (Cap 20, 27). The Environmental Management Agency is a statutory national institution that governs and regulates the operations of landfills in solid waste management in Zimbabwe.

Developing countries are characterised by rapid population growth due to rural-urban migration (Srivastava *et al.* 2015). Town planners have a role to plan, develop, manage and help prevent economic, social and environmental problems (Ashiru, Olugbenga, Oladimeji, 2015). Dumpsites are regarded as social and environmental problems World Health Organisation (2015: p 13-14) identifies health hazards associated with dumpsites that are negative on both the environment and public health. The health problems arise as a result of different ways of handling solid waste disposal or untreated waste which may result in leaks of waste contaminating soils and water streams. The water sources around Pomona dumpsites are likely to be affected by the waste leaks thereby making the water sources a health hazard for public consumption. The World Health Organisation indicates that living within landfill vicinity is a health hazard. The air is polluted through inhalation of substances emitted by the site. The Pomona dumpsite has a negative impact on the environment through uncontrolled littering that damage and deteriorates the natural landscape. Pomona`s open landfill dumping site is therefore a potentially a health hazard. There is a need thus for urgent attention to public health and the environment at Pomona dumpsite.

Studies were conducted on dumpsites but there is a dearth of knowledge in the dangers of open dumpsites to humans as a health hazard. The issue of dumpsites in managing solid waste has been a global concern. Various ways of disposing waste have been used ranging from open dumpsites, sanitary landfills to closed landfills (Chirisa, 2012). Despite the challenges that they encounter, developing countries like Ghana, Nigeria, and Zambia have attempted to attend solid waste disposal issues in so that they control and manage dumpsites in their countries.

The study assesses the sustainability of Pomona dumpsite as a health hazard in the city of Harare. The research further proposes a way forward to ensure the environmental safety in the light of a demographic swell and the physical expansion of the city. The Pomona landfill in the City of Harare if properly managed can sustain the population of Harare. The questions the chapter seeks to address are: Is there sustainability in the delivery of solid waste to Pomona dumpsite regardless of the expansion of the city? What health hazards are associated with the Pomona open dumpsite? What are the sustainable mechanisms that can be adopted to reduce solid waste pollution in dumpsites?

Theoretical Framework

The concept of sustainable development underpins several pillars which are ecology, social equity, economic growth, environmental protection and institutions (Kahn, 1995). Participatory approaches to community participation are either top down or bottom up approach to development. These approaches are suitable for the study so that we can have an appreciation of solid waste management at Pomona dumpsite, which is regarded as a health hazard to society and the environment. The UN (1987, pp. 5-10) defines sustainable development as development that meets the requirements of the present generation without interfering or compromising the needs of the future generation. The Brundtland report is defines sustainable development as development that meets the needs of the present without compromising the ability of the future generations to meet their own needs (International World Commission on Environment and Development (IWCED), 2007, p 1-2). The report discusses development and environment as a single inseparable issue. Economic sustainability can be measured by economic growth of developing nations reviving to equal the growth of developed countries (IWCED report, 2007, pp. 1-2). Social sustainability encompasses empowerment of society through employment creation, equal access to resources, that is, access to health, water, food, energy and sanitation. Social participation can be done through community involvement via ward councillors regarding social and health matters that concern them. Cultural identity plays a vital role in preserving the environment through social norms and values that are adhered to through indigenous knowledge systems. The institutions play a vital role in environment protection by implementing policies that protect the environment. Environmental sustainability ought to preserve the natural environment through biodiversity, ecosystem integrity and capacity (Kahn, 1995). Environmental sustainability promotes harvesting resources not more than the natural environment can generate.

Literature Review

Dumpsites are a global health and environmental concern in solid waste management. Developing countries widely use open dumpsites landfills in disposing solid waste (World Bank, 2012 P 4-7). The rural-urban migration has worsened the management of solid waste in the case of the City of Harare. The mushrooming of squatter camps around Harare illustrate this rural-urban migration. For example, the upmarket Gunhill suburb in Harare is now a neighbour to squatter camps with potential health hazards as squatters generally live in unhealthy conditions with no sewer systems, no clean safe water for drinking and no refuse collection, amongst others. Furthermore, the Harare City Council is failing to effectively manage solid waste because they are failing to fund the rapid increase and demand of solid waste services. This can be seen in the inconsistency of garbage collection by refuse trucks in locations and suburbs of the city of Harare (Tacoli, 2012: 19-23).

Studies from various scholars have indicated that dumpsites if properly managed can be effective in handling solid waste. The waste atlas (2014, pp. 18-72) report on the world's 50 dumpsites indicated that African countries have the biggest number of dumpsites followed by Asia, Latin America, the Caribbean and Europe. However, the report indicates that China was amongst the countries with the biggest dumpsites. Brazil has Estrutural dumpsite which is located in the capital city of Brasilia. The dumpsite occupies an area of 136 hectares and has been in operation for more than 50 years. About 21 to 30 million tonnes of municipal solid waste have been disposed of there with about 2500 waste pickers making a livelihood and a monthly income by collecting recyclable materials for resale. The dumpsite is located 10km away from the 1 million households and 500 metres away from the national park exposing a million people to health risks and deaths have been reported on the dumpsites (The Waste Atlas, 2014, pp. 18-72). Argentina has a dumpsite located in San Carlos de Bariloche called Bariloche dumpsite. The dumpsite is located 1.5 km from the nearest settlement and is located 3.5km away from the lake and has been in operation for 32 years (Waste Atlas report, 2014, pp. 18-72).

Developing countries in Africa with the biggest dumpsite include Ghana. There is a dumpsite called Agbogbloshie in Accra, Ghana. The dumpsite has been in operation for more than 13 years. More than 10 000 people process electronic -waste on the dumpsite to recover precious metals such as copper, iron and aluminium. The dumpsite is located 10km away from a population of 2.3 million people. There is open burning at the dumpsite which causes a thick black smoke that, according to the report, has been related to numerous breathing and chest problems, headaches and chronic nausea. The soils under the dumpsite have high levels of toxins due to the electronic- waste. South

Africa`s Arlington dumpsite in Port Elizabeth was also a health hazard to liquid hazardous waste in managing solid waste. The dumpsite has around 100 waste pickers working. Nigeria has a dumpsite located in Ibadan called Awotan (Apete) which is said to be the third metropolitan area in Nigeria (The Waste Atlas, 2014, pp. 18-72).

As a developing country, Zimbabwe is still advancing from open landfill towards closed landfill in the management of solid waste compared to first world countries. Several studies on environmental public health have established that solid waste pollution is a major problem in urban areas of Zimbabwe and other developing countries (Masocha and Tevera, 2003, pp. 9-19; Mapira and Mungwini, 2007, pp. 67-98). The studies indicated that municipal councils, stakeholders and the central government are still facing challenges of protecting the environment. This chapter acknowledges these studies and adds knowledge on the sustainability of Pomona landfill in solid waste management.

The challenges facing urban areas today can be traced back to the 1990s when the Harare city council had problems in solid waste disposal resulting in the communities' open dumps (Nhete, 2006, pp. 1-7). Zimbabwe`s urban growth was moving at a faster rate, crippling the already built infrastructure (Chidavaenzi, 2006, pp. 1-5). Solid waste disposal is a daily activity increasing the waste generation rate at dumpsites. During the rainy season, environmental conditions worsen as these open dumpsites are well known to release large amounts of hazardous chemicals that contaminate ground water and landfill gas.

Solid waste management in the city of Harare is deteriorating. This has resulted in the accumulation of solid waste pollution and disease outbreaks including diarrhoeal and typhoid. There is therefore a research gap to further investigate (Machiwenyika, 2012, p.1). There is therefore a need to research on the sustainability of Pomona landfill in Harare as an attempt to promote solid waste disposal that is environmentally friendly, with little or no health risks associated.

The city of Harare was once called the sunshine city because the town used to efficiently manage solid waste and delivery was reliable. The social and economic structure changes have made the state to neglect the built environment. This has impacted negatively on the local authorities, stakeholders and stakeholders in environmental management. Dumpsites have not only been a cause for concern to the local authorities alone but also an issue of concern to the residence who are living in areas proximity to Pomona dumpsite. Municipal councils face challenges in solid waste disposal. These include lack of provisions to the vehicles that amass waste and lack of fuel to carry out waste collection and disposal (Masocha and Tevera, 2003 p 9-19). Chidavaenzi postulates that the amount of solid waste generated has been reduced in its density volumes from 460 kg/m^3 to 230 kg/m^3 which is about 50% less density in the waste being generated but the volume of waste being generated has doubled in the communities (Chidavaenzi, 2006 p 1-5). The city council depends on various stakeholders for funding. This is because the council have limited funds to conduct a proper solid waste management. Pulling out of stakeholders mean that the city council is left crippled. During that period solid waste amounts had doubled causing problems to the expanding population (Chidavaenzi, 2006, pp. 1-5). This chapter however sought to bring out the gap of the sustainability of the Pomona landfill regardless of the expansion in managing solid waste.

The Harare City Council has encountered various problems in managing solid waste. Financial resources are another factor the local authorities have to explore with major problem and technicalities emanating from poor finances. Challenges in refuse collection and disposal are a key issue in managing landfills. These challenges facing the municipal council have been an on-going issue such that the Pomona open landfill has been the only dumpsite that is available to dispose waste in the capital City of Harare. Research has been done by the scholars and various people have dwelled on the inefficiency of the city council, poor budgets and mismanagement of funds, poor service provision in solid waste management. However, this research sought to the gap concerning the sustainability of solid waste disposal at Pomona dumpsite and whether that limits development of solid waste management.

Around the year 2000, solid waste management systems started collapsing as the country was facing severe economic crisis, foreign currency shortages causing hyperinflation to the environment and solid waste collection was amongst the most affected (Grover and Masocha, 2003, p11-19. Lack of adequate funding, poor planning, under payment of municipality workers, abuse of municipal funds and machinery have highly contributed to the lack of properly engineered and designed dumpsites in Harare. Dumpsites in many developing countries are poorly located.

The Harare metropolitan province is characterised by urban growth with leapfrog developments with infill and population expansions (Kamusoko, Gamba and Murakami, 2013, pp. 322-331). These infill and expansions have led to the developments of peri-urban settlements surrounding the city of Harare experiencing outbreaks of disease due to lack of planning and institutional integration (Chirisa, 2009). Lack of planning and institutional integration affect landfills due to the physical expansion of the city. This chapter therefore examines the sustainability of the Pomona dumpsite in light of the City of Harare`s expansion. The City of Harare is outgrowing the physical planning that was done during the colonial period so some of the urban challenges demand robust planning based on the city`s history (Chirisa, Kawadza and Muzenda, 2014, pp. 19-29). The increase in the urban population calls for rapid urban service provisions to align and keep pace with the Harare populations in terms of clean water supply, solid waste disposal, power supplies, refuse collection, roads maintenance, public transportation and other service provisions that are essential (Munzwa and Jonga, 2010, pp. 120-146). However, despite the city's physical expansion, there is only one dumpsite providing service for the City of Harare Metropolitan mandated to cater for the urban population.

Methodology

The overarching objective was to investigate the health hazards at Pomona dumpsite in managing solid waste disposal in environmental management. The research adopted the qualitative research design. A qualitative study was used for the research because the research involved oral communication with the respondents. Structured interviews with key informants were used because respondents would be very busy at work to fill in a questionnaire, making the structured interviews the best method for this research.

Secondary data, which is data sources from previous researches and government records, was suitable for the study because it allowed the researcher to solicit information on health effects on the residential areas surrounding the Pomona dumpsites. This was supported by direct observation, on-site measurements of the dumpsite and to get the reality of the day interactions from waste pickers who were the key informants familiar with the activities on the dumpsite. Direct observation was very important for the researcher to get to understand the respondents in their natural setting. The research set out to describe situations which prevailed at Pomona dumpsite from the perspective of the residents who live in proximity to the open landfill. The chapter sought to unveil the actual setting of the day to day operations at the landfill in which the site presented itself from observing independently making the data reliable.

The target population in this study was the waste pickers surrounding the Pomona dumpsite, the respondents from Pomona Barracks, Hatcliffe residents, Vainona and other residents from Mount Pleasant Heights. The sample size for the study was 30. Purposive and convenience sampling was used to select respondents for the key informant interviews. Purposive sampling was the best for the key informant interviews because it enabled the researcher to identify and interview the stakeholders who are the policy-makers and authorities in the management of solid waste. The key informants were from the Ministry of Environment, Water and Climate, Environmental Management Authority (EMA), Harare City Council, and representatives from the Combined Harare Residents 'Association. The key informants provided data that was based on their knowledge, expertise and responsibilities. Convenience sampling was adopted for selecting respondents to interview and it was suitable for the research because data were collected from the members of the population conveniently available to participate in the research study. Data were collected from primary sources interviews and onsite observation.

Direct observation was very reliable because it did not cause the Hawthorne effect, that is, once people knew they were being observed at the dumpsite performing their daily tasks they were likely to change their behaviours in their natural occurrences. In this regard, the researcher was covert when doing direct observation. The researcher used thematic analysis to analyse data obtained from the interviews and observations. The data were put into main themes, assigned codes, and responses were classified under the main themes (Cohen, Manion and Morrison, 2007, pp. 317-382). Data were coded verified and after coding data were reviewed, summarized and interpreted. The study maintained ethical consideration by asking respondents to sign an informed consent form before the interviews research were conducted.

Table 10.1: Sampling Plan

Structured Interviews	Number in sample
Waste Pickers on the Dumpsite	10
Experts	20
Total	30

Results

The results were obtained from the structured interviews conducted with participants and the researchers` on-site observations.

Sustainability of Pomona dumpsite in view of the city`s expansion.

One of the objectives was to examine the sustainability of delivery of solid waste to Pomona dumpsite regardless of the expansion of the city. The issue of sustainability of the Pomona dumpsite can be articulated from the physical, social, financial, environmental and economic sustainability. Application of these principles to development literally means that the location of Pomona dumpsite must be environmentally friendly to the future generation. Pomona dumpsite as an open dumpsite, exposed to scavengers who pick up waste for recycling and frequently visit the dumpsite anytime of the day. There is security at the entrance that monitors the movement of cars but the working conditions, as expressed by respondents, posed a health hazard. One of the respondents had this to say,

There is no water at the site and the toilets have since been closed. We rely on water deliveries to fill up the tank but the water is sometimes unavailable. The city council had since promised to drill a borehole.

Pomona open landfill does not have a bill board indicating that this was properly a designated dumpsite. The dumpsite does not have a weighbridge for waste trucks to pay dumping fees. Such toll fees could be used towards the servicing and maintenance of the dumpsite. An uncontrolled fire was once recorded at the Pomona landfill in October 2016. It took several days to stop the fire which was uncontrollable and causing massive black smoke. Respondents surrounding the landfill believed that the fire could have been started by the toxins while others were of the view that the fire was caused by the city council as a way of reducing the amount of solid waste. One of the respondents indicated that:

> Putting a fence does not help because it is not strong and people will come and steal the fence for personal use, so the city Council must put a drywall that is strong and durable.

Respondents' views were supported by one of the key informants who indicated that there was a need to look into security as a matter of urgency for the protection of the Pomona open landfill. Social sustainability is about understanding the social impacts which can harm society. As a health hazard, dumpsites must not be sited in proximity to residential areas. The interviews from key informants indicated that Pomona dumpsite is located close to Hatcliffe residential areas so that infringes on the people's freedom and right to clean air as the dumpsite burnings are a health hazard. There are also other indirect impacts on social sustainability that includes noise pollution from the waste disposal vehicles and air pollution from the solid waste. One of the respondents who were passing by the dumpsite expressed concerns over the dumpsite:

> *Tanzwa ne* noise everyday so we are now used to it, but if something can be done by the Municipality to reduce noise we would be happy.

To ensure social sustainability, dumpsites must not be sited close to settlements. These are critical factors that highly determine their social acceptability. Financial sustainability is another aspect that is of paramount importance to landfills. One of the broader challenges concerning dumpsites in developing countries is lack of adequate funds to improve their service delivery. The Unites States Agency for International Development (USAID) and World Bank report indicated that developing countries spend 20-50% of their budgets on solid waste disposal yet the budget is not enough to cover the entire population (Memon, 2010, pp. 30-40). This is true for the City of Harare which has 47 trucks on-site but the vehicle on the roads were very few. During the

213

interviews, the key informants expressed concern about the cost of maintenance service for the vehicles, with spare parts coming from as far as Japan. The costly vehicle service expenses resulted in fewer trucks collecting solid waste. The City of Harare has engaged in public–private partnerships with various organisations that have been assisting in service provision. These stakeholders provide bins for solid waste disposal, conduct anti-litter campaigns on waste disposal and waste separation. Despite this assistance, Pomona dumpsite still needs funds to convert the dumpsite into a landfill. This requires huge sums of money to operate.

Environmental sustainability includes creating and maintaining the aesthetic beauty of the local environs. It entails protecting the natural environs that sustain people. These can be rivers, dams, game parks and the natural vegetation. For example, Pomona dumpsite water was exposed to water leachate exposing the surrounding communities to the drinking water that is contaminated. The onsite observation was unbearable during the site visits. There were unbearable odours from the solid waste. This was because of the decomposing mix of garbage, with both biodegradable and degradable waste mixed together. Economic sustainability is defined by growth development in such manner that market allocation of resources trickles down to the poor (Kahn, 1995, p 2-13). In view of the dumpsite, Pomona can sustain its development by moving from an open dumpsite to a closed landfill that has been engineered and that meets the requirements of the Environmental Management Authority (EMA), that is, of not causing environmental pollution of underground and surface water bodies or causing soil and air pollution.

Health hazards associated with the Pomona dumpsite

There are health hazards that have been associated with the Pomona open dumpsite. Pomona dumpsite as an open dumpsite, generates environmental and health hazards. The decomposition of organic materials from the dumps produces methane gas which causes fire and explosions that can contribute to global warming. Uncontrolled fire breakouts generating air pollution from the smoke affects the residents surrounding the dumpsite (Martin, 2013, pp. 289-299). The waste pickers at the dumpsite are vulnerable to various diseases because they do not have any form of protective clothing. The respondents who were interviewed highlighted that the dumpsite was also a major breeding place for diseases like malaria and typhoid, amongst others. From the on-site observation, the researcher noted that there were some waste pickers wearing masks while others were not. They indicated that colds and coughing were amongst the most common diseases that they suffer as a result of the dust and exposure to various chemicals during waste picking. One of the waste pickers indicated that,

We make a living from picking waste so I am used to picking plastic containers without gloves. No one gives you the gloves so I have to work for me and my family for a living.

Sustainable measures to reduce solid waste at the Pomona open landfill

From the results obtained from the interviews, respondents expressed their views on some of the remedies that can be taken on board in reducing solid waste at the dumpsite. Zimbabwe is amongst the developing countries that are faced by crippling management of solid waste. So much can be taken from other developing countries who are involved in waste separation as a remedy to reduce solid waste at dumpsites. Households interviewed indicated that waste separation is very important because it made it easy for the City of Harare to collect waste according to the specifications. One householder had this to say on waste separation,

When I visited my daughter in London they had four bins one for plastics bottles, one for cans, one for paper and the other was for empty bottles or diapers. The solid waste was done very smart so if Zimbabwe could practice this mode of disposal we can reduce solid waste at the Pomona open landfill.

The other householder who was interviewed agreed with the above respondent and she indicated that in developed countries there are trucks that carry only disposable diapers. This could assist in the sustainability of open landfills as some of the solid waste could be taken for recycling. However, other respondents expressed their concerns over waste separation which they thought would require more refuse collections bins to enable the effective waste separation from the household. In addition, most residents have little knowledge about it. Most of the respondents indicated that acquiring more bins for households to reduce accumulation of waste at Pomona dumpsite was the most effective measure to ensure Pomona`s sustainability. The key informants from EMA indicated that a combined effort of corporates partnerships would produce positive results. The Ministry of Environment also indicated that they were involved in collaboration with Environment Africa, a private organisation to promote recycling as a way of reducing littering at Pomona dumpsite. The Harare City Council, in an effort to reduce solid waste pollution, indicated that they had engaged various companies in Zimbabwe to promote and enable waste separation by providing more bins to households and in the city centre. Amongst them include Nyaradzo Funeral Service, OK Zimbabwe and various organisations that had shown interest in reducing solid waste in Harare.

Discussion

The results obtained from the interviews conducted with the respondents, showed that the Pomona open landfill was not sustainable in light of the city`s expansion. The city council has experienced challenges in the supervision of the dumpsite. This was illustrated by the fire that occurred at the dumpsite in October 2016. The Pomona landfill did not have a borehole to stop the fire that occurred, and the city had to rely on the fire brigade to stop the fire. The City of Harare is expanding and faced by both the rural-urban migration and the natural population growth one dumpsite was not sustainable. The study revealed that there was no proper security and monitoring of the Pomona dumpsite so the physical variable available was solid waste. Social sustainability indicated that the local residents were exposed to air pollution as the dumpsite produced air pollution from the smoke and noise pollution from the trucks, infringing upon their human freedoms. Financial sustainability was a major problem as the City of Harare cannot afford to increase the very few vehicles which ferry solid waste to the dumpsite. Management of solid waste is difficult with a limited fleet of trucks. Furthermore, garbage collection trucks are stationed at the City of Harare`s works department in Graniteside, so they had to cross cut the city to the Pomona dumpsite which was costly in terms of its operations. The results revealed that poor service delivery has contributed to private organisation partnerships with the city council being formed to assist in disposing solid waste. The introduction of private trucks frequenting the landfill indicated that the city council was incapacitated to dispose of the solid waste. The results also revealed that environmental and economic sustainability of Pomona dumpsite was compromised as the landfill was an open dumpsite not a closed landfill. In addition, the lifespan of the dumpsite is no longer sustainable. The study established that the dumpsite has a mixture of degradable and bio-degradable waste.

The study established that health hazards are associated with the Pomona open dumpsite as it was a breeding place for rodents and diseases such as malaria and typhoid. There was leachate from the dumpsite to the surface water resulting in contamination of channels of water bodies. The study revealed that the Pomona open landfill was a source of livelihood to 15 waste pickers who were involved in accumulating empty plastic bottles for resale. The empty containers would be recycled. The waste-pickers however had no protective clothing as most of them were using their bare hands exposing them to health risks. Waste picking seems to offer financial sustainability to the young boys and girls who were supposed to be attending schools. Amongst the 30 respondents interviewed, 3 were orphans and 7 were school leavers who indicated that they were assisting their parents. Five out of the 30 participants were children

216

working together with their mothers as a sustainable mechanism to alleviate financial challenges. The study observed that scavenging work was a health risk. However, the work would have been made easier if the City of Harare and various stakeholders collaborate to educate the citizens of Harare to practise waste separation. The companies manufacturing and selling plastics could create more formal employment from waste picking and collection.

A modification by the environmental authorities from open dumpsite to a closed landfill and recycling would reduce the problem of solid waste disposal. The city of Harare made error in foresight as they did not take into consideration the population growth. The proposed new landfill site at Mount Hampden is also unsuitable as the city is expanding towards the west. Currently there are Fairview developers who are currently servicing residential stands. The Environmental Management Agency (EMA) regulations clearly stipulate that landfills must be further away from the communities. The City of Harare, Environmental Management Agency (EMA), and the Government of Zimbabwe must place initiatives to promote recycling among the communities. Poor waste management can be attributed to ignorance and lack of cooperation from the communities at large and the industrial sectors involved. Knowledge of waste separation should be disseminated at early ages in nursery schools to minimise reckless solid waste disposal.

Conclusion and Recommendations

The chapter is based on a study that sought to investigate the sustainable management of the Pomona dumpsite as an open landfill in the City of Harare. The results of this study have indicated that the Pomona landfill is a health hazard as people are exposed to ecological, physical and chemical dangers from the toxins emanating from the dumpsite. It can be concluded that the Pomona dumpsite is not sustainable in view of its inadequacy in handling the physical expansion of the town. Enhanced quality service delivery should be a priority in reducing threats in land, water and air pollution by shifting from open dumping to landfills of solid waste disposal. One of the recommendations proposed to ensure sustainability of the Pomona open landfill, is that the Government of Zimbabwe and the city fathers ought to encourage waste separation. This calls for more bins to allow separation of degradable and bio-degradable waste. Another recommendation is for the city council and stakeholders to embark on public information awareness campaigns seminars and workshops on the usefulness and importance of recycling of solid waste before disposal. The population growth demand more physical expansion as the city relies on one dumpsite. Furthermore, the study recommends that the planning system should allocate more land for new dumping sites. Landfills must be sited out of town far from the residential stands. It is also suggested that information on waste separation and landfills must be included in the school curriculum so that learners can have an appreciation of conserving the environment. The Environmental Management Agency (EMA) came up with a policy that penalises those who do not comply with the by-laws to pay a fine through the polluter pay principle. Developed countries like the United Kingdom, Brazil, Belgium and Germany practise recycling of solid waste. The city should engage inspection agency that enforces strict rules in disposing of the waste. The issue of dumpsites and sustainability needs further research in managing solid waste disposal due to the city`s physical expansion. Management of solid wastes can be made easy if the City of Harare incorporates the people in the community in decision-making processes. A bottom up approach to development is paramount to development as suggestions and ideas emanate from the people who are affected to where the policies are made. The City of Harare aim to attain its global city status by 2025 solid waste disposal and management of landfills is therefore one critical area the city fathers ought to consider. The gathered data will be of great help to service providers, stakeholders and other beneficiaries of waste management. There is room for the Environmental Management Agency (EMA), the police dog of environmental instruments in Zimbabwe, to revisit the acts, instruments, and policies on how best the Pomona landfill can be sustainable in view of the human population expansion of the City of Harare.

References

Ashiru, O.O. (2015). *The role of planners in the built environment.* Presented at the Academic Seminar of the Urban and Regional Planning Student Association of Nigeria Olabisi Onabanjo University. 16 September 2015.

Brundtland Report (2007). *Our common future framing sustainable development.* Oslo: United Nations World Commission on Environment and Development.

Chidavaenzi, M. and Kwenda, G. (2006). *Research and research gaps in waste management.* Proceeding of the emerging issues in urban waste management workshop organised by Practical Action for Southern Africa Newlands, Harare at Jameson Hotel 10 February 2006.

Chirisa, I. (2010). Peri-urban dynamics and regional planning in Africa: implications for building healthy cities. *Journal of African studies and development,* 2(2), 015-026.

Chirisa, I. (2012). Solid waste, the throw-away culture and livelihoods: Problems and prospects in Harare. *Zimbabwe Journal of Environmental Science and Water Resources,* 2(1), 001-008.

Chirisa, I., Kawadza, S. T., and Muzenda, A. (2014). Unexplored Elasticity of Planning and Good Governance in Harare, Zimbabwe. *International Review for Spatial Planning and Sustainable Development, 2*(4), 19-29.

Cohen, I., Manion, L. and Morrison, K. (2007). *Research methods in education* (6th edn,). City: Routledge.

Grover, V.I. and Masocha, M. (2003). Solid waste management and recycling in Victoria Falls, Zimbabwe. *J Sustain. Waste Manage, 91*, 11-19.

Kahn, M. (1995). *Concepts, definitions and key issues in sustainable development: The outlook for the future.* Proceedings of the 1995 International Sustainable Development Research Conference, Manchester, England, March 27/28, 1995, Keynote Paper, 2-13.

Kamusoko, C., Gamba, J. and Murakami, H. (2013). Monitoring urban spatial growth in Harare Metropolitan Province, Zimbabwe. *Advances in Remote Sensing, 2*(4), 322-331.

Machiwenyika, F. (2012, March 31.). Declare city sewage plants a national disaster-group. *Herald.*

Makwara, E.C (2011). *Work related environmental health risks: The case of garbage handlers in the city of Masvingo.* Saarbrucken: Lambert Academic Publishing.

Makwara, E. C., and Snodia, S. (2013). Confronting the reckless gambling with people's health and lives: Urban Solid Waste Management in Zimbabwe. *European Journal of Sustainable Development, 2*(1), 67-98.

Mapira, J. and Mungwini, P. (2007). River pollution in the city of Masvingo: A complex issue. *Zambezi, 32*(1 and 2), 95

Martin, G.L. (2013). The impact of interaction with students affairs on socially responsible leadership development in the first year of college. *Journal of College and Character, 14*(4), 289-299.

Masocha, M. and Tevera, D. (2003). Open waste dumps in Victoria Falls Town: Numbers 33/34. *Geographical Journal of Zimbabwe, 33-34*, 9-19.

Memon, M.A. (2010). Integrated solid waste management based on the 3R approach. *Journal of Material cycles and Waste Management, 12*(1), 30-40.

Munzwa, K.M. and Jonga, W. (2010). Urban development in Zimbabwe: A human settlement perspective. *Theoretical and Empirical Researches in Urban Management, 5*(14), 120-146.

Nhete, T. (2006). *Proceedings of the Emerging Issues in Urban Waste Management.* Workshop organised by Practical Action for Southern Africa, Newlands, Harare at Jameson Hotel, 10 February 2006.

Srivastava, V., Ismail, S.A., Singh, P. and Singh, R.P. (2015). Urban solid waste management in the developing world with emphasis on India. *Challenges and Opportunities, 14*(2), 317-337.

Tacoli, C. (2012). *Urbanisation, gender and urban poverty: Paid work and unpaid carework in the city.* London, UK: International Institute for Environment and Development: United Nations Population Fund.

Tevera, D.S. (1991). Solid waste disposal in Harare and its effects on the environment: Some preliminary observation. *Zimbabwe Science News, 25,* 9-13.

Tsiko, R.G. and Togarepi, S. (2012). A situational analysis of waste management in Harare, Zimbabwe. *A Journal of American Science 8*(4), 692-706.

UNEP. (2009). Solid waste: Generation, handling, treatment and disposal environmental guidelines for small scale activities in Africa, Chapter 15. UN Environment Programme.

United Nations. (2012). *The millennium development goals report 2010.* Geneva: United Nations Publications

USAID. (2009). Environmental guidelines for small scale activities in Africa. Available online: (EGSSAA) www.encapafrica.org.

Waste Atlas. (2014). *The waste atlas report 2014: Solid waste management in the world`s cities.* Available online:
https://www.iswa.org/fileadmin/galleries/News/WASTE_ATLAS_2013_REPORT.pdf

World Bank. (2003). Africa Malaria Day (2003). Washington DC: The World Bank Group.

World Bank. (2012). What a waste: A global review of solid waste management. Urban development series knowledge papers. Washington DC: World Bank.

World Health Organisation. (2015). *Waste and human health: Evidence and needs.* WHO meeting report. 5-6 November 2015, Bonn Germany.

ZIMSTATS. (2014). *The Zimbabwe National Statistics Agency Census preliminary report.* Harare: Zimbabwe National Statistics Agency.

Chapter 11

The Newlands Market in Harare: An Ecological Footprint Analysis of Forest Resources and Products

Aurthur Chivambe, Abraham R. Matamanda,
and Halleluah Chirisa

Summary:

The chapter features a study on our understanding of the nexus between market sources of natural resource materials, innovation, product development and marketing by exploring how small-medium entrepreneurs create establish niches and sell their products. This chapter brings to the fore issues including choice and innovative practices by these entrepreneurs, the challenges they face and how they cope as they establish a footprint and a brand for their products. Using an exploratory discourse analysis, based on in-depth unstructured interviews with the SMEs, officials from EMA and City of Harare, the study established that the conversion of natural resources in identified local areas such as the remote and arid areas like Birchenough and Buhera is linked to a critical ecological footprint of value addition which sees the establishment of backyard industries. Newlands Business Centre has become one of the markets where the products made by informal entrepreneurs are sold both to local and international buyers. The chapter uses a theory of economic development that includes the theory of core periphery. In relation to this present study, Harare is the core while the four corners of Zimbabwe represent the periphery. Specifically, the periphery areas include Mhondoro, Mt Darwin, Dete and Mutoko where the raw materials come from. These entrepreneurs juggle between a challenging macro-economic environment and competition to survive. To survive and eke a living, they become responsive to this highly competitive and elastic environment. In the periphery regions, efforts must be made to safeguard the natural resources to avoid their depletion. Moreover, the industry is also instrumental in the conversion of waste into usable products, that is, wastes recycle.

Introduction

The concept of "governance" has recently taken centre stage since it moved to the centre of debates on development in the 1980s (United Nations, 2012). By the mid-1990s environmental governance and sustainable development had become the major concepts influencing environmental management (Campbell, 1996). The Environmental Impact Assessment Policy of 1994 has been instrumental in integrating environmental and economic issues in various planning and development projects and programmes in Zimbabwe. Likewise, the Zimbabwe Environmental Management Act Chapter 20:27 Act 13 of 2002 spells out the strategies and policies that relate to natural resource management in the country. The preamble of the Act states that:

> 'An act to provide for the sustainable management of natural resources and protection of the environment; the prevention of pollution and environmental degradation; the preparation of National Environmental Plan and other plans for the management and protection of the environment (Government of Zimbabwe, 2002)'

The success of environmental management is partly attributed to devolution and participation. These two (devolution and participation) have remained the building blocks in development and environmental thinking (Finch and Omolo, 2015). The significance of devolution and participation is also cemented through the increasing concern by governments and non-governmental organisations anxious about the success of natural resource management resulting in a global trend of engagements with participatory approaches to governance (Mohammed-Katerere and Chenje, 2002; Mangena, 2014; European Union and Government of Zimbabwe, 2015:15-16). For example, section 73(b) (i-iii) of the Constitution of Zimbabwe provides that the natural environment must be protected to ensure sustainable development. Specifically, the environment must be protected through prevention of pollution, securing conservation and use of natural resources while promoting sustainable development (Government of Zimbabwe, 2013).

The chapter makes a case for creating and managing urban finance in Harare by pointing out the constraints and challenges embedded in the financial architectures of the city. Specifically, the chapter explores the untapped potential and options that can be used to exploit the financial resources that are part of the city's wealth. The main emphasis is placed on Harare because the capital city has become the core region while remote areas that include Buhera and Birchenough are peripheral. However, these peripheral centres serve as the major sources of raw materials. Most of entrepreneurs from the periphery come to Harare in search of greener pastures to support their families and subsequently improve their family incomes and standard of living (Feresu, 2010; Dube and Chirisa, 2012).

The national policy framework for natural resource management changed dramatically in the last two decades. The chapter demonstrates that there are two approaches that are used in environmental law, at both the national and international level. First, is the set of approaches which are designed to "ensure" compliance or conservation. These are prescriptive and more elaborate. Secondly, are approaches designed to "facilitate" better practice among citizens. These approaches are process oriented. Nevertheless, the processes and approaches impose a duty on the state to develop national legal systems that recognise such rights. In some instances, it encourages the development of private law rights such as traditional resource rights. These developments have occurred within the context of a growing body of human rights law dealing with socio-economic growth, justice, fairness and equity.

Background

When Zimbabwe gained independence in 1980, its citizens had prospects of a better life characterised by adequate employment opportunities and improved access to basic services and sources of livelihoods. Subsequently, the colonial laws such as Pass Laws, which restricted Africans from migration into urban areas, were removed (Patel, 1988: 23). Thus, there was a huge influx of people from the rural into urban areas in search of better living and working conditions (Feresu, 2010). Ironically, this large exodus of people into urban areas was not concomitant with economic development, especially industrialisation which is critical with regards to employment needs of the population (AFDB, 1997; Bandauko and Masvika, 2015). The droughts experienced in the early 1980s also exacerbated the socio-economic profile of the country (Kinsey, Burger and Gunning, 1998). Moreover, the post-colonial government also inherited the colonial economic system which had a lot of shortcomings. Therefore, by the mid-1980s it was apparent that the much-anticipated economic emancipation and freedom only remained a fallacy and pipe dream that required attention of the government.

By the late 1980s, the government was compelled to consider adopting the Economic Structural Adjustment Programme (ESAP) whose main thrust was on economic reforms. Although most critics argue that ESAP was a failure, it was successful in creating a macroeconomic environment conducive to the birth of the backyard industry and small scale-business sectors. Owing to the massive retrenchments that followed ESAP in the mid-1990 together with economic reforms, there was a proliferation of small industries which were heavily supported by the government. Presently, there are still many backyard industries in both middle and low-density suburbs in the major cities and towns of Zimbabwe (Dube and Chirisa, 2012; Gumbo, 2013). Matondi (2011) argues that unemployment in Zimbabwe has remained very high, while employment creation in both private and public sectors sector industries has remained depressed. Statistically, there have been some debates with regards the unemployment figures in Zimbabwe. According to the Zimbabwe National Statistics Agency (Zimstat), the nation's unemployment rate is 11.3% (Zimstat, 2014). However, other sources say unemployment is as high as 95% (Worstall, 2017). Africa Check, an organization that promotes accuracy in public debate and the media, states that most of the available unemployment figures are unreliable, because they are not based on primary data. However, events on the ground indicate that unemployment rates in Zimbabwe are extremely high and this has resulted in majority of people engaging in transitional economic activities which Matondi (2011) characterised as *ad hoc* economic activities. Consequently, the unemployment crisis has spurred informal, or backyard, businesses across the country (Matondi, 2011; Gumbo, 2013). According to a 2014 Zimstat survey of the labour status in Zimbabwe, 94.5 per cent of the population is engaged in informal employment. Since 2011, informal employment has grown more than 10 per cent, according to the same survey. Manufacturing is a fast-growing sector for informal employment (Zimstat, 2014). While the agency does not keep exact statistics on informal shoemakers, it says the trade is growing. Despite growth in the trade, the unstable economy means increased risks for entrepreneurs who face challenges due to lack of capital and weak customer bases.

Study Area

Harare, officially called Salisbury until 1982, is the capital and most populous city of Zimbabwe. Situated in the north-east of the country and in the heart of Mashonaland, the city currently has an estimated population 2.1 million people from the last official national census of 2012 (Zimstat, 2013).

Newlands is a middle density area situated in Harare. Its geographical coordinates are 17° 48' 29" South, 31° 4' 54" East. Figure 11.1 is a Google image which shows the aerial view of Newlands Shopping Centre. From the image, it is shown that the area is well served with roads which make it a strategic location for entrepreneurs. The site is located along Enterprise Road which stems off A2 Highway (Harare-Nyamapanda Road). Moreover, the site is also linked to other secondary roads which make Newlands easily accessible. In close proximity to the study site, are a number of retail and commercial facilities which help in providing a customer base for the market. Of utmost importance is TM Supermarket, Newlands Post Office, Murandy Square Mon Repos Building, Total Service Station and some food outlets. All these factors make Newlands a strategic site for the small-scale enterprises. The forthcoming section focuses on the conceptual framework guiding this chapter.

Figure 11.1: Study Area, Newlands Harare

Source: Google Images

Conceptual Framework

An understanding of the dynamics of the Newlands Market in Harare requires a conceptualisation through the urban-rural linkages. This is so because Harare is an urban area that thrives on the natural resources extracted from the rural areas and other smaller towns across the country. In this way there is justification for engaging relevant rural-urban linkage concepts that can illuminate the relationships between the urban and rural areas (cf. Andersson, 2001). The rural areas that supply Harare with natural resources include Buhera, Murehwa, Mutoko and Gokwe, among many others. The chapter adopts the core-periphery approaches as the guiding concept for this study.

The core-periphery concept attempts to explain the development that occurs between different regions, particularly the core and the periphery (Myrdal, 1957). The core region is basically characterised by urban areas that are based on tertiary production and commercial services. Overall, the core regions have large population which constitute a lucrative market for various commodities, innovation, high amounts of manufacturing industries and demand for raw materials as well as a well-established and complex transport system. The industries in the core region drive the economy and this helps to add value to the resources and products that are often imported from the periphery. On the other hand, peripheral regions are characterised by resource endowed regions that support the industries in the core regions. In this way there is a symbiotic relationship between the two regions as explained by Myrdal (1957) who introduced the concept of spread effects and backwash effects. Myrdal (1957) used the concept of 'spread effects' to describe the flows of capital, technology and consumer goods form the core to the periphery. On the other hand, the term 'backwash effects' was used to explain the flows of resources and labour from the periphery to the core. That being the case, the core regions develop by depending on the exportation of raw materials from the peripheries and hinterland regions (Matamanda and Chirisa, forthcoming).

In the same vein, the situation between Newlands Market in Harare is best conceptualised through the core-periphery model because Harare emerges as a core region due to the high concentration of population and a vibrant market for different goods and services, manufacturing industries that include numerous backyard industries and SMEs and functional transport networks. The core region of Harare depends on its hinterland regions such as Mutoko, Murehwa, Norton, Chitungwiza and Domboshawa which supply the industrial hubs of the city with natural raw materials and labour for the purposes of production. Natural resources such as wood and stones used for sculpting, honey, seeds used to make beads, grass and reeds are among the resources that are harvested in different rural areas. These resources are thus used to produce the products that are eventually sold at Newlands Market in Harare.

In as much as we would appreciate the significance of the core-periphery concept, there is need to factor in the aspect of sustainability in this discourse. It would be interesting to note the level of sustainability of the relationship that exists between the core, periphery and the natural resources. This is specifically so because issues that concern natural resources come with immense environmental implications through ecological footprints that require the factoring in of sustainability. Broadly, the concept of sustainability stems from sustainable development which focuses on efforts to ensure that development is undertaken in a way that helps to benefit present and future generations. Sustainability for this study will be conceptualised based on the three discourses proffered by Govannoni and Fabietti (2014) who argue that there is an environmental, business and social discourse to sustainability.

The environmental discourse mainly focuses on environmental conservation wherein processes by humans must not negatively impact on the biophysical environment. In as much as natural resources must be harvested, there ought to be a sustainable yield with emphasis on the simultaneous monitoring of the depletion of natural resources when utilising them (Sachs, 1984). The social discourse of sustainability places much emphasis on the needs of generations, for example, between the present and future generations. The extraction of the natural resources must be done in such a way that the future generations will also benefit from the same resources or even enjoy better than the present generation (Govannoni and Fabietti, 2014). There is also another dimension which looks at inter-generational equity which ought to be addressed (Campbell, 1996). Lastly, is the business discourse of sustainability which is defined as follows:

> " ...the capability of a corporation to last in time, both in terms of profitability, productivity and financial performance, as well as in terms of managing environmental and social assets that compose its capitals (Govannoni and Fabietti, 2014: 27)"

In this way the operations of the SMEs can be framed within this business discourse of sustainability which is mainly concerned with the operations of the business entities and corporate. This section has described the core-periphery concept and how it applies in the context of Harare. By so doing, it sets the tone for the literature review.

Literature Review

This section examines literature that considers the extent to which natural resources are usually managed. The section also focuses on how the informal sector uses natural resources to sustain livelihoods. Moreover, the section examines the role, in particular, of traditional markets and how the rights of participation and indigenous people are handled in natural resource management. Although the conservation success of a rights approach must be tested empirically, the principal argument made here is that rights must be recognised in themselves because of their centrality to human dignity and integrity.

In Zimbabwe, four sets of institutions have roles in natural resource management at the local level: specialist agencies, elected local government bodies, traditional institutions and state-initiated community management structures (Katerere, 2001). Legally, the role of tribal chiefs has been perverted – or in Mamdani's words the chief has been transformed into a "decentralized despot" (Mamdani, 1996). The colonial government used traditional leadership institutions to control local people. At independence, the government sought to reduce their power and role at all levels. A Prime Minister's Directive in 1984 on local government established a system of localized development committees; Village and Ward Development Committees (VIDCOs and WADCOs) (Kurebwa, 2015: 104-106). The purported objective of this Directive was to define the administrative structures at provincial and district level and the relationships and channels of communication between all participants in the development at provincial and district level in order to achieve the coordinated development of provinces and districts. With the adoption of the Traditional Leaders Act in 1998, government has done a near complete turn around and reinstated the power the chiefs held during colonialism. Village assemblies now exist alongside the VIDCOs and WADCOs (Katerere, 2001).

In the natural resource area, decentralization was further provided for through the development of the Communal Areas Management Programme for Indigenous Resources (CAMPFIRE) (Mutandwa and Gadzirayi, 2007). The Natural Resources Act of 1941 provided for the establishment of the Natural Resources Board, a national conservation watchdog comprising government appointed members. The act vested the board with broad and sweeping powers of intervention in the area of environmental conservation and, in native areas, these powers were exercised in a capricious and arbitrary manner: forced soil conservation works often relying on forced labour; restrictions on grazing; compulsory destocking; restrictions on cultivation.

In European areas, the enforcement of the provisions of the Natural Resources Act relied on voluntary regulation and the investment of large-scale grants, loans, machinery and other incentives to assist white settlers in implementing conservation measures (McGregor, 1991; Scoones and Matose, 1993). Voluntarily constituted conservation fraternities in European farming neighbourhoods received the designation of Intensive Conservation Areas (ICAs), which entitled their members to enhanced subsidy, land tax exemptions and pricing bonuses on agricultural produce (McGregor, 1995). In addition, a current draft Environmental Management Bill seeks to rationalise the country's fragmented environmental laws by integrating them to ensure consistency with each other. A close follow up on the evolution of the bill demonstrates how a patronising posture has been ingrained into the country's legislative culture. The first draft of the Environmental Management Bill (by a consultant on behalf of the ministry) was very democratic with regards to natural resource governance among peasant communities. It sought to extend 'appropriate authority' to user-defined groups at the sub-district level and not to Rural District Councils alone (Moyo, 1996).

Earliest forms of control in the woodland sector aimed at curtailing unprecedented woodland depletion associated with the opening up of land for settler agriculture and wood extraction for the energy and timber needs of the tobacco and mining industries (McGregor, 1995). The colonial government then imposed fees for the extraction of timber from mining zones, but the mining contractors avoided such tariffs by extracting wood from native reserves. In response to this overreach, the Native Reserves Forest Produce Act of 1928 was enacted. Table 11.1 indicates the different community based natural resource management in southern Africa. To ensure the sustainability of natural resource management efforts in vulnerable rural ecosystems, women must be engaged in planning and implementation and they must share the benefits of management outcomes.

Table 11.1: Examples of Large-scale Community-Based Natural Resources Management Programmes in Southern Africa

Examples of large-scale Community Based Natural Resources Management programmes in Southern Africa		
Country	**Programme**	**Comments**
Botswana	Formation of wildlife trusts	Started in 1989. Initially driven by USAID Natural Resources Management Project (NRMP) II. Sources of income: both hunting and tourism contracts. It is estimated that there are now over 100 community wildlife trusts.
Mozambique	Multiple programmes	Diverse local initiatives emerging following end of civil war in early 1990's and policy and legislative reforms in land and forestry and wildlife sectors. Substantial donor support since that time. Initiatives tend to be local, somewhat decentralized projects (e.g., Chipanje Chetu in Niassai Province and Tchuma Tchato in Tete Province).
Namibia	Communal Conservancy programme	Initial community initiatives in the 1980s led to formal development of CBNRM in wildlife policy process in early 1990's. Legal changes to enable formation of community conservancies passed in 1996 and first conservancy gazetted in 1998. Long term support since early 1990's provided by USAID. Formation of conservancies on communal land with rights over wildlife. Diverse sources of income including hunting, tourism, and non-timber products.
Zambia	Administrative Management and Design for Game Management Areas (ADMADE); Luangwa Integrated Resources Development Programme (LIRDP)	ADMADE national programme initiated in the mid- 1980s and supported by USAID and government wildlife agencies. Revenue-sharing scheme focused mainly on Game Management Areas (GMAs). LIRDP initiated in the Lupande GMA in 1988 with Norwegian support aimed specifically to link wildlife revenues with integrated rural development in the Luangwa Valley.

Zimbabwe	Communal Areas Programme for Indigenous Resources (CAMPFIRE)	Legislative reforms enabling granting of authority over wildlife to Rural District Councils passed in early 1980's after independence. CAMPFIRE programme design produced in 1986 and implementation started in 1988 and subsequently backed by USAID. Rights over wildlife decentralized to Rural District Councils. Main source of income from contracts with trophy hunters. Economic and political uncertainty placed severe constraints on community-based organisations and locally developed institutions but recent experience of resource rights agreements demonstrating considerable strength and resilience of these organisations.

Source: International Institute for Environment and Development (UK) (2009: 37)

SMEs require technical, financial and marketing support if they are to remain productive and sustainable (Odero, 2006). Looking at the events in Zimbabwe from 1998, the country was the world's thirteenth-largest producer of gold, which is the country's biggest mineral export. Throughout the late 1990s the mining sector continued to contribute significantly to the country's GDP. Other exports were from the agricultural sector which also had a huge share towards sustaining the country's economy during the same period. There was a thriving local, regional and international market for the country's commodities during the late 1980s. However, it seems there were some challenges with the marketing of the products from the informal sector (Matondi, 2011). Lack of markets tends to limit the performance and success of SMEs. The same argument is raised by SEDA (2016: 10) which state that the inability for SMEs in South Africa to access markets has been identified as a limiting factor to the longevity of the enterprises.

Subsequently, post-2000 the Government of Zimbabwe made attempts to increase the market of the SMEs with the view to promote the growth and development of the sector. Chingwenya and Mudzengerere (2013) highlight that the informal sector activities in Zimbabwe are not aimed at the local market only but are encouraged to participate in the regional and international market. In this regard, the government made great strides in simplifying procedures for exporting and importing goods to enable SMEs to benefit from the markets. This has been cemented through initiatives such as the Look East Policy which sought to capitalise on the big market of China, India and other Asian countries. Moreover, institutions such as Chamber of Small-Medium Enterprises provide platform for the informal sector to network and generate market linkages (Odero, 2006).

Owing to the debilitating effects of structural adjustment programmes such as ESAP, governments in Africa came to appreciate the informal sector as an important form of livelihood and employment particularly in urban areas (SEDA, 2016). This resulted in governments mainstreaming the informal sector into the local economy. This was made possible through various initiatives by governments aim at supporting the survival and growth of these SMEs. South Africa, through the 1995 White Paper on SMEs, tried to focus on creating a demand for the products and services provided by SMEs (The DTI, 2008).

Small and medium-sized enterprises (SMEs) or small and medium-sized businesses (SMBs) are businesses whose personnel numbers fall below certain limits. The abbreviation "SME" is used in the European Union and by international organizations such as the World Bank, the United Nations and the World Trade Organization (WTO). Small enterprises outnumber large companies by a wide margin and employ many more people. This is especially true for India where there are approximately 29.8 million enterprises that employ 69 million people and the SMEs are responsible for 45% of the country's industrial output and 40% of the exports (EISBC, 2017). Hence, SMEs are also responsible for driving innovation and competition in many economic sectors. A research conducted by Cacciolatti, Fearne, and McNeil (2011) indicated that SMEs that make good use of structured marketing information presented a higher probability of growth. The research of Mahmoud (2011) concluded that the higher the level of market orientation, the greater the level of performance in Ghanaian SMEs. Nguyen and Ng (2007) showed that there was a positive relationship between information utilization and the firm performance. Apulu and Latham (2011) found that the competitiveness of SMEs can be increased through adopting Information and Communication Technology. Subrahmanya, Mathirajan, and Krishnaswamy (2011) summed up that those SMEs which have technological innovation have a higher growth compared to the SMEs which are not creative in the sales turnover, investment and job.

The chapter reviews natural resource governance in Zimbabwe's peasant sector from colonial to post-colonial times. Governance is considered within the framework of power, process and practice and how these shaped peasant access, control and use of natural resources (Manungo, 1991). Colonial natural resource governance systems resulted in over-centralisation because they were crafted in the context of conquest and subjugation (Marongwe, 2003). Over the years, state visions of appropriate management and use of resources have largely been extended to the African peasant sector through a centrally directed structure and process (Sadomba, 2008). However, state control over the use and management of resources among the peasantry was and is largely ineffectual because the state lacks the resources and capacity to enforce such controls. Much of the colonial legislation was inherited piecemeal into post-colonial times, and amendments to date have largely de-racialised the colonial acts and policies without democratising them (Mandondo, 1997).

The introduction of the Forest Act of 1948 (amended in 1982) in Zimbabwe provided for the establishment of production and protection managed by the state for the conservation of biological diversity, watershed management and commercial hardwood extraction. The Act also vested the state forestry agency with the power to regulate the exploitation of indigenous hardwood timber from peasant areas, with the revenue accruing to Rural District Councils. Murphree and Cumming (1991) have called this Act double expropriation, where peasants are disempowered through displacement from the land, and the loss of control over resources in areas in which the peasant communities were relocated. However, the production and protection forests are not entirely free from tenurial and other pressures (Nhira *et al.* 1998). Most of these forests are surrounded by peasant communities or share common boundaries with them.

Box 11.1: Lessons from Diamond Mining in Chiadzwa, Zimbabwe

In Zimbabwe there was the introduction of Public-Private Partnerships (PPPs) during the period 2006 and 2008 in the exploration for and extraction of natural resources, and their subsequent processing and refining along production and supply chains to add value before they are marketed elsewhere. Chiadzwa is an extensive field of alluvial diamonds in the Marange district in the Manicaland province of Zimbabwe. Against the backdrop of capacity and resource constraints experienced by most African countries, African governments need to realise the benefits of partnering with the private sector in the exploitation and processing of natural resources. Consequently, in Zimbabwe, the government should facilitate and implement appropriate policies that promote joint ventures with the private sector. The private sector is technically equipped and financially resourced; it can stimulate innovation and improve productivity, wealth creation and distribution – critical achievements towards the realisation of the Sustainable Development Goals (SDGs) of poverty alleviation and eradication of hunger in poor communities, which are the main developmental issues in Africa.

Source: Gumbo (2013)

Box 1 indicates the challenges and opportunities that can be derived from using natural resources. From Box 11.1, it is shown that although natural resources, such as diamonds in Marange, Zimbabwe, have immense potential to transform communities, there remain a lot of challenges and ambiguities with regard their management. Ultimately, there are different models which may be used to manage the natural resource for example value addition in the supply chain will help to realise more returns from the natural resources. The next section provides a discussion on the methodology of the study.

Methodology

The study engages related literature, document review and in-depth interviews as sources of data critical in developing the present discourse. Semi-structured in-depth interviews were held with various informants who include the entrepreneurs operating in Newlands, officials from Environmental Management Agency (EMA), City of Harare and community leaders. Purposive sampling was used to select the respondents for each interview. Two officials were interviewed from each of the institutions, that is, EMA and City of Harare, while a total of 20 in-depth interviews were conducted with the entrepreneurs. The 20 respondents were sufficient for the study as Cresswell (2013) argues that, for qualitative researches, the respondents may range from 1 to 20. Specifically, interviewing the entrepreneurs was meant to track the record of where they get their raw materials and the type of materials which they use from the four corners of Zimbabwe. Document analysis was carried out to ascertain the implication of each independent factor towards the performance of SMEs in Zimbabwe. In the next section, focus is on presentation of the results.

Results

In interviews held with the entrepreneurs, it emerged that the majority of them are migrants who have come to Harare in search of better socio-economic opportunities. Although the small-scale entrepreneurs operating in Newlands come from all corners of Zimbabwe, fewer people came from the Matabeleland Provinces. One of the small-scale entrepreneurs from Matabeleland who was interviewed explained that most people in Matabeleland prefer to go and search for greener pastures in South Africa and Botswana instead of Harare. Adding on to this, the researchers observed that the artefacts that were being sold by the entrepreneurs showed that they were made in different parts of Zimbabwe or rather exhibited the cultures of the different parts of the country.

Plate 11.1: Chairs made by the local people of Zimbabwe near Newlands shopping centre
Source: Fieldwork (2017)

These small-scale entrepreneurs make these chairs, arts, metal animals of different names which include both domesticated and wild animals (Plate 2). Wood and metal are also used to make chair and table frames which are usually finished with a touch of reeds (Plate 1). The material used is called cane. These entrepreneurs source their raw materials from people in the rural areas of Muzarabani and Mutoko but the main stakeholders are those in authority such as the traditional chiefs and sub-heading. As a result, these vendors create employment for people in the rural areas and improve their standards of living. Taking this into consideration, it means that the theory of core periphery is still applicable in Zimbabwe. Most cities in Zimbabwe that include Harare, Bulawayo and Mutare are the major core for these vendors and are the places where they sell their products while rural areas such as Mutoko, Kwekwe and Masvingo to mention a few are the periphery areas. By so doing, these people promote the gross domestic product of the country but the government has relaxed to promote the informal sector. This is so because of the challenges which these rural areas face, for example, most of them lack proper infrastructure, poor lighting at night and parking facility is not available. During an interview one respondent said that:

> *We are so much affected by rainy season especially me a vendor who specialises in wood making good products since my products when rained can be damaged......the city council keeps empty promises saying one day we are coming to fix everything but in the mean time we have deficit budget .*

Plate 11.2 shows the type of wood products they make out of mahogany timber
Source: Fieldwork (2017)

The entrepreneurs also make different products using different types of stones namely soap stone, dolomite, green vedite, rapoko, black/green stone, spring stone, cobalt and fruit stone to mention a few. These stones are used to make different products namely giraffes, motor vehicles and people sculptures. They come from different areas that include Mutoko, Kwekwe, Guruve and soap stone usually taken from Christmas near Mutare. The market for these products is needs to be marketed widely and even internationally. During interview, one of the key informants, the Vice Chair for Arts and Craft association said that,

> *The government has improved the site where we operate and four hectares of land is going to be given for arts and craft to take place along Harare-Bulawayo road .... This is a good idea since some youths will be trained and venture into arts and crafting-making Zimbabwe a well-known country in the SADC region...*

Ii is clear therefore that, if these entrepreneurs operating in Newlands are promoted and given a chance, they can improve the country's GDP.

Plate 11.3: Products made by different art and craft stones
Source: Fieldwork (2017)

The study established that most of the wares that are sold in Newlands are locally made. In most instances, the wares are made using local natural resources. Of particular interest were the sculptors that were being sold by most entrepreneurs. Upon enquiry, the researchers gathered that these sculptors are carved using stones that are quarried from different areas in Zimbabwe. Soapstone and serpentine stones are the most common types of stones used. One respondent had this to say:

> I prefer to use soapstone for my carvings because it is soft and easy to carve. It also gives me good quality products that are highly sought by both local and international customers.

Another respondent said,

> Much of the stone used by most sculptors here is quarried in areas such as Mvurwi, Domboshawa, Chiweshe, Nyanga and Kwekwe. Some people like myself prefer to go to these areas and quarry the stones which and possibly carve them there then come here with the final products. Usually I have my customers most whites who make special orders on the sculptors that I produce.

In addition to the stone sculptors, there are also various products that are sold at Newlands produced from wood and reeds. It emerged that these raw materials are natural resources which include trees, stones that are quarried through unsustainable mining practices as well as reeds which are harvested from wetlands in and around Harare. In this regard, there is much ecological footprint which is associated with the production of the wares that are sold by the entrepreneurs at Newlands. Their main concern is to produce their final products, which they do with little regard for the environment and natural resources.

An official from EMA lamented that it is sad to note that these entrepreneurs depend on the natural resources from the environment which tend to exacerbate deforestation and damage of vegetation in wetlands and reeds in river banks. He went on to elaborate that:

> What these guys are concerned about is the final products and getting the ecosystem services that include grass, reeds and stones. The ecological footprints of these extractions tend to be so immense and with the worsening economic situation in the country it has been very difficult bring sanity and reprimand the offenders who eke their living from such practices.

The SMEs sector at Newlands is mainly dominated by men as the researchers observed that there were a higher proportion of men as compared to women. This was explained by the fact that the industry is mostly convenient for men who have the ability to produce the different kinds of products such as carvings from stone and wood. However, there have been some improvement in gender dimensions in the production of the raw materials, especially in the rural areas where most of the raw materials are produced. Many male respondents acknowledged that it is mainly women who provide them with raw materials such as grass, reeds and straw which they use to manufacture their final products.

The main reason for the migration of the entrepreneurs is due to push and pull factors in Zimbabwe which compel them to go and search for better livelihoods in urban centres such as Harare. These people come to manufacture the much-needed commodities which can be used by the local citizens as well as international tourists. In trying to explain the location of the entrepreneurs in Newlands, an official from City of Harare had this to say,

> Newlands is strategically located in Harare because of its connectivity to a road network and Newlands shopping area which is close by. The close proximity to Enterprise Road and Newlands Shops creates a higher threshold of customers which eventually sustains the SME's market. The Y-junction road shows the two major roads which can attract the residents of Newlands and the one going to the right have various use groups that include commercial and residential.

Beyond the production and location of the SMEs at Newlands, marketing is another critical activity that facilitates the success of the SMEs. One respondent highlighted the utility of marketing their products when she indicated that,

> This (product marketing) is to ensure that our business continue to grow and ultimately help to support the development of economy in Zimbabwe. Personally, I engage in marketing of my husband's products which include the chairs and some baskets which he makes. We mostly engage in informal marketing of our products mostly to local customers.

It was also observed that marketing was mainly done individually on a competitive basis. SME operators compete to maximise on their returns. This creates some tensions among them. However, it was interesting to note that despite the competition among the SME operators, there is some form of collaborations which exists with regards to marketing of the products. Overall, it was observed that the SMEs acknowledged the significance of marketing their products. The main issue which most of the SMEs raised was the way it was difficult for them to access markets beyond Newlands, a situation which greatly affected the growth of their businesses. The failure of the businesses to market their products was attributed to low education levels among most of the traders of which some of them were not even aware of the importance of marketing as they did not realise the value of their products beyond the Newlands Market. One respondent who was interviewed was aware of the value of his products. He indicated that he usually exhibits his products at Harare Agricultural Show and Trade Fair in Bulawayo. He also sells some of his carvings in South Africa. In this way, he highlighted that his business has been able to sustain his family and enabled him to develop his residential stand in Budiriro.

Based on the findings of the study, the following key lessons emerge:

- The entrepreneurs are most economic migrants from different areas outside Harare. This confirms the fact that there has been rapid urbanisation in Harare which is mainly attributed to rural-urban migration. Consequently, it shows that Harare remains the economic hub of the country.
- The products and artefacts produced are mainly from different natural resource harvested from the environment.
- There is spill-over effect to the rural areas resulting from the transactions which are made by entrepreneurs. The entrepreneurs go to the rural areas and pay for the natural resources which may be used for different community development projects.
- The small-scale industry has the capacity to pay just a significant amount.

- Males represent a larger proposition of the entrepreneurs.

Discussion

The chapter argues that women are the primary users and potential stewards of many natural resources that provide the means for basic survival (Rio Declaration, 1992; UNCED, 1992; CBD, 1993; Declaration on World Food Security, 1996). In Africa, women shoulder much of the responsibilities for example 80% of the food security and 90% of the water security in rural communities are their mandate (GWA, 2006; Madonsela, 2002). Moreover, women collect fuel wood for energy, plants and herbs for medicine, and utilize natural resources to support the economic stability of families and communities. Women assume these roles because the majority of the rural poor are women and their social roles and responsibilities require them to rely heavily on the goods and services that are provided by the natural world.

The degradation of natural resources impacts on everyone regardless of gender, race, age and level of income. This is so because human beings use the environment in different ways consciously or unconsciously, hence natural resources degradation negatively impact on almost everyone. However, the extent to which natural resources degradation affects individuals varies depending upon several key factors, most significantly economic status and gender. Considering that the majority of the world's poor are women, the links between economic status and gender are complex. An example is how deforestation to clear land to expand agriculture for exporting negatively impacted on women's income as they heavily depended on harvesting wood which they sold as charcoal.

Conclusion

In conclusion, in order to scale up natural resource management efforts that benefit women, gender disaggregated data must be acquired. This is so because, without a concerted effort to improve information and data collection, efforts to address the links between women, natural resource management and poverty alleviation will remain unaddressed. In this study, there are four determinants that are significant to affect the performance of SMEs. Based on the results from Newlands which stipulate that there is need for marketing of the products of the entrepreneurs, emphasis on sustainable use of natural resources and promotion of environmental stewardship, it emerges that effective entrepreneurship, appropriate human resources management, use of marketing information, and application of information technology are significantly related to the performance of SMEs. It was established that Harare is the focal point of entrepreneurship hence it emerges as the core region while the resources base rural areas resemble the periphery regions. The situation in Newlands therefore confirms the core-periphery model of development in Zimbabwe. The study also observed though these entrepreneurs play a critical role to support the economy, they need government support in terms of infrastructure so that responsible authorities could be empowered to collect tax to boost urban finance.

Policy Options and Recommendations

The results of this study lead to recommendations for the improvement for SMEs in Zimbabwe. First, SMEs entrepreneurs ought to actively search for the most favourable growth opportunities for their SMEs in the market. SMEs should embrace technology and accept change to that could help them in the development of their SMEs. Moreover, the use of integrated marketing information and appropriate human resource might also have a consequential impact on SMEs' growth probabilities. Firms are also encouraged to identify their threats, for examples competitors, who may push them out of business, changing consumer preferences as well as the socio-political environment and context. Such considerations will possible help to establish and guard against threats to the sustainability of their businesses. Overall, there is also need for each firm to pay attention to customer and supplier relations, personnel, quality, flexibility, and planning.

The conservation and development agencies are presented with a unique opportunity to streamline their current strategies. Working together across sectors to systematically engage women will not only further the protection of our terrestrial, marine, and freshwater resources, it will save the lives and improve the well-being of hundreds of millions of women and the communities that these women work to support.

Women have unique skills and experience that can improve the management of natural resources and yet they are not systematically engaged in natural resource management investments, policies and management decision making. More systematic inclusion of women and gender aspects into conservation efforts has the potential to create positive impacts on innovation, natural resource management and the empowerment of women. In addition to better understanding the links between natural resource management, innovation and product development and marketing, practitioners need to collect and use gender disaggregated data when designing and implementing conservation and natural resource management initiatives.

References

AFDB. (1997). *Zimbabwe: Economic structural adjustment programme project performance evaluation report.* Harare: AFDB. Available online: https://www.afdb.org/fileadmin/uploads/afdb/Documents/Evaluation-Reports-_Shared-With-OPEV_/06050223-EN-ZIMBABWE-ECONOMIC-STRUCTURAL-ADJUSTMENT.PDF.

Andersson, J. A. (2001). Reinterpreting the rural–urban connection: migration practices and socio-cultural dispositions of Buhera workers in Harare. *Africa, 71*(1), 82-112.

Apulu, I. and Latham, A. (2011). Drivers for information and communication technology adoption: A case study of Nigerian small and medium sized enterprises. *International Journal of Business and Management, 6*(5), 51-60.

Bandauko, E. and Mandisvika, G. (2015). Right to the city? An analysis of the criminalisation of the informal sector in Harare, Zimbabwe. *Journal of Advocacy, Research and Education, 4*(3), 184-191

Cacciolatti, L., Fearne, A. and McNeil, D. (2011*). Empirical evidence for a relationship between business growth and the use of structured marketing information amongst food and drink SMEs.* Academy of Marketing Conference (5-7 July 2011). University of Kent, Kent.

Campbell, S. (1996). Green cities, growing cities, just cities? Urban planning and the contradictions of sustainable development. *Journal of the American Planning Association, 62*(3), 296-312.

Chingwenya, A. and Mudzengerere, F.H. (2013). The small and medium enterprises policy in Zimbabwe: A narrative of strides taken to mainstream the informal sector activities in urban local authorities in Zimbabwe. *International Journal of Politics and Good Governance, 4*(4), 1-18.

Dube, D. and Chirisa, I. (2012). The informal city: Assessing its scope, variants and direction in Harare, Zimbabwe. *Global Advanced Research Journal of Geography and Regional Planning, 1*(1), 016-025.

EISBC. (2017). *Definitions of Indian SMEs.* Available online: http://www.eisbc.org/definition_of_indian_smes.aspx [Accessed on 3 July 2017]

Feresu, S.B. (Ed.). (2010) *Zimbabwe environmental outlook: Our environment, everybody's responsibility.* Harare: The Ministry of Environment and Natural Resources Management.

Finch, C. and Omolo, A. (2015). *Building public participation in Kenya's devolved government.* Nairobi: World Bank Group.

Gender and Water Alliance. (2003). *Tapping into sustainability: Issues and trends in gender mainstreaming in water and sanitation.* A background document for the Gender and Water Session, 3rd World Water Forum. Kyoto.

Giovannoni, E. and Fabietti, G. (2014). What is sustainability: A review of the concept and its applications. In: Busco, C., Frigo, M.L., Riccaboni, A., Quattrone, P. (Eds.), *Integrated reporting: Concepts and cases that redefine corporate accountability*. Geneva: Springer Publishing.

Government of Zimbabwe. (2002) *Environmental Management Act: Chapter 20: 27*. Harare: Government of Zimbabwe.

Government of Zimbabwe. (2013). *Constitution of Zimbabwe*. Harare: Government of Zimbabwe.

Gumbo, T. (2013). Public-private partnerships (PPPs) and sustainable natural resources exploitation in Africa: Lessons from diamond mining in Chiadzwa, Zimbabwe. *Africa Institute of South Africa Briefing No 88*.

IIED. (2009). *Community management of natural resources in Africa: Impacts, Experiences and Future Directions*. London: IIED.

Katerere, J.M. (2001). Participatory natural resource management in the communal lands of Zimbabwe: What role for customary law? *African Studies Quarterly, 5*(3), 1-27.

Kawerere, S.M. and Dibie, R. (2000). The impact of economic structural adjustment programmes [ESAPs] on women and children: Implications for social welfare in Zimbabwe. *The Journal of Sociology and Social Welfare, 27*(4), 79-107.

Keh, H. T., Nguyen, T. T. M., and Ng, H. P. (2007). The effects of entrepreneurial orientation and marketing information on the performance of SMEs. *Journal of business venturing, 22*(4), 592-611.

Kinsey, B., Burger, K. and Gunning, J.W. (1998). Coping with drought in Zimbabwe: Survey evidence on responses of rural households to risk. *World Development, 26*(1), 89-110.

Kurebwa, J. (2015). A review of rural local government system in Zimbabwe from 1980 to 2014. *Journal of Humanities and Social Sciences, 20*(2), 94-108.

Lambrou, Y. and Piana, G. (2006). *Gender: The missing component of the response to climate change*. Rome: Food and Agriculture Organization.

Madonsela, W. (2002). The impact of trade liberalisation in the agricultural sector on African women: Links with food security and sustainable livelihoods. Dakar: Paper prepared for Gender Institute at CODESRIA.

Mahmoud, M.A. (2011). Market orientation and business performance among SMEs in Ghana. *International Business Research, 4*(1), 241-251.

Mamdani, M. (1996). *Citizen and subject: Contemporary Africa and the legacy of late colonialism*. New Jersey: Princeton University Press.

Mandondo, A. (1997). Trees and spaces as emotion and norm laden components of local ecosystems in Nyamaropa communal lands, Nyanga District; Zimbabwe. *Agriculture and Human Values, 14*(4), 352-372.

Mangena, I. (2014). Environmental policy, management and ethics in Zimbabwe, 2000-2008. *The Journal of Pan African Studies*, 6(10), 224 – 240.

Manungo, K.D. (1991). The peasantry in Zimbabwe: a vehicle for change. In P. Kaarlsholm (Ed.), *Cultural struggle and development in Southern Africa* (pp.115-123). London: James Currey.

Marongwe, N. (2003). Farm occupations and occupiers in the new politics of land in Zimbabwe. In A. Hammar, B. Raftopoulos and S. Jensen (Eds.), *Zimbabwe's unfinished business: Rethinking land, state and nation in the context of crisis.* Harare: Weaver Press.

Matamanda, A.R. and Chirisa, I. (forthcoming). Dimensions, continuity and change in regional planning. In *Fundamentals of Planning and Real Estate Studies: A Primer for Zimbabwe.* Harare: University of Zimbabwe Publications.

Matondi, P.B. (2011). *Biofuels, land grabbing and food security in Africa.* Harare: Zed Books.

McGregor, J. (1991). *Ecology, policy and ideology: An historical study of woodland-use and change in Zimbabwe's communal areas* (Unpublished Doctoral thesis). Loughborough University of Technology.

McGregor, J. (1995). Conservation, control and ecological change: The politics and ecology of colonial conservation in Shurugwi, Zimbabwe. *Environment and History, 1*(3), 257-279.

McNeely, J.A. (1995). Partnerships for conservation: An introduction. In McNeely J.A. (Ed.), *Expanding partnerships in conservation, 1-12.* Washington D.C: Island Press.

Mohammed-Katerere, J.C. and Chenje, M. (2002). *Environmental law and policy in Zimbabwe.* Harare: Southern Africa Research Documentation Centre.

Moyo, S. (1996a). *Land and democracy in Zimbabwe.* Paper presented to the International Historical Dimensions of Democracy and Human Rights. University of Zimbabwe History Department, Harare.

Murphree, M.W. and Cumming, D.H.M. (1991). *Savanna land-use policy and practice in Zimbabwe.* Paper presented at the UNESCO/IUBS Conference on Savanna Land-use. Nairobi, January 1991.

Mutandwa, E. and Gadzirayi, C. T. (2007). Impact of community-based approaches to wildlife management: Case of the Campfire programme in Zimbabwe. *The International Journal of Sustainable Development and World Ecology*, 14(4), 336-344.

Myrdal, G (1957). *Economic theory and underdeveloped regions.* London: Duckworth.

Nhira, C. (1998). Land-use planning and woodland management: A case study of local control and regulatory capacity on household and communal woodland resources in Zimbabwe. *IES Working Paper 8.* Institute of Environmental Studies, University of Zimbabwe, Harare.

Odero, K.K. (2006). *SMEs and support systems in Zimbabwe.* IDS Seminar, University of Nairobi, July 2006.

Patel, D. (1988). Some Issues of urbanisation and development in Zimbabwe. *Journal of Social Development in Africa, 3(2),* 17-31.

Quang, D. V., and Anh, T. N. (2006). Commercial collection of NTFPs and households living in or near the forests: Case study in Que, Con Cuong and Ma, Tuong Duong, Nghe An, Vietnam. *Ecological economics, 60*(1), 65-74.

Sachs, I. (1984). *The strategies of eco-development. FAO Ceres, 17*(1) 17-21.

Sadomba, W.Z. (2008). *The impact of settler colonisation on indigenous agricultural knowledge in Zimbabwe: Fusion, confusion or negation?* Wageningen Agricultural University, Wageningen.

Scoones, I. and Matose, F. (1993). Local woodland management: Constraints and opportunities of sustainable resource use. In P.N. Bradley and K. McNamara (Eds.), *Living with trees: Policies for woodland management in Zimbabwe* (pp. 157-198). Washington, D.C: World Bank.

Small Enterprises Development Agency. (2016). *The small, medium and micro enterprise sector of South Africa.* Cape Town: The Small Enterprises Development Agency.

Subrahmanya, M.H.B., Mathirajan, M. and Krishnaswamy, K.N. (2011). Importance of technological innovation for SME growth: Evidence from India. *World Institute for Development Economics Research, 3.*

The DTI. (2008). *Annual review of small business in South Africa 2005-2007.* Department of Trade and Industry, Pretoria.

United Nations (2012) *Governance and development thematic think piece.* New York: United Nations.

Worstall, T. (2017). With 95% unemployment rate Robert Mugabe insists Zimbabwe in not fragile. [Online]. Available online: https://www.forbes.com/sites/timworstall/ 2017/05/05/with-95-unemployment-rate-robert-mugabe-insists-zimbabwe-is-not-fragile/#4d8679c368e8 [Accessed 22/ 06/ 2017].

Chapter 12

The Central Africa Building Society Project in Budiriro, Harare: The Cost of Low-cost Housing?

Claire Gutsa

Summary:

The provision for housing in the urban centres has been a challenge in the developing countries and continues to be. Accessibility is a major challenge for the low-income earners. This chapter examines the provision of housing for low-income earners in Zimbabwe. In Zimbabwe, low-cost housing existed before Zimbabwe obtained independence in 1980. Allocation of houses and its provision for the low-income earners was ruled as unfair as there was the exclusion of other individuals due to the rules and regulations that existed. The provision of low-cost housing for low-income earners by different participants has been debated in Zimbabwe since 1980 up to date. The involvement of the public and private stakeholders in the provision of low-cost housing in Zimbabwe has resulted in a disorganised situation as those that benefit from the proposed projects are not classified as low-income earners. This study was done taking into consideration the political, economic and social conditions in Zimbabwe, specifically looking at Budiriro, one of the low-cost urban dwellers suburb in Harare. Budiriro includes one of the recent low-cost housing projects that was initiated by Central Africa Building Society (CABS) under Old Mutual in partnership with the Harare City Council. The triangulation approach was used in order to blend qualitative and quantitative research methods. This involved the use of questionnaires, interviews, random sampling, secondary and primary sources and personal observation to capture all the status phenomena. The study directs recommendations to the Zimbabwean government to address housing policies and the private sectors to do a thorough research before project implementation.

Introduction

The provision of residential housing has remained one of the Zimbabwean government's priorities since independence 1980 (Crowley, 2003). While the demand for housing has increased in post-colonial Zimbabwe, the government, private sector and housing cooperatives have not succeeded in solving housing problems in all the urban centres. To address the housing problems, the

Government of Zimbabwe crafted policies such as National Housing policy as part of its national economic policy called the Zimbabwe Agenda for Sustainable Socio-Economic Transformation (ZimAsset). However, this failed to address the housing problems just like previous government policies. With the economic quagmire in Zimbabwe; there has been the need to provide affordable, well-planned and serviced residential areas with water reticulation, sewer, electricity and waste disposal system. According to Ruwende (2015), Zimbabwe is facing acute housing shortages with poor sanitation and service deliveries, compounded by inadequate mortgage lending. By 1999, the government in Zimbabwe could no longer provide serviced stands because of lack of resources while rural to urban migration escalated leaving the housing demand to reach a high number. The housing backlog presented by both local and central governments in Zimbabwe has been estimated to be 1.25 million people on the waiting list (ZIMSTATS 2014). This was a conservative estimation as other city councils did not record adequate information. Other than the government, community-based organisations and housing cooperatives have tried to provide housing for low-income earners. The financial sector has also intervened in the provision of low-cost housing.

This chapter is based on a study that sought to analyse housing delivery by low-cost housing schemes under financial institutions (CABS) and assess whether this low-cost housing is thus affordable and attainable by low-income earners in Zimbabwe. The specific objectives of the study were:

i) To assess and discuss the criteria used by agencies responsible for the provision of housing for low-income earners and the vetting of beneficiaries for the housing scheme

ii) To describe and comment on mortgages being offered by financial institutions and evaluate whether homeowners of urban low-income houses are low-income earners in Zimbabwe

Background to the study

Currently, there are 6 financial institutions in Zimbabwe that are offering mortgages and loans, and these include Central Africa Building Society (CABS), Central Bank of Zimbabwe (CBZ), Peoples Own Savings Bank (POSB), National Building Society (NBS) and Stanbic bank. Some of these banks such as Central Bank of Zimbabwe limited have been offering mortgages for commercial and industrial loans and mortgages (Shava, 2013). While there is need to plan affordable housing for low-income earners, this has become one of the main objectives in planning. Four models that have been implemented for housing projects have encompassed the government, cooperatives, community-based organisations and the financial institutions. The provision of

246

low-cost housing by the government, cooperatives and community-based organisations for low-income earners has been analysed in Zimbabwe. However, there is still a loophole in the provision of housing for low-income earners at a low cost and its success towards this goal.

The government has tried to address the housing issue by reviewing of the attendant housing policies and legislati0ns. According to the Constitution Amendment (No.20), housing is a basic human right. As noted before, the national economic blue-print, the Zimbabwe Agenda for Sustainable Socio-Economic Transformation (ZimAsset), was used to try to advance delivery of decent housing under the Social Services and Poverty Eradication cluster. Since 1980, the government has always been responsible for the provision of houses in Zimbabwe but failed. For some time until 1999, there was a noticeable increase in rural to urban migration, especially into big cities like Harare and Bulawayo. In 2003, the Ministry of Local Government, Public Works and National Housing further observed the inability of government to provide decent and affordable housing. It observed that the government plans for housing fell far short of the annual target of 162,000 units between 1985 and 2000 with actual production ranging between 15,000 and 20,000 units per annum (Human Rights, 2005). The government introduced National Housing Policy in 2000 brought about the intervention of cooperatives in trying to address the housing provision services. The National Housing Delivery Programmes (HNDP 2004-2008) introduced by the government further streamlined the role of cooperatives in leveraging resources for low-cost housing provision.

The housing cooperatives mainly focused on small to medium enterprises or business ventures. Cooperatives in Zimbabwe increased in popularity in the 1980s when the government strictly pursued the communist-socialist agenda foisted on the country in its first decade of independence (1980-1990) (Chirisa*et al.* 2014). Most of the housing cooperatives were introduced and became more popular in the 1980s when the government opt to engage other participants in the provision of low-cost housing. The housing cooperatives grew rapidly in the peri-urban areas and within open spaces and wetlands as government acquired land near urban areas, for example, in Whitecliffe to resettle those affected by Operation Murambatsvina. In Zimbabwe, corruption and other land barons led to the failure of cooperatives in the provision of low-cost housing. Only cooperatives that were launched in the early 1980s when the government was also providing houses were a success. According to Chirisa *et al.* (2014), these housing cooperatives have their identity in the ruling party, the Zimbabwe African National Union. This explains the politics of patronage and clientelism.

The urban poor within communities, formed community-based organisations (CBOs) which tried to intervene in the delivery of low-cost houses and services. The government underestimated the initiative as it was formed by the pro-poor while rural to urban migration increased. These organisations are currently being incorporated in programmes such as self-aided schemes. However, the government, cooperatives and community-based organisations failed to provide low-cost housing for low-income earners over the past 17 years.

Despite the failure by the Government of Zimbabwe and other non-state organisations to deliver housing for low-income earners, one of the financial institutions in Zimbabwe, the Central Africa Building Society made an attempt in the provision of low-cost housing services Budiriro 4. Other financial institutions such as banks have been offering mortgages and loans to help low-income earners to a basic housing commodity. This study aims to assess whether the provision of low-cost housing by financial institutions is benefiting low-income earners and affordable to the poor. The study further assesses how financial institutions have been able to help low-income earners in attaining houses in the period of economic hardships in Zimbabwe.

Theoretical framework

There are three theories, namely the Marxist theory, liberal theory and the positive theory of housing which were used in this research on the analysis of housing provision in a government. Modelling and urban planning theories became widely used and applied in urban planning in the early 1960s (Curley, 2005, 3). Modelling was adopted with a generalization that was characterized by the transformation of the urban form and urban planning as one identified as architecture-writ-large to one rooted less intuitively but grounded and more objectively (Batty, 1994). To summarize it, urban theories emerged as an effort to quantify and mathematically represent the conditions that determined decision-making in the planning sector (Curley, 2005). It was facilitated in a way which model developers began to poach analytical methodologies from other disciplines which include human ecology, mathematics, geography, operations research, linear programming, regional science, and economic modellers that were relentless in their pilfering of scientific techniques that might be applied to urban phenomena (Trussel, 2010). The theoretical framework that is going to be used in this study consists of three theories thus the Marxist theory, liberal theory and positive theories in housing.

The Marxist theory maintains that most governments worldwide use housing productivity as a means to guarantee a fair distribution of the country's natural and industrial resources and to sustain socio-political stability and loyalty to those governments (Curley, 2005.2). The Marxist approach defines housing as a necessary good for the reproduction of the labour force. The fact remains that housing productivity of the public sector in most governments in developing countries does not exceed 10-15 percent of the gross national housing productivity, and governmental housing productivity is not enough to satisfy all the work force of the country (Curley, 2005.2). The liberal housing theory views housing as determined by market forces, that is, the demand and supply in a country. The main aim of the mechanisms of the housing market lies in the development of the capital invested to obtain the maximum possible material return rather than the fulfilment of basic needs on the part of individuals who will occupy the housing unit (Curley, 2005, 2).

In the third approach, the positive housing theory, defines housing on three dimensions, namely the economic status, the public health situation, and the definition of housing as an item of consumption to be supplied by government authorities. Investing in real estate is a way of improving and developing the residential unit, relying on the fact that the price of the unit is increasing steadily with the passage of time (Curley, 2005.3). The positive theory mainly considers a public healthy environment within a community in which the public has access to the public goods and services. This is where in every housing provision scheme a health environment for the people has to be the first priority. Also, this view rests on the point that a housing unit is an item of consumption to be supplied by government authorities (Katz *et al.* 2003). The mandate of the government is to provide health environment suitable for human beings that will include provision of public services such as sewer and water reticulation, electricity and serviced areas with roads and all necessary facilities.

Literature review

The demand for low-cost housing is experienced worldwide although it is critical in the African and Asian continents that consist of developing countries (Rojas and Greene, 1995). The low-cost housing provision schemes exist in many countries around the world and very common in the developing countries. Although the government is usually considered to be responsible for the provision of houses to citizens, currently many governments have failed to do so. This has led to the intervention of the private sector which has resulted in the inclusion of the legal and illegal private actors. While the low-cost housing schemes have always been meant to benefit low-income earners, this is not always the case as the schemes are used to benefit people of great power and high government officials, especially in the developing countries. The formal mechanisms of housing production and financing do not reach all segments of the population while informal mechanisms tend to produce solutions that are either sub-standard or expensive (Rojas and Greene, 1995). They are expensive in the sense that the developments that are done may prove to be more costly in the long-run while others may face demolitions and or legal fees to legalise the informal settlements. The Marxist view maintains that most governments use housing as a means to guarantee a fair distribution of the country's natural and industrial resources and to sustain socio-political stability and loyalty to those governments. However, on the ground, government officials might be using housing for low-income earners for their benefit such as to gain support from the beneficiaries, and this has resulted in some governments failing to provide low-cost housing.

In all the models that were completed to address the housing problem, there have always been different criteria that were used to consider the beneficiaries. There have been conditions such as a marriage certificate, proof of employment, bank statements and mortgages. The criterion that has always been used differs from one model or organisation to the other. While different criteria have been used, some have resulted in the exclusion of low-income earners or the poor in urban areas. There are different requirements demanded by each different sector and requirements needed in a cooperative are different from those that are required by a building society.

There are several criteria that are used in the selection of beneficiaries of low-cost housing initiatives. One of these criteria is the waiting list. In its attempt to provide houses for low-income earners, the government used a criterion applicable before independence in 1980. The government designed low-cost houses in most cases would be a core house consisting of two bedrooms, a dining room, kitchen and a bathroom with a toilet. In Zimbabwe, most of the houses built before 1980 in areas such as Highfield and Mabvuku in Harare had room for extension. In many cases, some people often neglected to maintain their housing units. This brings us back to the criteria that was used and is used to consider applicants for low-cost housing in development of low cost housing units. The tenure conditions have left other people without hope of home ownership. This study also extends the discussion to the relationship between tenure conditions and standard of construction on one side and low-cost housing maintenance on the other (Arman *et al.* 2009).

There is need to address the criteria to be inclusive of the poor who are in the low-income bracket if the housing programme is to be considered low-cost housing. However, the bidding process by the City council, skyrocketing prices from cooperatives which have mushroomed everywhere around Harare and from land developers trying to obtain maximum profits have led to the problem land sold for residential purposes resulting in the demolition of these properties without compensation.

Mortgages offered by financial institutions

There are different terms and conditions that are put forward by institutions for mortgages. Financial institutions offer mortgages with terms and conditions that determine who will be able to obtain a house from the providers. Indeed, the predominant metaphors used to describe finance such as 'flow', 'movement' and 'circulation', position it above and beyond (and thereby differentiate it from) our everyday 'real' economic practices (Langley, 2006:2). The market normally determines the terms and conditions of a mortgage in any country as they are normally not constant and universal. In each state or country, the economy that affects the market will determine the terms and conditions that an institution will put forward to the interested part. Consideration of how everyday borrowing is closely bound to the capital markets through securitisation is overdue. This study thus further disputes the orthodoxy and revalue everyday spaces, practices and identities in our understanding (Crowley, 2003: 4).

While acquiring a house in Zimbabwe is expensive, the cost of constructing a building has also increased making it difficult for low-income earners. This has resulted in the use of other alternatives, for example, mortgages, other than salaries. A house in a medium density area such as Msasa Park is sold for between US$30 000 and US$40 000. According to Chifamba, quoted by Nyakazeya (2010), it costs about US$250 per square metre to build that can translate to about US$55 000, which is more expensive without including other unforeseen costs. With such an enormous amount, low-income earners may not be able to obtain a house in the city. According to Lohse (2002), effective shelter policies have to address the financing needs, and only then will a shelter delivery system allow everyone access to shelter, whether through purchase, renting, self-help construction, or through access to subsidies. The mortgages that are offered by financial institutions will be examined to ascertain if they meet the needs of the low-income earners in Zimbabwe.

The research highlights the weakness of the poor's claim to the right of permanent residency emphasizing insufficient state funding and poverty. In order to deal with housing problems in Zimbabwe, the government introduced the low-income urban housing policy. There is an examination of this policy and its implications on the low-income earners in Zimbabwe. Results of this study would help in shaping the direction of the ongoing debate on housing in Zimbabwe. Policymakers need to combine information gathered through land price surveys and household surveys to provide an up to date, accurate and detailed profile of land and housing market.

Housing lists and agencies behind the provision of low-cost houses

The issue of affordable housing has been a serious problem for both low-income earners and the local government authorities. The latter is confronted with keeping pace with the demands for low-income housing (Manikela, 2008). What this seems to suggest is that housing policies have a significant bearing in the living conditions of the low-income earners in urban areas, especially because such policies have an impact in terms of the type of houses, that is, its quality and the quantity. This study examines the impact of such policies on urban low-income earners. Specifically, it focuses on the urban low-income earners of Harare.

Sustainability encompasses various pillars that are social sustainability, economic, political and environmental sustainability with the freedom and security being provided for residents within an urban area. There is needed to take this into consideration for all regions and nations that have low-cost housing problems. According to Campbell (2003), sustainable development is balancing interests of social equity, economic growth and environmental preservation that are always in antagonism during stages of development. New urbanism promotes and considers social equity be adopted so as to provide low-cost housing in Zimbabwe. Beyond any doubt, the new urbanism concept advocates for small lots in stand sizes therefore it is land efficient (Nyakazeya, 2010).

The Zimbabwean government is responsible for the provision of low-cost housing for the public. The Regional Town and Country Planning Act Chapter 29: 12 stipulates that development within the urban environment is guided by statutory plans. Part V of the RTCP Act highlights on control of development. Furthermore, the Zimbabwe Layout Design Manual (1999) outlines the planning standards for residential areas from a point of view road hierarchy, stand sizes and social facilities that should be included within a residential area. Again, housing by laws clearly state the material to be used and the building procedures to be followed when building a house within the urban environment. The Environmental Management Act (Chapter 20:15) speaks of environmental protection regulations and standards to be followed in Zimbabwe. It forbids development on wetlands. All these statutes provide what ought to be done by the government and what needs to be provided for by the public.

Reality is that the housing output by the public sector in developing countries is very poor (Crowley, 2003). Due to poor provision of housing for the low-income earners, the government is responsible for the growth of informal settlements. Institutional factors, according to Fekade (2000), also result in the mushrooming of informal settlement. He further contends that mismanagement by institutions fuel the growth of informal settlement. This happens when the local authorities fail to allocate land properly to its residents. Furthermore, corruption and economic hardships fuel the existing problems. This reflects policy failure since institutions such as local authorities are organs responsible for translating national objectives (housing for all) into space (Crowley, 2003).

Methodology

In this research, the triangulation method was employed since there was use of both qualitative and quantitative data. This pragmatic method involved use of various methods of research that included qualitative and quantitative research methods. Consequently, interview, questionnaires and observations were used to gather data. Participants who were taken into consideration were the residents. The data that was obtained provide results such as income levels, state of home ownership, allocation of stands, the low-income bracket and those who benefited from the low-cost housing scheme. Mixed research methods were used to incorporate qualitative and quantitative research techniques so that all the data required, subjective and objective, was gathered. Observation of house occupation at Central Africa Building Society, City of Harare authorities' perspective and Old Mutual perspective on what low-cost housing is, and the residents' perceptions acted as a pond to gather both qualitative and quantitative data

The sample that was collected included both male and female residents who reside at the randomly selected houses. Out of the sampled population, 41% were females and the other 59% consisted of male counterparts. Many households are headed and owned by male residents except for other cases were women own the houses. The population sample consisted of people who rent, own houses and others that are under lease to purchase. The total number of correspondents was fifty two (52). The age of correspondents ranged between 20 years to above 50 years. The sample population of males and females is shown in Figure 1.2. Out of the 20 questionnaires that were administered to the people allocated house by the Central Africa Building Society in the low-cost housing project in Budiriro, 70% are on lease to purchase while 30% are renting. In total, out of the 50 questionnaires, 48% own houses in Budiriro, 28% are on lease to purchase and the remaining 24% are renting. While there was no selection concerning the age group, it was determined by the people who were interviewed. The researcher compiled, assembled and analysed all the collected data using manual methods basing on value judgment. The computer-based programmes which include Microsoft Excel together with SPSS (Statistical Package for Social Sciences) were used in the generation of diagrammatical illustrations of data in the form of graphs and tables. This gave a graphic and visual presentation of the results of the research. Household questionnaires were relatively quick and easy to create codes (manually) and interpret. As a result of the triangulation of data in this study, results were explored and presented thematically and graphically.

Results

While people in Zimbabwe wish to obtain low-cost housing, the research established that those who own houses date back between the years of 1980s to year 1999. Some purchased them through the city council, that is, the old residents. Some obtained the houses from a few individuals who sold their residential stands or houses after they had obtained them from the city council. From the results that were obtained, people who are living in the low-cost housing project built by the Central Africa Building Society (Old Mutual) are under the lease to purchase hierarchy of property rights.

Of the people who were considered to be eligible for the Central Africa Building Society low-income housing project in Budiriro, 85% of them earn $500US and above per month. Of the 20 interviewed beneficiaries of the housing scheme of the Central Africa Building Society housing project, 14 are under lease to purchase while the other 6 are renting the houses though owners were not mentioned. Considering those under the lease to purchase scenario under Central Africa Building Society, all of them have a salary that is above $500, who chose to stay there because of legitimacy than affordability. Under the lease to purchase agreement, many of the residents complained that they had no choice but to embrace the housing scheme since other modes proved to be under illegal operators. One respondent said:

> "There is nothing that is low-cost as they tell the nation, it is actually expensive and the cost is unbearable as we have to pay $460 per month for the next 10 years yet we have other bills to pay and families to look after so where will the low cost be in that situation where there are so many costs to be met" (respondent, 2017).

With the current economic, social and political situation in Zimbabwe, it should be taken into consideration what low-cost is and to whom does it apply to. Considering the targeted low-income earners, Central Africa Building Society seemed to have benefited land barons who are now renting those houses to other individuals.

Central Africa Building Society initially proposed the completion of 3102 houses in Budiriro to accommodate the low-income earners in partnership with the city council of Harare. Those who qualified had to be on the mandatory waiting list. The City council vetted 1661 applicants and, out of that number which they had accessed from their waiting list, 1224 people were recommended to Central Africa Building Society for further vetting (Gahadza, 2016). Bank approved 597 who met funding requirements and 500 houses were allocated to successful beneficiaries. Due to poor occupancy of the houses, CABS tenure mortgages increased from 10 to 20 years. With a housing backlog of 1.25 million, these houses have a very low occupancy than expected.

Table 12.1: Allocation of land and/or houses

Institutions	Number of people	percentage
Building societies	20	40%
Local authorities	19	38%
Cooperatives	6	12%
Political party, political member or self	2	4%
Bought from an individual	3	6%

Currently, the political conditions in Zimbabwe have also contributed to the increased rate of failure in the provision of land for low-income earners. While politicians use land for political gain, there are people who obtained land from political parties. One resident said:

"This property is now mine legally and no one can take it away from me. My political party said that we have the right to stay here thus it is now my property."

With such sentiments from some of the residents, the allocation of land in Harare has become controversial. Some of the cooperatives that exist are also a part of the scam that has always been misleading the public.

Considering the requirements of Central Africa Building Society, there are no low-income earners who own immovable properties yet the Budiriro project is termed low-cost housing initiative. The City of Harare strategic plan 2012-2025, state an objective of having decent and affordable accommodation for everyone in Harare. This was to be attained through the engagement of key stakeholders such as CABS and other financial institutions. However, the key stakeholders involved currently have housing projects which cannot be acquired by low-income earners in Zimbabwe as the economic conditions are stiff and many low-income earners do not have permanent employment. This has resulted in the need to come up with suitable strategies in the criteria used for low-cost housing initiatives in Zimbabwe.

Discussion

There have been misconceptions concerning low-income housing for low-income earners in Harare, Zimbabwe, where the low-income bracket is not specified, and the public is not informed. This has affected the provision of housing for the low-income earners in Harare. While the government has failed in the clarification and management of providers to provide for the low-income earners, the private sector has intervened with the false impression of low cost housing for low-income earners while they are trying to maximize their profits without consideration for the low-income bracket. This has seen initiatives such as Budiriro housing project by Central Africa Building Society which even civil servants such as teachers cannot afford.

There is a huge gap between the demand for low-income housing units and the provision of the houses to low-income earners. Currently the demand is 1,25 million people on the waiting list (ZIMSTATS 2014) while the houses that have been provided by Central Africa Building Society are only 3 102 houses. The housing delivery system for the low-income earners has been outwhelmed by demand which is more than the waiting list. Furthermore, there are other residents who are not registered on the waiting list but desire to own a house in the city. The housing backlog faced by poor housing delivery has resulted in the failure of the waiting list as a measure for fair distribution and order in the housing department. The housing waiting list is now seen as a waste of time and money as it is renewed annually without yielding any desirable results.

Regarding the research conducted at the Central Africa Building Society housing initiative for low-income earners, a remarkable number of beneficiaries, that is, 16 out of the 20 people interviewed, come from the income bracket that is higher than the stipulated income bracket of low income earners. There were participants that belonged to the middle and higher income bracket that obtained houses as low-income earners could not afford to meet the requirements by the Central Africa Building Society. Most of the urban low-income earners in Harare cannot afford the housing units and the terms and conditions stipulated by the bank. They rather opted for rental accommodation. The problem has escalated by the failure of the council to provide for low-income earners that has resulted in people waiting for the housing schemes that are illegal. Legit housing schemes such as that by Central Africa Building Society have high premiums the low-income bracket could not afford to pay. According to the Harare housing department, they have not been providing houses nor stands for the past 10 years now. The actors that are involved in the provision of housing do not adequately address the concerns of low to middle income bracket. This has resulted in the private and public sector displacing the low-income earners in low-cost housing initiatives.

Conclusion

The inadequate provision of low-income housing in urban centres of Zimbabwe has been characterized by economic, political, social and environmental constrains leading to the failure of meeting the housing needs of low-income earners. It is critical for all stakeholders and institutions in the provision of low-cost housing to come up with solutions. These solutions should be able to address the burning cases of corruption, illegal settlements, fraud and low occupancy of housing schemes. This calls for policy formulation that protects the public, and rules and regulations for actors in the provision of low-cost housing. There is need to find means to do away with the participation of the high-income earners in the schemes intended for low-income earners.

References

Arman, M., Zuo, J.L.W., Zillante, G. and Pullen, S. (2009). Challenges of responding to sustainability with implications for affordable housing. Ecological Economics, 68, 3034-3041.

Briassoulis, H. (2010). Who plans whose sustainability? Alternative roles for planners. *Journal of Environmental Planning and Management, 42*(6), 889-902.

Campbell, S. (2003). Green Cities, Growing Cities, Just Cities: Urban Planning and the Contradictions of Sustainable Development. *Journal of the American Planning Association, 62*(3), 457-483.

Chirisa, I., Gaza, M. and Bandauko, E. (2014). Housing Cooperatives and the politics of local organisation and representation in Peri-urban Harare, Zimbabwe. *African Studies Quarterly, 15,* 38-53.

Clarke, S. and Ginsburg, N. (1984). *The Political Economy of Housing.* London: Sage.

Crowley, S. (2003). The Affordable Housing Crisis: Residential Mobility of Poor Families and School Mobility of Poor Children. *The Journal of Negro Education, 72*(1), 22-38.

Curley, A.M. (2005). Theories of Urban Poverty and Implications for Public Housing Policy. *Journal of Sociology and Social Welfare, XXXII* (2), 98-119.

Gahadza, N. (2016, August 2). CABS to launch rent-to-buy Scheme. *Herald.* Available online: http://www.herald.co.zw/cabs-to-launch-rent-to-buy-scheme/

Group, W. B. (2012). Independent Evaluation Group (IEG). The World Bank Group. Available online: http://lnweb90.worldbank.org/oed/oeddoclib.nsf/DocUNIDViewForJavaSearch/4EF67E4EE2EE239C852567F5005D8BAE

GoZ, Regional, Town and Country Planning Act Chapter 29:12 (1996).

GoZ, Layout design Manual, Department of Physical Planning, Ministry of Local Government and National Housing (1999).

Johnson, M.P. (2006). Decision Models for Affordable Housing and Sustainable Community Development: The Futures of Housing. *Journal of the American Planning Association, 5,* 1-26.

Kamete, A.Y. (2006). The return of the jettisoned: ZANU-PF's crack at 're-urbanizing' in Harare. *Journal of Southern African Studies, 32*(2), 255-271.

Katz, B., Turner, M.A., Brown, K.D., Cunningha, M. and Sawyer, N. (2003). Rethinking local affordable housing strategies: Lessons from 70 years of policy and practice. The Brookings Institution Centre on Urban and Metropolitan Policy and Urban Institute.

Kippler, C. (2010). Exploring Post Development: Politics, the state and emancipation. The question of alternatives. *POLIS, 3,* 1-38.

Langley, P. (2006). Securitising Suburbia: The transformation of Anglo-American Mortgage Finance. *Competition and Change, 10*(3), 283-299.

Lindsay, C.M. and Feigenbaum, B. (1984). Rationing by waiting lists. *American Economic Review, 74*(3), 404-417.

Manikela, J.S. (2008). *Understanding the Peripheralisation of Low-Cost Housing Delivery in the Mbombela Local Municipality.* Johannesburg: University of the Witwatersrand.

Mansoori, M.J. (1997). Government Low-Cost Housing Provision in the United Arab Emirates: Implications of standards of construction and conditions of tenure. Available online: https://research.ncl.ac.uk/forum/v3i1/low-cost%20housing.pdf

Marongwe, N., Chatiza, K. and Mukoto, S. (2011). *Scoping study governance of urban land markets in Zimbabwe.* Johannesburg: Urban Land Mark.

Moyo, W. (2014). Urban Housing Policy and Its Implications on the Low-Income Earners of a Harare Municipality, Zimbabwe. *International Journal of Asian Social Science, 4*(3), 356-365.

Nyakazeya, P. (2010, January 14). Building Residential Properties Expensive. *Zimbabwe Independent.* Available online: http//www.theindependent.co.zw/2010/01/14/building-residential-properties-expensive/

Patton, M. Q. (1980). Qualitative Research and Evaluation Methods (3rd edn.). Thousand Oaks, California: Sage Publication.

Potts, D. and Mutambirwa, C.C. (2006). *High Density housing in Harare: Commodification and Overcrowding.* London: Liverpool University Press.

Rakodi, C. and Mutizwa-Mangiza, D.N. (1991). *Housing Policy and Production in Harare: Zambezia, XVII (i), 1-30.*

Herald. (2016, July 20). Council loses thousands to corrupt employee. *The Herald:* Available online: http://www.herald.co.zw/council-loses-thousands-to-corrupt-employees/

Human Rights. (2005, July). Housing Rights in Zimbabwe. *Human Rights Monthly, 37,* 6-9.

Rojas, E. and Greene, M. (1995). Reaching the poor: lessons from the Chilean housing experience. *Environment and Urbanization, 7*(2), 31-50.

Rosenbaum, J., Flynn, C. and Stroh, L. (1998). Lake Parc Place: A Study of Mixed-Income Housing. *Housing Policy Debate, 9*(4), 703-740.

Ruwende, K. (2015, February 27). CABS slashes deposit for Budiriro Scheme. *Herald.* Available online: http://www.herald.co.zw/cabs-slashes-deposits-for-budiriro-scheme/

Shava, T. (2013, November 12). Urban poverty increase in Zimbabwean Cities. *VOA* Available online: http://www.voazimbabwe.com/a/urban-poverty-increases-in-zimbabwe-study/1788633.html

Taylor, J. (2011). Landscape Architecture in the developing world: The growth of informal settlements. *Landscape Review, 14*(1), 7 – 10.

Tighe, J.R. (2010). Public Opinion and Affordable Housing: A Review of the Literature. *Journal of Planning Literature*, 25(1), pp.3-17.

Trussel, B. (2010). The bid Rent Gradient theory in Eugene Oregon: An empirical investigation. University of Oregon.

UNHABITAT. (2011). *Practical guide for conducting: housing profiles.* Nairobi: UNHABITAT.

New Zimbabwe. (2016, May 30). Chombo and the rot at Harare City Council. *New Zimbabwe.* Available online: http://www.newzimbabwe.com/news-29466-corruption+chombo+and+hre+city+council/news.aspx

Chapter 13

Public Sanitation Service Delivery in Harare Central Business District

Paidamoyo M Chikandiwa, Conillious Gwatirisa
and Liliosa G Musiyiwa

Summary:

The study focussed on women and public sanitation service delivery in Harare's Central Business District (CBD). The study sought to analyse the sustainability, functionality and efficiency of Harare's existing public sanitation facilities in the central business district with specific reference to impact on women. The study adopted Shortell's multi-level model and embraced the mixed methods research design. One hundred questionnaires were randomly distributed to women located at major bus termini with twenty-five questionnaires at each of the four sampled public toilet sites. Data was collected through participant observations of public sanitation facilities and sanitary practices. The research also collected data through key informant interviews with participants drawn from Harare City Council (HCC) and the Ministry of Health. The study's major limitations included hostilities by one group at Copa Cabana, delays in granting permission, falsification of data, reluctance to participate and failure to interpret the questionnaire. The findings were presented through tables and graphs. The study found out that women did not have access to facilities at night as public toilets were locked. It also established that most public toilets did not meet the international standards as they were vandalised with flushing equipment not operating. The research also established that there were more toilet facilities for men than women as suggested by the long waiting queues of women. The study recommends that Harare City Council (HCC) rehabilitates its public toilets, especially at Copa Cabana to improve access. Harare city council needs to promote collaboration by creating Sanitation Committees. Toilet cleaners ought to be deployed on a rotational basis to prevent users being denied access. To improve on service delivery and policy implementation, Toilet Inspectors and other HCC officials should regularly visit and use public toilets. Lastly, HCC needs to employ security to promote access to facilities at night.

Introduction

The study assessed whether Harare Central Business District (CBD)'s public sanitation facilities were gender sensitive in line with the international standards. The bias towards women stems from the observation that colonial planning had a bias towards the male population as they were the source of cheap labour with women being confined to the rural areas (Mukonoweshuro, 2014). As a result of the demand for cheap male labour, the colonial local authorities ensured that there was more service provision for males than female (Chirinda, 2014) The post 2000 era witnessed the rapid influx of informal traders into the central business districts (CBDs) of Zimbabwe's major cities such as Harare (Munzwa and Jonga, 2010). This influx of informal traders into Harare's CBD took place against a backdrop of declining revenue base and service delivery thus affecting policy implementation. The decline in Harare's City's revenue is evidenced by the fact that in 2017 Harare City council was accruing monthly revenue of between twelve million and 14 million against a budget of 24 million.

Background to the Study

MDGs targets called for the halving of people without sustainable access to safe drinking water and basic sanitation by 2015 (UNICEF, 2012). After failure to achieve MDGs, in July 2014, the United Nations Open Working Group (OWG) proposed the application of Sustainable Development Goals (SDGs) to ensure that there was availability and sustainable management of water and sanitation for all by the year 2015. Sustainable Development Goals 3, 5, 6 and 10, 11 and 17 were either directly associated or linked with improvements and accessibility to water and sanitation. The United Nations Open Working Group (OWG) viewed goal 6 as the panacea for improved water and sanitation as it was meant to ensure availability and sustainable management of water and sanitation for all. The slogan 'Sanitation for all was by 2030' was then coined so as to ensure that marginalised groups like women had access to adequate sanitation facilities such as public toilets. Before engaging in the 'Sanitation for all discourse' it is imperative for the researcher to define the concept sanitation. The Sustainable Sanitation Alliance (2011) defines sanitation as hygiene promotion through the provision of adequate faecal and urine disposal facilities with limited contact with hazards of human faeces. The slogan "Sanitation for all" in Zimbabwe implied that both the government and HCC had to ensure that all members of the public had access to public toilets at all public places such as the Harare CBD. The main goal aimed at fostering gender equality in the provision of sound sanitation for all with women having more public toilet facilities than men as they constituted more than half of the population and took more time in relieving themselves. Goal 3 covered water and sanitation and aimed also at promoting healthy lives and the well-being for all at all ages. By healthy lives, the goal called for an environment free from faecal contamination and diseases associated with improper public sanitary practices.

With specific reference to Zimbabwe the SDG called for the need for the Zimbabwean government and HCC to promote equal access for males and females, children and the disabled. Goal number 5 advocates for the need for an end to all forms of discrimination against girls and women in the access to public sanitary facilities and water. This Goal advocates for the construction of gender sensitive public toilet systems with facilities such as hangers, bathrooms and sanitary bins. Article 6.2 of Goal number 5 also calls for universal and equitable safe water and sanitation for all by 2030. The proposed SDGs were underpinned by a number of targets, which included to, 'support and strengthen the participation of local communities for improving water and sanitation management by 2030'. Another target was 'to achieve access to adequate and equitable sanitation and hygiene for all,' and 'to end open defecation, paying special attention to the needs of women and girls who happen to be in these vulnerable situations'. However, most studies in Zimbabwe's towns and cities have indicated that Zimbabwe has failed to achieve these MDGs (Mukonoweshuro, 2014; Munzwa and Jonga, 2010). Goal number 9 promotes the construction of resilient infrastructure (public toilets included) using modern technologies. In the Zimbabwean context, this implies that the Zimbabwean government (local authorities included) had to build standard public toilets with modern facilities.

SD goal number 11 petitions for the necessity to make cities and human settlements inclusive, safe resilient and sustainable. The element of cities being inclusive and safe hinges on the need for public toilets to cater for all public toilet users such as the disabled, women, pregnant women and children. The safety element implies secure from criminals, faeces and diseases such as cholera. Since Zimbabwe pledged to fulfil the requirements of these SDGs, it is of interest to establish whether the country is trying to meet the targets set on public sanitary facilities.

Studies in West Africa have shown that Ghana's women are the key players in implementing changes in hygiene and behaviour. However, despite the knowledge and experience that they bring, their contributions are often overlooked or under-utilised. Zambia's capital, Lusaka, is also experiencing typical urban problems such as poor sanitation.

In Zimbabwe, the Zimbabwean Public Health Act (PHA) has guidelines for the suppression of sanitary related infections such as cholera and diarrhoea and deals also with the rights of residents such as 'the right to access to a public sanitary facility' at all places where thousands of people converge daily and spend more than two hours waiting to receive a service. Mangwandu (2010) maintains that Part-(v) of the Public Health Act deals with the international sanitation regulations. These regulations spell out that public sanitation standards adopted by international institutions such as the American Restroom Association and the British Toilet Association campaigned for the construction of standard toilets with automated flushing equipment, automated hand driers and bathrooms. Issues covered by these sanitary standards include cleanliness standards, signage and the provision of public toilet facilities for special groups.

The Zimbabwe Standard (2010) observed that Zimbabwe's major urban centres of Harare, Bulawayo, Gweru, Mutare and Masvingo were plagued with inadequate water supply. A study in Harare by Musemwa (2004) found out that Harare's water and sanitation woes could be traced back to the late 1990's. Mtisi (2008) outlined several factors which hindered the provision of adequate sanitation and clean water in Zimbabwe's urban centres particularly Harare, Gweru and Mutare. Another study on barriers to water and sanitation service provision in Harare established that population growth, poor local governance structures, dilapidation in water and sanitary infrastructure and the sheer disregard of water and sanitation quality standards and by-laws were the major challenges (Mukonoweshuro, 2014). As a panacea for promoting socio-economic development, the Zimbabwean government crafted a blueprint named Zimbabwe Agenda for Sustainable Socio-Economic Transformation (ZIMASSET), ZIMASSET's service delivery infrastructure and utilities cluster was tasked with the rehabilitation of infrastructure and services related to water and sanitation such as public toilets.

Previous studies in Zimbabwe established that, despite Zimbabwe boasting of a plethora of blueprints, the Zimbabwean capital city of Harare was faced by a water and sanitation disaster due to the poor status of its public sanitation infrastructure (Manzungu, 2004). Chirisa and Dumba (2011) observe that the Regional, Town and Country Planning Act in Zimbabwe Chapter 29:12 was meant to provide for the planning of regions, districts and local areas with the objective of conserving and improving the physical environment as well as promoting health, safety, order, amenity, convenience and general welfare. Manzungu *et al.* (2004) assert that Harare is today a typical example of poor urban planning as political expedience takes precedence over good land-use and management, prudent infrastructure sense as well as a healthy welfare of people. They citedan example in which politicians meddled in the allocation of housing stands and settled people in designated wetlands. Besides this, the Ministry of LGPWNH has been accused of giving out land in Harare in contravention of the Urban Council`s Act chapter 15 regulations number 67 that empowers local authorities (Harare City Council included), to inspect public sanitation facilities. The Human Rights Watch Report released on November 19, 2013, acknowledged that the water and sanitation crisis in Harare places millions of residents at the risk of waterborne diseases as most of Harare's newly established settlements of Caledornia, Hopley and Ushewekunze lacked water and sanitation infrastructure with residents drawing water from wells.

Theoretical Framework

The research incorporated Shortell's theoretical framework (Figure 13.1). Shortell's theoretical framework was an organisational analysis of the major factors influencing public sanitation service delivery and public policy implementation (Shortell, 2004; Proctor, 2008).

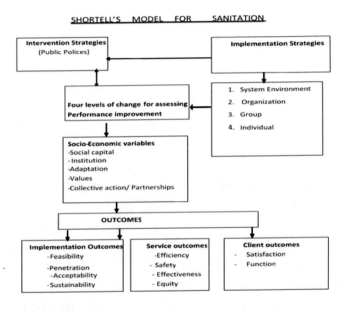

Figure 13.1: Shortell's Model for Sanitation
Source: Gwatirisa (2015), Adapted from Shortell (2007)

The framework posits that policy implementation is influenced by factors such as the policy environment, organisation, team or group and the individual (Conrad and Christianson, 2004). Basing on Shortell's theoretical framework, the policy environment under study refers to the physical, economic, socio-cultural, political and the technological environment affecting Harare City's public sanitation system. In the Zimbabwean context, groups and teams may refer to groups in the vicinity of major public toilets such as such as Copa Cabana's Grassroots and others such as UNICEF and Red Cross.

Shortell's model illustrates that individuals have a great influence on policy implementation through their values, culture and practices such as public urination, vandalism and open defaecation. The theoretical framework posits that these four levels of change are the pre-requisites for assessing the effectiveness of policy implementation and service delivery (Linder and Peters, 2017). The multi-level theoretical framework constitutes three pillars, namely, the intervention strategies, the implementation strategies and the outcomes (Proctor, 2008). The intervention strategies refer to strategies crafted so as to promote policy implementation and service delivery such as awareness campaigns, policies, taxes, levies, by-laws and legislation. The theoretical framework further posits that the four levels of change have a direct influence on the public sanitation outcomes as the status of the public toilet is influenced by the policy environment, the organisational factors, groups and individuals (Shortell, 2004). The theoretical framework further outlines that outcomes are further subdivided into implementation outcomes, service outcomes and client outcomes. The implementation outcomes are assessed through determining the feasibility penetration, acceptability and sustainability of the public sanitation facilities. These service outcomes, on the other hand, measure effectiveness, efficiency, safety and equity (Proctor, 2008).

In simpler terms, major policy implementation outcomes may include dissatisfaction by users, locked toilets, malfunctioning public toilets, and an inefficient public toilet system. The strength of Shortell's theoretical framework is its emphasis on the need for inclusivity in service delivery and policy implementation with the involvement of local authorities, groups, teams and individuals. Its emphasis on the inclusion of individuals in policy implementation is aimed at instilling a sense of ownership amongst public toilet users. In a nutshell, Shortell's model advocates for the participation of groups/teams and individuals (users) in the provision of security against vandalism and in the raising of awareness. In addition to this, Shortell encourages the formation of community-based groups such as Water and Sanitation Committees. This framework also encourages collaboration amongst all actors in public sanitation policy implementation. The theoretical framework's weakness is that it overemphasises the role of individuals in policy implementation forgetting that individuals at times resist to actively participate as they shoulder all the duties and responsibilities on local authorities.

Literature Review

Zimbabwe Public Health Act of 1996 provides that it is obligatory for all public toilets to have hand washing facilities. Section 2 of the Zimbabwe's Public Health Act Chapter 15:09 (1996) maintains that the absence of public toilets at locations where large volumes of residents frequent, such as bus termini, is a public nuisance. It further maintains that failure to provide public toilets at such places is considered as an infringement of the Public Health Act. Mangwandu (2010) affirms that Zimbabwe Public Health Act (1996:15) is divided into sections with part five of the Act encompassing international sanitation regulations. Chapter15 Section 9 of the Public Health Act dictates that every medical officer of health in a local authority is obliged to keep himself or herself informed about the public sanitary circumstances of his or her district, and is mandated to make such inspections and inquiries on the status of the public sanitary facilities.

It is of great interest to find out whether Harare's public toilets meet the above requirements or fall short of the minimum standards. Previous studies on Harare's public toilets revealed that they did not meet the minimum standards as some were characterised by over flowing raw human waste that stretched from the door to the squat holes (*Zimbabwe Standard*, 2015). In addition to this, the public toilets were either poorly lit or did not have any lighting at all. However, Creed (2010) argues that a well-designed lighting system in the public toilet aids in creating ambience which encourages more care and responsibility from users. Besides, materials used in the construction of public toilets should be durable and resistant to vandalism. In addition to this, a standard toilet should be built of good materials made of non-slip ceramic tiles or natural stone for floors, ceramic tiles or enamelled steel panels for walls and mineral fibre board or aluminium for ceiling (*Ibid.*). However, a study on Harare's sanitary facilities by Munzwa and Jonga (2010) mentioned that public toilets in the CBD did not have any of the observed modern features since they depicted technologies of the 1960s.

In some African countries such as Ghana, community-based organisations have played a critical role in policy implementation by actively participating in the rehabilitation, upkeep, maintenance and cleaning of the public toilets. Outman (2010) asserts that community-based organisations and NGOs should assist the Town Councils, and communities in the planning, funding and development of community sanitation infrastructure for the safe disposal of waste. As a way of improving public sanitation service delivery and policy implementation, The Environmental Policy of Ghana (2001) opines that the institutions concerned with implementing sanitation policy should be divided into principal and allied sectors. Under this arrangement, the principal sector had direct responsibility for aspects of sanitation while the allied sector agencies played a supporting role. To boost service delivery and policy implementation, Ghana's Environmental Policy also transferred some existing responsibilities from one institution to another as a way of empowering groups and teams (the private sector included) in public sanitation service provision, Plummer (2002) opines that the private sector should operate within policies, regulations, supervisory and licensing arrangements set up by the public sector to promote efficiency and competitiveness. As teams and groups are often overlooked when crafting policies, this study examines the roles of teams and groups in creating sustainable toilets.

WHO/UNICEF (2011) assert that lack of sanitation is an issue that affects women than man. UNDP (1990) argues that in areas without access to a public toilet, women lack privacy and are at risk of violence if they have to go outside and use the toilet often late at night. Cohre et al. (2008) mentions that women bear the brunt of the lack of toilets and other sanitary facilities and suffer the indignity of being forced to defecate and urinate in the open. In the absence of sanitary facilities, women have to wait until dark to go to toilet. Gender and Water Alliance (2003) observe that gender-specific failures occurred in scenarios were toilets with no doors faced the street thus making women feel insecure. UNDP (2009) points out that about 52% of the female population is of reproductive age and most of them are menstruating every month and need hand washing facilities in toilets. Dungumero (2007) argues that women needed to wash themselves during menstruation. House *et al.* (2012) opine that poor protection and inadequate washing facilities often increased susceptibility to infection with odour of menstrual blood putting women at risk of being stigmatised. A previous study by David (2005) observed that women had no safe place to dispose their sanitary pads, cotton or tampons as the public toilets were either malfunctioning or in a bad state. House *et al.* (2012) observe that failure to provide disposal facilities for used sanitary materials is resulting in latrines becoming blocked and quickly filling pits.

Methodology

The study focused on Harare CBD's public toilet facilities located at major bus termini. At these major bus termini/markets are found groups of toilets users that have the potential of accessing and using these public toilets on a daily basis. The non-pay public toilets that were targeted included the Copa Cabana, Fourth Street, Charge Office and the Market Square ones.

The study utilised the mixed research design which integrated qualitative and quantitative techniques. Livesey (2016) argues that the advantage of using the mixed method approach is that it offers strengths that counterbalance the weakness of both quantitative and qualitative research methods. To establish the role of groups, the study area was divided into distinct clusters such as the Copa Cabana, the Charge Office, and the Fourth Street. Snowball sampling was used to select authorities such as the Harare City Waste Management Superintendents, Supervisors and Toilet Inspectors. The researcher first approached the Harare City Council spokesperson who assisted to select other participants. Purposive sampling was also used to select Harare's CBD as the worst part of Harare affected by the convergence of the large influx of migrants day and night.

The researcher adopted the questionnaire method with one hundred questionnaires being self-administered to female informal traders located within the vicinity of the CBD's selected public toilet sites. Twenty-five questionnaires were randomly distributed to each of the four public toilet sites to eliminate chances of bias. The questionnaire method is credited for generating standardised data which can be analysed statistically (Creswell, 2014). To determine the role of groups in policy implementation, the researchers grouped the public toilet sites into clusters comprising informal traders around a particular public toilet site.

The researcher randomly selected twenty-five respondents per public toilet site targeting women sheltered at each of the four bus termini. Random sampling was used to eliminate chances of bias. The study targeted women operating in shelters within the vicinity of the public toilet sites to establish the role of teams and groups in promoting sustainable service delivery. In addition, these participants were anticipated to have valuable information on public toilets because they were likely to use them daily. Primary data was collected using key informant interviews, field observations and four focus group discussions that were held at the sampled sites. Secondary data on public sanitation facilities and policy implementation was collected from publications such as books, journals, newspapers, magazines, dissertations and the internet. The researcher carried out key informant interviews with six officials from Harare City Council's Departments of Waste Management, and Harare Water and Works Department. This was meant to get reliable information from authoritative sources. Babbie (2001) notes that secondary data has the advantage that it can be accessed in a relatively short time. Data was coded using SPSS and then analysed using descriptive statistics. Tables, pie charts and graphs were then generated from the captured data. Qualitative data was analysed in themes. To ensure informed consent, the researcher explained to participants why they were involved in the study. Participants were also assured that the information that they would provide would be used for academic reasons only. Confidentiality and privacy were assured to each participant. Interviews were carried out in private and no names were captured on the participant's forms.

Results

The majority (74%) of women participants were aged between 26 and 45 while 21% were aged 36-45. A few (5%) were aged 46 and above. A significant number (82%) had received secondary education.

Accessibility to places of convenience

On being asked about accessibility of public toilets, 65% of participants indicated that the facilities were not accessible. Very few (30%) acknowledged that they were accessible. On being asked whether they used their nearest public toilets, 54% agreed that they accessed them yet slightly less than half (45%) stated that they used alternatives. The responses on the reasons for using alternative facilities were that the public toilets were always locked (41%), malfunctioning (27%), and dirty (15%). Other respondents indicated that public toilets lacked privacy (13%), were usually soiled with human faeces (12%). However, Harare water officials stated that they did not use public toilets due to their unhygienic state. This confirms that truly these public toilets were not accessible due to lack of hygienic maintenance. On probing why some users used alternative toilets, the observations revealed that sites such as Fourth Street and Copa Cabana had very few cubicles for use to relieve oneself. For example, the facility at Copa Cabana had one male cubicle and three female cubicles. However, the site was congested with more than two thousand informal traders stationed around the public toilet site. The observations further revealed that, despite the Charge Office public toilet being functional, toilets users were at times denied access by the cleaning staff unless one happened to be known by the cleaner. It was also observed that at times some toilet cleaners stationed at the Charge Office and Fourth Street public toilet sites demanded money from users.

Organisational and policy factors influencing service delivery

The survey established that service delivery and policy implementation were influenced by a variety of organisational and policy related factors (See Table 13.1).

Table 13.1: Factors Influencing Public Toilet Sustainability

Variable	N=100	%
Policy environment		
Lack of prioritisation	56	56
Lack of enforcement	9	9
Polarised environment	13	13
Inadequate resources	20	20
Organisational factors affecting		
Lack of funding	45	45
Lack of maintenance	23	23
Lack of will	15	15
Sabotage	8	8
Neglect of consumers	6	6
Role of groups		
Maintenance	3	3
Funding	5	5
Security	8	8
Rehabilitation	15	15
Education	3	3
Public cleaning of toilets	5	5
Not at all	59	59

Source: Field Survey, 2016

Organisational factors influencing sustainability

The concept sustainability was borrowed from the concept sustainable development (SD) and is closely connected to the three pillars of SD, namely economic, social and environmental. The Sustainable Sanitation Alliance (2011; 34) asserts that, for a public toilet to be sustainable, it had to meet the following five criteria: be economically viable, socially acceptable, technically and institutionally appropriate and protective of the environment and the natural resources. In simpler terms, a sustainable public toilet is one that promotes human health and provides a clean environment that is free from diseases. The respondents indicated that the major organisational factors that influenced the sustainability of the Harare CBD's public toilets included lack of funding (45%), lack of maintenance (23%) and lack of will to provide service delivery (15%). Eight percent (8%) of the participants cited sabotage by staff while 5% stated that the current status was due to neglect. To illustrate how organisational factors were to blame for the lack of access at night, one of the key informants opined that the provision of access to public toilets at night was outside their organisation's mandate. The view that lack of funding was the major organisational barrier was shared by most of the key informants. One key informant highlighted that there is lack of prioritisation of public toilets by authorities.

Policy factors and service delivery

About half (56 %) of participants attributed the current unhygienic state of the public toilets in the Harare CBD to lack of prioritisation. Other responses on factors affecting the sustainability of public sanitation service delivery were issues such as the polarised political environment (13%), lack of policy enforcement (9%) and inadequate resources (20%). Key informants alluded to the fact that, although by-laws and policies meant to promote adequate sanitation were in, the former were not enforced while the latter were not implemented. On being asked whether Harare was complying with the standard 24-hour opening hours, one key informant revealed that there was no provision for council workers to work late in the CBD. Another key informant suggested that for Harare to provide 24-hour service the following conditions had to be met: (i) need for lighting; (ii) need for security; and (iii) need for attendants to man the toilets at night.

Groups and public toilet sustainability

When the participants were asked whether their group was actively involved in public sanitation service delivery, 59% indicated that their organisation was not at all engaged. Other responses on the contributions of groups were as follows: rehabilitation (15%), security (8%), public cleaning (5%) and funding (5%). The questionnaire responses indicate that the major groups stationed at these major public toilets contributed very little to public toilets service delivery. When key informants were asked about the role of groups/teams in public sanitation service delivery, most (67%) acknowledged that very few groups and teams were actively engaged in public toilet provision. The major groups that were involved in the refurbishment were Uniliver and Domi Stores which had refurbished the Charge Office and the First Street public toilets respectively. Meikles Hotel assisted in the maintenance of the Africa Unity Square public toilet. Key informants also stated that major groups located near public toilet sites had contributed very little in the painting, maintenance, cleaning and complete refurbishment of public toilets. Participant observations revealed that, despite the HCC leasing some of its public toilets to private players such as the Disruptive Innovations, very few public toilet users were using that facility probably due to that they could not afford the user fee of fifty cents.

Impact of individuals on sustainability

The responses on the role of individuals reflected that individuals had a great influence on the sustainability of public toilets.

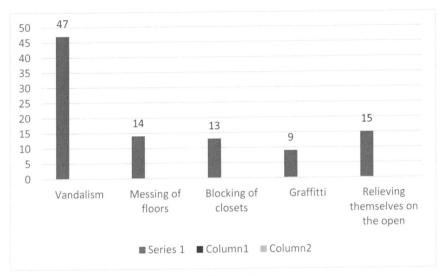

Figure 13.2: Responses on the Role of Individuals
Source: Field Survey, 2016

On being asked about the role of individual public toilet users in influencing the sustainability of these toilets, about half (47%) blamed members of the public for vandalism while 15 % blamed members of the public for using open spaces. Fourteen percent (14%) and 13% blamed users for messing floors and blocking public toilets respectively.

Figure 13.4: Vandalised Public Toilet at Charge Office
Source: From a Field Survey by Chikandiwa (2016).

The survey established that the Harare City Council cleaning staff were instrumental in both promoting or discouraging service delivery and policy implementation by locking public toilets, denying the users access or by scolding public toilet users (See Figure 5).

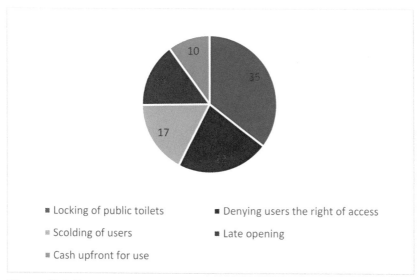

Figure 13.5: Responses on the Influence of Cleaning Staff

Basing on Figure 13.5 users blamed the cleaning staff for compromising sustainability of public toilets by resorting to the following: locking of public toilets 35%, denying users the right to access 22 %, scolding users 17 % and late opening 15%. Respondents also accused some cleaners of demanding cash up front. To illustrate how public toilet users were at times ill-treated and denied access, one user indicated that they would be told to use the public toilets for urination only and no defecation. The focus group discussion at Charge Office highlighted that women were denied access as evidenced by one user's sentiment when she retorted that,

> When I went to the toilet and found the cleaner mopping she told me to remove my shoes yet the floors were not yet dry'. She further argued that, 'because I could not control my bladder I removed my shoes and used the toilet disregarding the health hazards associated with going into a public toilet barefooted.

In response to the challenges the Charge Office public toilet users face at the hands of cleaners, another public toilet user, Mamoyo, narrated the following account,

When a public toilet user visits the toilet with the hope of relieving yourself, you are told to just urinate and not defecate.

To illustrate the magnitude of the level of harassment by cleaners, one female user Mandlovu stated that,

At times the cleaner would often move around and if one took time on the toilet seat they would be asked to slightly stand up so that the cleaner would confirm whether the user was not defecating.

Service Delivery Outcomes

Table 13.3: Responses on the Sustainability Outcomes

A Satisfaction	N=100	% Responses
Strongly Agree	5	5
Agree	6	6
Neutral	3	3
Disagree	18	18
Strongly Disagree	66	66
C. Functionality	**N=100**	**% Responses**
Strongly agree	6	6
Agree	4	4
Neutral	3	3
Disagree	17	17
Strongly Disagree	67	67
D Efficiency of HCC	**N=100**	**% Response**
Yes	21	21%
No	77	77 %
E. Safety of Toilets	**N=100**	**%**
Strongly Agree	6	6
Agree	12	12
Neutral	5	5
Disagree	16	16
Strongly Disagree	60	60
F Effectiveness	**N=100**	**% Responses**
Strongly Agree	9	9
Agree	5	5
Neutral	8	8

Disagree	12	12
Strongly Disagree	64	64
G Gender Equity	**N=100**	**% Reponses**
Yes	8	8
No	91	91

Source: Field Survey (2017)

Gender Equity

On being asked about gender equity, 91% of the participants indicated that public toilets were not gender sensitive as service provision for males was better than for females. Only 8% concurred that there was equity in the provision of public toilet service. The public toilet that was most gender insensitive was the Copa Cabana facility as observations indicated that after an interval of five minutes more than fifty men would have used the toilet while women would be in their snake like queues with some ending up going away without using the toilet. The observations revealed the distribution of the female cubicles as follows: Copa Cabana facility had three, Market Square Free toilet had three, Africa Unit Square toilet had three and Charge Office facility four cubicles (with only two functioning). Both the First Street and Fourth Street toilets had three cubicles. It was also observed that, despite the Charge Office having a functional flushing system, users were at times not allowed to flash after using the toilet with the cleaners flashing at once when they closed in the cleaning. However, the Charge Office public toilet was the most hygienic after rehabilitation by Uniliver.

Satisfaction

On being asked about the degree of satisfaction with the quality of public toilets, most respondents were dissatisfied as evidenced by 66% who strongly disagreed while 18% disagreed. As a result of the dissatisfaction, some users ended up using either toilets in cafes or open spaces. The field observations revealed that most public toilet users were dissatisfied by the poor state of the floors at Copa Cabana and Fourth Street that were always wet while closet floors were often soiled with human faeces. On being asked about their opinion of the cleaning process, 65% of the participants indicated that they were satisfied with the cleaning process.

The Copa Cabana focus group discussion established that women were dissatisfied by the lack of cubicle doors which deprived them of privacy, the lack of sanitary bins and the absence of bathrooms at these major toilet sites such as Copa Cabana. One female objected to the absence of sanitary bins arguing that since they could not carry some used pads in their bags they often dumped the pads in the pits. One focus group participant retorted that it was taboo for one's blood to be seen by people, so they carried their pads and burnt them home.

Efficiency

On being asked about the effectiveness of the HCC workforce, 77% stated that the cleaning workforce was inefficient while 21% stated that they were efficient. On being asked what they meant by inefficiency, most FGD members defined inefficiency as the failure by Harare City Council officials to provide public sanitation service provision to users usually at night, or during the weekends and periods of shutdowns of major waterworks such as the Morton Jeffreys. As evidence to prove the inefficiency of the public toilets, most users indicated that these public toilets had malfunctioning equipment such as taps, flushing equipment and sinks. Participant observations of the public toilets also established that during shutdowns, most public toilets were locked thus denying access to users. Interestingly, the field observations unearthed a malpractice by the Market Square cleaners who locked the public toilet under the guise that there was no water, yet the pay toilet located about one hundred metres away was functioning well. To illustrate the high degree of inefficiency, the focus group discussions concurred that some public toilets such as the Copa Cabana, Charge Office and Fourth Street had gone for years without replacement of vandalised equipment. One Waste Management Superintendent acknowledged that the maintenance division took long to repair malfunctioning and damaged equipment due to the bureaucracy associated with the long process of procuring equipment. Another key informant from the Waste Management Department attributed the poor status of equipment to division of responsibilities. For example, while public toilets were under the Waste Management Department, all maintenance fell under the Department of Works. Participant observations revealed the neglect at Copa Cabana, Market Square and Fourth Street public toilets which had broken septic tanks, malfunctioning water taps and cubicles without doors (See Figure 6).

Figure 13.6: Cubicles without Internal Doors at Fourth Street Public Toilet
Source: Field Survey by Chikandiwa (2016)

Health safety in the public toilets

On being asked about the health safety of public toilets, about half (60%) strongly disagreed and 16% disagreed that it was safe to use these public facilities. Those who acknowledged that there was health safety constituted 18% of the participants. Field observations by the researcher observed that that there was lack of health safety as public toilet users formed long queues and often came into contact with each other as they attempted to access the overcrowded public toilets. The only public toilet that had little contact between users was the Charge Office facility which had been renovated by Uniliver. At sites like Copa Cabana and the Fourth Street, public toilet users were exposed to criminal elements as drums that were meant to store water for hand washing acted as barriers to users entering the public toilets (Figure 13.6). The drums at Copa Cabana blocked the entrance resulting in users forming long queues outside. In addition to this, these drums (Figure 13.6) posed a great danger to users as there was a likelihood of users being tripped resulting in injury. The washing of hands by users using water from the drums also exposed users to water borne diseases. The lack of health safety was also evidenced by the malfunctioning lighting facilities at Copa Cabana, Market Square and Fourth Street at the time of collecting data for this study. The focus group discussions also concurred that, since all public toilets were locked at night, women who used open spaces and alleys as places of convenience were at risk of violence from criminal elements lurking in those places at night.

The status of Harare CBD's public toilets

On being asked about whether Harare CBD's public toilets were functioning well, 67% of the participants strongly disagreed while 17% disagreed. Only 10% of the participants either agreed or strongly agreed that the public toilets were functioning well. However, the field observations concurred with the responses from the key informants that the water system had broken down in most of these public toilets, so the authorities resorted to putting water in drums for use (See Figure 13.4).

Figure 13.7: Malfunctioning Public Toilet and Soiled Floors
Source: Field Survey (Chikandiwa: 2016).

Both the field observations and FDGs revealed that most flushing systems for the Copa Cabana, Market Square and Charge Office public toilets were not functioning well. Besides this, water taps in the three public toilets were malfunctioning with horse pipes being improvised to channel water for use even by outside vendors. However, at the time of writing HCC had started maintaining its water taps such as at the Copa Cabana facility.

Effectiveness of the HCC's public sanitation system

Responses to whether HCC's Waste Management and Public Sanitation Department was effective were marred by contradictions as 64% strongly disagreed, while 12% disagreed. A few (9%) strongly agreed while 5% agreed that HCC was effective. The participatory observations revealed that the cleaning staff at the Charge Office public site were ineffective at times as they took a longer time to clean and open the public toilets.

Conclusion, Policy Options and Practical Recommendations

The research found out that socio-cultural, economic, organisational and policy factors influenced accessibility of public sanitary facilities in the Harare CBD. In addition to this, it established that some stakeholders located near the public toilet sites did not actively participate in the rehabilitation, cleaning, maintenance and provision of security as expected of their social responsibilities. The study also established that some public toilets in the Harare CBD (Copa Cabana included) did not conform to the international sanitation standards that advocate for the establishment of gender sensitive facilities with more provision for females than males. The lack of sustainability was evidenced by the long queues of women trying to access public sanitary facilities as well as the restriction to access these facilities by some cleaning staff. At sites such as Copa Cabana, users were denied the right to privacy as cubicle did not have doors for concealment. The study found out that public toilets in the Harare CBD did not have basic facilities such as bathrooms, sanitary bins, baby changing facilities and hangers for women. The research also found out that participants were dissatisfied with public sanitation service delivery and regarded the system as inefficient, lacking in health safety and likely to endanger the lives of public toilet users due to unhygienic conditions. The study also established that women did not have access to public sanitary amenities at night as all public toilets were locked. Lastly, the research found out that, as a result of locking toilets at night, women were forced to use open spaces and alleys as places of convenience thus exposing them to risks of violence.

Since the study established that there was very little involvement of other stakeholders in the public toilets service delivery, there is urgent need for the Harare City Council to actively involve other groups to actively participate in the provision of security to curb vandalism. In addition, other stakeholders may assist in educational or awareness campaigns on the proper use of public sanitary facilities to foster behaviour change. Furthermore, there is need for stakeholder participation in the rehabilitation and maintenance of major public toilets. Public sanitation facilities paraphernalia in urgent need of rehabilitation include sinks, flushing equipment, tapes and cubicle doors. Since the Copa Cabana public toilet is very small, there is need for Harare City Council to either demolish it or renovate it to cater for the large population of users. Besides, organisations such as EMA and the Ministry of Health ought to assist HCC by carrying out more awareness campaigns on sustainable public toilet use. The Ministry of Health and Child Care should also enforce the public health and safety standards and guidelines. As the study established that the political environment was not conducive to service delivery, there is need for harmony between the Ministry of LGPWNH and HCC. In order to promote inclusivity, there is need for HCC to establish Water and Sanitation Committees comprising stakeholders located within the vicinity of major public toilets.

The Harare City Council should also partner water and sanitation organisations in the rehabilitation and provision of additional gender-sensitive facilities such as sanitary bins, cubicles, hangers, baby changing facilities and bathrooms. Another partnership strategy HCC may adopt is the twinning model with industry adopting specific public toilets. Lastly, since Harare is a twenty-four-hour city, the city council needs to provide night security at all major public toilet sites to promote access at night in line with the international standards.

References

Baker, J. (2013). *Urban practice: Innovations in Infrastructure Services*. New York: The World Bank.

Dornyei, Z. (2007). *Research methods in applied linguistics: Qualitative and mixed methodologies* (1st edn.). Oxford: Oxford University Press.

Dungumaro, E. W. (2007). Socioeconomic differentials and availability of domestic water in South Africa. *Physics and Chemistry of the Earth, Parts A/B/C, 32*(15-18), 1141-1147.

Gates, B. and Gates, M. (2013). *Water sanitation and hygiene strategy*. Boston: Bill and Melinda Gates Foundation.

Greed, C. (2013). *A code of practice for public toilets in Britain*. West England, University of West of England.

Guest, S. (2011). *Public toilets and poverty in Ghana*. Amsterdam, University of Amsterdam.

Gwatirisa, C. (2015). *Analysis of policy implementation Dynamics in Zimbabwe's urban areas: A case study of public sanitary facilities in Harare* (Unpublished PhD thesis). University of Zimbabwe.

Hove, M. and Tirimboi, A. (2011). Assessment of Harare water service delivery. *Journal of Sustainable Development in Africa, 13*(4), 61-84.

Manzungu, E. (Ed. (2008). *Towards a new creed, water management, governance and livelihoods* in *Southern Africa*. Harare: Weavers Press.

Morgan, P. (2001). *Ecological sanitation in Zimbabwe: A Compilation of Manuals and experiences* (Volume I). Harare: Sida,

Mulenga, M., Menase, G. and Fawcett, B. (2004). *Building links for improved sanitation in poor urban settlements: recommendations from research in sanitation in Africa*. Institute of Irrigation and Development Studies. Southampton, University of Southampton.

Outman, K.I. (2010). Community involvement in urban water and sanitation provision of improved service delivery in Ghana: The missing link in partnerships. *Journal of African Studies and Development, 2*(8), 208-215.

Plummer, J. (2002). *Developing inclusive public-private partnerships: The role of small-scale independent providers in the delivery of water and sanitation services.* London: GHK International, Prefontaine.

Richard, L. and Sicotte, H. (2000). *New models of collaboration for public service delivery.* Worldwide Trends, Cefrio.

Robinson, S. (2001). *Public conveniences: Policy, planning and provision.* London: Institute of Waste Management (IWM).

Owusu, G. (2010). Social Effects of Poor Sanitation and Waste Management on Poor Urban Communities: A Neighbourhood-Specific Study of Sabon Zongo, Accra. Journal of *Urbanism: International Research on Placemaking and Urban Sustainability*, 3, 145-160.

The Standard. (2014, March 4). Harare toilets: Every woman's nightmare. Harare: *The Standard.*

UNDP. (2006). *Human development report 2006.* New York: UNDP.

WHO/UNICEF. (2011). *Joint monitoring programme for water supply and sanitation.* New York: WHO.

World Health Organisation. (2007). *The world health report: World development report (WDR) 2003/4.* Workshop Held at Inseam Hall. Oxford 4-5 No 2002

.

Chapter 14

Groundwater Management in Greater Harare, Zimbabwe

Tamirirashe Banhire, Charlotte Muziri and Abraham R. Matamanda

Summary:

This chapter is based on a study that unravels the politics of groundwater management in Greater Harare, Zimbabwe. It is premised on the knowledge that underground water is a finite resource that requires sustainable management. Groundwater replenishment is a complex dynamic dependant on seasonal rainfall. The key players in the politics of groundwater are various stakeholders such as users of groundwater, the public and private suppliers of it, politicians and, most importantly, the various boards that observe, regulate and monitor groundwater use. Data were collected through document review, observation and interviews of stakeholders previously mentioned. The results show the complexity of politics of ground water management which arise from the fact that users, politicians and suppliers are also regulators and overseers on the matter. It is only natural that stakeholders act in their best interests hence the case of the tragedy of the commons which sees a common resource depleted as individuals act out of their own selfish interests and the game theory which sees several players being involved and maximising the situation. Greater Harare plays a big brother role where groundwater allocation to its constituents is concerned, and this has led to allocative inefficiency as reflected by the replacement of the 1976 Water Act (Chapter 20) by the 1998 Water Act (Chapter 20). The 1998 Water Act (Chapter 20) caters for new users. However, Greater Harare holds the power to allocate water to its constituents and water vending has also grown significantly posing threat to an already scarce resource. The key to solving the politics of groundwater management is co-management of the resource.

Introduction

This chapter explores and discusses the politics of groundwater management as a problem requiring the attention of policy makers and stakeholders in underground water resource management. Politics is inherent in groundwater management because the increase of groundwater usage is plagued by a variety of socio-ecological problems (Shah *et al.* 2000). Groundwater has several integral qualities that make it an increasingly exploited resource. Pollution and depletion of it are immensely important issues and well-recognised global problems. Groundwater management is also complex and dynamic particularly because of the manifold players in the matter and the issues on whether groundwater ought to be managed or just exploited (Davis and Hirji, 2014). As such, the politics of groundwater management has to do with the allocation of groundwater in terms of the body in charge, the amounts allocated and, especially, how efficiently. There is a need, therefore, not just for a paradigm shift in the handling of groundwater issues, but also an honest commitment from all stakeholders, including consumers themselves, to uphold groundwater development and management requirements in line with the law (ZINWA, 2015). Although Zimbabwe has a comprehensive institutional and legislative framework regulating the management of water system in the country, it seems there is inadequate attention paid to groundwater resources in the country. It has been highlighted that there are limited efforts towards the management of groundwater resources in the country, yet the use of such resources is increasing across the country (Davis and Hirji, 2014). The framework for allocation of surface water in Zimbabwe is very clear and often discussed. However, a just system of groundwater allocation that is clear to the entire population must also be put in place for the purpose of achieving its allocative efficiency. We therefore raise questions with regards to the politics of underground water, particularly in the urban areas across the country. Is the Zimbabwean nation underpinned by social justice for all, if so, what does the water allocation system reflect? Why has little attention been paid to underground water resources in the country despite their significance in water resources management? The framework for how water resources are managed is good to look at on paper, however, it is clear that it addresses surface water sources almost thoroughly but not groundwater resources. Perhaps groundwater sources often go unmanaged because these supplies can be replenished. However, the alarming increase in groundwater abstracted calls for deliberate groundwater allocation and management.

Background and Overview

While there is much attention for institutional development and more recently water governance, the power factor embedded in politics, is often left out of the equation (Mollinga, 2008; Zeitoun *et al.* 2012). The Greater Harare Metropolitan Area includes five settlements, namely Harare (urban and rural), Chitungwiza, Epworth, Ruwa and Norton. The municipal water required in the greater Harare area is drawn from the Manyame River system. The water is impounded at four main dam sites: Manyame (Darwendale), Chivero, Seke and Harava. Globally, the integrated water resource management (IWRM) and sustainable management are the critical concepts at the forefront of water management policies. Most African countries have adopted IWRM as their principal approach to water resource management (World Water Council, 2006). The concepts have been widely adopted to increase efficiency through participation and to counter Garith Hardin's tragedy of the commons which sees a common resource depleted as people over exploit it.

According to Thematic Paper 6 on groundwater governance, contemporary criteria against which water rules are measured including whether mechanisms created are accountable, transparent and participatory, and whether they deal with water resources in an integrated manner and enable sustainable management of renewable water resources. Zimbabwe also adopted these concepts as the country undertook its water sector reforms. It has been observed that one way of promoting more efficient and sustainable utilisation of water is through stakeholder involvement in water management at the catchment scale (Mugumo and Makurira, 2003). The idea behind this approach is to enhance greater participation at the catchment level, thereby increasing the sense of ownership among users and promoting sustainable and efficient use and environmental protection. Water management was decentralized to stakeholder-managed catchment councils (CCs) and sub-catchment councils (SCCs). However, this perfect framework for water management has not substantiated where allocation of groundwater resources is concerned and disparities in water allocation continue to be noted amongst Greater Harare and its constituents. It is critical to take due cognisance of the dire need to manage groundwater explicitly instead of the implicit attitude that has been adopted as well as acknowledge and deal with the politics embedded in groundwater management as it is a major contributor to the disparities in water allocation.

Theoretical Framework

The complexity in groundwater management arises from the manifold players involved, that is, the users of groundwater, the providers of it and those put in place to manage the resource. Members of the public often find themselves in conflict as they play two opposing roles, that is, as users as well as suppliers or regulators of groundwater use. Groundwater has also been managed implicitly, that is, it has been addressed under the all-encompassing term of water resources. There have been several working papers and reports on the management of water resources in greater Harare as listed by Eberhard (2015). These include: The Institutional Options for Improved Water and Sanitation Services in Greater Harare; Rapid Appraisal of Water and Sewerage Investment Priorities, Sanitation in Greater Harare: Current Situation and Future Directions; and The Greater Harare Water and Sanitation Investment

Plan Volume I (Main Report) and Volume II (Appendices), June 2014. All these working papers and reports point out to one common irresolute issue, that is, groundwater resources have not been explicitly given their individual due cognisance but have generally been addressed under the all-encompassing term of water resources. Groundwater and surface water are treated as part of one hydrological system and this is hindering effective groundwater management. Greater Harare plays a big brother role over its constituents where water allocation is concerned, and this centralisation of power has led to disparities in water supply. There are shortages of water supply in the city and as a result, it is only natural that Greater Harare maintains its own water supply at the expense of its constituents.

It has been observed that settlements such as Chitungwiza, Glendale, Norton and Ruwa do not have their own sources of water supply (Makurira and Tumbare, 2014). The settlements rely on the efficiency of other players to secure their own water. This complicates water supply management because, in the event of water scarcity, they receive less priority in water allocation which, in turn, increases water insecurity among their own consumers. As a country based on the principles of social justice, no one should take precedence when it comes to issues of water supply and therefore the little resources available must be fairly distributed. However, this is clearly not the case. As a result, the surrounding towns have to devise ways to become self-sufficient in the long-run. According to the Greater Harare Water and Sanitation Strategic Plan (2014), the supplies from City of Harare have become increasingly unreliable and are now virtually non-existent. Over the past ten years Ruwa has focused on its project to bring the town's water needs from Nora Dam, some 15.5km southeast of the town. This project was largely completed in 2014. This is a clear reflection of the disparities in water allocation that need to be addressed. Water allocation needs to remain fair as it is based on the notion of equity enclosed in national policy even when the nation is plagued by water scarcity.

Literature Review

The politics of groundwater management in Greater Harare is faced by a variety of challenges in Zimbabwe. Some of these challenges include the absence of effective implementation, mismanagement, poor allocation and mostly political interference (Nhapi, 2009; Musemwa, 2010). Some scholars have also observed the wide range of actors in the water sector in Zimbabwe and the dynamics between the many sector stakeholders. Given that water is a finite and generally scarce resource, it is in no way surprising that various conflicts exist in this sector (Nilsson and Hammer, 1996). The most important conflicts arising from scarcity, use and distribution of water resources are found between the mostly white commercial farmers and the smallholder and emerging black commercial farmers, between communities and government, between and within certain government ministries, particularly where coordination is either inadequate or non-existent. In a sector with so many different players, the division of responsibility for certain aspects of water resources development or management may be unclear or over-lapping, causing tension and conflict between agencies. The most worrying of these conflicts is between and within certain government ministries because distribution of water resources is within their jurisdiction and thus becomes inequitable in the presence of conflict (Muhangi and Mugisha, 2006).

Another major issue is that today's best practice in sustainable water management and integrated water resource management focuses on river basins as the units of management. However, this overlooks two fundamental realities in southern Africa. First, groundwater aquifer systems, while being an integral part of the overall water resource, seldom correspond with the surface water management unit the river basin. Second, in almost all cases, groundwater systems are, by their very nature, trans-boundary (Turton *et al.* 2006). This means that the explicit management of groundwater resources, if it is to increase efficiency, must holistically look at groundwater and surface water because they are under one hydrological system.

About a third (31 percent) of Zimbabweans live in urban areas, and the population is increasing at a rate of about 4% per year (World Bank, 2014). Many towns are unable to provide a reliable and continuous supply of water daily. It has been concluded that water supply challenges in urban areas in Zimbabwe are directly related to the way local authorities are running water services in their respective towns or cities (Makurira and Tumbare, 2014). This is similar to related to inequitable distribution of water in Greater Harare and its metropolis which also significantly reflects the power play and control embedded in water supply problems and politics.

As with surface water, groundwater access can be plagued by various challenges if the water rights are not defined or defined rights are not enforceable. Depending on the rate of recharge, open groundwater access can lead to conflicts among users, the marginalisation of users and to its depletion as a natural resource (Wegerich, 2006). The various stakeholders involved are the reason for the power play that results in grappling over groundwater resources hence the politics of groundwater management. The result is that the use and management of groundwater resources remains a highly contested terrain vulnerable to conflicts emerging from the diverging interests among stakeholders and the abuse by government officials and politicians (Nhapi, 2009; Tsodzo, 2013). Ironically, politicians exist as policy makers but many a time they end up assuming the role of technocrats which ends up compromising the good governance of groundwater resources (Muhangi and Mugisha, 2006).

While there is much attention for institutional development and more recently water governance, the power factor embedded in politics is often left out of the equation (Mollinga, 2008; Zeitoun *et al.* 2012, as cited by Steenbergen, Kumsa and Al-Awlaki, 2015). This risks an undesirable dichotomy of sorts where, on the one hand, much emphasis is given to developing institutions and formulating policies and, on the other, there is not much attention for the often manipulative business of ruling, balancing interests and securing resources, all part of politics, and even more basic issue of implementation (Steenbergen, Kumsa and Al-Awlaki, 2015). The power dynamics emerge as a result of financial muscles or through political powers which enable such individuals to make decisions which may affect the management of the groundwater resources (Mudenda, 2013: 21).

It has been observed that modern water legislation based on administrative water rights and a range of planning and monitoring tools has been introduced worldwide over the last decades (Mechlem, 2016). The legislation offers mechanisms to strike a balance between growing demand and the need to protect and preserve groundwater resources for current and future generations. Preparation and enactment of law takes into account the importance of sustainable management of resources and integrated water resource planning. As groundwater resources are becoming overly used and polluted, environmental concerns play a prominent role in groundwater legislation. The principle of sustainability has emerged as a key cross-cutting principle and cornerstone of modern groundwater legislation. In some instances, legislation determines the overall amount of permitted withdrawals per year. One example is the Edwards Aquifer Authority Act (Texas) which precludes the Edwards Aquifer Authority from authorising withdrawals from the entire aquifer exceeding 572,000 acre-feet (approximately 705,550 cubic meters) of water annually. Likewise, the Namibian Water Resources Management Act (2013) empowers the Namibian Minister of Water Affairs to restrict or limit groundwater abstraction so as to maintain certain standards and level of the quantity and quality of the water.

Numerous issues are raised in the groundwater legislations. Human right to water is increasingly recognized not only at the constitutional level but also in water resources legislation. There is a strong trend to treat groundwater as a public rather than as a private good attached to land rights. Administrative permit-based water rights systems are becoming a norm. They tend to work best in highly formalized water economies and always take into account local conditions, the existence of customary rules, and where applicable, existing administrative capacity. Developing countries with limited administrative capacity and high numbers of small-scale users face implementation challenges (Mechlem, 2016).

In some countries, for example, Australia, Chile and United States of America, users can trade groundwater abstraction permits. However, such exchanges are subject to some form of prior involvement of the water administration to protect both private and public interests and to mitigate negative impacts of such trades. Other countries, especially in South Asia, have informal water trading schemes. Worldwide there is no clear trend on the sensitive issue of trading water permits (Mechlem, 2016)

Zimbabwe also has its own legislative action and legal frameworks concerning water resources. The Ministry of Environment, Water and Climate is responsible for the Water Act and for the allocation of water rights through the water courts (Makurira and Vhiriri, 2017). Its mandate includes the development of underground water resources, and medium and large size dams. The overall objective of the programme is the sustainable, equitable and economically feasible use of water resources, taking into account shared waters. The Ministry of Environment, Water and Climate programme has two components, namely the institutional development and legal framework and the water resources management strategy project. Water management in Zimbabwe is currently governed by the Water Act (Chapter 20:24) of 1998. The Water Act is complemented by other Acts and policies. Before 1998, the Water Act of 1976 was in use to govern water use and development. Weaknesses in the Water Act of 1976 led to major water sector reforms. The Zimbabwe National Water Authority (ZINWA) operates under The Ministry of Environment, Water and Climate and precedes and provides technical support to catchment councils as well as sub-catchment councils.

Allocation of groundwater is a complex phenomenon because groundwater is difficult to account for in terms of amount, and the distribution of the resources is not uniform. Groundwater has remained a poorly understood and managed resource (Davis and Hirji, 2014). Groundwater is a common pool resource, and this makes it difficult to come up with effective government regimes towards its allocation and management. The complexity of groundwater resources is based on the fact that it is very difficult to establish its size and carrying capacity, the measurability of the resource, the temporal and spatial availability of resource flows, the amount of storage in the system, whether resources move (like surface water, wildlife, and most fish) or are stationary (like trees and medicinal plants), how fast resources regenerate, and how various harvesting technologies affect patterns of regeneration (Arai, 2010).

McPhee, Yeh and William (2004) argue that sustainability lacks a concise, agreed-upon definition. In most circumstances, sustainable development involves taking care of the needs of the present without compromising the ability of future generations to meet their own needs (WECD, 1987). Although there is great uncertainty about what future generations would want us to do for them, identifying the tradeoffs among current priorities and our guesses about future generations' priorities is an important component of any study involving sustainability.

Around the world, people are discovering the truth of Benjamin Franklin's dictum: "You don't value water till the well runs dry." In the most arid countries water is generally recognized for the precious resource it is and even though inefficient agricultural use of groundwater can be widespread (Foster *et al.* 2000). Hydro-geologists from China to Nigeria and from India to Mexico are realising that recognizing the problem and acting to correct it does not necessarily go hand in hand. Inaction, it seems, is generally a consequence of conflicting stakeholder claims, wrong-headed political decisions, and powerful interest groups. Unless governments in the developing world (and the international institutions that support them) can mobilize principal stakeholders, groundwater use will not be put back on a sustainable path.

Water use directly affects economic development because water utilisation impacts all the major national economic sectors. A sustainable water use resource management must stretch several decades into the future to assure the availability of adequate supplies of water to future generations without compromising the ability of the current generation to reasonable rates of economic development. In Botswana, for example, a series of cultural traditions and political constraints, coupled with bureaucratic managerial weaknesses, serve to maintain a system of water allocation that is unsustainable in the long-run and inefficient in the short term as well. Sustainability is thus present in Botswana's water policy though mostly in rhetoric only.

Shah *et al.* (2000) proposed that gearing up for resource management entails information systems and resource planning to find out groundwater availability, quality, withdrawal and other variables which enables allocation of the resource. It is impossible for a nation to begin to allocate groundwater resources equitably when the quantity and quality is unknown. An effective system for regulating the withdrawals should also be put in place. Past and upcoming work in IWRMI which advocates for sustainable management suggests that, like surface water, groundwater resources too need to be planned and managed for maximum basin-level for efficiency. It has been argued that sustainable management is critical to development (Muswe, 2016). This is the most important and yet the least thought about and understood, let al.one experimented with development.

Methodology

The study adopts a qualitative research approach where data were collected through observation of accounted for and unaccounted for groundwater use and interviews of the stakeholders. Unstructured interviews were also conducted with specific key informants which include officials from ZINWA, City of Harare and selected experts in water resources management. In doing so, it reviews the allocation and management of groundwater in Greater Harare as well as efforts to reform Zimbabwe's water supply and management. It then analyses the relevant legal frameworks and compliance issues propounded by various proponents. This is followed by secondary research by many authors who have written on various topics surrounding groundwater management.

Results

There are about 2.1 million people in Greater Harare (City of Harare and the four surrounding towns Chitungwiza, Epworth, Ruwa and Norton) (ZimStats, 2013). Following the economic problems in 2008 and early 2009, water and sanitation service delivery collapsed as a result of chronic power shortages, an inability to procure essential inputs such as chemicals to treat water, and significant disruptions in the pumping and treatment of water and wastewater. The increasing population continues to take a toll on the water supply services which prove to be unreliable and unable to cater for the populations of Greater Harare and its constituents and this has proved to be the core of water allocation and sustainable management problems. This has resulted in extensive groundwater Abstraction that is not on record for the purpose of monitoring. Households across Greater Harare continue to set up unregistered boreholes risking over Abstraction of groundwater yet no deliberate action to control the situation has been effective or fair (Davis and Hirji, 2014).

Illegal boreholes continue to increase and disparities in water allocation continue to be noted (Chirisa *et al.* 2014). The discovery was that most of the households with private boreholes hired private contractors to do the drilling hence why these boreholes are not officially accounted for (Mudenda, 2013: 47). ZINWA is the officially authority that is permitted to drill boreholes, yet private contractors are drilling boreholes across Harare which is illegal action requiring law enforcement.

Sustainable management has also been constantly laid out and discussed as an epitomic concern in water management in Zimbabwe (Nhapi, 2009). However, it has been a theoretical point of discussion that has been thoroughly analysed yet its implementation has not been significantly substantiated. The major issue that plagues sustainable water resource management is that the amount of groundwater available is not known and is not deliberately monitored. The question is: How can a nation sustainably manage and allocate a resource whose amount is unknown? This information gap is a hindrance to sustainable groundwater management in Greater Harare.

The results show that there is no information on current levels of groundwater as well as usage of groundwater; neither is there much accountability for groundwater resources as there is for surface water. This complicates groundwater resource allocation and management. The response which prevailed was that of corruption in water resource management. This goes against the legislative actions which led to the decentralisation of water resource management. Decentralisation was meant to curb corruption, yet this is not what has transpired (Mudenda, 2013). Corruption continues to distort groundwater management. The results are also a replica of the comment below by an official from ZINWA:

> The present system which sees water allocation and management of the resource decentralised to catchment councils and sub-catchment councils in Zimbabwe was not effective because the decentralisation was constrained by the political factor hence only selected responsibilities were passed down but authority and control remained with the original governing body.

A local user of groundwater commented that,

> Obviously, the present water allocation system is unable to provide a fair distribution of water in the present as well as future situations. The need for reallocation building on equity among all people is certain.

The study shows clearly that there is no improvement in the allocation of groundwater as Greater Harare continues to have more allocative power and precedence over its constituents regardless of the decentralisation of water resource management. It seems that equity among all people remains a dream.

A ZINWA employee who is a user of groundwater and a monitor of it commented that,

> Decentralisation of groundwater management has done nothing to curb corruption as is suggested by the notion of decentralisation. In fact, it has just worsened the groundwater Abstraction rate with all the bodies involved gaining from misusing groundwater unlike if one centralised body remained. Then at least corruption could have been contained and cut at the source.

The comment above is also supported by Negri (1989), as cited by Sarwa *et al.* (2010), who stated that another complication in the management of groundwater was that no single body was responsible for controlling the entire resource. In the absence of a single authority, it becomes difficult to implement policies that attempt to manage the resource in a long-term sustainable way.

The highlight of the results was the interaction between politics and groundwater governance and management. The political domain is the key to equitable groundwater allocation and management as discovered from the responses of the interviewees.

According to the ZINWA employee:

> Equity in groundwater allocation is not a major concern to leadership because it does not hold much political influence which tends to be the highlight of decision-making with politicians investing in only the things that expand their political influence.

Whether water issues are being given enough priority during budget preparations is another questionable issue. However, ZINWA has taken some commendable action towards management and control. Ten companies were penalised for various offences related to trade in bulk water in a joint operation between the ZINWA Groundwater Department and the Zimbabwe Republic Police from November 2 to November 11, 2015. The apprehension and penalisation of the companies was done in terms of Statutory Instrument 90 of 2013 (ZINWA, 2015).

It is clear that societal conflict and power struggles are inevitable. However, their inevitability does not erode the ability of a nation to rightfully deal with these factors. As governing bodies continue to play their part there is need also to reach compromises or resolution and reorientation of groundwater allocation and management can be given its due cognisance and actually realised.

More people in urban areas are increasingly relying on boreholes for their water needs. They have been forced to intensify efforts to monitor groundwater use with a view to ensure strict adherence to groundwater permit regulations as encapsulated in the Statutory Instrument 206 of 2001. The failure to meet increasing water demand in urban areas due to expanding urban population and increased industrial activity has led to the over Abstraction of groundwater. Groundwater resources now require assessment, planning, development and management to protect them from over-Abstraction which can lead to depletion of groundwater but mostly to come up with a feasible and fair allocation system. Over Abstraction of groundwater is an issue that is clearly examined yet the extent of this is unknown hence this knowledge gap creates a challenge.

Zimbabwean citizens clearly continue to undermine legislation partly because they do not face any retribution for breaking the law when it comes to environmental matters which seem to go unaccounted for. Due to increasing water shortage and the growing reliance of urban communities on borehole water, minimum groundwater development and utilisation standards have often been disregarded and, sadly, this has seen a prompt decline in the water table with boreholes in some suburbs drying (ZINWA 2015). Successful implementation of groundwater legislation depends on a number of factors including: the administrative set-up and the level of training of water administrators, a clear understanding of the institutional roles and functions at all relevant levels, an adequate level of public awareness and acceptance of legal provisions, political willingness to promote and attain sustainable groundwater management (Marcella *et al.* 2004).

The framework for a perfect water management system in Zimbabwe exists though the situation on the ground does not reflect this common belief (Makurira and Mugumo, 2003). The reform process has not taken off as expected owing to a combination of factors ranging from conflicting policies and weak institutional linkages, to insufficient funding. According to ZINWA, just as surface water usage and surface water storage for secondary purposes requires one to have a permit; it is also mandatory that, except for primary purposes, one must get in touch with relevant authorities and acquire a permit before tampering with groundwater. However, certainly not all consumers are registered; those registered are not paying levies (Makurira and Vhiriri, 2017).

Discussion

As put across in this chapter, various stakeholders have observed that politics is inherent in groundwater management and is a key contributor to the failure to efficiently allocate and sustainably manage groundwater resources. This has been the case in South Africa, Botswana and Zimbabwe. Knüppe (2011) postulates that South Africa's groundwater governance regime does not currently provide the capacity to assure effective and sustainable resource regulation and allocation. To date, the management of groundwater is hampered by a variety of uncertainties such as global climate change and socio-economic growth, as well as ineffective governance structures affecting resource use, regulation, protection and the implementation of alternative strategies needed to achieve sustainable management. Knüppe (2011) identified four key challenges to the development of adaptive and sustainable groundwater management and the successful implementation of current water legislation in South Africa. These include the undervaluation of groundwater importance and significance, the need for expertise and information at all scales, the centralisation of power and the disregard of ecosystems and the associated goods and services. There is need to promote equitable access to water for all citizens in Greater Harare because the right to water is guaranteed by these nation's constitutions which carry the sustainable development goal six which is, to ensure access to water and sanitation for all at all stages. According to The Global Framework for Action, to achieve the vision on groundwater governance, the effectiveness of groundwater governance will reflect the soundness of overall governance in a country and the level of engagement of political leadership as good groundwater governance requires both overall good governance and farsighted political commitment. Whatever directions groundwater governance takes, it is not isolated from the overall system of governance in a country and the political system that prevails.

Conclusion, Policy Options and Recommendations

In the mid-nineties, Zimbabwe formed participatory institutions known as catchment and sub-catchment councils based on river basins to govern and manage its waters. The city of Harare falls under the jurisdiction of the Upper Manyame Catchment. Derman and Manzungu (2016) submit that, in keeping with viewing IWRM as an apolitical or non-political activity, most participants in the water reform process rely on the best practices of water management to keep 'politics' out of water. However, external national political processes enable continued elite control while simultaneously limiting water reform. Despite significant efforts to alter the waterscape, fast track land reform which began in 2000 led to the undermining of the first phases of IWRM and water reform. The economic foundations for funding the new participatory institutions were lost through various corridors like the political crises that characterised the period from 2000 to 2010 (Derman and Manzungu, 2016). This helps in explaining why IWRM has struggled in Zimbabwe and particularly why Greater Harare and its constituents have not been able to equitably allocate groundwater resources under the jurisdiction of the Upper Manyame Catchment.

The fundamental problem with common property resources such as groundwater is that an individual's use of these resources is often associated with a "use it or lose it" leading to overuse. This is what results in the fundamental importance of managing the resource, monitoring its use and allocating it equitably. Greater Harare's water allocation system is challenged by inequitable groundwater allocation and management particularly due to the politics of groundwater, that is, the power play factor.

The indication of this chapter is perfectly summarised by the previously cited words of Steenbergen, Kumsa and Al-Awlaki (2015) who assert that, while there is much attention for institutional development and more recently water governance, the power factor embedded in politics is often left out of the equation (Mollinga, 2008; Zeitoun *et al.* 2012 as cited by Steenbergen, Kumsa and Al-Awlaki, 2015). This risks an undesirable dichotomy of sorts where, on the one hand, much emphasis is given to developing institutions and formulating policies and, on the other, there is not much attention for the often manipulative business of ruling, balancing interests and securing resources, all part of politics and even more basic, implementation.

The economic and humanitarian crisis in 2008 that included widespread cholera outbreaks prompted the Zimbabwean government and donors to begin dialogue on the modalities of financing relief and remedial efforts. The City of Harare requested the World Bank to support the development of a water supply and sanitation strategic plan for Greater Harare - the metropolitan area that includes Harare, Chitungwiza and the satellite towns of Epworth, Ruwa, and Norton. The purpose of the strategic plan was to assess the infrastructure requirements for the Greater Harare area as a single water and wastewater infrastructure system that could be managed as one entity (World Bank, 2014).

Groundwater has often been unaccounted for and used without consent or deliberate planning, however, the importance of the resource has been clearly noted by the increase in the users of groundwater and the conflict surrounding its allocation. Moench (2002) postulated that, initially, groundwater utilisation has often been perceived as a purely technical matter, but it also poses social and institutional questions such that researchers discussing groundwater in the developing world speak of its 'potential for social instability'. Clearly, what is needed most, but understood least, is competent groundwater resource management (Foster *et al.* 2000).

In the presence of policy frameworks and various legislative pieces, Zimbabwe has failed to sustainably manage water resources and equitably distribute these resources due to the lack of implementation skills. Nevertheless, the hope that nations can achieve social equity and sustainability in line with groundwater remains. Shah *et al.* (2000) postulates that, the water vision of a world that future generations will inherit will have to be the one in which groundwater plays its full developmental, productive and environmental role but in a sustainable manner; and the framework of action to realise this vision will mean eschewing the current free-for-all in groundwater appropriation and use, and promoting a more responsible management of this precious resource that is easy to deplete or ruin through depletion, salinisation and pollution. Most importantly, groundwater allocation will mirror social equity as embedded in the Zimbabwean nation's values and policies.

There is a clear line between what must be done in terms of suggestions, policies and legal frameworks and what is actually done on the ground. What should be in the end is not turned into reality. A nation's policy must be applicable and viable and must be carried to term. There are many policies and legislative frameworks regarding management of groundwater resources in Zimbabwe. However, Mechlem (2016) proposed that, in developing countries with limited administrative capacity and high numbers of small-scale users they face implementation challenges. The theory behind the Water Act (1998) for instance is commendable, however, when transformed to reality on the ground, the practice is not always so successful (Makurira and Mugumo 2003). These challenges need to be addressed to come up with a clear and equitable groundwater management and allocation system. There are also many policy options which can be adopted by Greater Harare and Zimbabwe at large. These policy options have been adopted by other countries or proposed in literature and can be modified to suit the Zimbabwean situation.

Zimbabwe's legislation needs to take on a participatory approach to groundwater management allocation after filling the knowledge gap addressed in the paragraph above. Makurira and Mugumo (2003) suggest that political influence should always be kept at minimum levels and that stakeholders will have different agendas, and it will take time for them to sit down to develop a management plan openly and honestly. The gravity of the groundwater situation demands the time and resources and it must be granted this, to secure the country's future. What is needed is an integrated approach to planning groundwater supply that marries stakeholder participation with technical expertise, together with a broad vision of present and future welfare. That approach implies community involvement in design, implementation, maintenance, and financing of projects, as well as reconciliation of communities' wishes with their willingness to pay for water at a rate that reflects full operating and capital costs.

Solving common pool resource problems involves two distinct elements: restricting access and creating incentives (usually by assigning individual rights to, or shares of, the resource) for users to invest in the resource instead of overexploiting it. Both changes are also needed in Zimbabwe. In some cases, the diagnostics may reveal that the general conditions and governance system are already in place, but in most cases, there are likely to be at best some gaps or need for improvement. Measures to improve the setup need to be tailored to the local context and their implementation planned as a coherent package.

References

Arai, K. (2010). Integration of groundwater management into transboundary basin, *Groundwater Management* 3(28) 59-83.

Braune, E. and Xu, Y. (2009). *Africa groundwater management issues in southern AFRICA: An IWRM perspective*. Department of Earth Sciences, University of the Western Cape, South Africa.

Chirisa, I., Matamanda, A. and Bandauko, E. (2014). Ruralised urban areas vis-à-vis urbanised rural areas in Zimbabwe: Implications for spatial planning. *Regional Development Dialogue, 35,* 65-80.

Derman, B. and Manzungu, E. (2016). The complex politics of water and power in Zimbabwe: IWRM in the Catchment Councils of Manyame, Mazowe and Sanyati (1993-2001). *Water Alternatives, 9*(3), 513-530.

Eberhard, R. (2015). Greater Harare Water and Sanitation Strategy: Summary note. In M. Tananni, S. Foster, H. Dumars, H. Garduño, K. Kemper and A. Tuinhof (Eds.), Groundwater legislation and regulatory provision from customary rules to integrated catchment planning. City: GW MATE Core Group.

Foster, S., Chilton, J., Moench, M., Cardy, F. and Schiffler, M. (2000). *Facing the challenges of supply and resource sustainability*. Washington DC: World Bank.

Groundwater Governance. (2016). Global Framework for Action to achieve the vision on groundwater governance. Rome: Food Agriculture Organization.

Knüppe, K. (2011). The challenges facing sustainable and adaptive groundwater management in South Africa. *Water SA, 37*(1), 67-80.

Makurira, H. and Mugumo, M. (2003). *Water sector reforms in Zimbabwe: The importance of policy and institutional coordination on implementation*. In Proceedings of the African Regional Workshop on Watershed Management, Chapter 14, ed. B. Swallow, N. Okomo, M. Achouri, and L. Tennyson, 167–174. Rome: Food and Agriculture Organization of the United Nations.

Makurira, H. and Tumbare, M.J. (2014). Water insecurity in Zimbabwe's towns and cities: Challenge for institutions. City: Publisher.

Makurira, H. and Vhiriri, N. (2017). Project country report. Water permit systems, policy reforms and implications for equity in Zimbabwe

McPhee, Y.J. and William, W. (2004). Multi-objective optimization for sustainable groundwater management in semiarid regions. *Journal of Water Resources Planning and Management-ASCE, 130*(6), 0733-9496

Mechlem, K. (2016). Groundwater governance: The role of legal frameworks at the local and national level—established practice and emerging trends. *Water, 8*(8), 347.

Moench, M. (2002). Water and the potential for social instability: Livelihoods, migration and the building of society. *Natural Resources Forum, 26,* 195–204.

Mudenda, M. (2013). Decentralization, private bulk water companies and urban domestic water supply: The case of Harare City (Unpublished master's thesis). Social Ecology, University of Zimbabwe.

Muhangi, D. and Mugisha, P.A. (2006). Local government capacity in the context of new management arrangements for water supply systems in small towns: Case from two councils in Uganda. Harare: Sable Press (Pvt) Ltd.

Muswe, V. (2016, April, 19). Sustainable water management critical to development. *The Zimbabwean*, 7.

Nhapi, I. (2009). The water situation in Harare, Zimbabwe: A policy and management problem. *Journal of Water Policy, 11*, 221-235.

Nilsson, A. and Hammer, A. (1996). Study of water resources in Zimbabwe. Available online:
https://www.sida.se/contentassets/266b0af39f644f9a97f0c52f75717711/study-of-water-resources-in-zimbabwe_1270.pdf

Rahm, D., Swatuk, L., and Matheny, E. (2006). Water resource management in Botswana: Balancing sustainability and economic development. *Environment, Development and Sustainability*, 8(1), 157-183.

Sarwar, Q., McCornick, P.G. Sarwar, A. and Bharat, R. (2010). Challenges and prospects of sustainable groundwater management in the Indus Basin, Pakistan. Water for Food Faculty Publications, 12. Available online: http://digitalcommons.unl.edu/wffdocs/12.

Shah, T., Molden, D., Sakthivadivel, R. and Seckler, D. (2000). The global groundwater situation: Overview of opportunities and challenges. Colombo, Sri Lanka: International Water Management Institute.

Tsodzo, C.C. (2013). Water service provision challenges in urban areas of Zimbabwe-Who is to blame? A case study of Harare and Chitungwiza (Unpublished dissertation). University of Zimbabwe. Harare.

Turton, A., Patrick, M., Cobbing, J. and Julien, F. (2006). The challenges of groundwater in Southern Africa. Available online:
www.wilsoncenter.org/water.

Van Steenbergen, F., Kumsa, A. and Al-Awlaki, N. (2015). Understanding political will in groundwater management: Comparing Yemen and Ethiopia. *Water Alternatives* 8(1), 774-799.

WCED (World Commission on Environment and Development). (1987). *Our common future,* World Commission on Environment and Development (the Brundtland Commission). Oxford University Press, Oxford.

Wegerich, K. (2006). Groundwater institutions and management problems in the developing world. In J.H. Tellam, M.O. Rivett, R.G. Israfilov and L.G. Herringshaw (Eds.), Urban groundwater management and sustainability. NATO Science Series (IV: Earth and Environmental Sciences) (Vol. 74). Dordrecht: Springer.

World Bank. (2014). *Main report.* Washington, D.C: World Bank Group. Available online:

http://documents.worldbank.org/curated/en/982261468196754920/Main-report

World Water Council. (2006). Water resources development in Africa. Africa Regional Document. 4th World Water Forum, 16-22 March 2006, Mexico City, Mexico

Zeitoun, M., Allan, T., Al Aulaqi, N., Jabarin, A., and Laamrani, H. (2012). Water demand management in Yemen and Jordan: addressing power and interests. *The Geographical Journal, 178*(1), 54-66. ZimStats. (2013). *Census 2012: Provincial Report Harare.* ZimStat, Harare

ZINWA. (2015). Alleviating water shortage using groundwater. Available online: http://www.zinwa.co.zw. Accessed 19/10/2017 at 1403.

Chapter 15

Smallholder Farmers' Adaptive Capacity to Climate Change and Variability in Zimbabwe

Hedwig Muronzi and Liaison Mukarwi

Summary:

The presence of negatively intervening factors in any environment can work both as a stimulator or barrier for the capacity of one to 'absorb' change and make it bring dividends to ensure a sustainable path of development. Literature seems to point to adaptation of farmers to climate change and variability. Climate change has been experienced in many parts of the world and has induced serious famines and eroded the livelihood capability of most households. However, almost absent in the same literature is a nuanced discussion of the dimensions, methods and measurement of the adaptive capacity of those smallholder farmers. This is a technical subject that requires a holistic 'model' that encompasses understanding the environment, the persona, the expected outcomes and the ability of the communities to 'do-it-themselves' to ensure sustainability rather than always relying on 'outside' interventions. Using primary and secondary data, this chapter seeks to proffer the pedagogics (and andragogics) of how smallholder farmers in Zimbabwe can adapt to the effects of climate change and variability. The data sought were analysed using thematic or content analysis.

Introduction

Many parts of southern and eastern Africa are currently experiencing rapid climatic variability. The pattern of climate variability includes episodic heat and cold coupled with some intense rains which, in most cases, induce flooding or its reverse. Globally, the issue of climate change has been discussed at length including at the 2012 Copenhagen Conference and Summit and the 2015 Paris Conference. The whole world agreed to reduce the global temperature by 2 degrees celsius with industrialised nations pledging to implement mitigation measures and the less industrialised regions like Africa engaging in adaptation measures. Why to the need for adaptation by developing countries? This is because, even though they are not the major instigators of the global warming and its impacts, they are on the receiving end and must therefore adapt to protect themselves from the harsh effects and consequences of climate change and the variable natural phenomena.

The worst affected communities are those that depend on primary and extractive industries that directly rely on natural resources for livelihood and these include farmers, fishers and foresters, among others. The major question is that of strategies to expand and enhance the affected communities' adaptive capacity to apprehend climate change and turn the fortunes out of the potential vagaries experienced due to climate change. Developing and enhancing one's capacity to adapt to a situation is not a simplistic task. It rather takes one's knowledge and skills in understanding the complexity of the matter being dealt with, willingness of the affected to cooperate, the availability of training institutions and extension, knowledge of the operating environment including the natural and institutional environment and the leadership, among others. For smallholder farmers, it is a matter of ensuring that the stated factors are in place and that they must also be ready to change their usual practices and engage new skills, technologies and even having a collective approach in learning through practice. In reality, achieving this is often easier said than done because they are numerous negatively intervening factors.

This chapter seeks to proffer the pedagogics (and andragogics) of how smallholder farmers in Zimbabwe can enhance their capacities to adapt. The aim of the study is to investigate the level of knowledge, perceptions and practices of smallholder farmers in Zimbabwe in the face of changing climatic conditions in their areas. In addition, the study aims to enhance the capacity of smallholder farmers to adapt to the changing climatic conditions and their strategies and everyday operations in their economic livelihoods. The objectives include to identify and classify the dimensions to adaptive capacity of smallholder farmers to climate change effects, to establish if the smallholder farmers have the capacity to adapt to the effects of climate change, to assess factors constraining the adaptive capacity of smallholder farmers in dealing with the effects of climate change and variability on their livelihoods, and to offer possible measures that can be used to boost the adaptive capacity of smallholder farmers to climate change and variability. The motivation for this study arose from that fact climate change is already negatively affecting smallholder farmers and there seems to be extrinsic rather than intrinsic interventions which seem not to be working. The interventions are not working because the smallholder farmers have not been coached towards contributing their own knowledge inputs to bring out meaningful results.

Definition of Key Terms

Smallholder farmers – means marginal and sub-marginal farm households that own or/and cultivate less than 2.0 hectare of land.

Climate change – refers to a change of climate that is attributed directly or indirectly to human activity that alters the composition of the global atmosphere and that is in addition to natural climate variability observed over comparable time periods (United Nations Framework Convention on Climate Change).

Community is a social unit (group of people) with diverse characteristics who are linked by social ties, share common perspectives such as norms, values, and identity, often engage in joint action in geographical locations or settings.

Adaptation refers to adjustments in ecological, social, or economic systems in response to actual or expected climatic stimuli and their effects or impacts; changes in processes, practices, and structures to moderate potential damages or to benefit from opportunities associated with climate change.

Adaptive capacity is the potential or ability of a system, region, or community to adapt to the effects or impacts of climate change; practical means of coping with changes and uncertainties in climate, including variability and extremes.

Livelihood comprises the capabilities, assets (including both material and social resources) and activities required for a means of living.

Conceptual Framework

Climate change is one of the main challenges faced by mankind in this century (Simoes *et al.* 2010; Speranza *et al.* 2014; Mubaya *et al.* 2012). Although developing countries have little historical responsibility for climate change, they are the most affected because of resource constraints to cope with or to adapt to its effects (Speranza *et al.* 2014). Adaption means adjustments in ecological, social, or economic systems in response to actual or expected climatic stimuli and their effects or impacts (Simoes *et al.* 2010). The activities include changing processes, practices and structures to moderate potential damages or to benefit from opportunities associated with climate change (*ibid.*). Adaptation to climate change has the potential to substantially reduce many of the adverse impacts of the same and enhance sustainable livelihoods. Adaptation is done to reduce vulnerability.

Climate change is ongoing and further significant impacts are now inevitable (Simoes *et al.* 2010; Speranza *et al.* 2014). The increase in losses due to climate change and variability indicate that autonomous adaptation has not been sufficient to offset damages associated with variations in climatic conditions (Simoes *et al.* 2010). Although climate change may affect agricultural sectors of different countries in different ways, what is clear is that these changes are causing substantial welfare losses, especially for smallholder farmers whose main source of livelihood derives from agriculture. Figure 15.1 shows the conceptual framework of this study. Figure 15.1 shows that, in responding to climate change, it is either mitigation or adaptation as it has come to the attention of many that the phenomenon cannot be reversed. In this study, the main focus is on adaptation of smallholder farmers to climate change and variability. Just like mitigation, adaptation seeks to reduce vulnerability of the community from the ravages of climate change which include droughts and high temperatures. These negatively affect conventional rain-fed crop and animal production, lead to water shortages for domestic use and livestock drinking, and occurrence of diseases, especially malnutrition. For effective adaptation, however, it depends on the adaptive capacity of the smallholder farmers at the local level and of the government at the national level. The determinants of the adaptive capacity include economic resources, technology, information and skills, social infrastructure and institutions devoted for the cause. It is also observed that people's perceptions also determine the success and strategies of adaptation hence is a determinant of the farmers' climate adaptive capacity. The willingness of the smallholder farmers to acknowledge and take climate change as a threat to livelihoods determines their responses hence the need to be taken into consideration when enhancing the adaptive capacity of the same. The adequacy of the adaptive capacity of the smallholder farmers is the road to successful adaptation to climate change which leads to climate change resilience and reduction of vulnerability.

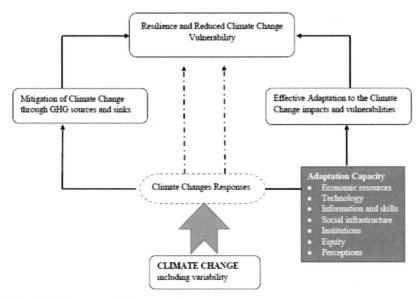

Fig 15.1: Conceptual Framework

Source: Authors' Creation (2017)

Theoretical Framework

The study draws reference from a capacity development model which is the "deficit model" to support the importance of capacity development to reduce climate change vulnerability. Enhancing the capacity in development is a noble process through which individuals, organizations and societies obtain, strengthen and maintain the capabilities to adapt from climate change. It also gives reference to the sustainable livelihoods framework to explain the smallholder adaptive capacity wherein the assets in this framework represent or influence the adaptive capacity.

The Deficit Model

The deficit model assumes that the problems facing communities are due, in large part, to their own lack of skills or abilities or capacity (Beazley *et al.* 2004). It is very much based on a social pathology understanding of communities and implies that they lack the necessary qualities and ingredients to propel sustainable development (*ibid.*). The focus and responsibility of change rests on the shoulders of the communities; it is their duty to become better informed and therefore engage more effectively in civic life. The focus of attention is that the capacity of the community needs to be enhanced in order for them to participate more effectively in existing structures (Tacoli, 2009; Beazley *et al.* 2004). It is not about changing the existing structures to be more sensitive and responsive to the needs of communities; it is about making communities fit the demands and needs of the structures. However, this model is top-down, paternalistic and deflects attention away from the need to change the existing institutional and economic structures (Beazley *et al.* 2004). For those in power, this model of capacity building is useful as it poses no threat. It is a view that serves and supports the status quo. It is a one-way street that places little pressure on existing institutions to review how they act and engage with communities.

In light of this model, adaptation can be achieved through the smallholder farmers themselves taking adaptive actions or by governments implementing policies aimed at promoting appropriate and effective adaptation measures (Laube *et al.* 2011). The model stresses the importance of capacity in community development with which, in such a view, its lack leads to community problems like food shortage, water shortages and poverty, among others. Enhancing their capacity in terms of knowledge, expertise, technology and information and financial resources would empower them to effectively respond to climate change and variability (Ziervogel and Calder 2003; Speranza *et al.* 2014; Scoones, 2009). Applying this to Zimbabwe, the theory holds water due to the presence of the above-mentioned problems which indicate a capacity deficiency in responding to climate change. Efforts underway are not effectively handling the effects of climate change (Mubaya *et al.* 2012). In gauging capacity, it is also important to know whether farmers respond to their perceptions of events. If they do, and if they recognize that climate change is occurring, then the state would simply need to help them overcome the constraints they face in implementing appropriate adaptation methods (*ibid.*).

Dimensions to Adaptive Capacity of Smallholder Farmers to Climate Change Effects

Adaptive capacity influence both vulnerability and resilience while others are more akin to the ability of systems to respond to specific hazards/vulnerabilities. Resilience and vulnerability refer to different but overlapping parts of system's ability to recover from both biophysical and social disturbances as a result of climate change. According to Sharma and Patwardhan (2008), as cited in Lemos *et al.* (2011), there are two dimensions to adaptive capacity, namely generic and specific. Generic adaptive capacity is defined as those assets and entitlements (endowments) that build the ability of different systems to cope and respond with a range of stressors. The generic adaptive capacity includes social, economic, institutional and financial capital that build the abilities of the smallholder farmers to respond to climate change. In this view, poor households are usually vulnerable to a number of overlapping and interdependent disturbances that shape their overall vulnerability. Lemos *et al.*

(2011:9) point out that poverty, lack of access to health and education, lack of political power, lack of financial and technical resources exacerbate vulnerability and the generic adaptation capacity.

Specific adaptive capacity refers to the conditions that prepare systems to cope and recover from a climate related events such as drought, floods, heat waves, hurricanes, tornadoes, and cyclones (*ibid.*). In practice, it refers to the range of risk management mechanism put in place by government or the small holder famers to decrease vulnerability (exposure and sensitivity) to climate change (Simoesa *et al.* 2010). Examples of specific adaptive capacity are emergency response plans, warning systems, design and construction of protective infrastructure and public works for example walls, dams or reservoirs (*ibid.*). One of the activities to enhance specific adaptive capacity include promotion of anti-poverty programmes, especially those that couple with education programmes. This positively influence the ability of smallholder farmers to take advantage of risk management mechanism, for example, use of social programmes and insurance and identification of effective drought response (Lemos *et al.* 2011). Rather than preparing for the expected climate change impact, as in the generic adaptive capacity, specific adaptive capacity entails coping. Most households cope with the shock in climate change by reducing expenditures, selling assets and borrowing so as to sustain lives in such times. Government usually provides immediate post-disaster relief programmes. For example, through Zero Hunger or Family Fund, the government of Brazil provided households with fungible cash resources and long-term access to education and health during the 2008 drought in northeast Brazil (Simoesa *et al.* 2010). These programmes fundamentally changed the relationship between exposure and sensitivity to drought and improving the ability of households to use monthly cash allowances for short-terms survival engendering long-term resilience through better health and educational access.

Smallholder farmers climate change adaptation strategies in developing countries

Adaptive capacity has the potential or ability of a system, region, or community to adapt to the effects or impacts of climate change, and manifests into practical means of coping with changes and uncertainties in climate, including variability and extremes (Speranza *et al.* 2014; Ziervogel and Calder, 2003; Herrmann and Hutchinson, 2005). Even though several factors have been put forward to explain the presence or absence of adaptation to climate change, the extent and efficacy of such adaptation vary from place to place. The strategies include changing crop varieties, irrigation, mixed farming, green revolution (ICTs and Technology), and livelihood diversification. Changing crop variety involves switching from one crop variety to another in response to climatic stresses and changes. This is demonstrated in adoption of climate-resilient crop varieties that are able to withstand a single or a range of climate stresses (Mubaya *et al.* 2012). In this scenario, as climate changes, less well-performing species in farmland are replaced by other crops that are better-suited to new conditions. For example, to increase productivity, smallholder farmers in Ghana are changing to crop varieties which are drought and insect/pest resistant. The reduction of planting time that comes along with the shift of the rainy season has led to the growing of short season varieties; types of cereals that have a long growth period are substituted by other types that mature faster (Alinovi, 2010; Descheemaeker, 2009).

The variability of rain and high evapotranspiration as a result of climate change has negatively affected natural rain-fed crop or animal production; negatively affecting the livelihoods of the smallholder farmers. In this view, most nations are going for irrigation systems. The expansion of irrigated agriculture came partly as the result of governmental efforts to enhance local agricultural production but is now becoming a farmer-driven development with many smallholder farmers having started the production of crops using water from perennial rivers and shallow groundwater aquifers (Speranza *et al.* 2014; Laube *et al.* 2011). This allows production of crops even in periods of prolonged droughts or during winter. However, this strategy is limited to an extent due to lack of irrigation facilities and limited knowledge of improving the same. Recent efforts in this regard include the construction of dams and reservoirs, education and extension services and provision of irrigation equipment.

Mixed farming is whereby the smallholder farmers grow crops and rear livestock at the same time. In order to reduce risk in agricultural production, the farmers now plant and intercrop different crop types across different growth periods and with diverse moisture requirements. They also cultivate farms in different locations (compound farm, family farm, bush farm) with different soil types to increase the chance that at least some crops will survive under extreme weather conditions (Laube *et al.* 2011). In addition, farmers in Africa also increasingly integrate crop growing with livestock husbandry, that is, the rearing of cattle, goats, sheep, donkeys, pigs and different varieties of fowl as it provides manure and animal traction (Speranza *et al.* 2014; Laube *et al.* 2011). It also serves important nutritional needs and is seen as a coping strategy, for example, in case of food shortages that may occur as a result of droughts or floods; the animals are sold to purchase food items during these times (Laube *et al.* 2011).

The smallholder farmers are embracing the green revolution in boosting agricultural productivity. According to Waugh (1998), green revolution is the application of modern or Western type of farming techniques in the developing countries. Green revolution encompasses the use of technology including fertilisers, insecticides, implements, water control and hybridises seed (*ibid.*). The aim is to adequately respond to the changing patterns of climate through the use of crop varieties or implements. Scientific weather forecast sensitises the farmers of such changes so that they put plans in place beforehand. Technology improves weather forecasts and predictions which might sensitise people on crop varieties which suit seasonal rainfall patterns (Speranza *et al.* 2014; Laube *et al.* 2011). The use of fertilisers, tractors, cultivators, insecticides or pesticides, among other modern farming practices, has been adopted to boost productivity. These technologies allow many smallholder farmers access to internet through cell phones, computers or tablets, and easy access of weather information. The wide of use of ICTs has increased the intensity and effectiveness of the climate change adaptation (Laube *et al.* 2011).

The smallholder farmers have responded to unreliable rain-fed cropping by diversifying their livelihoods including the off-farm livelihood strategies (Bernstein, 1996; Ashley and Maxwell, 2001). The off-farm livelihood strategies now represent the mainstay of the farmers' income. The income is mainly earned through labour migration, and small-scale commerce which include horticulture, selling livestock and crops usually in the urban areas (they form part of the informal sector). In addition to food, the money is used for clothing, medicine, tools and to meet social obligations like education (Ashley and Maxwell, 2001). It should be observed that, although most households in the village have managed to successfully diversify their livelihoods, some are still unable to meet their life needs due to climate change.

Factors affecting adaptive capacity

Adaptation to climate change depends greatly on the adaptive capacity of the affected region, or community to cope with the impacts and risks of climate change. The determinants of adaptive capacity relate to the economic, social, institutional, and technological conditions that facilitate or constrain the development and deployment of adaptive measures (Laube *et al.* 2011). The adaptation capacity depends on a range of variables which in turn affect the availability, accessibility and affordability of particular adaptation procedures. Several studies have identified specific variables which may positively or negatively affect the choice of particular adaptation methods. Deressa *et al.* (2009) conclude that farmers' knowledge, access to climate information, social capital, ownership and access to resources (financial, technical and natural) and agro-ecological settings greatly influence the adaptive capacity. These constraints may hinder farmers' uptake of other adaptation methods. Enhancement of adaptive capacity represents a practical means of coping with changes and uncertainties in climate including variability and extremes (*ibid.*). In this way, enhancement of adaptive capacity reduces vulnerabilities and promotes sustainable.

Information on the nature and evolution of the climate hazards faced by a society, both historical climate data and data from scenarios of future climate change, is key to enhancing adaptive capacity hence affect the same (Twyman, 2003). Farmers with more access to weather information will be more likely to make on-farm changes to adopt to climate change. Its lack signifies a weaker adaptive capacity hence enhancing access to information about climate and agronomy boost adaptation capacity. Ishaya and Abaje (2008) find that lack of awareness and knowledge about climate change and adaptation strategies is hindering adaptation, for example, in Jema'a, Nigeria.

Adaptive capacity or choice of adaptation strategies are also influenced by social factors such as social networks, values, perceptions, customs, traditions and levels of cognition (Kremen *et al.* 2012). Adaptation strategies will not be successful unless there is a willingness to adapt among those affected as well as a degree of consensus regarding what types of actions are appropriate. Social capital and social networks play an important role in the ability of the famers to manage risk and uncertainty, especially in the absence state aid as these facilitate collaboration and coordination among individual actors. For example, communities in Samoa in the south Pacific rely on informal non-monetary arrangements and social networks to cope with climate change damages, along with livelihood diversification and financial remittances through extended family networks (*ibid.*). This is because individuals are often interdependent through familial, social, and political interactions.

Assets and household wealth are necessary to allow adoption of adaptation strategies that may require access to capital, for example, key inputs such as improved seeds and fertilizer. Asset base is understood as the totality of human capital, liquid capacity and productive assets that household members deploy to reproduce and sustain the household. The implementation of adaptation strategies requires resources, including financial capital, human resources for, example labour, skills, knowledge and expertise and natural resources like land, water, raw materials and biodiversity. By this fact, adaptation to climate that requires these investments is, therefore, less likely to be carried out by the poor who are often budget constrained as poor access to resources means poor adaptive capacity (Scialabba *et al.* 2010; Tacoli, 2009; Gbetibouo *et al.* 2010). Given that previous studies have shown that increased assets improve the adaptive capacity of groups facing capital constraints (Meinzen-Dick *et al.* 2002) means that increased assets will be associated with increased potential adaptation. Although economic development may provide greater access to technology and resources to invest in adaptation, high income per capita is considered neither a necessary nor a sufficient indicator of the capacity to adapt to climate change (Scialabba *et al.* 2010).

Institutional frameworks manifesting as governance determine the adaptive capacity (Twyman, 2003). Democratic, participatory and transparent institutions signify a better adaptive capacity as people would be influencing policy decisions. Recent government policies and statements claim to embrace concepts of disaster risk reduction by building livelihood resilience to climate, economic and political disturbances and reforming mechanisms that transfer development benefits to the rural poor (Gbetibouo *et al.* 2010). The institutions which are committed to take deliberative approaches through supporting adaptive responses to climate related disturbances have potential in transforming local coping responses and collective activities in adapting to climate change (ibid.). Granting coordinated oversight in national planning strategies is central to integrating practical development agendas, especially those that stimulate agency for planned adaptation to climate change and variability across different scales. In order to provide oversight, prioritise rural development and provide early-warning forecasts, there is a need for well-resourced institutions for service delivery, monitoring and communication within the extension programmes which signifies that institutions are important factors which determine adaptive capacity.

Knowledge is an important determinant of adaptive capacity. Lack of knowledge affect the generation and use of the scientific knowledge on climate change and its adaptation hence a limitation in the adaptive capacity (Triomphe *et al.* 2007). The experience and technical knowhow of actors (smallholder farmers) are important factors which affect/ improve their adaptation potential. A knowledgeable farming community has a better adaptive capacity as it would be able to tailor, innovate, generate and use effectively scientific adaptive measures in response to the predicted climate change impacts beforehand (*ibid.*).

Methodology

The study was built from primary and secondary data collected using various methods. Primary data was collected using surveys that included administering questionnaires, interviews and field observations. The participating farmers were randomly selected in the purposively selected regions. The study purposively covered the natural ecological regions 4 and 5 of Zimbabwe since they are the worst affected by rainfall swings. Within each natural ecological region, 50 farmers were randomly selected. This made a total of 100 participants for the questionnaire surveys. Key informant interviews were done with officials from government (Ministry of Agriculture, Ministry of Environment, Water and Climate and Ministry of Local Government) non-governmental organisations

(CARE Zimbabwe; Food Agriculture Organisation of United Nations; Sustainable Agric Trust) and the local traditional leadership (15 village heads). From the organisations that participated, only one participant was purposively chosen. The participating key informants were purposively selected with the aim to get views from experienced and knowledgeable peoples pertaining farming in the selected jurisdictions. The study also made use of secondary data sought through literature review and document review. The secondary data assisted in creating benchmarks and getting lessons from other countries. The study also used newspapers which provided current debates on small scale farming and climate change on a national, regional and global scale. The qualitative data were analysed using statistical packages that include SPSS and Ms Excel. Qualitative data were analysed using thematic or discourse analysis.

Results and Discussion

Using primary and secondary data, this chapter sought to understand how smallholder farmers in Zimbabwe were and adapting to the effects of climate change and variability. The study sought data to establish if the smallholder farmers have the capacity to adapt to the effects of climate change, to assess the factor constraining the adaptive capacity of smallholder farmers in dealing with the effects which climate change and variability to their livelihoods and to offer possible measures that can be used to boost the adaptive capacity of the smallholder farmers to climate change and variability.

Adaptive capacity of farmers in Zimbabwe

Despite the fact that the smallholder farmers are aware of the changing weather patterns impacting their localities, they have limited capacity to adapt to the effects of that change. The findings indicated that smallholder's perceptions on climate change/variability are based mainly on temperature and precipitation events. All the farmers noticed changes in climate and pointed out that rainfall patterns have become highly unpredictable such that they could not predict the time of the onset of seasonal rainfall, and the prevalence of mid-season dry spells had increased. The majority of the smallholder farmers (93%) professed that, in the face of reigning climate change, they do not have the capacity to adapt to climate change. Only 7% indicated that the smallholder farmers are equipped to fully adapt to climate change and variability and therefore have the adaptive capacity. This indicates that farmers are still vulnerable to climate change and variability. Their vulnerability is exacerbated by poor access to agro-meteorological information which is very critical in facilitating decisions on potential coping and adaptation strategies. Lack of ready access to modern climate information leaves farmers with little options but to rely on indigenous/local knowledge indicators to plan cropping activities and respond to weather variations. Identification of strategies to integrate local knowledge with scientific findings could enhance adaptation as farmers were already coping with climate variability through use of suitable crop varieties, staggering of planting dates, multiple crop types and varieties and use organic nutrient resources.

The interviewed NGO staff indicated that they have been educating farmers about the changing climatic conditions and what the situation is likely to be in the future. They pointed out that, even though there had been trainings, the smallholder farmers are still at a loss because of climate change impacts. This also points to the fact that those educating about climate are also at loss as to what exactly should they tell farmers since current knowledge and models are not yet conclusive about the nature of change and its impact, especially at local levels. While climate change knowledge could help farmers to be more innovative and receptive of the advice that they get from these institutions, the thrust is to assist farmers to adapt to the drought conditions that have always been affecting them in their ward. There is limited knowledge on the magnitude of change and effective strategies to deal with such change.

The adaptive strategies by the smallholder farmers in Zimbabwe

Livelihood diversification has increasingly become an important adaptation strategy in the dry regions. It was reported that there are more climate change related migrations to the nearest and other distant towns and growth points in the country. Many young people are migrating to as far as South Africa and Botswana resulting in their families and other close relatives depending on remittances during periods of food shortages, as well as to supplement agricultural incomes. Other activities, such as vending, commercial brick moulding, firewood selling and selling labour are on the increase. The sustainability of these sources of income is still problematic considering that the job market has been shrinking over the years.

Soil and water conservation strategies such as water harvesting activities, which currently are practised by about 25% of smallholder farmers, are being intensified as NGOs promote such activities. NGO organisation are enthusiastic about promoting these practices because they are building on farmers' indigenous knowledge, skills, and experience acquired over the years as farmers were battling to survive the harsh climatic conditions that prevail in the area. If these practices are properly promoted and adopted, they promise to address some of the climate change challenges among smallholder farmers considering their poor resources and marginal location which makes conventional irrigation impossible.

The most popular adaptation strategies in Zimbabwe includes planting short season varieties, crop diversification, and varying planting dates. The main thrust of these strategies is increased diversification and escaping sensitive growth stages through crop management practices that ensure that critical crop growth stages do not coincide with harsh climatic conditions in the season, such as mid-season droughts. Crop diversification improves household food security since different crops are affected differently by the same climatic conditions. Given the high frequency of mid-season dry spells and shortening of the rain season, farmers are also growing short season and drought-resistant crop varieties such as sorghum, rapoko, and finger millet. For a staple crop such as maize, farmers have opted for hybrid maize that take a shorter period to mature and yield more than traditional varieties in good years. However, the hybridised seeds are difficult to acquire because of financial shortages.

Challenges of adaptive capacity

The challenges of adaption to climate change in Zimbabwe are as shown on Figure 15.2.

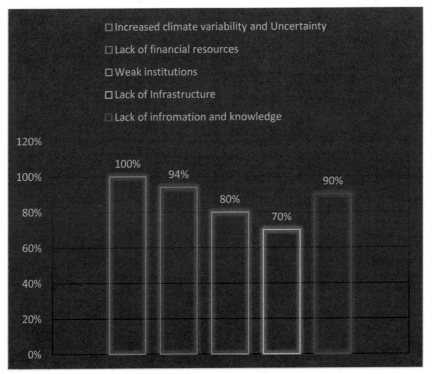

Figure 15.2: Perceptions on constraints affecting the adaptive capacity of the smallholder farmers in Regions 4 and 5 of Zimbabwe
Source: Fieldwork (2017)

Figure 15.2 indicates that the major constraint to smallholder adaptive capacity, among others, include increased climate change uncertainty. All farmers who participated mentioned that their strategies are ineffective since climatic conditions ware different altogether every season. It is also confirmed in literature that most of scientific projections of climate change and climate change impacts are highly uncertain, particularly at local and regional levels where many of the adaptation decisions have to be taken (Adger *et al.* 2005). This affects negatively the methods, scope and pace of adaptation capacities (*ibid.*). In the words of an official from the Ministry of the Agriculture, he said,

> ... climate has continually been changing with successive seasons having totally different climatic conditions. This has created unexpected risks to the farmers. This added to the lack of knowledge of the smallholder farmers who are unable to interpret most of the scientific projections of climate change (impacts), there has been low yields ...

The frequency of the unmanaged risks, significant exposure to variability in weather patterns marked by periodic droughts and floods on rain-fed agriculture indicate serious handicap/ limited capacity to manage variability or climate change effects. The smallholder farmers continue to suffer losses despite implementing strategies. For example, the abnormal rains experienced in the lowveld in the 2016-17 agricultural season left many crops waterlogged. The people in these dry regions have adopted the production of drought resistant crops as a response to low rainfall experienced in the previous seasons. The occurrence of such rains was a shocker and caught many farmers unaware resulting in significant losses.

Another challenge that emerged was lack or limited access to financial resources. This lack of finance plays as an adaptation barrier. The study revealed that 94% of the participants indicated that limited access to financial resources is a barrier to their adaption capacities. This is so because limited access to financing strategies or technologies, assets and household wealth are necessary to allow adoption of adaptation strategies that may require access to capital, for example, key inputs such as improved seeds and fertilizer. In literature, the asset base is understood as the totality of human capital, liquid capacity and productive assets that household members deploy to reproduce and sustain the household (Schmidhuber and Tubiello, 2007). One official from the NGO sector, said,

> ... the lack of financial resources led to under-investment in productivity-enhancing technologies in the region. Limited access to technology demand and delivery channels, with 60-75% of households estimated to have no contact with

agricultural research and extension services. This lack affects adaptation investments; poor access to resources mean poor adaptive capacity ...

The above sentiments confirm that the implementation of adaptation strategies requires resources, including financial capital, human resources, for example labour, skills, knowledge and expertise, and natural resources like land, water, raw materials, biodiversity. Above all, financial resources are critical in the accumulation of other resources. For example, smallholder farmers who would be wanting to start irrigation projects need finances to acquire land, equipment, seed and labour, among others. Limited access to such finance limits the ability of the same farmers to implement adaptive strategies.

Another challenge that emerged was weak institutions. The study revealed that 80% of the participants mentioned that weak capacity in policy formulation and implementation of public intervention, along with weak coordination among various actors in the public sector, is a key challenge in the adaptation to climate change. As published in literature, adaptation mainstreaming involves the need to integrate the notions of adaptation into existing structures and processes of decision-making. However, decision-making arms are marred with inefficiencies, corruption, maladministration and financial indiscipline, and are problems in boosting the capacity of local farmers. The institutions, in as much they are not well-resourced, are also blamed for financial abuse which affect their ability to carry out their mandates. In order to provide oversight, prioritise rural development and provide early-warning forecasts, there is need for well-resourced institutions for service delivery, monitoring and communication within the extension programmes, thus, this lack signifies poor adaptive capacity. Policy integration is also necessary to coordinate the adaptation measures of different regions, sectors, levels and actors to avoid conflicts and make use of synergies between different adaptation measures. Policy consistency and coherence in most cases are the challenges towards improving the plight of small holder farmers in the quest to climate change adaptation.

There is also lack of infrastructure that acts as a constraint to climate change adaptation. The study revealed that 70% of the participants mentioned that high transaction costs due to poor state infrastructure or its absence is another challenge in adaptation to climate change. Mostly, connectivity allows flow of raw materials, knowledge and out to and from the market or from area to the other. In Zimbabwe, infrastructure is a barrier which always create high cost of producing or taking the produce to the market. Under investment in roads, water, and electricity, to say the least, has tremendous cost implication on irrigation farming wherein smallholder farmers need electricity and water, which is highly priced and erratic in some instances. The distances and the state of the roads to access urban markets presents a major transaction, for example,

316

tobacco farmers who must transport their tobacco from distant rural areas to the urban tobacco floors. This erodes the adaptive capacity of the people as they cannot make any meaningful return out of their production thus increasing the vulnerability and poverty.

Conclusion and Policy Recommendations

The chapter illustrated that adaptive capacity to climate change included the ability of the natural or human systems to adjust in response to actual or expected climatic stimuli or their effects which moderates harm or exploits beneficial opportunities. It has presented the importance of adaptive capacity in the promotion and maintenance of sustainable livelihoods of smallholder farmers in the face of climate change. The dimensions of adaptive capacity and factors that affect the adaptive capacity have been shown to highlight the importance of such in enhancing the livelihoods of small-scale farmers in Africa. It emerged from the study that climate change resilience and adaptation can be promoted effectively by building communities' capacities to reduce their vulnerabilities to hazards. The level at which adaptation is achieved is dependent on the existing capacity of those taking action and the level of information available about the expected climate changes and their effect at local level. This calls for the prioritization of strengthening of existing capacities among smallholder farmers to lay the foundations for a robust management of climate risk and the rapid scaling up of adaptation through community-based risk reduction and effective local governance. The adaptation framework ought to enhance capacity for the development and implementation of corresponding local adaptation initiatives which align such initiatives to national and global targets; the authorities involved must promote public participation.

There must be public awareness programmes that teach smallholder farmers about climate change. This enhances the community capacity to understand climate risk issues, and use effectively available information and resources to develop the necessary ways to improve and protect their livelihoods. The major aim is to harness indigenous knowledge systems to mitigate the effects of climate changes. Given that climate change has brought about many problems, adaptation can be a form of addressing such problems. The problems of climate change also erode adaptive capacity of farmers; thus dealing with such manifestation of climate change assists in boosting the capacity of farmers, for example, drought lead to food shortages and food shortages further erodes the ability of such farmers to adapt to the ravages of climate change. The farmers cited precipitation and temperature-related weather events as real causes for concern in relation to their agricultural activities. The high frequency of excessive rainfall and drought have been the major challenges eroding farmers' assets, leaving them more vulnerable to the vagaries of these climatic events. Thus aid, material aid is essential in capacitating smallholder farmers. It emerged that there is financial crisis also affecting the ability of smallholder farmers to implement climate change adaptive measures. The government and other stakeholders ought to capacitate the Agricultural Bank and assist farmers to get access to cheap sources of capital. The capital ought to be used to acquire inputs, hire labour and equipment that can be used in farming.

References

Adger, W.N., Arnell, N.W. and Tompkins, E.L. (2005). Scales successful adaptation to climate change across scales. *Global Environmental Change, 15*(2), 77–86.

Alinovi, L., D'Errico, M., Mane, E. and Romano, D. (2010). *Livelihoods strategies and household resilience to food insecurity: An empirical analysis to Kenya.* Paper prepared for the Conference on "Promoting Resilience through Social Protection in Sub-Saharan Africa", organised by the European Report of Development in Dakar, Senegal, 28-30 June, 2010.

Allison, E.H. and Ellis, F. (2001). The livelihoods approach and management of small-scale fisheries. *Marine Policy, 25*(5), 377–388.

Ashley, C. and Maxwell, S. (2001). Rethinking rural development. *Development Policy Review, 19*(4), 395–425.

Bernstein, H. (Ed.) (1996). *The agrarian question in South Africa.* London: Frank Cass.

Chambers, R. and Conway, G. (1992). Sustainable rural livelihoods: Practical concepts for the 21st century. *IDS Discussion Paper 296.* Brighton: Institute of Development Studies.

Deressaa, T.T., Hassanb, R.M., Ringlerc, C., Alemud, T. and Yesufd, M. (2009). Determinants of farmers' choice of adaptation methods to climate change in the Nile Basin of Ethiopia. *Global Environmental Change, 19*(2), 248–255.

Descheemaeker, K., Amede, T. and Haileslassie, A. (2009). Improving water productivity in mixed crop–livestock farming systems of sub-Saharan Africa. *Agricultural Water Management, 97,* 579–586.

Gbetibouo, G.A., Ringler, C. and Hassan, R. (2010). Vulnerability of the South African farming sector to climate change and variability: An indicator approach. *Natural Resources Forum, 34,* 175–187.

Herrmann, S.M. and Hutchinson, C.F. (2005). The changing contexts of the desertification debate. *Journal of Arid Environments, 63*(24), 538–555.

Kremen, C., Iles, A. and Bacon, C. (2012). Diversified farming systems: An agroecological, systems-based alternative to modern industrial agriculture. *Ecology and Society, 17*(4), 44.

Laube, W., Schraven, B. and Awo, M. (2011). Smallholder adaptation to climate change: dynamics and limits in Northern Ghana. *Climatic Change, 111*, 753–774.

Margulis, S. Dubeux, C.B.S. and Marcovitch, J. (2010). *Economia da mudança do clima no Brasil: custos e oportunidades.* In S Margulis, C.B.S. Dubeux and J. Marcovitch (Eds.), *Economia da Mudanç̧a Climaˊ tica no Brasil: Custos e Oportunidades.* Sãˇo Paulo: IBEP Graˊfica,

Mubaya, C.P. Njuki, J. Mutsvangwa, E.P. Mugabe, F.T. and Nanja, D. (2012). Climate variability and change or multiple stressors? Farmer perceptions regarding threats to livelihoods in Zimbabwe and Zambia. *Journal of Environmental Management, 102*, 9-17.

Schmidhuber, J. and Tubiello, F.N (2007). Global food security under climate change. *Global Perspective Studies Unit, Food and Agriculture, 104*(50), 19703-19708.

Scialabba, N.E. and Mu ̈ller-Lindenlauf, M. (2010). Organic agriculture and climate change. *Renewable Agriculture and Food Systems, 25*(2), 158–169.

Scoones, I. (1998). *Sustainable rural livelihoods: A framework for analysis. IDS Working Paper, 72.* Sussex: Institute of Development Studies.

Simoesa, A.F., Kligerman, D.C., La Rovere, E.L. Maroun, M.R., Barata, M. and Obermaier, M. (2010). Enhancing adaptive capacity to climate change: The case of smallholder farmers in the Brazilian semi-arid region. *Environmental Science and Policy, 13*, 801– 808.

Smit, A.B. and Wandel, J. (2005). Adaptation, adaptive capacity and vulnerability. *Global Environmental Change, 16*, 282–292.

Speranza, C.I., Wiesmann, U. and Rist, S. (2014). An indicator framework for assessing livelihood resilience in the context of social–ecological dynamics. *Global Environmental Change, 28*, 109–119.

Tacoli, C. (2009). *Crisis or adaptation? Migration and climate change in a context of high mobility.* Paper prepared for the Expert Group Meeting on Population Dynamics and Climate Change, London, 24–25 June, 2009.

Twyman, C., Sporton, D. and Thomas, D.S.G. (2003). Where is the life in farming? The viability of smallholder farming on the margins of the Kalahari, Southern Africa. *Geoforum*, (35), 69 - 85.

Ziervogel, G. and Calder, R. (2003). Climate variability and rural livelihoods: Assessing the impact of seasonal climate forecasts in Lesotho. *Area* 35(4), 403–417.

Chapter 16

Wetlands under the Impact of Urban Development in Zimbabwe

Charlotte Muziri, Tamirirashe Banhire
and Abraham R Matamanda

Summary:

This chapter centres on the effects of urban development on wetlands in cities and Zimbabwe at large. In Zimbabwe, wetlands cover approximately 4.6% of the land and they are found in different states and condition of development. Some of the wetlands are still open spaces while others are now sites of housing and infrastructural developments. It ought to be noted that development on wetlands induces structural failure of buildings and houses. In this study, data were collected through observation and interviews. The interviews with stakeholders included the Ministry of Lands, Environmental Management Agent, City of Harare and the Zimbabwe Institute of Regional and Urban Planning. Results from the study indicate the depletion of the water table, and underground water pollution because of over extraction of groundwater and improper waste disposal methods. The indiscriminate exploitation and ultimate degradation of wetlands are negatively affecting ecological functions. The measures to arrest wetland destruction caused by urban development include awareness campaigns which are pro-wetland, preservation of virgin wetlands in cities and educating urban dwellers about the relationship between the city and wetlands. The study calls for urban planning and policy development which engage serious participation and consultation on the utilisation of wetlands. Wetlands conservation and management need to be made a public policy issue with the objective of developing an integrated and comprehensive wetland policy that helps to curb wetland degradation.

Introduction

Urban development, particularly in the Global South, is recently becoming a global phenomenon associated with various environmental challenges which include the degradation and destruction of wetlands (Matamanda *et al.* 2014; Chikosha and Kadziya, 2013). Urban development negatively impacts on the wetlands because it is a resource-efficient, socially connected and profitable investment which compel people to engage in natural resources extraction and subsequently degradation (Hansen, 2015). On the other hand, the demand for land to spearhead urban development projects has seen town authorities parcelling out land in wetlands, some of which are not fit for construction (Sithole and Goredema, 2013). Within the last 50 years, wetland ecosystems have been altered more rapidly and extensively than in any other period of history (Millennium Ecosystem Assessment (MEA), 2005).

Although wetlands are highly productive and ecologically important systems (Zedler, 2003), they are increasingly and continuously threatened by human disturbance such as urban development. For example, 39% of wetlands in the metropolitan area of Portland, Oregon, were lost between 1981/1982 and 1992, and the remaining wetlands were most often located in recently developed suburbs (Holland *et al.* 1995). It is only recently that wetlands have become a hot-issue in urban studies because their continued degradation and destruction compromise sustainable urban development which raises alarm bells (Muderere, 2011; Skiyi *et al.* 2016). It is in this light that Zimbabwe's rapid urban growth, which is among the highest in the world, has at times been criticised for seemingly casting a blind eye on the developments occurring in wetlands (Muderere, 2011; Sithole and Goredema, 2013).

It seems that wetland management is an understudied area in global environmental research. In Zimbabwe, various scholars have raised alarm bells with regards the conservation of wetlands in the country. Kamete (2002) profiled the urban poverty and environmental dilemmas nexus, while Muderere (2011) focused on the destruction of biodiversity in wetlands through housing construction. Matamanda *et al.* (2014) examined the stakeholders' awareness of wetlands ecosystem services and Skiyi *et al.* (2016) proposed the integration of wetlands in land-use management. The fact of the matter is that urban development in Zimbabwe greatly impacts on wetlands which call for some scrutiny and possible way forward to mitigate the misuse and destruction of wetlands and promote their wise use in the urban context.

The primary objective of this chapter is to study the impact of urban development on wetlands revealing the consequences and effects. This study seeks to examine the danger posed by the spread of urban development wetlands and proffers solutions that would check the incursion into these essential natural habitats. In this chapter we first examine existing literature on wetlands, including the contemporary world views on such ecosystems as well as their multiple ecologically relevant functions. We also examine the threat posed by population growth and the attendant urban development on the wetlands. At the end, it is recommended that policies and strategies that can be applied towards the conservation of wetlands in relation to urban development.

Background and Overview

Globally, wetlands cover less than 9% of the earth's land surface but provide habitat to disproportionately high numbers of species (Zedler and Kercher, 2005; Dudgeon *et al.* 2006), such as water birds, amphibians, fish, invertebrates and variety of flora (Mitsch and Gosselink, 2000). In the past, wetlands have been regarded as "wastelands" which harbour disease vectors and were not supposed to be integrated in urban land-use planning and management (Hettiarachchi *et al.* 2013). Wetlands were therefore subject to large-scale drainage and conversion for alternative uses without giving regard to ecological and socio-economic values (Guto, 2010). In the past decades, despite realising the value of wetlands, the demand for urban land has often resulted in the destruction of wetlands which were often considered as waste lands (Boyer and Polasky, 2004). As a result, over the years urban wetlands have been faced with much destruction, a situation which compromises their value (Emerton *et al.* 1999).

The conviction is that the socio-economic benefits of wetlands are not fully appreciated by communities. The precise functions and services provided by wetlands depend on their size, type, and location within an urban community. Urban development and urbanisation can therefore have direct and indirect impacts on the environment which include wetlands that are particularly susceptible to negative change (UN-HABITAT, 2009). The increased development on urban wetlands threatens the water quality, habitat for animals, reduces amount of provisioning services available for use as well as exacerbate climate change, among other issues. In light of this, various proponents have argued for the integration of wetlands in the urban system such that their benefits are maximised. A good example is the Nakibuvo wetlands in Kampala, Uganda, which have been integrated into the city land-use such that they contribute to wastewater treatment, urban agriculture, biodiversity conservation among many other uses (Emerton *et al.* 1999). In Zimbabwe, urban wetlands are continuing to face exploitation despite efforts from various institutions to conserve and preserve them (Skiyi *et al.* 2016; Matamanda *et al.* 2014). It becomes critical then to examine the best approaches to managing wetlands in the context of urban development considering that urbanisation is occurring at unprecedented rates in Zimbabwe.

Conceptual Framework

Urban development is a process which is synonymous with various activities and human needs. First, as urban development takes place, people need land for accommodation and construction of other structures. Considering that land is usually scarce in urban areas, especially for multiple land-uses associated with urban development, wetlands are often viewed as potential land for housing development. Second, urban development is the livelihood of urbanites and is usually diverse hence some people use wetlands for fishing, harvesting reeds and sedges for handicrafts, etc. Urban agriculture is another livelihood strategy adopted by urban citizens to augment their food supply and improve food security (Mbiba, 1995).

Water and food sustain human life and, the demand for these resources increase when urban development occurs. Some people, especially the poor who are not connected to city water mains resort to the extraction of water even in wetlands (Chirisa *et al.* 2014). Furthermore, human beings need recreational and leisure facilities, and these ought to be integrated in urban development. Overall, wetlands provide a multiplicity of ecosystem services which are critical in sustaining urban development. Hence there are linkages and connections at various levels between urban development, human needs, ecosystem services and wetlands as shown in Figure 16.1.

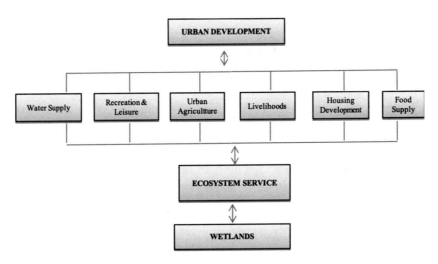

Figure 16.1: Conceptual framework showing the relationship between urban poverty and wetlands

Source: Authors' creation (2017)

Literature Review

This section reviews the literature relating to urban development and wetland management drawing lessons and insights from different regions around the world. First, it highlights on the definitions of wetlands and their characterisation. Secondly, it focuses on urbanisation and urban development. Thirdly, it discusses the utility of wetlands in urban areas and the need for managing them considering their continued degradation and deterioration. Cases are also drawn from some countries and cities where wetlands have been managed in urban development.

Wetlands defined

The Environmental Management Act (Chapter 20:27), Section 113 of Zimbabwe adopts the Ramsar definition where wetlands are defined as "… areas of marsh fen, pet land or water, whether natural or artificial, permanent or temporary, with water that is static or flowing, fresh or salty including riparian land adjacent to wetlands." Wetlands are therefore ecosystems which are characterised by abundance of water and biodiversity which are sustained throughout the year. Although the water may not be visible above the soil, the soil may be saturated with water as some wetlands act like sponges which absorb and retain water throughout the year. Hence, there are instances where a piece of land may be deemed fit for development yet the infrastructure, if not well-planned and designed, will end up being compromised.

Wetlands are of importance to both human species and the natural ecosystem. The importance of wetlands is in the benefits that arise from the ecological functions associated with wetlands. For example, they provide natural water quality improvement, flood storage, aesthetic appreciation, ground water recharge, shoreline protection and they cause groundwater to discharge to the land surface or prevent rapid drainage from the land surface so that soils are saturated for some time (Daniels *et al.* 2006; Akwetaireho, 2009; Amaniga, Ruhanga and Iyango, 2010). The value of wetlands has been categorised into four broad groups basing on the ecosystem services derived from the particular wetlands. These include provisioning services, cultural services, regulating and supporting services (MEA, 2005). To be more specific, wetlands may be categorised broadly basing on their value which may be direct, in-direct or potential. Direct value of wetlands refers to the tangible benefits which people enjoy from the wetlands, while the in-direct refers to the intangible benefits which may include flood protection. Lastly, is the future value which refers to the bequest value of the wetlands usually resulting in conservation and preservation of the wetlands for future generations. Although wetlands provide those benefits to the society and the ecosystem, they are still under pressure from developers and the local people in any urban setting. The knowledge base about wetland resources, status and key management problems is limited and no proper policy guidance is in place (Khroda, 2002).

Urbanisation and Urban Development in the African Context

The twenty-first century has been called the urban century with more than half the world's population living in towns and cities. In the Global South, the demographic shift to a majority urbanised state is expected to be reached before 2020 (WUP, 2005), and in Africa not before 2030. In the next two decades, cities in the developing world will absorb 95% of urban growth (UN-HABITAT, 2006). The trend, however, is clear that 'the urban' is continuously outgrowing 'the rural'. Hansen (2015) defined urban development as the integration of careful planning by civil and design engineers, project managers, architects, environmental planners and surveyors, to produce large cities, towns and even small neighbourhoods. It is a system of residential expansion that creates cities usually into unpopulated areas.

Urban development should not compete with the available land because it needs to be sustainable so as to secure the needs of the next generation. Moreover, the rapid rates of urbanisation have led to the growth of megacities of over 10million in developing countries. In 1975, there were three megacities in the world: Tokyo, New York and Mexico City. The speed and scale of urban development bring challenges, including meeting accelerated demand for affordable housing, well-connected transport systems, and other infrastructure, basic services, as well as jobs, particularly for the nearly 1 billion urban poor who live in informal settlements to be near opportunities (Matamanda and Chirisa, 2014).

Urban development is a major component of every developing country and is normally seen as a sign of progress resulting in environmental imbalance through development on wetlands. Some proponents have labelled urban development in most African cities as chaotic, associated with squalor poverty and irregularities. Chief among these challenges has been the proliferation of urban poverty, poor governance and limited land which has resulted in various approaches being adopted by citizens as they try to navigate their way in the urban space with the aim to eke a living. Considering that wetlands have for long been regarded as wastelands, they are usually open spaces which make them easy targets for various delinquencies such as illegal settlement, unauthorised water extraction, unsustainable agricultural practices and solid waste disposal.

Wetlands and Urban Development Nexus

About 13% of global urban settlements are found in wetlands hence there is great need to examine the nexus between wetlands and urban development (Obia et al. 2015). The fate of wetlands and human settlement has been linked inextricably for a millennia (Maltby, 1986; Coles and Oliver, 2001). From prehistoric times man has viewed wetlands as wastelands, disastrous realms, custodians of diseases and obstacles to meaningful development (Matthews, 1993; Barbier et al. 1997; EPA, 2006). It is widely accepted that more than 50% of specific types of wetlands have been destroyed in parts of New Zealand, North America, Europe and Australia (UN-HABITAT, 2006). This loss of wetlands and their dependent species continues despite the fact that when both the marketed and non-marketed benefits of wetlands are included, the total economic value of uncovered wetlands is often greater than that of converted wetlands (Constant *et al.* 1997; MEA, 2005).

Urbanisation is a major cause of impairment of wetlands (USEPA, 1994). According to Boadi et al. urban growth and rapid urbanisation have been the major drivers diminishing the land resource in sub-Saharan cities. Urbanisation has resulted in direct loss of wetland acreage as well as degradation of wetlands. Construction activities are a major source of suspended sediments that enter wetlands through urban runoff. As roads, buildings and parking lots are constructed, the amount of impervious surface increases. Impervious surfaces prevent rainfall from percolating into the soil. Rainfall carries sediments organic matter, pet waste, pesticides and fertilizers from lawns, gardens and golf courses into urban streams and wetlands (USEPA, 1993). Increased salinity, turbidity and toxicity and decreased dissolved oxygen all affect aquatic life and, therefore, the food web (Crance, 1988).

The maintenance and use of roads contribute many chemicals into the surrounding wetlands. Rock salt used for de-icing roads can damage or kill vegetation and aquatic life (Zetner, 1994). Herbicides, soil stabilisers and dust palliatives used along roadways can damage vegetation and aquatic life (Zetner, 1994). Herbicides, soil stabilisers and dust palliatives used along roadways can damage wetland plants and the chemicals may concentrate in aquatic life or cause mortality (USEPA, 1993). Runoff from bridges can increase loadings of hydrocarbons, toxic substances and de-icing chemicals directly into wetlands. Landfills can pose an ecological risk to wetlands. Landfills construction may alter the hydrology of nearby wetlands. Landfills may receive household hazardous wastes.

Globally, wetlands are under threat due to altered hydrology, destruction of vegetation, fragmentation, dumping of waste, being drained and/or filled for 'development', receiving contaminated storm water, exploitation and local extinction of fauna, invasion by feral animals and plants, excessive nutrient loading, pressure for recreation infrastructure and vandalism (MEA, 2005; Van Asselen *et al.* 2013; Davidson, 2014). Europe, the most recent overview of the extent of wetland loss, indicates that overall wetland loss exceeds 50% of the original area (UNEP, 2005). This is reported in areas like Netherlands, Germany, Spain, Greece, France, Italy and parts of Portugal (Judith, 2007). Bai *et al.* (2013), mention that most cities in Sub-Saharan Africa have not been able to develop the basic utilities for water and environmental services to keep pace with the rapid growth. As a result, people have been susceptible to water borne diseases such as typhoid, dysentery, cholera among others. Wetlands are habitats for mosquito breeding; hence they create a place which is good for disease propagation. Wetlands have been turned into illegal dump sites, and with the increased pace of sewerage burst run-off, such water eventually makes its way straight into wetlands.

The case of Lagos in Nigeria is also very pertinent. Metropolitan Lagos is situated in a narrow coastal territory which once consisted of wetland ecosystems (mangrove swamps). According to UN-HABITAT Report (citing Adelekan, 2009), "to facilitate city development, rapid and unplanned land reclamation have been achieved by infilling coastal swamps and floodplains" (UN-HABITAT, 2009). During construction, direct work process on wetlands included, for example, use of caterpillars and dredgers to build foundations and filling up wetlands so that they build easily. The final effect of the enormous wetland loss that occurred in Lagos has been the incessant and excessive occurrence of floods in the coastal parts of the metropolitan region of Lagos ever since. McGranahan *et al.* (2007) posit that, while economic activity and urban development often increase the environmental pressures that lead to flooding, it is usually the low-income settlements and poorest groups within the urban settlements that tend to be vulnerable the most.

Indirect impacts are caused by increased storm water and a pollutant generated by land development within a wetland's contributing drainage area that stresses the plant and animal community. These originate outside the wetlands through the alteration of the hydrological system. Three main processes associated with land development significantly change the hydrology of the land. First, native vegetation that once intercepted rainfall is removed, and soils are compacted. Secondly, impervious cover is created when roads, rooftops, and parking lots are constructed, which greatly increases runoff volumes. Lastly, efficient storm drainage systems are installed to quickly convey runoff to downstream waters, including wetlands. As a result of these changes, infiltration and recharge of groundwater is diminished. The construction of roads across streams and wetlands can also cause hydrologic changes that extend a significant distance upstream and/or downstream. Crossings of an individual wetland can cause direct wetland impacts, which may be regulated under Section 401 or 404 of the CWA. However, wetlands can also be indirectly impacted by roads that cross the wetland, tributaries to the wetland in the CDA, or just downstream of the wetland. The primary indirect impact is flow constriction.

Harnessing Value from Wetlands in Urban Development

Despite the persistent negative and hostile attitudes to wetlands, humans have consistently enjoyed the immense benefits that wetlands offer since the establishment of the earliest urban conurbations in Mesopotamia nearly five millennia ago (UN-HABITAT, 2009). There are some cities which have made great strides in incorporating wetlands in urban development and this has proved to be very success to the extent that some cities have engaged in the construction of artificial wetlands so as to maximise the benefits from the wetlands.

The case of Nikivubo wetlands in Kampala, Uganda, demonstrates how wetlnds are useful in urban development. The wetlands cover an estimated are of 5.5 km² and a catchment of over 40 km² (Emerton *et al.* 1999). Previously, plans were made to drain and reclaim the wetlands and pave way for residential, industrial and commercial infrastructure development. However, after some assessment and evaluations of the value of the Nakivubo wetlands, the proposed plan to reclaim and drain the wetlands were reversed since it emerged from the assessments that the ecosystem services provided far outweighed the development that had been proposed in the plan (UNDP-UNEP 2002). The assessment and evaluation established that the wetlands were economically efficient in wastewater purification and nutrient retention as compared to establishment of new sewage treatment plants in the city. The wetlands were therefore reserved in its natural state as part of the city's greenbelt zone. At the present moment, the wetlands form part of the city's space and contributes to urban development through the provision of livelihoods to communities who practice urban agriculture, fishing, harvest reeds and sedges as well as its role in purifying waste water.

Urban wetlands have long been used for recreation and leisure purposes. This is so because humans require recreational facilities which have to be incorporated in urban land-use plans. Considering that wetlands provide much more than aesthetic values, there have been instances where wetlands have been designed for parks and tourism development. Examples include the establishment of the Urban Wetland Recreation and Eco-Tourism Park in Nyandungu Valley, Kigali City in Rwanda (Gakuba, 2012). Wetlands have thus been preserved as nature reserves thereby providing much needed ecological functions in urban development. Other examples include the Toronto Music Garden Park in Canada, Parc de la Villette in Paris, France, and Wetland Park in Hong Kong. On the whole, it is evident that wetlands may be conserved as public open spaces which may help to promote eco-tourism and thereby raise revenue for local authorities and may then be used to support other urban development initiatives.

There is growing attention being given to the construction of wetlands in urban areas. This shows that wetlands are critical ecosystems hence there are various proponents who are advocating for the construction of wetlands which may be used for wastewater treatment (Mthembu *et al.* 2013). It follows that when allocating land-uses for urban development, some space may be set aside for wetland construction which may then be used for wastewater treatment, fish farming, aquaculture and agriculture. In this way, urbanites will benefit substantively from the wetlands. Wetlands serve as a critical line of defence from flooding, and act as filters for pollution. Wetlands play beneficial roles in climate regulation and mitigation of the impacts of climate change. Although peat lands cover only 3-4% of the land surface of the earth, they are responsible for about 1.5% of total global carbon storage (about 540 gig tons of carbon), amounting to 25-30% of the global carbon storage in terrestrial ecosystems (MEA, 2005).

Methodology

This study is qualitative in nature and in designing the methodology for the study we were informed by previous studies by Gakuba (2012) which adopted the same research design in efforts to establish urban wetland tourism in Kigali. Data were collected through observation and interviews. Documentary review was the first stage we undertook so as to understate the complexity of the matter. Observation was a starting point of the research, which was followed by in-depth interviews. The interviews were held with officials from the Ministry of Lands, Environmental Management Agency, local authorities such notably City of Harare, citizens and civic organisations.

Results

Urban Wetlands in Zimbabwe an Overview

Zimbabwe has a large inventory of wetlands which are mostly located in urban areas. Zimbabwe's wetlands cover about 4.6% of the land and there are approximately 1 117 wetlands across the country. From these 1 117 wetlands across the country, 7 have been designated as Ramsar sites and these are Monavale Vlei, Cleveland Dam, Mana Pools, Lake Chivero, Lake Manyame, Chinhoyi Caves, Victoria Falls National Park, and Driefontein Grasslands. Harare, the capital city of the country, is home to three Ramsar wetland sites, namely Lake Chivero, Cleveland Dam and Monavale Vlei. In addition to these Ramsar sites, Zimbabwe has various wetlands spread across the country, for example, in 2013 over 30 wetlands were gazetted in Harare (Chikosha and Kadziya, 2013). More than half of the capital is built on wetlands but soon there could be nothing left as development, urban agriculture and pollution threaten their very existence (Magwada, 2014).

It is imperative to examine these wetlands and identify the best practices in relation to urban development. Although wetlands provide many benefits to the people of Zimbabwe they are still being targeted and exploited for development purposes. They are being targeted because some of these wetlands are found in areas where there is large market for accommodation space and because urban areas are running out of space to accommodate more urban development, thus, they opt for wetlands (Chikosha and Kadziya, 2013).

Urban Development in Zimbabwe

Zimbabwe is characterised by rapid urban development which is triggered by high urbanisation rates (ZimStat, 2013; Mhofu, 2015). Urban development in Zimbabwe is synonymous with sprawling. As Zimbabwean cities and towns are sprawling, they are extending outwards on the surrounding wetlands slowly destroying them through infrastructure development, especially housing. According to EMA officials' real estates developments is encroaching into wetlands threatening their existence. Bindura's main plan on real estate's indicates that there is intention to encroach into some wetlands in the town. Urban growth is therefore negatively impacting on wetlands. Construction that is taking place in and around wetlands results in permanent changes on wetland status (Chikosha and Kadziya, 2013).

Unfortunately, the local authorities of many cities have turned a blind eye on the environmental and social consequences of building in wetlands. However, there are some cases worthy applauding, for example, Mutare city officials are also up in arms with preserving their wetlands from exploitation by property developers. In Gweru, the Minister of Wildlife and Resource Management, Oppah Muchinguri, also postulated that the increase in wetland occupation is destroying the ecosystem and strict laws ought to be implemented. Land is still being allocated and developed on wetlands while the increase in population and demand for land continue to threaten wetland status and functions. Surprisingly, councils which are expected to safeguard these ecologically vital areas needed to secure future water supplies are at the forefront of running them down (Sithole and Goredema 2013). In Zimbabwe, residential and business stands are still allocated on wetlands. For instance, the new suburbs of Westlea is a wetland area of 123 hectares (304 acres). It has 87 houses, the first of which was built in 2008, according to the Harare Residents Trust, a nongovernmental organization (Kadirire, 2014).

Urban Development and Wetlands in Zimbabwe: Experiences from Practice

Wetlands are principally protected by the laws of Zimbabwe and it is illegal to cultivate or build on wetlands before getting approval from EMA. Section 113 of the Environmental Management Act (Chapter 20:27) states that the Minister may declare any wetland to be an ecologically sensitive area and may impose limitations of development in and around that area. Any activity conducted on a wetland without a licence, is subject to a prison sentence or a heavy fine. Building cities that "work", are inclusive, safe, resilient and sustainable, requires intensive policy coordination and investment choices. Once a city is built, its physical form and land-use patterns can be locked in for generations, leading to unsustainable sprawl.

Zimbabwe's laws on wetlands are very comprehensive as the country is also part of the Ramsar Convention in relation to proper utilization of wetlands. Wetlands are protected areas as they are of importance in the Zimbabwean ecosystem. Environmental Impact Assessment and Ecosystems Protection Regulations (SI) 7 of 2007 provides for the protection of wetlands. However, EMA claims to have their hands tied when it comes to stopping any developments on these marshes. Environmentalists in Zimbabwe are up in arms trying to promote and achieve a sustainable use and management of wetlands. EMA spokesperson said the agency was trying to spread awareness of the importance of not constructing on wetlands.

Through various Acts, which include the Urban Councils Act (Chapter 29:15), the Rural District Councils Act (Chapter 29:13), and the Regional Town and Country Planning Act (Chapter 29:12), local governments in Zimbabwe have the powers to ensure that the environment is managed in a sustainable manner. Sithole and Goredema (2013) argue that wetlands are principally protected by the laws of Zimbabwe and it is illegal to cultivate or build in wetlands before getting approval from the Environmental Management Agency (EMA). Wetland utilisation is governed by Section 113 of the Environmental Management Act Chapter 20:27 in Section 113 which states that:

> … the minister may declare any wetland to be an ecologically sensitive area and may impose limitations on development in or around such area. Any activity conducted on/in a wetland, without a licence from the agency is considered illegal, and is punishable with a level 10 fine and or a prison sentence of no more than six months.

It is therefore a legal requirement to apply for wetland utilisation from the nearest EMA offices. Zimbabwe's numerous wetlands that can be identified in and around Harare have since been converted to stands, most notable being the Monavale wetland where houses now stand, the Belvedere wetland by the National Sports Stadium where construction of a multi-purpose centre (hotel and wholesale) was recently completed, while a school was built on the Ashdown Park wetland. Wetlands in Ballantyne Park, Borrowdale (opposite the race course), Budiriro 3 and 4, Tynwald, Glen Lorne, Eastlea, and many in Chitungwiza also face imminent danger in the face of constructions taking place on them (Masara, 2012). The effects are more in the urban areas due to the rapid urbanisation that is estimated at an annual growth rate of 1.6% (UN, 2009).

In Zimbabwe, environmentalists are up in arms about the construction of shopping malls and residential housing on wetlands which, they argue, will affect water supplies in urban areas (Mhofu, 2105). Authorities argue that rural-to-urban migration, puts pressure on the country's urban land resulting in the buildings on wetlands. Sithole and Goredema (2013) postulated that the city of Harare will run dry or will need more money to purify its water from open sources as commented by one environmentalist. Wetlands are productive environments that provide countless ecosystem services to humanity and biodiversity. Many species of plants, birds and animals, including the humans who live in and around the city, depend on the exceptionally biodiversity, seasonally inundated and open grassland swamps for survival (Hettiarachchi *et al.* 2013). But construction on wetlands is posing a major threat to the future of natural vital habitats.

ZINWA groundwater department official, revealed that the construction of houses on wetlands coupled with a sharp increase in the use of borehole water has contributed to the depletion of Zimbabwe's cities water table, especially Harare which is built on half of the wetlands. This evidenced by drilling of boreholes in many urban residential stands. Majority of developments are taking place without any EIA being done, because a house cannot be developed a few metres from a stream in a flooding zone. To sum up the topic, different policy approaches and institutional arrangements in place for urban wetlands governance have to be studied comparatively to obtain a better understanding of the current issues.

Local governments are responsible for the approval of construction plans, provision of building permits and the inspection of construction including on wetlands. The unique state of their soil composition makes them unfit to accommodate urban human settlements (Sithole and Goredema, 2013). The shortage of land in the urban areas has led to encroachment of urban development on urban wetlands which has adverse impacts on it. It contributes to the degradation of the wetland environment and reduction of area coverage of the wetland and reduction in water quantity. There is loss of biodiversity during the clearance of vegetation to pave way for residential developments. Construction and industrial activities on wetlands are also giving rise to pollution of underground water.

Despite all the legislation another mall dubbed southern Africa's biggest is set up to shape up on wetlands in a posh suburb of Borrowdale, east of Harare. Development is crucial to the country but the shopping malls and any form of development should be situated on high grounds and away from wetlands. A consultative workshop on the development of wetland utilization gridlines was conducted in Harare. This workshop included representatives of residents, researchers, environmentalists, surveyors, physical planners, local authorities, among other involved stakeholders. This shows the attempts by the Government of Zimbabwe to support investing in sustainable management of wetlands.

All the officials who were interviewed highlighted similar implications of building on wetlands. They made it clear that infrastructural developments on wetlands increase surface runoff and thus exacerbating chances of flooding. The residents who have houses located in wetlands have witnessed the depreciation of their houses. There is evidence that building on wetlands results in structural failure to precast walls, fences and buildings; tilting of electricity poles. This structural failure poses a threat to human safety, while it remains a looming threat to sustainable housing provision.

Discussion

In this study, we found that wetland cover and impervious cover have independent effects on wetland quality variables, with the effect of wetland cover generally stronger than the effect of impervious cover, at least within the ranges of wetland cover and impervious cover. Almost all stakeholders agreed that urban development is one of the major causes of wetlands degradation in Zimbabwe and globally. Houses built on wetlands depreciate at a faster rate because building on wetlands results in structural failure to precast walls, fences and buildings; tilting of electricity poles, thus posing a threat to human safety, while it remains a looming threat to sustainable urban development. There are dangers associated with urban development on wetlands which include cracking of walls and reducing building life spun.

Wetlands are complex ecosystems whose direct and indirect contribution to humanity is not obvious (Campell and Luckert, 2002). Education ought to help people to appreciate more values of wetlands. In essence, as noted by Muchapondwa (2003), education would make it easier for households to comprehend negative externalities and passive user values of natural resources. Ideally, decisions pertaining to wetland utilisation are expected to be influenced by education level of households. Intuitively, a positive correlation was expected.

The Government of Zimbabwe has turned a blind eye on the environmental consequences of building in wetlands because land is still being allocated and developed in low lying for instance the approval of the construction of Long Chen Plaza in Harare and this continues to undermine marshlands status and functions. The Government of Zimbabwe should also put huge fines on the law breakers as EMA"s laws are not stringent enough to stop construction of houses on wetlands. It appears that EMA lacks the capacity to protect the wetlands from land developers. The failure by the EMA to protect the country's wetland effectively betrays the commitments made under the Ramsar Convention to promote the conservation of wetland areas.

Conclusion, Policy Options and Recommendations

In conclusion, the study has illustrated that wetlands are among the most important ecosystems on earth and function as the "kidneys" of the earth, which play an important role in maintaining ecological service functions (Bai *et al.* 2013). The study also illustrated that wetlands are constantly under threat from human activities, especially through urban development. Results from the study indicate that wetlands are essential to both the community and the ecosystem as they provide ecological services. They are vital water sources for human settlements and wildlife within their catchment areas and they also help in the recharge of water sources. Urban development on wetlands leads to structural failure, flooding and many negative impacts. However, this problem can be solved through awareness campaigns, stricter urban policy and other recommended actions mentioned above. Moreover, this study demonstrated that significant progress can be made in expanding the knowledge on wetland management. It was shown that with the appropriate policy and management settings and strong community involvement, wetlands can be protected in Zimbabwe. Furthermore, the presence of wetlands enhances the liveability of the surrounding city by offering a convenient way for residents and tourists to connect with the natural environment along with the attendant physiological, psychological and social benefits. Lastly, wetland management is a global issue which needs to be addressed continuously for effective results to be achieved.

This study calls for a stricter urban planning policy development which engages stakeholder participation and consultation on the utilisation of wetlands. The policies for the protection of natural resources require an international approach because they cannot be accomplished by local and national approaches to sustainably manage the utilization of natural areas (Sithole and Goredema, 2013). To protect wetlands, various treaties, protocols and conventions were designed. According to McInnes (2010), February 2 marks the date assigned to wetlands and is known as World Wetlands Day (WWD) commemorating the Convention of Wetlands that was signed on the 2nd of February, 1971, in Ramsar, Iran. WWD was first celebrated in 1997 and now each year government agencies, nongovernmental organizations, conservation organizations, and groups of citizens can help raise public awareness about the importance and value of wetlands. In relation to the Ramsar Convention, different provinces in Zimbabwe commemorate the World Wetlands Day on the 2nd February of each year.

In Zimbabwe, wetlands and other environmental issues are overseen by the Environmental Management Agent (EMA). The UNHSP (2009) highlights that, there is an acute shortage of virgin land in some areas, but the issue of shortage of serviced land pervades all local authorities in Zimbabwe. Conversely, the Government of Zimbabwe has turned a blind eye on the environmental consequences of building in wetlands because land is still being allocated and developed in low lying areas, for instance, the approval of the construction of Long Chen plaza in Harare. This continues to undermine marshlands status and functions. It is therefore important to look more closely into some of the policy measures and strategies that have been put in place to deal with the problems (as well as to tap on the opportunities put forward) by urban growth pressure on wetlands.

Zimbabwean authorities recognise the significance of wetlands and laws are in place to prevent its degradation. The country's Environmental Management Act restricts development works on wetlands. The law requires that developers obtain an Environmental Impact Assessment Certificate from the agency managing the environment before they are issued a permit to carry on with a project on any wetland in the country. However, this law is not always respected. "Wetlands in Zimbabwe are protected on paper but are being destroyed, compromising water availability and the quality of fresh water for sustainable development" observes Julia Pierini, BirdLife Zimbabwe Chief Executive. "Loss of wetlands in Harare equals loss of water for the city".

To sum up the topic different policy approaches and institutional arrangements in place for urban wetlands governance have to be studied comparatively to obtain a better understanding of the current issues. Overall, wetlands need a comprehensive approach to their management and sustainable use. Environmental organisations like EMA and the government ought to formulate policies and tools or concepts to supply adequate information on wetlands so that they can be used sustainably.

Educational campaigns also need to be enhanced and done regularly to keep reminding and telling the various stakeholders interested in urban development the benefits of wetlands and the effects they can cause when disturbed and their impact on the developed property. EMA should work closely with the ministry of lands and the city councils to ensure that wetlands are not allocated for any form of development. The city councils should improve their waste collection system to avoid the dumping of wastes on wetlands.

EMA should also make sure that any form of development on wetlands undergoes social impact assessment (SIA) and Environmental impact assessment (EIA). This will help in the conservation of wetlands. EMA ought to work together with the department of Geographic Information System in order to undertake remote sensing for monitoring and evaluation of wetlands.

It is asserted that, for wetlands to be respected, government must put a price value on them to show just how much is being depleted by human activity. In some countries like the United States, New York City bought their wetlands and have since valued them to be over $1 billion, which they guard jealously. Zimbabwe could also put monetary value on any of the country's wetlands so that the government will not give any considerations to anyone building on wetlands. Magwada also contends that, by putting a value on wetlands and indicating the loss value of depleting the area, the country may get somewhere.

References

Akwetaireho, S. (2009). *Economic valuation of Maramba Bay wetland system of international importance, Wakiso District, Uganda.* Alps-Adriatic University of Klagenfurt, Klagenfurt.

Bai, J. Cui, B. Cao, H. Li, A. and Zhang, B. (2013). Wetland degradation and ecological restoration. *Scientific World Journal,* 2013(1), 1-3.

Barbier, E. B. (1993). Sustainable use of wetlands; valuing tropical wetland benefits: Economic methodologies and applications. *Geographical Journal, 159*(1), 22 – 32.

Boadi, K., Kuitunen, M., Raheem, K. and Hanninen, K. (2005). Urbanisation without Development: Environmental and health implications in African Cities. *Environment, Development and Sustainability, 7,* 465-500

Campbell, M. and Luckert, M. (2002). Uncovering the hidden harvest: Valuation methods for woodland and forestry resources. London UK: Earthscan Publications.

Chikosha, F. and Kadziya, L. (2013). Wetlands and urban growth in Bindura, Zimbabwe, *2*(6), 195-199.

Chirisa, I., Matamanda, A. and Bandauko, E. (2014). Ruralised urban areas vis-à-vis urbanised rural areas in Zimbabwe: Implications for spatial planning. *Regional Development Dialogue, 35,* 65-80

Comer, P. K. Goodin, A. Tomaino, G. Hammerson, G. Kittel, S. Menard, C. Nordman, M. Pyne, M. Reid, L. Sneddon, and K. Snow. 2005. *Biodiversity Values of Geographically Isolated Wetlands in the United States.* NatureServe, Arlington, Virginia, USA.

DCM. (2007). Wetlands: Their functions and values in Coastal North Carolina. Morehead City: DCM Printers.

Emerton, L., Iyango, L., Luwum, P. and Malinga, A. (1999). *The economic value of Nakivubo Urban Wetland, Uganda.* Uganda National Wetlands Programme, Kampala and IUCN – The World Conservation Union, Eastern Africa Regional Office, Nairobi.

Finlay, C. *et al.* (1988). Wetlands of Northern Territory. A.J. McComb and S. Paul (Eds.), Lake the conservation of Australian wetlands. Sydney: Surrey Beatty and Sons.

Gakuba, A. (2012). Study for establishing urban wetland Recreation and Eco-tourism Park in Myandungu Valley, Kigali City (Rwanda). Kigali: Rwanda Environment Management Authority.

Gopal B. (2003). Perspectives on wetland science: Application and policy. *Hydrobiologia, 490*, 1–10

Government of West Bengal. (2006). West Bengal Act VII of 2006.

GOZ. (1996). Rural District Councils' Act. (1996). (Chapter 29:13). Harare: Government of Zimbabwe.

GOZ. (2007). Statutory Instrument No 6 of 2007 Effluent and Solid Waste Disposal. Harare: Government of Zimbabwe.

GOZ. (2000). Constitution of the Republic of Zimbabwe. (2000). Harare: Government of Zimbabwe.

GOZ. (2002). Environmental Management Act. (2002). (Chapter 20:27), Harare: Government of Zimbabwe.

GOZ. (1996). Regional, Town and Country Planning Act. (1996). (Chapter 29:12). Harare: Government of Zimbabwe.

GOZ. (2007). Statutory Instrument No 7 of 2007 EIA and Ecosystems Protection Regulations. Harare: Government of Zimbabwe.

GOZ. (1996). Urban Councils' Act (1996). (Chapter 29:15). Harare: Government of Zimbabwe

Guto, S.N. (2010). Impact of residential development on urban wetlands: The case of Watiti Wetland, Kangemi Estate, Nairobi County. Nairobi: Unpublished Doctoral Dissertation, Kenyatta University.

Hettiarachchi, M., McAlpine, C. and Morrison, T.H. (2014). Governing the urban wetlands: A multiple case-study of policy, institutions and reference points. *Environmental Conservation,* 41(3), 276 – 289.

Kadirire, H. (2014, July 24). Harare's wetlands under threat. *Daily News*, 8.

Matamanda, A., Chirisa, I. and Mukamuri, B. (2014). Stakeholders' awareness of and perceptions of ecosystem services provided by wetlands in Harare, Zimbabwe. *Zambezia, 41*(1/2), 107 – 122.

McInnes R. (2010). Urban Development, Biodiversity and Wetland Management: UN- Habitat (pp 3- 21). Expert Workshop Report 16 to 17 November 2009, Kenya Wildlife Service Training Institute, Naivasha.

MEA (Millennium Ecosystem Assessment). (2005). *Ecosystems and human well-being.* Washington, DC: Island Press.

Mitsch, W.J. and Gosselink, J.G. (2007). Wetlands. New York, NY, USA: John Wiley and Sons

Mthembu, M.S., Odingo, C.A., Swalaha, F.M. and Bux, F. (2013). Constructed wetlands: A future alternative wastewater treatment technology. *African Journal of Biotechnology Review, 12*(29), 4542-4553.

Muchapodwa, E. (2003). The economics of community-based wildlife conservation in Zimbabwe (Unpublished PhD thesis). Department of Economics. Göteborg University Sweden and University of Zimbabwe, Harare

Ramsar Convention Secretariat. (2007). Wise use of wetlands: A conceptual framework for the wise use of wetlands. Ramsar handbooks for the wise use of wetlands (Vol. 1.) (3rd edn.) Switzerland: Ramsar Convention Secretariat.

Sarukhán, J. and Whyte, A. (2005). Millennium ecosystem assessment, ecosystems and human well-being: Wetlands and water synthesis. Washington DC: World Resources Institute.

Sithole, A. and Goredema, B. (2013). Building in wetlands to meet the housing demand and urban growth in Harare. *International Journal of Humanities and Social Science, 3*(8), 1-9.

Sithole, A. and Goredema, B. (2013). Building in wetlands to meet the housing demand and urban growth in Harare. *International Journal of Humanities and Social Science.* 3(8): 193 – 201.

Skiyi, V., Matamanda, A. and Chirisa, I. (2016). *Constraints and opportunities in integrating wetland ecosystem services in urban land-use planning, Harare, Zimbabwe.* The Proceedings of the 2016 ILASA Conference 55-63, Institute for Landscape Architecture in South Africa (ILASA). University of Pretoria (UP), Pretoria

Smardon, R.C. (2009). Sustaining the world's wetlands. London, UK: Springer.

The East Kolkata Wetlands (Conservation and Management) Act. (2006). Available online: URL http://www.elaw.in/ wetland/ecwact.html Greenberg

Tiner, R.W. (1984). Wetlands of the United States: Current status and recent trends. US Fish and Wildlife Service. Washington, DC

UNDP. (2009). Community Action Plan Dzivarasekwa Environmental Restoration through Integrated Environmental Management. Harare:

UNEP. (2005). Millennium development goals needs assessment report requirements for Goal No.7, Target! 0: Providing sustainable water and sanitation services. Nairobi: UNEP

USEPA. (1993). National health and environmental effects research lab. Carvallis: Western Ecology Division 2005 SW.

USEPA. (1994b). National health and environmental effects research lab. Carvallis: Western Ecology Division 2005 SW.

USEPA. (2007). Nutrient criteria technical guidance manual. Wetlands. Washington, DC, USA: US Environmental Protection Agency. USEPA (2013) Clean Water Act, Section 404.

World Resources Institute. (1995). Millennium Ecosystem Assessment. Ecosystems and human wellbeing: Wetland and Water synthesis. Washington: WRI

Zedler, J.B. and Kercher, S. (2004). Causes and consequences of invasive plants in wetlands: Opportunities, opportunists, and outcomes. *Critical Reviews in Plant Sciences.* *23*(5), 431-432.

Chapter 17

Smart City Development as an Aspect of the Real Estate Advancement: Evidence from Harare

Chiwota Tatenda

Summary:

The aim of this chapter is to examine the potential contribution of the real estate sector towards the development of smart cities. It further sought to examine the proposition that in order to be competitive, cities ought to be sustainable, have intelligent transportation systems, and have high-density, mixed-use and efficient infrastructure with low carbon emissions since cities are growing at an alarming rate. The major literature gap which this chapter sought to fill relates to the underestimation stakeholders have of the contribution that the real estate sector can make towards the development of smart cities. The chapter can therefore be useful for policy makers who design new policies and strategies for smart cities. Methodologically, the chapter employed interviews with officials and some relevant stakeholders for data collection. From the study, the following results are noted: most stakeholders support the view that real estate sector has a lot to contribute in form of smart buildings and smart environment in and outside those smart buildings to contribute and can do so if property resourced and governed since they contribute a lot through infrastructural development. It is therefore recommended that the private sector and the public sector should come together when approaching the issue of smart city development. The real estate sector ought to contribute to the changes in the city infrastructure and the public sector ought to provide with the right environment or framework to make them happen.

Introduction

Cities are the main pillars of human settlement and economic activity. They hold the potential to create synergies allowing great development opportunities for their inhabitants. However, they also generate a wide range of problems that can be difficult to tackle as they grow in size and complexity mainly due to urbanisation and natural growth (Chourabi *et al.* 2012). Today's world is a space with numerous challenges like terrorism (e.g., the infamous 9/11 2001 World

Trade Centre terrorist attack in the USA) which clearly manifest that the real estate sector is supposed to invest in smart security. Socio-economic challenges are a corruption, some economic like inflation and negative growth, others environmental like high rates of pollution, natural disasters to name but a few are also amongst those morden challenges (Chirisa and Dumba, 2012). All these make the global village a sceptical place to live. Nevertheless, the development of what are called smart cities may help to control these problems with the help of the real estate sector since a large number of people spend much of their time in built environments. There is a wide variety of definitions of what a smart city could be in the approach of the smart cities concept. Sufficient water supply, guaranteed power supply, sanitation, including strong waste administration, effective urban mobility and public transport, affordable housing, particularly for poor people, vigorous IT availability and digitalisation, good governance particularly e-governance and national support, economical condition, wellbeing and security of citizens, especially women, youngsters and the elderly, health and education make up the core infrastructure elements in a smart city (Barrionuevo et al. 2012).

The real estate sector has a major role to play when it comes to development of smart cities and its contribution is enormous since most of the population lives in urban areas where they spend much of their time in real estate components such as buildings and land (Batty et al. 2012). This chapter examines the contributions that the real estate sector can make towards smart cities development. Developments in smart technology may attract price premiums as well as enhance desirability by tenants. Smart developments are attractive to real estate buyers as they enable efficient utilisation of buildings and lower operating costs. With the technology sector booming, the development of districts and supporting businesses in this industry may result in the creation of jobs thus attracting professionals who need housing. In addition, population growth also creates demand for housing, which is further stoked by amenities wrought by a smart city: high salaries, excellent public transit, and access to expedient services as well as easy communication with government officials via social media. With the rise of smart cities comes an increase in the standard of living – and residents will follow. With lowered operating costs, smart cities have the flexibility to redirect funds to other projects, allowing such resources to be invested in cities and attracting developers who like to market their properties using local amenities as an appealing element (Harrison and Donnelly, 2011).

In Columbus, an aggregation of high-tech firms into a district formed after the receipt of a $40 million U.S. Department of Transportation grant and an additional $10 million from Vulcan Inc, spearheaded by investor Paul Allen. With smart investments made by the city's business community, those monies were multiplied tenfold. Physical safety and emotional fulfilment are two major aims of the smart-city function which, despite its high-tech roots, is ultimately designed to address the needs of people. This shows itself in many ways, including the rise of micro-apartments for Baby Boomers and Millennials. With continued investment in infrastructure, community, and efficient, people-centred functionality, government entities will enhance their abilities to look out for their constituents, even spotting potential problems in real estate before they occur (Batty *et al.* 2012).

Buildings make a city, and grid connected smart buildings make a smart city. If a transition into a smart urban is to be undertaken, the world must develop smart buildings alongside the grid in smart cities, and crucially focus on the interconnection between the two. Cities are expanding at an unprecedented rate and so is their complexity. By 2050 the world will be populated by an estimated nine-billion people. Seventy percent of people will live in urban areas, many of them in new towns and mega-cities (Harrison and Donnelly, 2011). To support their vast urban populations, cities will increasingly rely on smart infrastructure which the real estate sector should embrace to efficiently deliver vital services, such as power, water, public transit, distribution of goods and services, waste management and security within the built environment and the area around. There are several reasons that smart cities should be of interest to developers, long-term investors and corporate real estate professionals. Perhaps the most obvious reason is that smart, sustainable cities command higher land and property values, which attract large-scale investors. However, the real estate industry needs to understand that the buildings sector plays a huge role in helping to make cities smart. The key to smart cities is data analytics – an important element of which relates to the millions of buildings and the huge masses of population that they accommodate (Hancke and Hancke 2012). To gain maximum value from owning or managing real property in a smart city, the real estate itself should also be 'smart'

Theoretical Framework

A range of conceptual variants often obtained by replacing "smart" with alternative adjectives, for example, "intelligent" or "digital". The label "smart city" is a fuzzy concept and is used in ways that are not always consistent. There is neither a single template of framing a smart city, nor a one-size-fits-all definition of it (O'Grady and O'Hare, 2012). Being a smart city means using all available technology and resources in an intelligent and coordinated manner to develop urban centres that are at once integrated, habitable, and sustainable (Barrionuevo *et al.* 2012).

In the approach of the smart cities concept, the objective is to promote cities that provide core infrastructure and give a decent quality of life to its citizens, a clean and sustainable environment and application of 'smart' solutions. The focus is on sustainable and inclusive development and the idea is to look at compact areas, create a replicable model which will act like a lighthouse to other aspiring cities. It is meant to set examples that can be replicated both within and outside the smart city, catalysing the creation of similar cities in various regions and parts of the country. Accordingly, the purpose of the smart cities is to drive economic growth and improve the quality of life of people by enabling local area development and harnessing technology, especially technology that leads to smart outcomes (Batty *et al.* 2012). Area-based development would transform existing areas (retrofit and redevelop), including slums, into better planned ones, thereby improving liveability of the whole city. New areas (greenfields) will be developed around cities in order to accommodate the expanding population in urban areas. Application of smart solutions would enable cities to use technology, information and data to improve infrastructure and services. Comprehensive development in this way would improve quality of life, create employment and enhance incomes for all, especially the poor and the disadvantaged, leading to inclusive cities (Chourabi *et al.* 2012).

A smart city has a number of dimensions which include smart people, governance, living, environment, economy, and mobility. Figure 17.1, extracted from Giffinger *et al.* (2007), can help to explain these dimensions.

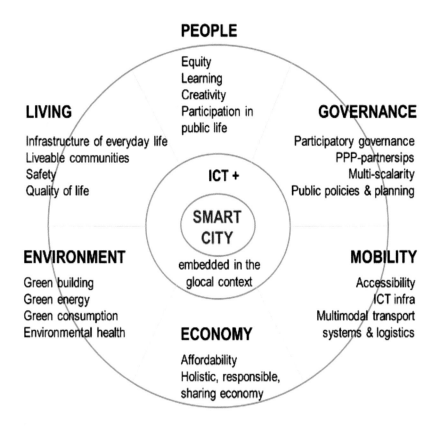

PEOPLE

Equity
Learning
Creativity
Participation in
public life

LIVING

Infrastructure of everyday life
Liveable communities
Safety
Quality of life

GOVERNANCE

Participatory governance
PPP-partnersips
Multi-scalarity
Public policies & planning

ICT +

SMART CITY

embedded in the
glocal context

ENVIRONMENT

Green building
Green energy
Green consumption
Environmental health

MOBILITY

Accessibility
ICT infra
Multimodal transport
systems & logistics

ECONOMY

Affordability
Holistic, responsible,
sharing economy

Figure 17.1: Dimensions of Comprehensive Development of Smart Cities

Some typical features of comprehensive development in smart cities are described below. Cities can adapt this program through promoting mixed land-use in area-based developments, planning for 'unplanned areas' containing a range of compatible activities and land-uses close to one another in order to make land-use more efficient. The states would enable some flexibility in land-use and building bye-laws to adapt to change. Mixed land-use involves a range of complementary land-uses that are located together in a balanced mix, including residential development, shops, employment community and recreation facilities and parks and open space (Chourabi *et al.* 2012).

Housing and inclusiveness expand housing opportunities for all is the other feature. The pricing of houses should be set in a way that allows every member of any income group to be able to buy one. In addition, related features include creating walkable localities, reducing congestion, air pollution and resource depletion, boosting the local economy, promoting interactions and ensure security. The road network is created or refurbished not only for vehicles and public transport, but also for pedestrians and cyclists, and necessary administrative services are offered within walking or cycling distance (Shapiro, 2006).

The other feature is preserving and developing open spaces such as parks, playgrounds, and recreational spaces in order to enhance the quality of life of citizens, reducing the urban heat effects in residential areas and generally promote eco-balance (Hancke and Hancke 2012). Given the cost and complexities involved in purchasing and setting aside green, open space, no one type of organisation can go it alone.

Making governance citizen-friendly and cost effective increasingly rely on online services to bring about accountability and transparency, especially using mobiles to reduce cost of services and providing services without having to go to municipal offices should be a character inherent in smart cities (Harrison and Donnelly, 2011). Giving an identity to the city based on its main economic activity, such as local cuisine, health, education, arts and craft, culture, sports goods, furniture, hosiery, textile, dairy, et cetera, is also the other element of smart cities. There is need to apply smart solutions to infrastructure and services in area-based development in order to make them better. For example, making areas less vulnerable to disasters, using fewer resources, and providing cheaper services (Barrionuevo *et al.* 2012).

"Smart cities should be regarded as systems of people interacting with and using flows of energy, materials, services and financing to catalyse sustainable economic development, resilience, and high quality of life; these flows and interactions become smart through making strategic use of information and communication infrastructure and services in a process of transparent urban planning and management that is responsive to the social and economic needs of society" (European Innovation Partnership on Smart cities and Communities - Strategic Implementation Plan. 2013).

This final definition is the one most common today. Technologies are now regarded as "force multipliers" for achieving targeted results. a smart city as a high-tech intensive and advanced city that connects people, information and city elements using new technologies in order to create a sustainable, greener city, competitive and innovative commerce, and an increased life quality (Bakıcı *et al.* 2012).

Literature Review

At the Smart City Expo World Congress 2017 (SCEWC) in Barcelona, Spain, experts hailed ICT as the "nervous system" for the successful implementation of the smart city solution, a comprehensive system that features top-level design, integration, operations, service applications and new ICT infrastructure (IT news Zimbabwe, 2017). The smart city concept is growing everywhere, driven unstoppably by megatrends such as demographic change, resource scarcity, and climate change. It has also proven to be successful in most of these cities such as Berlin in Germany. Cities have to make themselves smart to tackle these challenges (Deakin, 2013). It comes as no surprise, then, that most of the problems that Zimbabwean cities are facing can be best solved by the smart city concept. Cities in Zimbabwe, particularly Harare, is begging for the smart city concept.

Real estate sector as a whole can contribute to smart city development through being involved in smart mobility, smart governance, smart environment, smart people and smart economy which are clearly described and explained below. The objective of this strategy is to have a city with connected technology-enabled infrastructure for multiple modes of mobility that innovates towards future transport modes and prioritises walking and cycling through the smart mobility scheme. The smart mobility theme focuses on how people move around the city and use technology to support transport network design and function and to promote active and multi-modal travel (Barrionuevo *et al.* 2012). The real estate sector can contribute through introducing building with smart transport such as elevators and escalators, they can also help through constructing building that are easy to move within, in and out of the premises. Easy mobility within buildings can be done through increasing the number of exits or entrances to streets and nearby buildings. Other simple means is to introduce fewer steep steps for quicker mobility, GIS maps can be introduced building for easy movement to a needed location so as to reduce confusion which cause poor flow of pedestrians and traffic. From smart parking to transportation to green and automated office space to the locations of the municipal data centres themselves, real estate is central to the very notion of a smart city (Harrison and Donnelly, 2011).

Smart governance is the other strategy that can be applied. Real estate sector-led action smart city with coordinated leadership and collaboration across may need to be employed to improve governance of both smart cities and the real estate sector as well (Giffinger *et al.* 2007). The objective would be a global industry and business, which leads the way and connects with its tenants, clients and citizens. The smart governance theme also focuses on how real estate sector operates and sets policy to achieve the smart city vision (Maglaras *et al.* 2016). Smart governance has got its sub-strategies as well like digital transformation and e-services strategy in which it adopts digital technologies and service platforms across the sector to improve real estate project planning, property management, valuation and service delivery. Open data strategy creates and adopts policy frameworks, open standards and information technology platforms to make appropriate real estate datasets accessible and available to increase productivity and growth (Kitchin, 2016). Collaborative city strategy develop partnering frameworks that create opportunities for city and real estate industry stakeholders to partner effectively and efficiently with council across a range of initiatives, for example, housing and amenities development. So, the real estate sector can adopt these technologies and put in place frameworks to control the same. Frameworks can also be put in place to employ quality and honest professional who knows proper governance, training of workers on the issues of proper governance may also be undertaken.

Smart living involves smart city infrastructure programs like greener places strategy in which the real estate sector can develop and deploy city-scale technology infrastructure to improve the amenity of the city and the lives of its tenants, residents and visitors. Digitally interactive places strategy which have interactive technologies into a high-quality public domain to create well loved, active, safe places of interest, education, and discovery (Kitchin, 2016) can be employed by the real estate sector. Virtual city strategy which involves investing in digital applications to improve planning processes, infrastructure delivery and maintenance and citizen engagement simply setting up an email or WhatsApp platform for suggestion can help.

Smart environment is also another key strategy in implementing a smart city concept. The smart living theme will identify, deploy and leverage technology and digital applications to improve the liveability, amenity and experience of the city. It hinges foremost on the development of advanced digital connectivity and smart technology in the city centre, which enables sensors and devices to connect and share information, and to generate insights from this data to identify further opportunities for city improvements and community ingenuity. The smart environment theme aims to enhance the use of innovative technology and data in natural, aquatic and built environment management (Cocchia, 2014). The real estate sector can include accelerating adoption of renewable, especially for real estate development, creation of a future energy centre, encouraging a higher quality of building design and a greener building, and getting smarter about our resources, including water sensitive design and re-use of waste within and around buildings. Real estate developers ought to be involved to provide urban design and development advice since they are the one who are involved in making sure that there is a high quality of urban design and high-quality buildings.

Greener places strategy under the smart environment develop and deploy city-scale technology infrastructure to improve amenities of the city and the lives of its residents and visitors, and this strategy deliver technology interventions that enhance sustainability in urban places, parks, waterways and building management (Barrionuevo et al. 2012). Smarter waste strategy is about using technology and data to encourage sustainability in resource use and improve the efficiency of waste collection and processing. The real estate sector can work with the Environment Management Agency and Ministry of Health can help by providing relevant information on how the environment can be managed sustainably, for instance, in issues such as waste management and pollution control within and around buildings (Mudzengerere and Chigwenya, 2012). Real estate developers should also incorporate green energy in their developments, for instance, they should mainly use natural air-conditioning systems instead of artificial ones.

The real estate sector can produce technologies that help monitor building performance, maintain its operational functions, track data, and help with maintenance. On a granular level, building data collected can be turned into analytics that help fine-tune the processes at a greater number of building systems to lower energy and maintenance costs (Hancke and Hancke, 2012). The built environment can provide better indoor air quality, cleaner water to the occupants. As costs decline, prices would no longer deter property owners from implementing smart building solutions. As the corporate sector increasingly demands smarter, greener office space, owners may be more willing to invest in upgrading their premises to secure good-quality tenants.

The other inherent strategy in implementing smart city concept is smart people. Real estate sector ought to invest in people and attract talent to the sector. This would create opportunities through emerging smart technologies and enable everyone to participate which may also improve the city as a whole. A smart city is ultimately about people, cities together with real estate sector can actively promote its assets and facilities to engage and retain smart people. As a result, the main stakeholder is the public who may provide their expertise and talents toward the development of the city contextually real estate development (Harrison and Donnelly, 2011). The theme of the strategy is to deliver initiatives that aim to address the digital divide and ensure an inclusive city environment which can involve ensuring inclusive real estate environment. This would work to equip community with skills to engage fully with the smart city and create opportunities for creative expression and economic growth through provision of open access technology and data platforms (Cocchia, 2014). A look at countries that are successful in smart-building development reveals a combination of private sector willing to make changes and the public sector providing with the right environment or framework to make them happen.

Smart economy is the other strategy whereby a city invests in innovation and provides a roadmap and infrastructure to support successful business outcomes and attract industry and investment in smart sectors. Different stakeholders such as the Ministry of Finance and the Ministry of Small and Medium Enterprises could be involved by providing advice on planning how to attract investment and boost the economy, not forgetting the real estate sector as a stakeholder as well. The smart economy theme would work to further encourage diversification of the city and regional economy towards the growth areas of the 21st century (Cocchia, 2014). Real estate sector can strengthen economy through diligent collaboration with the financial sector, government, local businesses and the community. This would enable collaboration and growth in the real estate innovation ecosystem, create a real estate sector environment conducive to the digital and technology-led sectors, and develop business attraction and promotional strategies to bring the industries of the future which can be done through construction of buildings which encompass other smart city strategies.

Green leasing can also be introduced by the real estate sector to enhance the smart city concept. Green leasing offers a lot of potential for resolving 21st century property management and operational challenges (Mudehwe *et al.* 2016). A 'green lease' is a lease of a commercial or public building which incorporates an agreement between a landlord and a tenant as to how a building is to be occupied, operated and managed in a sustainable way. It links sustainable building design with post-constructive obligations for both the landlord and tenant of commercial property to achieve environmentally sustainable development objectives. In other words, a 'green lease' reflects the parties desire to improve and be accountable for energy efficiency at a building. It also provides a legal framework for the ongoing sustainable operation of a building in accordance with its environmentally sustainable design (Hinnells *et al.* 2008)

The real estate sector may further contribute through the creation of a digitally connected innovation buildings in city centres to attract businesses and industries working in the digital economy and creative industries. Real estate sector can also adopt a collaborative living lab strategy to develop a model of collaborative industry led innovation to fast-track real estate research, development and deployment of technology prototypes and solutions. Private information technology institutions can he involved as stakeholders who will help by providing technology advice, prototypes and solutions, by so doing contributing to the development of smart cities (Deakin, 2013). All these contributions may make real estate services more affordable to clients which is one of the aims under the smart economy strategy as indicated in the diagram above.

Zimbabwe is begging for the smart city concept since there are elements of corruptions and poor governance which can be manifested by poor service provision in cities. So, to address this situation a smart governance strategy can be employed to improve governance of cities in Zimbabwe. Huawei has been at the fore in promoting smart cities initiatives across the world. In February 2016, the company pledged to assist Zimbabwe with technology advancement in this digitalisation era. With the Internet of Things (IoT) gaining traction, impacting every area of our lives and quickly turning everything to be smart, for example, smartphones, smart TV, smartwatches, if these smart technologies are properly used, they may improve the governance of cities.

Growing heights of rubbish heaps can be noticed in almost all of the cities in Zimbabwe, particularly Harare. So, it is evident that city officials might be facing challenges in keeping their environment clean, so they might need to employ the smart environment strategy to control and manage their environment well. Dilapidating buildings with poor service provision, not forgetting ill maintained equipment, are also indicators that are begging for the smart infrastructure strategy in order to overcome these problems.

Zimbabwe's property sector is seriously under siege as the economy continues to face significant headwinds resulting in increased space surrenders and rent defaults. The pressure on rentals and occupancy levels has forced many property-owning companies in Zimbabwe to make downward reviews of rentals in order to retain tenants as well as downward fair value adjustments of investment properties. High vacancy rates in residential properties are experienced everywhere in Harare including in upmarket areas with no takers (Ajibola, 2011). Real estate companies are grappling with a myriad of challenges stemming from economic problems which have left businesses battling for survival and struggling to pay rentals. This has resulted in growing defaults and property voids, forcing the sector to adopt survival tactics such as offering rent holidays to new tenants, reducing rentals and offering free internet services in the face of de-industrialisation that is threatening viability of Zimbabwe's real estate.

Harare has been experiencing problems with traffic congestion and road accidents and these may be smartly solved by implementing the smart mobility strategy. The economy of Zimbabwe may also be best harnessed using the smart economy strategy which helps to draw investments into these cities at the same time manage these investments and economies smartly with the help of technology. If all these strategies are employed strategically, either using the comprehensive approach to this smart city concept or any other, then the public may feel satisfied with their cities and that satisfaction can be multiplied by employing the smart people strategy mentioned before (Shapiro, 2006).

Methodology

A mixed research approach which uses both quantitative and qualitative approaches was employed in this study. The use of mixed method research provided several advantages that offset the weaknesses of both quantitative and qualitative research methods. In addition, this provided a more complete and comprehensive understanding of the research problem than either quantitative or qualitative approaches alone. A mixed research approach provides an approach for developing better, more context specific instruments. For instance, by using qualitative research it is possible to gather information about a certain topic or construct in order to develop an instrument with greater construct validity, that is, that measures the construct that it intends to measure. Furthermore, it helps to explain findings or how causal processes work. However, the research design can be very complex. It can also take much more time and resources to plan and implement this type of research. It may be difficult to plan and implement one method by drawing on the findings of another. It may be unclear how to resolve discrepancies that arise in the interpretation of the findings when a mixed research approach is used (Creswell, 2007).

A desktop study was also undertaken to make the research firm. Desktop study involves the summary, collation and/or synthesis of existing research. Desktop study is contrasted with field in that field research involves the generation of data, whereas desktop study uses field sources as a source of data for analysis (Gallivan *et al.* 2003). This study used the survey method based on all the four listed property companies which are Zimre Property Investment Limited (ZPI), Pearl Properties, Mashonaland Holdings and Dawn Property Limited, the general public and the Harare City Council. The survey was conducted through issuing out questionnaires to selected respondents as well as undertaking interviews mainly with key informants such as the founder of Zim Smart Cities. In combination, secondary data from property reports and company reports from these companies provided valuable data. Members of the public were consulted using interviews since there was also a need to explain and clarify the concept to them. The main question was: 'Can the real estate sector contribute to development of smart cities and how?' On the overall, the response rate was acceptable given the technical nature of the research topic. This was evident since those who partially responded were not well acquainted with the concept of smart cities.

Results

Property market is the safest investment in an economic environment with limited investment options so most investors and many stakeholders like government prioritise it (Case *et al.* 2004). In Zimbabwe, Harare has witnessed an increase in population due to a number of factors such as rural to urban migration. Harare has a population of 1.56 million people and the demand for land for housing development is increasing, and so is the significance of the real estate market.

This section shows the results obtained from the questionnaires and interviews in which households, realtors, planning officials and practising town planners shared their view. City of Harare town planners acknowledged their knowledge of the concept of smart cities and encouraged its implementation. One city council official clearly said that:

> ... a smart city is an urban area that uses different types of electronic data collection sensors to supply information which is used to manage assets and resources efficiently and so it is imperative to emphasise that technology is not an end in itself but a tool to realise the potential that real estate have in development of smart cities.

The town planners cited it as a solution to numerous problems faced by the city council and the real estate sector, namely poor governance and corruption. However, they mentioned the issue of lack of resources such as finance being one of the drawbacks that might be faced.

The local authority planners from Harare City Council admitted that it never secured alternative solutions to some of the security and environmental problems they are currently facing, and they have opined that the smart city concept might be a possible solution. There were complaints concerning resource constraints, since it is generally difficult to allocate scarce resources amongst different smart city strategies since each strategy might need its own resources. One planning official opined that:

> ... the concept of smart cities cannot bring immediate improvement to the spatial planning of land and other urban management problems, but smart city concept would only be achievable in Zimbabwe's capital city if adequate finance was, is or will be unveiled.

Planning consultants acknowledged that data-keeping systems were not yet computerised, therefore mistakes in interpretation and data capturing could occur resulting in situation such formal housing being mistaken for informal housing. Some council officials were not comfortable discussing whether it would be feasible to implement the smart city concept.

Real estate professionals applauded the idea since it might also help improve their workload also making their properties command higher land and property values, which attract large-scale investors. However, some mentioned that it may strain both their infrastructure and financial resources. One property consultant, Mrs Lynn Chigwada, supported the initiative by saying that the smart initiative is a great initiative and she would love to see how it goes. She believes in it and would be willing to invest start-up resources in the concept.

Technology experts, particularly telecommunication engineers from the wireless and telecommunication industry also contributed ideas since they play a pivotal role in the development of smart cities. On the 17th of February 2018, Huawei Zimbabwe Public Relations Manager Mr Lightman Lai articulated that cities like Harare can be turned to smart cities.

> For safe city, we don't have the digital national ID system in Zimbabwe. So, I think that is the fundamental we need to initiate. After that we need to have the surveillance system. With this you can tell whether someone is going to break into a house, a going to have an accident. Huawei is definitely willing to make Harare a smart city. From a technical perspective, we are willing to share our wisdom of the successful case we have in China, Kenya and other countries globally. To teach you how to deploy from a technical perspective. To tell you who should play the leading role, in this case, the Government.

Zimbabwe's cities have the capacity to build smart cities provided quality of data is high, a Huawei official has said.

The public expressed lack of knowledge about the concept but nevertheless a brief explanation was given to them. Those who understood the concept showed that they liked the idea since it might help to reduce problems such as congestion and pollution currently being faced by cities. However, most of the public feared for their jobs since they mentioned the fact that the smart city concept might come with technologies that might replace their manual jobs. Some also mentioned the need to get proper training and education on how to use technologies as well as on the concept itself. During an interview on 4 April 2018, a member of the public, Mr Maramba, proposed that perhaps the conversations around designing a smart city should be carried out in vernacular languages, to allow for a wider spread and understanding of the mind-set and competency development that would need to take place in order to successfully transition cities like Harare towards smart city statuses.

Households indicated that if the local government officials solicit financial contributions to help implement the smart city concept, it would be successful. Some suggested that city authorities and government should solicit individuals, donors and international banks. However, many households interviewed felt that it would benefit both parties to formalise informal settlements rather than demolishing them because it would be less costly and added value in terms of developing cities. Most citizens mentioned that this concept should not be left to the market as it might end up negatively affecting them. The government should therefore be involved and have the courage to control its implementation and operation.

The smart city concept was supported by EMA since it makes it easy to manage waste through technological initiatives. However, the environmental agency emphasised the need for the real estate sector to take into consideration the issue of the environment when implementing the concept. They also encouraged the need to involve these agencies when implementing this concept so that wastages of resources and conflicts might be reduced.

Most of information technology officials suggest that the smart city concept, if well implemented, is cheap and sustainable in long term. It was also suggested that this concept goes a long way in reducing the financial burden on the government's budget. Some states that the smart city concept encourages investment in their sector, since the smart city concept incorporates a lot of digitalisation. It also helps to curb problems of errors in data capturing and issues such as corruption and fraud can be controlled as mentioned by some responders.

Technology experts stress points that the focus of the concept of smart cities may lead to an underestimation of the possible negative effects of the new technological and networked infrastructures needed for a smart to be smart.

From the desktop study, the following information was obtained: Officially opening an information and communication technology (ICT) workshop in Harare on behalf of Acting President Joice Mujuru, Khaya Moyo in May 2014, said the adoption of ICT in urban transport management systems would halt the "kombi wars" and traffic congestion. "To solve these problems, let us learn from others' best practices and add value to other people's knowledge of how the smart city solutions can promote more harmonious cities," he said (*Newsday Zimbabwe,* May 2014).

As clearly noted in *The Chronicle* of 15 February 2018, Mr Thulani Moyo, Terracotta Trading Private Limited Director and Egodini Mall Developer, said that for having a smarter city, African countries have to go there and do it. They do not have a choice. It is not about the possibility of it, they have to do it, because of sustainability and self-reliance issues.

Discussion

Cities are expanding at an unprecedented rate and so is their complexity. By 2050 the world will be populated by an estimated nine-billion people. Seventy percent of people will live in urban areas, many of them in new towns and mega-cities. In order to be competitive, cities will need to be sustainable, have good transportation systems, and have high-density, mixed-use and efficient infrastructure with low carbon emissions. To support their vast urban populations, cities will increasingly rely on smart infrastructure to efficiently deliver vital services, such as power, water, public transit, distribution of goods and services, waste management and security. There are several reasons that smart cities should be of interest to developers, long-term investors and corporate real estate professionals. Perhaps the most obvious is that smart, sustainable cities command higher land and property values, which attract large-scale investors. However, the real estate industry needs to understand that the buildings sector plays a huge role in helping to make cities smart. That is because the key to smart cities is data analytics – an important element of which relates to the millions of buildings and the huge masses of population that they accommodate. To gain maximum value from owning or managing assets in a smart city, the real estate itself should also be 'smart'.

Conclusion and Recommendations

In the final analysis, the real estate sector has a lot to contribute to the development of smart cities as noted in this chapter. Nonetheless, there is a need to take into consideration that initiatives need to be backed by adequate finance for them to be successful. It is necessary that smart security should be smart city strategy on its own since the issue of security is now of concern nowadays. Issue of security can encompass the issue of cyber security and physical security such as safety from terrorism. Cities are expanding at an unprecedented rate and so is the complexity of security which may invite the need of using technologically advanced methods of ensuring high security within cities (Cocchia, 2014). So, the real estate sector should ensure security within and around its buildings as well as their property management, valuation and agency software and emails. Security can be ensured through establishing a department which deals with security within the real estate sector. It should also deal with defence which includes detection, prevention and response to threats through the use of security policies, software tools and IT services. Real estate developers should put technologically advanced systems in their building, for instance, fire alarm systems, fire sprinkler systems and all stakeholders including the public should be well informed about these systems.

Local authorities need to adopt smart city and i-transport solutions to tame the traffic jungle that has seen innocent citizens caught up in the crossfire as traffic police fought running battles with public transport drivers which is resulting in the death of some innocent public civilians. To solve these problems, there is need to learn from others' best practices and add value to other people's knowledge of how the smart city solutions can promote more harmonious cities.

The real estate sector ought to embrace the Geographic Information System (GIS), a system designed to capture, store, manipulate, analyse, manage, and present geographic data. This system will help the organisation to capture buildings/properties for valuation property management and selling, billing purposes and this will provide a visual interpretation of data so saving time, providing easier understanding so improving efficiency of real estate organisations. GIS is a very useful tool because of its massive collaborative effort of OpenStreetMap and auto-generated location tags in social media you can be located exactly where a property is.

Households ought to be educated on the smart city concept. It is recommended that the government work to implement the smart city concept since it seems that they are fundamental for human settlements and proper urban management. It is acknowledged that technology is dynamic, and therefore it needs to be continuously reviewed. It is therefore recommended that the Ministry responsible for planning in Zimbabwe should work towards implementing the smart city concept.

A look at countries that are successful in smart-building development reveals a combination of private sector real estate sector willing to make the changes and the public sector providing with the right environment or framework to make them happen. So, the contributions of the private real estate sector also need support from the public sector.

The adoption of goals for sustainable urban development requires an assessment of the effect of development on both the natural and human environment as noted by (Brown, 2001). So, this point suggests integrated approaches to urban development, which combine social, economic, and environmental considerations, to give equitable access to resources both within and between generations.

References

Bakıcı, T., Almirall, E. and Wareham, J. (2013). A smart city initiative: The case of Barcelona. *Journal of the Knowledge Economy, 4*(2), 135-148.

Barrionuevo, J.M., Berrone, P. and Ricart, J.E. (2012). Smart cities, sustainable progress. *IESE Insight, 14*(14), 50-57.

Batty, M., Axhausen, K.W., Giannotti, F., Pozdnoukhov, A., Bazzani, A., Wachowicz, M, and Portugali, Y. (2012). Smart cities of the future. *The European Physical Journal Special Topics, 214*(1), 481-518.

Brown, A. (2001). Cities for the urban poor in Zimbabwe: Urban space as a resource for sustainable development. *Development in Practice, 11*(2-3), 319-331.

Chirisa, I. and Dumba, S. (2012). Spatial planning, legislation and the historical and contemporary challenges in Zimbabwe: conjectural approach. *Journal of African Studies and Development, 4*(1), 1-13.

Chourabi, H., Nam, T., Walker, S., Gil-Garcia, J. R, Mellouli, S, Nahon, K, and Scholl, H. J. (2012). Understanding smart cities: An integrative framework.

In *System Science (HICSS), 2012 45th Hawaii International Conference on* (pp. 2289-2297). IEEE.

Cocchia, A. (2014). Smart and digital city: A systematic literature review. Department of Economics, University of Genoa, Genoa, Italy.

Cohen, L., Manion, L. and Morrison, K. (2000). Research methods (5th edn.). New York: Flamingo Press.

Creswell, J.W. and Clark, V.L.P. (2007). Designing and conducting mixed methods research. Los Angeles: University of Nebraska-Lincoln.

Deakin, M. (Ed.), (2013). *Smart cities: Governing, modelling and analysing the transition.* New York USA: Routledge.

Gallivan, G., Margraf, T., Preston, L. and Gallwitz, G. (2003). *U.S. Patent Application No. 10/142,028.* United States: Philadelphia.

Giffinger, R., Fertner, C., Karmar, H. and Kalasek, R. *et al.* (2007). Smart cities: Ranking of European medium-sized cities. Centre of Regional Science, Vienna University of Technology.

Hancke, G.P. and Hancke Jr, G.P. (2012). The role of advanced sensing in smart cities. *Sensors, 13*(1), 393-425.

Harrison, C. and Donnelly, I.A. (2011). A theory of smart cities. In Proceedings of the 55th Annual Meeting of the ISSS-2011, (Vol. 55, No. 1), Hull, UK.

Hinnells, M., Bright, S., Langley, A., Woodford, L., Schiellerup, P. and Bosteels, T. (2008). The greening of commercial leases. *Journal of Property Investment and Finance, 26*(6), 541-551.

Kitchin, R. (2016). Getting smarter about smart cities: Improving data privacy and data security. Dublin, Ireland: Data Protection Unit, Department of the Taoiseach.

Kothari, C.R. (2004). Methodology: Methods and techniques (2nd edn.). New Delhi, India: New Age International Publishers.

Maglaras, L.A. Al-Bayatti, A.H. He, Y. Wagner, I. and Janicke, H. (2016) "Social Internet of Vehicles for Smart Cities", Journal of Sensors and Actuators Networks, vol. 5, issue 3.

Mudehwe, R., Chirisa, I. and Matamanda, A.R. (2016). Green leasing in Zimbabwe: Lessons from Harare commercial property market, *International Journal of Real Estate Studies* 10(2), 1-12.

Mudzengerere, F.H. and Chigwenya, A. (2012). Waste management in Bulawayo city council in Zimbabwe: In search of sustainable waste management in the city. *JSDA, 14*(1), 228-244.

Ndhlovu, L. (2018, February, 15) Smart cities a possibility for Sub-Saharan Africa, *The Chronicles. Zimpapers.* Harare. http://www.chronicle.co.zw/smart-cities-a-possibility-for-sub-saharan-africa/

O'grady, M. and O'hare, G. (2012). How smart is your city? *Science, 335*(6076), 1581-1582.

Samukange, T, (2014, May, 20). Adopt smart-city solutions to fight kombi wars' *The News Day. Zimpapers.* Harare. Available online: http://www.chronicle.co.zw/smart-cities-a-possibility-for-sub-saharan-africa/

Shapiro, J.M. (2006). Smart cities: Quality of life, productivity, and the growth effects of human capital. *The Review of Economics and Statistics, 88*(2), 324-335.

Chapter 18

Greening the Construction Industry in Zimbabwe

Shamiso H. Mafuku

Summary:

The chapter sought to evaluate the implementation of green construction in the construction industry in Zimbabwe and its contribution towards enhancing sustainability in construction practice. It also highlights the concepts/principles of green construction and how they are applied in Zimbabwe and assesses the challenges hindering its implementation in the country's construction industry. To achieve these objectives, the study mainly focused on small to large construction companies and relevant practitioners within the construction industry. The study employs a descriptive and analytical effort and uses both quantitative and qualitative methods of data collection. To acquire this data, the study used questionnaires distributed to target respondents as well as interviews carried out with professionals from The Green Building Council of Zimbabwe, Environmental Management Agency and the Ministry of Local Government, Public Works and National Housing. Evidence drawn from literature highlights that even though sustainable development is placed high on many developing countries' agenda; very little effort has been made towards its implementation (Adebayo, 2014). Reviews of green construction within Zimbabwe have found that only a small proportion of buildings can claim to be green. Despite the availability of a number of policies and guidance on sustainable construction, the adoption of this concept and its achievement is not happening fast enough. The study reveals that, although the concept of green construction is still very low in Zimbabwe, the country is a pioneer in the use of green building technologies. The concept of green design and construction was used exclusively in the construction of Batanai Gardens, Hurudza House, Chinhoyi Hospital and Eastgate Centre in Harare, amongst others. A lot of regeneration of buildings has been noted in Harare CBD as owners are moving slowly towards greening of existing buildings, through the use of modern and more durable materials. However, the concept has proved to grow on a slow scale in Zimbabwe's construction industry as a whole as the continued use of conventional methods and materials is persistent among contractors and owners. Among the challenges facing the implementation of green construction are lack of financial capital, lack of green culture in the Zimbabwean construction industry and low commitment by top management officials and clients, among others. The study also highlights that there is a lack of appropriate tools and methods to evaluate the sustainability of buildings that are being constructed.

Introduction

The construction industry is a major contributor to the global economy through its provision of facilities and utilities (Dania *et al.* 2013). Facilities are designed, built or installed to serve a specific function and to afford convenience or service to the users. Construction provides facilities such as transportation facilities, educational facilities and residential facilities and so on. Utilities are more of services, such as a telephone or electricity systems and the like. The construction industry can be linked with the processes of industrialisation and urbanisation. These economic activities are highly dependent on the development of infrastructure for the provision of investment opportunities and job creation. However, with all the economic and social benefits associated with the construction industry, the process of building has a negative effect on the natural ecosystem (Du Plessis, 2007). The negative effects of construction on the environment are seen through deforestation, land degradation and carbon emissions which have contributed greatly to the ozone depletion and climate change. The construction industry is also characterised by excessive use of natural and energetic global resources resulting in their depletion. Adebayo (2014) points out that while sustainable development is placed high on many developing countries' agenda as an effort to preserve the environment for future generations and while extensive research and recommendations have been done in the area of green construction, very little or no effort has been done towards its implementation. The challenges of lack of capital, lack of knowledge of the green construction concept, low commitment by top management officials and clients among others, which are facing developing countries in the implementation of green construction, have also not spared Zimbabwe as a developing nation. Furthermore, there has been little effort by the regulatory authorities, such as Environmental Management Agency, to combat the scourge of excessive consumption of natural resources and extensive environmental pollution by the construction industry. While the construction industry is fundamentally linked to efforts to achieve sustainable construction targets, the changes and improvements in the industry practices that are needed to realise this are not happening fast enough (GVA, 2011).

Reviews of green construction within Zimbabwe and most African countries have found that only a small proportion of buildings can claim to be green in any way (Halliday, 2008). Despite the availability of a number of policies and guidance on green construction, the adoption of this concept and its achievement is yet to be seen in the industry. Green construction is concerned with creating and operating a healthy built environment based on resource efficient and ecological principles. The study recognises the problem that green methods and materials of construction are not being utilised in the local construction industry, yet that is the key to achieving sustainable development. The chapter therefore seeks to evaluate the level of implementation of green construction in Zimbabwe by assessing the extent to which contractors are implementing sustainable methods in building projects, highlighting the challenges being faced and how they can be overcome in order to increase the adoption of the concept.

Background

According to Adetunji (2005), the pursuit of sustainable development in Africa and the world at large has put the built environment and the construction industry under the spotlight. The term built environment refers to the man-made surroundings that provide the setting for human activity in which people live, work, and recreate on a daily basis. The construction industry, on the other hand, is the major facilitator in creating and building infrastructure that constitutes the built environment including buildings, roads, electric and telecommunication systems, entertainment and leisure centres and other important services required in the running of business and other activities important to humans. The construction industry is a significant part of any economy and contributes both positively and negatively to the quality of life (Al-Yami and Price, 2006). According to the Worldwatch (2001), the industry accounts for 40% (approximately three billion tons) of the total flow of raw materials such as wood, sand, iron and fossil fuels into the intertwined economies of the world's individual countries which are highly dependent on each other (i.e., global economy) every year. The production and processing of raw materials such as wood into timber and iron into steel has great impacts on the natural landscape and can cause air pollution through the burning of fossil fuels in order to acquire energy. Processing of metals may also result in toxic runoff into water bodies and extraction of pit sands and cutting down trees for wood may result in loss of agricultural land and forests (Crossley, 2002). The construction process from excavation to erection of the building and the operation of the building also require a great amount wood, energy and water use and the process can generate significant quantities of solid waste. Construction activity also demands a significant amount of transportation of building materials from different points to the site of construction. Transportation consumes a significant amount of fossil fuels which are formed naturally from decayed plants and animals that form crude oil, coal or natural gas by exposure to heat and pressure in the earth's crust over many years. Fossil fuels are a major source of carbon dioxide and other polluting substances causing global warming (Adetunji, 2005). The construction industry is therefore one of the largest end users of environmental resources and one of the largest polluters of man-made and natural resources (Ding, 2007). However, Powmya and Abidin (2014) note that there has been little, or no attention given to the importance of selecting more environmentally friendly designs during the project appraisal stage, the stage where environmental matters are best incorporated.

A number of practices that threaten the environment have been common in the construction industry of Zimbabwe without looking into the adverse effects on the environment. Some of the issues include the use of sites such as wetlands for construction of buildings. Areas that consist of wetlands such as Cold Comfort and Long Cheng Plaza area are now being utilised for construction of residential houses as well as shopping centres. A lot of land degradation has been noted as people extract pit sand for building construction. Most commercial buildings use air conditioners instead of natural ventilation systems resulting in a lot of energy consumption. There is therefore concern about how to improve local construction practices in order to minimise their negative effects on the natural environment and this can be done through the application of green construction principles. Green building includes not only interior, exterior and site considerations, but also off-site considerations, i.e., local, regional, and global (Adetunji, 2005). Locally and regionally, for example, unsustainable building practices can put stresses on communities and government services by filling up landfills exacerbating flooding, spreading the demand for road building and utility infrastructure, and so forth (Mbohwa and Mudiwakure, 2013). On a global level, construction practices are affecting climate primarily because of our use of greenhouse gas-producing energy sources for heating, cooling, ventilation, and lighting, and our use of building materials and equipment that contain ozone layer depleting chemicals (Landman, 1999). The aim of this chapter is to evaluate the implementation of green construction towards enhancing sustainability in the Zimbabwean construction industry.

Conceptual Framework

The main principles of green construction form the framework for integrating sustainability principles into construction projects right from the conceptual stage as they inform decision makers during each stage of the design and construction process throughout the whole life cycle of a building (Kibert,

2005). The following illustration, Figure 18.1 highlights the framework for implementing sustainability in building construction.

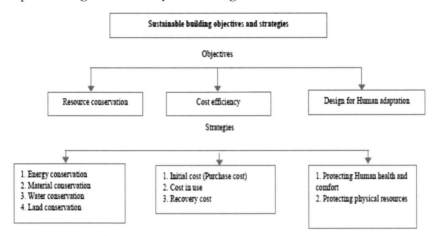

Figure 18.1: Framework for implementing sustainability in building construction
Source: Griffith, A. (1994)

To obtain optimal solutions to current construction and infrastructure problems, it is vital to consider environmental, social, and economic aspects, their synergies and the inevitable balances between them. The framework in Figure 18.1 indicates that the environmental and social issues are as important as economic issues in terms of the sustainability of a building. In terms of the environment, Figure 18.1 illustrates that the whole building process must ensure that there is conservation of water, energy, land and materials to ensure that there may be no waste of the resources. In terms of the economy, green buildings ensure that there is cost efficiency which is achieved by using more affordable materials in construction, which may be acquired locally, as well as durable materials in order to minimise maintenance costs. Buildings which are green attract more occupants and a higher economic value due to comfortable conditions for tenants. In addition to the social aspect is that green buildings ensure the protection of human health and promotes the comfort and well-being of occupants, which may lead to more productivity. Sustainability in this way expresses solutions with regard to a whole system, with an entire combination of outcomes, as these are interdependent of each other (Ferng and Price, 2005).

Literature Review

Green construction is quite a broad concept which has grown to be one of the major issues in the construction industry. Green construction is often referred to as "sustainable" or "environmentally sound" construction

(Landman, 1999). This chapter will refer to it throughout as 'green or sustainable". The term sustainable construction generally describes the application of sustainability in the construction industry. The Bruntland Report (1987) defines sustainable development as "meeting the needs of the present without compromising the ability of future generations to meet their needs". In 1994, the Conseil International du Batiment (CIB) defined sustainable construction as "creating and operating a healthy built environment based on resource efficient and ecological principles" (Kibert, 2005). According to Sarkis *et al.* (2008), green construction is therefore an emerging field of science that aims at incorporating the general sustainable development concepts into conventional construction practices. The concept of green construction in the broader view addresses the issues of economy, society and the environment for the future generation. In order to be sustainable, construction initiatives must be economically viable through the use of more affordable, recyclable and durable materials and methods of construction, socially and environmentally compatible through the use of construction materials that do not harm the environment or the health of occupants in the building (Bakar 2006). The environmental compatibility of green buildings is then seen in the improvement of air and water quality, minimization of energy and water consumption and reduction of waste disposal. On the other hand, the economic viability of green buildings is noted in the reduction of operation and maintenance cost and in increasing revenue from sale price or rent. Social viability is seen in health and community benefits which include occupant comfort. Al Yami and Price (2005) concur that green construction is the design and construction of buildings using resource efficient methods and materials that will not impact negatively on the environment or the health and well-being of the building's occupants, construction workers, the general public, or future generations.

Emerging Trends in Green Construction

Numerous green technologies and practices are emerging in the implementation of green construction around the world. These include bio-mimicry, retrofitting and living walls, among others.

Retrofitting involves greening existing buildings by upgrading and renovating (Gunnel, 2009). This includes the adoption of energy-efficiency strategies within existing buildings. Energy-efficiency retrofitting strategies may include introducing the use of solar-water heating and use of geyser blankets (CIDB, 2009). The increase in use of retrofits in the built environment is the easiest way of greening buildings provided that it involves less cost.

The increasing awareness climate change has forced a focus towards carbon neutrality in all spheres of human activity. For the built environment, this means a trend towards buildings that emit less or no carbon at all (Bertschmann, 2010). This involves building in such a way that the building will release less carbon emissions over a given time period, e.g., a year. The carbon emissions may emanate from different materials that may have been used for construction or for use within the building, for example, wood as a building material releases less carbon into the atmosphere as compared to metal and concrete. Carbon emissions from buildings are a result of energy consumption from the services of a building such as heating, ventilation and air-conditioning. The energy is mainly acquired through the use of fossil fuels such as gas and coal for heating and cooking which then emit greenhouse gases such as carbon into the atmosphere. Carbon emissions can therefore be used as one of the relative measures of the environmental friendliness of a building.

Green construction has moved towards a philosophy of being in harmony with the natural environment, in terms of form and function (Gunnel *et al.* 2009). A green roof is a roof of a building that is partially or completely covered with vegetation and soil, or a growing medium, planted over a waterproofing membrane (Du Plessis, 2009). This type of roof has several advantages, including its beauty, its ability to assist the house with blending into the environment and providing climatic stabilization. A living roof reduces heating (by adding mass and thermal resistance value) and cooling (by evaporative cooling) loads on a building; reduces storm-water runoff; filters pollutants and carbon dioxide out of the air; and increases wildlife habitat in built-up areas, among other advantages (Gunnel *et al.* 2009). It is believed that if 8% of roofing in the city is green then the ambient temperature in the city can be reduced by up to 2 degrees. That significantly cuts the effects of global warming and city "heat islands" (Cooper, 2008).

Living walls are also called bio-walls or vertical gardens (Gibberd *et al.* 2009). Vertical gardens can be grown on just about any type of wall with or without the use of soil, and they can be placed both on outdoor and indoor walls. This is another green way of naturally ventilating buildings (Gibberd *et al.* 2009).

Bio-mimicry is the concept of copying designs and innovations found in nature. Bio-mimicry can be referred to as strong ecological design because it advocates using exactly the same materials and processes utilized by nature (Kibert, 2010). The Eastgate Centre in Harare, Zimbabwe, is an example of a green building that has mimicked strategies used by termites in termite mounds for temperature control.

Benefits of Green Construction

There are several benefits that come along with green construction and these include the following:

Green buildings are designed with environmental protection in mind. Green construction aims at ensuring safety and sustainability of the eco-system and promotes the use of materials, methods, and technology that favour objective (Obediyi, Subramanian and Braimoh, 2010). The following sections clearly elaborate the environmental benefits of green building.

a) Resource conservation: Green buildings help conserve and protect our natural resources by using building products and materials that are more easily restored or do not extremely affect the ecosystem to a point of no return.

b) Pollution reduction: Green buildings minimise or eliminate the use of products that can pollute the air, water or land. They promote the use of natural building materials that require less processing.

c) Waste management: Green buildings are designed to minimise solid waste generation as they promote recycling and reuse (Sustainable Buildings Industry Council (SBIC) Guide, 2012).

d) Greenhouse gas emission reduction: Green buildings aim at using systems and materials that emit less or no greenhouse gases at all. Green buildings try to use more natural alternative methods of heating, cooling, ventilation, energy and so on in order to reduce the use of fossil fuels which emit greenhouse gases into the atmosphere. This can contribute to the mitigation of climate change (Obediyi, Subramanian and Braimoh, 2010).

e) Improving energy efficiency: Green buildings use less energy to operate and support the use of buying local materials to reduce transportation energy consumption, thereby reducing the burning of fossil fuels (SBIC Guide, 2012).

Healthier Indoor Environment

a) Indoor air quality: Green buildings limit the use of products and materials that emit toxins into the atmosphere. Also, moisture control is a key design strategy for the building exterior in order to help prevent the possibility of deterioration and moulds (EIA 2008).

b) Day lighting: Natural lighting is incorporated through transparent roofing materials and glazing to enhance energy savings (SBIC Guide, 2012).

c) Acoustics: Noise from inside and outside the building is controlled (SBIC Guide, 2012).

Economic Benefits

a) Reduced operational costs: Green buildings promote lower operating costs from energy and water savings. There is also less maintenance required as a result of the use of more durable materials and better building technology. (SBIC Guide (2012).

b) Increase in building value: Environmentally-sensitive features on a building enhance its quality and add value. Lower operating costs also make buildings more attractive to potential buyers. (Landman, 1999).

Challenges in Green Construction Implementation

Developing countries have faced various challenges in the implementation of sustainable construction. The challenges are discussed in the following sections:

Financial Challenges:

Contractors often fear and anticipate higher investment costs for green buildings compared with traditional buildings and the risks of unforeseen costs are another common barrier for green construction (Häkkinen and Belloni, 2011). Green building solutions may be thwarted because clients are concerned about the higher risk based on unfamiliar techniques, the lack of previous experience, additional testing and inspection in construction, a lack of manufacturer and supplier support, and a lack of performance information (Hydes and Creech, 2000). According to Bartlet and Howard (2000), cost consultants often overestimate the capital cost and underestimate the potential cost savings. Even though it is a known fact that sustainable practices in construction are estimated to increase initial capital cost generally in the range of 1-25%, this can often be offset by significant savings in the operational costs (Kats, 2003).

Capacity/Professional Challenges:

Another critical challenge to green construction is the lack of capacity of the construction sector to actually implement sustainable practices (CIB Report, 1999). Häkkinen and Belloni (2011) reiterate that green construction can be hindered by ignorance or a lack of common understanding about sustainability in the built environment. Rydin *et al.* (2006) postulate that professionals within the built environment need to be fully acquainted with sustainable construction principles in order to implement its practice. Not only are they supposed to be knowledgeable, these professionals need to form an integrated team from conception to inception with the best available information on products and tools to achieve sustainable construction.

Steering Barriers:

The construction industry is characterised by a large number of players ranging from clients to the contractor, thus an effective steering strategy will be required to implement sustainable construction (Al Yami and Price, 2006). Steering challenges include, but are not limited to, the lack of building codes, government policies/support and measurement tools, amongst others. Building authorities and other public actors in the building sector ought to play a pioneering role in this regard (Rohracher, 2001). Measurement tools have been developed in some advanced countries to measure the application of sustainable principles in buildings such as United States of America's LEED (Leadership in Energy and Environmental Design) and United Kingdom's BREEAM (Building Research Establishment Environmental Assessment Method).

Lack of Awareness:

According to Zanuil (2012), public awareness is one of the significant factors affecting the lack of responsibility towards nature. He further asserts that greater involvement and constructive interaction from the demand side which include clients, buyers and users, will inevitably improve good practice initiatives, drawing closer linkages to the supply side and consequently in the delivery of improved sustainable construction. The lack of knowledge, information and understanding are another worrying barrier to the success of delivering sustainable buildings (Porter, 1991). It is important for construction practitioners to understand sustainable construction sufficiently to be able to ensure that their actions and decisions add as little as possible to the total burden on the environment.

Legal Framework Affecting Sustainability in Construction

Environmental Management Act (Chapter 20:27): The law forms a broad legal statement on environmental management in Zimbabwe and is a consolidated piece of legislation on environmental matters in the country. It is an Act to provide for the sustainable management of natural resources and protection of the environment and the prevention of pollution and environmental degradation. It also provides for the formulation of environmental quality standards and environmental plans, environmental impact assessments audit and monitoring of projects and for other matters relative to environmental management.

Agenda 21: The Agenda 21 is an international blueprint for sustainable development, a comprehensive plan of action to be taken globally, nationally, regionally and locally by the UN, governments, interest groups, businesses and society in general (Du Plessis, 2001). The Agenda 21 for sustainable construction was published by the International Council for Research and

Innovation in Building and Construction (CIB) in 1999. According to the CIB (1999), the Agenda document provided a detailed overview of concepts, issues and challenges of sustainable development and sustainable construction, and posed certain challenges to the construction industry. However, the development priorities, the capacity of the local industry and governments, as well as the skills levels are radically different and there are also certain cultural and worldview differences between the developed and developing world countries that impact on the understanding and implementation of sustainable development and construction (Du Plessis, 2001).

Role of Government in Promoting Sustainable Construction

According to Landman (1999), one purpose of government is to compel individual actors to make collectively wise decisions in the interest of public health, safety, or welfare through regulatory policy (requiring and prohibiting certain actions) or non-regulatory policy (creating incentives for or simply encouraging and facilitating certain actions). Also, Hakkinen and Belloni (2011), argue that government involvement can lend legitimacy to the environmental advocacy efforts of non-profit organisations since government is expected to have a more objective or conservative perspective than advocacy groups.

Obediyi, Subramanian and Braimoh (2010) highlight that education activities including seminars, workshops, and conferences can be very useful in enhancing the implementation of sustainable construction. Developing and distributing curricula that include sustainable building concepts is yet another effective way of spreading the message. More information in standard high school and college curricula about the effects and solutions of the building industry can also contribute positively towards the sustainable construction goal.

Djokoto, Dadzie and Ohemeng-Obabio (2014) postulated that economic incentives will also be necessary to boost the interest of those people who will never be compelled by the environmental reasoning behind sustainable building, and to even the playing field for those who are compelled. Economic incentives can be used to promote voluntary action (e.g., conservation) where it might not occur otherwise. Tools include tax credits and rebates, as well as financial assistance, such as loans with favourable terms or outright grants (Wargocki, 2000).

Many of the changes that will need to be made to overcome current barriers (both educational and economic) will best be achieved through non-governmental action. For example, professional associations and environmental groups can offer workshops on sustainable building. Professional groups can also sponsor more sustainable building competitions and awards programmes to encourage and publicly recognize model projects. They also are the logical locus for efforts to reform fee structures towards performance-based compensation as well as to reform specifications that are accepted as the industry standard, and to make the team process a more integrated, less linear one. As mentioned before, non-governmental groups play an important role in bringing sustainable building stories to the attention of the media. Government can tap into and support many of these activities (Landman, 1999).

Methodology

Quantitative methods were useful in classifying certain aspects of the research and quantifying them in an attempt to explain the extent of prevalence, importance or severity. Primary data was collected using interviews, questionnaires and case studies and secondary sources of data were also useful for this research.

Results and Discussion

The main aim of the study was to assess the extent to which green construction is being implemented in the Zimbabwean construction industry and how it is being implemented by different property developers, architects and contractors. The following findings were drawn.

About 12 (52%) out of 23 respondents, including small to large construction and property development companies and other relevant practitioners within the construction industry (i.e., architects, engineers, quantity surveyors, town planners), indicated that they had existing policies that support sustainable construction within their organisations. For example, Old Mutual has a clearly laid out property development policy that highlights acceptable and sustainable construction methods as well as ensuring safety and health in their property development processes. Nine (39%) out of 23 of the respondents indicated that their company policies had no specifications on green construction practices and methods that were expected of them. In addition, 2 (9%) out of 23 of respondents were not sure concerning the existence of sustainable construction policies within their organisations. The fact that at least 52% of the visited organisations have internal policy specifications on green construction practices highlights the level at which the technology is being considered in the industry. The incorporation of organisational internal policies on sustainable construction is likely to spearhead the implementation of green construction technology. During interviews, some key informants highlighted that, though policies may be existent in organisations, the problem is with the uptake and implementation of the policies rather than the drafting. This is because many of the policy guidelines are not mandatory and it is largely up to the building owners to adopt them. There are also issues to do with the financial capacity of developers to implement the given best practices, among other reasons, which will be discussed under challenges encountered in green construction implementation.

Green construction practices being employed in Zimbabwe

This section serves to explain how green construction is being incorporated and implemented by property developers and small to medium enterprise contractors as well as architects and planners in Zimbabwe, and the methods being employed. A list of green construction practices obtained from Gunnel (2009) was reviewed by the researcher and respondents were asked to highlight which green practices they applied in projects they had worked on.

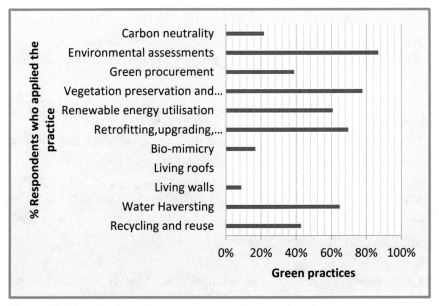

Figure 18.2 Application of green construction practices by contractors

The survey results showed that environmental assessments (87%), vegetation preservation and planting (78%), retrofitting, upgrading and renovating (70%), water harvesting (65%), as well as renewable energy utilization (61%) were amongst the most commonly applied green construction practices by respondents as illustrated in Figure 18.2. This shows a significant growth of green construction culture in Zimbabwe as higher percentages of professionals such as contractors and architects are adopting more sustainable practices of construction.

Among the least applied practices were living walls (9%), bio-mimicry (17%), carbon neutrality (22%), green procurement (39%), recycling, waste reduction and reuse with 43% of the respondents having applied it in some of their projects. The survey revealed that none of the respondents had applied living roofs in any of their projects before. This indicates that some of these methods have not yet been embraced in the construction industry in Zimbabwe, and this has a negative impact on the sustainability of construction projects and their impact on the environment and human health.

From the findings presented, the study reveals that the implementation of green construction in Zimbabwe is still at infancy level. Generally, the construction industry is aware of the concept of green construction and some organisations have drafted policies to incorporate them; however, the main issue is with practice and implementation. Quoted on *The Herald* newspaper, urban environmental planning expert, Mr Percy Toriro, pointed out that, although the concept of green building is still very low in Zimbabwe, the country is a pioneer in the use of green building technologies. Toriro also pointed out that the concept of sustainable design and construction was used exclusively in the construction of Batanai Gardens, Hurudza House and Eastgate Centre in Harare. However, the concept is slowly catching up in the construction industry as a whole.

Challenges of Implementing Green Construction

There are many hindrances in the Zimbabwean construction industry affecting the implementation of green practices amongst key stakeholders. Having discussed the several challenges facing green construction implementation in literature review, challenges were compiled, and the respondents ranked them according to their level of severity. A severity index tool was employed for this purpose, as shown in Table 18.1.

Table 18.1 Severity Index of the challenges to green construction implementation

Challenges	Frequency of Ranking					Percentage	Ranking
	1	2	3	4	5		
Lack of knowledge/understanding and ignorance of the concept	0	2	5	6	10	80.86%	3
Lack of demand/promotion for Green Construction	10	6	3	2	2	42.60%	8
Resistance to change in current practice	10	6	3	2	2	42.60%	8
Lack of initiative by government and professional bodies	5	4	4	5	5	60.86%	6
Belief that cost of construction will be higher	2	3	4	5	9	73.91%	4

	1	2	3	4	5		
Lack of Investment Capital	3	3	4	5	7	**66.08%**	**5**
Lack of legal enforcement by the government	0	0	0	7	16	**93.91%**	**1**
Poor commitment by the top management of organisations	0	0	4	5	14	**88.70%**	**2**
No organisational culture for sustainable construction	5	4	4	5	5	**60.86%**	**6**
Lack of green construction resources	8	5	3	3	4	**51.30%**	**7**

The researcher employed the Likert scale to test the severity of each challenge on a scale of 1-5, with 1 being the least severe and 5 being the most severe. This was done in order to find out how severe the reviewed challenges encountered in green construction implementation are, according to respondents' perceptions. The following formula extracted from Jamieson (2004) was used to compute the severity percentage of each challenge as illustrated in Table 39.1.

$\sum$ [r*n] /N *100/5

Where r=rating level (i.e. 1-5), n=frequency of rating, N=total number of respondents (23 in this study)

A severity ranking test was carried out. The research used this test to determine the extent to which challenges are affecting the implementation of green construction by using rankings of the challenges given by respondents. The level of severity of a challenge will show its impact on the level of implementation of green construction technology in the Zimbabwean construction industry.

Lack of legal enforcement by the government

In Table 18.1 above, lack of legal enforcement by the government was ranked as the most highly severe challenge to the implementation of green construction by the respondents at 93.91%, among all the other factors. This shows that the government has played a major role in the low implementation level of green construction technology in Zimbabwe provided that no strict regulations have been established by local government to facilitate and enforce the implementation of green construction. This is in line with literature reviewed, that regulations can encourage or discourage the adaptation of innovation, as asserted by Gann, Salter and Whyte (2003).

Poor commitment by the top management of organisations was ranked second most severe challenge at 88.70%. This is another serious hindrance to the green technology application in construction since it is the role of top management officials in organisations to approve new innovations and developments. Their negative perceptions towards new technology may become a challenge. According to Sarkis (2009), top management commitment has the ability to influence and support actual formation and implementation of green initiatives across the construction organisations.

The respondents in the construction industry ranked lack of knowledge and understanding of green construction and lack of awareness about environmental impacts of construction as the third most severe challenge at 80.86%. It is another challenge slowing down the adoption of green technologies since stakeholders seem ignorant to the impacts of the construction industry to the environment and the health and well-being of occupants. Mbowa (2014) highlights that in a situation where impacts of construction are not known, precautions will not be taken against them hence becoming a challenge to attaining sustainability in construction.

From the severity index test, respondents highlighted that the belief that cost of construction for implementing green technologies may be higher than conventional methods is another severe challenge to the implementation of green construction and sustainability. This challenge was ranked as the fourth severe one at 73.91%. This is in line with Häkkinen and Belloni (2011)'s assessment that the fear of higher investment costs for green buildings compared with traditional building and the risks of unforeseen costs are often addressed as barriers for green construction.

The fifth ranked severe challenge from the respondents was lack of investment capital by project owners or clients and it was ranked at 66.08%. According to Kats (2003), it is a known fact that sustainable practices in construction are estimated to increase initial capital cost generally in the range of 1 - 25%, however, this can often be offset by significant savings in the operational costs. This poses a challenge of the need for higher capital which most clients are not willing encounter because of the higher investment risk associated with higher capital.

Respondents ranked lack of initiative by government and professional bodies as the sixth severe challenge that impacts on the implementation on green construction. Lack of culture for sustainable construction was also given the same ranking. These factors were ranked at 60.86% according to the severity index. It is important for the government to facilitate for the growth of green construction practices; this will in turn cater for the growth of a culture of green construction in Zimbabwe.

The eighth ranked severe challenge from the respondents is lack of green construction resources at 51.30%. Scarcity of necessary resources for green construction is impacting on the slow development of green construction implementation. This is becoming a challenge since some stakeholders are lacking necessities to invest in green construction technology hence reducing the implementation level.

The least ranked challenges that impact on the level of implementation of green construction were resistance to change in current practice, as well as lack of demand for green construction. These were ranked at 42.60%.

Benefits of Implementing Green Construction

Several benefits were listed by the researcher and respondents rated them according to their level of importance on a scale of 1 to 5. Table 18.2 below shows the importance index and the ranking of the benefits according to data collected through questionnaires. A total of 23 respondents participated.

Table 18.2 Importance Index of the benefits of green construction

Benefit	Frequency of ranking					Percentage	Ranking
	1	2	3	4	5		
1. Natural resource conservation			1	4	18	94.78%	1
2. Minimisation of solid waste generation		3	6	4	10	78.26%	7
3. Greenhouse gas emission reduction		3	4	5	11	80.87%	6
4. Improving energy efficiency		2	3	4	14	86.09%	4
5. Healthier indoor environments			2	5	16	92.17%	2
6. Reduced operational costs		1	4	6	12	85.22%	5
7. Increased building Value			4	3	16	90,43%	3

The following formula extracted from Jamieson (2004), was used to compute the percentage ranking of importance each benefit as illustrated on Table 39.2.

$\sum [r*n] /N * 100/5$

Where r=rating level (i.e. 1-5), n=frequency of rating, N=total number of respondents (23 in this study)

Natural resource conservation was ranked the most important benefit by respondents with a ranking of 94.78%. Green buildings conserve and protect natural resources by using products that are more readily replenished, reforested, or do not adversely affect the ecosystem. Several key informants pointed out that environmental preservation is a global concern and green construction is beneficial in enhancing sustainability in the construction industry as well as built environment.

The second most important benefit of green construction, according to the survey, was that of healthier indoor environments with a ranking of 92.17%. Green buildings are beneficial to the well-being of their occupants as they promote a healthier indoor environment such as improved air quality through natural methods of ventilation and lighting, also noise from inside and outside the building is controlled. Respondents also scored increased building value as one of the most important benefits of green construction at 90.43%. Several clients elaborated that it is highly advantageous to own structures that cater for worker productivity and satisfaction to ensure high uptake from tenants. Building green will therefore benefit all interested stakeholders, that is, clients, tenants and workers from a commercial point of view. This reiterates Hill (2010)'s assertion that it is important for owners and developers to remember that the cheapest development is not necessarily the most profitable. Putting environmentally-sensitive features into a building enhances its quality and adds value, just as putting in typical amenities does. Lower operating costs and environmental features make buildings more attractive to potential buyers.

Improvement in energy efficiency was ranked the fourth most important benefit of green construction with a ranking of 86.09%. Green buildings use fewer resources over their lifecycle thereby reducing energy consumption, which is a remarkable economic benefit. Such benefits are already being enjoyed at Eastgate Mall in Harare with reduced operational costs scored 85.22% on the importance scale according to respondents. This reduced level of operational costs can be as a result of energy and water savings, low cost of facility maintenance and repair due to the use of durable materials, and improvement in water and energy efficiency.

Greenhouse gas emission reduction had a percentage ranking of 80.87%. It was noted that green construction promotes pollution reduction by minimising or eliminating the use of products that can emit toxins into the air, water or land. The least ranked benefit was minimisation of solid waste at 78.26%. Green buildings are designed to minimise solid waste generation and promote recycling and reuse, which is beneficial to the environment.

A survey was carried out to find out the frequency of audits carried out by Environmental Management Agency on construction procedures being employed by contractors on site and to what extent they impact the environment. Audits may include waste management procedures as well as issues of land degradation during construction. The results reveal that 70% of the interviewed construction companies were inspected by the authorities at most twice a year, 30% had three to four inspections done in a year. This shows that there is need for improvement in the enforcement of regulations. In an interview, one Environmental Management Agency official pointed out that the few visits are due to the reduced number of officers to do the work as many of them have been retrenched. One respondent pointed out that, of all the projects he had worked on in the past 5yrs, only one project had a license from EMA and there was no time an EMA officer visited any of their sites in the past one year to check on the construction methods, materials or damage to the environment. There is therefore very little or no enforcement of the regulations.

The study also revealed that 80% of the respondents of questionnaires were not aware of any local building assessment methods but were only aware of international building assessment methods such as the United States of America's LEED (Leadership in Energy and Environmental Design) and United Kingdom's BREEAM (Building Research Establishment Environmental Assessment Method). In addition, 5 (20%) out of 23 of the respondents were not familiar at all with any of the environmental building assessment methods, whether in Zimbabwe or internationally. Several respondents highlighted concern over the fact that some of the standards of international building assessment methods may not necessarily be suitable in a developing country like Zimbabwe. It is therefore important that environmental building assessment methods suitable for the local context are drafted by responsible authorities, so as to have a basis for measuring the extent of sustainability of buildings.

Conclusions and Recommendations

There is a lack of appropriate tools and methods to evaluate the sustainability of buildings that are being constructed. This is evidenced by the fact that there are no existing environmental building assessment tools or criteria in place within the regulatory framework or existing by laws. It is therefore difficult to determine the extent to which a building can be considered green when the assessment standards are not clearly laid out. There also exists a lack of methods to evaluate the extent of environmental impact posed by existing buildings as well as the environmental impact of different construction technologies used in the construction of buildings. Currently the level of implementation of green construction in Zimbabwe is low and there is slow adaptation of the concept due to various challenges that include lack of financial capital, lack of awareness of the long-term benefits, lack of green products on the local markets, lack of commitment from top management, among other challenges. This is mainly because the industry is dominated by small to medium enterprises who find high capital requirements as a major challenge to adopt green construction methods. Many contractors have continued with the utilisation of traditional methods and materials such as brick masonry and reinforced concrete in the construction of buildings. This is because new technologies such as bio-mimicry require some changes in processes, and these come with different risks and unpredictable costs as argued by Häkkinen *et al.* (2011). However, several large companies involved in bigger construction projects, such as Old Mutual, have been evidently applying green construction methods to some of their development projects such as Westgate shopping centre and Eastgate Mall due to their financial muscle to contract great architects and contractors. The use of bio-mimicry and living walls, among other green practices, has been noted in their developments. Other contractors in Harare have resorted to greening through regeneration and renovation of existing buildings to make them more comfortable for occupants, as is evident in the renovation activities taking place in Harare CBD.

Though the industry professionals are aware of the general principles of green construction, there is still a need to enhance the level of understanding and the knowledge to the clients, investors, developers and engineering consultants involved in the construction industry to enable the implementation of sustainable practices in all disciplines of the construction industry. Design consultants and project managers should involve specialized contractors to advise on realistic time frames and economic solutions for construction works, and to incorporate green construction specifications for these works.

Housing unions and cooperatives, community-based organisations and non-governmental organisations should work together with the government in spearheading the educating of all segments of society about the need for adopting green buildings. Training building professionals in green construction concepts and methods are also the most essential ways of encouraging the widespread adoption of green building practices. Seminars, workshops and lectures should be organised for all stakeholders in construction to address issues on efficient waste management, environmental management systems, and design for flexibility, durability, adaptability and the use of renewable construction materials. Such education could create a greater demand for sustainable building products and services, which would boost markets, thereby spurring more innovation and bringing prices for green products down. There is a need for regulatory bodies responsible for environmental protection such as Environmental Management Agency and the recently established Green Building Council of Zimbabwe to come up with local environmental building assessment tools for assessing the level of sustainability of buildings economically, environmentally and socially. Existing international building assessment methods should be evaluated, and the most effective ones should be adopted and replicated. Taking advantage of the existing knowledge base requires more collaboration amongst all key players in the construction industry.

References

Adebayo A.A. (2014). *Sustainable construction in Africa: Africa position paper.* Durban, South Africa: School of Architecture, Planning and Housing.

Adetunji, I. (2005). Sustainable construction: A web-based performance assessment tool. Hampshire: Loughborough University.

Akadiri, P. O., Chinyio, E. A., and Olomolaiye, P. O. (2012). Design of a sustainable building: A conceptual framework for implementing sustainability in the building sector. *Buildings, 2*(2), 126-152.

Al-Yami, A. and Price, A.D.F. (2005). Exploring conceptual linkages between value engineering and sustainable construction In SOAS, Proceeding of the 21st annual conference of the association of researchers in construction management (ARCOM), 7-9 September, (Vol. 1) (pp.375-384).

Bakar, A.H.A, Razak A.A., Abdullah, S. and Awang, A. (2006). Project management success factors for sustainable housing: A framework. Available online: http://eprints.usm.my/16076/1/ICCI09-_14_aidah_awang.pdf (Accessed: 10 May 2016).

Cooper, I. (1999). *Sustainable construction: The policy agenda.* London: CEPG, LSE

Ding, G.K.C. (2007). Sustainable construction – The role of environmental assessment tools. *Journal of Environmental Management, 86,* 451-464

Djokoto, S. D., Dadzie, J., and Ohemeng-Ababio, E. (2014). Barriers to sustainable construction In the Ghanaian construction industry: Consultants perspectives. *Journal of Sustainable Development, 7*(1), 134.

Du Plessis, C. (2007). A strategic framework for sustainable construction in developing countries. *Construction Management and Economics, 25*(1), 67-76

Ferng, J., and Price, A. D. (2005). An exploration of the synergies between Six Sigma, total quality management, lean construction and sustainable construction. *International Journal of Six Sigma and Competitive Advantage, 1*(2), 167-187.

Gibberd, J. (2002). *The sustainable building assessment tool: Assessing how buildings can support sustainability in developing countries.* Pretoria, South Africa: CSIR.

Griffith, A. (1994). *Environmental management in construction.* The MacMillan Press Ltd: London, Kent.

GVA Properties. (2011). *Stimulating sustainable construction in the UK - Do we need a scrappage scheme for buildings?* London: GVA.

Häkkinen, T., and Belloni, K. (2011). Barriers and drivers for sustainable building. *Building Research & Information, 39*(3), 239-255.

Halliday, S. (2008). *Sustainable construction.* Oxford: Butterworth-Heinemann.

Hydes, K. and Creech, L. (2000). Reducing mechanical equipment cost: the economics of green design. *Building Research and Information, 28*(5/6).

Jamieson, S. (2004). Likert scales: how to (ab) use them. *Medical education*, *38*(12), 1217-1218. .

Kats, G., Alevantis, L., Berman, A., Mills, E., and Perlman, J. (2003). The costs and financial benefits of green buildings. *A report to California's sustainable building task force*, 6(8) 200-*134*.

Kibert, C.J. (2005). *Sustainable construction: Green building design and delivery.* Hoboken, New Jersey: John Wiley and Sons, Inc.

Landman, M. (1999). *Breaking through the barriers to sustainable building: Insights from building professionals on government initiatives to promote environmentally sound practices.* Boston: Tufts University.

Miyatake, Y. (1996). Technology Development and sustainable construction. *Journal of Management Engineering, 12*(4), 1-18.

Obediyi, S.O. (2010). Green architecture: Merits for Africa (Nigerian Case Study). *Journal of Alternative Perspectives in the Social Sciences, 2*(2), 746-767.

Rydin, Y., Amjad, U., Moore, S., Nye, M. and Withaker, M. (2006). *Sustainable construction and planning: The academic report.* . London: London School of Economics.

Zainul Abidin, N., and Pasquire, C. L. (2005). Delivering sustainability through value management: Concept and performance overview. *Engineering, Construction and Architectural Management, 12*(2), 168-180.

Chapter 19

The Case for National Database towards Sustainable Property Management in Zimbabwe

Henry T. Gurajena

Summary:

In the context of sustainable property management practices, this chapter sought to answer the question: How can profile information on prospective tenants be obtained in the selection process of new tenants when property managers are leasing out space? This question arose as a result of poor management of properties which led tenants defaulting on the payment of rentals. Furthermore, defaulting tenants of the local real estate industry would simply relocate their businesses to new operating sites to avoid paying the ballooned rental arrears. In the end, the property owners would end up facing the consequences of high service charges such as water and electricity bills and high rental arrears. As tenants move from one building to another other, property managers face challenges vetting reputable tenants. For purposes of recording these observations, the research inquired on the benefits and potential changes that could be realised by using a software that assesses prospective tenants with national statistics of tenants to monitor movements and payment history of tenants. The study was initiated by the need to understand if advancement in use of a national database of tenants in property management could improve the sustainability and the effectiveness of the practice of property management in Zimbabwe. Data was obtained from various property management institutions in Zimbabwe and their regulator Real Estate Institute of Zimbabwe (REIZ). Data collection tools used were interviews and questionnaires which property managers in property companies completed. This study adds value in property management, especially in the advancement of the real estate management industry in Zimbabwe and other developing countries like Zambia, Botswana and Lesotho.

Introduction

In a depressed economy such as Zimbabwe, many industries normally encounter operational challenges (Mangudhla, 2016). Stakeholders in the industry therefore struggle to operate even at break-even point (Mangudhla, 2016). In Zimbabwe, though with little documentation, it has been observed that from the period 2013 going forward, the economic conditions started to deteriorate leading to underperformance of the property sector (Mangudhla, 2016). Furthermore, the economic environment has been characterised by recession that resulted in a low demand for rental space and ultimately reduced rental incomes. This is evident from the lowering of rental yield from 8% in the last year to 7%. Likewise, occupancy rates of commercial properties decreased from 85% to 82% during the same period (Mudehwe, Chirisa and, 2016). With the existing background, this chapter sought to apprise stakeholders in property investment about the peripatetic propensity of some tenants who rent space from one building to the other owned by different property owners. Their tenancy is only for a temporary period of time after which the tenant will then migrate to the next premise when they have accumulated rentals and building operating costs such as cleaning, water and electricity charges. The migration to the new premises is therefore motivated by attempting to avoid paying commission and rentals due to the property manager and the landlord respectively. By running away from paying rentals, the tenants remain in business just because they are successful in running away from operating costs. In other words, tenants continue to operate as a result of creating savings by avoiding paying operating costs of rentals. As a practical solution to improve the practice of property management in Zimbabwe, this study sought to establish a permanent solution that could help property owners and management agents to keep track of potential new clients and existing tenants. A general proposition made by the research is that, if an information technology system in the form of a national database for all the existing tenants is used by all property managers to keep track of all the tenants, it may make it difficult for tenants to escape the obligation to pay rentals when they fall due.

The first section of this chapter is mainly anchored on property management challenges. The background and context section describe the challenges of property management from the period when Zimbabwe gained her independence in 1980 to 2016 deliberating its economic performance in the period under review. The theoretical framework section introduces the theory underpinning this study, namely the agency theory and described its features and how it applies in the study. This chapter also reviewed the existing literature on property management considering both the national and international context. Methodology section shows how researchers collected data, the sampling method used and the justification for using the techniques used. Finally, after carrying the research, results and discussion section shows what was obtained, giving a direction for the policy options, recommendations and practical implications section. Finally, the conclusion section gives perceptions from the study results with aim at improving the practice of property management in Zimbabwe. To complement this chapter, the researcher has engaged software developers that are working on creating a model sample of the tenant management software that has been proposed in this study. The following section introduces history of tenants and property management in Zimbabwe since 1980.

Background and Context

The performance of the real estate property market in Zimbabwe has been unstable since independence in 1980. It has been constantly characterised by fluctuations with the graph slowly changing downwards from the period 1980 – 2016. This can be attributed to government policy inconsistencies which have led to various aspects of the economy continuously changing. Zimbabwe's economic meltdown commenced in 2000 (Mudehwe, Chirisa and Matamanda, 2016). From that point, the real estate sector never performed to full potential. In the real estate property management industry, the main elements affected included the commercial retail and office leasing space (Mudehwe, Chirisa and Matamanda, 2016). This is because, when employment decreases in the economy, households' spending patterns also decrease hence a few are prepared to spend on fancy goods; consequently, companies relinquish the leasing space to lower their operating costs represented by rental charges. Mushayakarara (2014) reports that, in the commercial property portfolio, most tenants have struggled to discharge the lease's main obligation of paying rental on time since 2013 (Mudehwe, Chirisa and Matamanda (2016). Furthermore, asset values in the real estate sector shed off some of the value accumulated since dollarization. The regulator of property management agents, Estate Agency Council of Zimbabwe pointed that the economic depression resulted in the flight of quality tenants in the hyperinflation period prior to the dollarization of the economy in 2009. Generally, all these observations show that the real property industry had been under a serious depression. However, there is a consensus that the economic recovery and growth trends since the dollarization of the economy have resulted in property sector boom, particularly in the retail space. Although, speculations on the existence of a boom and recession are there, it can be argued that what has not been clear is how the tenants managed to survive or rather how they are surviving in the difficult trading environment.

Observations have been shown from the laid-out background of the practice of property management in its relationship with tenants. It can be generally deducted that difficulties in property management in the depressed economy of Zimbabwe has led to tenants inventing different survival strategies so as to remain in business. Some of the common survival strategies being used by tenants operating businesses include delaying and sometimes even failing to pay wages for their workers. Tenants are also delaying paying suppliers of their

385

stock. In some instances, tenants are also dismissing employees and cutting down salaries. Some desperate tenants are evading the taxman and relinquishing rental space to property managers. In many occasions, some businesses are moving from building to building so as to run away from ballooned rental arrears. The last strategy has motivated the development of this chapter. With all these survival strategies, this chapter concentrated mostly on the main challenges of high rental arrears in which tenants have been moving from one property to the other running away after accumulating rental arrears and fleecing property owners and property managers of the necessary income.

This study is justified as it conscientises property managers of unethical tenants who are in the practice of going around and fleecing property owners and managers thousands of dollars in unpaid rental arrears. These arrears are quickly converted to bad debts and written away by property owners and managers. In addition, the study aims at warning property owners and managers to avoid falling prey to unscrupulous tenants. This study therefore makes a practical contribution in the real estate management industry by advocating for the establishment of a software system that can be developed to keep national statistics of tenants in the form of a 'national database'. This will go a long way in creating a sustainable property management culture in Zimbabwe.

Theoretical Framework

The main theory that underpins this study is the agency theory that was propounded by scholars such as Ross (1973), Eisenhardt (1989), and Shapiro (2005). Agency relationships arise from a number of sources that includes the division of labour (Mitnick, 1984). In this case, property managers are appointed by property owners to lease out space to tenants on their behalf. The structure-agency theory is far more constitutive and complex than the mere interaction between two individuals in society. Giddens (1984) is more realistic in his discourse on the ontological contours of structure-human agency in his treatise "The Constitution of Society". The agency theory is interested in explaining the relationship that materialises when two parties are working together. Scholars, for example, Ross (1973), argue that agency is one of the long-standing contractual relations which are old and common and a way of interaction in a society. Agency is a special relationship in that it is entered into by two or more parties. The first party is regarded the agent and is responsible for representing and acting on behalf of the other party who is called the principal. The decisions made by the agent bind the principal and, often at times, the terms of relationship may be implied or specified in a management contract (Ross, 1973; Shapiro, 2005). The agency theory was propounded by scholars such as Eisenhardt (1989) and Shapiro (2005). This theory aims at eliminating two problems in the relationship between agents and principals. The challenge for the principals is that, in the first problem, there is no yardstick to measure performance of the agent. Secondly, a problem materialises when both parties, that is, the principal and agent have different approaches pertaining to risks in business. Agency theory therefore tries to resolve and minimise these two problems. Since the purpose of this study is anchored on the management of real estate by property managers acting as agents of owners, the agency theory should be encompassed as the proposed system is a measure that is meant to improve effectiveness of property managers hence reducing principal-agents problems in the agency theory.

Literature Review

With the theory underpinning this study, one can argue that although agents act on behalf of the property owners, the tenants are taking advantage due to negligence of agents in carrying out a background check on all prospective tenants. Failure to conduct checks is leading to tenants accumulate rental arrears in many properties. At the end of the day, the property owner suffers since they fail to realise the expected rentals. The agency theory and its problems eventually escalate. Generally, it can be agreed that whenever two parties, one being the principal and the other being the agent, conduct business in which the agent is acting for the principal, the agency relationship is established (Ross, 1973). A macroscopic investigation into the matter can show that all the problems created by agency problems could be avoided if agents formulate a tenant database system that contains history and information on all tenants and their previous rentals. This would enable property managers to conduct further investigations when issuing out rental space. The agency doctrine defines the legal obligations that principals have with the third part for actions that agents take on their behalf (DeMott, 1998). For example, the principal can enter into a binding contract with the agent and this contract may have a negative impact on the principal if the agent represents, or act on behalf of the principal in a manner that destroys both the image and reputation of the principal (DeMott, 1998).

Agency relationships arise from a number of sources that includes the division of labour (Mitnick, 1984). For example, there are property investors such as pension funds like National Railways of Zimbabwe Pension Fund which has a main mandate to pay pension benefits to members when they retire. However, these organisations have made significant investments in commercial real estate properties around the country. The pension fund cannot directly engage in the management of their entire commercial real estate properties, so they can engage a renowned property manager or agent such as Knight Frank to help in the management of their real estate assets thereby creating an agency relationship. It has been observed that humans do not have time to do everything they need because other complex tasks often require more than one actor (Mitnick, 1984). Mitnick (1984) terms this division of labour practical or structural agency. Furthermore, Mitnick (1984) has noted that agency relationships arise from the acquisition of expertise or access to specialized knowledge and he labelled this content full agency. Agency relationships also arise from the bridging of physical, social and temporal distance. Lastly, agency relationships also materialise when parties amalgamate in a bid to enjoy benefits of operating collectively, for example, economies of scale and a great minimisation of risks. This is referred to as systemic or collective agency (Mitnick, 1984). This is evidenced when the property manager amalgamates various properties owned by several firms and starts to manage them internally for a commission.

The agency theory is concerned with resolving two problems, explained above, that can occur in agency relationships. This special relationship needs control since problems can easily be created. Two problems exist, first, is the problem when the principal cannot account for the productiveness or usefulness of his agent thus the principal is not be able to account for what his agent is doing in relation to the specifications of their management contract (Eisenhardt, 1989; Shapiro, 2005). Secondly, when both parties have different attitudes and behaviours towards risk, a problem materialises (Eisenhardt, 1989; Shapiro, 2005). Apart from the principal-agency problems, the principal's control should be exercised effectively on the agents because when they are empowered to act on behalf of the principal, they might engage in activities that leave the third parties at loss of which the principal would be expected to reimburse the third parties and claim damages from the agent (Shapiro, 2005). This calls for supervision of agents by the principals. These reasons altogether call for special arrangements to be made in-order to ensure that the principal-agent problems are always under control. Although principal-agent problems have been proven to exist by sociologists, for example, Shapiro (2005), principals and their agents many a time carry same interests. Agents are more likely to be even honest when entrusted with responsibilities.

The main problem experienced in this regard is between the property manager, who is the agent, and the property owner, who is the principal. The problem is experienced because of the first principal-agent problem if it is becoming difficult for the principal to believe that the agent is representing him well when he is failing to collect rentals from tenants and when many tenants are evading paying rents. When accrued rental arrears are converted to bad debts, it is the principal who gets to suffer more in operating costs and unpaid rentals and this represents a loss to the investor. This has created a great challenge to the relationship between principals, who are property owners, and the agents, who are property managers. This challenge is attributed to the tenants' failure to pay their rental as they fall due. The agency theory underpins this study due to the disputes and tensions between property owners and managers caused by tenants evading to pay their rentals.

Methodology

The research objective of this study involves finding out if alternative measures can be taken by property managers to correct the mishap in property management. The question underpinning this study is: Why tenants are evading their rental obligations and what must be done to stop this development? The study sough to establish the perspectives of tenants for evading paying rent to property owners and the rationale behind that move. The approach used in this study included consultations with main stakeholders in property management. Two main groups of tenants exist, namely residential and commercial groups. This study is mainly interested in commercial tenants. This group normally rents out space for income generating activities such a shop, an office or retail space.

Total tenants in Zimbabwe are estimated to be over one million. The researcher only administered 50 (fifty) questionnaires to tenants because of inadequate financial resources and time constrains. Stakeholders in property industry such as landlords, managing agents, estate agents, and council members answered questions following an interview guide that was created by the researcher. The entire study created quantitative and qualitative responses and data. The quantitative data was analysed using figures and tables in the results sections while the qualitative data was analysed textually and thematically. The art of real estate management is encompassing, therefore several stakeholders contributed in the study so that the chapter could have an intimate appreciation of true matters on the ground. Three main stakeholders were interviewed. The stakeholders included the property managers, the property owners and tenants. The move to consult all stakeholders was initiated by the need to get perspectives and perceptions of different parties in a real estate management agreement. The researcher mainly wanted to establish the viewpoint of property managers and their reactions when tenants with very large rental arrears moved from rented premises without an eviction order. This was important as it was the basis of the entire study.

The researcher enquired from agents if it was indeed true that sometimes tenants with large rental arrears could leave rented premises without notice. The researcher also wanted to establish if tenants relocated to new premises after leaving their previous rented sites. If this was the case, the researcher wanted to establish the steps taken by property owners and managers to mediate and deal with such cases. Finally, the researcher wanted to identify tenants who moved from one premise to another after accumulating significant arrears. However, only tenants operating small businesses admitted to such misdeed. The researcher ended up administering a questionnaire to general tenants and asked them to respond assuming that they had significant rental arrears. To blend the responses obtained from various stakeholders directly involved in the management contracts and leasing of space, the researcher also inquired from board members of the real estate industry regulator, Real Estate Institute of Zimbabwe (REIZ). Tools used for the purposes of data collection were interviews and questionnaires. The researcher however maintained high ethical considerations and did not name any of the respondents in the chapter. Challenges were mainly faced in identifying tenants who moved from one premise to another and after accumulating arrears. Generally, with the employed methodology, the researcher knows that the obtained data, if interpreted correctly could become useful and important in the advancement of the real estate management practice in Zimbabwe and other developing countries who are also facing challenges in their real estate industries.

Results and Discussion

This section brings about the main thrust of this study. The section contains four main subsections. The subsections include input from tenants, landlords, the property managers and, lastly, the Estate Agents Council. Basically, these subsections give a summary of the main findings that were obtained at the data collection stage. The data represents the results that were obtained from the research. The researcher presented the data as it was originally intended and no alterations whatsoever were made by the researcher. The errors in laying down results or even from the data collection stage remain the responsibility of the researcher. Through support for shared knowledge and learning, the researcher presents what was obtained to get the practical aspect of this study.

Perspectives of tenants

A total of 50 tenants engaged in different trades completed the questionnaires. These trades ranged from small phone accessories shops, boutiques, office space, food outlets and hair saloon shops. The following Figure 19.1 shows the groups of tenants who completed the administered questionnaire. Initially, it was targeted that each group of tenants was expected to complete 10 questionnaires. However, because of difficulties in locating tenants caused by mobility, different groups ended up completing more and some less than the initially allocated 10 questionnaires. All the tenants who completed the questionnaires are based in Harare and operate at various buildings selected purposively throughout the Harare Central Business District.

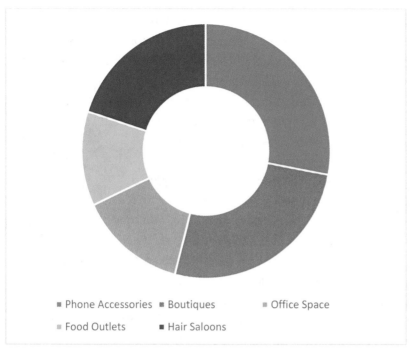

Figure 19.1: Respondents and Business Nature
Source: Survey, (2017)

- **Phone Accessories Shops**

The 14 respondents (28%) represented phone accessories shop operators who responded. This group highlighted that they are mostly interested in operating in strategic positions to attract much clientele traffic so that their phone accessories could be able to push more volumes. Most of the tenants occupy the downtown part of the CBD where bus termini generate a huge volume of traffic of people. The interviewed tenants (93%) who carry business of selling phone accessories did not have registered companies and they did not pay any returns to the Zimbabwe Revenue Authority (ZIMRA). When asked about their views towards high rentals and issue of rental arrears, 21% of this group of operators noted that the sales they make in rented premises are inadequate to meet all their business expenses so they sometimes resort to extending opening hours, set up some selling points even in streets and underselling their competitors so that they can meet break-even point. Of this group, 57% admitted that they sometimes leave rented premises when they noted that the rental arrears have ballooned, and they moved to other new rented premises. This was the main interest of the researcher and it was clear that, generally, tenants involved in selling phone accessories can easily move to new premises since their business is small and can operate anywhere since the clientele they serve can be obtained in nearly every street corner.

• Boutiques

Boutique tenants (13) selling fashioned clothes have occupied nearly all the streets in Harare Central Business District. Of the total tenants that were consulted, those involved in selling clothes represented 26% of all tenants who completed the questionnaires. Of the total boutiques operators who were interviewed, 77% were registered companies that were contributing returns in the form of PAYE (pay as you earn) and tax returns to the tax collector, ZIMRA. Since many of these operators represent a significant number of tenants in the Central Business District, it can generally be agreed that their business is performing well. The questionnaire completed by this group proved that, despite having a viable business plan, the team is suffering high space costs from property managers and property owners. The boutiques operators argued that property owners expect them to pay for all property expenses including all the vacant space in upper floors of business which in most instances will be reserved for office use. These operators noted that it was difficult for them to move from premises to premises running away from accumulated rentals because their business was based on reputation and confidence of the public since on many occasions, their business allowed them to sell goods on lay bye. This therefore meant that, generally, these tenants cannot abruptly leave their premises because they mostly consider their clients and their established relationships with the public.

• Office Space

Besides big reputable organisations that occupy more than 1000 square metres of office space, there are also other smaller offices that are involved in consultancy business in office buildings. Fourteen percent (14%) representing 7 tenants who completed the questionnaire were tenants at buildings using their rented premises for office business use. Organisations that occupy most office space are normally registered companies. Of these organisations, 57% admitted that they had ballooned rental arrears and were struggling to keep track with the demanded rentals. These organisations were significantly affected by the difficult economic conditions that were affecting the country. The economic performance was not matching high rental charges in office space. Tenants who occupy office space are registered companies and they are willing to protect their reputation and consistency to continue pursuing business from the same address. Furthermore, tenants noted that it could be too costly to change operating addresses. Managers in the offices noted that the organisations are expected to reprint stationery which matched with their new addresses if they move from premises to premises in a bid to evade rental arrears.

- **Food outlets**

Fast food outlets shops have remained in business despite the economic meltdown in Zimbabwe. These are necessary since they provide a basic good without human beings cannot survive. The 6 tenants interviewed basically form 12% of the entire population of the tenants that were interviewed. Although this figure is generally low, the responses that were obtained generally represents an intimate appreciation of the responses mainly noted on the ground. Fifty percent (50%) of interviewed operators using space as food outlets expressed concerns over high rental charges. The charges were reported to be unsustainable. More than half of the interviewed operators (66%) using rented premises as food outlets noted that because they are selling food, which is a necessity for the working class that spends the whole day in town, they are able to make enough sales that are able to cover the basic expenses including the high rentals. The group however pointed that they cannot easily relocate to new premises since they will not easily find a good site to establish their business. It was also noted by the researcher that this business prioritises location since it is the main determinant for them to achieve higher sales volumes.

- **Hair Saloons**

As initially expected, the researcher managed to interview the planned 20% representing 10 tenants of the population sample of tenants. This group of tenants is running its business single-handed. On many occasions the tenants sometimes group themselves in batches and open up a single shop were each member of the group rents a single chair so as to service individual clients. One unique characteristic of this business is that each hair designer usually has contact details of their clients so that in case of change of address, it is easy for the operator to invite clients to the new trading address. Of the interviewed barbers, 80% admitted that each time they feel that they are being charged unfair rentals, they normally pay the landlord amounts they consider to be current "fair" rents. In the event that their rental arrears have ballooned, these operators admitted that they simply move on to new premises and leave behind outstanding huge rental arrears. It is therefore difficult for property managers to keep track of the debt and, eventually with time, the agent recommends to the property owner that the debt be treated as bad debts. The following sections detail the results obtained from the other important stakeholders.

Perspectives of the principals

This group represented owners of real estate properties throughout Zimbabwe. Property owners range from large pension funds, insurance companies, banks and other individual property firms also including few private individuals. Basically, property investors own real estate because they expect a reasonable return so as to make profits and meet their trade obligations. The study revealed that property firms have also been affected by the difficult economic conditions. Most firms highlighted that they have shifted attention from rental collections to other sources for them to continue in existence. Commercial real estate has been underperforming characterised by very high default and less occupancy rates. This has led to property owners opt to maintain real estate investments as they store in value and are an effective hedge against inflation. Landlords however noted that, for the buildings that are occupied, tenants have accumulated high rental arrears. The property owners who manage their buildings in-house have reported that they have tried to take legal action against their tenants and, in many instances, tenants move away from the properties and leave behind nothing. It had also proved to be fruitless to them even if they appoint debt collectors as some business had accumulated rental arrears that were larger than the capital structure of the tenant. In many occasions, the property owners pointed that they are left with the option of taking forgoing rentals and just return real estate assets by writing off the rental arrears.

With the current economic performance, 60% of principals are convinced that their appointed property management agents are trying to bring the best results they can in a depressed economy. For other principals that are managing their properties internally, they noted that it was actually better for them to collect all rentals and avoid leakages represented by paying agent's commission. To curb the challenges landlords are facing of tenants who run away, 60% of interviewed landlords pointed out that they have employed property managers to administer their real estate assets. This move was as result of noting that it was difficult to manage tenants without proper property management systems and expertise of how to handle ever constant features of management disputes. This was a strategy to make sure that they collect the maximum possible from their real estate investments. Generally, with the interviews carried on with the property owners, it emerged that these stakeholders are the ones who suffer most as they would be the one expected to pay operating costs for buildings that are not occupied. They also suffer greatly at the hands of unscrupulous tenants who run away from one premise to another trying to avoid paying accumulated rental arrears to the previous landlords. Overall, this group pointed out that they have employed massive selection criteria each time when they are selecting a tenant to lease their space. However, they admitted that, on many occasions, they ended up lowering their standards since they may also let out space to reduce their void levels.

Perspectives of agents / property managers

A total of 10 property management firms and agents with different sizes were interviewed by the researcher. The quest to interview players with different sizes and experience was initiated by the need to uncover the correct experiences in the industry. The research revealed that property managers are also facing the problem of tenants who run away from their rental arrears. Agents are only able to claim their commission from rentals that would have been paid. This means that they can only charge and be rewarded their commission from the collected rentals. Agents explained that, because of such an arrangement, they are fighting hard to collect very high amounts so that their income can also significantly improve. Property managers are aware of the proclivities of some unscrupulous tenants who, after accumulating rentals, abruptly leave premises in a bid to defrauding property managers and property owners of their commission and rentals respectively. One mitigating strategy being employed by agents is that of vetting all tenants before giving them space to rent in their buildings. Furthermore, other managing agents are getting details and surety forms signed by directors of small companies so that, if the company tries to run away without settling rental arrears, the property manager can pursue legal action against the directors and the surety of the organisations. Property managers pointed that their job was very difficult as it included collecting rentals at the same time trying to maintain the value of the property. Many operators submitted that the selection strategy has proved to be fruitful since they are only admitting reputable organisations into their premises under their management.

Perspectives of the Estate Agents Council (EAC)

The researcher managed to get hold of a board member that sits on the panel of EAC board. An interview guide was administered to the member who responded giving his own personal opinion and opinions of the Council. The member showed that, while he appreciates that the real estate industry was not performing to capacity, the challenges that were faced by property owners and managers in recovering ballooned rental arrears was a technical challenge. The member showed that if the practice had good systems that could allow them to keep track of operations and memberships, some of these challenges would have been avoided. He pointed out that the market has a system of self-adjusting pointing out that whenever an anomaly is noticed, it should be seen as an indicator to the conscience of the policy maker to give attention to the new development. Prior to the interview, the researcher had indicated to the informant the purpose of the study. So, during the interview, the informant kept on refereeing back to the main thrust of the study that there was actually a need for a database which could be accessed by all registered property managers so that they could use and keep track of the tenants and their past history when issuing out rented spaces. The overall conclusion obtained by the researcher from perspectives of EAC is that the council is willing to allow developmental innovations that would make the practice of registered property managers easy and more transparent.

Policy Options, Recommendations and Practical Implications

The findings from the study show that tenants are avoiding paying rentals, as a result, a national database for all tenants in Zimbabwe is needed. This is also supported by Tsai, Ruan, Sahu, Shaikh, and Shin (2007) in 'Virtualization-based techniques for enabling multi-tenant management tools'. Furthermore, it can be added that such a system may improve some of the common challenges that are experienced in the practice of real estate management in Zimbabwe. The system that should be created should have particular facilities. First, it should be online and be updated by various users in different geographical locations. This ability makes it unique and easily accessible by all intended users. Secondly, the system should only be used by all registered estate agents so that tenants should not have access to it because they may alter information. The system should be able to have a high-powered database to keep information of every registered tenant, trading names and names of directors such that when a property manager searches on a particular client, the system should be able to show out the full history pertaining to the tenant. Such a property management system ought to capture all the relevant particulars of tenants and landlords, for example, duration of leases so that one can easily know if a particular tenant has a current valid lease with other property owners elsewhere or not.

The proposed and recommended system has proven theoretically to be able to yield massive returns for both the property managers and property owners. It is therefore important that when the researchers finish developing the system, the industry should be willing to try out the exciting new development which ought to improve property management system. Just as property management firms use property management systems like SAP and MD property manager, there is also a need for systems that manage all tenants in the industry. Unless this system is designed and adopted by all property managers in Zimbabwe, the real estate management industry will continue to have tenants who succeed in defrauding property owners evade to pay their rental arrears. In addition, these errant tenants may still be able to move to other new trading premises without any action being taken against them.

Conclusion

The study concluded that the property management industry needs to have a national database system that stores all the background and history of tenants. This national database ought to be accessed and used by all property managers in Zimbabwe. The national database ought to have the capacity to register all tenants in buildings. Property owners ought to share information about their current tenants so that they can all be entered into the system. This would enable other property managers to carry out a background check on a prospective tenant. The national database should be specific in relation to the data it shows, for example, it should share the details of tenants and their current and rental arrears. If the national database can be used and be accessible to all property managers, it can become a vital tool used by all property firms as the main source of reference when a tenant is seeking new rental space. The study has shown that tenants run away from one premise to the next one trying to avoid payment of rental arrears. With a national database for all tenants, it will be easier to show one's accumulated rental arrears which is taken as a bad record only to be cleared by updating accounts with the previous landlord.

References

DeMott, D.A. (1997). A revised prospectus for a third restatement of agency. *UC Davis L. Rev, 31*(1), 1035 - 1064.

Eisenhardt, K.M. (1989). Agency theory: An assessment and review. *Academy of Management Review, 14*(1), 57-74.

Giddens, A. (1984). The constitution of society: Outline of the theory of structuration. Berkeley: University of California Press

Mangudhla, T. (2016, March 11) Property market hits a new low. Zimbabwe Independent. In Available online: https://www.theindependent.co.zw/2016/03/11/ property-market-hits-a-new-low/.

Mitnick, B.M. (1984). Agency problems and political institutions. Presented at Annu. Meet. Am. Polit. Sei. Assoc, 80th, Chicago.

Mudehwe, R., Chirisa, I. and Matamanda, A.R. (2016). Green leasing in Zimbabwe: Lessons from Harare commercial property market. *International Journal of Real Estate Studies, 10*(2), 13-24.

Ross, S.A. (1973). The economic theory of agency: The principal's problem. *The American Economic Review, 63*(2), 134-139.

Shapiro, S. P. (2005). Agency theory. *Annual. Rev. Sociol, 31*, 263-284.

Tsai, C.H., Ruan, Y., Sahu, S., Shaikh, A. and Shin, K.G. (2007, October). Virtualization-based techniques for enabling multi-tenant management tools. In *International workshop on distributed systems: Operations and management* (pp. 171-182). Berlin, Heidelberg: Springer.

Chapter 20

Rubber from Euphorbia Matebelensis Latex

Samuel Mudzviti and Jeofrey Matai

Summary:

The chapter assesses the suitability of latex obtained from Euphorbia Matebelensis species in rubber manufacturing as a way of promoting local economic growth by capitalising on local renewable natural resources which form the economic base of particular localities as well as to meet the demand of the growing rubber market with locally manufactured and cheaper rubber than imported products. It has been argued that failure to tap on local natural resources to trigger development of localities is one of the reasons for regional imbalances and high levels of poverty experienced in most rural areas. Although some localities are endowed with such resources in large quantities, lack of scientific knowledge on how such resources can be processed into finished products that can be exported to other regions in exchange for income is one of the major challenges facing certain localities resulting in these localities lagging behind with their inhabitants languishing in poverty and consequential negative externalities. Using rural Buhera as a case study, laboratory tests were done in which characterisation of the tapped latex in terms of chemical and physical parameters, structure and functional groups using an infrared spectroscopy were made to ascertain the suitability of Euphorbia Matebelensis latex for rubber production. The Euphorbia Matebelensis tree species were purposively selected and then a tree within the Euphorbia Matebelensis specie was then picked randomly for the purposes of carrying out the tests, that is, to find out if the latex from Euphorbia Matebelensis meets the standard requirements that are suitable for rubber manufacturing. The study revealed that the physical parameter results analysed for the raw latex falls within the permissible standard ranges of natural rubber, thus, it meets all the characteristics of good rubber. Recommendations were made that research should be done on how the Euphorbia Matebelensis tree species can be grown commercially to increase the resource base for the production of rubber. It was also recommended that new technologies that can be used for the production of rubber Euphorbia Matebelensis tree species in large quantities be explored.

Introduction

Lack of knowledge and suitable equipment for the processing of raw materials into finished and useful products hinder many developing countries from capitalising on their abundant natural resources and address poverty related issues in the countries' rural localities and the nations at large. In Zimbabwe, the economic challenges that the country is going through has, of late, worsened the situation as any efforts to invest in research and development are thwarted by lack of finance thereby impacting on the technical capacity for innovation. However, if the locally available resources are tapped into and processed, opportunities may arise to better the livelihoods of the communal people, an activity that can reduce regional imbalances and boost the economy of the country. Researches have been done on how local resources can be processed into finished products, for example, gold and fruits among others, as a way of adding value to the products and subsequently improving the livelihoods of the local communities, (Campbell, Luckert and Scoones, 1997; Aragón and Rud, 2013; Chong et al. 2016). However, none have attempted to investigate the physical parameters of latex extracted from *Euphorbia Matebelensis* to determine whether it can be used for the production of rubber and unlock opportunities for the improvement of local communities. This study characterises the raw latex from *Euphorbia Matebelensis* in terms of chemical and physical parameters to determine the functional groups and compound constituents of latex in order to assess the suitability of the latex in the manufacturing of rubber products as per specified standards as well as to analyse the physical, chemical and mechanical parameters of produced rubber products. The motivation behind this is to assess the suitability of the latex obtained from *Euphorbia Matebelensis* species in rubber manufacturing as a way of adding value to local resources and address livelihood issues in local areas focusing on rural Buhera where the *Euphorbia Matebelensis* plant species are plenty.

Background

Latex is made up of 5% of dry mass and other materials such as proteins, fatty acids, resins and inorganic materials (salts) found in natural rubber (Madhavan,2004). The world's first supply of rubber came from the evergreen rubber trees called *Hevea Brasiliensis* which are scattered throughout the Amazon forest in Brazil (Suzuki, 2004). Natural rubber is obtained from latex which exudes from the bark of the *Hevea* tree when it is cut. During that period, the demand for rubber was low and commercialisation was not thought of as an option. However, the invention of the motor car and the manufacturing of rubber tyres and utilisation of rubber as insulation material for electrical cables and wires gave rise to an increase in the demand for rubber. It soon became obvious that indigenous trees had to be grown in Brazil in order to meet the escalating demand for rubber. As a result of the rising demand, rubber seeds were germinated in greenhouses, and the seedlings were sent to various parts of the world such as Sri Lanka, Malaysia, Indonesia, and Thailand where plantations were developed (Thomas *et al. 2007*). This growth in demand and the corresponding response to calls for increased supply of rubber brought positive impacts to the local communities as these unlocked opportunities for employment and improved livelihoods (Suzuki, 2004).

Natural rubber producing countries developed new ways of preparing rubber for commercial purposes. Usually the natural rubber latex collected from the tree exists as a colloidal suspension. The synthesis of natural rubber is done either as concentrate latex, known as skim latex or as coagulated latex. Fresh latex is preserved by ammonia solution from coagulation. Skim latex is a material resulting from the production of concentrated latex in the centrifugation process. After centrifuging the fresh latex, about 5-10% of total rubber, together with an enhanced proportion of the non-rubber constituents remains the serum phase of the skim latex (Tabb, 2011). The raw latex collected from the tree is also treated with acetic or formic acid to coagulate the suspension rubber particles within the latex. The coagulated latex is then pressed between rollers to consolidate the rubber into 0.6μm thick slaps or thin crepe sheets. The rubber is then air-dried or smoke-dried. Currently rubber is sold with a guarantee of quality, so grading each sheet or block by eye is no longer necessary (Gazeley *et al. 2008*).

Natural rubber is also treated with chemicals such as sodium hydrogen thio-sulphate ($NaHSO_3$), to bleach the rubber and then produce rubber of pale colour named pale crepe (Kalpakjian, 2004). The world's largest producers of natural rubber are Malaysia and Indonesia and they produce 70% of the world's production (Hertzog, 2005). Sri Lanka and Thailand produce nearly 15% of the world's production. The other countries outside Asia which are significant rubber producers are Nigeria and Liberia. The industrial countries of Western Europe, the U.S.A., Russia, China and Japan are the main rubber consumers (Smith, 2009).

In India, the government launched rubber development programs in some parts of the country in order to effectively rehabilitate tribal communities in the region and meet the ever-growing domestic demand for natural rubber by introducing the growing and production of rubber to smallholder farmers (Viswanathan, 2007). This approach has also provided a dominant contribution to the gross household income of the rubber growers and provides the smallholders with ample capabilities for resilience during difficult times and ensure a sustained flow of income for their families. However, although rubber production can be a source of livelihoods, as is the case with some parts of India, and a national economic base as in Thailand, Jawjit, Pavasant and Kroeze (2015) argue that this is done at the expense of the environment. Measures should therefore be in place to keep an eye and combat the likely negative externalities to the environment.

Euphorbia Matabelensis species are mostly found in hot and humid climatic conditions such as the Savanna lands. The plant grows to height of about 5.3metres with spiny branches which are in inflorescences. The plant can be grown either from seedlings or grafted buds (Adams, 2010). The Shona name is *Chisimbo* and the botanical name is *Euphorbia Matabelensis*. In Zimbabwe, *Euphorbia Matebelensis* is found abundantly in Buhera district, a dry region in Manicaland Province, Zimbabwe. The specie has little value in the local area as people generally extract the latex from the tree for minor purposes such as trapping birds to complement their food. However, the plant has potential to improve the livelihoods of the local people if it is exploited in a manner that adds value to the latex and options for commercialisation of the plant species is to be provided.

Figure 20.1: *Euphorbia Matabelensis* **tree species and closed up flowers (2014)**

Study Area

Makuvise Village at Chiurwi School is in Nyashanu rural area, Ward 23, Buhera District, in Zimbabwe. Buhera District is in the Savanna lands (Surveyor- General, 2012). Tree types are mainly deciduous, and the soil is loose and sand with patches of red and black cotton soils. The annual rainfall is between 250mm- 400mm and temperature is in the range of 250C- 300C and may be relatively higher between the months of October and January. The geographical location of Makuvise Village is in the southern part of Buhera District. The village is situated in the Middle of Save Catchment area (ZINWA, 2009).

Literature Review

Most of the world's rubber trees are grown either on small holdings or on large farms known as estates or plantations and the majority of the trees are propagated by bud grafting (Buist, 2007). Countries such as Indonesia, Malaysia, Thailand and India have experienced rapid structural transformation in terms of growth of the smallholding sector under various socio-economic, political, and institutional contexts, (Viswanathan, 2007), and today smallholdings account for almost 90% of rubber production in Thailand and 89% in India. Such practices result in the improvement of people's lives as farming of the rubber producing trees creates employment in the various sectors associated with rubber tree farming to rubber processing and manufacturing of rubber products. However, institutional arrangements play a significant role in the success or failure of smallholder rubber farming.

Euphorbia Matabelensis species are widespread throughout the Savanna lands of Zimbabwe (Hiller, 2005). The shrub is mainly found in semi-dry and bush land and many types of woodlands, stony slopes, and reverie coastal thickets. The species grow on different soil types. Specific growing conditions include uniform temperatures of above 26^0C, an annual rainfall of over 200mm, well-drained heavy soils and plenty of shade during its early stages of growth which is provided by tall trees (White *et al.* 2008). Since the world's first supplies of rubber was obtained from the wild and ever-green tree called *Hevea Brasiliensis*, which is a native to Brazil, the plant produces a regular supply of a white milky fluid called latex which is the same stuff being obtained from *Euphorbia Matabelensis* plant in Zimbabwe (Jinno, 2007).

From studies done by Basslers *et al.* (2010), the *Hevea Brasiliensis* tree, as compared to *Euphorbia Matabelensis,* grows very well in hot, humid climatic conditions of equatorial lowlands. For its commercial cultivation, it requires uniform temperatures of above 26^0C, an annual rainfall of over 2000mm which should be fairly evenly distributed throughout the year; well-drained heavy soils, plenty of shade during its early stages of growth that is provided by inter-planting with banana plants and abundant cheap labour for weeding and tending the young trees and later for tapping trees to extract the latex. Other trees which have shown promises as sources of natural rubber include *Focus Elastica* (rubber fig); *Castilla Elastica* (Panama rubber tree) and *Taraxacum Officinale* (Dandelio) (Basslers *et al.* 2010).

Presently, natural rubber suppliers are Malaysia, Indonesia, Sri Lanka and Nigeria. The production of natural rubber begins at the plantation where a slit is made into the bark of the rubber tree to allow the flow of a milky sap. With growing research and innovation, attempts have been made to extract natural rubber from certain plants such as *Perthenium Argentatum* and that proved to be of economic success (Griffths, 2008). Latex extracted from *Hevea Brazilliensis,* a native plant of Brazil, proved to have an elastic parameter that eventually led to a multi–billion dollar of rubber processing industry. This has improved the lives of vast majority of people of this planet (Graham, 2010).

The uses of rubber range from house-hold to industrial products. Examples are motor vehicle tyres which are on high demand from the motor industry, surgical gloves that are used in the health sector by medical practitioners, electrical cable insulations, pencil markings erasers, condom manufacturing, shoes soles, gaskets slurry pump liners, rubber springs, vibration mounts and impellers (Archer *et al.* 2005).

Latex extracted from trees exists as a colloidal suspension which is mainly harvested in the form of latex, a sticky, milky colloid drawn off by making incisions into rubber trees. Natural rubber consists of suitable polymers of the organic compound isoprene with minor impurities of the other organic compounds plus water. It constitutes neutral lipids (2.4%), glycolipids and phospholipids (1.0%), proteins (2.2%) carbohydrates (0.4%), ash (0.1%) and compounds (0.1%). The forms of poly-isoprene, which are useful as natural rubber, are known as elastomers (Senntheshannmugana *et al.* 2005).

Products made from rubber have flexible and 3-dimensional chemical structure and are able to withstand large force under deformation. So, rubber exhibits unique physical and chemical properties. The stress-strain behaviour of rubber exhibits the Mullins effect which is often modelled as hyper-elastic. Owing to the presence of double bond in each repeat unit, natural rubber is susceptible to vulcanization and sensitive to ozone cracking. Therefore, two main solvents for rubber are turpentine and naphtha (petroleum). Since rubber does not dissolve easily, the material is finely divided by shredding prior its immersion. An ammonia solution is used as a preservative for coagulation of raw latex while it is being transported from collection site (Sweet, 2009). Ultimate Tensile Strength is the maximum tensile stress reached in stretching a test piece usually a flat dumb-bell shape to its breaking point. By conversion, the force required is expressed as force per unit area of the original cross-section of the test length (Marlies, 2005). The other property is vulcanization. Natural rubber is often vulcanized, a process by which rubber is heated such that sulphur, peroxide and bisphenol are added to improve resistance, elasticity and prevention of degradability. The effects of vulcanization are to transform an elastomer from a weaker thermos-plastic mass without useful mechanical properties into a strong and elastic tough rubber (Jacob, 2005).

Latex is a dispersion of rubber particles in aqueous phase. Most types of rubber, both natural and synthetic are made into an aqueous form (Duerden, 2004). Latex can be used in specialized application such as those requiring oil, solvents and flame resistance and various mixing techniques to produce different grades of dispersions, that is, ball-milling or ultrasonic for fine particle dispersions and simple stirring or colloid milling for coarse dispersion. Latex can be processed either as concentrate for the manufacturing of thin goods such as surgical gloves, balloons, condoms, bladders, hot water bottles and very fine rubber products or as coagulated under specified conditions by using formic or acetic acid. The coarser particle-sized dispersion known as slurry is acceptable latex foam used mainly for carpet backing (Blow, 2006). Therefore, when a rubber product is made, the primary raw material is a polymer. There is some elasticity, but not always. The raw material is mixed with certain chemicals and reagents such ethanoic acid, sulphur, peroxide or biphenyl to produce a rubber compound which is then subsequently vulcanized. A rubber compound obtained by mixing a base polymer with series of additives is the one referred to as rubber by the industry. The choice of the base polymer and additives is therefore closely linked to the type of properties to be achieved and the quantity of additives varies as a percentage on the weight (Sweet, 2006).

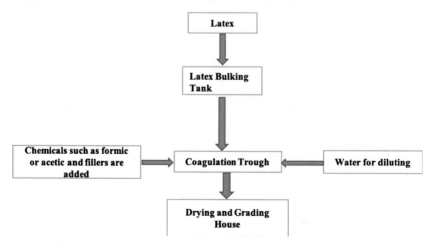

Figure 20.3: Latex Processing Flow Chart; Source (Ceiesielski, 2010)

Latex dipping and casting are procedures of rubber processing. The procedure uses a porcelain or aluminium mould that is repeatedly dipped in the latex compound. Once set, the coated former is washed, air-dried and vulcanized in a steam autoclave before the product is removed. In order to increase the thickness of the deposit obtained per dip, the former is immersed in coagulant before and after each latex dip (Korana *et al.* 2006). Latex casting is a similar technique to dipping but is used to make hollow seamless articles. The product formed on the inside of the mould will give a better definition (Tarachiwin *et al.* 2007). The processing of rubber provides mechanical processes involved in the production of various types of rubber goods for commercial purposes. As the latex is gathered, a small amount of ammonia is added as a preservative. The latex is later coagulated by addition of 5% solution of acetic acid. Then the coagulum is later washed and dried. The industry uses very powerful machinery with the potential to cause fatal and serious injuries Therefore, there are established industry safe-guarding standards for certain machinery (Nandi, 2005).

Crepe rubber results if a small amount of sodium bisulphate is added to bleach the rubber. The coagulum is rolled out into thin sheets about 1mm thick and dried in air at about 50^0C. If smoked sheets are to be made, the bleaching process is omitted, and somewhat thicker sheets are rolled. These are dried in smoke-houses at about 50^0C in the smoke from wood. The mastication process, according to discovery by Hancock (2004), describes the procedure of making the rubber a soft, gummy mass when subjected to severe mechanical working. The addition of compounding ingredients such as sodium bisulphate is greatly facilitated by that treatment, which is usually carried out on roll mills or internal mixers or plasticators. Mastication is accompanied by a marked decrease in the molecular weight of the rubber. Oxidative degradation is an important factor in mastication since the decrease in viscosity and the other property changes do not take place if the rubber is masticated in the absence of oxygen. Poly-isoprene, especially when chemically modified by vulcanization process has the remarkable ability to substantially return to their original shape after being stretched considerably. Therefore, any material which fulfils this requirement is entitled to be called rubber. So, vulcanization of rubber creates disulphide bonds between chains, thus it limits the degree of freedom. As a result, the chains tighten more quickly for a given strain, thereby increasing the elastic force constant and making rubber hard and less extensible. Natural rubber is often vulcanized, a process by which rubber is heated to such that sulphur; peroxide and bisphenol are added to improve resistance; elasticity and prevention of degradability (Hartley, 2005).

Particular care is greatly required in storage areas to ensure that the incompatible materials such as carbon black and sulphur are adequately segregated. However, many rubber compounding additives are known to be highly explosive when in finely divided state such as Azodicarbonamide, calcium and zinc steer ages. A good design dust extraction and collection systems should be fitted and good housing-keeping should be maintained in order to minimize the risk of secondary dust explosion (Maurice, 2011). Once the compound ingredients have been weighed out, they are mixed together using specialized machines capable of dealing with the high stresses involved in shearing rubber. So Mixing can be by internal or external/open milling (Gorton, 2006).

Before the rubber is being added into the mixer, it may require cutting into small pieces on a bale cutter or guillotine. These are usually down stroking machines which should be securely fenced with interlocking access gates (Tanaka, 2005). Most of rubber industry uses the mechanical handling such as the vacuum bale cutter lifter. It is reliable and low-cost option for handling standard 33.3 kilograms (Hoffman, 2009). Internal mixing involves the feeding of the compound ingredients into the enclosed mixing chamber via the feed hopper and then mixed by the shearing action of two winged rotors the walls of the mixing chambers resulting in a continuous nip. Furthermore, a powered ram of floating weight in the feed throat forces ingredients into the mixing chamber which is usually water-cooled. The mixed compound is then discharged via a sliding or hinged door which is set below the mixing chamber. The procedure is usually onto a two-roll mill, then roller die, twin-screw extruder, conveyor and slip hoist or wheeled truck (Gan, 2005). External mixing refers to mixing operations using horizontal two roll mills. It is operated by the mill man who places the various ingredients in the nip formed between the rolls and mixes the compound by cutting it off the rolls re-feeding it into the nip until all the ingredients are added (George, 2005). Extrusion as a process involves forcing uncured rubber through a die under pressure to form a shaped profile or sheet. This is where rotating knives (or die face cutters) can then convert extruded materials into pellets slugs for a further processing (Lee *et al.* 2009).

Mechanical hazards and safety issues on machines must be considered.

- *Screw (Scroll) extruder:* The machine conveys uncured rubber forwards down the barrel and through the die by the action of a rotating extruder. It produces continuous extruded sections such as cable covering. Screw extruders can be either hot fed with warmed pre-heated or cold-fed. Therefore, the main hazards on screw rubber extruder include the trap between the rotating screw and the fixed parts of the machine at the feeding opening and the feed systems can create additional trapping hazards such as a crammer feed device (Weng, 2008).

- *Fire and explosion hazards:* Many of the rubber compounding additives are fire sensitive, particularly sulphur and organic peroxides used as curing agents, and azodi–carbonamide also used as a blowing agent in some celled rubber or lattices (Kabuko, 2007).
- *Cleaning and maintenance hazards:* The greatest hazard at internal mixers is during the maintenance and cleaning, including cleaning of blockages. This is where operators may need access to the mixing chambers or rotors, via the discharge opening. Due to the size of internal mixers, operators could be working at three levels, which include the rear inspection door on the feed platform, the discharge door at the motor platform and the dump chute access at the floor level. Communication is therefore difficult with the potential to increase risks. In addition, stored electrical, hydraulic and pneumatic energy as well as potential energy from gravity fall of floating weight and inertia from run-down of the rotors may be released if the correct run-down procedures are not properly followed (Gregg, 2003).

The following range of additives can be mixed with latex dispersion or emulsion:

- *Fillers:* There are two types namely reinforcing or non-reinforcing. For instance, carbon black is commonly used as reinforcing filler and that is why some rubbers are black. Calcium carbonate is also used as non-reinforcing filler (Davey, 2007).
- *Plasticizers:* These play a major qualitative role in building a rubber compound. They improve the flow of rubber during processing and improve filler dispersion on physical properties of vulcanized rubber at low temperatures. Examples are mineral oils and paraffin (Backhaus, 2003).
- *Vulcanization chemicals:* Vulcanization is the process whereby the gum-elastic raw material is converted into rubber-elastic end-product by subjecting under heat. Vulcanizing agents commonly used are sulphur; peroxide or bisphenol. They are added to improve the elastic force constant and making rubber harder and less extensible (Alenius, 2006).
- *Accelerators:* They increase the rate of cross-linked reaction and lower the sulphur content necessary to achieve the optimum vulcanization properties (Palosuo, 2003).
- *Curing agents:* The most common usually used is sulphur (Tangpakdee, 2004).
- *Thickeners:* They include casein; glue and cellulose derivatives (Nithi-Uthai, 2008).
- *PH adjusters:* These include ammonia; sodium hydroxide; potassium hydroxide and formaldehyde (Murari *et al.* 2003).

- *Biocides:* Mostly used are halogen derivatives for suppression of bacterial decay and fungal infection (Sekhar, 2008).
- *Activators:* They activate the vulcanization process and assist the accelerators to achieve their full potential (Blackey, 2005).
- *Ant-degrading Agents:* They increase the resistance to attacks of ozone; UV light and oxygen. These include waxes; substituted phenols; and amines based anti-oxidants.
- *Processing aids (Coagulants and gelling agents):* These are chemicals that improve the process ability, including calcium; magnesium salts; aluminium salts; acetic and formic acid; cyclohexyl-amine acetate and ammonium acetate (Nishiyama, 2003).

Pigments: These are organic and inorganic substances used to colour rubber compounds (Mooibroek, 2005).The calendaring process involves the passing through of rubber material under pressure through horizontal rolls when either heated or unheated. The rolls can either create a rubber sheet of required thickness or apply a thin layer onto a cloth liner by the process known as combining or frictioning. Calendars can have two, three or four rolls of various sizes and configurations (Fulton, 2003). The main mechanical hazards of calendars are caused by nips between the rolls for both the rubber and fabric feed. This is a particular problem during threading up, cleaning and maintenance. There is also a running nip at the take-off or wind-up devices. Depending on the design, there are other mechanical hazards caused by cooling drums; cutting devices; stock guides and auxiliary rolls for embossing on tensioning. The simplest way of preventing finger access to the nips is to use a fixed nip bar that extends the length of the rolls, positioned on more than 6mm from the surface of the roll to prevent a trapping point. There is also a risk of the operator getting entangled with materials and dragged over the table towards the nip. To prevent this risk, there is need to position.

Methods and Materials

The research adopted a case study approach in which Buhera was purposively selected for the study due to the abundance of the *Euphorbia Matebelensis* species and the general high prevalence of poverty in the area which can be addressed by the extraction of rubber from the *Euphorbia Matebelensis* plant. The research was quantitative in nature in which tests for parameters for latex extracted from *Euphorbia Matebelensis* tree were done to determine whether they can produce rubber of the expected quality. Using purposive sampling, the trees were randomly selected for the extraction of latex that was tested in the laboratory. The following equipment was used such as the cutting knife for stripping the bark of the tree. A cut was made halfway through the bark, extending about two thirds around the tree. An aluminium cup was used to receive the oozing raw latex. The flow of latex from the cut diminished in time necessitated the removal of another thin layer of bark. The cutting process was repeated several times until the cup was full. A storage container was used for keeping the raw latex. Then a small amount of ammonia solution was added as a preservative after collecting enough raw latex ready for transportation to the laboratory for analysis. The latex was first diluted with water, and then poured into a mixing container. It was then coagulated by adding 5% acetic acid in small quantities with continuous stirring by a glass rod.

The coagulum was then placed into a mould containing 2cm by 8 cm separators placed at intervals across the trough. The latex then became hard and strips of 2cm by 8cm were formed. The strips were dried into an oven set at 400C. The strips were graded by holding to the light to check whether they contain any holes or bits of foreign materials such as wood. Different mixtures were formed using additives such as carbon black and calcium bicarbonate peroxide.

The coagulum was then placed into a mould containing 2cm by 8 cm separators placed at intervals across the trough. The latex then became hard and strips of 2cm by 8cm were formed. The strips were dried into an oven set at 400C. The strips were graded by holding to the light to check whether they contain any holes or bits of foreign materials such as wood. Different mixtures were formed using additives such as carbon black, calcium bicarbonate and peroxide.

Dried strips were graded by holding them to the light to check whether they contained holes or bits of foreign materials such as wood as described by Basslers (2005). The strips were first weighed before placed in the oven set at 40^0C. After one hour the strips were then taken from the oven and cooled for twenty minutes, then re-weighed. The difference in masses before and after drying was determined then as the moisture content. The procedure was repeated for other samples. A sample was placed in water in a basin so that the water covered the sample completely. The sample remained fully immersed in water for a continuous period of24hours. After immersion, the sample was removed from the water and allowed to drain for a few minutes. Then the wet mass was determined (mass A). The sample was then placed in an oven set at 400C for a continuous period of 24 hours. The sample was removed from the oven and cooled for 20 minutes in a desiccator. The sample was re–weighed and the mass determined (Nanashiyama, 2006).

The tensile strength was determined by using an extensometer whereby a specimen with known length was placed on the instrument and clamped both ends. The instrument was switched on and the process continued until the specimen reached the moment of rupture. The procedure was repeated for more samples and different tensile strengths were determined using the same procedure as employed by Crafts (2004). Elongation or strain was determined using an extensometer whereby an extension between bench marks was produced by a tensile force applied to the sample under test. The initial length of sample was observed and then the sample was placed on the instrument and clamped both ends. The instrument was switched on and the test proceeded to the breaking point, that is, the ultimatum elongation at the moment of rapture. The final length at moment of rupture was observed expressed as a percentage of the initial length between the marks as described by Howard (2006).

The potential of hydrogen (pH) of the raw latex was determined using a pH meter. 50ml of raw latex sample was placed in a beaker and the probe was dipped into the sample, and then the pH reading was observed. The procedure was repeated for other mixtures of samples. In the investigation of natural products, compounds are particularly isolated and then analysed. Likewise, when carrying out a synthesis or preparation of a desired compound or test reaction, unexpected compounds are sometimes isolated. Then analysis and identification become important and desirable procedures (Miller *et al.* 2010). The organic nature of a compound is determined by complete oxidation of the compound to carbon dioxide (CO_2) and water (H_2O), using the process called carbon–hydrogen analysis. Then the presence of carbon dioxide is determined by conducting the effluent gas through limewater (saturated calcium hydroxide solution). If a precipitate of calcium carbonate is formed, this indicates the presence of carbon dioxide. The procedure is made quantitative by simply weighing sample of the unknown and then the water and carbon dioxide evolved from combustion are absorbed and weighed in absorption tubes of known weight. Then the percentages of carbon and hydrogen can be calculated. Once the percentage composition is known, the empirical formula, that is, the simplest atomic ratio formula can be also calculated. The equation for the reaction is as follows: CO_2 (g) + Ca $(OH)_2$(aq) $CaCO_3$(s) +H_2O (l) (Berglund, 2010).

Once the molecular formula of a compound is known, the structure of the compound should be determined, and the presence of functional groups could be determined by a variety of test reactions. When organic compounds are exposed to radiation, they absorb part of the radiation and a spectrum appeared. Therefore, the structure determination for the sample was carried out using an Infrared Spectroscopy technique whereby 5.0ml sample of raw latex was placed in a sample holder or cell tube. The cell tube was positioned in the path of an IR beam in order for the sample to absorb characteristic frequencies of IR radiation. The instrument was switched on, the process was allowed to reach the end, and the structural elucidation was identified. The IR information was presented in the form of a spectrum with wave-numbers as the x-axis and absorption intensity (percent transmittance) as the y-axis. The spectrum was matched with the spectrum of already known compound structures (Ansell, 2004).

IR spectroscopy is the common spectroscopic technique employed in organic and inorganic samples analysis. The main goal of IR spectroscopic analysis is to determine the chemical functional groups in the sample. 5.0ml raw latex sample was placed in a cell tube and then positioned in the path of an IR beam. The instrument was switched on, then the process allowed to reach the end and multiple functional groups gave rise to multiple-characteristic absorption in the region between 4000 and 400cm-1. The appearance of strong absorption bands in different regions revealed stretching vibrations which occurred between hydrogen and some other atoms with a mass of 19 or less. Thus, the spectra interpretation was done by matching it with the spectrum of known functional groups (Sherman, 2005). Infrared Spectroscopy is an important and popular tool for structural elucidation and compound identification. Infrared radiation spans a section of the electromagnetic spectrum having wave-numbers from roughly 13,000 to 10cm-1 or wave-length from 0.78 to 1000 μm. It is bound by the red end of the visible region at high frequencies and the region at low frequencies (Nair, 2008). Infrared absorption positions are generally presented as either wave-numbers (v) or as wavelengths (Scoffed, 2006). Wave-number is the number of waves per unit length. Thus wave-numbers are directly proportional to frequency, as well as the energy of the IR absorption. However, the wavenumber (cm-1, the reciprocal centimetre) is more commonly employed in modern IR instruments that are linear in the cm-1 scale (Katon, 2006). In contrast, wave-lengths are inversely proportional to frequencies and their associated energy. Currently, the recommended unit of wave-length is micrometre (μm). Generally, IR absorption information is presented in the form of a spectrum with wavelength or wavenumber as the x-axis and absorption intensity or percent transmittance as the y-axis (Sakami, 2003).

Results and Discussion

Rubber strips were graded by visualizing through light to observe for any foreign material. No foreign material was detected.

Table 20.1: Percent Moisture Content of Natural Rubber Samples of Different Compounds.

Sample Type	Percent Moisture Content
NR1	0.01
NR2	0.01
NR3	0.02
NR4	0.02
NR5	0.02
NR6	0.03
Average	**0.02**
Standard Deviation	**0.008**

Table 20.2: Water Absorption Percent for Natural Rubber Sample

Sample Type	Absorption Percent
R1	0.0002
R2	0.0003
R3	0.0002
R4	0.0003
R5	0.0003
R6	0.0002
Average	**0.00025**
Standard Deviation	**0.00447**

Table 20.3: Percent Strain Test Results for Natural Rubber Samples.

Sample Type	Percent Strain
NR1	1.80
NR2	1.82
NR3	1.79
NR4	1.82
NR5	1.85
NR6	1.83
Average	**1.82**
Standard Deviation	**0.02**

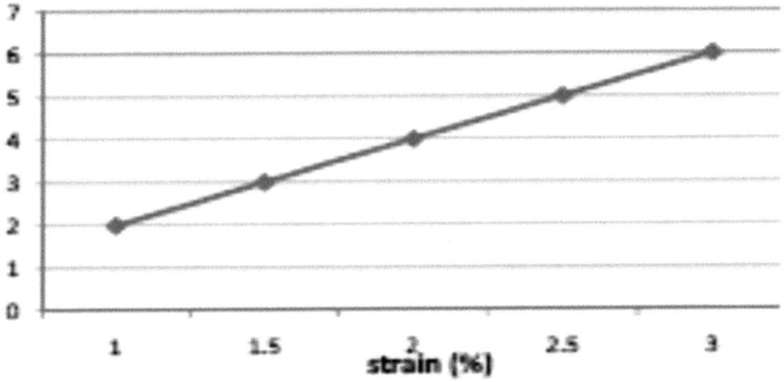

Figure 20.4: Stress-Strain Results for Rubber Compounds.

Table 20.4: pH Test Results for Latex Mixed with Different Additives.

Sample Type	pH Reading
A	5.90
B	5.91
C	5.90
D	5.92
E	5.92
F	5.91
Average	**5.91**
Standard Deviation	**0.01**

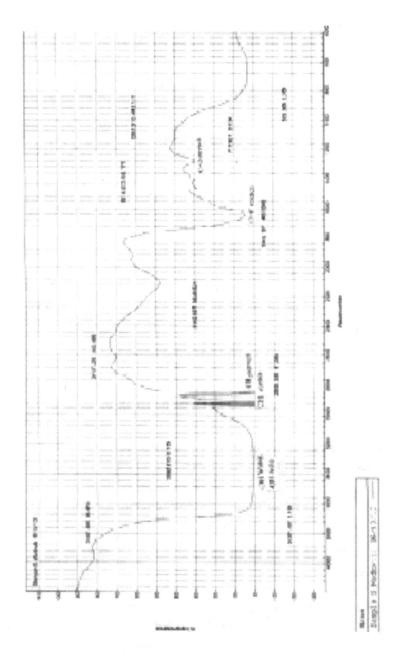

Figure 20.6: Infrared absorption Spectrum of Natural Rubber, $H_2C=C-C=CH_2$, CH_3

Infrared Spectroscopy, Digilab Merlin type was used for functional groups identification. The absorption peaks (or maxima) were portrayed on the recorder chart, such as those shown in figure 2. By examining the spectrum of natural rubber shown in figure 4.2, the compound have -OH (for water), CH_2, CH_3 and C=C stretches or groups which are the same as those appearing on the natural rubber structure. Therefore, Infrared Spectroscopy results for functional groups revealed same functional groups as indicated in literature review figure 2.1. The functional groups and infrared absorption relative height of peaks and intensity which appeared on the spectrum are shown in table below.

Table 20.5: Functional Groups for Natural Rubber Sample

Compound Class	Structure	V, cm^{-1}(Range)	Intensity	Assignment
Alkenes	RCH=CH$_2$	3000-3140	m	=CH Stretch
		1655	m	C=C
	R2CH=CH$_2$	3000-30140	s	=C-H stretch
		1650	m	C=C stretch

Intensity of Absorption (relative height of peak) is keyed by letter: m – medium s – short.

Table 20.5 above also shows the frequency ranges at which functional groups in the sample absorbed the infrared radiation which resulted in the spectrum that made possible for the identification of unknown compounds by matching the spectrum with the already known one.

Conclusion

The physical parameter results analysed for the raw latex were found to be impacting on the permissible standard ranges of natural rubber. Similarly, the chemical parameter results analysed for the raw latex were found to be within the standard ranges for natural rubber. The mechanical test results for the rubber revealed that it stretched rapidly and considerably under tension. It exhibited tensile strength and stiffness when fully stretched it retracted rapidly. It recovered its original dimensions fully on the release of the stress, that is, it exhibited the phenomena of resilience and low permanent set. The rubber showed characteristics of a high polymer, which resulted in it being above the glass transition temperature (TG). The rubber showed to be amorphous in its stable state and it contained a network of cross-links in order to restrain gross mobility of its chains. The analysis results by the Infrared Spectroscopy showed that the latex produced by the *Euphorbia Matabelensis* species plants contain functional groups which are found on natural rubber chemical structure. As such, it can be concluded that latex from the *Euphorbia Matabelensis* species plant is a resource that remains untapped, yet it has potential to substitute the importation of rubber in the country if it is done at commercial level. It would be logical and very interesting to try synthesising natural rubber using our natural resources such as plants which produce latex provided the latex is not a health hazard.

Recommendations

The following recommendations are suggested when employing latex from *Euphorbia Matabelensis* latex. *Euphorbia Matabelensis* latex can be employed in natural rubber synthesis since the physical and chemical parameter for the analysed results are within the recommended standard ranges. The mechanical properties of the rubber synthesised from *Euphorbia Matabelensis* latex revealed same properties such as those attained by products synthesised from other species of plants such as the *Hevea Brasiliensis*. *Euphorbia Matabelensis* is locally available. Generally, the latex produced by the *Euphorbia Matabelensis* species is friendly user, an attribute which is attained by the latex produced by nearly five hundred different species employed for natural rubber manufacturing in the past. It is also recommended that the government and interested stakeholders explore the possibility of manufacturing rubber from Euphorbia *Matabelensis* plant species at commercial level and as a way of solving livelihood challenges in Buhera and the country at large.

References

Adams, A. (2004). *The cultivation of rubber.* Sungai Buloh, Rubber Research Institute, Malaysia.

Alenius, C. and Audley, B.G. (2006). *History of rubber in natural rubber technology.* New York: Interscience Publishers, a Division of John Wiley and Sons.

Ansell, R. (2004). *Molecular structure of natural rubber.* New York: John Wiley and Sons.

Archer, B.L. (2005). *Biosynthesis of rubber in natural rubber science technology* London: Oxford University Press.

Augustine, S.M. (2003). Spectroscopy analysis. *Spectroscopy, 9*(8), 28.

Azuay, D. (2007). *Rubber development.* New York: Chapman and Hall.

Backhaus, D.N. (2003). *Stabilization of polymers.* London: Chapman and Hall.

Backmann, F.A. and Neilsen, L.E. (2005). *Progress in high polymers* Nielsen BookData UK

Basslers, G.C. and Morrill, T.C. (2010). *Spectroscopic identification of organic compounds* (74th edn.). New York: John Wiley and Sons.

Berglund, R.A. (2010). Applications of in-situ FT-IR in pharmaceutical process. *RandD Spectroscopy, 8*(8), 31.

Bhownick, J.J. and Graig, D. (2008). *Rubber chemical technology,* London: Oxford University.

Billmeyer, G. (2005) *Elastomer technology.* New York: John Wiley and Sons.

Blackey, C.D. (2005). *High polymer science* (Volume1). London: Maclaren and Sons.

Blow, C.M. (2006). *Silicone rubber in rubber technology manufacture.* London: Butterworths.

Briston, S. (2006). *Rubber testing methods.* New York: McGraw-Hill Book Co.

Bristow, G.M. and Stephens, I.S. (2006). *Natural rubber resources. Oxford, United Kingdom. Oxford University Press*

Buist, J.M. (2007). *Rubber materials.* Proceedings of Institute of Materials International Rubber Conference, IRC 96 Manchester, U.K, Paper no.1.

Burgoyne, E.E. (2004). *Short course in organic chemistry.* City: McGraw – Hill.

Campbell, B.M., Luckert, M. and Scoones, I. (1997). Local-level valuation of Savanna resources: A case study from Zimbabwe. *Economic Botany, 51*(1), 59. doi: 10.1007/BF02910405

Ceiesielki, A. (2010). *An introduction to rubber Technology.* Shrewsbury: G.B.R. Smithers.

Coats, J.P. and Friedman, D. L. (2006). Quality control analysis by infrared. *Spectroscopy, 18*(11), 40.

Cornish, K. (2008). *Compounding and processing rubber and resins.* New York: Schildknecht, Interscience Publishers.

Corradini, P. (2006). *Structures and properties of polymers.* New York: St Martin's Press.

Crafts, R.C. (2004). *Natural rubber technology.* London: Oxford University Press.

Daniel, F. (2007). *Rheology and mechanical properties of polymers.* New York: Inter-science Publishers, a division of John Wiley and Sons.

Davey, D.R. (2006). *Chemistry and physics handbook.* Lide: CRC. Press.

Dole, M. (2004). *Advances in polymer science* (7th edn). London: Chapman and Hall.

Duerden, F. (2004). *Natural rubber technology.* New York: St Martin's Press.

Fern, K. (2014). Useful tropical plants database. Creative Commons Attribution-NonCommercial-Share Alike 3.0 Unported License. New Delhi, India: Amerind Publishing Co, 254-271.

Fred, A. (2004). *The study of rubber-like substances by X-ray diffraction methods.* New York: John Wiley and Sons.

Fred, G. (2003). *Applied chemistry of rubber.* New York: McGraw-Hill Book Co.

Fulton, S.W. (2003). *Avoiding the problems of odour during rubber processing.* New York: Reinhold Publishing Corp.

Gan, N.S. (2005). *Trends in polymer science.* New York: American Scientific Publisher.

Gazeley, K.F., Gorton, A.D. and Pendle, T.D. (2003). *Latex concentrates properties and composition in natural rubber science and technology.* London: Oxford University Press.

George, D. (2005). *Methods of testing elastomers and plastomers*. New York: Reinhold Publishing Corp.

Gorton, A.D.T. (2006). *Latex concentrates properties and composition in natural rubber*. New York: Reinhold Publishing Corp.

Graham, M. (2010). *Rubber material and their compounds* (Volume111). New York: Elsevier Publishing Co.

Gregg, E.C. (2003). *Rubber chemical technology* (Part1). New York: Inter-science Publishers.

Griffths, P.R. (2008). *Fourier transform infrared spectroscopy*. New York: Publishers.

Hancock, K. (2004). *Natural rubber and other poly-isoprene*. New York: Reinhold Publishing Corp.

Hartley, D.P. (2005). *History of natural rubber technology,* Benin **City**, Rubber Research Institute of Nigeria.

Haseith, A. (2010). *Natural rubber synthesis*. New York: John Wiley and Sons.

Haven, H. (2008). *Introduction to rubber technology*. New York: McGraw-Hill Book Co.

Heaton, A.C. (2003). *Industrial chemistry*. Glasgow, London: Blackie and Son.

Hines, R.A. (2005). *Polymers derived from Dienes*. New York: Reinhold Publishing Corp.

Hoffman, B. (2009). *Introduction to rubber processing and safety issues*. Munich, Germany: Carl Hanser Verlag.

Hofmann, W. (2005). *Rubber technology handbook*. Munich, Germany: Hanser Publishers.

Hoven, P.V. (2008). *Rubber chemical technology*. Available online: http;//www.agsci.ubc.ca.

Howard, B.J. (2006). *Polymeric materials*. New York: John Wiley and Sons.

Isono, T.C. (2008). *Rubber processing and world trade. Kansas City, (Humana Press, c/o Springer Science+Business Media, LLC.*

Jacob, J.L. (2005). *Natural rubber science and technology*. New York: Inter-science Publishers.

Jinno, S.T. (2007). *Rubber materials*. New York: John Wiley and Sons.

Jitladda, D. and Yeoh, H.O. (2004). *Fundamental characteristics and properties of natural rubber* (pp. 6). Education Symposium no. 35, Philadelphia, Rubber Division, ACS.

Kabuko, Z. (2007). *Rubber chemical technology*. New York: St Martin's Press.

Kalpakjian, A.A. (2004). *History in rubber technology and manufacture* Motor City: Addison-Wesley Educational Publishers Inc.

Katon, J.E. (2006). IR *Spectroscopy: Routine IR sampling methods, extended to microscopic domain–analytical chemistry*. New York: John Wiley and Sons.

Korana, P. (2006). *Synthetic Rubber*. Rubber City, Arcadia Publishing press.

Lee, C.Y. and Whitaker, J.R. (2009). *Processing rubber technology* (2nd edn.). Manchester: University of Manchester and UMIST.

Madhavan, S. (2004). *Plant physiology.* Australia: CSIRO Publishing press.

Marlies, A.C. (2005). *Composition of pure-gum vulcanization of natural rubber.* City Press Ltd., Letchworth, England,

Maurice, M. (2011). *Rubber technology.* Cambridge, England: Heffer, W. and Sons.

Miller, J. (2010). *Instrumental methods of analysis.* New York: McGraw-Hill Book Co.

Mooibroek, H. (2005). *Applied microbiology biotechnology.* New York: John Wiley and Sons.

Morrill, T.C.; Silverstein, R.M. and Basslers, C.G. (2011). *Spectroscopic identification of organic compounds.* New York: Inter-science Publishers, a Division of John Wiley and Sons.

Murari, R.; Wedmid, Y. and Bauman, J.W. (2003). *Organic chemistry.* New York City: McGraw-Hill.

Nagdi, K. (2005). *Rubber as an engineering material guide-lines for users.* Munich, Germany: Hensers Publishers.

Nair, S. (2003). *Characterisation of natural rubber for greater consistency.* New York: John Wiley and Sons.

Nakade, S. (2008). Natural rubber resources. *Journal Natural Rubber Resources, 12,* 33-42.

Nandi, W. (2005). *Polymer science.* London: City.

Nishiyama, N. (2005). *Rubber science and technology handbook.* : Oxford, England, UK Imprints: Clarendon Press

Nithi-Uthai, B. (2008). *Elastomers.* Proceedings 7Th Seminar on elastomer, Bangkok.

Norrish, I. (2005). *Natural rubber chemistry technology.* New York: St Martin's Press.

Palosou, C.T. (2003). *Accelerators of vulcanization in rubber materials.* London, Science Publishers Ltd.

Sakami, J.L. (2003). *FIT-IR spectra of biochemical and related organics in hardbound books.* New York: Inter-science Publishers.

Sakdapipanich, J.T. and Tanaka, Y. (2005). *Bio-macro-molecules.* New York: Inter-science Publishers, a Division of John Wiley and Sons.

Sekhar, J. (2008). *Rubber technology.* Germany: Hanser Pub Inc.

Senntheshannmuganathan, S. and Brydson, J.A. (2005). *Constituents chemistry of natural rubber.* New York: John Wiley and Sons.

Smith, G.M. (2009). *Rubber technology.* New York: John Wiley and Sons.

Stern, S. (2006). *History of rubber technology.* London: Butterworths.

Surveyor- General (2012). *Map of Nyashanu Rural area, Buhera District, Zimbabwe.* City: Publisher.

Suzuki, D. (2010). *The tree that changed the world.* Ottawa, Canada: Publisher.

Tabb, L. (2011). *Rubber world.* New York: St Martin's Press

Tanaka, Y. (2005). *Applied polymer science.* New York: John Wiley and Sons.

Tangpakdee, J. (2004). *Long-chain poly-phenols and rubber in young leaves of Hevea Brasiliensis, Physio chemistry.* John Wiley and Sons, Inc., Hoboken.

Tarachiniwin, L. and Sakdapipanichi, J.T. (2005). *Rubber chemical technology.* Machidol University, Thailand: RILCA Mahidol University Press.

Thomas, E. and Joseph, J.K. (2007) *Cultivation of rubber plants and synthetic rubber.* Ampang, Kuala Lumpur Malaya: Rubber Research Institute.

Viswanathan, P.K. (2007). Emerging smallholder rubber farming systems in India and Thailand: A comparative economic analysis. Retrieved from https://core.ac.uk/display/6231836 (Accessed: 27 April 2018).

Weng, K. (2008). *Hazardous area classification for exposable ducts in rubber and industry.* Via Beato: Cisa Publisher - Eurowaste Srl Press.

ZINWA (Zimbabwe National Water Authority) (2004). *Zimbabwe Catchment Boundaries Map.* Harere: IWA Press.

Chapter 21

The Sustainability of Diamond Mining in Zimbabwe

Solomon Muqayi and Oripha Chimwara

Summary:

Several studies and literature on the Zimbabwean diamond industry have focused on the impact of Multinational Corporations (MNCs) in the diamond industry in the country. As a result, the importance of sustainable development strategies in diamond mining has been under researched. The aim of this chapter is to evaluate the importance of sustainable development strategies both in terms of policing and mining methods to counter the resource curse in Zimbabwe and to give recommendation on the ways to improve sustainability of diamond mineral resources. This study was guided by the resource curse theory and sustainable development concept, and provides a suitable analytical foundation upon which whether diamonds in Zimbabwe have sustainably contributed to the development of the country. The study used qualitative methodology particularly observations, key informant interviews and documentary search. Data were analysed using thematic analysis. Data for this study was analysed in themes that were created in resonance with the major findings of this study. Thematic analysis has been especially selected in this study due to its power in giving enhanced clarity to concepts under review. Diamond mining has the potential of transforming economies and fuelling or inciting conflict between the various actors involved in the industry. The history of diamonds in developing countries has been characterised by conflicts due to the enormous market value of the stones. Due to the market value of diamonds, these precious gems have been marred by corrupt tendencies in their extraction and management. The potential of diamonds in helping states towards a development path has therefore been greatly compromised. Consequently, several studies have focused on the relationship between diamonds and conflict, especially with the emergence of such terms as 'blood diamonds' which is a literal deductive interpretation of conflict diamonds. Diamonds associated with conflicts and human rights abuses have been delegitimized in order to enforce international standards and transparency on the extraction and management of diamonds. The concept of whether diamonds were to be legitimately considered fit for sale on the international market has usually been associated with multinational corporations (MNCs) taking a leading role in defining whether diamonds mined in a particular country qualify as 'blood diamonds' or not in order to legitimise them on the market.

Introduction

This chapter interrogates the various sustainability and development factors in the diamond mining sector in Zimbabwe. The topical question that this chapter seeks to answer is: How sustainable is the diamond mining sector in enhancing national development in Zimbabwe? The main scope of the chapter is to identify hurdles and challenges to sustainability and development in the diamond sector in order to ensure that the resource contributes to the general development of the economy at the same time giving leverage to for future use. The chapter underpins the conceptual framework that guides sustainability and development in the diamond mining sector by giving clear and functional definitions of sustainability and development. The resource curse theory will then be used to discuss and create a theoretical foundation and template upon which sustainability factors in the diamond sector can be interrogated. The chapter then presents a brief review of literature to incorporate the various and corresponding views concerning sustainability of the diamond mining sector on development. This section helps in evaluating the scholarly perceptions vis-à-vis the findings of the study to see if there is any direct correlation of views so as to generalise conclusions. After a brief literature review, the chapter presents the findings of the study through comprehensive themes for an easy flow of the various views that were proffered during interviews.

The scope of our investigation in this chapter is Chiadzwa diamond mining in Marange district in Zimbabwe as shown by the map below.

Figure 21.1: The Zimbabwean map showing Marange diamond field location in the Manicaland Province of Zimbabwe

In June 2006, a United Kingdom-based mineral exploration company called Africa Consolidated Resources (AFCR) discovered massive deposits of alluvial diamonds in an area called Marange, near Zimbabwe's eastern border with Mozambique. According to De Beers (2012), the Zimbabwean government "could generate significant amounts of revenue from the diamonds, perhaps as much as USD$200 million per month, if Marange and other mining centres were managed in a transparent and accountable manner" (Human Rights Watch, 2009). Media and industry reports suggested that the diamond deposits in Chiadzwa in the Marange district in Zimbabwe could be worth as much as USD$800 billion (Sprinks, 2011). This was the period when Zimbabwe was experiencing dreary economic challenges and impasse, and the discovery of diamonds brought shreds of renewed hope of regeneration, economic recovery, improved human welfare and national development among other things. However, the Chiadzwa diamonds, up until now, have failed to live up to their billing. They have significantly failed to transform the Zimbabwean economy from collapsing. Since the discovery of diamonds in Chiadzwa, Zimbabwe has experienced contemptible levels of corruption in its economic history where fifteen billion United States dollars from diamond revenue as well as raw diamonds were alleged to have disappeared without trace into the international informal markets (*Financial Gazette,* 2016). The discovery of diamonds, instead of being supplementary to other development sectors like agriculture and the manufacturing industry, led to the neglect of other relevant sectors which are equally integral to the development of the economy. This has seen other important sectors of the economy being given nominal attention by the government. Agriculture has continued to falter despite government efforts as espoused by the Zimbabwe Agenda for Sustainable Socio-economic Transformation (ZIMASSET) and the command agriculture of 2016 (Makochekanwa, 2016). There exists a diversion of investment interests among most foreign investors since the discovery of the precious mineral. The diamond sector has become a target for investment by investors at the expense of other sectors, thus creating an unbalanced investment environment in which other sectors of the economy are sacrificed. According to the Zimbabwe Chamber of Commerce (ZCC) (2016), there has been an increase in the number of investments in the mining sector, particularly diamond mining, in Zimbabwe since 2009. ZCC further noted that 63% of new investments in Zimbabwe have been targeting diamond mining and the mining sector in general since 2009. The three aspects of sustainable development in the diamond sector: social, economic and environment, have not been fully taken into account by both the government and diamond extracting companies in Zimbabwe (Chindori-Chininga 2013). Since the advent of formal extraction of diamonds in Chiadzwa in 2009, displaced families from the Marange community have not been given adequate compensation by either the government and companies operating in the area through various initiatives of corporate responsibilities in which companies are expected to develop and initiate programmes that ensure community development in the areas they are operating in (De Beers, 2014). There has been massive degradation of the land around Marange area as a result of operations by heavy machinery in the area. As consequence, the extraction of diamonds in Chiadzwa has not been adequately sustainable in ensuring social and environmental protection.

The Conceptual Framework

Sustainable development concept

In an effort to link environmental stability with economic development, the Brundtland Commission issued a report, "Our Common Future." The report provided the frequently cited definition of sustainable development as "development that meets the needs of the present without compromising the ability of future generations to meet their own needs" (United Nations General Assembly, 1987:43). In Zimbabwe, sustainable development in the diamond mining sector is generally unbalanced as more emphasis is placed on economic advancement and progress while neglecting the long-term value of conserving the environment; diamond mining in Zimbabwe has principally ignored the framework for the integration of environmental policies and development strategies" (UNDP, 2015). Before the late 20th century, scholars argued that there ought not be a trade-off between environmental sustainability and economic development.

In addition to substitutability, the definition of sustainability is also founded on several other important principles. Beutros (2009) defines sustainability as development that meets the needs of the present without compromising the ability of future generations to meet their own needs. Contained within this common definition of sustainable development, intergenerational equity recognizes the long-term scale of sustainability in order to address the needs of future generations (Dernbach, 1998; Stoddart, 2011). Also, the polluter pays principle states that "governments should require polluting entities to bear the costs of their pollution rather than impose those costs on others or on the environment" (Dernbach, 1998:58). Thus, government policy should ensure that environmental costs are internalised wherever possible; this also serves to minimize the environmental problems such as land degradation, water and air pollution that might emanate from irresponsible mining practices. Extracting companies in the diamond mining sites such as Chiadzwa in Marange district have been reported to be disposing liquid waste into the rivers such as Odzi River thereby polluting water sources for the community and endangering aqua and wildlife (KPCS, 2010). The companies have been blamed for failing to reclaim their shafts in the Chiadzwa and this, according to De Beers (2014), has led to land degradation including formation of gullies, and this has been viewed as a direct threat to sustainability of diamond mining in Marange and Zimbabwe. The key principle of sustainable development underlying all others is the integration of environmental, social, and economic concerns into all aspects of decision-making. All other principles in the sustainable development framework have integrated decision-making at their core (Dernbach, 2003; Stoddart, 2011). It is this deeply fixed concept of integration that distinguishes sustainability from other forms of policy. The Government of Zimbabwe is typically organised into sectoral ministries and departments. In practice, sustainable development requires the integration of economic, environmental, and social objectives across sectors, territories, and generations. Sustainable development therefore requires the elimination of fragmentation, that is, environmental, social, and economic concerns must be integrated throughout decision-making processes in order to move towards development that is sustainable. To buttress the above arguments, the study discusses the theoretical foundations which underpin extraction and management of diamonds. In this study, the resource case theory was found to be the most suitable theoretical basis upon which diamond mining and sustainable development can be explained in clearer terms.

Resource curse theory

The resource curse theory denotes the paradox that countries with an abundance of natural resources like fossil fuels and certain minerals tend to have less economic growth, less democracy and worse development outcomes than countries with fewer natural resources (Di John, 2010). The major assumptions behind the 'resource curse' are that mineral and fuel abundance in less developed countries (LDCs) tends to generate negative developmental outcomes, including poor economic performance, growth collapses, high levels of corruption, ineffective governance and political violence. According to Biti (2012), the emergence of diamonds in Zimbabwe did not bring significant impact to economic development as they have, since their formalisation, contributed nominally to the Gross Domestic Product in Zimbabwe. He further argues that Zimbabwe has over the years suffered from budget deficit despite high expectations of an improved economy from diamond revenues. Diamond mining has received more government priority at the expense of other key economic sectors such as agriculture and manufacturing leading to a decrease in maize production and closure of industries over the past decade from 2007 (Makochekanwa, 2017). Corruption in the diamond sector has been a major developmental setback. Zimbabwe has raw diamonds and diamond revenues from Chiadzwa have been reportedly diverted and externalised into international black-markets (De Beers, 2014). This observation was buttressed by Kadenge (2017) when he argued that the disappearance of US$15 billion worth of diamond revenues could have transformed the economy and living standards of Zimbabweans in a very significant way. Informal diamond miners in Chiadzwa faced multiple challenges including gross human rights violations in the hands of state security apparatus. The violence against informal miners is reported to have claimed 200 lives of perceived illegal miners (KPCS, 2016). According to KPCS (2010), the violence that characterised Chiadzwa between informal miners and security forces culminated into the resource being classified under conflict and blood diamond framework by the international community.

Natural resources, for most poor countries, are deemed more of a 'curse' than a 'blessing' (Di John, 2010). The negative outcomes of diamond booms world over have been considered to be more detrimental to the balanced growth of the economy. This aspect is clearly captured in the Dutch disease concept which explains the economic imbalance that would occur in the event of rapid inflows of money due discovery of large deposits of natural resources such as oil and diamonds among others. Dutch disease is the negative impact on an economy of anything that gives rise to sharp inflow of foreign currency such as the discovery of large oil reserve (Di John, 2010). The currency inflows lead to currency appreciation making the country's other products less price competitive on the export markets. It also leads to higher levels of cheap imports and can lead to deindustrialisation as industries, apart from resource exploitation are moved from cheaper locations. The economic concept of Dutch disease refers to the potential negative effects natural-resource windfalls and accompanying appreciations (value growth) of exchange rates can have for the rest of the economy (Khan and Jomo, 2000). One of the potential dangers of diamond booms, for example, is that exchange-rate appreciation renders the non-diamond-tradable sectors such as manufacturing sector and agriculture less competitive and thus can generate de-industrialisation due to potential shifts in investment interests to more competitive sectors such as diamond mining. The emergence of Marange diamonds and the anticipation that diamond reserves could be the biggest in Africa, if not in the world, and worth billions of fortune by geologists led to the deflation and neglect of other formerly key economic sectors such as agriculture (Mashakada, 2012). As a consequence to this windfall in the diamond-mining sector, the government, corporate world and foreign investors seemingly turned a blind eye on other economic sectors and expend more investment in the mining sector at the expense of other continually depressed sectors.

The rentier-state model is a concept whereby the state derives all or a substantial portion of its national revenues from the rent of indigenous resources to external clients (Mahdavy, 1970). Rentier-state models move beyond economic models of the resource curse, such as Dutch disease models in which sharp inflows of foreign currency has a direct and negative growth impact on other sectors of the economy, by attempting to indigenise policy-making and institutional formation. In particular, they attempt to explain why state decision-makers in natural resource-rich economies create and maintain growth-restricting policies (Mahdavy, 1970; Karl, 1997; Auty, 2007). These models are part of a growing trend of reviving the 'staples thesis,' the notion that natural factors endowments or technology shape the relations of production, or institutional evolution of a society (Engerman and Sokoloff, 1997). In the rentier-state model, the principal view is that mineral/resource driven economies such as Zimbabwe are subject to a higher level of rent-seeking and corruption in comparison with non-mineral abundant economies (De Beers, 2014). This observation by De Beers (2014) has been vividly reported about the tendering processes of prospective mining companies in Marange, a development that has been alleged to be corruptible and lacking transparency thus leaving no room for accountability of diamond revenue.

The proposition that natural resource abundance induces extraordinary corruption, rent-seeking and centralised interventionism and that these processes are necessarily productivity and growth-restricting is not supported by comparative or historical evidence (Khan and Jomo, 2000). In the Central African Republic (CAR), a brutal civil war erupted in 2013 with both sides, the Muslims and the Christians, fighting for the possession of diamonds in that country. The KPCS banned the CAR diamonds citing violence in the diamond sector and other unorthodox practices in the sector. Diamonds from CAR have been, according to De Beers (2014), smuggled into the international black markets. These leakages and embargoes which were set on CAR diamonds by the KPCS have had a negative impact on the overall development of the economy of CAR. Despite their overwhelming abundance in that country, diamonds have, as such, fallen short in transforming lives of the people but have rather been the source of conflict and, consequently, underdevelopment. In 2008, the Government of Zimbabwe took over the control of Chiadzwa alluvial diamonds by imposing heavy military security in the Chiadzwa area (Moyo, 2010). In 2016, the then president of the Republic of Zimbabwe, Robert Gabriel Mugabe made a public pronouncement that US$15 billion worth of diamond revenue was missing. Masunungure (2016) argues that the US$15 billion could have changed the economic fortunes of Zimbabwe had it been expeditiously and accountably used. The extent to which mineral abundance, particularly diamond, generate developmental outcomes depends largely on the nature of the state and politics as well as the structure of ownership in the export sector, all of which are neglected in much of the resource-curse literature (Di John,

2010). Much more research is needed to examine why Zimbabwe has failed to effectively use diamond rents in productive ways.

Literature Review

This section of the study presents a review of literature that is relevant in helping to explain sustainability and development issues in the diamond mining sector. It further discusses sustainable development vis-à-vis diamond mining. Literature on the diamond sector in Zimbabwe and the various policy and legal challenges affecting that sector also find expression in this central section of the chapter.

Sustainable development and diamond mining

Mining by nature is inherently unsustainable in that the life of the mine is limited and will eventually end (Di John, 2010). However, the linkages it forms with other sectors of the economy can ensure its sustainability. Sustainable development as defined by the World Commission on Environment and Development (WCED, 1987) is "development that meets the needs of the present generation without compromising the ability of future generations to meet their own needs". However, this widely used definition focuses on intergenerational equity and a further expansion of the standard definition was made during the 2002 World Summit on Sustainable Development, using the three pillars of sustainable development: economic, social, and environmental (UNDP, 2003). The Johannesburg Declaration created,

> a collective responsibility to advance and strengthen the interdependent and mutually reinforcing pillars of sustainable development at local, national, regional and global levels (Amnesty International, 2004:17).

The next section presents the various challenges which are affecting the diamond mining sector ion Zimbabwe. The section commences by giving a brief explanation of the genesis of the multiple challenges in the sector. The section explains sustainability and development challenges that characterize the diamond mining and management in Zimbabwe.

Marange diamonds: An exegesis of the problem in Zimbabwe

The problems that afflict the diamond sector in Zimbabwe cut across the whole diamond supply chain, from allocation of mining rights to the trade and export of rough diamonds. In a number of African countries, alluvial diamond production and trade have fuelled and fanned conflicts and gross human rights abuses. Zimbabwe has not been an exception as during the initial years of diamond discovery in Marange district, the Government of Zimbabwe orchestrated a reign of terror on illegal miners with independent monitors having recorded high levels of gross human rights abuses (CRD, undated). Furthermore, literature and statistics have it that the proceeds from the alluvial diamonds in Marange and other places have not been channelled towards national development initiatives but were rather unscrupulously smuggled out of the country and traded on illicit markets for the benefit of few government officials (Moyo, 2013). That is why the Kimberley Process Certification Scheme Core Document states that trade in conflict diamonds has over the years had an adverse and devastating impact on peace, security of people, systematic and gross human rights violations as well as negative outcomes on economies (KPCS, 2002).

The United Nations (2004) defines conflict diamonds as "diamonds that originate from areas controlled by forces or factions opposed to legitimate and internationally recognized governments and are used to fund military actions in opposition to those governments or in contravention of the decisions by the [United Nations] Security Council." While the KPCS has largely defined conflict diamonds as 'rough diamonds used by rebel movements or their allies to finance conflict aimed at undermining legitimate governments', this definition is problematic in that the nature of conflicts in the diamond sector has changed since the KPCS was formed in 2002. The conflicts are no longer solely caused by rebel movements seeking to unseat governments but rather fuelled by governments and non-state actors like diamond mining companies that disregard the rights of host communities where diamond mines are located. The state may act through state security forces, the military and police, while the mining companies normally contract private security companies. In this case conflicts arise out of disrespect of community rights through wrongful displacement and failure to pay compensation for loss of property, land and livelihoods. Added to this are limited opportunities for participation in mining, environmental pollution and degradation. The Marange diamond mining fiasco fits the bill of conflict diamonds as it exposed the legal, policy and administrative deficiencies in Zimbabwe and how the country's internal control measures are not in tandem with KPCS minimum requirements. According to Global Witness (2016) and Partnership Africa Canada (2015), the Zimbabwean government falls short of a specific diamond policy that helps regulate the mining and management of diamond in Zimbabwe. The involvement of security forces to regulate the mining activities in the Chiadzwa area had two challenges that it created: 1) The involvement created a human rights crisis in the area due to the militarisation that characterised the formalisation of the mining in

Chiadzwa (De Beers, 2014); 2) The soldiers and police officers helped as conduits for illicit smuggling diamonds to external traders (Global Witness, 2016).

According to the United Nations (2004), diamonds become a curse when they fail to benefit the generality of the people and economic systems of the country in which they are extracted. The diamond curse commenced in 2008 when the government in Zimbabwe seized power over the Marange diamond fields in the East of the country. In so doing, the Government of Zimbabwe was not reluctant to use the police, the army and two attack helicopters to get rid of the remaining freelance diamond diggers, who had been based in Marange (Zimbabwe Lawyers for Human Rights, 2015; Partnership Africa Canada, 2015). According to the Centre for Research and Development based in Mutare, Zimbabwe, approximately 200 people were killed in the 2008 attacks (Perry, 2010; Spinks, 2011). The allegations of state-sponsored killings led NGOs such as Human Rights Watch and Global Witness to send research teams to the Marange fields in order to investigate government practices around the mines. The outcomes of these investigations were as shocking as expected. Zimbabwe's military, stationed in Marange, was part of grave human rights abuses. Moreover, soldiers were actively engaged in diamond smuggling practices by managing syndicates and by securing cross-border smuggling operations to Manica in Mozambique (Global Witness, 2010). The Human Rights Watch reported similar practices. According to the NGOs team of inquiry, the Zimbabwean army used syndicates of local minors to extract diamonds, thereby forcing children to work in the mines. The army further recruited people from outside Marange to join the army-run diamond mining syndicates and killed young men who tried to hide raw diamonds (HRW, 2009).

Zimbabwe was suspended from the Kimberley Process in November 2009 on the basis of reports which were presented by civil societies concerning human rights abuse and corruption by state apparatus in the Chiadzwa diamond mines. Nevertheless, the Zimbabwean government advocated quite clearly that without Zimbabwe, one of the biggest diamond producers, the Kimberley Process would be worthless and not functioning (CRD, undated). Thus, despite the pressure from civil society and several government participants of KPCS, a compromise deal was agreed, attempting to bring the country into line with Kimberley Process standards. This deal allowed Zimbabwe to continue the sale of its diamonds after the Kimberley monitor, Abbey Chikane from South Africa, had declared the mines to comply with the KPCS (Global Witness, 2010; Perry, 2010). In the view of the Marange diamond mines, conflict diamonds per definition and the resource curse theory are virtually meaningless concepts that are not equipped to separate human rights abuses from the diamond trade and sustainable economic development in general. The human right violations in the

Marange diamond fields are on-going and national economic development remains a pipe dream despite diamonds being mined in the Marange region and other areas, nevertheless, the diamonds from the area are allowed into the global system (Warnica, 2012).

Methodology

This study employed the qualitative research methods in the collection, presentation and analysis of data for this study. McNabb (2010:34) submits that qualitative research design is a scientific method which involves observing and describing the behaviour of a subject without manipulating it in anyway. Qualitative research design is generally based on social constructivism perspective and research problems become research questions based on prior research experience (Creswell, 2003). The difference between qualitative and quantitative research design is that quantitative research design is employed for the purposes of quantifying the research problem through generation of numerical data or data which can be transformed into usable statistics. However, qualitative research design is primarily exploratory and is used to gain an understating of underlying reasons, opinions and motivations. It provides insights into the problem or helps to develop ideas or hypotheses. The study employed the descriptive research design which, according to Greene (2006), is a scientific method which involves observing and describing the behaviour of a subject without influencing it in any way. Descriptive research design uses both qualitative and quantitative research methods which make it very suitable in creating a springboard of choices of data collection and analysis methods. The method has been selected for this study as it presents a unique means of data collection. Case studies can be based on various sources such as secondary data, that is, journals, reports and academic documents, as well as primary data like interviews. The study used face to face interviews, questionnaires as well as observations as data collection tools. Face to face interviews are data collection tools in which the researcher directly communicates with the respondent (Lavrakas, 2008). This data method allowed researchers to clarify research questions to respondents as well as seeking further clarification of responses they proffered. Questionnaires are a set of research or survey questions prepared by the researcher to extract specific information (Mugenda and Mugenda, 1998). Consequently, researchers had the advantage of profiling and examining associative relationships among various individuals and institutions of concern. Descriptive survey affords different researchers to observe a similar phenomenon yet still come up with different findings. Thus, descriptive survey scrutinizes the actual situation in a chosen setting. In this study, data was drawn from Marange Diamond Mining Companies, Zimbabwe Mineral Development

Corporation, Minerals Marketing Company of Zimbabwe and civil society organisations. The Ministry of Mines and Mining Development and the Ministry of Finance were also referred to as part of pursuing ministerial intervention and interface as well as to solicit their views which pertains to diamond revenue management and utilizations. The researchers preferred chief executive officers from diamond mining companies in Chiadzwa and diamond regulatory companies as respondents for this study. Furthermore, 40 residents from the Chiadzwa community were also chosen to represent various opinions of residents of Marange District and its satellite areas that were directly impacted by diamond mining activities. Four experts from Transparency International Zimbabwe and the Zimbabwe Anti-Corruption Commission were engaged in the focus group discussions. Since the population in this sensitive study area is usually elusive and consequently small, stage sampling or whole population sampling was used to select respondents who took part in the study.

Diamond management in Zimbabwe remains opaque and lacks transparency (Transparency International, 2015). As a result, respondents were not at liberty to disclose sensitive information of corruption, mismanagement and misappropriation of diamond revenue due to fear of reprisal and other unknown consequences for disclosing such information. As result of this inherent fear, the population in this area was generally elusive, uncooperative and not easy to come by. Purposive sampling was used to select stakeholders who participated in this study. Purposive sampling is a non-probability sampling technique that is used to select a population with special characteristics and in line with the objectives of the study (Babbie, 1998). The study opted for purposive sampling because it allowed researchers to collect data from respondents with expert and relevant information that helped to identify sustainability factors in the diamond mining sector and how these have affected national development. Five stakeholders from Marange diamond mining companies, Zimbabwe Minerals Marketing Corporation, line ministries and the civil society were selected under this method through random selection. Lastly, snowball sampling had been used to group respondents into distinct categories. The first category comprised respondents from diamond extracting companies, and the second category comprised respondents from government ministries and enterprises; the other category comprised respondents from the Marange community, and a last category of respondents from civil society. According to Saunders (1998), quota sampling is a sampling method through which representative respondents are selected from a specific sub-group to ensure that the population under study is fully represented.

Data was presented using themes, tables and graphs. Themes are defined as recurring ideas that are central to the understanding of the subject matter (Mugenda and Mugenda, 1998). Data for this study was analysed using thematic

434

content analysis. Thematic content analysis is a method of examining themes within data and coding to create meaningful patterns (Creswell, 2003). Thematic analysis is performed through the process of coding in six phases to create established and meaningful patterns. These phases are familiarization with data, generating initial codes, searching for themes among codes, reviewing themes, defining and naming themes and producing the final report. The following section presents the results and a discussion of the results for this study.

Results and Discussion

The International Monetary Fund's Natural Resources per Capita Index (per individual statistical aggregate that measures change) claims that Zimbabwe is one of the countries with the highest natural resources per capita in the world. This data is disputable since it seems there is nothing to show for this. Resource based development in the country on the contrary has not mirrored any sustainable exploitation of this potential. The country is still rated 136 in terms of investment attractiveness (Cross, 2011). It is claimed that the nation commands large diamond and platinum reserves, which can be used to turn around the fortunes of all Zimbabweans and over 40 exploitable minerals with potential to turn Zimbabwe into a jewel of Africa. There are conflicting figures regarding the economic potential of Chiadzwa diamonds. *Business Times Africa Magazine* (2012) puts the potential output of the Marange diamonds deposits at 60 million carats a year - worth about $3 billion, or more than 15% of the global diamond supply. Canadian jeweller, Brilliant Earth, suggests that the total value of Marange gems may be as high as $800 billion, making them the richest fields ever found. The economic valuation of the deposits remains unknown given the shadowy arrangements under which they are being exploited. Unfortunately, however, all these claims are without basis as there has not been adequate exploration to establish the exact diamond endowment of the fields. The question that remains unanswered is to what extent are the local communities benefitting from the diamond mining irrespective of the endowment?

Performance of diamond sector in Zimbabwe

Since 2009, there has been a lot of brimming assumption on the potential revenue from the Marange diamond fields. Emphasising the potential diamond benefits, in the 2012 budget announcement after the Kimberley Process Certification, the Government of Zimbabwe said it projected US$600 million in additional revenue from diamond sales in 2012. In a face to face interview with a respondent from the Ministry of Finance and Economic Development, it was highlighted that in 2010 the government earned US$80 million from Marange diamonds and in 2011 it is assumed that the government received US$174 million dollars of diamond revenue, a figure which is believed to be too low in view of expectations (Interview, 14 February 2017). The Ministry of Mines had indicated that it anticipated an income of more than US$1 billion for the year 2012 and that this would rise to US$3 billion in subsequent years. The projected revenue did not materialise. People are wondering where the revenue from diamond mining is going to since the government is only receiving a tiny fraction of what the companies are getting, and nothing is going to the local communities. Respondents from Chiadzwa community that were interviewed did not understand why government is not getting adequate remittance from the mining companies (Informant Interview, 10 February 2017). Local members of the community expressed that all mining operations were taken over by government. There seems to be some truth in this claim. Statistics show that diamond output in Zimbabwe stood at 152 475 carats in the first quarter of 2016, compared to 639 377 carats produced during the same period in 2015, as shown in the Figure 21.1.

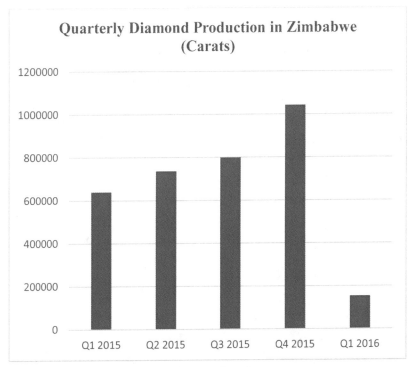

Source: Ministry of Mines and Mining Development

Diamond mining at Marange fields is undergoing a transition under which the existing mining firms are being consolidated into one state-owned Zimbabwe Consolidated Diamond Company (ZCDC), which now holds all the diamond claims in the country. The Zimbabwe government wholly owns Marange Resources and has a 50% stake in Mbada Diamonds, which it co-owns with South African investors. Another miner, Anjin Zimbabwe is a 50-50 joint venture between the Zimbabwean and Chinese governments. Through the ZMDC, the government also wholly owns the claims previously run by Sino-Zimbabwe, a Queensway Group appendage. Government also has a 50-50 share arrangement with Diamond Mining Corporation (DMC) (Amnesty International, 2016). In spite of the joint venture arrangements of these companies, the public has not been exposed to the character of the partners government has chosen to deal with.

Based on unconfirmed diamond endowment of Chiadzwa fields there were two estimates of the total revenue that the state was supposed to get from the diamonds (De Beers, 2004). The first estimate was that Chiadzwa diamonds should provide over US$1 billion per month in revenue' (Roger, 2008). The other estimate is from sentiments such as a lack of proper institutional, orderly and legal framework for diamond miners which has resulted in the country loosing at least US$1,2 billion per month (Interview, 13 February 2017). The annual income from diamonds therefore was estimated to be at least around US$12 billion dollars (Ministry of Finance and Economic Development, 2016). Some respondents in this study nonetheless considered this a conservative figure. They believed that with proper management of the diamond mining, the expected revenue was supposed to be higher.

Respondents from the civil society pointed out that the anticipated revenue from diamonds alone was greater than any previous Gross Domestic Product (GDP) figures for Zimbabwe even during good years of the 1980s and 1990s. Given these figures and, if diamond is managed with due fiduciary commitment it deserves, most respondents concurred that the country would be in a position to finance its economic recovery programme which needs at least US$8.3 billion if the diamond industry was managed properly. A respondent from the Ministry of Mines and Mineral Development pointed out that the Marange alluvial diamonds fields could be producing in excess of $100 million a month in raw, uncut diamonds. Presuming that 75% of the gross revenue from these sales accrued to the state, then, this source of revenue, by itself, could double civil service salaries. Nevertheless, this is not happening as lives of many economically active citizens continue to vacillate far below the poverty datum line that is currently set at $500. Diamonds are being smuggled out of the country and new wealth is accumulating in India, China, Mozambique, Malaysia, Dubai and China to mention but a few (Interview, 15 February 2017).

Zimbabwe diamond sector and sustainable development

In an interview conducted in Harare with a ZANU PF official, he stressed that it has always been a matter of policy to address comprehensively the challenges of formal and informal miners in Chiadzwa and, at the same time, ensuring sustainable livelihoods for villagers and national economic recovery have been primary agendas in the public domain. The intrusion of mining in Chiadzwa displaced the cultural and social mosaic while privatising the commons and subjecting the villagers to several risks and harms with minimal benefits. The clandestine involvement of the state and its stakes in the formal and informal diamond economy, as indicated by the existence of clandestine networks, makes underhand diamond economy injurious to the prospective diamond-anchored economic resurgence. There is a general outcry at local, national and international about the opaque nature of the diamond mining proceed and the benefit sharing arrangements (Interview, 12 February 2017).

A respondent from Marange community warned that there is evidence that the Chiadzwa diamond deposits could really transform the national and local economic fortunes of Zimbabwe and Chiadzwa respectively. Demilitarisation, close monitoring of the diamond trade, appropriate declaration and repatriation of diamond revenues together with normalisations of relations with the Western diamond markets will certainly see the Zimbabwean diamonds turning around the economy. The extractive nature of the diamond industry, however, should be accompanied by appropriate observance of environmental laws, appropriate corporate social responsibility, legislative reforms and transparent accountability by all stakeholders (Interview, 9 February 2017).

The respondents from civil society concurred that the government, in partnership with the private sector, should attempt to create mechanisms that ensure transparency and fiduciary commitment in the extraction, management of diamonds and revenue to ensure sustainability in the sector that would in turn foster national development. They reiterated the need to create an independent committee and building capacity of the parliamentary portfolio committees on mines and energy to ensure that they operate independently and efficiently in ensuring transparency and fidelity in the diamond mining sector. Although their responses lacked a properly specified theoretical basis, the researchers deduced that they were indicating a "production function" for good governance. This is a function of: (i) an accountable executive; (ii) an efficient civil service; (iii) the rule of law; (iv) participation of "civil society" in policy making; and (v) an open and transparent policymaking process. The respondents said that other inputs such as property rights and contract enforcement must also be taken into cognizance. In précis, the rule of law, strong civil society and quality of bureaucracy tends to be the most important institutional characteristic in explaining human development, particularly in Zimbabwe. One of the more important policy conclusions that respondents gave pertaining to this study is that institutional capital is important, but it can be accumulated, and the stock altered following appropriate political choices (Interview, 10 February 2017).

Sustainable development and resource curse in relation to the Zimbabwean diamond sector

The study found that the question whether mining corporations share enough of their profits with their host countries and communities remains a contentious issue. Zimbabwe's legislation provides for mining companies to pay royalties to the state. The key issue is how much is paid in royalties and other taxes? Furthermore, what is the criterion that is used by the government in the allocation and distribution of mineral revenue? To what extent does that criteria benefit the mineral bearing community, in this case Marange? While the central government might be benefiting, many mining communities in Zimbabwe complain about the lack of development and investment in their areas by both mining companies and the government. The mining companies often leave a trail of damage to the environment which they cannot or are unwilling to rehabilitate. For instance, despite huge profits made over the past years, diamond-mining companies are unable to rehabilitate the Marange district besieged by their degrading operational activities. While most of the corporations involved accept responsibility, they simply claim inability to finance the clean-up costs (Interview, 12 February 2017).

Furthermore, the Government of Zimbabwe has been at conflict with itself concerning control of the revenue streams from Marange diamonds often with inconsistent numbers being indicated by the actors involved (Interview, 12 February 2017). Thus, pertinent questions can be asked about the role civil society and the public could play in monitoring revenue and promoting transparency. A question whether this is possible without accountability and information disclosure regarding contracts concluded between the state and corporations being made public comes to the fore. The response to these pertinent questions is negative considering the history and trends of regulation of diamond mining in Zimbabwe.

Another respondent from the Ministry of Mines and Mineral Development noted that the major problem is the absence of effective legislative provisions in mining or fiscal laws to ensure transparency and accountability in how governments decide and collect taxes, royalties and other revenue from mining companies. In particular, the public often does not know how much profit mining companies make and what proportion of that goes to the state. Compounding this problem, most mining laws do not require mining companies and the government to disclose the terms and conditions of mining concession contracts they enter into. The access to information laws in Zimbabwe have proved ineffective as tools to obtain such information are usually inaccessible. Transparency and openness in the management and handling of diamonds as well as revenue by the government and diamond companies would enable the public and local communities to demand that the government provide social services and funds to address environmental problems caused by mining. The impenetrability of diamond revenue has led to allegations that dishonest politicians in Zimbabwe are pilfering such revenue (Interview, 14 February 2017).

Strategies to promote Sustainable Development on the Zimbabwean Diamond Sector

Legal and policy reformation

The respondents concurred that the Government of Zimbabwe should also respect its own laws and not just enforce or ignore them when it is convenient or inconvenient to do so. The essence of the rule of law is that laws should be applied equally to all citizens to democratise diamond ownership there is need to pass legislation that bans serving members in Zimbabwe's security sector from exerting any control over mining companies, including being the beneficial owners of subsidiaries of companies operating in the country's mining sector.

Mineral law reform

Efforts to amend the Mines and Minerals Act ought to consider the merits and demerits of introducing the long-awaited Mines and Mineral Amendment Bill. The Mines and Mineral Amendment Bill sought to introduce several reforms in the mining sector. Inspiring these reforms are issues such as the system of issuing mining rights, indigenisation of the mining sector, inclusion of environmental impact assessment reports as a requirement before mining rights holders are granted a certificate of inspection, and establishment of an Environmental Rehabilitation Fund (Interview, 15 February 2017). Legislators should therefore incorporate Corporate Social Responsibility (CSR) as a legal prerequisite in the mining sector, include provisions that ensure that communal residents displaced by mining operations receive adequate compensation and are notified and consulted on the relocation exercise, advocate for environmental protection as well as the economic, social and cultural rights of communities. A good mining law ought to protect the rights of mining communities by ensuring that they participate and draw economic benefits from mining activities. The bill ought to guarantee transparency and accountability in the management of revenue from mining operations as well as in the awarding of mining contracts (Interview, 15 February 2017).

Revenue and contracts disclosure

Respondents from civil society and the opposition party agreed that the information concerning diamond revenue and contracts must be open to the public. The Minister of Finance and Economic Development, citizens, corporate world and the civil society in Zimbabwe deserve to be provided with transparent accounting systems, the names and structure of mining firms, their directorships and their investment and declaration of revenue so that all parties monitor resource use and reduce corporate obscurity. Proposals for a diamond law and its endorsement ought to be expedited given the suspected revenue losses through undercover dealings. The Zimbabwe Revenue Authority ought to play its part in the "entire value chain of diamonds from mining, marketing, to distribution and collection to the government" (Interview, 14 February 2017)

Transparency and accountability

The study established that access to information is a vital tool to prevent corruption and conflicts. The civil societies suggested that government and private companies should be obliged by law to disclose, publish and subject to public scrutiny all mining contracts and agreements. People should access information on the revenue generated, its distribution, the names and ownership structures of private companies given mining contracts. It would be imperative to make mining contracts public and making mining companies accountable. Such efforts should seek to promote accountability and transparency in the exploitation of natural resources. Consistent with the Extractive Industries Transparency Initiative (EITI) (Alao, 2007), Zimbabwe's diamond industry needs to establish tight check and balances to ensure that diamond revenue impacts on the lives of its citizens. The presence of effective checks and balances will minimise corruption and illegal leakages of diamonds into international black markets. Checks and balances improve the diamond sector performance in contributing to national economic development through enforcing fiduciary commitment. Production and sales were erratic and progressively declined from 2010 to 2015 as shown in Table 21.1.

Table 21.1: Zimbabwe Diamond Sales

Year	Payments to Government from Diamond Sector (US Dollars)
2010	125,278,522
2011	168,534,967
2012	142,478,766
2013	93,246,239
2014	84,396,414
2015	23,400,956
Total	**637,335,956**

Source: Ministry of Mines and Mining Development (1 December 2016).

Improving monitoring of diamond resources and revenue

A respondent from Movement for Democratic Change – Tsvangirai (MDC–T) emphasised that the oversight role of Parliamentary Portfolio Committees should be strengthened and respected by Parliament or the Executive so that they can effectively discuss extractive sector contracts and agreements as a mechanism to ensure transparency and accountability. The respondent from MDC-T further explained that Parliamentary Committees should continue to use their powers to request government officials and private companies to account for their actions by requesting to see every natural resource exploitation contract signed with government. The respondent further explained that revenue from natural resources like diamonds generally risks being misappropriated and spent on projects that do not change people's livelihoods and ensure economic recovery if proper measures to foster transparency are not put in place (Interview, 15 February 2017).

Diamond wealth economic valuation

A respondent from the Zimbabwe Mining Development Corporation (ZMDC), in corroboration with the reservation made by a respondent from MDC-T, stressed that with increased evidence of large diamond deposits in Zimbabwe in Mutare, Beitbridge, Tsholotsho, Lupane, Murehwa, Chipinge and Masvingo, the Ministries of Mines and Mineral Development and its department of Geological Survey, in close partnership with the Ministry of Finance and Economic Development, ought to conduct a detailed survey to the approximate amount of diamond wealth in the country. This resource valuation allows for future planning of the diamond industry and the sustainable exploitation with future generations in mind (Interview, 10 February 2017).

Capital flow tracking

A respondent from Minerals Marketing Company of Zimbabwe (MMCZ) stressed that the national economic and financial intelligence systems should track both the diamond exports and revenues to secure repatriation of profits and reduce externalisation. This follows the cases in 2011 when the India Revenue Intelligence Director intercepted 9.72 kilograms of diamonds worth US$2 million. In 2012 an Israeli citizen was also apprehended at the Harare Airport in possession of diamonds worth US$2 million. These figures of economic losses alone speak volumes about the revenue the country is losing through smuggling to other countries at the expense of national development, and due to these losses, the diamonds in Zimbabwe become a curse instead of a boon (Interview, 9 February 2017).

Beneficiating the diamonds

A respondent from ZANU PF pointed out that there is evidence that most of Zimbabwe's diamonds exported are sold to the Indian diamond industry in Surat. Surat is assumed to be polishing over 90% of the world's diamond and employing thousands of Indians. This highlights the number of jobs Zimbabwe has created for other countries. By polishing the diamonds locally, Zimbabwe could considerably improve the unemployment situation and other positive multipliers. An estimated twenty companies have been granted polishing licences by May 2012 but the direct contributions to Marange and Manicaland are not known. Investments into the diamond polishing are suspected to be directed to Harare, further centralising development and economic empowerment (Interview, 10 February 2017).

Diamond mining and environmental sustainability

The respondents for the diamond mining recommended several environmental concerns but the most important are the following recommendations by respondents.

Environmental impact assessments (EIAs)

Prior to engaging in mining, companies ought to secure an impact assessment certificate proclaiming what they anticipate to be the risks and benefits that would arise from their activities. The assessment should also lay down the mining company's commitment to address the environmental risks and negative impacts arising from its activities. In Chiadzwa, the EIA process was supposed to have been done in consultation with the villagers (Interview, 9-10 February 2017).

Shaft reclamation

Respondents from Marange lamented the negligence that some companies show in their operations and that such dangerous level of disregard for the environment would cause untold repercussions to the community. Consistent with conservation requirement of mining and the EIAs, mining companies ought to rehabilitate and restore environmentally degraded landscapes. It may be advisable for most mining companies to start afforestation programmes which would restore habitats and ecological diversity (Interview, 9-10 February 2017).

Effluence reduction

All respondents emphasised the need for reduction of pollution of the environment as this had long lasting implications to society. Respondents stressed that measures to reduce pollution should include tailing ponds to lessen sediment laden runoff through infiltration. Environmental Management Agency ought to monitor the mining operations and periodically appraise the public. The pollution of water resources is a worrying issue with severe negative impacts on downstream communities. Similarly, mining companies also ought to maintain high air quality standards to reduce the risks of air borne infections and diseases (Interviews, February 2017).

Conclusion and Recommendations

This study showed a strong nexus between factors leading to the resource curse and factors leading to a decline of sustainable economic development. There is extensive practical evidence that economies principally dependent on their natural resources are characterised by slower economic growth. This so-called resource curse is generally traced back to the fact that natural resources generate rents independent of economic performance, leading to sub-optimal reinvestments of this consumed natural capital. The study observed that weak political and economic interactions causing poor macroeconomic and public expenditure policies increase consumption rather than investment. This depends in part (but not exclusively) on the quality of participating institutions as this effect is even possible within strong institutional structures. The level of corruption, either in the form of rent-seeking or in patronage has the worst effect on investment behaviour. Resource rents constitute an easily attainable source of income and, in addition, corrupt agents, either private or public, have easier access to natural resource rents for consumption rather than investment. Respondents from opposition parties in this study identified what they termed "tenderpreneurship" in which ZANU PF ministers would be bribed by foreign mining companies to grant tenders and concessions. This, according to Transparency International (2015), constitutes rent-seeking and corruption in the diamond sector thereby compromising transparent operations of the companies.

Political leadership usually rules resource-rich countries with fragile acceptability or legitimacy and narrow oversight institutions. This combination lends itself to circumstances where leaders are effectively auctioning off a country's national resource treasure for personal aggrandisement. In Zimbabwe, this has been done through granting concessions to surrogate companies that are owned by political leadership (Transparency International, 2016). According to Global Witness (2017), the Zimbabwe Mineral Development Corporation is owned by President Robert Mugabe of Zimbabwe under the guise that it is a state-owned company. Whereas unaccountable governance forms the epicentre of the resource curse, it should be acknowledged that even reform-minded governments face arduous challenges in bringing multibillion-dollar predatory networks like the Queensway Group and other multinational corporations to account. Pursuant to this, are recommendations aimed at addressing some of these systemic problems in the extractive sector, particularly the diamond sector in Zimbabwe. These are presented across the three overarching enabling structures of the resource curse: weak domestic accountability institutions, limited home-country oversight of predatory investment, and a self-righteous international regulatory environment. Remedying this systemic exploitation will also require addressing linkages between these three processes as the cumulative effect of their impact is more damaging than any one element of this equation on its own.

a. Parliamentary and private sector oversight role

In addition to asserting authority to approve every natural resource license and contract, Zimbabwean legislature can enhance layered oversight by spreading responsibility over natural resource governance across multiple committees. Some African parliaments have deftly used the tools at their disposal to enhance transparency and accountability. Notably, the case of Tanzania's shows how country's Parastatal Organisations Accounts Committee can be an effective tool for parliamentary oversight of the executive branch. The Zimbabwean Parliamentary Portfolio Committees are usually ignored and underfunded and therefore incapacitated to effectively conduct their oversight mandate. In Tanzania, these types of committees, often known as a Public Accounts Committees (PAC), are usually chaired by opposition members of parliament. This safeguards integrity and ensures that opposition parties have a voice, are able to challenge senior government officials, and push for alternative courses of action. In parliament, for example, the Parliamentary Portfolio Committee on Public Accounts and the Parliamentary Portfolio Committee on Mines and Energy in Zimbabwe can be effective mediums for reviewing audits and assessing government expenditures (Houngnikpo, 2012). In addition, the existence of private actors playing an oversight role helps mitigate some of the negative repercussions of domestic and international actors aiming to exploit the country's natural resource wealth. The Zimbabwean parliament ought to empower such committees and private organisations such as civil societies and NGOs to conduct annual evaluations of state-owned diamond mining companies.

b. Creation of effective oversight mechanisms within the value chain in extractive industries

The key reason for the contrast between outcomes for successful commodity exporters and for the majority of Africa's resource-rich states is effective oversight institutions. Natural resources are invariably plundered, wasted, or mismanaged when individuals or small élites control the extractive industries. Significantly, no particular institution can alleviate the destructive impact of natural resource revenues on governance. Too often, governments enact cosmetic reforms that merely enhance oversight at one stage of the natural resource extraction process while neglecting to close loopholes at other stages. In addition, anticorruption commissions that are established in graft-ridden states often amount to an effort to pay lip service to reform in order to pacify donors but ultimately fail to reduce public sector corruption (Heilbrunn, 2004). Corrupt officials and illicit entrepreneurs have proven that they are nothing if not innovative and can adapt quickly if reforms are not comprehensive. Effective management of the natural resource sector requires a system of independent, capable, and accountable institutions that spans every stage of the extractive industries value chain (Alba, 2009).

This study observes that the Natural Resource Charter (NRC) developed by international economists, lawyers, and natural resource governance experts provides a useful framework for reformers seeking to improve governance of the extractive industries. Launched in 2010, and adopted by the AU Heads of State steering committee in 2011 and by the New Partnership for Africa's Development (NEPAD) in 2012, the NRC is a set of 12 economic principles (referred to as "precepts") that outline best practices for equitably managing the extractive industries (see "The Twelve Precepts of the Natural Resource Charter"). The Natural Resource Governance Institute offers expert advice, training, and courses that facilitate reform and institution-building based on NRC precepts. NRC partnerships with the University of Zimbabwe and other prominent learning institutions in Zimbabwe to host an intensive course for senior officials responsible for mineral management are very crucial. This is in order to outline the major policy choices officials must confront throughout the extraction process. A coterie of strategies ought to be advocated and advanced to ensure that resource revenues are allocated equitably, including the establishment of natural resource funds, direct cash payments to citizens, and resource-for-infrastructure swaps. While each has its merits, it is the criterion that key decisions are subject to review by an independent body representing the interests of stakeholders from civil society, government, and the private sector that is crucial.

c. The need for a policy review

In order to improve governance in the Zimbabwe's diamond industry, a good policy provides a fecund starting point. Nonetheless, the mineral management policy needs to be reviewed so as to address questions of revenue transparency, mine closure, investor identification and access to information, community participation and environmental impacts, among other pertinent issues. A transparent, professional and consistent criterion for identifying investors and awarding licences is the linchpin upon which a robust diamond sector can be established in Zimbabwe. The discretionally powers of the president and the responsible minister regarding the identification of investors and issuance of licences must be significantly reduced and spread to various institutions such as the Parliamentary Portfolio Committee on Mines, the Precious Stones Commissioner and the Diamond Board, among other actions.

A parallel law, a Diamond Act, is a requisite necessity for the policy to be efficient. The Diamond Act ought to address the inadequacies characteristic in the Mines and Minerals Act as well as to precisely deal with matters peculiar to the diamond industry. In coming up with a Diamond Act, the Zimbabwean Government must seek expert and technical support from relevant stakeholders such as the Zimbabwe Chamber of Mines, Kimberly Process Certification Scheme, mining experts, Zimbabwe Lawyers for Human Rights, Partnership Africa Canada and other states that have instituted successful policies in managing their diamond industries such as South Africa, Namibia and Botswana, among others. The current mineral policy depends more on a faulty Mines and Minerals Act (CAP 21:05) for its enactment. The Act has demonstrated to be exceptionally derisory in addressing the governance problems in the diamond sector. It provides too much power to the Minister of Mines and Mineral Development at the expense of institutions, making it principally accountable for the governance challenges in the diamond sector. The study also acknowledges the pertinence of the oversight role of parliament. In the essence of separation of powers, parliament should be allowed unfettered access to diamond mines and to all information pertaining to diamond mining activities.

References

Alao, A. (2007), *Natural resources and Conflict in Africa: The tragedy of endowment.* NY: University of Rochester Press.

Alba, E.M. (2009). *Extractive industries value chain: A comprehensive integrated approach to developing extractive industries*, Africa Region Working Paper No. 125. Washington, DC: World Bank.

Amnesty International. (2013, February 14). *Zimbabwe: Arrest of peaceful protestors casts doubt on possibility of credible referendum. Title of Newspaper.* Date, page.

Andrews, A.E. (2006). Diamond is forever: De Beers, the Kimberley Process, and the efficacy of public and corporate co-regulatory initiatives in securing regulatory compliance note. *South Carolina Journal of International Law and Business, 2*(1), 177-214.

Brodhag, C., and Talière, S. (2006, May). Sustainable development strategies: Tools for policy coherence. In *Natural Resources Forum* (Vol. 30, No. 2, pp. 136-145). Oxford, UK: Blackwell Publishing Ltd.

Cerin, P. (2006). Bringing economic opportunity into line with environmental influence: A discussion on the Coase theorem and the Porter and van der Linde hypothesis. *Ecological Economics, 56*(2), 209-225.

Cooper, P.J, and Vargas, M. (2004). *Implementing sustainable development: From global policy to local action.* Lanham, MD: Rowman and Littlefield Publishers, Inc.

Dernbach, J.C. (1998). Sustainable development as a framework for national governance. *Case Western Reserve Law Review,* (49)1, 1-103.

Di John, J. (2009). *From windfall to curse? Oil and industrialization in Venezuela, 1920 to the present.* University Park, PA: Penn State University Press.

Falls, S. (2011). Picturing blood diamonds. Critical arts. *A South-North Journal of Cultural and Media Studies, 25*(3), 441-466.

Fearon, J.D. (2004). Why do some civil wars last so much longer than others? *Journal of Peace Research, 41*(3), 275-301.

Fennell, T. and Lovgren, S. (1999). *The diamond war.* Available online: Research/Chiadzwa%20diamonds%20%20Blessing%20or%20cur se%20.htm

Heilbronn, J.R. (2004). *Anti-corruption commissions: Panacea or real medicine to fight corruption?* Washington, DC: World Bank.

Houngnikpo, M.C. (2012). Africa's militaries: A missing link in democratic transitions. *Africa Security Brief, 17*(5), 1-9.

Human Rights Watch. (2009, June 4). *Diamonds in the rough: Human rights abuses in the Marange Diamond fields of Zimbabwe.* New York: Human Rights Watch.

Keblusek, M.E. (2010). Is EITI really helping improve global good governance? Examining the resource curse, corruption, and Nigeria's EITI implementation experience. *Niger Delta Professionals for Development,* 1(5) 1-29.

Khan, M, and Jomo, K.S. (Eds.). (2000). *Rents, rent-seeking and economic development.* Cambridge: Cambridge University Press.

Kimberley Process Certification Scheme. (2002). Kimberley process certification scheme core document, adopted at Interlaken, 5 November 2002.

Kimberley Process Certification Scheme. (2010). KPCS report of the follow-up mission to Zimbabwe (9-14 August 2010).

Neary, P. and van Wijnbergen, S. (1986), *Natural resources and the macro economy.* Cambridge, MA: MIT Press.

Open Government Partnership. (undated). How it works: Requirements. Available online: http://www.opengovpartnership.org/ (Accessed 20/07/2017).

Partnership Africa Canada; Diamonds and Clubs. (2010, June). *The militarised control of diamonds and power in Zimbabwe.* Cape Town: Zebra Press.

Pigou, A. (1920). *The economics of welfare.* London, England: Macmillan and Company.

Porter, M. E., & Van der Linde, C. (1995). Toward a new conception of the environment-competitiveness relationship. *Journal of economic perspectives, 9*(4), 97-118.

Porter, M.E. and van der Linde, C. (1999). Green and competitive: Ending the stalemate. *Journal of Business Administration and Politics,* 215-230.

Rosenblum, P. and Maples, S. (2009). *Contracts confidential: Ending secret deals in the extractive industries.* New York: Revenue Watch Institute.

Sachs, J. and Warner, A. (1995). Natural resource abundance and economic growth. NBER Working Paper nr 5398. Cambridge, MA: National Bureau of Economic Research.

Siegle, J. (2012). Overcoming dilemmas of democratisation: Protecting civil liberties and the right to democracy. *Nordic Journal of International Law,* 81(4), 471–506.

Spinks, R. (2011). Export of Zimbabwean diamonds threatens ethical jewellery trade. *Ecologist,* 9-11.

Stoddart, H., Schneeberger, K., Dodds, F., Shaw, A., Bottero, M., Cornforth, J., & White, R. (2011). A pocket guide to sustainable development governance. [London United Kingdom] Stakeholder Forum 2011.

United Nations Conference on the Human Environment. (1992). *Rio Declaration on Environment and Development.* Rio de Janeiro, Brazil: United Nations.

United Nations General Assembly. (1987). *Report of the world commission on environment and development: Our common future.* Oslo, Norway: United Nations General Assembly, Development and International Co-operation: Environment.

Chapter 22

Indigenous Knowledge in Beekeeping and Education for Sustainable Development in Zimbabwe

Peter Kwaira

Summary:

This chapter is based on a study founded upon an on-going community development project launched around 2006 in Makonde Rural District (North-Western Zimbabwe). Since implementation of the land reform in early 2000, several re-settlement villages have emerged. So far, the project has gone through Phase 1 (Food production and processing at Long Valley Farm focusing on maize, ground nuts, soya-beans and sun-flowers), and Phase 2 (Design and development of post-harvest technology at Muungwe Farm, focusing on the care, management and storage of maize-grain). The currently study is part of Phase 3, focusing on beekeeping issues at Muungwe Farm, where farmers have approached a researcher at the Department of Technical Education at the University of Zimbabwe seeking educational and technical assistance. The farmers have expressed the desire to develop a more productive and sustainable system of beekeeping. The long-term intention has then been to develop a specimen program designed to address identified needs. The challenge is to identify the existing knowledge base guiding farmers in their activities before introducing any new knowledge. Data collected through observations, interviews and discussions revealed that farmers mainly rely on indigenous knowledge, passed and shared from generation to generation over the years. The study sought to address the question: In what way could indigenous knowledge be accommodated in modern-day beekeeping for the sake of sustainable development in Zimbabwe? Addressing this question is expected to later help inform the design and development of the intended specimen programme.

Introduction

Beekeeping, also known as *apiculture,* is an activity in which one rears honey-bees and acquires their products. So long as bees are considered among other creatures, there is a sense in which apiculture is generally treated as a form of animal husbandry and, consequently, supervised under the livestock industry (JAICAF, 2009). Bees produce valuable products which include honey and wax.

They also pollinate various crops and fruit trees, thereby promoting agriculture and forestry. In fact, a close relationship existed between bees (insects) and plants, well before human beings appeared on planet earth. By the time human beings featured, the bee had already been around for about 40–50 million years or more; evolving from its hunting-wasp ancestors to become a strict vegetarian (Cramp, 2008:1). While this is debatable, it is interesting to note that Goulson (2014) even estimates the advent of bees on earth to have been around 130 million years ago. Recent studies at Cornell University revealed surprises, reporting on the discovery of a 100-million-year-old bee fossil. DNA evidence from the fossil suggest bees to having originated in the northern rather than the southern hemisphere, and from a different family of bees than previously thought (Cornell University, 2006).

Bees and flowering plants have evolved together in a remarkable relationship that has changed and coloured the world in which we live today (Cramp, 2008:1-2). This evolutionary symbiotic relationship between bees and plants appears to have been probably the most important reason why our world looks like it does today; and still, the vital work of bees continues unabated. It is at this point that one imagines a situation where all human beings disappear from the earth's face, only to find the world probably reverting to its rich, ecologically balanced state that existed some 10,000 years ago. On the other hand, if bees and other pollinating insects were to disappear, humans and other animals would feel the impact; losing most of the plant-based food items from flowering plants (Cramp, 2008:2).

Since the bottom line is really for bees and other insects to pollinate plants in order for them to reproduce, one sees the value of bees in nature. This explains why we need these insects and why governments around the globe spend so much protecting them, besides investing in ecological research. Actually, because of their activities, bees are among the most economically important insects on earth and certainly the most studied (Goulson, 2014). Honey production is essentially a side issue and the bee and beekeeper's role in all this is therefore more important and valuable by the day as most of our farming activities dramatically eradicate the habitats of bees and other pollinating insects. According to Cramp (2008:2), some insects can only survive by eating the pollen of specific plants and, if these were to be removed in favour of crops, bees and other pollinating insects would perish, resulting in an unbalanced ecosystem. This shows how important apiculture is to the survival of all living organisms, especially human beings, who appear to be the most vulnerable in the face of starvation.

From a global perspective, as already observed, human involvement in life on earth was much later than the interaction between insects (especially bees) and plants (Goulson, 2014). After bees and plants had been in interaction for more than 50 million years, human experience of beekeeping only started with the arrival of our ancestors 1.8 million years ago (JAICAF, 2009). Extraction of honey started in a manner similar to the one by which, chimpanzees today lick honey from sticks by inserting them into wild bee hives. The development of tools and techniques for honey hunting appears to have continued since then. Records from ancient Egypt, where the so-called traditional beekeeping is thought to have originated, show the first domestication of bees dating back to around 5,000 years (JAICAF, 2009:3). The first apiaries were established in clusters of clay beehives, which were also discovered later across the Middle and Near East (JAICAF, 2009:3).

Modern beekeeping, dating back 200 years has continued to develop and improve globally although Africa, supposedly the original home of beekeeping, has in many respects lagged behind; mainly maintaining traditional methods (JAICAF, 2009:3). While a lot of research has been conducted on bee races, very little has been done in Africa. There has actually been evidence of African bees being unpredictable in their defensive behaviour. Deaths reported every year on people and domestic animals have resulted in a lot of fear among farmers (JAICAF, 2009:9).

The history of beekeeping in Zimbabwe is very closely related to most of what has been reported in the other African countries including Angola, Ethiopia, Kenya, Uganda and Tanzania. There are similarities from country to country, as confirmed by European records of traditional beekeeping in Africa dating back to 1594 (Clauss, 1992). After coming across log and bark hives in the upper Zambezi, David Livingstone also confirmed the same records in 1854 (Clauss, 1992).

Beekeeping has become widespread in Zimbabwe, with outstanding projects located in Bondolfi (Masvingo), Chipinge, Murehwa, Gokwe and Makonde where it has helped to supplement incomes. It has also become a perfect model of sustainable agriculture, benefiting communities by providing additional food and medicine apart from income (Illgner, *et al.* 2010). In light of the economic constraints currently prevailing, self-reliance strategies drawing on local knowledge and skills have gained renewed importance. In fact, like in many other African countries, desperate economic realities in the country have resulted in communities seeking solutions to the circumstances in which they find themselves. According to the United Nations, "for almost 900 million people; approximately one-sixth of mankind, the advance of human progress has become a retreat (Illgner, *et al.* 2010). Several countries are experiencing a reversal after decades of steady economic advance, with many relapsing back to poverty (Gooneratne and Mbilinyi, 1992). For most of Africa, this has meant effective collapse of social services due to vast debt burdens, coupled with hyperinflation and the disastrous effects of global trade and structural adjustment packages (Taylor and Mackenzie, 1992). This situation militates against any significant socio-economic intervention, on the part of governments. Apart from the usual tokenistic interventions by aid agencies and non-governmental organizations, many communities are forced to look inward at their own resources and potential in order to carve some form of future for themselves (Gooneratne and Mbilinyi, 1992). In most cases, this has led to a rediscovery of traditional forms of livelihood and income generation; hence the renewed interest in beekeeping. Given this scenario, there appears to be a critical need to determine the extent to which traditional and indigenous knowledge systems could be accommodated in modern-day beekeeping for the sake of sustainable development in Zimbabwe.

Background (Insight to the Problem)

The study leading to this chapter is part of a major on-going community development project, launched around 2006 in Makonde Rural District. Since the land reform program in 2000, several resettlement villages have been established in this part of Mashonaland West Province in North-Western Zimbabwe. The project has so far gone as follows: Phase 1 (food production and processing at Long Valley Farm); Phase 2 (addressing post-harvest issues at Muungwe Farm); and Phase 3 (addressing problems being encountered by beekeepers at Muungwe Farm). Since the whole project has been at the request of the farmers, these phases have been aimed at addressing specific needs and problems as presented by the farmers.

Focus in this study was on Phase 3, where farmers approached the Department of Technical Education at the University of Zimbabwe, seeking assistance in their endeavour to develop a more productive and sustainable system of beekeeping. Being under pressure from government to contribute to national development through their activities, they have realized the need for appropriate education and technical know-how regarding productive beekeeping. For example, Table 1 of the ZimAsset policy document shows agriculture as one of the economic growth targets, where beekeeping/apiculture is identified as part of animal husbandry (Government of Zimbabwe, 2013:28). Besides providing various products together with honey, bees play a crucial role in pollinating crops and other plants thereby contributing to food security. This then qualifies beekeeping as an ecologically appropriate form of income generation for some of the poorest communities in the country. The role of apiculture in promoting economic self-reliance and the need to enhance this role are highlighted in the Banjul Bee Declaration of 1991 (Bradbear, 1991).

Considering the farmers' needs in terms of education and training, one could see the long-term solution lying in the development of a prototype programme comprising several specimen course outlines in selected areas. From literature (Rutgers, 2017), the following possibilities were identified: theory and practice of apiculture; principles of bee business management; bee biology; integrated pest management; hive management; apiary design; introduction to carpentry; introduction to welding; rules and regulations; product processing and packaging; marketing, and first aid training. For the purpose of this study, it is in view of such courses that one had to explore into the possibility of accommodating traditional/indigenous knowledge in modern-day beekeeping for the sake of sustainable development in Zimbabwe.

Preliminary investigations through interviews and discussions revealed that nearly all farmers relied heavily on indigenous knowledge in their day to day beekeeping activities; mainly passed on from generation to generation. Such knowledge was evident in their hive and apiary designs, where traditional knowledge guided their beliefs and practices. Given this background, the challenge for this study was to establish the current/existing knowledge base guiding farmers in their activities before introducing any new forms of knowledge. The question then was: How can traditional and indigenous knowledge systems be accommodated in modern-day beekeeping for the sake of sustainable development in Zimbabwe?' Addressing this question meant unpacking it as follows:

- Under what aspects/areas of practice in beekeeping are the beekeepers of Muungwe exhibiting elements of indigenous knowledge?
- How effective and sustainable are the current systems?
- What aspects/areas of the current practices need improvement for the sake of sustainable productivity?
- How best could one take advantage of existing forms of knowledge in the development of new knowledge under modern-day beekeeping?

A Review of Some Pertinent Theoretical Perspectives

To contextualise this study within the appropriate theoretical framework, there was need to revisit the following:

- Indigenous knowledge in beekeeping;
- Tradition and modernity in beekeeping;
- Sustainability in beekeeping; and
- Design and technology in beekeeping.

Indigenous knowledge in beekeeping

As already observed under 'Introduction', the history of beekeeping in Africa, like in the rest of the world dates back millions of years. Much more recent recorded history shows farmers engaging in organized beekeeping as a side-line activity from 3500BC, particularly in Egypt and Ethiopia. It is then within this situation, spanning over centuries, that it is presumed farmers, then turned beekeepers, started developing indigenous knowledge through accumulated experiences to a valuable resource for community development (Shiferaw, 2011). In this study, one had to be conceptually clear about indigenous knowledge and how it benefits the community.

'Indigenous knowledge' is about knowledge that is unique to a given culture/society (Shiferaw, 2011). In most cases, it is contrasted with scientific knowledge generated in universities through research. All over the world, indigenous knowledge has been used at local levels for decision-making on matters pertaining to food security, human/animal health, education, natural resource management, and other related activities (Gorjestani, 2000). Unfortunately, this valuable knowledge accumulated over generations, is often neglected by researchers, despite being important for developing sustainable life systems at community levels (van den Ban and Hawkins, 1996).

Indigenous knowledge is the basis for self-sufficiency and self-determination for at least two reasons (IIRR, 1996): First, people are familiar with local practices and technologies, which they can understand, handle, and maintain better than anything from outside. Secondly, indigenous knowledge draws on local resources; human and otherwise, where people are less dependent on costly and scarce outside supplies. According to Gorjestani (2000), adoption of technology by communities is high when it is a product of familiar experiences. Hence, indigenous knowledge is more adoptable since it relies on locally available skills and materials. This is why Workneh *et al.* (2008) advise researchers and development organizations to identify and document existing indigenous technical knowledge of farmers (beekeepers) before integrating it optimally into improved or modern practices. In this study, the identification and documentation of indigenous knowledge within beekeeping was therefore deliberately meant to ensure the accessibility of such knowledge and related skills which would, in turn, contribute to improved beekeeping.

Tradition and modernity in beekeeping

From the outset, the belief in this study was that the so-called indigenous knowledge and modern knowledge could be bridged together, resulting in a more sustainable system of beekeeping. The two were also assumed to have their own individual sets of advantages and disadvantages; hence the need to complement each other. Although modern beekeeping technology meets the needs for improved product quality and for the expansion of market for processed products, traditional beekeeping technology still holds sufficient potential value, regarding sustainability (Bradbear, 1991).

The advent of beehives allowing for inspection/management of multiple honeycomb frames has enabled beekeepers to carry out various management tasks, including dividing colonies, adding frames to create larger colonies and inversely thinning out surplus frames to build more compact colonies. Because of this type of beehive, the trading of live bees has become a reality. In addition, standardised beehives allow for the movement of colonies for purposes other than honey harvesting; for instance, the conveyance of colonies exclusively for the pollination of target crops. In short, versatile modern beehives enable the efficient use of bees in various applications. With modern technology, honey is now easily harvested whenever needed; hence the possibility of producing particular kinds of honey from specific sources (Bradbear, 1991). Nowadays beekeepers produce honeys bearing specific flower names with diversified and controllable quality. Similarly, other products like wax and royal jelly are these days produced in greater quantities than ever before due to beehives that are easily modified to meet specific production requirements (Bradbear, 1991). All this appears to have been possible due to the flexibility and innovation owing to the high adaptability of honey-bees that has allowed beekeepers to develop intermediate technology systems putting indigenous and modern forms of knowledge together.

Sustainability in beekeeping

Among other things, beekeeping has been found to be one of the most environment friendly enterprises in farming, promoting the planting and maintenance of trees. In the process, besides farmers producing food from livestock and crops, several other sectors also benefit from related activities. For example, carpenters, builders, tailors and blacksmiths are also promoted when they produce hives, bee houses, bee suits and other pieces of beekeeping equipment. According to the thinking in this study, these practitioners/tradespersons comprise the human resource base that could be developed through technical education. Now, dealing with industrial production, such as we have in agriculture in general and beekeeping in particular, one can hardly avoid addressing issues relating to sustainability and sustainable development.

Among several tenets, sustainable development is about advocating for technological choices meeting human needs while at the same time preserving the environment for future generations. Accordingly, technology should be both socially appropriate and environmentally sustainable (Pearce, 2012). Technology that is 'appropriate' and 'sustainable' is also likely to be durable, besides being functional and relatively cheap. Such technology is usually suitable for the purposes for which it is designed, and where it becomes sustainable in the sense of being maintained at a steady level without exhausting natural resources or causing permanent ecological damage (World Bank, 2011). In many ways, this technology appears suitable for small-scale, grassroots and people-centred economics such as we have in much of the developing world.

Sustainable development is about being mindful of our actions and the consequences of those actions regarding the exploitation of natural resources within our environment (World Bank, 2011). Working bottom-up (not top-down) to meet grassroots economic needs is the foundation of sustainable living (Kates *et al.* 2005). This contention is agreeable to the fundamental perspective where appropriate technology is about caring and forward-thinking. It is as much a philosophy as it is a way of seeing and doing things, particularly in relation to problem-solving (McKeown, 2002). Schumacher (1973) advocates production from local resources to meet and satisfy local needs. Production, he argues, should be a means to an end, increasing well-being. The goal, therefore, should be to achieve that end with a minimum of resources and environmental degradation. While efficiency is still important, it must be defined by the propositions that nature is priceless, and that finite resources, which get depleted over time, should be treated as capital assets to be carefully husbanded rather than as income accruing anew every year (Pearce, 2012). This appears to imply that technologies are environmentally sustainable based primarily upon renewable resources such as energy from the sun, water, and wind, as opposed to such non-renewable resources as fossil fuels. According to Schumacher (1973) and Pearce (2012), most of the earth's resources are limited and difficult to replace.

Today, the Intermediate Technology Development Group (ITDG) is a typical example of non-governmental organizations that have continued to work on several projects in rural and urban areas to foster sustainable improvements (World Bank, 2011). With offices in several countries (Bangladesh, Kenya, Nepal, Peru, Sri Lanka, Sudan, Zimbabwe and the United Kingdom), they have been working in the areas of energy, transportation, manufacturing, water/sanitation, construction, mining, and food production. In all their activities, they advocate and promote features such as low-cost, low usage of fossil fuels, use of recycled materials and use of locally available resources (World Bank, 2011). It is actually these ideas that have underpinned the philosophy behind this study, where one could see the important role that could be played by design and technology (D and T) in community development (CD).

Design and technology in beekeeping

In this study, there was need to clarify on the meaning of design and technology (DandT). To do that, one had to define 'design' and 'technology' separately before uniting them into one composite process referred to 'design and technology'. According to Roberts and Zanker (1994:5), the view that 'technology' encompasses 'design' is misleading. They suggest an understanding of these terms individually before coalescing them into one connected whole concept of DandT. In this study, it was therefore necessary to take heed of Roberts and Zanker's (1994) advice for the sake of clarity.

In line with Roberts and Zanker's position, Stables (2014) maintains that 'design' is a process in which a wide range of experiences, knowledge and skills are used to find optimum solutions to given problems within specific contexts and constrains. Accordingly, the process involves identifying and clarifying a problem, making a thoughtful response, and then creating and testing one's solution. After testing and evaluating a solution to a particular problem, one might need to modify it in such a way that the process of designing begins again, depending on the results of the tests. For example, if the solution has been successful, the process is rested for a while. If not, the process resumes and continues into more circles until an acceptable solution is achieved. Stables (2014), also describes design as a creative activity where one may use known facts or solutions to solve a given problem. However, the way one puts these together in problem-solving requires creative thinking thereby resulting in design being more than just problem-solving. It involves the whole process of producing a solution, from conception to evaluation (Wong and Siu, 2011). Perhaps this is why designers are found working in almost every area of life; for example, product design, graphic design, interior design, engineering and environmental design.

While 'design' has to do with creative thinking in problem-solving, 'technology' on the other hand, has to do with the hardware/equipment used in problem solving (Baynes, 2006). It is not enough to just think creatively and coming up with good ideas without applying those ideas. This is where it becomes necessary to consider the link between 'design' and 'technology' resulting in the composite process of DandT as already indicated. The need for such a link is justified by the belief that we cannot have a complete solution to a problem without the two combined (Kwaira, 1998).

Methodology

Being part of a major on-going community development project, this chapter has been part of a continuous process approached through developmental research (DR). Since the task was to find out how indigenous knowledge could be accommodated in modern-day beekeeping for the sake of sustainable development in Zimbabwe before coming up with a program designed for education/training in beekeeping, the approach was found appropriate. It was also hoped the findings would help to inform further research for the sake of intervention aimed at meeting the needs of beekeepers in Mashonaland West Province, specifically focusing on Muungwe Farm in Makonde Rural District. Such an approach was typical of DR, often initiated for complex and innovative tasks where very few validated principles are available to structure and support given developmental activities (Van den Akker *et al.* 1999; Lijnse, 2000). Typical activities in DR found applicable in this study include literature review, participatory research and case studies of current practices. Since the activities started in this study are developmental in nature, they are likely to continue for a foreseeable future. This is because there is a need to keep abreast of the changing circumstances of the beekeepers involved as they continue to grow and develop experientially. Data captured from discussions during meetings were later reinforced by data gathered through interviews with key informants. Observations of specific beekeeping practices and methods were captured on camera in preparation for analysis. More data were also collected through document analysis of relevant reports and minutes, in addition to a detailed literature review. Gathered through interviews, discussions, observation and document analysis, all data were mainly analysed qualitatively. Since all interviews, discussions and observations were captured on camera, analysis of data was done with the aid of transcripts and check-lists. For document analysis, only check-lists were applicable.

Results

These were presented in line with the thematic issues emerging from the research questions and going as follows:

Aspects under which beekeepers exhibited elements of indigenous knowledge

Investigations culminated in evidence of beekeepers at Muungwe Village being actively guided by a lot of indigenous knowledge in their activities and practices. Typical examples of some of the indigenous technical knowledge exhibited by these beekeepers were identified in the following: bee-hive designs; honeybee management techniques; honey season identification; swarm catching and attractant methods; swarm control methods; identification of honeybee enemies and methods of protection; protection against stings (reduction of pain) and honey harvesting techniques. In short, the beekeepers were found to have plenty of appreciable indigenous knowledge. Hence, what was only left was to verify and decide on which elements to adopt and integrate into mainstream knowledge development and management in line with the need to promote sustainability.

Effectiveness of current beekeeping practices regarding sustainability

Careful observation of the beekeepers at work showed a lot regarding their activities in relation to specific practices. Most of their practices were low-cost and simple. Unfortunately, some of these practices were quite harmful to both bees and the environment. A typical example of a situation where some of these harmful practices were closely observed was during honey harvesting. There was a lot of destruction since many bees were killed in the process. Open flames would actually be forced into hives to burn off the bees before removing all the honey combs, including even those containing larvae. The process appeared extremely violent and barbaric. In most cases, the hive was also destroyed in the process. The open flames that were used also posed the risk of veld fires, rendering the process dangerous and unsustainable.

Observations also showed parents teaching and showing their children how to go about several beekeeping activities. This was supposed to be really good, had the curriculum been good. In a way, children were being taught the wrong practices, particularly in relation to honey harvesting. One other observation was the gender balance when it came to some of the activities. Again, using evidence acquired during honey harvesting, no women or girls were allowed in the vicinity. In this case, the reason was very simple and clear; the men actively involved in the process would do it naked. Upon investigation, it was revealed that one would remove all clothes and then smear special herbs and soil preparations/mixtures for protection against bee stings. This was comparable to similar experiences elsewhere in Africa, as observed in literature on beekeeping in Zambia and Mozambique (Clauss, 1992).

Aspects of current practices needing improvement for the sake of sustainable productivity

As already indicated above, one aspect that really needed urgent attention was 'honey harvesting' that was found extremely destructive to both the bees and the environment. The removal of honey was also not orderly resulting in both the honey and the wax being of inferior quality. Another area requiring attention was beehive construction. The use of green barks was destructive to the vegetation where trees were left to dry and die-off. The problems identified here called for relevant course outlines within the intended program/curriculum.

Taking advantage of existing forms of knowledge in the development of new knowledge

This study revealed the strengths and weaknesses of the current beekeeping practices at Muungwe Farm, consequently justifying the need for specific intervention strategies to improve the situation. One key strategy was to come up with an overall action plan and allowing for the design and development of a program to enable beekeepers to improve their activities. The plan involved identifying key areas for the program given the need at hand. The following aspects were therefore identified for course development: knowledge of the honeybee; knowledge of bee hives; management of bees; assembly of bee hives; honey harvesting techniques, and processing of honey products. Course outlines were to be designed out of these broad areas.

Discussion of Conclusions and their Implications

From the results and findings, the following conclusions were drawn and subsequently followed by a discussion of their implications:

- Some of the current beekeeping practices at Muungwe are unsustainable and there is need for improvement.
- There is a lot that can be adopted and adapted from the indigenous knowledge system currently used by beekeepers at Muungwe Farm into modern beekeeping.

The fact that beekeepers at Muungwe continue to practise traditional methods of beekeeping is not that they are not aware of modern methods. They indicated an awareness of modern methods and wiliness to adopt them. However, the main obstacle was lack of knowledge and resources, hence the need for assistance from the Department of Technical Education at the University of Zimbabwe. This resulted in this study searching for the specific points at which the challenge could be handled. The Department has the capacity to assist in terms of both knowledge and technical skills. Out of the six disciplines in the Department (Agriculture, Home Economics, Building Technology and Design, Wood Technology and Design, Metal Technology and Design and Technical Graphics), Agriculture was found to be the most suitable host.

In most agriculture curricula, beekeeping is one of the sections. However, in Zimbabwean schools and tertiary institutions, this area has in most cases been underplayed, if not avoided altogether. Although agriculture has been identified as the most obvious host for beekeeping, opportunity for possible subject integration could also be explored. Subject integration is where all subjects could contribute towards this innovation. Going by the philosophy of DandT guiding all activities in the Department, all the six subject areas could have a role to play since the whole task is a problem-solving issue. Just like the involvement of several sectors in the production of hives, bee houses, bee suits and other pieces of beekeeping equipment, one could see all the subjects in the Department sharing responsibility in problem-solving aimed at benefitting beekeeping.

Recommendations

From the results, findings and conclusions in this study, several recommendations could be made. However, being part of an on-going project, the following were found specifically pertinent at this stage: First, now that several course outlines have been found possible, there is need for further research where individual courses are trial run at pilot levels with the intention to determine their relevance and appropriateness, given the target group. The idea is also to find out the extent to which they could also be used with groups of beekeepers from other parts of the country. Secondly, since there is also a need to assist beekeepers in the design and development of selected pieces of beekeeping equipment such as bee-hives, it will be necessary to determine their individual levels of technical and manipulative skills. Research in this regard could actually go as far as identifying those aspects of material science that could be relevant for the purpose. At this stage, it would also be necessary to inculcate elements of education for sustainable development (ESD) within the program with the intention to help beekeepers appreciate environment related issues. A typical example here could be the sustainable extraction and application of materials.

References

Baynes, K. (2006). Design education: What's the point? *Design and Technology Education: International Journal, 11*(3), 7-10.

Bradbear, N. (1991). Banjul Bee Declaration. In N. Bradbear (Ed.), *Proceedings of the First West African Bee Research Seminar* (pp.80-82). Bakau, Gambia: Bees for Development.

Clauss, B. (1992). *Bees and beekeeping in the North Western Province of Zambia.* Ndola, Zambia: Forestry Department.

Cornell University. (2006). Two studies on bee evolution reveal surprises. *Science News.* Available online: https://www.s.ciencedaily.com/htm.

Cramp, D. (2008). *A practical manual of beekeeping: How to keep bees and develop your full potential as an apiarist.* Mt Vernon, Lawrence: Spring Hill House, A Division of How to Books Ltd.

Gooneratne, W. and Mbilinyi, M. (1992). *Reviving local self-reliance: People's responses to economic crisis in Eastern and Southern Africa.* Nagoya, Japan: United Nations Centre for Regional Development.

Gorjestani, N. (2000). *Indigenous knowledge for development: Opportunities and challenges.* Paper presented at the United Nations Conference on Trade and Development (UNCTAD) Conference on Traditional Knowledge, November 1, 2000, Geneva.

Goulson, D. (2014). The beguiling history of bees. New York: Scientific American.

Government of Zimbabwe. (2013). Zimbabwe Agenda for Sustainable Socio-Economic Transformation (ZimAsset). Harare: Government Printers.

Illgner, P.M., Nel, E.L. and Roberson, M.P. (2010). Beekeeping and local self-reliance in rural southern Africa. *Geographical Review, 88*(3).

International Institute for Rural Reconstruction. (1996). *Recording and using indigenous knowledge*: A manual (IIRR). Cavite, Philippines: Silang.

Japan Association for International Collaboration of Agriculture and Forestry (JAICAF). (2009). *Development of beekeeping in developing countries and practical procedures: Case study in Africa.* Tokyo: Agriculture and Forestry.

Kates, R.W., Parris, T.M. and Leiserowitz, A.A. (2005). *What is sustainable development? Goals, values, indicators and practice.* New York: Digital Vision.

Kwaira, P. (1998). Problems experienced by teachers in their efforts to implement the Design and Technology approach in the teaching of technical subjects. In J.S. Smith (Ed.), *IDATER'98* (pp.224-229). Loughborough University: Dept. of Design and Technology.

Lijnse, P. (2000). Didactics of science: The forgotten dimension in science education research? In R. Millar, J. Leach and J. Osborne (Eds.), *Improving science education: The contribution of research.* Buckingham: Open University Press.

McKeown, R., Hopkins, C. A., Rizi, R., and Chrystalbridge, M. (2002). *Education for sustainable development toolkit.* Knoxville: Energy, Environment and Resources Center, University of Tennessee.

Pearce, J.M. (2012). The case for open source appropriate technology. *Environment, Development and Sustainability, 14,* 425-431. Available online: http://dx.doi.org/10.1007/s10668-012-9337.

Roberts, P. and Zanker, F. (1994). NADE response to the SCAA national curriculum: Design and technology. *The Journal Association for Design Education, 2,* 4-5.

Rutgers. (2017). *Beekeeping courses*. Office of continuing professional education. The State University of New Jersey, New Jersey. Available online: http://www.cpe.rutgers.edu/programmes/beekeeping.html

Schumacher, E.F. (1973). *Small is beautiful: Economics as if people mattered*. New York: Harper and Row.

Shiferaw, A. (2011). Identification and documentation of indigenous knowledge of beekeeping practices in selected districts of Ethiopia. *Journal of Agricultural Extension and Rural Development, 3*(5), 82-87.

Stables, K. (2014). Designerly well-being: Implications for pedagogy that develops design capability. *Design and Technology Education: An International Journal, 19*(1), 9-20. Available online: http://ojs.lboro.ac.uk/ojs/index.php.

Taylor, D.R.F. and Mackenzie, F. (1992). *Development from within: Survival in rural Africa*. London: Routledge.

Van den Akker, J. *et al.* (1999). *Design approaches and tools in education and training*. Dordrecht: Kluwer Academic Publishers.

Wong, Y. L., and Siu, K. W. M. (2012). A model of creative design process for fostering creativity of students in design education. *International Journal of Technology and Design Education, 22*(4), 437-450.

Workneh, A., Ranjitha, P. and Ranjan, S.K. (2008). *Adopting improved box hive in Atsbi Wemberta district of Eastern Zone, Tigray Region: Determinants and financial benefits*. Addis Ababa, Ethiopia: International Livestock Research Institute (ILRI).

World Bank, Natural Resources Institute, and FAO. (2011). *Missing food: The case of postharvest grain losses in sub-Saharan Africa*. Washington, DC: The World Bank.

Chapter 23

The Green Economy Potential in Zimbabwe

Easther Chigumira, Idah Mbengo, R. Chitopo
and M. Chigumira

Summary:

The concept of green economy has gained prominence in international and regional policy tractions due to increasing pressure for identification and deployment of sustainable development pathways and improved welfare of people. The global landscape has placed the concept of green economy and green growth strategies at the centre of development agenda. The chapter provides a situational analysis of Zimbabwe's potential to transition to a green economy. Using a political ecology framework, the study analysed academic and research documents, grey (the country's legislation, policies, economic instruments) literature, and interviews with key stakeholders from the public and private sectors and civil society. Snowballing and purposive sampling were used to identify key stakeholders and relevant government officials for the study. The main findings show that Zimbabwe is has appropriate legislation, policies and economic instruments that can enable the country to transition from a brown to a green economy. Although deindustrialisation has had a negative impact on the country's economy and the welfare of its citizens, we argue that it actually paves a way for a regeneration of industries that follow green principles and strategies, and which can allow for a sustainable development pathway. We found amongst other aspects that there is potential for industries to transition to a green economy through a strategic focus on renewable energy production and instilling energy efficiency. We position the informal sector as a strategic area for pursuing green growth strategies since many Zimbabweans are working in these informal channels. This informal sector is very brown and both economically and environmentally unsustainable. The chapter concludes by suggesting opportunities, risks as well as recommendations for supporting a green economy context in Zimbabwe.

Introduction

In recent years, the concept of green economy has gained prominent international and regional policy traction due to increasing pressure for the identification and deployment of more sustainable development pathways

(Houdet and Chikozho, 2016) and improved welfare of citizens. In literature green economy is interchanged with concepts of green growth (UNEP, 2011; Deloitte, 2012). Following deliberations at the UNFCCC Rio +20 Conference of Parties (COP) and agreements at COP 21 in Paris (2015) for low carbon development and climate resilient pathways, the global landscape has placed the concept of green economy and green growth strategies at the centre of the development agenda. In order to understand the dynamics and potential for a green economy in the country, the study provides a situational overview and contextual discussion of Zimbabwe's socio-economic, institutional, policy and legal frameworks related to the environment, climate change, and energy nexus to map out the country potential to transition to a green economy.

Green economy refers to an economy that pursues inclusive economic growth through policies, programmes and projects that encompasses sustainable infrastructure, better natural resource utilization and management, builds resilience to natural disasters and enhances food security (AfDB, 2012). Green economy has been defined as one whose growth in employment and income is spearheaded by public and private investments that facilitate reductions in pollution and carbon emissions. In addition, green economy prevents loss of biodiversity and ecosystems as well as enhance resource and energy efficiency (UNEP, 2011). A green economy therefore encompasses the three pillars of sustainability, which are economic, social and environment (Gonzalez, 2015). Green economies are characterised by improved human wellbeing, social equity, and reduced environmental risks and ecological scarcities (UNEP, 2011). Transitioning to a green economy is viewed as a catalyst that will ensure the viability of environment and economic growth that enhances human wellbeing for the present and future generations.

It is expected that pursuing a green economy paradigm will facilitate the attainment of the Sustainable Development Goals (SDGs) (Silveira, 2015). This notion is based on the fact that green economy strategies are implemented in parallel to initiatives centring on the three pillars of sustainability (Barbier, 2011) and green growth through green jobs. Focusing on green growth will lead to a green economy. Green growth is defined as economic progress that fosters environmentally sustainable, low carbon and inclusive development using an ecosystems approach to agriculture, forestry, and fisheries management (UNEP, 2012). It integrates values of natural capital into decision-making and reduces or avoids natural capital depletion and environmental risks. This development paradigm is considered a more action-oriented approach to sustainable development with operational policy agenda that can help achieve solid measurable progress of the economy and environment (Barbier, 2009).

South Korea's green economy policy is one of the most successful cases. It has been driven by centralization and strong top down leadership that links long-term development objectives with the greening of its economy (Lee and Ahn, 2015). Examples of strategies used included an establishment of a green economy organisation that develops implements and coordinate green economy efforts of different agencies (OECD, 2015). Another strategy aimed at ensuring green economy activities are tracked in an organised and systematic manner within budget benchmarks. Passage of legislation on national greenhouse gases emissions trading schemes and inventory report system enabled the reduction of greenhouse gas emission. Ireland also had a national plan from 2007-2013 that fostered success in their green economy journey. The plan set out indicative financial allocations for investment priorities aimed at providing better quality of life, bring together sectoral investments policies into one framework, promote coordination and alignment as well as deliver implementation of public investment (OECD, 2015). A substantial amount of about EUR 1 billion was invested in programmes and projects that directly promoted environmental sustainability. These projects included pollution prevention controls, restriction of hazardous substances and energy end use efficiency. Other strategies included continual encouragement of companies to adopt efficiency initiatives in the natural resources renewable sector. Furthermore, the increase in societal and business demands for firms to behave in an environmentally friendly way has aided the green economy pathway.

Studies undertaken by the UNEP (2011) point to generation has generated an estimated 3 million jobs and 6 billion products plus services respectively in the United States of America under its green economy strategy. This translates to 4.2% of the county's GDP (UNEP, 2011). Sales of organic food increased by 15.8%, which is three more times than any other food sector around the world. The green sector in Germany contributes 4.8% of the country's GDP (Grigoleit and Lenkeit, 2012). German is a world leader in exporting eco-friendly goods and services, for example, it sells 12% of the world's climate control equipment. In addition, Germany reduced greenhouse gas emissions by 80-90 percent as a result of green strategies.

African countries like Rwanda are charting the green agenda in their economic development and poverty alleviation strategies. Focus of their green economy strategy has been in the land and forest sector. In Kenya, green economy transition has been categorized into rapid transit systems, sustainable natural resources management as well as integrating green economy issues into all level of education. Furthermore, categories also include efficient management of public finances and generating alternative activities through resilience building. Promoting employment creation for youth, women and people with special needs to achieve social inclusion and sustainable livelihoods has been part of green economy in Kenya. South Africa has focused its green economy strategies on cities which are considered the great emitters of greenhouse gases.

Literature Review

A review of literature on Zimbabwe shows little reference to the concept of green growth and green economy, which is an indication that these concepts are relatively new to the country. The commonly used concepts are sustainable economic development, climate change adaptation and mitigation, and renewable energy development. The study therefore seeks to assess the potential for Zimbabwe to transition to a green economy by mapping areas and strategies that could be put in place to chart forth this development paradigm.

Methodology

This chapter is grounded in a post-structural political ecology framework which provides for the exploration of both discourse and narratives around the green economy in Zimbabwe. In addition, this paradigm allows for an exploration of the drivers of a green economy paradigm through situating the analysis in the socio-economic, political and ecological context in the country. The research design involved the collection of qualitative data through in-depth interviews with 20 key stakeholders from civil society organisations (CSOs), government officials at the national level, donor agencies, consultants and the private sector. Snowballing and purposive sampling were used to identify stakeholders and relevant government officials. An interview guide was developed and administered to understand the nature and dynamics of institutional frameworks governing the triad (environment-climate change-energy) from different stakeholders considered to have a high influence in the green economy. Questions in the guide were designed to provide insight into policy-making strategies, and issues considered important for the environment, climate change and energy nexus.

An extensive desk review of secondary data that included academic and grey literature (national, regional and international), and analysis of policy and strategy reports was undertaken. This data included national legislation such as the Constitution of Zimbabwe, Environment Management Act, Forest Act, and Mines and Minerals Act. In addition, country's policies and strategies such as the National Environment Policy and Plan, and National Climate Change Response Strategy, draft Climate Policy, Energy Policy, Disaster Risk and Management Strategy were reviewed. Furthermore, the study relied on reviews of reports and literature such as the Zimbabwe's State of the Environment Outlook report and other resources on Zimbabwe's socio-economic and physical environment; current press releases and pamphlets related to climate change, energy and other environmental concerns; and various frameworks of institutional and administrative structures for environmental governance in the country.

Data collected was entered into a database in NVivo where both content analysis of the interviews and textual analysis of secondary data were undertaken. Key themes emerged and were used in the interpretation and analysis of this study.

Overview of Zimbabwe potential to transition to a Green Economy

Zimbabwe has a long history of government concern for, and involvement in environmental issues. This concern is reflected in the number and diversity of laws on the statute books governing access to, and the conservation and use of natural resources, and in the country's active role in a range of international environmental conventions (Frost, 2001). Zimbabwe was among the first countries to sign and ratify the United Nations Framework Convention on Climate Change (UNFCCC) in 1992 and accede to the Kyoto Protocol in 2009 and submit to National Development Goals as their Intended Nationally Determined Contribution (INDCs) in 2015.

Following deliberations at the UNFCCC Rio+20 Conference of Parties (COP) and agreements at COP 21 in Paris (2015) for low carbon development and climate resilient pathways, the global landscape has placed the concept of green economy and green growth strategies at the centre of the development agenda. The concept of green growth and the green economy is relatively new, and Zimbabwe does not have a national green growth policy framework or strategy. However, the Government of Zimbabwe (GoZ) recognises the need for green growth and the movement away from a brown to green economy. In the *Future We Want'* communique at the Rio +20 Conference of Parties (COP), the GoZ positioned green growth as a goal to "achieve growth that is social as well as environmentally sustainable so that all citizens enjoy sustained improvement in their quality of life" (Government of Zimbabwe, 2012). This communique indicates that the potential for green growth lies in renewable energy, green buildings, clean transportation, water management, waste management, and sustainable land management. The GoZ proffered the following as reasons for embarking on a green growth pathway:

i.   The livelihoods of the majority of Zimbabweans are directly dependent on natural resources, which are vulnerable to climate change, and other ecological disruptions;

ii.   It provides the opportunity and mechanisms for reducing waste, pollution and destruction of natural resources and other environmental risks;

iii.   Pays attention to equity, sustainability and viability issues; and

iv.   Provides a basis for meeting growing demands for affordable food, more renewable energy and energy efficiency, and transportation.

The foundation for green economy in the country is already embedded in several existing policies and strategies, legislations and regulations, economic instruments (Pigovian taxes), awareness activities and voluntary agreements. An opportunity thus exists for the harmonisation of the aforementioned, which will enable and/or provide a roadmap and indicators for Zimbabwe's transition to a green economy.

Legislative foundations for a green economy

Successful transition to a green economy requires governments to put in place environmental legislation and Acts, policies, strategies and frameworks that provide an enabling environment for mainstreaming this development pathway. The main findings show that Zimbabwe is embedded with appropriate legislation and policies and economic instruments that can enable the country to transition from a brown to a green economy.

The Constitution and various pieces of legislation, Acts, statutory instruments, conventions to which Zimbabwe is a signatory, frameworks, policies and strategies provide the necessary framework for a green economy context in the country (Figure 3.1). The Constitution which was adopted in 2013 provides for the necessary grounds for a green economy in Zimbabwe. The Constitution embraces environmental rights and encourages environmental protection through Sections 48, 73, 76 and 77. These sections of the Constitution enshrine the principles required for green growth and the transition from a brown to a green economy. Section 73 provides every person the right to an environment that is not harmful to their health or wellbeing. Although Zimbabwe does not have a green economy policy and framework, there are however several existing Acts and statutes shown in Table 23.1 that support a green economy and provide for its foundation. These legal provisions are binding and violations or failure to abide by them is actionable in a court of law (ZELA, 2013).

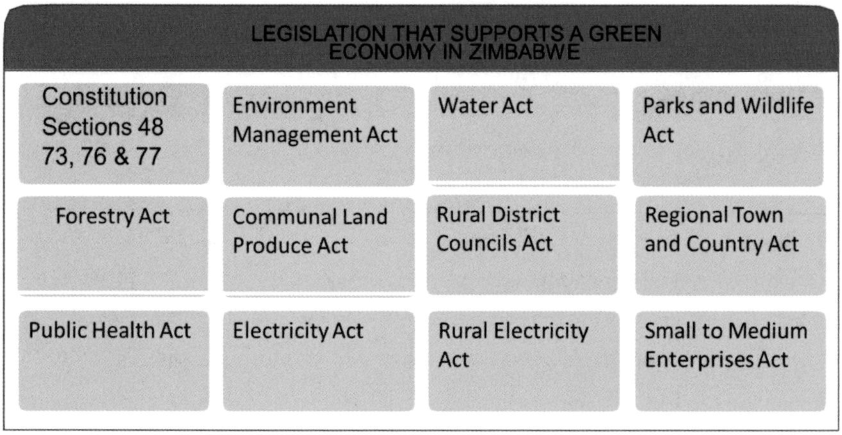

Figure 23.2: Key Legislation that Supports a Green Economy in Zimbabwe.
Source: Chigumira (2016)

Table 23.2: A Summary of Key Legislation and Provisions that Supports a Green Economy in Zimbabwe.

Legislation	Key Provisions
Environment and Natural Resources	
Environmental Management Act (2002), amended in 2006	Sustainable management of natural resources, the protection of the environment – including protection of wetlands and the prevention of pollution and environmental degradation; and establishment of environmental quality standards on air quality, water pollution, waste management, noise, noxious smells and radioactive wastes. Provides legal framework for transitioning to a green economy. It mandates the undertaking of Environment Impact Assessments (EIA) before any prescribed project activities. This has implications for any green projects (e.g. renewable energy development of solar and hydro plants and wind farms).
Forestry Act (1949), amended in 1996	The establishment of forest areas for sustainable utilization of timber, as reservoirs of wildlife and water catchment and for the conservation of biological diversity

Communal Land Forest Produce Act (1988)	Regulation of the exploitation of wood resources in communal areas through Rural District Councils
Parks and Wildlife Act	Preservation of plants and animals, including specially protected animals and indigenous plants. A consequence of this provision is that no construction and development should engage into activities which violate this Act. Stringent environmental controls will need to be enforced and adhered to.
National Water Act (2003)	The establishment of water catchment councils and sub-catchment council, granting of water permits and control of water use when it is in short supply as well as protection of the environment, the prevention and control of water pollution
Climate and Climate Change Policies – Provide for:	
Meteorological Services Act (1990)	The production and dissemination of climate information
Civil Protection Act (1989)	Response to climate change in disaster reduction
Energy	
Electricity Act	The Act requires that a license be sought from the Zimbabwe Electricity Regulatory Commission (ZERC) for transmission and distribution of electricity in excess of 100kV. The licensee should ensure that: the natural environment is protected. The licensee should cause as little detriment and inconvenience and do as little damage as possible and pay compensation to any person who suffers loss or deprivation of rights.

Rural Electricity Act	Provides for funding of the programme through levies, loans, fiscal allocations, grants and donations. At present, the Rural Electrification programmes are primarily funded by 6% levy, levied on all electricity consumers as well as fiscal allocations.
Health and Economic	
Public Health Act	Legal framework for the protection of public health in Zimbabwe. Provision for maintenance of cleanliness and prevention of nuisance, which include premises that promote the spread of infectious diseases, pools of water that may serve as breeding places for mosquitoes, polluted domestic water and accumulation of refuse and overcrowding in dwellings.
Small to Medium Enterprises Act	Promotes the development of micro, small and medium enterprises operationalizing in both informal and formal sectors. Allows for the widening of the sphere of economic activities.
Governance	
Rural District Council Act	The powers of the Rural District Council, among other things, include conservation of natural resources, prevention of bush fires, grazing, animal diseases, sewerage works, pollution, and effluent or refuse selection and disposal etc. Empowers RDCs to plan for the overall development of the Districts and guide of all development activities by governmental, CSOs and the private sector in their jurisdiction.
Regional Town and Country Act	Provides for the planning of regions, districts and at the local level in order to conserve and improve the physical environment.

Source: (Chigumira, 2016)

Given these supporting policies and legislation, an opportunity exists to develop a green economy/ green growth strategy or framework to guide this green development pathway. However, while Zimbabwe has comprehensive legislation related to the environment and sustainable development, the country has a very weak multi-sectoral approach to mainstreaming environmental issues and policies. Environmental functions, as shown in Figure 3.2, are fragmented across more than 10 government ministries, which often leads to poor coordination and implementation of rules and regulations. The lack of coordination amongst government departments and research institutions weakens the capacity of the country to successfully transition to a green economy. Furthermore, the effectiveness of such legislation is constrained by a poor regulatory system amongst law enforcement agencies, perceived lack of transparency and political will to enforce the laws.

Lessons drawn from international and regional experiences in transitioning to a green economy point to synergistic growth between economic development and environmental management, which are driven by strict adherence to policies and legislations and supported by economic instruments such as environmental taxes, and implementation of and compliance with rules and regulations. For example, South Korea's success in transitioning to a green economy was based on this synergy and characterized by a combination of stringent regulations and economic instruments such as different emission charges, eco-labelling and green public purchasing. South Korea gave local governments a bigger role in implementing environmental policies and expanded environmental information and public participation. This effective citizen engagement resulted in public support for research and development and commercialisation of environmental technologies, especially in small and medium enterprises.

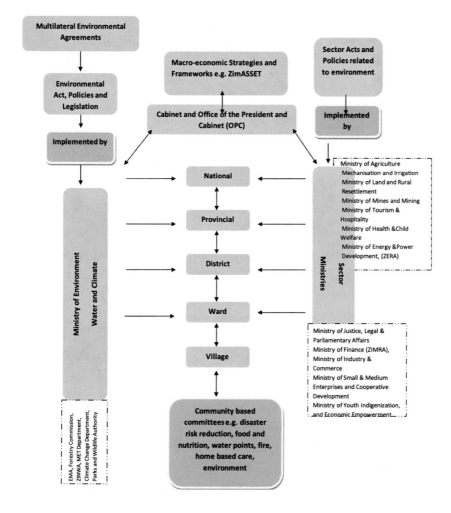

23.2: An illustration showing how the different government ministries, departments, agencies and policies in Zimbabwe relate to each other and how each level of governance is connected.
Source (Chigumira, 2016).

Institutional and human capacity for a green economy

Zimbabwe is one of the few countries in the Global South with a high literacy rate that has potential to be transformed into human and intellectual capital for advancing the green agenda. Unfortunately, primarily due to the poor macroeconomic environment, Zimbabwe continues to lose its technical and skilled experts to other countries in the region and abroad. Weak institutional capacity to implement policies and strategies is the gravest risk to curbing Zimbabwe's environmental challenges such as the impacts of climate change and losses in biodiversity and ecosystem services and in turn effective transition to a green economy. The barriers that affect Zimbabwe's capacity to respond effectively to these environmental challenges are related to skills migration in key government departments, limited financial resources and human capacity, obsolete equipment and infrastructure in the private sector. This brain drain has further weakened both public and private sectors' institutional capacity for innovation in green technology and cleaner production. There is therefore need for enhanced human and institutional capacity (technology, skill-set, financing) in the country.

Greening the energy sector

This section provides insight into the energy sector in the country by mapping the various actors, initiatives/projects that can contribute toward a low carbon and green economy development pathway. It further emphasizes the importance of greening the energy sector for human wellbeing, particularly for women and children, who are mainly affected by energy poverty and the ill-effects of traditional fossil fuel usage.

The main sources of energy used in Zimbabwe are electricity (from coal-fired stations, hydroelectricity and solar energy), petroleum products (including kerosene/paraffin), propane gas and fuel wood. Thermal power generation, which uses coal as combustible, and hydro-electricity dominate electricity generation. The energy sector is the greatest emitter of GHG in the country. The sector produces 49% of carbon emissions compared to agriculture, industry and waste (GoZ MEWC, 2015). The COP +21 climate deal to reduce GHG emissions hinges on the country's pledge and contribution communicated in Zimbabwe's NDCs. In this NDC, Zimbabwe pledged a 33% annual reduction in energy emissions by 2030 (GoZ MEWC, 2015) and pointed to the energy sector as a crucial area for the reduction of GHG emissions. Greening the energy sector is key to economic growth in Zimbabwe. The National Energy Policy (NEP) guides the planning, development and implementation of energy-related projects in the country. The implementation strategy in the NEP aims to achieve socio-economic development, increased productivity in productive sectors and environmental sustainability. While one of the objectives of the NEP takes the environment into consideration, it is, however, silent on renewable energy as an alternative to fossil-based energy consumption.

Exploiting renewable energy sources is key to advancing a green economy pathway and green growth. There are several renewable resources that remain under explored in the country, such as geothermal generation in the Eastern Highlands. Tapping into such renewable energy sources can generate green jobs that are not just located in the energy producing sector "but also in value chains that encompass renewable energy equipment, renewable energy project development, construction and installation work associated with renewable energy capacity; operation and maintenance of renewable energy facilities and other cross cutting activities…" (LEDRIZ, 2015:10). The energy sector in the country is a strategic area for green growth and low carbon development requires a renewable energy policy and regulatory framework and an energy efficiency policy and strategy. Zimbabwe has a long history with renewable energy, dating as far back as the mid-1970s when the country commercialised ethanol fuel blending (10 – 20%). The country was the second in the world after Brazil to commercialise biofuel for its fuel blending.

The donor community has also taken an active role in the energy sector in Zimbabwe. Notable programmes that have been set up in the region are The EU Sustainable Energy for All initiative (SE4ALL) project and Power Africa Challenge. The SE4ALL project targets 26 countries in East and Southern Africa power pool. The purpose of the programme is to: (a) harmonise regulatory energy frameworks in COMESA, SADC and the East African Community (EAC); (b) provide technical assistance facilities in the area of energy (c) set performance standards in all 26 countries and (d) create an autonomous electricity market in the two power pools SADC and EAC. Zimbabwe is one of the 26 countries under the SE4ALL projects. Several CSOs in Zimbabwe participate in renewable energy initiatives. These include SNV, HIVOS, Oxfam, Practical Action, FES, ZELA and Zimbabwe Regional Environment Organisation (ZERO). The CSOs created dialogue platforms with the public sector (Zimbabwe Electricity Regulatory Authority (ZERA), Rural Electricity Agency (REA), Zimbabwe Electricity Distribution Company (ZETDC) and Zimbabwe Power Company (ZPC)) in order to influence the public sector on energy policy formulation, interrogation of existing frameworks and action plans, and the implementation thereof (ZELA 2015).

The private sector participates in the energy sector through independent power producers (IPPs) retail and infrastructure installation. The renewable energy projects undertaken by IPPs vary from hydroelectricity power generation, solar farms to biofuels. The key IPPs presently involved in renewable energy production include Nyangani Renewable Energy (NRE) operating in Honde Valley, Great Zimbabwe Hydro operating in Masvingo (funded by MOL Power Zimbabwe, Industrial Development Cooperation South Africa and NU Planet), and Chisumbanje green fuels. Fifteen projects proposed to ZERA by licensed IPPs since 2011 are not yet developed or operational. This is attributed to IPPs failing to secure finances from local banks or guarantors, regional and international investors. The findings show that current activities in the renewable energy sector are not supported by law nor policies making it difficult for large-scale investments to occur. Currently, Zimbabwe is considered to have inconsistent investment policies, in particular, the indigenisation policies which restrict investments. Policies provide the backbone for the successful implementation of green initiatives. The GoZ, however, commissioned in 2015 the drafting of a renewable energy policy that can provide guidance and strategies to enable the development of this alternative and sustainable energy resource.

Financial mechanisms and approaches to support a green economy

Studies on how Kenya, Rwanda and South Africa are transitioning to a green economy point to substantial financial investments into this sector (Nhamo, 2011). In light of deindustrialization, coupled with job losses and economic meltdown, the conditions for leveraging capital investment for a green economy in Zimbabwe are limited. Zimbabwe continues to experience shortages of foreign direct investment (FDI) due to low investor confidence caused by political and policy uncertainties (World Bank Outlook, 2016). However, there are local financial institutions in Zimbabwe that promote financing green activities. These institutions include the Zimbabwe Agricultural Development Trust (ZADT), the Infrastructure Development Bank of Zimbabwe (IDBZ), and the African Development Bank (AfDB). The other financial mechanisms that could support a green economy, include multi-donor trust funds such as ZimRef and ZUNDAF. The focus of ZimRef and ZUNDAF on strengthening livelihoods and resilience, climate change, and water and infrastructure development contributes to the green economy. The IBDZ has a statutory mandate to spearhead the mobilisation of funding for infrastructure in all sectors of the economy, with energy being one of the priority areas. The IBDZ has no green policy but has an interest in financing green buildings and infrastructure.

Support for the energy sector is crucial for the green economy due to its contribution to GHG emissions. Most energy projects in the country were not operational due to lack of funding and investment in this sector. However, there is a strong regional and international focus on supporting and financing renewable energy and climate-smart agricultural programmes. Regional support from financial institutions like the AfDB and DBSA have focused on greening the energy sector by improving energy efficiency and funding of renewable energy projects. Government can access finances from two key financial facilities. These include the African Union Extreme Climate Facility and the UNFCC Green Climate Fund. Furthermore, the African Development Bank (AfDB), World Bank, European Investment Bank, Development Bank of Southern Africa (DBSA), Export-Import Bank of China and the Islamic Bank provide funding, especially in the energy sector that is available to independent power providers (IPPs). The GoZ, for example, through a US$202 million loan from Export-Import Bank of China backed an IPP, Intratrek Zimbabwe, to construct a solar power project in Gwanda in partnership with CHINT Electrics.

Conclusion

We position transitioning to a green economy as an opportunity for key players (public and private, civil society and donors) to reconcile the need for economic growth and development within the parameters of a sustainable environment, maintenance of healthy ecosystems, and good governance and accountability. This transition requires a movement away from orthodox development which has negative environmental and social consequences and associated ecological debts for the future (Houdet and Chikozho, 2016). In the mainstream vision of a green economy, growth in income and employment are driven by economic activities that reduce carbon emissions, enhance energy and resource efficiency, and reduce losses in biodiversity and ecosystem services in both public and private sectors (Houdet and Chikozho, 2016). This concept has expanded further to include social and economic dimensions such as human wellbeing, poverty reduction, social equity and green job creation (Nhamo, 2013).

The chapter points to the legislative foundation that can enable green initiatives that allow for a transition to a green economy paradigm. It highlights funding constraints that are related to Zimbabwe's macroeconomic and policy environment and the lack of capable human resources. There is therefore an opportunity for capacity building of human resources in government as well as collaborative approaches that include working with academics in order to facilitate Zimbabwe's ability to green the economy. This study argues that, an enabling macroeconomic environment characterised by economic growth, re-industrialisation and improved investor confidence, could act as a catalyst for green growth and transitioning from a brown to a green economy. The opportunity exists for introducing cleaner green technologies which are in-line with green economy principles when the macroeconomic environment stabilises, and re-industrialisation takes place. It is imperative therefore that a green growth policy framework and strategy be set in place in anticipation of industrial growth.

References

CDC. (2015). CDCS planning and integrating gender concerns. Washington, D.C: USAID.

Chagutah, T. (2010). *Climate change vulnerability and adaptation preparedness in Southern Africa.* Cape Town: Heinrich Böll Press.

Chigumira (2015). Addressing issues of climate change and scope for green growth in Zimbabwe: A situational assessment (Unpublished Danida Report).

Chigumira (2016). Climate change, livelihoods, and gender in resilience building, Zimbabwe. Unpublished report prepared for the UNDP Zimbabwe resilience building project. (Unpublished Danida Report).

Chimhowu, O. and Manjengwa, J.S (2012). Drivers of poverty in Zimbabwe: Emerging lessons for wealth creation from the protracted relief program, Harare, Zimbabwe.

Clark, J, and Carney, D. (2008). Sustainable livelihoods approaches – What have we learnt? A review of DFID's experience with sustainable livelihoods. ESRC Research Seminar Paper.

Davis, C.L. (2012). Climate risk and vulnerability: A summary of Zimbabwe needs. In Handbook for Southern Africa. Pretoria, South Africa: Council for Scientific and Industrial Research.

Davis, R. and Hirji, R. (2014). Climate change and water resources planning, development and management in Zimbabwe. World Bank. Available online: htt://documents.worldbank.org/curated/en/2014/10/23839207/climate-change-water-resources-planning-development-management-zimbabwe

Dube, C., Abel, S. and Mugocha, E. (2013). Access to bank credit as a strategy to re-industrialisation in Zimbabwe: The issues Zimbabwe Economic Policy Analysis and Research Unit (ZEPARU) Discussion Paper.

Frost, P. (2001). Zimbabwe and the United Nations Framework Convention on Climate Change. Working Paper, Overseas Development Institute.

Governance and Social Development Resources Centre. (2009). *Helpdesk research report: Climate change and Zimbabwe.* Harare: DFID Zimbabwe.

Government of Zimbabwe (2013c). *National budget statement for 2014.* Harare: Ministry of Finance and Economic Development.

Government of Zimbabwe. (2011a). *Zimbabwe medium term plan (MTP) 2011-2015.* Harare: Ministry of Economic Planning and Development.

Government of Zimbabwe. (2012). Zimbabwe Second National Communication to the United Nations Framework Convention on Climate Change.

Government of Zimbabwe. (2013a). Constitution of Zimbabwe. Amendment (No 20) Act 2013. Harare: Fidelity Printers.

Government of Zimbabwe. (2013b). Zimbabwe agenda for sustainable socio-economic transformation (ZimAsset): Towards an empowered society and a growing economy. October 2013- December 2018. Harare.

Gwimbi, P. (2007). The effectiveness of early warning systems for the reduction of flood disasters: some experiences from cyclone induced floods in Zimbabwe. *Journal of sustainable development in Africa, 9*(4), 152-169.

IASC (2007). Women, girls, boys and men different needs equal opportunities, IASC. IFAD (2011). Rural Poverty Report 2011. Rome.

ILO-green International Labour Organisation (ILO). (2012). Working towards sustainable development: Opportunities for decent work and social inclusion in a green economy. Geneva: International Labour Office.

International Labour Organisation (ILO). (2012). The green jobs programme for the ILO. Available online: www.tinyurl.com.

International Labour Organisation (ILO). (2015). *Green equality and green jobs: A policy brief.* Geneva, Switzerland :ILO.

International Labour Organisation. (2012). Global Employment Trends for Women, Available online: http://www.ilo.org/wcmsp5/groups/public/---dgreports/---dcomm/documents/publication/wcms_195447.pdf.

International Republican Institute. (2015). Survey on Local Governance and Constitutionalism: Zimbabwe International Trade Union Confederation, 2009, gender (in) equality in the labour market: An overview of global trends and developments. Available online:
http://www.ituc-csi.org/IMG/pdf/GAP-09_EN.pdf.

Kanyenze, G. (2014). The Zimbabwean economy. Presentation made at the Crisis Coalition Zimbabwe Workshop, Bronte Hotel, Harare, and 17 June 2014.

Manjengwa, J., Kasirye, I. and Matema, C. (2012). *Understanding poverty in Zimbabwe: A sample survey in 16 Districts (2012).* Paper prepared for presentation at the Centre for the Study of African Economies Conference 2012 "Economic Development in Africa". March 18-20, 2012; Oxford, United Kingdom.

Mass Public Opinion Institute. (2015). Afrobarometer Round 6 Survey in Zimbabwe. Available online:
http://afrobarometer.org/sites/default/files/publications/
Summary%20of%20results/zim_r6_sor.pdf.

Masson, V.L., Norton, A. and Wilkinson, E. (2013). Gender and resilience. Working Paper. BRACED Knowledge Manager.

Ministry of Finance. (2012). Budget estimates for the year ending December 31, 2012. Harare: Ministry of Finance Blue Book.

Ministry of Finance. (2013). Budget estimates for the year ending December 31, 2013. Harare: Ministry of Finance Blue Book.

Ministry of Finance. (2014). Budget estimates for the year ending December 31, 2014. Harare: Ministry of Finance Blue Book.

Ministry of Finance. (2015). Budget estimates for the year ending December 31, 2015. Harare: Ministry of Finance Blue Book.

Ministry of Finance. (2016). Budget estimates for the year ending December 31, 2016. Harare: Ministry of Finance Blue Book.

Moyo S. and Yeros, P. (2005). Reclaiming the land: The resurgence of rural movements in Africa, Asia and Latin America. London, United Kingdom: ZED Books.

Moyo. S. and Yeros, P. (2007). Reclaiming the nation: The return of the national question in Africa, Asia and Latin. London, United Kingdom: Pluto Press.

Muyengwa, M. L (2015). Youth employment, empowerment, participation and sustainable livelihoods: A report for UNICEF, Harare. Zimbabwe.

Muzamwese, T. (2014) Green *economy and energy sector: Towards a sustainable development model in Zimbabwe in exploring Zimbabwe's green economy potential (The energy sector)*. Harare: Unpublished Report.

Namukombo, J. (2016). Information and communication technologies and gender in climate change and green economy: situating women's opportunities and challenges in Zambian policies and strategies. *Jàmbá: Journal of Disaster Risk Studies, 8*(3), 1-7.

Nhemachena, C. and Mano. R (2007), 'Assessment of the Economic Impacts of Climate Change on Agriculture in Zimbabwe: A Ricardian Approach' CEEPA discussion paper 11. Available online: http://www.ceepa.co.za/docs/cdp11.pdf.

Quisumbing, A. R., & Pandolfelli, L. (2010). Promising approaches to address the needs of poor female farmers: Resources, constraints, and interventions. *World Development, 38*(4), 581-592.

Reeler, T. (2014). Women and Democracy in Zimbabwe. Insights from Afrobarometer, Policy Paper. Available online: http://afrobarometer.org/sites/default/files/ publications/Policy%20paper/ab policypaperno14.pdf.

Rurinda, J., Mapfumo, P., Van Wijk, M.T., Mtambanrengwe, F., Rufino, M.C., Chikowa, R. and Giller, K.E. (2014), Sources of vulnerability to a variable and changing climate among smallholder households in Zimbabwe: A participatory analysis. *Climate Risk Management, 3*(1), 65-67

SADCC (2015). SADC Gender protocol barometer 2015: Zimbabwe gender links. Available online: http://www.genderlinks.org.za/article/sadc-protocol-barometer-2015-zimbabwe-2015-05-05.

SARUA. (2013). Climate change counts: Country background information document. University of Cape Town ... SARUA Climate Change Counts Mapping Study: Zimbabwe

Shiney Varghese, S. (2012). Looking through a gender lens: Water in the green economy, Henrich Boll Stiftung. Available online:

http://www.iatp.org/files/Varghese_WomenWater.pdf.

Skinner, E. (2011). Gender and climate change: Overview Report: *BRIDGE cutting edge pack on gender and climate change.* Brighton: Institute of Development Studies.

Sultana, F. (2013), Gendering climate change: Geographical insights. *The Professional Geographer, 66*(3), 372–381.

Thomson Reuters Foundation (2015). Workforce Development Theory and Practice in the Mental Health Sector. Available online: http://www.trust.org.

UNDP. (2012). *Overview of the linkages between gender and climate change.* New York: UNDP.

UNDP. (2015). *Briefing for countries on the human development report, Zimbabwe.* New York: UNDP.

Unganai, Initial. (1996). Historic and future climate change in Zimbabwe. *Climate Research, 6*(2), 137-145.

USAID. (2015). *USAID Zimbabwe 2016 climate change matrix.* Harare: College Press Publishers,

USAID. (Year). Gender analysis and assessment for FIF programming. Available online: http://pdf.usaid.gov/pdf docs/PA00JT8C.pdf.

Vincent, V. and Thomas, R. (1960). *An agricultural survey of Southern Rhodesia: Part I: agro-ecological survey.* Salisbury: Government Printer.

Walker, B.H., Ludwig, D., Holling, C.S. and Peterman, R.M. (1969). Stability of semi-arid Savanna grazing systems. *Journal of Ecology, 69*(2), 473-498.

World Bank. (1995). Kenya poverty assessment. Report No. 13152-KE, Population and Human Resources Division, Eastern Africa Department, Africa Region. Washington, DC: World Bank.

World Bank. (2009). Kenya poverty and inequality assessment. Report No. 44190-KE, Poverty Reduction and Economic Management Unit, Africa Region. April, 2009.

World Bank. (2010). Running on one engine: Kenya's uneven economic performance. Kenya economic update, Ed. no. 2. Poverty Reduction and Economic Management Unit, Africa Region. June, 2010.

World Factbook. (2015). Zimbabwe. Available online: https://www.cia.gov/library/publications/the-world-factbook/

ZEPARU. (2013). Building agriculture competitiveness in Zimbabwe: Lessons from the international perspective. Available online: http://elibrary.acbfpact.org/acbf/collect/acbf/index/assoc/HASHdf2f.di r/doc.pdf.

ZEPARU. (2013). The nexus between growth, empowerment and poverty in Zimbabwe. The economics of employment creation in Zimbabwe. Available online:

http://elibrary.acbfpact.org/acbf/collect/acbf/index/assoc/HASH0182/
48b68517.dir/doc.pdf.

ZEPARU. (2014). Zimbabwe: Cost driver analysis of the Zimbabwean economy. Harare: MCSER Publishing Press.

Zimbabwe Climate Change Response Strategy. (2015). Participatory development and arrangements of the National Strategy and Action Plan for low-carbon water and sewage industry . Harare: Government Printers.

Zimbabwe Democracy Institute. (2015). Governance, politics and the shifting political economy in Zimbabwe. Harare: Government Printers.

ZIMSTAT (2013). 2012 Population census results. Final Report. Harare: ZIMSTAT.

ZIMSTAT (2013). Poverty income consumption and expenditure Survey 2011/12 Report. Harare: ZIMSTAT.

ZIMSTAT (2014). Multiple indicator cluster survey (MICS). Harare: ZIMSTAT.

Printed in the United States
By Bookmasters